THE
MIND OF THE NEGRO:

An Intellectual History
of Afro-Americans

By

EARL E. THORPE

ISBN: 978-1-63923-840-8

Printed: March 2023

Published and Distributed By:
Lushena Books
607 Country Club Drive, Unit E
Bensenville, IL 60106
www.lushenabks.com

ISBN: 978-1-63923-840-8

THE MIND OF THE NEGRO:
AN INTELLECTUAL HISTORY OF
AFRO-AMERICANS

TO

MY SISTERS AND BROTHERS

ACKNOWLEDGMENTS

For permission to quote from works published by them grateful appreciation is hereby extended to the following: Alfred A. Knopf, Dryden Press, Rinehart and Company, University of North Carolina Press, Little, Brown and Company, Harpers, Dodd, Mead, American Historical Association, Columbia University Press, Citadel Press, W. E. B. Du Bois, Rayford W. Logan, Association for the Study of Negro Life and History, Albert and Charles Boni, *Quarterly Review of Higher Education Among Negroes*, *Phylon*, Macmillan, Harcourt, Brace, Grosset and Dunlap, The Free Press, University of Wisconsin Press, University of Chicago Press, Yale University Press, Viking Press, Prentice-Hall, Chapman and Grimes, Houghton-Mifflin, *Negro History Bulletin*, Cornell University Press, *American Journal of Sociology*, Ronald Press, Doubleday, University of Oklahoma Press, and The Dial Press.

For special kindnesses extended in connection with his efforts at scholarly productivity, the author is indebted to Twiley W. Barker, Jr., John B. Cade, Sr., Felton G. Clark, Henry E. Cobb, James S. Galloway, Elton C. Harrison, Rodney G. Higgins, Sr., Blyden Jackson, Ralph J. Lowery, Robert E. Moran, and William S. Smith.

INTRODUCTION

THE TASK

Any attempt at writing an intellectual history of the Afro-American has as a model such works as Vernon Louis Parrington's *Main Currents in American Thought*,[1] Henry Steele Commager's *The American Mind*,[2] and Wilbur J. Cash's *The Mind of The South*.[3] That the mind of the Negro is not completely subsumed under topics treated by these scholars is predicated on the fact that the Afro-American has held a status, hence played a role in the national drama, which is in some ways unique. No other segment of our society was held in chattel slavery for over two centuries, and no other group has been the object of the same brand of segregation and discrimination. Because he has held a unique status, he has an intellectual history which is in a number of ways unique.

The author hopes that this volume will have interest not only for the general reader, but that its coverage of the main facts of Negro History is so comprehensive that the work will find use as a text in courses on the Negro in American history. It is partly with this in mind that he adopted the procedure of allowing Negro spokesmen and leaders to speak for themselves as often as was practical.[4] This study does not purport to be either exhaustive of the general subject or definitive in any way. That the chapters herein are by no means exhaustive of the topics treated is obvious. Perhaps a full-length book could be written on each chapter, as indeed already has been done in a few instances.

The central theme of Negro thought has been the quest for freedom and equality. Where theory on the race issue is concerned, from beginning to end Negro thought is basically accommodation and attack thought, just as much of the thought of the white South is similarly defensive. Among other things, the white South generally has defended states-rights, secession, slavery, segregation, the agrarian way of life, and the rights of a minority section. On a number of these, the Negro often has been on the opposite side from the white South, attacking, equally as confident that God, the Bill of Rights, the Constitution, and right are on his side. In addition to protest against his status, much of the defensive element in Negro thought has derived from the felt need of defending the race against the charge of biological or racial inferiority.

The mind of the Negro herein outlined is drawn primarily "from the record." This record does not show the Negro to have been either arrogant or insolent in his quest for equality of citizenship, but rather it shows the dominant aspects of his "nature" to have been modesty, kindness, humility, frustration, and faith. These virtues were extolled even by the rulers of the Old South. The portrait does not show the Afro-American to be without faults. True to the sociological concept of polarization, the Afro-American has manifested his nation and section's dominant virtues and vices in exaggerated degree. Among his more pronounced faults have been a too-often restriction of his *Weltanschauung* to the narrow confines of race, hypersensitivity, and an inferiority complex which displays itself in a thousand and one ways.

While writing this volume, the author constantly has been aware that he was engaging in considerable generalizing, and of the well-known dictum that all generalizations are false. Still, far from being able to do without generalizations, we commonly aim at them. Such is the goal of all inductive and scientific thinking. Individual facts and statements have no pattern or meaning until grouped together. Since interpretation is an essential part of historical writing at its best, such grouping and generalizing must be done. What should be insisted on is that a writer shall be aware that there are exceptions to practically every generalization and that he shall offer evidence to support his statements. It is hoped that these rules have been adhered to in this work. Despite his precautions, the necessity which the writer has had of relying heavily on the written record may well have given this volume a too-strong middle-class coloring.

In one sense, thoughts comprise or reveal the soul of any individual or group. In this volume the author hopes that he has, in some small degree, bared the soul of the American Negro, to one end, at least, that not only shall white America and the world know him better, but that the present-day Negro may know himself better. No person of African descent needs to be ashamed of that phenomenon which we have chosen to call "The Mind of the Negro."

THE NEED FOR AN INTELLECTUAL HISTORY OF THE NEGRO

The history of ideas, or intellectual history, is a fairly new field in which there is considerable current interest. John Herman Randall, Jr.'s *Making of the Modern Mind* has become something of a classic.[5] With *The Idea of Progress*,[6] J. B. Bury earlier had shown how fruitful and revealing this approach to history can be. *The Heavenly City of the Eighteenth Century Philosophes*, by Carl Becker, used the "ideas" approach.[7] For American history, Vernon Louis Parrington's *Main Currents in American Thought* still stands as perhaps the best effort to date over the period covered, while in *The American Mind*,[8] Henry Steele Commager ably covers the period since 1880, the terminal date of Parrington's treatise. In his *The Growth of American Thought*,[9] Merle Curti ably has traversed the whole of American history, and R. H. Gabriel has done the same in his *The Course of American Democratic Thought*.[10] These titles alone reveal that intellectual history, or the tracing and analyzing of ideas, is by no means a completely new endeavor. What is relatively new is the effort to establish this as a separate field or area of specialization. One of the broadest and most concise statements of what this effort involves is to be found in the Introduction to Crane Brinton's volume entitled *Ideas and Men*.[11]

As surprising as it may seem, no previous study has been published, the main burden of which is to analyze the Negro mind in the United States. It is true that studies have been made of various aspects of Negro life and thought. Among these studies, some which stand out have been *The Negro Family*[12] by E. Franklin Frazier; *Negro Labor*[13] by Charles Wesley and others; *The Negro's God* by Benjamin Mays; *The Negro Author*[14] by Vernon Loggins; *The Negro in Drama*[15] by Frederick W. Bond; *Negro Art* by Alain Locke,[16] as well as studies of the historian,[17] the Church,[18] the poet,[19] and education.[20] Although Carter Woodson was interested in the thought theme when he edited *The Negro Mind as Reflected in Letters Written during the Crisis*,[21] that work is scarcely more than a compilation. The same is true of Herbert Aptheker's recent *Documentary History of the American Negro*.[22]

The interest by Howard Odum and other scholars in analyzing slave songs may be said to have culminated in Miles Mark Fisher's *Negro Slave Songs*, which appeared in 1953.[23] Beginning in a big way with the interest of Joe Chandler Harris, numerous writers have collected, analyzed, and criticized the folk literature of this people. Scholars have studied jazz, the slave, the Afro-American press, and other areas of the life and thought of the race. In one degree or another, the Negro mind was a consideration of practically all of these writers, yet, to tackle the job of sifting through all of these diverse manifestations of history, to the end of telling the general and broad story of the evolution of the Negro mind, no one had done.

The question may be raised as to whether there is a need for tracing the mental development of any one segment of the population. One reply would be that this is a long and accepted procedure. The Puritan mind has been studied again and again. The same is true of the Plainsman, or the Frontiersman, or The Mind of the South, or the rural as against the urban dweller.

Such a question as the above probably would be based on the premise that the Negro group in its development has not deviated from the majority of the population, or that any existing deviations are not significant. Further, in such a question the assumption would have to be made that almost from the beginning of its history here, the dark-skinned minority was more-or-less thoroughly Americanized; even now, however, there is some disagreement as to whether so-called Negro culture is basically Western or "African." Such a question also would have to be based on the assumption that in their larger studies, Parrington, Commager, Gabriel, Cash, and others did not overlook or slight such sources as songs, poems, sermons, histories, speeches, plays, novels, and drama done by the Afro-Americans. The latter conclusion would be far from the truth. "Except for an occasional Nat Turner, Booker T. Washington, or George Washington Carver," states Richard Bardolph, "the Negro as a person is missing from the textbooks from which the millions learn their history."[24] Bardolph goes on to point out that the treatment which this minority has received in the literature of this country is "largely preoccupied with Negroes *en masse* and as a 'problem,' and has rarely extended to the individual, creative Negroes and their contributions to American society."[25] Bardolph's study of the distinguished Negro revealed that persons of color make up only about six-tenths of one percent of the entries in the *Dictionary of American Biography*, and that in the 1950's *Who's Who in America* carried less than one percent of such entries.[26]

CLASS DISTINCTIONS AND NEGRO THOUGHT

American Negroes long have belonged to fairly large and distinct groups. For the ante-bellum period there were the free persons of the North, free persons of the South, domestic or other skilled slaves and field slaves. First in independence, freedom, education, militancy and Westernization were the free Negroes of the North. Their spokesmen asked and fought doggedly for social and political equality. In such urban and cosmopolitan centers as Philadelphia, New York, Cincinnati, and Boston, members of this group were as vigorous and modern in their denunciation of slavery, race or class prejudice and other forms of tyranny of man against man as any John Locke, Jean Rousseau, Voltaire, Benjamin Franklin, or Thomas Jefferson. With its numbers enlarged by fugitive slaves, especially after 1830, this group formed the substantial body of Negro abolitionists.

There are several reasons why the northern free Negro was more militant and articulate than his southern counterpart. In the first place, he had less to fear from his white neighbors, who even when they were not abolitionists, at least usually believed in the right of all Americans to exercise such freedoms as the right to speech and assembly. Too, the free Negro absorbed the dominant political and social faith of the North, a faith which was typified by such documents as the Declaration of Independence, the Constitution, and the Bill of Rights. Finally, the northern free Negro was at almost all times consciously and actually closer to the genuine citizenship of his state and the nation than his southern counterpart. Numerous studies of modern revolutions have shown that the most revolutionary classes and groups are not those farthest down, but those closest to the top. It is this fact, in large part, which explains in part the post-World War II militancy of the southern Negro. He is now too near the top to keep quiet and complacent or to continue the somewhat traditional Uncle Tom role.

In both the pre-Civil War and post bellum periods until his death in 1895 Frederick Douglass was the main spokesman for northern militancy. After his death, W. E. B. DuBois, though he worked for years in the South, assumed the primary leadership of this group and retained it until he broke with the NAACP in the 1930's. Since then the NAACP has retained the leadership, with Walter White holding the limelight until his death in 1955. In 1960 it appeared that newer more militant groups might be usurping the NAACP position.

Within the South, which after 1830 became the almost exclusive home of and a synonym for slavery, the free Negro class came first in degree of Westernization and education. The largest numbers of this class were centered in the large cities, with Charleston and New Orleans holding top positions. There was much white blood in this class, and sometimes fairly close social ties existed between members of the ruling class and their colored blood relations. The latter usually were proud of their white blood and light complexions, while both despising and loving their dark-skinned brethren in bondage. In general, free mulattoes everywhere probably hoped for an early end to slavery and a subsequent uplifting of the freedmen through the acquisition of property, education and culture.

Members of the free class participated in almost all of the major slave plots and rebellions. This, plus the fact that their mere existence in the South stirred desires and hopes of freedom in the slaves, caused southern states, especially after 1831, to proscribe the freedom, rights, and opportunities of this class.

Among the slaves, field hands constituted a distinct group from those who worked at such occupations as valet, butler, cook, maid, overseer, and artisan. Of this, a former slave stated:

There was a social distinction with the slaves. The house and personal servants were on a higher social plane than the field slaves, while the colored persons, who would associate with the 'po white trash' were practically outcasts, and held in very great contempt. The slaves who belonged to the lower class of white folks, were not considered on the same level as those belonging to the 'quality folks' and the slaves of these families were the most proud of and bragged of their connection with the better families.[27]

In the post-bellum period one finds this same tendency prominent among the freedmen. For example, today, the Negro maid, butler, or chauffeur who works for the more affluent white families is held in higher esteem than those who work for persons who do not belong to the first families in the locale.

Non-field hands had a more intimate social relation with the master class and hence absorbed its culture and civilization quicker. Scarcely was force needed in the relations between these two groups, whereas with field hands the language of the lash was the main one spoken. Having an enviable status within the institution, non-field hands were prone to expose slave plots and attempts at insurrection or escape. It was the generally docile and contented non-field hand class that Ulrich Bonnell Phillips and other "pro-slavery" historians of the South have depicted as possessing characteristic behavior for the Negro in general. On the other hand, abolitionist and other "anti-slavery" writers sometimes have generalized almost exclusivly from the attitudes toward the institution which were depicted by the free Negro of the North. However, of the total colored population in the nation, field hands were most numerous. By virtue of their circumstances they were forced to be more other-worldly in their hopes and aspirations, and to concentrate keenly on the matter of sheer survival. If one must utilize the *strictly erroneous* approach of generalizing about the race from the characteristics of one of its classes, because they represented the largest group or class, the field hands would be the most logical choice. They were definitely not the persistently militant creatures depicted by Herbert Aptheker and other Marxist-oriented historians, nor were they always or often the contented, docile, semi-buffoons delineated by Ulrich Phillips and scholars of similar biases.

There was no single outstanding and common spokesman for the conservative ante-bellum tradition of the southern slave. This is because, while the slaves had common hopes and aspirations, they possessed no common action or program. For the slave, realities of the southern geography, economy, and political considerations made group action impossible.

The existence of groups or classes within ante-bellum Negro society indicates that one might more rationally entitle an intellectual history of the race, "The Minds of the Negro." This, however, is no more true of the colored American than would be the case with such volumes as H. S. Commager's *The American Mind,* or John H. Randall, Jr.'s *Making of the Modern Mind.* In either case the plural would be more exact. But as with all such works, there are so many similarities and basic patterns of thought until one is justified in using the singular "mind" so long as he does so with caution, and with an awareness of class, sectional, and other differences. It is neither more appropriate nor inappropriate to speak of "the Negro" than it is to speak of "the American," or the "Westerner," or "the Asiatic."

The deluge of civil war did not destroy class divisions among Negroes. The South's old free class and non-field hands now merged to form an "upper" class which represented a highly Westernized group which was proud of its light complexion and relatively high degree of civilization and culture. Often more cautious and conservative than the masses, they continued the pre-war attitude which saw them both despising and loving the descendants of field hands. As the latter still constituted the majority of the race, this contempt often had, and has today, the character of contempt for the race in general. Thus, the disparagement which Negroes sometimes have shown for their race stems in part from an upper class view of the crudeness and backwardness of the lower majority class, as well as being in part an unconscious acceptance of the attitude and views of the white dominant majority.

Until recently the masses of Afro-Americans have been descendants of field hand slaves. As in the dark days of slavery, oppression and lack of opportunity were the diseases which mainly explain their plight. E. Franklin Frazier has shown well how crime, illegitimacy, desertion by fathers and husbands, and matriarchy were some of the malign characteristics among these "folk culture"[28] individuals. That their lot long presented a brighter side, however, there can be little doubt, still it was mainly the plight of this large group of lower-class persons which led Booker Washington realistically to advocate as a program for his race "industrial" education, "character" training, thrift and abstinence from agitation for political and social equality. The slave tradition of advance through conservatism, seemingly broken by the brief period of Radical Reconstruction, a period when so-called Carpetbaggers and Scalawags actually dominated the stage, was epitomized by the Washington leadership from 1895 until his death in 1915. Though it lacked a dominant personality after the latter date, this tradition remained strong in the South until the World War II period, when a number of forces combined to cause the mind of the southern Negro to lose much of its old distinctiveness and to merge with that of the militant northern tradition.

While the Negro of the North generally has represented the vanguard of the race's militancy, liberalism, culture, and Westernization, and has provided much of the leadership in such thought and action, his feelings and convictions probably have represented the highest aspirations of the southern colored masses. Of necessity the southerner's methods have been different, but not his goals. It is no exaggeration to state that almost all Negroes of the ante-bellum period despised the institution of slavery and wished its early demise, or that given a good opportunity, they worked in some small way to hasten its over-throw. Since 1865 practically all colored Americans have desired as their ultimate condition complete social, economic, political, and civil equality. Practically all constantly have viewed this country as their home, and have not wished to be expatriated or colonized. Their political and social faith has been the traditional faith of America, and they speedily and unhesitatingly have risen to the colors when the nation was imperilled by war. By and large, they have been basically American since the early days of slavery, and their so-called racial traits are simply American traits, accentuated here and there by historic circumstance. Their behavior is to be explained in terms of the national culture. This does not deny the survival of certain African words, dances, and similar idioms, but these survivals have become a part of the total national culture.

That the Negro masses, southerners always, have been directly influenced by many of the same geographical and cultural factors which W. J. Cash so excellently outlined in his *The Mind of the South* is not to be denied. The same hardship, poverty, and long distances between farms and plantations has helped to create in the Afro-American the spirit of southern hospitality. The same primitive unlettered existence so long characteristic of the white southern masses has helped to give the Negro a bent toward a hedonistic, unrealistic, romantic, dreaminess about life. The same is true of some other southern characteristics, but differences, too, there have been in the thought of the two races. At times the mind of the South outlined by Cash is the Negro mind only in broadest outlines. For example, the love of the latter for the South is not expressed in the same mood as is that of the white native of the section. The love of the Negro is more often mixed with feelings of disappointment and bitterness. This obviously is so because the South is the dark-skinned Americans home, but it has been, and still is at times his oppressor also. Too, the early and lengthy frontier environment of the South has not imparted the lynch-law spirit to the Afro-American, as Cash so well shows that it has done for the white South, and the realities of slavery and oppression often have shocked the colored southerner out of his romantic and dreamy attitude toward life. The black man had to be more realistic and objective to survive. Another example of difference is the fact that the Negro does not "hate" the "damned Yankee" as does the white southerner, but often, though not always, regards the Yankee as a friend and humanitarian.

Just as, in Frederick Jackson Turner's learned opinion, the existence of the West did much to make the frontiersman American, so the present writer believes slavery and oppression did the same for the Negro. The realities of slavery, and oppression, perhaps as much as any other factors, forced the race to be patient, gradualistic, legalistic, pacifistic, egalitarian, in-genious, and resourceful. Too, as was the case with the Western frontier, in addition to causing a negation of democracy, the presence of the Negro in the United States has been a great catalyst to and creator of American democracy. Central to the "color problem" in this country always have been vital questions on the nature of human freedom, dignity, the nature of man, democracy, and the Christian religion, the resolution of which has produced not only such obvious results as the thirteenth, fourteenth, and fifteenth amendments to the Federal Constitution, and the May 17, 1954 Supreme Court decision against compulsory segregation in public school education, but in many less obvious ways has forced the nation to re-think and sharpen its concept and practice of Christianity and democracy. With the rise of the colored masses of humanity which the twentieth century is witnessing, having to resolve a racial and color problem on the domestic scene may yet prove a blessing in disguise for the nation.

THE MIND OF THE NEGRO:
AN INTELLECTUAL HISTORY OF
AFRO-AMERICANS

THE AGE OF SLAVERY

It is perhaps well known by now that the first Negroes to come to America were not slaves. As servants, laborers, sailors, and fighters, they were with Balboa when he discovered the Pacific Ocean, with Cortez when he overthrew Montezuma, with DeSoto on his epic exploration, with Mendez at the founding of St. Augustine, perhaps even with Columbus. But it was as slaves that they first came in significant numbers, almost a million in the sixteenth century, almost three million in the seventeenth, and over twice that number in the eighteenth century. Practically everyone knows, too, that Negroes were first brought to the English settlements in 1619, and that from Virginia they slowly appeared in all of the colonies.

Probably the first slaves to be brought to what is now the United States of America came in 1526. This was a Spanish settlement in South Carolina headed by the colonizer, Lucas Vasquez de Ayllon, and it included about six hundred persons, one-sixth of whom were Negro slaves. Within eight months, disease, dissension, and Indian hostility caused this project to be abandoned, the Spaniards going to Haiti, while the slaves were left among the Indians. The latter thus became the first permanent, non-Indian settlers within the present limits of the United States of America.

Although it is true that before Negroes were brought to America they had known slavery in Africa, Arabia, and medieval Europe, nowhere had they known it on such a large scale and with such disregard for anything save the profit motive. Over-population and absence of the plantation system in Africa, Arabia, and Europe usually had made slavery impractical save as an ornament of wealth, but the labor shortage which the Occident knew from 1500 A.D. - 1900 A.D. was the greatest that history had ever known. It was to supply this labor need that the Negro was brought from Africa to America.

Recent research has pointed out that West Africa, which supplied most of the New World's slaves was not as isolated in the middle ages as has been popularly thought, and that the culture of West Africa's Negroes at the beginning of the modern period was considerably higher than that of the New World's aborigines. Thus we are led to believe that the Negro survived midst New World slavery not because he possessed any physical advantages over the Indians, but because the Negro's culture was advanced to a point where it could withstand the economic, social, and political demands placed on it in the Occident. Too, the fact that Negroes had long practiced chattel slavery in Africa and the medieval Arab slave trade probably made it easier for them to accept in America. Although the agricultural and oligarchichal nature of their culture in Africa probably helped prepare Africans for these same conditions in America, as bondsmen here some would erect the fiction that before the white man came to Africa all was equality, democracy, harmony, and brotherhood.

The slave trade increased and intensified wars in Europe, America, and Africa, as from five to fifteen million Africans were brought out of Africa. Negroes often compared the manner of their enslavement with piracy, and they were very elevated when on January 1, 1808 the federal act went into effect prohibiting the slave trade. Little did they realize then how close the newly invented cotton gin would come to making this law virtually a dead letter, for so great became the South's need for labor that the smuggling in of slaves from Africa continued to the very eve of the Civil War. Further, legislation against the African trade, coupled with declining profits from tobacco-raising in the upper South while cotton was booming in the lower South, erected a very large domestic slave trade. In 1836 Virginia alone exported approximately 120,000 bondsmen to the lower South.

In 1650 there had been only about 300 Negroes in Virginia. By 1700 the number was increasing so rapidly that before the end of the slave era, Virginia's slave population would number around one-half million, more than in any other state. In 1724, with a total population of less than 200,000, the Carolinas had three times as many slaves as white persons. Although none of the lower southern states had entered the Union when the first census was taken in 1790, by 1830 the lower South had 604,000 slaves.

Slaves in the U.S.A. increased from 700,000 in 1790 to over 2,,000,000 by 1830, hence more than doubled in less than a half century. In the thirty years after 1830 the slave population again doubled, and was one-half of the South's total population. This tremendous increase, all coming within the lifetime of a few long-lived bondsmen, must have had a great effect on the thought of the bondsmen, increasing their doubts that such a thriving institution ever would fall, while on the other hand, hopes were increased by the dynamism of such rapid change.

In the South the Society for the Propagation of the Gospel in Foreign Parts had opened schools for the slaves during the 17th century. During this same century, in New England, John Eliot and Cotton Mather, among others, were interested in teaching the slaves. Although restricted to a relatively small number of Negroes, education was to be a prime force behind the race's resistance to slavery.

The Haitian revolt began in 1791, and was dominated by the personality and leadership of Toussaint L'Ouverture from 1794-1800. The effect of this revolt on slavery in the United States was much more widespread than is commonly known. In the fear of domestic insurrection which the Haitian revolt engendered in this country, schools, where they existed, were closed to the slaves, tougher slave codes were passed, and more careful observation of slave behavior began. On the mind of the slave the Haitian revolt had a similarly large effect, increasing their faith that freedom was at hand, and that they, through their own militancy, would have to play a part in bringing it about.

It is to the twentieth century's heroes of such hell-holes as Belsen, Daschau, and Buchenwald that one has to turn to find lessons in man's strength-in-adversity comparable to that strength which the Negro slave exhibited when, out of the depths of despair and sorrow, they gave forth their spine-tingling rhythm, laughter, gaiety, and the heavenly music of the spirituals. Reflecting on these gifts today we know again that nowhere is any tragedy ever absolute or complete.

Chapter I

THE FRONTIER AND SLAVERY

The Problem of Inevitability

Because of the light which it may shed on the problem of why slavery was fated to disappear in the United States[1] and the Western world, the present essay proposes to examine the frontier theory as it may be related to the slavery question. As traditionally stated by its proponents, this view holds that the frontier is the rock on which slavery broke.[2]

Although the moral, economic, and cultural determinists hold that the Civil War was inevitable, the present writer believes that only the demise of slavery was inevitable. In the fact that the institution might have been eliminated without war, as was the case of abolition by England and France, lies justification for the theory that inept leaders in both sections blundered into war. While slavery was fated to disappear, the Civil War was not inevitable, but was, like most wars, a tragedy which resulted when men failed to find and act with sufficient resolve on more intelligent alternatives. Wars originate not with the gods, or fate, or some other inevitability, but with men who always have alternatives.

As to that other inevitability, for too long we in the United States have committed the error of seeking locally for the reasons why slavery was doomed. That any purely or largely domestic answer is wholly inadequate is seen in the fact that the disappearance of slavery in the nineteenth century was not a phenomenon peculiar to this country, but was rather general over the whole of Western civilization. Since the phenomenon was general, the cause must be general. Once this cause is ascertained, in order to solve that other riddle of why in the United States the institution's disappearance was attended by war, it would be necessary only to determine what special factors existed here which were absent from other places. Although we do not propose to make a full investigation of this latter inquiry, already it appears that the most significant difference lies in two facts. The first is that in most places, when heavy assaults were made on the institution, profits from the slave-grown produce were declining.[3] In the United States, on the contrary, these heavy assaults were attended by the constantly rising price of cotton, the chief slave-produced staple. The second fact is that outside the United States both heavy assaults upon the institution and the decision to end it came from a source whose preponderance of power was so great as to present no prospect of a successful resort to arms by the defendants. Within the United States, however, the South had a reasonable chance of making good its threat of secession. For the British and French colonists *vis-a-vis* the mother countries, there was no such probability.

Walter P. Webb has pointed out that everywhere slavery appeared with the opening of the frontier and ended when the frontier age approached its end.[4] According to this view, the frontier sired the institution of slavery which readily presented itself as a most practical means by which the vast economical potential presented by a virgin world could be speedily realized. Without slavery, Eric Williams has declared, "the great development of the Caribbean sugar plantations, between 1650 and 1850, would have been impossible."[5] The same is true throughout the colonial world where slavery appeared. Exploitation of the frontier was essentially an economic problem. Slavery was primarily an economic institution. The latter fact is often obscured by the moral and racial implications which still loom large to those of us so little removed in time from abolitionists and civil war. Of this, William states:

> A racial twist has thereby been given to what is basically an economic phenomenon. Slavery was not born of racism: rather, racism was the consequence of slavery. Unfree labor in the New World was brown, white, black, and yellow; Catholic, Protestant and pagan.[6]

The system of unfree labor in the New World did not originate with the Negro, but with white Europeans and Indians as its first object. Negroes, writes U. B. Phillips, "were late comers fitted into a system already developed."[7] Not his color, but the availability, cheapness, and efficiency of his labor explains why the black man came to be the chief object of slavery.

It is true that the frontier not only gave rise to slavery but, for a time, fed the vitals of the institution and prolonged its life. Thus the frontier had a dual effect on the institution. Those who see no significant effect of the frontier on slavery are usually guilty of taking the short view. In this area, if one is to speak with validity of results of the frontier, an indispensable precondition is that he shall take the long view.[8] When the long view is used, it readily can be seen that several factors, which drew much of their impetus from the frontier, worked mightily to bring the institution to its demise. Then can it be seen that the disappearance of slavery was but one phase of the democratic and technological revolutions which have been wracking the modern world during the past two centuries. Among other things, the democratic revolution has seen growth of the idea that no man is inherently inferior to another, hence no man has the right to degrade another. The technological revolution has seen archaic and inefficient forms of economic and social organization constantly eliminated in favor of more efficient ones. Substitution of the power of steam, electricity, atom, and machine for that derived from relatively inefficient human muscles is one aspect of this technological revolution. But as we hope to show, contrary to the general view of proponents of the frontier hypothesis, rather than being a direct cause, the frontier was the cause behind the cause behind the cause, and there were further causes behind the frontier cause.

With the long view it may be seen that the frontier doomed slavery by providing a powerful stimulus to the growth of commercial and industrial capitalism in the United States in general and the Western World in particular. Present economic development of this nation reveals that the early concentration of this phenomenon in the Northeast was temporary only. Industrialization is now national in scope and there seems to have been a strong element of inevitability in the inexorable manner which this dynamic force relentlessly crushed agrarianism into subordination, North and South, East and West.

Also, the frontier doomed slavery by giving rise to the modern corporation, which is the institutionalization of the process of work originally done by individuals. Any corporation is the group at work. "The corporation," declares Walter P.

Webb, "moved into the position occupied by the individual, taking over most of the work, most of the tools, and most of the substances. Its success piled up wealth succeeding all bounds."[9] This gargantuan success made it possible to "finish off" the frontier faster, and as a consequence finish off the institution of chattel slavery, which was born of and fed on, the frontier. The corporation made chattel slavery backward and outdated, for the latter remained too near the original individualistic work basis, to survive in a society which had evolved to a higher level. As the corporation helped kill the laissez-faire theory and practice, so it helped sweep chattel slavery into oblivion.

The frontier doomed slavery again, because, when it made available a plentitude of land and economic opportunity, land monopolies and other types of monopoly became anomalous. Monopoly has no place in a society of great and open opportunity. It is peculiarly characteristic of societies of scant or closed opportunity. While the frontier lasted, the abundance to which it gave rise made it unnecessary that either the state should prey heavily on its subjects or that subjects should prey heavily on one another. Wealth generally tends to be a liberating influence. Just as no poverty-stricken man is free, most subjects in a poverty-stricken state are not free. Herbert Aptheker has shown that under the slave regime the treatment of slaves and their restiveness varied as the fortunes of the Old South went repeatedly from famine to prosperity.[10] Perhaps enough economic prosperity in the South ultimately would have freed the slave,[11] for then he would not have been needed. Despite the constantly increasing price of cotton, the section's continued over-all poverty kept the institution alive, much as this poverty later gave rise to and fed such phenomena as share-cropping, lynching, segregation, and race riots. In the mid-twentieth century, economic prosperity is contributing greatly to a solution of the South's race problem.

While the plantation system had its origins in abundance of good farm land and scarcity of labor, in the South this system found itself in conflict with democratizing frontier forces almost as soon as it became well organized. Slavery was inimical to the frontier ethos which capitalism epitomized.

Adam Smith, chief spokesman of this spirit, denounced slavery and declared that: "A person who can acquire no property can have no other interest than to eat as much, and to labour as little as possible."[12]

The frontier ethos emphasized "freedom, independence, individualism, self-reliance, courage, initiative, aggressiveness, and finally industry."[13] Of this, Webb states:

> All the high words the frontier man used to describe himself and to express his egoistic ideal meant *work* of one sort or another . . . independence, freedom, self-reliance, and individualism mean that each man expects to act for himself. It is *I* who possess these attributes; every man on the frontier is an *I* because society has been atomized down to its elemental particles each of which is an *I*.[14]

To be dependent on the labor of another, as was the slave-owner, was contrary to this spirit.

The frontier not only doomed slavery by helping create the individual but by serving as a magnet which for four centuries drew millions of oppressed peoples across the ocean in quest of a new measure of opportunity, freedom, security, and self-respect. The deep-seated cravings and ambitions of these millions were diametrically opposed to all that slavery represented. A republic in which all men are free and equal before the law existed in their minds and hearts long before they, in Civil War, took a major step toward making the dream a reality. Slavery was a clear-cut violation of their image of America, and it may be doubted that any major institution which is antithetical to this dream can ever long endure.

The increasing tide of immigration worked in still another way to doom this institution. Slavery was the outgrowth of one of history's greater labor shortages. Just as early white male immigrants at times used Indian and Negro women as concubines because there was a shortage of white women in the colonies, they used forced red, brown, black, and yellow labor in their mines and fields because there was an acute shortage of manpower. Immigration ended the acuteness of the labor shortage.

Also, because this type of labor and economic exploitation

generally is quick to burn out the soil, the institution required ever newer fertile land. "Expansion," writes Eric Williams, "is a necessity of slave societies."[13] For a while the ever-receding West or frontier supplied the institution with the vitally needed room for expansion. But what was to happen when the available room was exhausted? The South knew that without ever-newer fertile land the system would have become economically impractical, and its aggressive expansionism frightened the North into believing that the house-divided was in danger of becoming considerably less than half-free.

Still in another way the passing of the frontier spelled doom for slavery. Walter Webb points out that with the passing of the frontier must come a renunciation of the profit motive. He states that the masses in Europe and America already have been forced to renounce the freedom they once owned to use their tools and labor directly for profit, and that the corporation is the last great stronghold of the capitalistic ethos. The corporation too, he believes, must surrender the profit motive in favor of what John Dewey called a "shared culture," or some form of socialism.[16] Inasmuch as chattel slavery existed primarily as a capitalistic profit - making enterprise, this trend toward a non-profit shared culture may be said to have doomed slavery.

Too, the frontier doomed slavery by dictating that ours would be a highly fluid society. Geoffrey Barraclough has declared: "The open spaces, the moving frontier, the flow of population, stood in the way of the formation of stable social and regional groups."[17] In another place Barraclough points to yet another trend into which slavery could not fit. "The conquest of the frontier," he writes, "for good or for evil, has made the whole world one."[18] One might add that as this trend doomed slavery, many contemporary events indicate a comparable fate for all programs of racial discrimination.

Of the many tremendously important changes evident when the pre-1939 world is compared with that of post-1945, Barraclough singles out the most "overshadowing" of "all else" to be "the starting change in relations between the white and the coloured races." "May it not be," he concludes, "that, in a couple of centuries, the war of 1939-45 will appear not as the last in a long succession of successful struggles to prevent a European hegemony, but rather as the decisive conflict in which Europe . . . surrendered mastery to the coloured peoples?"[19] If there can be validity in this viewpoint, might it not also be valid to consider the emancipation of slaves in the American Civil War of 1861-65 as but one of the steps by which the hegemony of the white race was transferred to that of the colored? At least emancipation from slavery and colonialism were pre-conditions for the possibility which Barraclough raises.

The Frontier and the South

In view of the above-stated position relative to the potency of frontier-derived anti-slavery factors, the question may well be raised as to why they seem to have had so little effect on the South. While it is true that the most conspicuous manner in which these forces hit the South was indirectly, through the North as an instrument, they had considerable direct influences. As Wilbur J. Cash has shown,[20] the ante-bellum South itself was largely a frontier. Thus, from within and without frontier forces beat upon the section, and in both instances they were often frustrated by the southerners' dogged determination to hold time still and maintain a static culture. Leaders of the section were convinced that they had achieved Plato's republic, Imperial Rome, and the Middle Ages of Sir Walter Scott all rolled into one, and it took the ruthless will and might of a section almost completely moved by the frontier impulse to force the South to give up the past and live in a present which was, to a very large extent, a one-sided creation of a one-sided frontier. Yet, as stated, even while it was consciously resisting aspects of the frontier impulse, unconsciously the South was accepting and adopting many other of its aspects. Here is a source of some of the paradoxes which have been so persistent in southern life.

Because of the existence of one or more powerful institutions which hold antipathy to a new on-rushing force, the effect of the latter may be slowed, if not negated altogether. In the United States the frontier impetus was only slowed and modified by the medieval way of life of the ante-bellum South, but in Latin America, even to the present day, aspects of this way of life practically negate much of the frontier impetus. A similar case is seen in the Russia of 1100-1800 A.D. where, partly through the influence of a church which had grown hostile toward the pretensions and practices of Roman Catho-licism, the nation successfully beat back waves emanating from the Renaissance, Reformation, and Enlightenment. Even more ancient is the case of Greece and Rome. After the seventh and sixth century B.C. colonization, a strong frontier impulse came resounding back upon Greek life and thought. The same is true of Rome following her conquest of Carthage and the remainder of the Mediterranean world. Yet so firmly was slavery en-trenched in these societies that in neither instance was the frontier impetus sufficient to dislodge it.

In the South the equalitarian urge bred by plentiful op-portunity actually helped to fasten slavery more firmly on the section. Enterprising lower and middle class persons came to feel that the number of acres and slaves possessed constituted a mark of distinction, and, wanting to be equal to the top "aristocrats" in their area and those of the Tidewater region, these persons sometimes began with a few acres and slaves and in fifteen or twenty years were great planters and slave-owners. Ironically, it was their desire and opportunity to rise in the economic and social scale—a democratic phenomenon—which caused the incubus of slavery—an undemocratic phenomenon—to grow to gigantic proportions.

The Frontier and the Slave

Just as it affected slavery through the mental and institu-tional forms which it birthed in white America, the frontier also had a profound impact on the mind of the slaves them-selves. The frontier helped mould the slaves into a force which contributed significantly to the demise of the institution which long held them in a vise-like grip. Here another problem is encountered, for a major difficulty in considering the southern frontier is that in the eighteenth and nineteenth centuries it was never isolated enough for the indigenous elements of the culture to develop in anything like a pure form. Thus, to ele-ments in the mind of the slave which had their source in the South, there was constantly being added those acquired from the North and Toussaint L'Ouverture's Santo Domingo constantly beat upon the mind of the slave, ever modifying and altering it. Two streams, one liberal and the other conservative, met in the mind of the slave. Here is one source of many subsequent paradoxes in Negro thought and behavior.

There can be little doubt that midst his misery and degradation, the bondsman caught the hope and optimism which the nation's great economic boom and opportunities for the individual afforded. For too long only the pessimistic and other-worldly aspects of slave thought have been emphasized. However, the spirituals show pessimism and optimism, and mundane matters and materialistic considerations often dominated slave thought just as they did that of white America.[21] Although they had their moments of doubt and despair, the pre-Civil War thought of Frederick Douglass, William Wells Brown, James W. C. Pennington and others of the Negro Abolitionist group was often optimistic. Later Booker Washington would epitomize this optimism, even while telling the members of his race that they should fight on fronts other than the political and civil rights ones.[22]

Like the rest of America, and especially the white southerner, the Negro received much of his love of freedom, egalitarianism, boisterousness, disdain for things intellectual and cultural, combative proclivity and love of violence, individualism, garrulousness, and contempt for thrift from the frontier. Also for substantially the same reasons, the same religious denominations which found the frontier especially fertile soil also found great favor with the slave. As is well known, these were largely the Baptist and Methodist denominations.

The fluidity and dynamic character which the frontier imparted caused the slave to see that little in American society remained long unchanged. His awareness of this, plus abolitionist sentiments and activities here and abroad, caused the bondsman to sing—"I'm so glad, trouble don't last always," and "Stand the storm, it won't be long, we'll anchor by and by." Proof that this optimism was sometimes very impatient is seen in the well-known actions of Gabriel Prosser, Nat Turner, Denmark Vesey, and the significant host whose story is told so well in Aptheker's *Negro Slave Revolts*. Thus it may

be seen that the frontier worked through the slave, black abolitionists, and black troops of 1862-65 to help pull down the
nefarious institution.

The Frontier and the North

By 1861 the North had become completely a frontier creation. The will of the frontier was thus the will of the North,
and through this instrument slavery and the whole static and
archaic southern way of life were brought to their end. Capitalism, industrialism, immigration, the gospel of work and the
profit motive, equalitarianism, initiative, self-reliance, industry,
all of these reached their high point of development in the
North.

To the view that the frontier impetus created desires, institutions, and a state of mind in America which doomed
slavery, the objection can be raised that neither in the North
or South did a majority favor abolition. But majorities almost
never decide the course of history. Of one significant minority,
Peter Geyl states: "The accusation of the Abolitionists was such
a painful hit because in it there spoke the spirit of the times."[23]
On this, Geyl continues:

> Behind that little group of fanatics there stood the
> silent condemnation of the free North, of Europe, of
> the world. By clinging to its 'peculiar institution' the
> South cut itself adrift from the modern development
> of Western civilization, isolated itself in an obstinate
> and wilful self-righteousness, and fell under the spell
> of its wildest, blindest, and most reactionary ele-
> ments.[24]

Thus it is that Yankeedom was a willing mistress to her frontier
suitor and adopted so many of this impulsive lover's thoughts
and ways that they came to see eye-to-eye and ceased for a
time to quarrel. Not until the furthermost extent of that virgin
land farther and farther Westward had been reached did the
West-Northeast marriage of 1830-1865 show clear signs of
being headed for the divorce court. And the fact that the North
"went frontier whole-hog," adopting frontier greed, narrow-
mindedness, often-reckless individualism, and contempt for
things cultural gave the South a valid reason for her refusal
to be seduced by Yankee wiles.

CHAPTER II

AFRICA IN THE THOUGHT OF
NEGRO AMERICANS

The continent of Africa is daily growing in economic, political, and cultural significance. In the late 1950s a Negro newspaper in St. Louis, Missouri contained the statement that the newly independent state of Ghana holds significance for Negro Americans which is comparable to that which Israel holds for Jewish Americans. How much truth is there in such a statement? Or better still, what does Africa and its history mean to American Negroes? Opinions on this vary greatly, for in an opposite vein from that contained in the St. Louis newspaper, the most eminent of all Negro Sociologists stated that most educated Negroes have little but contempt and disdain for Africa and its peoples. This sociologist, Professor E. Franklin Frazier, wrote:

> The black bourgeoisie have shown no interest in the 'liberation' of Negroes except as it affected their own status or acceptance by the white community. They viewed with scorn the Garvey Movement with its nationalistic aims. They showed practically no interest in the Negro Renaissance. They have attempted to conform to the behavior and values of the white community in the most minute details.[1]

When the Negro press shows an interest in Africa, Professor Frazier avers, this interest is limited to the social life and other activities of the educated elite in the African states, hence, does not extend to the masses of Africans. Writing one year earlier than Professor Frazier, Margaret Just Butcher apparently agreed with Donald Young that "the ordinary Negro knows little or cares less about African ways of life."[2]

What is the truth between these two rather extreme views? While the following does not give a categorical answer to this question, such a survey of the statements which Afro-Americans have made from time to time respecting that continent and its peoples may shed light on the question.

15

Those millions of slaves who were brought to America from Africa would have been less than human if they had not experienced intense grief and heart-rending desire to return to their homes and kindred. Doubtless, for most, the passing years diminished both the grief and desire, and many took their new land and its people to heart.

Phillis Wheatley and Benjamin Banneker are perhaps the best known of all Negroes who lived during this nation's Colonial Period. Although both have been criticised by Afro-Americans for a seeming lack of interest in their race and in Africa, more recently an effort has been made to show that they were race conscious and militantly interested in the cause of their group's advancement. In this connection it is now claimed that in 1789 Banneker authored a militant treatise under the pseudonym of "Othello." Also, it is known that in 1791 Banneker wrote a lengthy letter to Thomas Jefferson which was militantly anti-slavery. Some persons believe that this letter helped mould Jefferson's liberalism on the slavery issue.[3]

In a letter dated May 19, 1772, Phillis Wheatley expressed thanks to God for bringing her to America. She wrote: "Let us rejoice in and adore the wonders of God's infinite love in bringing us from a land semblant of darkness itself, and where the divine light of revelation (being obscured) is in darkness. Here the knowledge of the True God and eternal life are made manifest; but there profound ignorance overshadows the land."[4] Showing that she accepted the current myths regarding her race, she commented; "Your observation is true, namely, that there was nothing in us to recommend us to God."[5] Arthur P. Davis is among those who have refuted the contention that Miss Wheatley was completely estranged from Negro culture and consciousness. Davis has shown that at times she was quite race conscious. Like many Negroes in America, Miss Wheatley felt that education was the phoenix of her race. She wrote in her poem, "On Being Brought from Africa to America"—"Remember, Christians, Negroes black as Cain, May be refined, and join the Angelic train."[6] Her poem entitled, "To the Right Honorable William Earl of Dartmouth," Davis calls her "strongest and most forthright utterance on slavery." Here Miss Wheatley referred briefly to Africa. She wrote:

> Should you my Lord, while you peruse my song,
> Wonder from whence my love of freedom sprung,
> Whence flow these wishes for the common good,
> By feeling hearts alone best understood,
> I, young in life, by seeming cruel fate
> Was snatched from Africa's fancied happy seat;
> What pangs excruciating must molest,
> What sorrows labor in parent's breast! . .. .
> Such, such my case. And can I then but pray
> Others may never feel tyrannic Sway?

"She writes upon two levels," Davis informs us. "As a little African girl it was cruel to be snatched from her parents, but to find Christ as a result of this misfortune was more than ample compensation for this "seeming cruel fate!" "She is definitely race conscious in her writings," Davis concludes.[7]

During the long slavery era Negroes often compared their bondage in the United States with that of the ancient Hebrews in, Egypt and Babylonia. In his famous *Appeal*, David Walker made this allusion and urged that Negro leaders should be of the disposition of Moses in their resistance to slavery. Both Nat Turner and Denmark Vesey were inspired by the slavery of the Hebrews and the leadership of Moses.

AFRICAN SURVIVALS

Considerable controversy has arisen over the extent to which the thought and actions of Afro-Americans constitute persistence of African traits. Perhaps in this controversy may be seen evidence of attitudes held by Negro Americans toward Africa and the African. In his book *Africanisms and The Gullah Dialect*, Professor Lorenzo Dow Turner has emphasized that Africanisms may be seen in numerous words which survived and have become a part of the American language. Turner indicates that a number of African habits, as dances, chants, and shouts also remain,[8] while Margaret Just Butcher feels that African rhythm was one of the most significant survivals.[9] In his book *Negro Slave Songs in the United States*,[10]

Miles Mark Fisher interprets the slave songs in terms of African survivals. With Melville Herskovits and R. A. Park, Fisher believes that much of the culture of Africa, which he terms "Oriental," persists among Afro-Americans. Though he attempts no clear-cut definition of this African culture, Fisher makes it plain that he considers the following as being African traits: (a) the wearing of elaborate dress for worship, (b) secret meetings held by slaves, (c) sporadic violence, (d) singing for almost all occasions, (e) a materialistic outlook on life, (f) polygamous practices, (g) "shouting" in church, and (h) belief in reincarnation. The author variously refers to these traits as "Africanisms" or as comprising an "African cult." Again and again he writes of "the traditional Orientalism of Africans," or "an Oriental race living under Occidental slavery." Fisher believes that the American Negro's religion always has been Mohammedanism with a thin veneer of Christianity. Among his many statements in this vein are:

> "Negroes expressed strong desires to be reincarnated in Africa." (p. 144)
> "Christianity rarely occurred as an element in antebellum Spirituals . . . . The characters mentioned in slave songs were to be sure, oriental." (p. 108)
> "Not one spiritual in its primary form reflected interest in anything other than full life here and now." (p. 137)

Indicative of the disagreement here is the contrary judgement of Benjamin Mays, another outstanding student of the religious thought of Negro Americans. In his *The Negro's God* Mays has declared:

> "The majority of the spirituals were compensatory and other-worldly." (pp. 24, 28)
> "The Negroes' ideas of God are those of traditional Christianity, but they are the most lofty of the traditional ideas." (p. 126)

E. Franklin Frazier is numbered among the scholars who deny that there are significant African survivals among Negro Americans.[11] "Most antebellum slaves," states Kenneth Stampp, "showed a desire to forget their African past and to embrace as much of white civilization as they could."[12] Stampp recounts the experience of a Tennesseeian who tried to teach slaves an African dance which he knew. The Tennesseean found that the slaves "felt insulted by the insinuation which his effort conveyed."[13] Also, when slaves newly-brought from Africa were placed in groups which had been in this country for quite some time, the new slaves were laughed at because of their awkward foreign speech and ways of acting. Thus it can be seen that even during the days of bondage, Negroes were beginning to feel superior to their ancestors in Africa.

Among the slaves, belief in such things as good luck charms, voodoo spells, and quick and fanciful cures for diseases were widespread. To many observers, the long and persistent belief of many Negroes in voodooism and other superstitions is proof of the continuation of a strong African heritage, however, what seems to be peculiarly African in these superstitions is often naught but the general, common, world-wide folk-belief pattern of all cultures. Stampp further concludes:

> How substantial and how durable the African heritage was is a question over which students of the American Negro have long disagreed. But the disagreement has been over the size of what was admittedly a fragment; few would deny that by the end of the antebellum period slaves everywhere in the South had lost most of their African culture.[14]

Despite the unsettled nature of this controversy, the bulk of evidence and opinion seems to indicate that Negroes in this country are today thoroughly Americanized. So much is this the case that many resent any discussion of Africa as their homeland, and are ashamed of their slavery-dominated past and want to forget it. Although there are other explanations for these phenomena, some Afro-Americans probably deny African survivals in their thought and behavior because they do not want either a cultural or biological connection with Africa. Alain Locke has pointed out that acceptance by Negroes of many strong African survivals, by giving the impression of non-assimilability of the race, would probably increase prejudice between the races in America.[15] After studying the relations of the Negro with the Communist Party, Wilson Record concluded: "The Negro has shown that he is an American in the most fundamental sense."[16]

THE COLONIZATION SOCIETY

In the early decades of the nineteenth century, the work of the American Colonization Society and the founding of Liberia projected Africa into the thought of Negroes in America as never before. In the 1820's and 30's the colonization question was *a dominant issue in the minds of free Negroes and slaves alike.* Through an analysis of the slave songs, Miles Fisher shows that many slaves became possessed by the dream and hope of being freed and sent to Africa. He believes that many spirituals which seem to indicate this dream and hope through references to ships, captains, and sailing were composed during this period. Among these were "Old Ship of Zion," "My Ship is on the Ocean," "Roll Jordan Roll," "Fare You Well," "Don't Stay Away," "Jesus is My Captain," and "I Ask My Lord Will I Ever be the One."

But if the slave regarded expatriation to Africa as a welcome eventuality, the majority of free Negroes, many of whom were active abolitionists, did not share this attitude. Through mass meetings, orations, petitions, editorials, letters, and other means they remonstrated against the effort to remove them from the United States. Yet the free Negroes revealed ambivalence in their attitude toward Africa. When they were describing the kidnapping of their forebearers from the ancestral home and the horrors of the slave trade, they painted the continent and its people in beautiful glowing terms, but when efforts were made to force free Negroes to "return" to Africa, the overwhelming majority refused to go there and depicted Africa and its people in a quite different light.

As for the beautiful picture of Africa which the Negro abolitionists drew, the direction which their arguments would take may be seen in Benjamin Lundy's 1831 appeal to Americans of color. He exhorted:

> Rouse ye' and show to your traducers, beyond the power of contradiction, that the African bosom yet glows with the generous emulation that erst nourished

the arts and sciences to maturity in Ethiopa and
Egypt . . . while Asia made less pretensions to knowledge and moral grandeur, Europe was in barbarism
and America was unknown to the civilized world.[17]

Throughout the course of American history, Negro historians constantly have pointed with pride to the black king-
doms with high cultures which existed in Africa during the
eleventh, twelfth and thirteenth centuries when European
civilization was at a low ebb. A number of the nineteenth
century Negro historians sought to show that several outstanding ancient Greeks and Romans were of African ancestry.[18]

The first Negro newspaper in the United States, John B.
Russwurm's *Freedom's Journal,* stated in its initial editorial—
"Useful knowledge of every kind and everything that relates
to Africa, shall find a ready admission into our columns." This
editorial contained the author's belief that the African had a
history worthy of high commendation.[19] In a speech delivered
January 1, 1808, after describing the horrors of the slave trade,
Reverend Peter Williams, Jr., of New York City cried out:

Oh, Africa, Africa! to what horrid inhumanities have
thy shores been witness; thy shores, which were once
the garden of the world, the seat of almost paradisa-
ical joys, have been transformed into regions of woe;
thy sons who were once the happiest of mortals, are
reduced to slavery, and bound in weighty shackles,
now fill the traders ship.[20]

At another point Williams declared:

Before the enterprising spirit of European genius ex-
plored the western coast of Africa, the state of our
forefathers was a state of simplicity, innocence, and
contentment. Unskilled in the arts of dissimulation,
their bosoms were the seats of confidence; and their
lips were the organs of truth. Strangers to the refine-
ments of civilized society, they followed with implicit
obedience the (simple) dictates of nature. Peculiarly
observant of hospitality, they offered a place of refreshment to the weary and an asylum to the unfortunate. Ardent in their affections, their minds were

susceptible of the warmest emotions of love, friendship, and gratitude.[21]

Years later, in a Commencement Address at Paine College,
Augusta, Georgia, Bishop R. A. Carter voiced similar feelings
about Africa, and contended with those who would deny the
Afro-American's kinship with that continent. Bishop Carter
declared in 1923:

> Since the discoveries of the former greatness of the
> ancient Egyptians and Ethiopians, it has suddenly
> been discovered that they were not Negroes. . . .
> The Negro has been called 'Sons of Ham,' 'African,'
> and Ethiopian in scornful derision for all these years
> and it is too late to try to make him somthing else
> when it is discovered that these designations link him
> with the greatest civilizations of the past. As Negroes,
> therefore, we claim kinship with the Ancient Ethio-
> pians, and all colored races, and share the greatness
> and glory of their achievements and history.[22]

As earlier indicated, however, at other times the Afro-
American has thought of Africa and its people in less commendable terms, and has tended to look down on them as wild,
barbarous pagans who were sorely in need of the blessings of
Western civilization. At such times, the Negro Americans'
attitude has come close to that which Rudyard Kipling expressed in his epic poem, "White Man's Burden." When offered
the chance of returning to Africa by the American Colonization
Society, free Negroes in Philadelphia stated in January, 1817:
"That without arts, without science, without a proper knowledge of Government, to cast into the savage wilds of Africa
the free people of color, seems to us the circuitous route
through which they must return to perpetual bondage."[23] This
attitude was typical as free Negroes throughout the North
used annual conventions, petitions, forum, and editorials in a
vigorous opposition to the colonization movement.[24] While
praising Negro progress in a 1905 address, another Bishop gave
his quite different impression of the ancestral home of his racial
group. He declared:

> Remembering the sacrifice of benefactors whose mem-
> ory is embalmed in history's urn, we mark the vast

step from savagery of ancestor to the prdouct of the school today. From chattering jargon and fetish adoration on native heath four centuries ago, we rung by rung have come to poets, painters, scholars, of aesthetic tastes and a reverence for the Christian's God.[25]

Even in the antebellum period, Afro-Americans evidenced a desire to help lift Africa to a greater respectability through extending Christianity to the continent. In his 1827 address on the occasion of New York's emancipation of slaves, the Reverend Nathaniel Paul hoped that his race might yet produce "one whose devotedness toward the cause of God, and whose zeal shall cause him to leave the land which gave him birth, and cross the Atlantic, eager to plant the standard of the cross upon every hill of that vast continent, that has hitherto ignobly submitted to the baleful crescent, or crouched under the iron bondage of the vilest superstition."[26] In 1867, J. Sella Martin stated:

> A civilized and converted population of Africans in America means the civilization, in no very distant day, of Africa itself. England and France spend every year their millions to maintain squadrons on the coast of Africa, but the slave-trade still goes on. The whole civilized world has sent missionaries to Christianize the Africans, and but little headway has been made in the work, because of the deadly nature of the climate to the white. But if our labors are aided as they ought to be, by the good people of every country, we shall send educated Christian coloured men from America proof against the deadly diseases of the climate, possessing a claim to the confidence of the natives in sameness of complexion, and carrying the principles of truth against those of error to an ardent-natured people, with natures of their own as ardent to dry up the fountain head of the slave-trade, and to stop the stream for ever, and to attack superstition with the strongest weapon next to truth itself—the ability to live where it prevails, and to command the confidence and sympathy of the natives.[27]

Previous to W. E. B. DuBois, George Washington Williams was the most distinguished of all Negro historians. Together with the Colored abolitionists and most Negro historians of the nineteenth century, Williams accepted many of the then-current stereotypes about his race.[28] However, Williams and others tended to assign to Afro-Americans only the stereotypes which were favorable, and to leave the remainder for Negroes who were still in Africa. Thus Williams said of the colored soldiers in the Civil War that: "Endowed by nature with a poetic element, faithful to trusts, abiding in friendships, bound by the golden threads of attachment to places and persons, enthusiastic in personal endeavor, sentimental and chivalric, they made hardy and intrepid soldiers." But of the African, he declared:

> The Negro type is the result of degradation. It is nothing more than the lowest strata of the African race. . . . His blood infected with the poison of his low habitation, his body shrivelled by disease, his intellect veiled in pagan superstitions, the noblest yearnings of his soul strangled at birth by the savage passions of a nature abandoned to sensuality, the poor Negro of Africa deserves more our pity than our contempt.[20]

Support by planters of the American Colonization Society's founding and efforts was not the first indication that they regarded free Negroes as a menace to their human property. Even before the founding of this organization in 1816, several states passed laws restricting the growth of the class. In some places, laws specifically proscribed manumission or the allowing of slaves to work for wages.[30] Many forces had combined to produce the colonization movement. The humanitarian sentiments unleased by the Revolutionary period caused a wave of abolitionism to sweep the nation from which even the South was not exempt. In the North, farms could be operated successfully around family size units, and commerce and industry were dominant activities. Gabriel's plot of 1800 and other evidences of interracial antagonism and violence in the South convinced many northerners that they did not wish to fasten this incubus more securely around their necks.

With the conviction that the United States was their only and proper home, most free Negroes opposed and fought this organization. A few, however, because they agreed with the philosophy and program of the society, supported it and emigrated.[31] From its inception in the second decade of the 19th century to its demise in the 1850's, the American Colonization Society transported over one hundred boat loads or approximately 12,000 Negroes to Liberia, mostly southern free persons. This considerable activity caused a great deal of hope to spread among the slaves that here at last was God's way of delivering them. It is not difficult to believe that most slaves desired colonization even at the North or South Pole over remaining in bondage.

When the Colonization Society was scarcely a year old, and long before the leading white abolitionists turned from acceptance to rejection of colonization, approximately three thousand free Negroes met in Philadelphia and vigorously denounced the colonization proposals. These free Negroes, led by such distinguished personages as James Parker and Richard Allen, were especially suspicious of the many slave owners who were loud in their support of the society.

At a January 24, 1817 meeting in Richmond, Virginia, some free Negroes said:

> We perfectly agree with the American Colonization Society that it is not only proper, but would ultimately tend to the benefit and advantage of a great portion of our suffering fellow creatures, to be colonized; but while we thus express our approbation of a measure laudable in its purposes, and beneficial in its designs, it may not be improper in us to say, that we prefer being colonized in the most remote corner of the land of our nativity, to being exiled to a foreign country.[32]

Also at a January, 1817 Philadelphia meeting devoted to the colonization question, the free Negroes noted: "Whereas our ancestors (not of choice were the first successful cultivators of the wilds of America), we their descendants feel ourselves entitled to participate in the blessings of her luxuriant soil, which their blood and sweat manured; and that any measure or system of measures, having a tendency to banish us from her bosom, would . . . be in direct violation of those principles, which have been the boast of the republic."[33] The persistent desire of the Negro to remain in this country is one more proof that he was early Westernized and Americanized. If Miles Fisher were right in his thesis that the Negro's culture remains to this day strongly African, one could expect a more favorable response to colonization schemes than has been the case. Yet most bondsmen saw little hope of an early end to slavery, and they did not regard themselves as American citizens as free Negroes did. Thus, unlike the masses of free persons slaves were willing to accept colonization as a worthy alternative to bondage. Before the rise of the colonization movement, and no doubt long afterward, in slave songs such words as "Heaven," "Zion," "Home," often referred to the North or to Africa.[34]

The Vesey plot of 1822 and the Nat Turner revolt of 1831 intensified the white South's fears of free Negroes and increased the activity to either force them out of the South or out of the nation. As they began to flee the South, the North raised barriers to them. Of the colonization proposal, James Forten said for free Negroes: "We have no wish to separate from our present homes, for any purpose whatever."[35] Speaking for the slaves, Forten again opposed this idea. On this he said:

> If this plan of colonization now proposed is intended to provide refuge and a dwelling for a portion of our brethren, who are now held in slavery in the South, we have other and stronger objections to it, and we entreat your consideration of them.
> The ultimate and final abolition of slavery in the United States is, under the guidance and protection of a just God, progressing. Every year witnesses the release of numbers of the victims of oppression, and affords new and safe assurances that the freedom of all will in the end be accomplished.[36]

Negroes felt betrayed and alone now that even some of their former friends wanted to take away their homes and property and be rid of them. They felt that in the colonization move-

ment their white friends were now working with the slave-
holders. The Rev. Theodore S. Wright of New York City
declared before the New York State abolition society in 1837
that it had become difficult to identify a true abolitionist any
more. There was one test which still stood, however, he declared. On this, he opined:

> Unless men come out and take their stand on the
> principle of recognizing man as man, I tremble for
> the ark, and I fear our society will become like the
> expatriation society; everybody an abolitionist....
> The identity of the human family, the principle of
> recognizing all men as brethren—that is the doctrine,
> that is the point which touches the quick of the
> community. It is an easy thing to ask about the vile-
> ness of slavery at the South, but to call the dark
> man a brother, heartily to embrace the doctrine ad-
> vanced in their moral worth, to treat the man of color
> in all circumstances as a man and brother—that is
> the test.[38]

The speaker stated that several colonization societies needed
to catechize new members on this point and to revise their
constitutions to take cognizance of it. "Abolitionists must
annihilate in their own bosoms the cord of caste," he declared.

In an 1862 speech before the Massachusetts Anti-Slavery
Society, Dr. John S. Rock, noted abolitionist, castigated the
efforts of northern whites to colonize his race outside the
United States. He stated that the Afro-American was more
afraid of the northern white men than of the slaveholder because the latter's motivation was simple and easily understood.
Rock continued:

> The Northern pro-slavery men have done the free
> people of color ten-fold more injury than the Southern
> slave-holders. . . . In the South, it is simply a ques-
> tion of dollars and cents. The slave holder cares no
> more for you than he does for me. They enslave their
> own children, and sell them, and they would as soon
> enslave white men as black men. The secret of the
> slave-holders attachment to slavery is to be found in
> the dollar. There is no prejudice against color among
> the slave-holders. Their social system and one million

of mulattoes are facts which no arguments can demolish. They [slave holders] believe in their institution because it supports them.[39]

The first of the annual Conventions of Afro-Americans was held September 20, 1830, at Bethel Church, in Philadelphia and was attended by many outstanding free Negroes of the day, including James Cornish, Junius C. Morel, Benjamin Paschall, and Richard Allen. The second Negro Convention, headed by Henry Sipkins and Philip A. Bell, met in Philadelphia, June 4-13, 1832. In attendance were 29 delegates from 8 states, with Maryland the only southern state represented. The convention resolved to raise money for refugees in Canada, to form temperance societies, to boycott slave-made products, to petition state and national legislatures against slavery and discrimination, to employ a Negro lecturer on the question of Negro rights, and to continue the efforts for an industrial school. It arranged and heard a debate on colonization between William Lloyd Garrison and the Reverend R. R. Gurley, Secretary of the American Colonization Society, as a result of which was reaffirmed their opposition to emigration schemes. Forten held that a Negro colony in Africa would fail because the ex-slaves would be ignorant and untutored. Too, he felt that to allow some bondsmen to go to Africa would fasten slavery more securely on the remainder whose reduced numbers would be less dangerous to the owners, and only the non-militant slaves would remain in slavery. Thus, he believed that the colonization schemes would prolong the life of what he felt was already a dying institution. But it was August 10, 1817 that Forten uttered these optimistic sentiments, which the rise of the cotton kingdom would soon kill.

As southern slave owners made much of the benefits of Christianity which they transmitted to the slave, so did the northern free Negroes. Forten felt that colonization in Africa would cut the Negro off from Christianity which would be shut out by the clouds of ignorance. But Forten's chief opposition to colonization was that "it will stay the cause of the entire abolition of slavery in the United States, . . . and may defeat it altogether."

In a 4th of July address in New York in 1830, Peter

Williams declared that the prejudice - inspired colonization movement was responsible for the waning anti-slavery efforts of white liberals and the declining civil rights of free Negroes in the North. This movement, he declared, aimed at making the United States a white man's country. Throughout the controversy over colonization, free Negroes of the North felt that the white press was either too hostile or too silent. When the Rev. Samuel E. Cornish began his *Freedom's Journal* to give the free Negro a voice, one speaker declared that "it came like a clap of thunder."[37] This same speaker declared that when W. L. Garrison took up the cudgel in defense of the black man, "it was like the voice of an angel of mercy! Hope, hope then cheered our path." After listening to the arguments of the Reverend Gurley in behalf of the societies program, Negroes were more convinced than ever that they should oppose these efforts. Those present vowed "that the doctrines of said society, are at enmity with the principles and precepts of religion, humanity and justice, and should be regarded by every man of color as an evil for magnitude, unexcelled, and whose doctrines aim at the entire extinction of the free colored population and the riveting of Slavery."[40] This remained the unbending sentiment of the overwhelming majority of free persons throughout the history of the colonization society.

Out of a total free population of one-half million persons, by 1865 the colonization movement led to approximately 25,-000 Afro-Americans having emigrated to Africa, the Caribbean, and various Latin American republics. One reason that free Negroes resisted all colonization schemes was that they owned millions of dollars worth of houses and other property in the United States. Though the literature does not indicate how important a factor this was in their resistance to schemes to get them to leave the country, that Afro-Americans were aware of their immediate economic interests is clear.

In his epic *Appeal*, David Walker wrote: "Let no man of us budge one step, . . America is more our country, than it is the white—we have enriched it with our *blood and tears.* The Americans have got so fat on our blood and groans, that they have almost forgotten the God of armies."

From a January 25, 1831 mass meeting in New York,

organized by Samuel Ennals and Philip A. Bell, came, the following statement on colonization—"We are contented to abide
where we are. We do not believe that things will always continue the same. The time must come when the Declaration of
Independence will be felt in the heart, as well as uttered from
the mouth. This is our home, and this is our country. Beneath
its sod lie the bones of our fathers. Here we were born, and
here we will die."[41] The third national Negro Convention met
in Philadelphia in June, 1833. The same eight states as before
were represented. Sixty-two persons attended. The same stand
against colonization was taken as in 1832, and the same interest
in vocational education was voiced. Here Negroes carried the
arguments for colonization to one of their logical extremes.
"If shades of difference in complexion is to operate to make
men the sport of powerful caprice," they asserted, "who can
pretend to determine how long it may be before, on this principle, the colonists may be again compelled to migrate to the
land of their fathers."

During this period one highly nationalistic and chauvinistic group of Afro-Americans who denounced the United
States Constitution as a hopelessly pro-slavery document, favored emigration and colonization of their race in some remote
part of the United States, or in Africa or South America.
Prominent among this group were William P. Quinn of Indiana, Mrs. Mary E. Bibb of Canada, Dr. Martin B. Delany of
Ohio, H. Ford Douglass of Ohio, and William C. Monroe of
Michigan. At an 1854 National Emigration Convention held
by this group at Cleveland, Ohio with 102 delegates present,
H. Ford Douglass stated: "Is not the history of the world, the
history of emigration? The coming in and going out of nations, is a natural and necessary result. . . . Let us then be
up and doing. To stand still is to stagnate and die."

Few indeed are the theoretical works dealing with the
race question, and written by Negroes, prior to the Civil War.
One of the most significant of these is the book, *The Condition,
Elevation, Emigration and Destiny of the Colored People of the
United States Politically Considered,* by Martin R. Delany.[42]
In the appendix of this volume, Delany pointed to the over
four million Negroes who were in this country, and like Fred-

erick Douglass and other colored Americans, he realized that this was a very significant number. He called for a national Negro convention to form an emigration association for the purpose of re-settling Negroes in a nation of their own, preferably in Eastern Africa, but perhaps in South America, Mexico, the West Indies, or any other favorable place. He felt that the nations of Europe would seek the trade and friendship of such a black republic. Africa he stated, was rich in minerals and metals. "The land is ours—there it lies with inexhaustible resources; let us go and possess it. In Eastern Africa must rise up a nation, to whom all the world must pay commercial tribute," he declared. We must *make* an *issue, create* an *event, and establish a national position for ourselves* and never may we expect to be respected as men, and women until we have undertaken, some fearless, bold, and adventurous deeds of daring contending against every odd—regardless of every consequence," he concluded. No doubt Delany was influenced in his emigration schemes by the firm control which the Slavocracy seemed then to have over national affairs, but also very probably he was influenced by the nationalistic movements and spirit which swept Europe and the Western World in the wake of the overthrow of the Napoleonic hegemony.

In his 1852 annual message to the New York legislature, Governor Hunt proposed that funds be appropriated to the American Colonization Society. Speaking before the State Convention of Colored Citizens, Reverend James W. C. Pennington attacked the suggestions. Pennington assailed the proposed grant as a violation of the Constitution of New York. The American Colonization Society he called "a gigantic fraud . . . a moulder of, and a profiter by a diseased public opinion, [which] keeps alive an army of agents who live by plundering us of our good name."[48] Finally, he stated that he was against the proposed appropriation because free Negroes of New York could never forsake those of their race still in bondage in the United States. "May evil betide us," he asserted, "when the hope of gain, of the fear of oppression, shall compel or persuade us to forsake them to the rayless good of perpetual slavery."

Negro leaders seemed more willing to view with favor

colonization to countries in the Western hemisphere than to Africa. Particularly, did some of them, of whom Martin Delany was one of the most prominent, view with favor the idea of colonization in Canada, the Caribbean, and Central and South America. Several religious leaders, among whom were Lott Cary and Daniel A. Payne, were friendly toward the move to colonize Negroes in Africa because they believed the race had a duty to carry Christianity to that continent.

In his 4th of July, 1830 address against colonization to Africa, Rev. Peter, Williams of New York City urged his listeners to support the effort to build up a strong Negro community in Canada just in case economic, legislative, and other pressure should force free Negroes out of the United States as he felt already was being done in Cincinnati, Ohio, New Orleans, Louisiana, and other places. He asked that his listeners contribute the money which they normally would spend in celebration of the 4th of July to this cause. Years later, in 1957, the Negro Mardi Gras clubs of New Orleans would be asked to forget their annual balls and dances in order that this money might be contributed to the NAACP's fight for equality of citizenship.

With the overthrow of slavery in the fire of Civil War, the American Negro soon found, for various reasons, he was scarcely more than half-free. In the 1870's and 80's two ways that the Negro reacted against the Klu Klux Klan and other violence and repressions incident to the restoration of native white rule of the South were by emigrating to the North and West in considerable numbers, and by talk of "returning" to Africa. In 1886 the African Emigration Association petitioned Congress for funds to aid any colored Americans who desired to go to Africa, and settle. The petition stated that sixteen thousand persons already had gone to Africa and that there were thousands more who desired to go there and erect a "United States in Africa," modeled after the United States of America. One reason for desiring this emigration, stated the petitioners, was "for the perpetuity of our race, which is here losing its identity by inter-mixture with the white races."[44]

In December, 1895, Bishop Henry M. Turner, a staunch and long-time advocate of emigration, stated:

I believe that the Negro . . . has been free long enough now to begin to think for himself and plan for better conditions than he can lay claim to in this country or ever will. There is no manhood future in the United States for the Negro . . . I believe that two or three million of us should return to the land of our ancestors, and establish our own nation, civilization, laws, customs, styles of manufacture, and not only give the world . . . the benefit of our individuality, but build up social conditions peculiarly our own, and cease to be grumblers, chronic complainers and a menace to the white man's country or the country he claims and is bound to dominate.[45]

As earlier indicated, the Negro American's attitude toward the so-called Negro type is indicative of his attitude toward Africa and Africans. Although Africans vary greatly in physical type, the Afro-American's contempt for a dark skin, thick lips, flattened nose, and frizzled hair at times may reveal contempt for the African. When, around the turn of the century, the dialect poetry of Paul Lawrence Dunbar and James Weldon Johnson became popular, some educated Negroes objected to this emphasis on folk expression as degrading. They similarly demanded and got much of the dialect removed from the Negro spirituals.[46]

After the brief flurry of talk in the 1880's and 90's about emigration to Africa, and a mild protest against late nineteenth century imperialism, Afro-American interest in the so-called "Dark Continent" appears to have subsided until the 1920's, when, coincident with the Harlem Negro Renaissance, interest in Africa burgeoned anew. W. E. B. DuBois led in the sponsorship of meetings designed to bring Negroid peoples closer together. The first Pan-African Congress, held in Paris in 1919, resulted when DuBois was sent to Europe by the National Association for the Advancement of Colored People to investigate the treatment of tan G.I.'s. He used this opportunity to organize the Congress, which was attended by fifty-seven delegates from the United States of America, the West Indies, and Africa. Racial concord and advancement were the primary objectives. In 1921 a second Pan-African Congress was held which drew 113 delegates to Europe, two years later a third was held, the fourth Congress met in New York City in 1927, and the fifth met in Manchester, England in 1945.[47] American Negroes showed little interest in Pan-Americanism.

In art and literature, the new interest in the Negro and Africa was part of a larger primitivist movement of the 1920's. This movement partly reflected the frustration of the "Lost Generation," partly the growing interest in anthropological and archeological studies, and partly the movement toward naturalism in art and literature which began around 1912. Among others, these interests could be seen in such diverse media as the writings of the Europeans Jean Cocteau, Blaise Cendrars, and Guilliame Apollinaire; the Americans Waldo Frank, Eugene O'Neill, Carl Van Vechten, Vachel Lindsay, DuBose Heywood, and Howard Odum; the paintings of such renowned figures as Matisse and Picasso; and the music of Milhaud and Honneger. These movements also saw, for the first time, a keen interest in Negro Art and sculpture. The Negro's new-found appreciation for things African, was reflected in a race consciousness which now tended to be based more on pride and less on shame, and once more Negroes depicted Africa in glowing terms. One of the leading writers of the Harlem Renaissance, Claude McKay, wrote a sonnet entitled "Africa," in which he said of this continent:

> The Sun sought thy dim bed and brought forth light,
> The sciences were sucklings at thy breast;
> When all the world was young in pregnant night
> Thy slaves toiled at their monumental best.
> Thou ancient treasure land, thou modern prize,
> New peoples marvel at thy pyramids!
> The years roll on, thy sphinx of riddle-eyes
> Watches the mad world with immobile lids.

Yet when one of his patrons in this period wanted Langston Hughes to concentrate on the African theme in his writings, he refused to do so. Of this experience, Hughes observed

> She wanted me to be primitive and know and feel the
> intuitions of the primitive. But unfortunately I did
> not feel the rhythms of the primitive surging through

me, and so, I could not live and write as though I did. I was only an American Negro—who loved the surface of Africa—but I was not African. I was Chicago and Kansas City and Broadway and Harlem.[48]

Few Negro poets of the twenties would write of Africa in a more nostalgic and romantic vein than Arna Bontemps.[49] Bontemps poems paint beautiful images of African drums, rivers, jungles, tropical nights, desert palms, rainfalls, and romantic images of the Afro-American's black ancestry before the ravages of the slave trade.

In the twenties Negro historians also showed a keen interest in Africa. In his little volume entitled _Miseducation of the Negro_, published in 1923, Carter Woodson stated: "The 'educated Negroes' have the attitude of contempt toward their own people because in their own as well as in their mixed schools Negroes are taught to admire the Hebrew, the Greek, the Latin and the Teuton and despise the African.[50]

While most Afro-Americans have wished to be a part of the mainstream of the national life and culture, not all have wanted this integration. A few, either because they felt that the race actually is inferior and could not compete with whites, or because they went to the opposite extreme and came to believe that Negroes were superior and would lose their distinctive qualities, or for other reasons, have desired continued segregation in some form, either here or abroad. Marcus Garvey belonged to the latter group, and in the late 1950's the Reverend Clennon King, former History Professor at Alcorn College, testified before a Congressional Committee that funds should be made available and American Negroes encouraged to "return to Africa."

The Garvey Movement and Race Consciousness

The Garvey Movement revolved around an organization called the Universal Improvement Association. Centered in the North, though by no means limited to it, this movement had its genesis in the World War I stimulus to the desire of equality. But while it originated out of the desire for a full share in democracy, the movement fed on the lynchings and racial strife which characterized the twenties, color consciousness

among Negroes and on the growing maturity of the race.
Sharing the pessimism and disillusionment, as well as the optimism of the period, Marcus Garvey became convinced that
the position of his race within the United States was eternally
without hope. Thus he advocated a "back to Africa" movement, and in step with the new appreciation which artists and
scholars were beginning to show for African culture, Garvey
created a veritable cult of blackness. Reacting against the contempt for dark complexions which many white and Negro
Americans held, he often attacked mulattoes and proclaimed
that black is actually the best and "superior" color. Since it
coincided with the efforts of Carter Woodson and other scholars
in the social sciences, as well as with the aforementioned trends
in literature, the movement "put steel into the spine of many
Negroes who had previously been ashamed of their color."[51]
Especially did Garveyism appeal to lower class Negroes, and
even yet it represents the nearest semblance to a mass movement which has existed among Afro-Americans. Most Negro
organizations and intellectuals opposed the movement, however.[52] Garvey often spoke of the "Four-hundred Million Negroes" in the world, and set up branches of various organizations in a number of countries which had large Negro populations. Though born in the West Indies, Garvey was distinctly
Negroid in appearance. He had lived in Europe for a while and
came to the United States of America during the World War
I period along with many other West Indians, who later formed
in New York the nucleus for his movement.

Both Garveyism and the Harlem Renaissance were in a
sense results of the urban impact on the peasant folk culture
of the Negro. Though these movements signalled the birth of
the militancy of the Negro folk, they were also dying-gasp
efforts to save the rural-based folk culture which was falling
before the onslaughts of urbanization. The same rural-urban
clash evoked from southern whites the sentiments and convictions of the noted volume, *I'll Take My Stand*. It was ironic
and perhaps even humorous that in the Garvey "Back to
Africa" movement Negro race pride was taking a form that
even the Ku Klux Klan could enthusiastically support. The
Garvey movement was fed also by the great migration of

Negroes, from the South, especially. In Garveyism, together with the Holiness movement in the religion of the period, for the first time since they served as troops during the Civil War, lower class Negroes really flexed their muscles and felt their strength. Garveyism and the Holiness and general sect revolt in religion were counter-parts of the revolt by the Negro intellectuals or middle class which is evidenced in such phenomena as the NAACP, Urban League, Negro History Movement, and the Talented Tenth literary and artistic movement.

Garvey was imprisoned in 1925 for using mails to defraud, and, deported two years later, he died abroad in 1940. How much the almost unanimous rejection of the Garvey movement by the Negro middle class implied a rejection of the race's African heritage is debatable.

Along with Garvey, other Afro-Americans have taken intense pride in their race, and some have even believed that Negroes are "God's chosen people." In a speech made in 1916 R. R. Moton said that members of his race represent "God's most perfect handiwork, and any lack of appreciation on our part is a reflection on the great creator."[53] Benjamin Brawley was one of the most outstanding Afro-American proponents of the notion that "every race has its peculiar genius." This conviction runs through all of his published studies on Negro literature, and was capped in 1937 by his volume entitled *The Negro Genius*.[54] Claude McKay, while often pessimistic in his poems, in one statement expresses a belief that God has set the black man on earth to be a light for true Christianity before the white man destroys himself and civilization. In this vein, McKay asked the lynchers of Negroes in the twenties:

Think you I am not fiend and savage too?
Think you I could not arm me with a gun
And shoot down ten of you for every one
Of my black brothers murdered, burnt by you?
Be not deceived, for every deed you do
I could match-out match; am I not Africa's son.
Black of that black land where black deeds are done?
But the Almighty from the darkness drew
My soul and said: Even thou shall be a light

Awhile to burn on the benighted earth,
The dusky face I set among the white
For thee to prove thyself of highest worth;
To show thy little lamp; go forth, go forth!!

In the sense of true conviction, many Negroes have never consciously accepted the idea that they were inferior innately to Caucasians or any other group. But even these often have accepted the notion that they are innately different. They have believed that members of their race can run faster, sing better, live closer to God, have more patience, and so forth. From the very beginning, however, they have denied that the race is inferior. Many Negroes have accepted some of the white man's stereotypes about the race, often when these stereotypes were favorable and desirable attributes, but also when they were unfavorable. Probably most Afro-Americans have believed that the explanation for their race's shortcoming was environmental and due to lack of opportunity rather than to lack of ability. Many, however, have been aware of lack of effort on the Negro's part as one factor. In the ante-bellum period free persons of color often complained that they could make a more creditable showing if they had the opportunity of being full and equal citizens.[55] "At the bottom of his heart" Robert R. Moton declared, "the Negro believes that he has capabilities of culture and character equal to that of any other race; he believes that his gifts and endowments are of equal worth to those of any other people; and even in the matter of the mingling of racial strains, undesirable it might seem to be from a social point of view, he would never admit that his blood carries any taint of physiological, mental, or spiritual inferiority."[56] In 1842 Charles Lenox Remond, speaking to a legislative committee of the Massachusetts House of Representatives stated: "It is said we all look alike. If this is true, it is not true that we all behave alike. There is a marked difference; and we claim a recognition of this difference."[57]

In his 1843 call to the slaves to rise up and strike for their freedom regardless of the cost, Henry Highland Garnet revealed his intense racial pride and voiced some disgust at the bondsmen. He stated: "you are a patient people. You act as though, you were made for the—

special use of these devils [slave-holders]. You act as though your daughters were born to pamper the lusts of your masters and overseers. And worse than all, you tamely submit while your lords tear your wives from your embraces and defile them before your eyes. In the name of God we ask, are you men? Where is the blood of your fathers? Has it all run out of your veins?

Although the attitude of this nation's majority group sometimes has caused many colored Americans to be ashamed of their dark skins, use bleaching creams, and to be proud when they or their sweethearts or relatives had light complexions, many Afro-Americans have felt that the white man often had an unfair attitude toward race and color. Since these are aspects of an individual's person fixed by God, the Negro has felt that, being all-wise and all-good, God did not intend for color or race to be degrading badges. "Complexion," stated Charles Lenox Remond in 1842, "can in no sense be construed into crime, much less be rightfully made the criterion of rights. Should the people of color, through a revolution of Providence, become a majority, to the last I would oppose it upon the same principle."[58] Negro leaders or spokesmen generally have voiced no shame or regret at having dark skins, rather, they have voiced pride in their color, partly because it was the work of a Benevolent God, and partly because they were aware of the positive contributions of their race to civilization and history.

The 1854 National Emigration Convention of Colored People meeting at Cleveland, Ohio resolved:

That no people, as such can ever attain to greatness who lose their identity, as they must rise entirely upon their own native merits. That we shall ever cherish our identity or origin and race, as preferable, in our estimating, to any other people; That the relative terms Negro, African, Black; Colored and Mulatto, when applied to us, shall ever be held with the same respect and pride; and synonymous with the terms, Caucasian, White, Anglo-Saxon and European, when applied to that class of people.[59]

Not until the twentieth century, with the rise of an edu-

cated group not directly connected with slavery, did a significant number of Negroes show many clear and unmistakable
signs of being ashamed of their race and the desire to discourage use of such terms as Negro, Black, and African. It would
seem that even more than ante-bellum racial propaganda, a
measure of success and progress, plus education acquired
through books written by white Americans imparted to the
Negro race in America considerable contempt for its biological
heritage. Twentieth Century Negroes have shown considerable
evidence of being ashamed of their race; a shame that is, to be
sure, often strongly mixed with pride. They have bleached to
lighten their color, straightened their hair, and sometimes refused to read books on Negro history, or to read so-called
Negro newspapers. In their thoughts and appearances these
individuals try to get as far as possible from identification with
their race. Evidence along this line moved Carter Woodson to
pen the little volume entitled, *The Miseducation of the Negro.*
Still another characteristic of the twentieth century Negro has
been his sometimes bitterness. The nineteenth century Afro-
American reflected less of this particular attitude. Color prejudice and discrimination have made many Afro-Americans
hyper-sensitive, thus, their novelists and historians generally
have steered clear of "anything other than a flattering portrayal
of the race."[60] R. R. Moton wrote in the 1920's that Negroes
were so race conscious that "the strongest appeal to activity
among them is [the] vision and interpretation of the signi-
cance of their endeavors in lessening the disadvantages and removing the handicaps which the whole race suffers in its present
condition."[61] Almost everything," he concluded, "is looked at
by Negroes from this angle."

As previously stated, the race has tended to attribute its
shortcomings primarily to slavery and lack of opportunity.
Commenting on their lack of equal achievement with white
persons of the city of Philadelphia by 1841, one author stated:
"but this is the fault of circumstances—the offspring of exig-
encies which they [Negroes] had no agency in producing—
and which they have never been able to surmount."[62] In 1856
some Ohio Negroes utilized this argument in petitioning for
citizenship rights. "Our want of intelligence is urged as a

reason against our admission to equal citizenship," stated these petitioners. "The assumption that we are ignorant is untrue; but, even if it were true, it really affords an argument for the removal of the disabilities that cramp our energies, destroy that feeling of self respect, so essential to form the character of a good citizen."[63] The first issue of the first Negro newspaper in the United States sounded this theme. "We are aware that there are many instances of vice among us," wrote the editors, "but we avow that it is because no one has taught its subjects to be virtuous; many instances of poverty, because no sufficient efforts accommodated to minds contracted by slavery, and deprived early education have been made, to teach them how to husband their hard earnings, and to secure to themselves comfort."[64]

In 1834 David Ruggles raised the question of whether the person of the black or white race possessed the most character. If a man's character depends upon the color of his skin, he asked, which of the two groups would come out on top. "The whites," he wrote, "have robbed us . . . . for centuries—they made Africa bleed rivers of blood!—they have torn husbands from their wives—wives from their husbands—parents from their children—children from their parents—brothers from their sisters—sisters from their brothers, and bound them in chains—forced them into holds of vessels—subjected them to the most unmerciful tortures: starved and murdered, and doomed them to endure the horrors of slavery!" There he rested his case. Again, David Walker thundered:

> Millions of [white Americans] are this day, so ignorant and avaricious, that they cannot conceive how God can have an attribute of justice, and show mercy to us because it pleased Him to make us black—which color, Mr. Jefferson calls unfortunate!!! As though we are not thankful to our God, for having made us as it pleased himself, as they are for having made them white. They think because they hold us in their infernal chains of slavery, that we wish to be white, or of their color—but they are dreadfully deceived— we wish to be just as it pleased our creator to have us, and no avaricious and unmerciful wretches have

any business to make slaves of, or hold us in slavery. How would they like for us to make slaves of, and hold them in cruel slavery, and murder them as they do us.[65]

Since the 1920's

With the depression of the thirties and the events leading to World War II, in many ways Afro-American thought gained a new international concern, and Africa, long the focal point of the international interests of Negro Americans, became more integrated in a larger world setting. By 1960 the interest of the American Negro in the world's underprivileged peoples was diffused, but despite this broader interest in the world's people of color, among them Africa and Africans always have loomed largest in the Afro-American mind.

Ethiopia always has been a cherished land and symbol to the American Negro.[66] The Mussolini-led Italian invasion of Ethiopia was particularly disturbing to Afro-Americans, and evoked a protest movement which was centered in New York City. During the thirties Negro historians reflected a continuing interest in Africa. Appearing in this general period were Carter Woodson's *The African Background Outlined*[67] and *African Heroes and Heroines*.[68] "History should be reconstructed," declared Charles Wesley, "so that Africa . . . . shall have its proper place."[69] This was a major theme with Negro historians of the period. The first attempt of W. E. B. DuBois to write the history of Africa was entitled, *The Negro* and appeared in 1915.[70] About one-third of DuBois' *Black Folk Then and Now*, published in 1939,[71] deals with the African background of Negro-Americans, and in 1947 this same author's, *The World and Africa*, was published.[72] The latter book bore the sub-title, "An Inquiry into the Part which Africa has played in World History," and with the volume the author stated that he was seeking to "remind readers of the crisis of civilization, of how critical a part Africa has played in human history, past and present, and how impossible it is to forget this and rightly explain the present plight of mankind."[73] In 1931 George Schuyler published *Slaves Today: A Story of Liberia,* in which he took up the cudgel against the sufferings of natives of Afrca.[74]

In this period the Federal Theatre Project organized a special unit which was to feature African Culture, and Hampton Institute and Fisk, Howard and Atlanta Universities led in establishing creative art and dance units which gave considerable attention to African culture. With this same medium the concert dancers Pearl Primus and Katherine Dunham achieved international reputations. The above-named universities, along with Tuskegee Institute, established outstanding library collections on the Negro which included African history and culture, and the Carter Woodson-led Association for the Study of Negro Life and History was instrumental in getting the noted A. A. Schomburg Collection turned over to the New York Public Library.[75] In his poem, "Heritage," written in this period, Countee Cullen proudly admits that he is a descendant of black Africa. Also in the thirties William Grant Still wrote an African ballett, *Sahdji*, and Asadata Dafora Horton's dance opera featuring Africa, *Kyunkor*, was performed before appreciative New York audiences.

With the coming of World War II, like others, Afro-Americans were caught up in the war effort, and the earlier concern with Africa was submerged by more pressing issues. Still the prominence of the African theatre of battle during the early years of the war, participation of native African troops in the allied cause, and the possible demise of colonialism as a consequence of the war kept Africa prominent in the thought of Negro Americans. With the return of peace, the old race consciousness and pride were bolstered not only by the phenomenal overthrow of imperialism and colonialism by yellow, brown and black people in Asia and Africa, but by the dramatic achievements in racial integration within the United States, and just as the personality and efforts of Mahatma Gandhi had inspired Afro-Americans in the twenties and thirties, he, Kwame Nkrumah, Jomo Kenyatta, Gamel Nasser, Tom Mboya and other nationalist leaders in Asia and Africa were great sources of inspiration to them in the post-world war II era. It seems almost paradoxical that rampant nationalism in Asia and Africa have evoked a greater internationalism in the thought of Afro-Americans.

As earlier indicated, Africa and Africans are still dominant among the international interests of the Negro-American.
In the fifties, in *Black Power*, Richard Wright lifted his cudgel
in defense of nationalist aspirations in Africa,[76] while Era Bell
Thompson struck a similar note in her *Land of My Fathers*.[77]
As was the case with Schuyler's *Slaves Today*, both Wright and
Thompson based their convictions on direct observation of
conditions in Africa. Indeed, a dominant characteristic of the
mid-twentieth century Negro vis-a-vis Africa is the greatly
increased number who have visited that continent, many under
auspices of the Point Four and other federally sponsored programs. This travel is helping to dispel much of the ignorance
about Africa and Africans which has been evident among
Negro Americans. Thus many of the old stereotypes once
commonly accepted are now rapidly being discarded. In July,
1951 *Poetry* carried Melvin Tolson's "Libretto for the Republic
of Liberia," a work which was commissioned for the Liberian
Centennial, and, though commenting on a narrower theme, in
1956 Margaret Just Butcher ably summarized the past and
present attitudes and thoughts about Africa and Africans held
by Negro Americans. She wrote:

> In the dislocating process of being transplanted from
> Africa to America, Negro art and the Negro Artist
> were somehow separated; it was generations before
> they came together again. In the interval, African
> art was forgotten; Negro themes and subject matter
> were neglected by artists generally and many Negro
> artists regarded 'Negro art' as ghetto restriction and
> fled from it in protest and indignation. Now African
> art is both recognized and prized.[78]

As a consequence of the degradation of slavery, Negroes
have been unique among Americans in the rejection of the
land of their fathers. Now a greater maturity and developing
race pride are bringing an end to this rejection, and it would
not be surprising, to the present writer at least, to see the
masses of Afro-Americans soon embrace Africa with a force
somewhat comparable to that which the Irish and Jewish
Americans show for the lands of their fathers.

CHAPTER III

SOME ATTITUDES OF NEGROES TOWARD SLAVERY AND FREEDOM

ON SLAVERY

Among the statements on slavery and freedom made by Afro-Americans are eloquent definitions, as well as numerous ideas about the nature and consequences of both. Slavery was a scar which the freedmen would wear for decades, and the dark heritage of the fathers probably will be passed on to the sons and grandsons through countless generations. Doubtless the fact of his enslavement would have weighed less heavily on the mind of the bondsman had he been denied his freedom in a society, which put no high premium on individual rights and freedom.

That slave labor was "unrequited toil" has held a high place among the items of denunciation which Negroes have brought against the institution, and on the natural love of liberty, Henry Highland Garnet said:

> Slavery! How much misery is comprehended in that single word. What mind is there that does not shrink from its direful effects? Unless the image of God be obliterated from the soul, all men cherish the love of liberty. The nice discerning political economist does not regard the sacred right more than the untutored African who roams in the wilds of the Congo. Nor has the one more right to the full enjoyment of his freedom than the other. In every man's mind the good seeds of liberty are planted, and he who brings his fellow down so low, as to make him contented with a condition of slavery, commits the highest crime against God and man.[1]

In 1851, speaking to an Ohio Convention of Negroes, H. Ford Douglass said:

> Every man is inspired with a . . . deep and abiding love of liberty. I care not where he may dwell . . . whether amid the snows of the polar regions or weltering beneath an African sun, or clanking his hot

iron fetters in this free Republic and I care not how
degraded the man, that Prometheran spark still lives,
and burns, in secret and brilliant grandeur, upon his
inmost, and the iron-rust of slavery and uninterrupted
despotism, can never extinguish it.[2]

The Reverend Hosea Eason of Masssachusetts stated,

Were I capable of dipping my pen in the deep-
est dye of crime, and of understanding the science of
the bottomless pit, I should then fail in presenting to
the intelligence of mortals on earth, the true nature
of American deception.[3]

Another abolitionist exhorted:

Let us view this demon, which the people here
worshipped as a God. Come forth, thou grim monster, that thou mayest be critically examined! There
he stands. Behold him, one and all. His work is to
chattelize man; to hold property in human beings.
Great God! I would as soon attempt to enslave
Gabriel or Michael as to enslave a man made in the
image of God, and for whom Christ died. Slavery
is snatching man from the high place to which he
was lifted by the hand of God, and dragging him
down to the level of the ox.[4]

Early in the nation's history an Afro-American declared slavery
to be "repugnant to the feelings of nature, and inconsistent
with the original rights of man."[5] This writer, who used the
pen-name "Othello," declared that by acquiescing in slavery
the nation was violating the tenets of its own faith as expressed in the Declaration of Independence, and would surely
suffer the wrath of an angered God. The then legal slave trade
he termed "one of the greatest defects" in the federal system,
a system which he praised on most other points. "Othello"
asked of the institution of slavery, "can anyone say that this
is doing as he would be done by?," and he equated the American slave-trade with the piracy which was then being practiced
by the barbary states of North Africa. He praised the latter
for preying upon the shipping of strong states while Americans
preyed only on the defenseless Africans.[6]

As to why he championed the cause of the slave, Charles Lenox Remond said:

> It is not because the slave is a poor man, nor an ignorant man, nor a lowly man, a despised man, an outraged man, a trampled man, a brutified man. It is because I know that He who has promulgated to us all truth—who is Himself the fountain of justice—the source of truth—the perfection of loveliness—has announced from the hill of Sinai, that man cannot attempt the bondage of his fellowman without being guilty of a deadly crime.[7]

"Where is the man," Remond asked, "who, if asked to become a slave, would not hurl back the offer indignantly in the teeth of the oppressor? Nay, where is the woman—where is the child?"

To the Negro there was little middle-ground in the slavery issue. Charles Lenox Remond declared:

> Many there are, I grieve to say, who are deterred from the consideration of this subject through a vain and silly thought that the question is an elaborate and complicated one, and that in the discussion of it they would become bewildered and mentally blinded, as it were. 'Tis false, most corruptly false, to say so. There is no complication in the matter. The road lies before us, clear, straight, and unwarped as in the path of truth and justice. The question is resolved into two words only—liberty or slavery?[8]

Frederick Douglass spoke of "three millions of human beings deprived of every right, stripped of every privilege, ranked with four-footed beasts and creeping things, with no power over their own bodies and souls, deprived of the privilege of learning to read the name of the God who made them, compelled to live in the grossest ignorance, herded together in a state of concubinage—without marriage, without God, and without hope."[9] And again:

> Slavery . . . is the granting of that power by which one man exercises and enforces a right of property in the body and soul of another. The condition of a slave

is simply that of the brute beast. He is a piece of property—a marketable commodity, in the language of the law, to be bought or sold at the will and caprice of the master . . .; he is spoken of, thought of, and treated as property. His own good, his conscience, his intellect, his affections, are all set aside by the master. The will and the wishes of the master are the law of the slave. . . . Whatever of comfort is necessary to him for his body or soul that is inconsistent with his being property is carefully wrested from him, not only by public opinion, but by the law of the country.[10]

M. C. B. Mason labelled human slavery "that iniquity of all iniquities."[11] J. C. Price called it "that wrong, that iniquity, that hydraheaded monster,"[12] while to Nathaniel Paul, slavery was "a hateful monster, the very demon of avarice and oppression, the scourge of heaven, and the curse of the earth."[13] M. J. Butcher termed slavery, "democracy's greatest antithesis."[14]

Just as the Afro-American has had his days of gloom and despair, such as the day the colonization movement was launched, or the day of the 1850 fugitive slave act, or the days of the Dred Scott and negative civil rights decisions, so there have been days of jubilee. Such a day of jubilee occurred when in 1827 New York state abolished slavery. Significantly, the state chose July 4th to proclaim the end of human bondage. At a mass meeting in Albany, July 5th, 1827, the Reverend Nathaniel Paul spoke in commemoration of the event. He praised the manner in which it had come about.

> Not by those fearful judgments of the almighty, which have so often fallen upon the different parts of the earth, which have overturned nations and kingdoms, scattered thrones and scepters, nor is the glory of the achievement tarnished with the horrors of the field of battle. We hear not the cries of the widow and the fatherless; nor are our hearts affected with the sight of garments rolled in blood; but all has been done by the diffusion and influence of the pure, yet powerful principles of benevolence.[15]

The mistreatment of Negro women under slavery has been an especial source of rancor to Negroes. In this connection, Charles Lenox Remond wrote:

When I see a woman condemned to wear an iron collar, as it were cruelty to bind around the neck of a dog, working in that collar, eating in it, aye, even sleeping in it, for no other crime than merely that of having asked permission to visit her child in an adjoining plantation—when, I repeat, I look on sights like these, my frame shudders with disgust—my blood freezes, and my heart bursts with indignation as I exclaim, 'If these things be the result of Christianity or of patriotism, may heaven deliver me from the influence of either!'[16]

On the impact of slavery on the nation, Frederick Douglass wrote:

The existence of slavery in this country brands your republicanism as a sham, your humanity as a base pretense, and your Christianity as a lie. It destroys your moral power abroad: it corrupts your politicians at home. It saps the foundation of religion; it makes your name a hissing and a by-word to a mocking earth. It is the antagonistic force in your government, the only thing that seriously disturbs and endangers your *Union*. It fetters your progress; it is the enemy of improvement; the deadly foe of education; it fosters pride; it breeds insolence; it promotes vice; it shelters crime; it is a curse to the earth that supports it; and yet you cling to it as if it were the sheet anchor of all your hopes. Oh! be warned! be warned! a horrible reptile is coiled up in your nation's bosom; the venomous creature is nursing at the tender breast of your youthful republic; *for the love of God, tear away*, and fling from you the hideous monster, and *let the weight of twenty millions crush and destroy it forever!*[17]

During the height of the abolitionist movement, Frances Ellen Watkins Harper wrote:

Make me a grave wher'er you will,
In a lowly plain or a lofty hill;
Make it among earth's humblest graves,
But not in a land where men are slaves.

The colored abolitionists fought to get slavery recognized
as a sin, not just an evil or wrong. In the strongly religious
nineteenth century, the word "sinner" was often a fighting
word. This is a major reason for the deep bitterness which existed between abolitionists and slave-holders. Frederick Douglass gave utterance to this view while speaking in Glasgow,
Scotland, May 29, 1846, when he said—

> The abolitionists of the United States have
> been laboring, during the last fifteen years to estab-
> lish the conviction throughout the country that slav-
> ery is a sin, and ought to be treated as such by all
> professing Christians.[18]

Previous to the abolitionists, Douglass averred, only the Society
of Friends and the small body of Reformed Presbyterians regarded slavery as a sin. The abolitionists, he stated, wanted
slaveholders expelled from the churches, and "the antislavery
sentiment not to sit in communion with slaveholders and to
warn the slaveholders not to come near nor partake of the em-
blems of Christ's body and blood, lest they eat and drink dam-
nation to themselves," Douglass declared, "is become very
prevalent in the free States."[19] Douglass repeatedly called the
slaveholder a sinner and a thief and a robber, "for what is a
thief? what is a robber? but he who appropriates to himself
what belongs to another. The slaveholders do this continually.
They publish their willingness to do so. They defend their
right to do so."[20] Slavery he called "a foul blot upon Christianity." Douglass attacked those Christians who would denounce
slavery, but not the slaveholder. Of these, he said: "While they
would denounce theft, they would spare the thief; while they
would denounce gambling, they would spare the gambler; while
they would denounce the dice, they would spare the sharper.
. . . Well may the thief be glad, the robber sing, the adulterer
clap his hands for joy."[21] Douglass wanted the doer and the
deed given the same tag. For "Slavery—I hold it to be an in-

disputable proposition—exists in the United States because it
is respectable. The slaveholder is a respectable man in America.
All the important officers in the Government and the Church
are filled by slaveholders . . . one of the most direct, one of
the most powerful means of making him a respectable man, is
to say that he is a Christian."[22] Almost needless to say, it was
the growth of the sentiment in the North that the slaveholder
was indeed a "sinner," "thief," and "robber" which led the
South to secession.

Afro-Americans have tended to believe that for them
slavery was not all bad, that it taught them reverence for God,
patience, love, humility, and in some ways, made them morally
and physically stronger than white people. When in 1843 he
asked bondsmen to rise and overthrow slavery, even at the risk
of death, Henry Highland Garnet alluded to these aspects of
the institution. "You will not be compelled to spend much time
in order to become inured to hardships," he stated to the slaves,
and continued: "From the first moment that you breathed the
air of heaven, you have been accustomed to nothing else but
hardships. The heroes of the American Revolution were never
put upon harder fare than a peck of corn and a few herrings
per week. You have not become enervated by the luxuries of
life. Slavery has prepared you for any emergency."[23]

Frederick Douglass states that "the very first mental effort" that he remembered as an adult was an attempt to solve
the riddle of why the Negro in America was the slave of the
white man. His first understanding of this matter was that
God had ordained this. But, how God could so arrange things
and "still be good," left Douglas puzzled. He thought and
wept over this matter many times, until having overheard
some elderly slaves discuss how their parents were stolen from
Africa by white men, Douglass saw the answer which satisfied
him. Slavery was not then the will of God, but the result of
human avarice and greed.[24]

William Wells Brown shared the conviction that slavery
degraded the oppressor as well as the oppressed. On this, he
wrote of the institution:

It is regarded as an offense in the sight of God,
and opposed to the best interests of man. There is a

proverb, that no man can bind a chain upon the limb
of his neighbor, without inevitably fate fastening the
other end around his own body. This has been degrad-
ingly verified by the slaveholders of America. While
they have been degrading the colored man, by en-
slaving him, they have become degraded themselves.
In withholding education from the minds of their
slaves, they have kept their own children in comparative ignorance.[25]

"The immoralities which have been found to follow in the
train of slavery in all countries and all ages," he continued,
"are to be seen in their worst forms in the Slave States of
America."

In 1837, Reverend Hosea Easton stated of slavery and
prejudice, that the "whole system is founded in avarice." "I
believe the premises to be the production of modern philosophy,
bearing date with European slavery," he continued.[26] He concluded with the well-known statement that "The love of
money is the root of all evil." Interesting in the thought of
Afro-Americans on the subject of slavery is the failure of acceptance of the notion, so much advanced by the Slavocracy,
that chattel slavery was ordained by God. One searches the
literature in vain for evidence that even a small minority of
Negroes accepted this dictum. However, human credulity
being what it is, some bondsmen must have accepted this
dictum. The abolitionists overwhelmingly blamed their race's
enslavement on the avarice and sinfulness of the Caucasian,
who sought to use his superior numbers and force to profit
from the toil of others. Inasmuch as many of the Afro-Americans originally came from a land of primitive and animistic
faith, where the gods were blamed for many things, good and
bad, the failure to accept this particular argument of the
Slavocracy must be taken, in part, as further proof of the
Negro's early Westernization. The Declaration of Independence, the arguments of the patriots of the Revolutionary War
era, and the Constitution provided the foundation of the
Negro's outlook on slavery and society.[27]

On Freedom

Most bondsmen had an intense desire for freedom. One ex-slave said: "We all had freedom in our bones."[28] They often prayed for freedom. One ex-slave said: "I thought it was foolishness then, but the old-time folks always felt they was to be free. It must have been something 'vealed unto 'em."[29]Booker T. Washington said: "I have never seen one who did not want to be free or one who would return to slavery."[30] That slaves had a deep-seated desire for freedom was to be proved in their jubilant reaction when the news of emancipation would finally come.

The desire to escape from slavery, it has been noted, constituted a major theme of Negro slave songs.   J. S. Bassett thought that with the beginning of the radical abolitionist movement of 1830, at least 2,000 slaves fled to the North each year. Doubtless, these figures are too conservative for the 1840-60 period. That thousands of bondsmen escaped annually is well known, but how many more made the attempt each year only to be captured and kept in bondage cannot be known. Evidence that between 1831-61 there was a considerable and constant exodus of Negroes to the North is seen, in the many advertisements for fugitives that appeared in southern newspapers, and the persistent agitation which southern congressmen carried on for ever more stringent fugitive slave laws.

Slaves ran away for many reasons. The threat of punishment, separation of families through the sale of one or more members, or the threat of such, news of the Toussaint's insurrection, congressional debates on slavery, the nearness to free areas such as the North or to Florida, Mexico, or Western Indian territory; the encouragement of fellow slaves or of fugitives or of free Negroes or friendly southern whites; and the hard work of hot frenzied summer months are among the many things which spurred bondsmen to make the break for freedom.

Free Negroes participated in numerous of the slave plots, rebellions, and abscondings, but their own precarious freedom kept them from making open assertions in favor of freedom for the bondsmen. There can be little doubt, however, that their sympathies lay primarily with the members of their own race. Only when they possessed freedom and acceptance by the majority group to such an extent as existed in New Orleans, Louisiana, did the Free Negro populace occasionally feel very estranged from and hostile toward the slave. It seems probable that the slave generally was not aware of the true extent of the sympathy which the free person felt toward him, and that lack of awareness caused the bondsmen to view the free person with considerable suspicion.

Of running away, one ex-slave reported: "Canada was popular then [with runaways] because all of the slaves thought it was the last gate before you got all the way *inside* of heaven. I don't think there was much chance for a slave to make a living in Canada, but didn't many of 'em come back. They seem like they rather starve up there in the cold than to be back in slavery."[31] Stimulated by their participation in the War of 1812 and campaigns in Canada, Negroes had increased their efforts to settle there after the war, and Canada became a sort of "heaven" in Negro thought. That England soon abolished slavery in her empire, and that Canadians were quite friendly to the migrants, coupled with the fears of staying anywhere in the United States which the fugitive slave law of 1850 engendered, the Negro population of Canada had grown to considerable proportion by the outbreak of the Civil War. Negro abolitionists solicited funds to aid the fugitives who settled in Canada, and the African Methodist Episcopal Church organized a Canadian conference almost a generation before the Civil War came. Yet that approximately 50,000 Negroes were in Canada in 1860 compared with only around 20,000 in the post World War II period reveals that many of the migrants, because of lack of job opportunities, home-sickness, and increasing racial bias in Canada, returned to the United States in the decades following the Civil War.

The slave, George Moses Horton, wrote during the height of the abolitionist movement:

> Come, Liberty! thou cheerful sound,
>   Roll through my ravished ears;
> Come, let my grief in joys be drowned,
>   And drive away my fears.

In his epic 1843 address to the slaves, Henry Highland Garnet declared: "Liberty is a spirit sent out from God, and like its great Author, is no respector of persons."

The Negro abolitionists certainly knew that freedom had restrictions and limitations for even in the North they were only quasi-free. Yet they appear to have held the conviction that human beings universally and naturally choose freedom or liberty over all forms of dependency. The twentieth century, which has seen the majorities in several nations either choose or acquiese in various forms of totalitarianism, is inclined to be more skeptical of this so-called natural inclination of all men toward freedom. Doubtless, many of the black abolitionists would be rudely shocked if they could return to earth and witness the twentieth century retreat from freedom. Doubtless, too, their own personal acquaintance with slavery would be yet so vivid in their minds that even the analyses of Erich Fromm's book *Escape From Freedom* would be insufficient explanations for the twentieth century's acceptance of totalitarianism.

Most of the abolitionists believed that God ordained and gave freedom to man, and that those who restricted it or denied it to others were blaspheming God. Also, the abolitionists based the claims of their race to freedom and equal rights on their American nativity.

In 1847, Charles L. Reason wrote:

> O Freedom! Freedom! Oh, how oft
> Thy loving children call on Thee!
> In wailings loud and breathings soft,
> Beseeching God, Thy face to see.
>
> With agonizing hearts we kneel,
> While 'round us howls the oppressor's cry,
> And suppliant pray that we may feel
> The ennobling glances of Thine eye.

One ex-bondsman said he had vowed that if he ever got free, he was just going to lie in bed and never get up.[52] Another reported of the 1850s.

> We knowed freedom was on us, but we didn't know what was to come with it. We thought we was going to get rich like the white folks. We thought

we was going to be richer than the white folks, 'cause we was stronger and knowed how to work, and the whites didn't, and they didn't have us to work for them anymore. But it didn't turn out that way. We soon found out that freedom could make folks proud, but it didn't make 'em rich.[33]

Another showed jubilation:

My mistress said to me when I got back home, 'You're free. Go on out in the orchard and git yourself some peaches.' They had a yard full of peaches. Baby, did I git me some peaches. I pulled a bushel of 'em.[34]

Freedom meant different things to different persons. Some hated to see the old order change, while a few were indifferent. Some thought emancipation meant freedom from work, and others saw it primarily as a chance to go any place they wished. One Negro in Vicksburg, Mississippi believed that his race was scheduled to assemble in New York City and "have white men for niggers."[35] Doubtless, most were glad because they believed that they were now going to be treated more "like white folks" and have the tangible and intangible goods which the better class of whites possessed. These different reactions notwithstanding, to most if not all of the ex-slaves, freedom was a precious jewel indeed. In 1876, Frederick Douglass spoke of "our blood-bought freedom,"[36] and the freeman John Mercer Langston declared:

Liberty is the whitest and brightest jewel in the firmament, and . . . the greatest heritage of American citizenship is to be free. . . . Virtue is the very essence of popular liberty; but equally so is liberty the essence of public virtue.[37]

J. C. Price averred: "freedom implies manhood."[38]

On the occasion of the emancipation of slaves in New York, July 4, 1827, Reverend Nathaniel Paul had pointed out that freedom alone was not a worthy goal. He stated:

While we rejoice at the thought of this land's becoming a land of freemen, we pause, we reflect. What, we would ask, is liberty without virtue? It tends to lasciviousness; and what is freedom but a curse, and even destruction, to the profligate? . . . Brethren, we have been called into liberty; only let us use that liberty as not abusing it. This day commences a new era in our history; new scenes, new prospects open before us, and it follows as a necessary consequence that new duties devolve upon us; duties, which if properly attended to, cannot fail to improve our moral condition and elevate us to a rank of respectable standing with the community; or if neglected, we fall at once into the abyss of contemptible wretchedness. It is righteousness alone that exalteth a nation, and sin is a reproach to any people.[39]

Later the Emancipation Proclamation, the Thirteenth Amendment, even the supreme court decision of May 17, 1954, and related decisions would cause these same convictions to be uttered by other Afro-American spokesmen.

CHAPTER IV

NEGRO THOUGHT ON CRUELTY AND PLEASURE DURING BONDAGE

One primary source of Negro thought has been the cruel aspects of slavery. Apologists for the institution have sought to minimize and excuse away the lashings, sometimes unto death, brandings, mutilations, improper and inadequate diets, rapes, breaking up of families, and other types of cruelty to which slaves were subjected. No doubt Northern abolitionists, by concentrating on these aspects of slavery almost to exclusion, gave a picture of the institution that was out of focus. Still, it is undeniable that a characteristic feature of the institution was cruelty. Fear, not love, was the primary weapon used to control slaves. To keep people working long hours in the southern sun solely for minimal food, clothing, and shelter dictated that fear had to be the chief weapon used. Cruel treatment caused thousands of bondsmen to risk their lives in such actions as flight to freedom or, in desperation to plot and attempt insurrection and rebellion, or to commit suicide. The record of cruelty has caused Negro historians pondering it to shed tears during their researches, and belongs to the blackest chapters in the long story of man's inhumanity to man.

Amazing as it may seem, news of practically all major national and international debates and events concerning slavery reached the ears of bondsmen shortly after the occurrences and caused considerable unrest among them. There is evidence that, at times, such news inspired directly plots and insurrections. Testimony at the trial of the conspirators involved with Denmark Vesey of South Carolina shows that among other things, the slaves had been aroused by anti-slavery sentiments voiced in Congress during debates over the Missouri Compromise questions. Similar unrest among slaves followed the abolitionist sentiments voiced during the heated 1840 presidential campaign, and the 1856 candidacy of John C. Fremont.

As early as the Revolutionary War many slaves came to feel that God and friendly men were asking them to rise and strike a blow for their freedom. Stirred by the talk of freedom and human rights which filled the air on every hand, slave plots and uprisings were numerous during and shortly after the War for American Independence. This pattern of behavior was repeated during the War of 1812, Mexican War, French Revolution, Haitian uprising led by Toussaint L'Ouverture, revolutions of the Latin American republics during the early nineteenth century, as well as the democratic revolutions in post-Napoleonic Europe. Slave revolts started early. In 1741 there was a "conspiracy" in New York in which New York "bondsmen" destroyed many buildings by fire. For this over thirty persons were executed.

Miles Mark Fisher concluded that, "Overlords did not see or care that field slaves dropped tears which watered the ground they cultivated. Indeed, the opinion of no less a person than George Washington was that slaves required brutal treatment."[1] Henry Bibb, fugitive living in Detroit, wrote that had his master treated him better, he probably would not have run away.[2]

It is perhaps unfortunate that the friendly paternalism of which the South boasted was not more often the real basis of relations between black and white. Perhaps it could not have been otherwise, but the fear basis of race relations and cruel repressive measures set black and white up as enemies of one another. While it often created "respect" one for the other, this could be scarcely more than formality. Thus it is probably safe to say that in the Old South only the Negro who was a house servant or artisan or held some other privileged position ever really loved members of the Caucasian race with Christian love. All the rest appear to have only feigned admiration and love. Thus was born Uncle-Tomism. Slaves often seemed delighted to pretend to be to the white man what they were not. As this was also their joke on the Caucasian, their way of getting even without being suspected, it is small wonder that many Negroes have enjoyed playing the role of Uncle Tom. This has been their secret and private revenge for many physical and mental abuses and insults. Many slaves feigned stupidity. Many believed that the planter did not want a slave of intelligence and integrity, and that the more child-like they behaved,

the less likely would be their chance of angering "the boss."
Of slaves being newly broken in, one planter said:- "Let a
hundred men show him to hoe, or drive a wheelbarrow, he'll
still take the one by the Bottom and the other by the Wheel.[3]

Cruelty to slaves must be viewed against the larger background of the eighteenth and nineteenth centuries which saw
child labor, factories which commonly worked people twelve
and more hours per day, saw sailors flogged, and prisoners, or-
phans, and the insane often brutally treated..

There were no slave overseers, only slave assistants to the
white overseer, called drivers. Coming from the poor white
class as they usually did, overseers often hated the plantation
system and vented their anger against the slave, the symbol
which they could abuse with less danger of retaliation.

The types or forms of cruelty which were in the slave
system seemed to be legion. Slave women often resented doing
work which they termed men's work,[4] while many bondsmen
were highly sensitive about being cursed. All resented the whippings. "They wouldn't whip horses half as hard as they would
whip darkies," commented one ex-bondsman.[5] Slaves always
said that owners or overseers treated them like dogs or mules.
Being placed in the same category with farm animals was one
of the most often-mentioned of all resentments which slaves
felt toward their situation.

Mistresses of the plantation were neither as often loved
or as often hated as was the case with the masters or overseers.
Doubtless this is because the mistresses usually played a more
passive role in the slave system. When they actively tempered
the cruelty of masters or overseers, the mistresses tended to
be loved and respected, but when they encouraged or participated in the cruelty, they too were hated.[6] Some mistresses beat
their slaves habitually until blood ran down their bodies.[7]
One ex-slave said of his mistress—"well, she was good as most
any old white woman. . . . They all hated the po' nigger."[8]
Suspecting that they were her husband's progeny, some mistresses were more cruel to mulatto children on the plantations
and would not let them serve as house servants or insisted that
they be sold. Sometimes the mistresses whipped male adult
slaves.[9] Of one mean mistress, her bondsman reported that he

laughed when she died.[10] One type of cruelty domestic slaves held against some mistresses was their not giving or allowing the slaves to have enough to eat. The cruelties which loomed largest and almost exclusively in their minds had to do with physical necessities. Only the black abolitionist complained much about cruelties involving such things as the right to vote, hold public office, or use public facilities without being discriminated against.

Being sold away from friends and relatives was one of the cruelest aspects of slavery, but that being sold meant leaving relatives and friends was not the only reason many slaves hated to be sold. They deeply resented the manner in which the sales were conducted. They disliked being placed on a platform, partly or wholly nude, while prospective buyers examined their physiques and peered into their mouths as if they were cattle on sale. One ex-slave said of his being sold: "They stands me up on, a block of wood, and a man bid me in. I felt mad. I don't know what they sold me for, but the man what bought me made me open my mouth while he looks at my teeth . . . like you sell a horse."[11] To some bondsmen selling a mother from her children was "like taking a mother from her pigs."[12] One slave child felt no cruelty in slavery until her parents were sold. One mother threatened to kill her infant by holding it by the feet and striking its head against a tree rather than be sold separately.[13] One ex-slave pointed to the irony involved in inter-racial relations in the Old South. On his plantation, he said, "The white folks sold one colored woman, to send their boy to school to be a doctor. They sold her away from her husband."[14]

The Lower South states were places of horror in the minds of slaves who had never been there, and Afro-Americans still feel, along perhaps with most northern white Americans, that race relations are still infinitely worse in the lower South. In slavery many recalcitrant or captured runaway slaves were sold into the Lower South and the threat of being "sold down the river" was often used to control slaves.

How many slaves felt about their status may be gleaned from words of Frederick Douglas on this topic. In a letter to his master, with which Douglas celebrated in 1848 the tenth anniversary of his flight to freedom, he describes briefly his feelings as a slave. He writes of himself as then trembling at the sound of his master's voice "lamenting that I was a man, and wishing myself a brute."[15] "When I saw the slave driver whip a woman," he averred, "cut the blood out of her neck, and heard her piteous cries, I went away into the corner of the fence, wept and pondered over the mystery."

On one farm, because of cruel treatment, a large group of slaves plotted to throw themselves in a nearby river. They stayed off the farm until after mid-night and said concern for their children caused them to reconsider. Doubtless one ex-bondsman unwittingly spoke for many others when he said of slavery—"There wasn't much fun to be had in them times. Didn't have no time for yourself."[16] "Slavery was the worst days was ever seed in the world," one ex-slave declared.[24] Another, reminiscing, said: "Yes, Lawd, there is a mighty whole lot of people today what had they been through what I been through they would be crazy as a bed bug."[17] Of the first realization that he was a slave, one ex-bondsman said, "I knew I was a slave after I got big enough to know that I couldn't do the things that I wanted to do."[18]

One aged ex-slave said in the 1940's: "I have sho' seen some bad days, and heard all about them. Times are bad enough now, but you ain't seen nothing. White folks will always be hard on niggers and niggers will never have a chance. I hope God will help the niggers and they will help theirselves."[19] The 1864 National Negro Convention which met at Syracuse, New York said that the race in the U. S. A. had been "cruelly wronged by people whose might constituted their right; we have been subdued, not by the power of ideas, but by brute force."[20]

The late nineteenth and early twentieth century myth that Negroes were happy under slavery, has been exploded for the most part. Contributions by such persons as Herbert Aptheker, Henrietta Buckmaster, Carter Wodson, W. E. B. Dubois, and John Hope Franklin have shown that while slaves made an adjustment to their condition, they were not happy in it. Apologists for the institution, led by the ante-bellum planters and post-bellum writers such as Ulrich Bonnell Phillips and the

W. A. Dunning School, sometimes have called adjustment and accommodation blissful enjoyment. They failed to realize that Uncle Tomism and humor were the slave's defense mechanisms. Any objective examination of the spirituals reveals that in them sadness and longing for a better life are dominant themes, and it matters little whether the better life was envisioned as being in this world, in Africa, or in the North, as some interpretations of the spirituals hold, or whether it was to come in life after death. Of course the persons who fled the institution spoke out in unison in bitter denunciation of it.

In *American Negro Slave Revolts,* Herbert Aptheker has shown that many of the worst slave plots and insurrections followed economic depressions which necessitated shorter slave rations or the master breaking up families and selling some of his human property in order to pay bills.[26]

That the United States witnessed no large scale slave revolts such as the one led by Toussaint L'Ouverture in Haiti would appear to be adequately explained by a lack of opportunity for laying of plans, the elaborate system of control which planters exercised, opportunity of escape to the North, and the patient hope which Christianity brought. The same may be said for the lack of an even larger number of runaway slaves. However, these conditions notwithstanding, sporadic local revolts were legion and continuing and the number of fugitives who either escaped or attempted to do so is quite large. Frederick Douglass stated that nothing could keep the Negro satisfied in slavery. "Give him a *bad* master," Douglass declared, "and he aspires to a *good* master; give him a good master, and he wishes to become his *own* master."[21]

Less dramatic than the slave plots, rebellions, and absconding was the day-by-day resistance to slavery. This resistance took many subtle and sometimes vicious forms. Of one type of resistance, Kenneth Stamp writes:

> Slaves sought to limit the quantity of their services in many different ways. At cotton picking time they carried cotton from the gin house to the field in the morning to be weighed with the days picking at night. They concealed dirt or rocks in their cotton baskets to escape punishment for loafing. They fixed

their own work quotas, and master had to adopt stern measures to persuade them that they had been unduly presumptuous. Where the task system was used, they stubbornly resisted any attempt to increase the size of the daily tasks fixed by custom.[22]

They also would not work hard when the over-seer wasn't near, often refused to compete among themselves, sometimes refused to learn skilled trades when offered the chance, damaged crops and farm implements and animals, stole from the smokehouse, and feigned illness.[23] One slave-holder felt aggrieved when he saw that the small patches which his Negroes cultivated for themselves were better cared for and more productive than his own fields. They also maimed themselves, committed suicide, feigned pregnancy, ran away, helped fugitives with food, refused to inform on one another, even held a few sit-down strikes, poisoned their masters, and set fires.[24] For the most part the slaves who thus provoked masters and overseers were the meek, smiling ones whom many thought were contented though irresponsible.[25] Of those slaves who "waged ceaseless and open warfare against their bondage" Kenneth Stamp says —"As the American Revolution produced folk heroes, so also did southern slavery—heroes who, in both cases, gave much for the cause of human freedom."[26]

Frances A. Kemble reported that every southern woman with whom she talked admitted to her that the planter class lived in constant fear of slave insurrection. She stated that southern men usually denied the existence of this fear.[27] Frederick L. Olmstead made a similar observation in his A Journey In The Back Country. Poisonings, arson, plots and conspiracies which existed, and those hundreds which never happened but which whites expected, charged the southern air with fear. Fear has ever been a major mainspring of cruelty and hate, and the major factor which created prejudice and hatred between blacks and whites in the South was not the Reconstruction era, as is commonly thought, but the slave regime. Clearly both races were victims of the institution and both were enslaved.

For most bondsmen, death was the only release from their lot. The likelihood of escape to the North did not loom large until the rise of militant abolitionism and the Underground Railroad around 1830, and even then, bondsmen in the lower South could scarcely hope to travel the road to freedom. Still, after 1830, there were friends all along the route to the North, and the traffic grew annually.

A number of bondsmen petitioned the colonial and state governors and legislatures for their freedom. Some used the legal ground that the will of a former master had so ordained. Others, on moral grounds, appealed to the consciences of the governors and legislators. In such petitions, the slaves generally stated that they were very unhappy because of their degraded and non-propertied status. These petitions came from all sections of the country.[28]

For many slaves Christmas was the only holiday in the year, and perhaps for just as great a number Saturday afternoons and Sundays were not free from required labors, for although work might cease in the fields, many had weekly personal chores to perform both for themselves and their owners. By ten years of age and often earlier, childhood was over for slaves. By then plowing and all sorts of hard tasks became common. Slaves had almost no mirrors. Many never saw themselves in good likeness until they were adolescent or older. Dressing up for Sundays or dances was a very special joy to them because they usually went ragged and dirty. Lice and other vermin were common. It was not unusual for the Fourth of July to be a holiday for slaves, at which time much dancing and feasting went on.

There is abundant evidence that slaves regarded the dirty rags which they commonly wore as one of the most hateful badges of their degradation. One of their happiest occasions came when in the fall or early winter they were given their annual clothing allowance. Crude and cheap though they were, slaves cherished these bits of new clothing as well as any cast-off hat, gloves, coat, dress, or trousers which were given by their masters. That their shoes seldom fitted accounts in large part for the stereotyped notion that all Negroes are innately cursed with corns, bunions, and other manifestations of "bad feet." Commenting on slave clothing, one freedman said—

"shoes was the worstest trouble."[29] Considering their long experience in slavery, there can be little wonder that to many
bondsmen and freedmen fine-looking shoes and other items of
clothing became an end rather than a means.

Slaves missed not having salt for their food. Ex-slaves
very often commented that "The only salt we ever got . . .
was what dropped down on the ground from the meat that
was hanging up. It was just the color of brown sugar. We
never knowed about no other kind."[39] One of the greatest
delights of slaves was the hot biscuits which some received on
Sunday mornings.

One ex-slave said of table delicacies during slavery—
"white folks would give them [slaves] a rooster and an old
hen for supper sometimes."[31] Also slaves were sometimes given
and regarded as delicacies hogs' feet, heads, tails, and entrails
(chitterlings). "Ham was white folks meat, and if you got
any you would have to steal it,"[32] one ex-bondsman reported.
Also—"The white folks would not give us no butter and things
like that."[33] Slaves stole jellies, sugar, chickens, ham, and other
delicacies. Slave children were seldom given meat. They commonly received "pot-likker," buttermilk, beans and cabbage
soup. Meat usually went to adults because they had to work.

A pleasure which most bondsmen desired to no avail was
the opportunity and joy of acquiring knowledge. One ex-slave
said: "When I was a little boy I always wanted to know what
was on a piece of paper."[34] Another ex-slave said—"Don't
know much about education. All I got I got it out in the field.
That was my fountain pen and pencil, the blade of the hoe,
and my slate was the ground."[35] Another commented—"The
only writing a nigger ever git am when he git born or marry
or die, then Marse put the name in the big book."[36] Slaves believed that whites did things much worse than most slaves had
ever seen. They talked of whites taking infants by the heels
and beating their brains out against trees, killing slaves and
chopping their bodies up. Apparently one instance of extreme
brutality went a long way among slaves. Many slaves believed
that the master or overseer on the next plantation was always
meaner than their own. Reminiscing on the cruelties of slavery, one aged freedman said: "Oh, white folks have done every-

thing. I can't hardly hold the tears back. It's just awful to think about it, and it was awful to be there. . . . God is a forgiving God, but sometimes I don't think he has forgiven the white people for the way they treated the poor black folks."[37] Another ex-slave declared: "I don't know what made the white folks have such hard hearts; it sho was awful."[38]

After emancipation the most recurrent remembrance of unpleasantnesses was the beatings administered to slaves. Even allowing for exaggerations on the part of the freedmen, this feature of the bondage stands out as one of its most inhuman aspects. Slaves were sometimes completely incapacitated for two or more days as a result of these whippings, and the mere threat of a whipping was enough to cause a slave to make the always perilous and little-likely-to-succeed effort at running away. Almost always the slaves definition of a good master was one who neither used nor allowed much use of the lash. Especially did the slaves resent that generally before being lashed, they had to remove all or part of their clothing, and that often the beatings were given before unwilling slave audiences.[39] Some plantations had a regular day on which beatings were given, and sometimes all slaves were whipped, regardless of whether they had committed any offense. One ex-slave reported—'I lays in the bunk two days, gitting over that whipping, gitting over it in the body but not in the heart. No, sir, I has that in the heart till this day."[40] Slaves being whipped to death was common enough so that almost every slave had "knowledge" of such experience. One aged ex-slave with failing memory said—"I don't know nothing they done before the war but whip niggers. They whipped them all the time."[41] If bondsmen received lashes when they were innocent of any offense, they were unusually resentful of the blows, and at such times might either strike back or silently plot some revenge.

One of the greatest fears of slaves were the bloodhounds or "Nigger Dogs" which were features of plantation life. In their wrath at the trouble which a runaway slave had caused them, masters or overseers sometimes allowed the dogs to give the caught slave a "working over," and the dogs might tear off the ears of slave men or the breasts of slave women. All bondsmen felt intense respect and fear at the ingenuity and cruelty of these dogs.

SLAVE PLEASURE

The Afro-American ever has felt an incumbency to minimize or deny the pleasures and joys which his race had in slavery. To affirm this side of slavery has seemed to him an acceptance and approval of slavery itself; thus the only image of slavery which has been acceptable to the mind of the Negro has been the image of the unhappy slave. This, of course, is the same psychological pattern which has caused southern whites, both ante and poste-bellum to blot out of their minds the image of the unhappy slave and avidly to maintain that only the jubilantly happy slave existed, for apparently it has seemed to southern whites that to accept the picture of the unhappy slave is to accept the abolitionists condemnation of slavery.

On all major holidays or social events such as weddings, election days, militia muster, or a fair, some benefits of the holiday seeped down to slaves in the form of lessened work. In the colonial period New England had mock slave "elections" and slave "Governors."

The Mississippi black codes did not allow slaves to beat drums or blow horns. Throughout ante-bellum America the Negroes, slave and free, were required to keep the white notion of the Sabbath. Yet, so enjoyable a day was it generally that slaves could sing of the Sabbath—

> Oh laugh an' sing an' don't git tired.
>   We's all gwine home, some Mond'y,
> To de honey pond an' fritter trees;
>   An' ev'ry day'll be Sund'y.

But of the other six days of the week, Joseph S. Cotter, Sr., a twentieth century Negro, would utter what most slaves must have thought and felt. Cotter wrote:

> I will suppose that fate is just,
> I will suppose that grief is wise,
> And I will tread what Path I must
> To enter Paradise.

Kenneth Stampp has written:

> The average bondsman lived more or less aim-
> lessly in a bleak and narrow world. He lived in a
> world without schools, without books, without learn-
> ed men; he knew less of the fine arts and of aesthetic
> values than he had known in Africa; and he found
> few ways to break the monotonous sameness of all
> his days.[42]

Stampp states that the "culturally rootless" slaves devoted much of their leisure time "to the sheer pleasure of being idle." "The slaves," he continues, having lost the bulk of their African heritage were prevented from sharing in much of the best of southern white culture."[43] And—

> In slavery the Negro existed in a kind of cultural
> void. He lived in a twilight zone between two ways
> of life and was unable to obtain from either many of
> the attributes which distinguish man from beast.[44]

Again Stampp points up this degradation when he discusses the slave's source of leisure-time pleasure through "alcohol in its crudest but cheapest and most concentrated form." "To be sure," he opines, "these bibulous bondsmen merely indulged in a common vice of an age of hard liquor and heavy drinkers: but they, more than their masters, made the periodic solace of the bottle a necessity of life."[45] Bondage moulded the Negro into "a fatalist and futilitarian, for nothing else could reconcile him to his life."[46]

Religion was one pleasure or safety valve which was some-times afforded the bondsman. Just as some masters encouraged religious exercises for the slave, they also provided such things as Saturday night dances which followed an afternoon of loaf-ing, special prizes of food, drink, money or judicious praise for tasks well done; feastings and alcoholic beverages at Christmas and other holidays; much sexual license, and occasional slave weddings. When the crop was laid by there was another period of feasting, and at Christmas slaves were sometimes rewarded with a cash bonus and new clothes. Encouraging slaves to de-velop small gardens for extra foodstuffs not only served to help the planter by keeping the health of the slave up while his grocery bill went down, but this also served to keep the slave more contented. The threat of withdrawal of some or all of these privileges was a means of control over slave behavior. Indeed manipulation of these privileges sometimes took precedence over the lash as a means of control. With some masters the lash was probably a last resort.

As stated, planters in the Upper South sometimes threatened to sell their slaves into the lower South. They painted gruesome pictures of conditions in the rice swamps or sugar plantations. So effective was this propaganda until in the twentieth century many Negroes who reside in the upper South not only paint unrealistically dark pictures of race relations in the lower South, but imagine that they are in some way superior to members of their race who reside in the lower South.

"Slaves yearned for some recognition of their worth as individuals," states one observer, "if only from those in their own limited social orbit for to them this wholly human aspiration was, if anything, more important than it was to the whites. Each slave cherished whatever shreds of self-respect he could preserve."[47] Some slaves felt important because they were looked up to as persons possessing unusual intellectual or physical strength. At times slaves of exceptional intellect and religious bent became preachers of the gospels. Sometimes the master allowed the slave to preach in religious services, while at other times the preacher just gave informal advice as a sort of community elder. It was not uncommon for female slaves to hold this position. At times the practice of voodoism or other manifestations of magic were coupled with preaching. As in the case of Nat Turner, some slaves claimed that they had visions and received messages from God or His angels.[48]

Slaves boasted of the wealth possessed by their masters and got ego satisfaction out of belonging to very wealthy owners. "To be a slave, was thought to be bad enough," wrote Frederick Douglass, "but to be a *poor man's* slave was deemed a disgrace, indeed."[49] "I have heard of slaves objecting to being sent in very small companies to labor in the field," wrote one ex-slave, "lest that some passer-by should think that they belonged to a poor man, who was unable to keep a large gang."[50]

Bondsmen also received self-respect and esteem from such achievements as being the best cotton picker, out-doing one another in some form of athletic competition, and from stealing successfully or in some way outwitting the master or overseer. "Everybody, in the South," declared Frederick Douglass, "wants the privilege of whipping somebody else."[51] Fanny Kemble stated that slavery gave the bondsmen an attitude of "unbounded insolence and tyranny" toward each other.[52]

Not only did slaves derive ego satisfaction out of the high status and wealth of their masters, but they boasted about the high prices which the latter paid to purchase them. If the master had paid $1500.00 for a slave, he sometimes felt superior to one who had been purchased for $1000.00.

Corn-shuckings had great appeal to the slaves. The competition, cameraderie, food and liquor of such occasions provided much entertainment for them. After the work was done and food and drinks consumed, fights sometimes broke out among the bondsmen. After dances or corn-shuckings encounters were sometimes encouraged in the same manner as fights between dogs or roosters, and it seems that the slaves shared heartily the love of physical encounter which W. J. Cash, John Hope Franklin and others have ascribed to southern whites.[53]

While Negroes have been regarded by many persons as having complacent easily satisfied natures, evidence shows this stereotype like so many others, to be false. It appears that where the colored man has asked for little, it is because he was realistic enough to know that at best, he could get only a litle, and often his "satisfaction" has been only a mask to hide his true feelings. The mask which the Negro traditionally has worn presents an interesting study. The Negro often laughed when he was sad, sang to express practically all emotions, and often smiled and feigned love and admiration when he felt hatred and contempt.

The planter was sometimes rationalizing when he depicted the adult slave as an indolent, irresponsible, playful child, and yet, there was considerable truth in this description. Many slaves were well-nigh perfect prototypes of the planter's characterization, and for these the latter erred only in stating that the attributes were innately racial. They were, of course, cultural in origin. Slave pleasures were essentially those of the child—food, sex, play, song, laughter, at times even work. Regarded and treated as a child, the bondsman often acted as one. Seeing that it was in many ways good for the institution of slavery, the planter encouraged this child-posture at every turn, but here the bondsman was being encouraged to do what was not only good for an institution but what in some ways was good for him. The mid-twentieth century knows well that many adults age quickly and die young because they do not sing, play, dance and laugh enough. Modern social science knows that —"Except ye become as little children, ye cannot enter the Kingdom of Heaven," has many deep meanings. In the Old South the planter saw this and often envied the joy of the bondsman, and some persons observed that Jean Jacque Rousseau's happy noble savages might well have been the blacks of the American Southland.

But just as slavery's oppression warped and dwarfed the character and personality of many Negroes, making children of what should have been adults, this same oppression moulded other persons into characters of sterling silver and high carat gold. Oppression and wretchedness did not drive these latter into drink, playfulness, and living for the mere moment, but forced them to seek refuge in the world of the spirit, and this flight from a harsh outer world led to a strengthening and sharpening of that inner world. This amazing slave-formed character can be seen in a Frederick Douglass, James W. C. Pennington, William Wells Brown, Sojourner Truth, and Harriet Tubman before 1865 no less than in Booker Washington, William Hooper Councill, and Similar Souls after 1865. These knew that wretchedness and oppression were not only the sources of their shortcomings, but also the mainsprings of their strength, and many of those who lived into the 1880's and 90's would complain that easy living was destroying the moral fibre of the race.

From the foregoing it is clear that bondsmen found both unhappiness and happiness in the system, and that the amount of each varied according to section, owner, time, and other factors. Slavery was no more the same everywhere than the South itself was the same everywhere, and it is somewhat misleading to write as we often do of "*the* slave regime," "*the* planter," or "*the* slave-owner." There were different types of slave-owners, systems and regimes, and the "typical" here is often little more than myth.

Especially should any objective consideration of the "peculiar institution" take into account the periods through which it passed. This is seldom done, especially by persons who wish to evaluate the effect of the institution on the bondsman. Yet from its beginnings in 1619 until approximately 1800, cotton figured very little in the economic forces which provided sustenance for slavery. Throughout this period there was a fairly strong abolitionist movement, South and North, which must have had considerable to do with how slaves were treated by their masters. No class of human beings is ever completely immune to public opinion. The slave era previous to 1800 was quite different from that of the next sixty years, and within these years the institution was different in the 1800-1820 period from the years 1820-1860. The brief years from 1820-1860 constitute the true cotton kingdom of classic memory, and of course slavery of the period 1861-65, when masters were away at war and there was hope on the part of the slave that a northern victory would bring emancipation, was different from anything that preceded it.

The Old South of which most people are conscious is the one created by the cotton gin and which was in its hey-day for the brief period of about 1820-1860. It is in these forty years that cotton was "king" and during which, in a quest for ever greater profits, the slave system became geared to a feverish pitch. It is in these four decades that cruelties mounted, free Negroes had their liberties most proscribed, and the bondsman was driven and lashed as never before. It is here that the great plot of Denmark Vesey and the bloody uprising of Nat Turner occurred. Perhaps it is in this period also that the most sorrowful of the spirituals were "composed." Certain it is that this era produced the Underground Railroad in high gear and the greatest of all anti-slavery outcries in Garrisonism.

It seems odd that an institution which lasted in this country approximately two and one-half centuries should be stereotyped and judged almost exclusively by a character and nature which was peculiar to it for only four decades. As W. J. Cash and others have shown, this legend of the Old South has determined the popular picture of the planter also. Perpetuated and cherished by southern whites partly because of the aristocratic ideal which it contained, fate has decreed that the stereotyping of the planter at his "best" also should preserve and stereotype slavery at its worse.

HOSTILITY, REVENGE, AND PROTEST AS ELEMENTS IN NEGRO THOUGHT

Among historians, though not necessarily among sociologists, one of the most persistent myths about the mind and personality of Negro Americans is the one which declares that, in and out of slavery, they felt only love for white folk. According to this myth Negro Americans, true to the Uncle Tom-Uncle Remus pattern, have unusually Christian and forgiving natures and could never feel or exhibit hatred toward whites. Attention given by the press and other news media to the number of assaults on and murders of whites by Negroes has done little to do away with the myth in some quarters. Yet, a study of aggression, revenge, and protest as elements in Negro thought reveals that there is more fancy than fact in the traditional picture of the Negro who cannot hate or exact revenge in any way, a picture which some historians have done much to perpetuate.[1]

John Fiske contended that Negro slaves were remarkably contented and happy.[2] James Schouler described Negroes as "a black servile race, sensuous, stupid, brutish, obedient . . . and childish."[3] J. G. Randall, Claude H. Van Tyne, and Ulrich B. Phillips are among the sizeable list of scholars who have held similar notions. Phillips believed the Negro to be innately stupid, docile, submissive, unstable, and negligent.[4] Another stereotype of the same vein would appear to be the type related by the sociologist John Dollard. This scholar has written:

A highly placed white man expressed a widely-held view when he said that Negroes have neither malice nor gratitude; they will do anything in the heat of passion, but once rage is burnt out they do not carry grudges. It is this sudden blind 'passion' which the whites fear in Negroes, and against which they feel they must defend themselves.[5]

Of the mind of the slave, Herbert Aptheker concluded that the sources on the institution are filled with "exaggera-

75

tion, distortion, censorship."[6] Almost a hundred years before
Aptheker arrived at this conclusion, the Negro Martin R.
Delany wrote:

> The colored people are not yet known, even to
> their most professed friends among the white Ameri-
> cans for the reason that politicians, religionists, col-
> onizationists, and Abolitionists, have each and all, at
> different times, presumed to think for, dictate· to,
> and know better what suited colored people, than
> they knew for themselves; and consequently, there
> has been no other knowledge of them obtained, than
> that which has been through these mediums.[7]

Carter Woodson based his life-long crusade to establish Negro
history as a respectable area for scholarly study on the conviction that his race was not known by most Americans.[8] "The
dominant historiography in the United States," wrote Aptheker
in 1951, "either omits the Negro people or presents them as a
people without a past, as a people who have been docile, passive,
parasitic, imitative."[9] "This picture," he concluded, "is a lie."
Further evidence that the Afro-American is too often misun-
derstood is found in the glaring mis-readings of the Negro
mind of which the American Communist Party has been guilty.
These mis-readings constitute one reason why that party failed
to recruit more colored members during the 1930s and 40s.[10]

As is true of a number of stereotypes, some Negroes have
accepted the judgment that their race could bear no grudges
or hates. In his poem "Ode to Ethiopia," Paul Laurence Dunbar
declared—-

> No other race, of white or black,
> When bound as thou wert, to the rack,
>   So seldom stooped to grieving;
> No other race, when free again,
> Forgot the past and proved them men
>   So noble in forgiving.

In a speech before the Forty-first Congress, Hiram Revels declared of his race immediately after the Civil War—"They
bear no revengeful thoughts, no hatred, no animosities toward
their former masters."[11] In 1905 Bishop W. T. Vernon would
say of his race that it felt no resentment nor bitterness about

past treatment, "nor do we cherish resentment for those who harm or strive to harm us now."[12] Further, he opined:

> Omniscience alone may dare to visit the mistakes of buried sires on breathing sons or adjust accounts between the living and the dead. Time, public sentiment and God will finally reward this patient courage and make all things right.[13]

The notion that colored Americans are very forgiving where their oppressors and traducers are concerned is prominent in Negro literature. In *Fire in the Flint*,[14] although the hero's sister's honor and his brother's life have been sacrificed to race prejudice, the author, Walter White, has this hero decide to minister to the physical ills of a critically sick white girl in the town of these mis-adventures. Similar instances of this chivalrous behavior are numerous in Negro literature. Benjamin Mays sees the race's view of God as one explanation for its penchant for forgiveness. Believing as they do about God, he states, Negroes in many instances have stood and suffered much without bitterness, without striking back.[15]

Today, among the more discerning students of the Negro, the supposed innate docility of the colored man is apt to be interpreted as a mask behind which he hides his true feelings. In other words, his docility, meekness, and humor were often, though not always, insincere. They were adjustment and survival techniques in a society where education, economical, political, and military power were overwhelmingly against him. On this, Robert R. Moton, observed:

> Properly to interpret the Negro one should understand at the outset that the psychology of the Negro is protective. The Negro everywhere has a steadfast purpose of survival. . . . It [the race] has long been subject to adversity; this has made the race cautious. . . . this has made it secretive in the presence of preponderant power and general animosity.[16]

Moton calls the Negro's "artful and adroit accommodation of his manners and methods to what he knows to be the weakness and foibles of his white neighbor" the race's defense mechanism."[17] "The white man does not know the Negro so well as he thinks he does," said a post-bellum South Carolina white man.[18] A Georgia planter said—"So deceitful is the Negro that as far as my own experience extends I could never in a single instance decipher his character. . . . We planters could never in a single instance get at the truth."[19] Another planter said:

> The most general defect in the character of the Negro is hypocrisy: and this hypocrisy frequently makes him pretend to more ignorance than he possesses; and if his master treats him, as a fool, he will be sure to act the fool's part. This is a very convenient trait, as it frequently serves as an apology for awkwardness and neglect of duty.[20]

Hortense Powdermaker has indicated well the revenge element in the Uncle-Tom pose which many Negroes have assumed around whites. Calling this type "the unaggressive Negro," she has noted that he enjoys and feels superior to whites in this role because, (1) through this masochistic suffering he atones for guilt feelings that are induced by his hatred of whites, (2) he feels that he is fooling whites with his posture of meekness and humility, (3) taking personally the injunctions "Blessed are the meek," and "Blessed are those who suffer," he feels that his Christianity is superior to the kind that is practiced by whites, and, (4) taking personally the idea, "the first shall be last, and the last shall be first," he believes that the ultimate triumph belongs to the colored and not the white man.[21]

For too long even the opponents of slavery and oppression have thought of the bondsman and freedman as victim and hapless prey whose every danger came from the outside world, without realizing, perhaps, that in so doing they were accepting the biased southern white man's view of the slave and the Negro. In other words, both friend and foe of the Negro too often have thought of him as a helpless, passive, submissive, sub-human creature. Yet, though otherwise enslaved, the human being who has the opportunity to work and play is never completely without defenses. As is the case with freedom, human bondage is never absolute.[22] The slave had more freedom than is commonly realized, one of which was the freedom to hate.

Psychologists inform us that being thwarted in our desires is the root of almost all hatred. Today, no one should seriously deny that, in an otherwise democratic society, to deprive a person or group of freedom and opportunity is to thwart the desires of that person or group. Although hatred between Negroes and whites always has existed, its existence is a taboo which both races generally have denied. While even Negro scholars genereally have chosen to disavow the existence of this hatred, Edgar Thompson, John Dollard, Gunnar Myrdal, Arnold M. Rose, Gordon Allport, Hortense Powdermaker and other white scholars have accepted it for what it actually is. Of the Negro's hatreds, Gunnar Myrdal noted:

> Physical attack [by Negroes] upon the whites is suicidal. Aggression has to be kept suppressed and normally is suppressed. It creeps up, however, in thousands of ways. The whites do not get as wholehearted a response from their Negroes as they would if the latter were well satisfied with the necessity of accommodation. Only occasional acts of violence but much laziness, carelessness, unreliability, petty stealing and lying are undoubtedly to be explained as concealed aggression. The shielding of Negro criminals and suspects, the dislike of testifying against another Negro, and generally the defensive solidarity in the protective Negro community has a definite taint of hostility.[23]

Of one type of his "examples of Negro hatred of whites" and Negro self-glorification, Arnold Rose states that "in general they are very much like what is encouraged in the armed forces of a nation as 'pride in outfit,' 'loyalty to the nation,' and 'hatred of the enemy'."[24] "There is," he stated, "regular indoctrination in these attitudes among Negroes, even though it is more informal than that practiced in the armed forces."[25] Among some groups, he states, the stronger one's avowed hatred for whites the more acceptable he is in the group. "This hatred of white people is not pathological—far from it," Rose avers. "It is a healthy human reaction to oppression, insult, and terror," which "should not be surprising" to anyone, he concludes. Rose indicates his belief that, at least some of the time, most Negroes hate whites. "Hatred of the white man who has humiliated and frustrated him" is the "predominating feeling" of the Negro toward "the strong dominating group" says Helen V. McLean.[26] John Dollard adds:

> [The Negro's] situation . . . is one of frustration.
> . . . The usual human response to frustration is aggression against the frustrating object. In this case the frustrating object is the American white caste which maintains its dominance over the Negro caste in various ways. . . . The white caste . . . means all white people in America, since the caste line is drawn in the North as effectively, if not as formally, as in the South.[27]

That some Negro sociologists have been willing to call hatred by its real name is evident from the following observations by Horace Cayton.

> There is a close analogy between Negroes living in America and a soldier under battle condition. . . . The Negro has had to learn, like the war-hardened veteran, to adapt himself to fear in order to survive. He has developed, because of this constant presence of fear, a sort of immunity to it. . . . I am convinced that at the core of the Negro's mentality there is a fear-hate-fear complex.[28]

Although they often have been reluctant to admit its existence, southern whites have sensed the hostility present in many words and acts of the Negro, and it is this awareness which accounts, in large part, for much of the vicious brutality which whites have inflicted on Negroes.[29] In their superficial observation, many persons have not seen this hatred producing hatred, and have charged that the "meek, humble, helpless, benign" Negro has been object of such brutality because too many white southerners are depraved barbarians. Probably the success and popularity which Booker Washington had with southern whites was due not only to his compromises, as important as these were, but in considerable part to the fact that whites sensed no veiled hostility in his protestations of friendship. Washington could not hate whites, but probably felt considerable veiled hatred for his own race.[30] Although the origin of the Negro's hatreds is understandable, through the hostility and aggression which he has never been able completely to veil, the Negro has been the cause of some of the vicious and brutal treatment to which he has been subjected. Often when he has thought that he was fooling the white man, his dissembling was fooling only himself. It should be obvious, however, that since he did not create the conditions which caused him to hate whites, the Negro cannot be considered the *primary* cause of the viciousness and barbaric treatment here alluded to. Too often in the history of the South both the white and colored man have been pathetic victims of cruel circumstance.

THE SLAVE'S AGGRESSION, REVENGE, AND PROTEST

In his famous *Appeal* the ex-slave David Walker referred to southern whites as the "natural enemies" of his race, and Gabriel Prosser, Nat Turner, Denmark Vesey and other leaders of slave plots and rebellions planned to kill as many whites as possible. Usually, however, slave aggressions and revenge were less direct and more veiled than what these men proposed or did. In his revenge against whites the slave resorted to such means as loafing when the planter or overseer was absent, being cruel to the farm animals, damaging tools and the agricultural produce being worked, making jokes about and adversely criticizing whites when they were not present, despoiling the food being prepared for their consumption, setting fire to their property, stealing their hams, chickens, and other items, attempting to conjure them and their farm animals, poisonings, bodily assault,[31] feigning illness, mimicrying whites in speech, dress or mannerisms, consigning their souls to an eternity in flaming hell, playing with tongue in cheek the meek, obedient "good darky" role, absconding, or even committing suicide.[32]

Many Negroes always have believed that both in this life and the one to come God will punish anyone who mistreated them.[33] To one another as well as to whites who "mistreated' them, they have said openly or silently, "I'm going to pray for you," meaning that they were going to ask God to exact retribution. They have believed that no "mean white folk" will be admitted into Heaven, but instead will surely burn pitiously and mercilessly in hell. In this hell-going category Negroes have tended to place many southern whites. In ante-bellum days, even when "Ole Marster" or his wife or the over-seer died of natural causes, bondsmen sometimes thought that the death was God's vengeance for wrongs which had been visited upon them. The same conclusion was often reached about any other calamity such as drought, plague, fire, or acci-dent which befell whites.

The Afro-American has been keenly aware that, like the press, Supreme Court, Congress and other institutions, at times the Christian church has sided with slavery and racial segre-gation and discrimination. Slaves were sometimes compelled to sit and listen to ministers of the gospel defend slavery and the actions of the planter. Despite frequent injunctions to "obey your masters" and "wait on the lord," many bondsmen re-mained unconvinced. They continued to sing that, "Everybody talking 'bout Heaven ain't a-goin there," and slave plots, in-surrections, and absconding were fairly frequent. Although a number of the spirituals do reveal this protest and hatred of whites, Robert Kerlin, a close student of Negro music, chose to accept the myth of the non-hating Negro. "There is no prayer for vengeance in the Spirituals, no vindictive spirit ever suggested," Kerlin wrote.[34] The true religious feelings of slaves often were manifest only in the secret meetings which they would hold in the woods or in some other secluded place after singing "Steal Away to Jesus."[35]

Many persons have viewed the Negro's religiosity as aris-ing primarily out of his need to find understanding and hope in his plight. In this view, the shortcomings of his external environment created the slave's great need for the Christian religion and determined that he would embrace it with great fervor. Largely neglected to date, however, is consideration of the possibility that the fears and hopes which drove the bonds-man and freedman to religion were not due *directly* so much to the cruel and inhumane treatment to which he was sub-jected by his external environment, but that his compelling need for Christianity may well have derived more from the rage and hostility which he carried within himself.[36]

Revenge in Tales, Wit and Humor

It is well recognized that, among other uses, wit and humor are age-old devices used by human beings to work off their hostilities. Thus it is that jokes on the mother-in-law, or about "my sweet little wife," or about the preacher, police-man, or boss are universal and legion. Jokes in which a slave or freedman makes the white man look foolish are common among Afro-Americans.[37] Of this, one sociologist wrote in 1949 that among Negroes:

> Jokes at the expense of white people are made and passed around with an intensity of effort that shows they are not merely jokes. Some of the jokes are so bitter as almost to lack humor, thus revealing their kinship to hatred.[38]

Slave-owners generally overlooked that a number of the "harmless" tales which they delighted to hear from slaves had subtle undertones of a less benign character. Bondsmen de-lighted in such stories as those of the fox and the hare, the fox and the tar-baby, the race between the hare and the tortoise, of a magic hoe which worked itself, and of flying Africans who escaped whippings and bondage by magically changing into birds and flying away to the Dark Continent. Other tales poked fun at the Irish and poor whites, as well as at the "Po hard-working Nigger" and his unhappy lot. In these tales the slaves usually identified themselves with the victorious under-dog. With the omnipresent hare outwitting the fox the bonds-men were saying to themselves that the stone that was rejected should eventually become the corner-stone.[39]

Commenting on Bernard Wolfe's study of the Uncle Remus tales, Arnold Rose writes that Wolfe shows that "Ne-groes expressed their hatred of the white man through these stories."[40] "Wolfe shows," Rose continues, "that [Joel Chand-ler] Harris was aware of this but camouflaged the hatred with the stereotyped Uncle Remus and with the statement that the stories originated in Africa."[41] Wolfe himself declared that, "A Negro slave who yielded his mind fully to his race hatreds in an absolutely white-dominated situation must go mad; and the function of such folk symbols as Brer Rabbit is precisely

to prevent inner explosions by siphoning off these hatreds before they can completely possess consciousness."[42]

REVENGE IN STEALING

Slave masters often complained that stealing was a habit
of the Negro, and many members of the ruling caste came to
feel that this was a racial characteristic. Usually, however, the
slave did not think that he could steal from his owner. Since
the latter paid him nothing for his labors, and since most of
the physical wealth which the master possessed was the direct
result of the slave's labor, the latter felt that he was exacting
revenge and only taking a portion of that which was owed to
him. One "took" from whites, but "stole" only from fellow
slaves. Travellers in the South were quick to notice the "taking" habit of the slave, and contemporary sociologists have
attested to the continuation of this practice among freedmen.[43]

One planter said that bondage made slaves "callous to the
ideas of honor and even honesty," and that bondsmen were
"heedless, thoughtless."[44] Another planter said that the slave's
feeling of indebtedness to his master "is of so flimsy a character
that none of us rely upon it."[45] While it is true that many
slaves lied, pretended, loafed and stole, like the planters they
were merely acting in what they conceived to be their best interests. Often neither planter nor slave could claim that any universally acceptable moral code constituted the basis of his
thought and actions. On questions of morality, Kenneth
Stampp asserts that "many slaves rejected the answers which
their masters gave. .. . . The slaves did not thereby repudiate
law and morality: rather, they formulated legal and moral
codes of their own."[46] "No slave would betray another," Stampp
states, and informers were held in the lowest esteem.[47] In one
instance slaves were told by a fugitive brother:

> Numerous as are the escapes from slavery, they
> would be far more so, were you not embarassed by
> your misinterpretations of the rights of property.
> You hesitate to take even the dullest of your master's
> horses—whereas it is your duty to take the fleetest.
> Your consciences suggest doubts, whether in quitting
> your bondage, you are at liberty to put in your packs

what you need of food and clothing. But were you better informed you would not scruple to break your masters' locks, and take all their money. You are taught to respect the rights of property. But, no such rights belong to the slaveholder. His rights to property is that of the robber-right. . . . You are prisoners of war, in an enemy's country. . . . by all the rules of war, you have the fullest liberty to plunder, burn, and kill.[48]

Of his own escape, Frederick Douglass wrote his former master, "In leaving you, I took nothing but what belonged to me, and in no way lessened your means for obtaining an *honest* living."[49] On February 20, 1860 a slave owner, Mrs. Sarah Logue of Tennessee, wrote to one of her fugitive slaves then residing in Syracuse, New York, complaining that partly as a consequence of his running away and stealing one of her fine mares, she had come upon hard times. She felt that the fugitive could square matters by sending her one thousand dollars, then she would give up all claims to him. He refused and called her a wretched old woman. "Have you got to learn that human rights are mutual and reciprocal, and if you take my liberty and life, you forfeit your own liberty and life?" he asked.[50] Of her husband, this fugitive asked Mrs. Logue: "Is it a greater sin for me to steal his horse, than it was for him to rob my mother's cradle, and steal me?" Everywhere in the Negro's utterances of the *ante-bellum* period is the omnipresent sentiment that to eat the fruit of his own toil, to clothe his person with the work of his own hands, is not considered stealing.

Crimes, Threats of Crimes, and Attacks on the Nation's Idealism

Hortense Powdermaker has pointed to the aggressive element in stealing and other crimes. She states:

Crimes committed by the slaves are . . . evidence of lack of acceptance of status and of aggressive feelings toward whites. . . . The fact that these crimes were committed in the face of the most severe deterrents, bears witness to the strength of the underlying aggression.[51]

The large list of crimes committed by slaves included "murder, rape, attempted rape, arson, theft, burglary, and practically every conceivable crime."[52]

There is indication of a revenge element even in the bitter denunciations by Negroes of many of the nation's ideals, and in their threatened as well as actual lawlessness and violence. Was there revenge in Frederick Douglass' rejection of the national holidays? Addressing the citizens of Rochester, New York for the Fourth of July celebration in 1852, Douglass used the topic, "What to the Slave is the Fourth of July?" To whites, he concluded: "This Fourth of July is *yours*, not *mine*. You may rejoice, I must mourn."[53] On a similar occasion in 1857 Charles Lenox Remond said:

> Today, there are, on the Southern plantations, between three and four millions, to whom the popular Fourth of July . . . is a most palpable insult; and to every white American who has any sympathy whatever with the oppressed, the day is also a mockery.[54]

The first date which Nat Turner selected for his famed insurrection was the Fourth of July, 1831. He took his ensuing illness, however, as a sign that he should change the date.

During the ante-bellum era, among the forms of organized protest were the Underground Railroad; such plots and rebellions as the 1739 Cato conspiracy near Charleston which resulted in the death of approximately thirty white persons, the 1741 "conspiracy" to burn New York city, the 1800 Gabriel plot and 1831 Nat Turner insurrection in Virginia; and the Denmark Vesey-led plot in South Carolina; periodic national Negro conventions; founding of separate Negro churches and schools, and participation in the abolitionist movement. From the very beginning Negroes were prominent in the founding, organizing, and continuous activities of the American Anti-Slavery Society, which was throughout an interracial enterprise. Among the early Negro leaders of this organization were Robert Purvis, Samuel Cornish, Christopher Rush, Charles B. Ray, Peter Williams, James McCrummell, James W. C. Pennington, and George Whipple.

Appealing to European audiences for help with the American race problem has been one form of Negro protest. Of Negro abolitionists who took the bondsman's cause directly to European audiences were William Wells Brown, Ellen and William Craft, Alexander Crummell, Frederick Douglass, Henry Highland Garnet, Nathaniel Paul, Charles Lenox Remond, and Samuel Ringgold Ward.

Speaking in celebration of New York's abolition of slavery in 1827 the Reverend Nathaniel Paul indicated what his revenge would be if slavery did not end all over the nation. He wrote:

> Did I believe that it [slavery] would always continue, and that man to the end of time would be permited with impunity to usurp the same undue authority over his fellows, I would disallow any allegiance or obligation I was under to my fellow creatures, or any submission that I owed to the law of the country; I would deny the superintending power of divine Providence in the affairs of this life; I would ridicule the religion of the Saviour of the World, and treat as the worst of men the ministers of the everlasting gospel; I would consider my Bible as a book of false and delusive fables, and commit it to flame. Nay, I would still go further: I would at once confess myself an atheist, and deny the existence of a holy God.[55]

During the Mexican War period, Frederick Douglass had said:

> I should welcome the intelligence tomorrow, should it come, that the slaves had risen in the South, and that the sable arms which had been engaged in beautifying and adorning the South were engaged in spreading death and devastation there. . . . Why you welcomed the intelligence from France, that Louis Philippe had . . . [achieved a victory] by Republicanism over Royalty. .. . . and should you not hail, with equal pleasure, the tidings from the South that the slaves had risen?[56]

The 1850 fugitive slave act, 1854 Kansas-Nebraska Act, and 1856 Dred Scott decision joined with other seeming south-

ern victories in the sectional struggle to make the 1850s a particularly depressing period for Negro abolitionists. Although
they continued to protest through such meeans as participating
in the Underground Railroad and writing and speaking against
slavery, a new and strong note of threatened disloyalty and
violence entered their utterances. Reflecting the northern spirit
which produced the personal liberty statutes and open violation
of the fugitive slave law, some colored persons passed resolutions stating unequivocally that they disapproved of the law
and had absolutely no intention of obeying it. "We will repudiate all and every law," said one group, "that has for its
object the oppression of any human being, or seeks to assign
us degrading positions."[57] This same group formed a vigilance
association "to look out for the panting fugitive, and also for
the oppressor, when he shall make his approach."[58] In a similar
vein, Frederick Douglas exhorted:

> Without appealing to any higher feeling I would
> warn the American people, and the American gov-
> ernment, [that] . . . there is a point beyond which
> human endurance cannot go. The crushed worm may
> yet turn under the heel of the oppressor. . . . Those
> sable arms that have, for the last two centuries, been
> engaged in cultivating and adorning the fair fields of
> our country, may yet become the instruments of ter-
> ror, desolation and death, throughout our borders.[59]

At another point, Douglass declared: "Slaveholders have made
it almost impossible for the slave to commit any crime, known
either to the laws of God or the laws of man. If he steals he
takes his own; if he kills his master, he imitates only the heroes
of the revolution. . . . Make a man a slave and you rob him
of moral responsibility."[60]

Douglass pointed out that should the nation find itself
involved in a life and death war with a European power, three
million slaves might use this as an opportunity to strike for
their freedom. To Douglass, this was "a fearful multitude to
be in chains." While opposing the Mexican War, Douglass had
said two years earlier:

> For my part, I would not care if, tomorrow, I should
> hear of the death of every man who engaged in that

bloody war in Mexico, and that every man had met the fate he went there to perpetrate upon unoffending Mexicans.[61]

At an 1851 state convention of Ohio Negroes Charles H. Langston and H. Ford Douglass were among those present who agreed that the United States Constitution was a pro-slavery document. Langston said, "I would call on every slave, from Maryland to Texas, to rise and assert their liberties, and cut their masters' throats if they attempt again to reduce them to slavery."[62] Robert Purvis suggested that, in reply to the Dred Scott decision, for Free Negroes to continue to support the United States government was "the height of folly and the depth of pusillanimity."[63] Calling American democracy 'piebald and rotten," "the only duty the colored man owes' to the Constitution, he declared, "is to denounce and repudiate it."[64] C. L. Remond held similar views. In 1857 Remond told a meeting of the Massachusetts Anti-Slavery Society:

> The time is coming when a larger number than is gathered here today will subscribe to the idea of a dissolution of the Union as the only means of their own safety, as well as of the emancipation of the slave.[65]

Perhaps because he was a fugitive Remond feared that he would be returned to slavery. He regretted intensely that after 1850 Massachusetts was no longer a safe place for fugitives. A genuine revolutionist like David Walker and William Lloyd Garrison, Remond called for immediate uncompromising abolition of slavery.[66] So bitter was he in 1858 that he recommended slave insurrections as proper action, and "boldly proclaimed himself a traitor to the government and the Union."[67] As early as 1843 Henry Highland Garnet had issued a burning call for all bondsmen to rise, demand immediate emancipation, and back the demand with the price of their lives and blood if this were necessary. "There is not much hope of redemption without the shedding of blood," he declared.[68] In this period the figure of Toussaint L'Ouverture loomed larger than ever in Negro thought. In 1857 James Theodore Holly gave an especially eloquent plea for the L'Ouverture type of leadership.[69]

Out of a total of eighteen persons, five Negroes were direct participants in John Brown's "raid" at Harpers Ferry. Negroes showed their feelings in favor of the "raid" through mass meetings, letters to Brown and to friends and newspapers, and in other ways. They voted their endorsement and hearty approval of the spirit shown by Brown, and their regrets that he did not succeed. One group declared: "We will teach our children to revere his name . . . as being the greatest man in the nineteenth century."[70] Commenting on Brown's venture, Frederick Douglass wrote:

> I am ever ready to write, speak, publish, organize, combine, and even to conspire against Slavery, when there is a reasonable hope for success. Men who live by robbing their fellow men of their labor and liberty, have forfeited their right to know anything of the thoughts, feeling or purposes of those whom they rob and plunder.[71]

If the thinking of Remond and others that only militant action would end slavery was radical, it must be remembered that the institution actually was eliminated in the most radical action imaginary—civil war. And the Free Negro was by no means alone as he drifted toward more radical thinking in the 1850s. This was an age of radicalism which saw the birth of the Republican party, William Seward's "Irrepressible Conflict" utterances, Harriet Beecher Stowe's epic indictment, and the daring of John Brown all well-matched by the incendiary proposals of such southern Fire-Eaters as R. B. Rhett and William H. Yancey.

Revenge in Civil War and Reconstruction Eras

During the Civil War bondsmen were to get revenge in such ways as loafing more than ever, being openly impudent and sassy, telling Yankee soldiers where "Ole Missy" hid the silverware and other valuables, or running away to fight or work for the Federals. In his book, *Black Reconstruction*, W. E. B. Du Bois declared that the slaves went on a virtual sit-down strike during the war.[72] This conclusion is doubtless an exaggeration, although Bell I. Wiley has stated that slave unruliness was "far more common than postwar commentators

have usually admitted."[73] Also, no doubt overdrawn is the
picture which Herbert Aptheker, a Marxist like Du Bois, has
drawn of slave militancy during the war.[74]

Negroes saw the war, not only in terms of their own revenge acts and thoughts, but they were convinced that through
the war God was using the North to punish the South, and
using the suffering and casualties to punish the entire nation
for the wrongs which the white man had visited upon the black.
That Negroes were not alone in this latter thought can be seen
in the words of President Lincoln's Second Inaugural Address.
Here the President declared that it might be God's will that the
war should continue until every drop of blood drawn with the
lash should be repaid by one drawn with the sword. In the
mind of the slave the planter was "Satan," who was getting
his due punishment.

That revenge was not the uppermost thought in the mind
of the Negro soldier is clear. One ex-slave Union soldier visited
his former mistress in Tennessee while on a furlough. She reminded him of the manner in which she had nursed him as a
child and said, "Now you are fighting me." The ex-slave answered: "No'm, I ain't fighting you, I'm fighting to get free."[75]
Another ex-bondsman said—"I fought to free my mammy and
her little children all through Nashville and Franklin and
Columbia, Tennessee, and all down through Alabama and Augusta, Georgia."[76]

When the planters returned home from the battlefields
and saw the poverty, desolation and wretchedness which their
gamble had wrought, the despair, remorse and guilt which
many felt could be assuaged by nothing short of self-destruction. Looking backward, the planter knew that even with the
abolitionists, high-tariff men, and internal - improvementers,
the world of 1831-1861 was heaven compared with the hell
which secession had wrought. And try as he might to blame
Abe Lincoln for tricking the South into war, deep down inside
the planter knew that the decision to secede and fight if need
be was the South's alone. While he looked around for scape-
goats, the planter could not escape an awful sense of personal
guilt nor the human need to punish himself in atonement.
Thus it is said by the freedmen that scores of ex-slave owners

took to malingering and died of strokes, heart attacks, or slowly wasted away in awesome silence.[77] Remorse and guilt, however, are not all that the planter felt. "With fear, bitterness, and rage in their hearts," Dollard says of them, "the white people of the South set out to salvage what they could of the old order,"[78] and—"Reconstruction was in a sense a prolonged race riot."[79]

But midst his jubilation the ex-slave, too, felt some guilt for the desolation brought upon the South. Despite his lowly estate, even while a bondsman he, too, loved the section. He, too, loved its rivers, hills, valleys, woods, climate, cotton, to-bacco, and epic watermelon, chicken, pork, and hominy. The South had long since seeped into his heart and bones, and he felt guilty at being the central issue in the controversy which had brought a proud section to its knees. In part it may have been as atonement for guilt feelings which prodded the freed-man to vow to share willingly the sufferings and hardship which were the price of lifting the section to its former eminence, wealth, and pride. Still there was probably a revenge element, albeit again mixed with and often submerged by other motives, in such acts as the freedman's refusal to work for "Ole Mars-ter,"[80] being lazy on the job, joining the Union League and voting the Republican ticket, dressing "fancy-like," refusing to attend religious services if he had been compelled to do so in bondage, migrating from southern farm to the city or to some western or northern city, serving as strike-breaker, vio-lating the laws of urban communities, or even aspiring to get an education,[81] wealth, or a white collar job[82] so as to poossess in freedom those attributes and material things which bondage had scrupulously withheld. Also, Dollard sees aggression in the "withdrawal of deference forms and prestige acknowledge-ments to white people,"[83] frequent moving from one share-cropping farm to another,[84] and "telling tales about southern white people to northerners and other democratic sympathiz-ers."[85] Dollard points out that in their dreams Negroes get off aggressions against whites, and he gives actual cases.[86] Freed-men would also get revenge by, where possible, making whites use the titles "Mr." or "Mrs." when addressing them, and in-sisting that whites take off their hats while inside their homes, not trading wth stores whose clerks are impolite to Negroes, or by automobile driving which threatens to run over white pedestrians, going out of their way to pick fist fights, suing white businessmen, telling tales on whites to whites in an effort to get one fired from his job or otherwise start trouble, and by exhibiting prejudice against poor whites and Jews, Chinese, Mexicans, "Dagos," "Polocks," and other minorities, or, indeed, against other Negroes.[87] Too, Negroes have been criticized for contributing so meagerly to their own charitable, educational, and similar enterprises. On this, Arnold Rose states— "There is a certain amount of protest involved in this lack of charity—'If the whites want segregation, let them pay for it',"[88] they seem to say. Related to this, probably present in the readiness with which some Negroes have been willing to become public charges or even spend time in jail, or with which some slave and free un-married Negro girls accept public aid for repeated pregnancies is a revenge motive. Perhaps relevant here is the song, popular during the depression of the 'thirties, which had as its theme the words—"Let Jesus lead you, and the welfare feed you."

Charles S. Johnson told of Negroes who "get the white man's nerves" by maintaining in their presence a posture of cold politeness, and he stated that some Negroes get revenge by avoidance of contact with whites.[89] During bondage, in addition to the sheer thrill of "conquest," to outwit the white man often carried the reward of a stolen bit of ham, watermelon, or some other denied delicacy, or of respite from work. While this game was so dangerous that bondsmen played it only occasionally, there would be freedmen who would regard living by their wits as the only smart way to live. Now in their revenge against "the white man's work," they could render part-time service for full-time pay, or steal money or other material goods from the white employer, or if they refused to work at all they had to live by crimes in which members of their own race were exploited as well as whites. Perhaps many have viewed all forms of "revenge against work" as revenge against whites.

In the post-bellum period, the prevalence of lynching in the South and nation has focussed considerable attention on the rape of white women by Negroes. Recent research has shown that rape was not a charge in most lynchings, that the antebellum period was by no means free of instances of rape, and that in the rape of white women by Negroes there has sometimes been present the revenge motive. Here the rapist, by despoiling that which the white man seems to prize most, may think of himself as exacting the revenge *par excellence.*

During the Reconstruction period, mingled with the Negro's joy of freedom was remorse and pity for the planter.[91] Some freedmen believed that the younger whites were ashamed of the licentious and cruel behavior which their parents and grandparents too often had been guilty of during slavery, and most freedmen ardently desired that there should be peace between the races in the South.[92] Examples of this spirit are numerous. During the first session of the Forty-second Congress Representative Benjamin S. Turner of Alabama introduced a bill to remove all political and legal disabilities from southern whites.[93] He also sought to get the cotton tax money refunded to the South. Other Negro congressmen sponsored similar legislation, and in some instances Negro politicians holding state and national offices lost favor with their own race because they were thought to be too friendly toward southern whites. Although the enactment of such a program would seriously jeopardize his political future, Senator Hiram Revels fought for general amnesty. In the Senate he never showed either bitterness or vindictiveness and sought to advance the interests of all Mississippians.[94] He never joined in the popular villification of Jefferson Davis and once declared: "The white race has no better friend than I," and it is generally agreed that he matched word with deed in this regards.[295] Representative Charles E. Nash of Louisiana said of white southerners:

> We are not enemies but brethren. . . . This country is our joint inheritance. . . . Over brothers' graves let brothers' quarrels die. Let there be peace between us that swords which we have learned to use so well, may strike only at a common foe.[96]

There were times, however, when, focussing in their speeches on the uglier facts of slavery and Reconstruction,

Negro congressmen and other politicians appeared to be anti-South and filled with bitterness. In his defense of Radical Reconstruction measures Robert B. Elliott, South Carolina congressman, made bitter assaults on the class of former slave holders.[97] But even Elliott worked for measures which benefited southern whites exclusively.[98] In a speech in support of the Force Bill Representative Thomas E. Miller of South Carolina bitterly castigated the South. In bitter language, reminiscent of H. L. Mencken's famed indictment, he declared of white southerners:

> There is no people in the world more self-opinionated without cause, more bigoted without achievements, more boastful without a status, no people in the world so quick to misjudge their countrymen and to mis-state historical facts of political economy and to impugn the motives of others. History does not record a civilized people who have been contented with so little and who can feed so long on a worthless, buried past.[99]

Among Negro congressmen of this period Miller's attitude and record is one of the closest to the most radical of the Radicals. Also in support of the Force Bill, Representative John M. Langston of Virginia said: "I would pass bills and pile up penalties and put behind every bill soldiers with bayonets until they rose to the top of mountains and kissed the stars" to protect Negro rights.[100]

Impudence or "sassiness" has been one long-standing form of revenge which the Negro has exacted. Because of the rise of revenge in this and other forms some freedmen felt that the work of the Ku Klux Klan was largely good. Klansmen whipped many white and colored men for mismanaging their farms through laziness, for commiting adultery or otherwise mistreating their families, and for other forms of immorality. One freedman opined that, "any nigger that behave hisself and don't go running round late at night and drinking never had no trouble with the Kluckers."[101] Another averred: "I think the Ku Klux Klan was a good thing. . . . The darkies got sassy, trifling, lazy. They was notorious—they got mean. The men wouldn't work. . . . They woulda starved the whites out and theirselves too."[102] Another opined: "Seems like there wa'n't no trouble 'mongst the whites and blacks till after the war. Some white mens come down from North and mess up with the niggers."[103]

REVENGE IN THE EXODUSES

In the late 1870s around forty thousand freedmen left the South and moved to the North and West, with Kansas as the main goal of emigration. Although there were many motives behind this exodus and subsequent ones from the section, revenge against southern whites probably has been one of these motives.[104] As one "Pap" Singleton wrote a pamphlet on "The Advantage of Living in a Free State," as inspiration for the exodus which began in the seventies, the *Chicago Defender* would provide similar and greater encouragement and help for the great exodus of the World War I era which saw around one million Negroes move from South to North. Reporting on the role of the *Defender*, one leading sociologist states.

The *Chicago Defender* . . . not only propagandized for migration but printed train schedules, railroad rates, and gave other detailed information that migrants would need to know. It described in glowing and exaggerated terms the advantages of the North; it printed advertisements of specific jobs.[105]

Analyzing the exodus, this sociologist also has noted:

Migration was not a temporary response to the needs of Northern war industry; it was also a permanent expression of the Negro protest. Escape from the South was a protest against the South, and the escape allowed an increase in protest.[106]

With many Negroes the hatred which they have been compelled to suppress while in the South has come out in marked fashion after migration to the North. It seems that the long period of suppression has increased the intensity of the reaction. This is probably one source of the strength of the assaults on slavery made by Frederick Douglass and other fugitives from slavery who participated in the abolitionist movement. Also, the mounting scope and intensity of Negro protest since 1920 is partly to be explained by this fact, Part of the explanation for Richard Wright's strong and eloquent protest can be acquired from a reading of his autobiographical *Black Boy*, giving particular attention to the hatreds which he was forced to suppress while living as a youth in the South.[107] The last two pages of this volume, in which he gives his reasons for leaving the South, indicate that he saw an element of revenge in his leaving.[108]

REVENGE IN SPORTS

It is generally recognized that individuals may direct their hostilities and aggressions against themselves in diverse self-destructive ways or else they may direct them against society in destructive ways. Similarly, hostilities and aggressions may be channeled into socially useful activities in recreation or in some competitive work, business, or political action. Long largely excluded from the worlds of politics and business, and taught contempt for work by his bondage, sports or recreation has been an ideal area in which the Negro could work off his hostilities. Here, as in few other areas, he could endeavor to "beat" the white man. With his energies so channeled into this area, there can be small wonder that the Negro has had such a prominent role in boxing, track, football, basketball, and whatever sport he has turned his attention to, or that the Negro masses have participated vicariously but enthusiastically in the victories and defeats of their outstanding athletes.[109] "It is probable," one eminent sociologist has stated, "that when a Negro prize fighter knocks out a white opponent, many Negroes are pleased not only because they feel he is showing white people that a Negro has ability, but also because a Negro is hitting and hurting a white man."[110] Some persons have viewed the legal battles of the National Association for the Advancement of Colored People and other race protest organizations in the same way. On this, Arnold Rose notes that, "In fighting the bully, the protest organization acts as a big brother to the average Negro."[111]

BOOMERANGS FROM THE URGE TO REVENGE

The Negro's hate-induced revenge urges have led not only to his making mental, verbal, and bodily assaults on the white man and on the national culture, but, in a number of ways, the Negro himself has been an object of his own hatreds.

One scholar has noted that hate leads to a flight-fight pattern in human behavior.[112] This is doubtless one source of the Negro's desire to flee from himself through such devices as "passing" for white, bleaching his skin, straightening his hair, or denying that there is a distinct and valid Negro history, press, business, or culture. Contrary to popular belief, the Negro's self-hatred is not all absorbed from the negative views of his race held by many whites. A number of psychologists hold that in human behavior there is a frustration—hate—revenge—guilt—atonement syndrome. The individual can effectively rid himself of oppressive guilt feelings derived from hating and revenge thoughts and acts only through some form of punishment,[113] either self-administered or coming from an external source. Thus it is probable that some of the Negro's self-degradation is self-punishment administered to atone for guilt feelings derived from hostility and revenge thoughts and acts directed at whites.

If some Negroes have felt a revenge element in passing for white, it would seem that the opposite is also true. "One way of expressing hatred of whites," writes Arnold Rose, "is to avoid becoming white when the opportunity offers itself."[134]

Aggression by Negroes Against Negroes

Fighting is the overt physical expression of hating, and there are countless ways of fighting. Gunnar Myrdal and other scholars have held that deflected hatred of the white man is a primary reason that Negroes fight one another in notorious fashion. Among forms of Negro aggression against Negroes because of hatred of whites, Dollard lists excessive sexual jealousy, gambling, boasting and banter (playing the "dozens"), gossip, and economic exploitation.[116] Arnold Rose has noted the bossy attitude which some Negroes have toward members of their race. Of this penchant in Booker Washington, Rose comments:

> The 'Tuskegee Machine' was ruthless toward any Negro who tried to voice the Negro protest or go against Washington in any way. Forced to be weak

in the presence of whites, Washington was arrogant toward other Negroes.[117]

Myrdal notes that while the lower class Negro may take out his aggressions against whites in fighting other Negroes, generally middle and upper class Negroes are hindered from this outlet by "caste, prudence, and respectability," and hence "they have to store up their aggression."[118] This, he concludes, "is probably another cause of their greater sensitivity."[119]

Impact of Hate on the Health of Slave and Freedman

Freudian psychologists have long held that always present with human beings is a wish to "die" and a wish to "live," and that when the former is predominant the individual is prey to suicide, malingering, martydom, asceticism, polysurgery, alcoholism, psychosis, and other forms of self-destruction.[120] Study of Negro spirituals and other sources have shown that the wish to die was sometimes strong with both the slave and freedman. It is known, too, that actual suicide has been rare among Negroes.[121] Considering, however, the close relationship between the mental and the organic, might not this strong wish to die account for much of the high incidence of mental and physical illness to which bondsmen and freedmen were so prone, thereby contributing to the high death rate for which the race has been notorious? Usually the high incidence of physical illness and death have been blamed exclusively on such factors as poor diet, clothing, and housing, a purely physical explanation. Might there not also be valid psychological explanations for some of these phenomena?[122]

The Negro male or female with the "misery" in the arms, back, or legs is legendary. How much of this neuralgia, rheumatism, or arthritis was of emotional origin can never be known, but it may be suspected that much of it was psychosomatic in nature. Calling hypertension "one of the most typical of all the psychosomatic diseases," a leading physician and scholar stated in 1947:

> The African Bush Negro does not have hypertension. His brother who was brought to America as a slave, however, quickly developed it and has outstripped the

southern white in the incidence of high blood pressure. The southern white, on the other hand, suffers considerably less from it than his northern brother. But when the southern Negro moves North to live, his hypertension rate jumps quite sharply.[123]

According to this view, appendicitis also should be common to the Negro. Ulcers, often called the most common of psychosomatic illnesses, should also have been very common with both slave and freedman except that, according to some scholars, to be a "true ulcer type" one has to be an ambitious, driving, inner-directed personality.[124] In slavery and freedom many Negroes have been deprived of drive and ambition by an oppressing culture, hence have shown more tendencies of the "colon type" of personality which is non-ambitious and other-directed.[125] Thus spastic and ulcerative colitis and related ailments said to be common to this personality type should and have been prevalent among Negroes. Also, guilt feelings derived from hate and revenge thoughts and acts directed at whites, and the need for atonement by self-punishment, probably account for much of the recklessness and devil-may-care attitude, accident proneness, criminality, addiction to alcohol, sex, and dope, as well as asceticism and martyrdom which have been common among some elements of Negroes.[126]

A major factor which kept the slave and masses of freedmen from suffering and dying even more of psychosomatic illnesses than actually occurred, was their lack of urbanity and sophistication. They were thus able to give vent to their emotions by laughing, yelling, singing, crying, and working instead of repressing them completely. Only under the eyes of the overseer or planter did they have to repress their thoughts and emotions, and even then they had to repress only anger, hostility, resentment or hatred. Because it was believed that a "happy" slave was a safe one, and a good worker in addition, any and all expressions of joy or gladness were encouraged in the slaves, who, not only with impunity but actual approval, could thus laugh, sing, and dance with abandon. Here is a major source of the laughing, singing, dancing characteristic which has become a well-known stereotype of the race.

Although the Negro's singing, joking, laughing, dancing, and working got rid of a considerable amount of his aggressions, this did not completely rid him of the boiling volcano of hostility deep in his subconscious, hence did not in the long run save him from psychosomatic disease. In slavery and since, this volcano has been an important contributing factor to such psychosomatic illnesses among Negroes as hypertension, heart disease, arthritis, rheumatism, strokes, kidney ailments, ulcers, diabetes, dementia praecox, asthma, headaches, backache, purposive accidents, and tuberculosis, as well as to other malign tendencies.[127]

THE FLIGHT FROM HATRED TOWARD LOVE

As it was impossible for Negro slaves not to hate their white masters, it was also impossible for these same bondsmen not to love their masters. It is probably impossible for human beings not to feel a considerable degree of love for whomever provides the only food, shelter, clothing, and security they possess, regardless of how meager these provisions may be. When human beings hate those whom they also love, figuratively bite the hand that feeds them, it is then that resultant guilt feelings are especially intense. Perhaps, however, only through such long-term bitter hating and being hated as they have been subjected to could Afro-Americans develop the mature realism about the nature of hate, and hence such a proper fear of and flight from it toward love as many have exhibited. Hatred and revenge are usually childish reactions which often do greater damage to the hater than to the hated. Too, the social consequences of hatred are very serious. Many Afro-American leaders have seen this and have urged their race not to succumb to hate. Booker Washington often wisely said that no man could make him stoop so low as to hate. The majority of Negroes, slave and free, always have had strong guilt feelings about their hatred for white people and, for several reasons, have sought to suppress, restrain, and eliminate it. This is a major source of the "forgive the former slave-holder" talk of the Reconstruction era, and the theme is common in the writings and speeches of the descendants of the ex-slaves. In the

1920s this tradition caused Margaret Adelaide Shaw to write in her "Closed Doors":

You who find closed doors before you
Turn not bitter while you wait:
Work and grow, for nothing shrivels
Up the soul like burning hate.

Reflecting in verse in the same period on his races' "trampled rights" and on "caste," in a poem entitled "The Feet of Judas," George Marion Horton urged his race not to forget that "Christ washed the feet of Judas." In his poem "Judas Iscariot," written in the same period, Countee Cullen even found it in his heart to exculpate Judas and make room for him in Heaven. Beginning in the late 1950s this tradition would provide perhaps the largest source of the Reverend Martin Luther King's famed emphasis on love.[128]

Already mentioned is the manner in which the glorification of blackness and the Negro physical "type" became a medium of revenge. This is especially to be seen in the Marcus Garvey movement of the 1920s. According to Garvey black is the most beautiful color and one which even God and His angels in Heaven bear. While denouncing the earlier-exalted mulatto, Garvey praised and flattered the darker-skinned Negro masses. That there was some precedent for his type of thinking may be seen in a pre-Civil War statement by the noted abolitionist, Dr. John S. Rock. In 1858 Dr. Rock had declared:

> The prejudice which some white men have, or affected to have against my color gives me no pain. If any man does not fancy my color, . . . I shall give myself no trouble because he lacks good taste. . . . I will not deny that I admire the talents and noble character of many white men. But I cannot say that I am particularly pleased with their physical appearance. . . . When I contrast the fine tough muscular system, the beautiful, rich color, the full broad features, and the gracefully frizzled hair of the Negro, with the delicate physical organization, wan color, sharp features and lank hair of the Caucasian, I am inclined to believe that when the white man was created, nature was pretty well exhausted.[129]

On this Arnold M. Rose has stated: "While whites are more inclined to select a light Negro, the Negro group itself, when the choice is up to it, is more inclined to select a dark man."[130] Adverse criticism by Negroes of the person of the white man has extended to such area as the assertion that characteristically whites have a bad body odor and are "cold-natured."

With the rest of the nation, Negroes turned in the 1930s to a much closer consideration of the nation's economic and social problems, and as a consequence their thought became somewhat less race-centered. Their aggressions became less directed at the white man and more toward the economic and social system, and as Afro-Americans came to view themselves more as co-victims with whites—members of the same "proletariat," there was, perhaps, less hatred of "the white man."

During the thirties, and since, rising living standards, superior education on both sides of the racial front and attacks on racial bias by the Urban League, NAACP, CIO, scholars in various fields, and numerous other organizations and persons, have served to reduce hatreds, hence also the felt need for revenge, between colored and white Americans. In the thirties the rise of totalitarianism and tyranny abroad served to shift some of the Negro Americans' aggressions away from the white man at home. Especially did Benito Mussolini's "rape" of Ethiopa, and the British persecution of Mahatma Gandhi and his brown-skinned followers combine with Adolf Hitler's racism to work as catalysts to this end. In the post-World War II era, integration in industry, sports, the military, and other areas of American life also have worked to this end. Despite the stubborn efforts by some persons—South and North—to preserve the old order of things, the trend in race relations would seem to indicate that the day may not be too distant when the type of revenge herein discussed will not be a significant aspect of the mind of the Negro.[131]

THE NEGRO'S CHURCH AND GOD

Discounting the changes in belief and practice which always occur when a religion is transmitted from one group of people to another, the master—slave relationship was not an ideal posture for white Americans to introduce transplanted Africans to the Christian religion. Despite this very serious difficulty, an effective transmission was made, and this religion became not only the dominant thought stream in the mind of the Negro, but a major vehicle for transmitting Occidental culture to this alien race.

Once he absorbed the basic tenets of the Christian faith, the Negro's religion would be affected not only by his own peculiar past and present, but by almost every major historical current which swept across the nation. This was true of the 1764-1789 revolutionary fervor which created a new nation. The eighteenth century Great Awakening also had a significant impact on slaves just as it did on white Americans. In New England, and probably elsewhere, this movement, among other things, resulted in the conversion of many more slaves to Christianity. During this century Negroes began to establish segregated churches. Ex-slave Richard Allen, with Absalom Jones organized the Free African Society, and in 1794 organized Bethel African Methodist Episcopal Church in Philadelphia. Allen became the second AME Bishop. In 1796 some New York Methodists separated from the whites and formed the African Methodist Episcopal Zion Church. In 1822 James Varick was elected first Bishop of this church, which also numbered among its early leaders George Collins and Christopher Rush. Beginning around 1806 Negro Baptists began to separate from whites, and the African Methodist Episcol Church began its great contribution to Negro journalism and thought in 1847 when it began to issue the *Christian Herald*. In 1852 the name of this publication was changed to *The Christian Recorder*.

Afro-Americans have held slavery and racial oppression to be foul blots on the white Americans' religion, and they have been especially critical because the white clergy usually either has supported or been silent on these topics. As recently as the 1920's one Negro declared: "The colored races the world over will have even more doubt in the future than they have had in the past of the real Christianity of any church which holds out to them the prospect of being united in heaven after being separated on earth."[1] In 1923 James Weldon Johnson echoed an oft-repeated strain when he said: "The Negro stands as the suprme test of the civilization, the Christianity and the common decency of the American people."[2]

The slave received religious indoctrination from ministers who told him that his highest duty on earth was to be faithful, obedient, and hard-working. His plight was explained to him as indeed a hard one, but a condition ordained by God and not to be rectified by man. Rosy pictures were painted of Heaven as the reward for being "good,' and Biblical authority was cited as proof of all conclusions about the institution of slavery. Bondsmen sometimes stole away, however, and held illicit religious meetings of their own, at which they were given a contrary doctrine by "preachers" among their own group. Here they learned that the deity had not ordained slavery and that the evil system would soon be overthrown by the combined efforts of God and man. These secret meetings held at night, often were announced by clever code systems, during the work day, in full view of white overseers. Often improvised words sung in the tune of a popular spiritual was the means of passing the information around that a meeting was to be held that night. Slavery schooled the Negro in duplicity and deceit, and the eagerness of the ruling class to believe that slaves were happy, contented, obedient, child-like creatures, made the deceit easier to put over. Without these code systems and secret meetings it may well be doubted that such a large-scale conspiracy as that of Denmark Vesey could have been organized. Of religious training, M. M. Fisher states that: "Negroes soon learned that their plantation teachers [Missionaries] were interested primarily in making slavery more secure, and slaves paid their missionaries scant attention."[3] But that the indoctrination had considerable success, there can be little doubt. "I have met many religious colored people, at the South," wrote Frederick Douglass, "who are under the delusion that God requires them to submit to slavery, and to wear their chains with meekness and humility. I could entertain no such nonsense as this; and I almost lost my patience when I found any colored man weak enough to believe such stuff."[4] Whether religious indoctrination and other emoluments which the institution afforded the bondsman brought him happiness is a much debated question. On this, Frederick Douglass observed:

> We are sometimes told of the contentment of the slaves, and are entertained with vivid pictures of their happiness. We are told that they often dance and sing; that their masters frequently give them wherewith to make merry; in fine, that they have little of which to complain. I admit that the slave does sometimes sing, dance and appear to be merry. But what does this prove? It only proves to my mind, that though slavery is armed with a thousand stings, it is not able entirely to kill the elastic spirit of the bondsman. That spirit will rise and walk abroad, despite whips and chains, and extract from the cup of nature, occasional drops of joy and gladness.[5]

'Why is it," Douglass continued, "that all the reports of contentment and happiness among the slaves at the South come to us upon the authority of slave-holders, or (what is equally significant) of slave-holders' friends? Why is it that we do not hear from the slave direct? The answer to this question furnishes the darkest features in the American slave system."[6] This was a persistent argument with Douglass against the myth that the slaves were contented and happy with their lot. Douglass was a great believer in the right of individual expression, and lamented constantly that the slave was not allowed to speak for himself. "If there were no other fact descriptive of slavery," he wrote, "than that the slave is dumb [silent], this alone would be sufficient to mark the slave system as a grand aggregation of human horrors."[7] Douglass admitted that religious services, often surrepticious ones, brought considerable happiness to the slave. "We were at times remarkably buoyant, singing hymns, and making joyous exclamations, almost as triumphant in their tone as if we had reached a land of freedom and safety,"[8] he wrote. But that these meetings were dangerous to the system, even the planters came to know. For here slaves were alone, could express their grievances unrestrainedly, and plot rebellion and insurrection. Douglass stated of the buoyant singing about "heaven" and "Canaan Land," "A keen observer might have detected in our repeated singing of:

> 'O Cannan, sweet Cannan,
> I am bound for the land of Cannan'

something more than a hope of reaching heaven. We meant to reach the North, and the North was our Canaan."[9] Douglass conceived and planned his escape during one of these meetings. The ruling class prohibited these religious meetings, but still slaves would often sing, and act on their singing: "Steal away, steal away, steal away to Jesus, Steal away, steal away home, I ain't got long to stay here." Thus did the meetings continue.

Perhaps most bondsmen were convinced that to take Christianity literally and live a meek, lowly, uncomplaining, hard-working, hard-suffering life was the best path for them to follow. Many felt this way partly because such is one side of the spirit of Christianity, and partly because wisdom dictated this as the best course in the face of overwhelming odds. It is this effect of Christianity on people which caused Rome to oppose it for her soldiers, and brought Lenin to characterize it as the opiate of the proletariat. Since 1865 several Afro-Americans have denounced religiosity as a primary source of the continued degradation of their race.

Fisher shows that even the "Uncle Tom" slave often felt that he was acting in the best interests of Christianity and his race. R. R. Moton tells how these persons, commonly called "white folks' niggers" have always been "thoroughly disgusting and humiliating to all thinking members of their race."[10] In his volume, *The Wife of His Youth and Other Stories of the Color Line*, Charles Chesnutt includes a story entitled, "The Passing of Grandison." Here a slave pretends to hate abolitionists and their movement, only to trick his master so that he wins freedom in Canada for himself and his family.

The already-mentioned controversy over the extent to which the thought and action of Afro-Americans is a persistence of African traits involves the religion of the Negro.

In his *Negro Slave Songs in the United States* Miles Mark Fisher (see Chapter I) interprets the slave songs in terms of African survivals, and concludes that the American Negro's religion has long retained numerous pagan and Mohammedan, or "Oriental" elements. The error which Dr. Fisher makes is to mistake general characteristics of many different primitive groups for peculiar Negro traits. The traits which he considers to be peculiarly African have been characteristics of various ethnic and geographical groups in the United States and in many other countries; many primitive groups dress elaborately for worship, and certainly no one has shown that the Mormons practiced polygamy because of African influence. Alfred Kinsey never argued that present day "polygamous" tendencies among whites in the United States have been learned from Negroes.

Fisher appears to believe that the primary reason why many slaves were gradually denied the right to worship with whites was the slaves' habit of "shouting." Slaves, he writes, "disturbed quiet and dignified Methodist worship by beating out the rhythm of songs with feet patting and hands clapping, in place of African instruments . . . . until their odors were quite repulsive." He hints that American whites learned the shouting habit from Negroes, but the author fails to marshal any evidence to support this belief which is so divergent from accepted opinions. Most scholars hold that shouting, stamping of feet, and other such spirited behvior in worship was fairly typical of many lower class white Americans, especially in the West and South. Kenneth Stampp has declared that "slave superstitions did not all originate in Africa, and it would even be difficult to prove that most did. For the slaves picked up plenty of them from the good Puritans, Baptists, Methodists, and other religious" groups. "Indeed," Stampp continues, "more than likely Negroes and whites made a generous exchange of superstitions. There is no need to trace back to Africa the slave's fear of beginning to plant a crop on Friday, his dread of witches, ghosts, and goblins, his confidence in good-luck charms, his alarm at evil omens, his belief in dreams, and his reluctance to visit burying grounds after dark. These superstitions were all firmly rooted in Ango-Saxon folklore."[11] Of the "shouting" traits, Stampp notes:

> But again it is not easy to tell how much of their 'heathenism' the slaves learned in the white churches and at white revival meetings. One Sunday morning, in . . . Virginia a visitor attended a Methodist Church where the slaves were permitted to hold their meetings before the whites occupied the building. Such a medley of sounds, I never heard before. They exhorted, prayed, sang, shouted, cried, grunted and growled. Poor Souls' they knew no better for I found that when other services began the sounds were similar, which the white folks made; and the Negroes only imitated them and shouted a little louder.[12]

"In the Americas," Fisher declares, "the institution of the African cult [secret meetings] rather than the home . . . . was relied upon by adult Negroes to train their children to take every step in life," and that this was the chief reason for "continuing the African institution of the secret meetings." He concludes that the Negro churches of the twentieth century were founded on doctrines which were "superficially Christian, but in truth they were the traditional beliefs of the secret meetings."

In America pondering the slave-trade, Negroes would conveniently forget the large and essential role which African chiefs played in the capture and sale of slaves, and erect the myth that all slaves were stolen by whites in a form of wanton piracy. The ugly inhumanity of the Middle Passage has been bitterly criticized by Afro-Americans. Reflecting on it Kelly Miller wrote in the second decade of the twentieth century— "I see the ocean basin whitened with bones, and the ocean current running red with (their) blood."[13]

It is well-known that slave owners discouraged and "killed," as much as possible, such African customs as conflicted with the pattern of slavery. Among these discouraged customs and practices were secret meetings, the practice of sorcery, use of African languages, and the sending of messages by code. Other customs, harmless to the institution were not discouraged but rather were sometimes encouraged.

Magic, like much of religion, is a propitiation of feared threatening forces within and without man himself. The arbitrariness and cruelty of the world of the slave heightened his fear and gave him great need for any and all supports which were at hand. Religion and magic were two of his greatest supports. Rabbits' feet, horseshoes, four-leaf clovers, and the potions of the "Hoodoo" man were all meant to give the benighted beleagured bondsman a greater feeling of security, hence comfort and happiness. The domestic and skilled slaves were not less superstitious than the field-hands because they were more intelligent, but rather in large part because there was less arbitrariness, cruelty, and fear in their lives. The Negro slave lived in an age where faith in witchcraft was very widespread. The infamous Salem witch trials were not perpetrated by Negroes, and even in the twentieth century a considerable number of white Americans believe in witchcraft.

David Walker, perhaps the most outspoken colored radical of the pre-1830 era, was born in Wilmington, North Carolina in 1785. Offspring of a slave father and free mother, Walker early left the South and settled in Boston, Massachusetts, where he acquired the rudiments of an education and was caught up in the abolitionist fervor which was sweeping New England and the North. In 1829 his famous APPEAL was published. The consternation which this work caused in the South is reminiscent of the furor later raised over Harriet Beecher Stowe's famed volume. Leaders of southern states demanded that the APPEAL be suppressed and offered ten thousand dollars for the capture and delivery of Walker. To his race Walker said: "The man who would not fight under our Lord and Master Jesus Christ, in the glorious and heavenly cause of freedom and of God . . . . ought to be kept with all of his children or family, in slavery, or in chains, to be butchered by his cruel enemies." In the most intemperate language, Walker poured out an intense hatred against all justifications for human bondage, as well as against those who, for any reasons, would not see slavery immediately overthrown regardless of the means which might be necessary to accomplish this end. Walker based his recommendations on strong personal religious convictions. Before 1831 there was probably one or more Negro preachers on every plantation. Shortly after the Nat Turner insurrection Negro preachers were generally outlawed. In places where slaves were allowed to attend churches with whites, sitting in back or in the gallery, this was sometimes done because of the fear that at separate religious gatherings of slaves rebellions were too easily fomented.

There is still considerable controversy as to whether the early slave songs or spirituals are essentially secularistic or other-wordly in tone. Sterling Brown has indicated the difficulty of interpreting the slave ways and other expressions of the Negro folk mind. "The field of folklore in general," he has written, "is known to be a battle area, and the Negro front is one of the hottest centers. One sharply contended point is the problem of definition of the folk; and then that of origin."[14]

Perhaps no scholar has interpreted the day-by-day message of spirituals with the thoroughness of Miles Mark Fisher.[15] Although one may well quarrel with the over-all thesis behind Fisher's interpretation of these songs, no one has so skillfully fitted them around the major historical events of the ante-bellum period. Fisher probably goes much too far when he says, "not one spiritual in its primary form reflected interest in anything other than a full life here and now."[16] "Christianity," Fisher continues: "rarely occurred as an element in antebellum spirituals." And—"The characters mentioned in slave songs, were to be sure, Oriental."[17] In the effort to prove his exaggerated thesis, Fisher makes several erroneous statements. For example, he contends that Frederick Douglass "was indebted to secret [slave] meetings for his total ideology."[18] It is difficult to see how one can rationalize away the other-wordly aspect of the spirituals, as Fisher attempts to do. "The other-wordly idea of God," Mays has noted, "finds fertile soil among the people who fare worst in this world; and it grows dimmer and dimmer as the social and economic conditions improve."[19] Although he concludes that the dominant note of the spirituals is other-wordly, Mays correctly observes that purely secularistic emphases are present. In two separate statements on the message of the spirituals, Mays reflects both the other-wordly and secularistic emphases. Here he concludes:

The ideas reflected in the spirituals may be briefly summarized: God is omnipotent, omnipresent, and
omiscient. In both Heaven and earth God is sovereign.
He is a just God—just to the point of cruelty. In the
very nature of things sinners will be punished by God.
He will see to it that the wicked are destroyed. God
is revengeful. He hardened the heart of Pharaoh for
the express purpose of trapping him and his host in
the Red Sea. This indicates that God is a warrior and
He fights the battles of His chosen people. 'Go Down
Moses' and 'Joshua Fit De Battle of Jerico' are filled
with the confidence that God takes care of His own.
He will also see to it that the righteous are vindicated
and that the heavily laden are given rest for the troubles of the world. The spirituals, 'Mos' Done Toilin'
Here' and 'Members, Don't Git Weary,' are illustrative of the assurance that God will give rest to those
who toil here below. This rest comes after death. God
saves for Heaven those who hold out to the end. He
provides golden crowns, slippers, robes, and eternal
life for the righteous, the principal reward comes in
the other world.[20]

"The Negroes' ideas of God," in the period 1760-1860,
Mays found, "are those of traditional Christianity, but they
are the most lofty of the traditional ideas . . . . It is clear
that these early Negro writers exercised a keen sense of selec-
tivity and chose those ideas of God that supported their claim
for social justice and complete emancipation."[21] Even M. M.
Fisher makes some slight concession to the other-worldly interpretation of the slave songs. On this he states:

Possibly, the originals of other worldly spirituals
were not in existence when the first collectors made
their search. There can be no doubt, however, that
slaves like other people, transferred their earthly desires to the other world when they were frustrated.
Negroes expressed strong desires to be reincarnated in
Africa.[22]

Although he is correct in pointing out that late nineteenth
and early twentieth century Americans of color often resented
spirituals as hateful "plantation melodies," R. R. Moton errors

somewhat in asserting that by 1929 Negroes had come to accept them. On this, Moton states that the race had begun. "To sing them with a zest and abandon that was previously known only amid the scenes of their origin."[23] The truth is that even today there are many colored Americans who feel that the fewer Negro spirituals their choirs sing, the better.

In *Native Son*, Richard Wright's portrayal of the mother of Bigger Thomas is of the unlettered submissive person who willingly bears the extreme burden of life with the sole consolation of a happier life in Heaven. In *Native Son* Wright reacts against this other-wordly consolation, as he later does even more effectively in his autobiographical *Black Boy*. Reaction against the other-wordly thought of many lower class Negroes has caused a number of middle class persons to be against organized religion, just as the passivity of the Russian peasantry caused Communists to view religion as the opiate of the people. Of his early religious experiences, Frederick Douglass states:

> Many slaves rejected the religious ideas which planters sought to drill in them. By some means I learned from these inquiries [questions about God when a child], that God, up in the sky, made everybody; and that He made white people to be masters and mistresses, and black people to be slaves. This did not satisfy me, nor lessen my interest in the subject. I was told, too, that God was good, and that He knew what was best for me and everybody. This was less satisfactory than the first statement; because it came, point blank, against all my notions of goodness. It was not good to let old master cut the flesh off Esther, and make her cry so. Besides, how did people know that God made blacks to be slaves?[24]

Later Douglass concluded about slavery: "I was not very long in finding out [that] it was not color, but crime, not God, but man, that afforded the true explanation of the existence of slavery"[25] [And] "I was just as well aware of the unjust, unnatural and murderous character of slavery, when nine years old, as I am now. Without an appeal to books, to laws, or to authorities of any kind, it was enough to accept God as a Father, to regard slavery as a crime."[26]

The spirituals give insight into attitudes and ideas which the bondsmen had toward such topics as human rights, cooperation, and security. The thought of the race was rooted in religion. To the Negro, God has been the Father and creator of humanity, and all men brothers made of one flesh. The Creator had no favored children, hence could not be the author of racial inequality; all of His children ought to have the same privileges and immunities. "Whence, then, the actual and very real inequalities?", many have asked. "Why freedoms for white, and not for black?" The record of his efforts to find a satisfactory answer to these queries presents a mottled picture born of the colored Americans' confusion.

With the attitude of the race toward cooperation, the religious note is again struck first. Slavery made group consciousness acute and these outcast Americans often thought of themselves as a despised race or band. They were to "walk together Children and Don't Get Weary," for "Dere's a Great Camp Meeting in de Promised Land." During the ante-bellum period security to the black man did not have the same economic implications that it was to have in the twentieth century. Then the quest was primarily for emotional and physical security, and in a sense, the Heavenly Father and His Son constituted the main sources of security. The spirituals are replete with the attitude, "I Got a Home in Dat Rock, Don't You See," or "Jesus is My Friend, He'll Keep Me to De 'En," or "My Soul's Been Anchored in De Lord."

Like that of most Americans, the thought of Negroes has tended toward the materialistic emphasis. Even as slaves they were caught up in the Great American Dream which centered around possession of an abundance of worldly goods. This desire, then as now, they could not help but absorb from the cultural milieu of which they represented the lower order. But plainly, as slaves their status precluded ownership of goods in this world, for not even possessing their own bodies, how could they hope for mundane fortune? The answer lay in Heaven, the city of golden streets and pearly gates. There, "I Got a

Robe, You Got a Robe, All-a God's Chillun Got A Robe," And they sang: "Deep River, My Home is Over Jordan," and "I Know De Udder Worl' is Not Like Dis."

Rather than something to be avoided as today, to the bondsman suffering generally was something to be borne patiently. As with Job, this suffering would be rewarded on earth and in Heaven. The constancy of this outlook reveals that pessimism usually out-weighed the buoyant optimism which the black American sometimes expressed, and shows that he saw no early escape from his miserable condition. God's help was sure, but slow and distant. The slave-owner would never willingly give him his freedom, and the slave was too wise to believe that his own effort could overthrow the hated institution. Still, in his despondence, he sang: "De Harder de Cross, de Brighter de Crown."

Thus a primary burden of the spirituals was to impart encouragement and hope. Conditions were bound to improve the slaves sang. An omnipotent and all-wise God still reigned in Heaven and everything proceeds out of His divine plan. He will right all wrongs, if not in this world, then surely in the world to some. So, "Don't Git Weary, A Better Day's A'coming"; "Just a Little Talk Wid Jesus Makes It Right." Then, "Steal Away, Steal Away to Jesus." A slave working in the cotton fields, barefooted and dressed in battered simple clothing longs for the fine clothing seen on the white members of the master class. The slave begins to sing: "I got shoes, you got shoes, all God's chillun got shoes. When I get to heab'n gonna put on my shoes, and shout all over God's heab'n." Or another, recently whipped, overworked, and constantly abused, begins to sing: "Nobody knows de trouble I've seen, nobody knows but Jesus"; Sometimes I'm up, sometimes I'm down, O' yes Lord! Sometimes I'm almost to the ground, O' yes Lord!", while still another sings, "I'm so glad trouble don' las' always." Often with this beleagured people hope bordered on despair, and they sang—"Sometimes I feel like a Motherless Child."

If faith and hope had the virtue of sustaining slaves, they also often kept them obedient, submissive, and humble. So it was intended by the ruling class.

The impact of the story of Jewish slavery and deliverance has had a great impact on Afro-Americans, who have seen themselves as Daniel in the Lion's Den and as the three Hebrew children in the fiery furnace. From their earliest utterances, Afro-Americans appear to have believed that God is love, and that under no circumtances should they hate even their oppressors. When the teaching efforts of Daniel A. Payne, a Charleston, S. C., free Negro, were curtailed by law in 1835 it seemed as if life and God had closed a door in his face. He began to question the very existence of God. In this dark hour the scripture sustained him as he recalled: "With God one day is as a thousand years and a thousand years as one day. Trust in Him, and He will bring slavery and all its outrages to an end."[27]

Contrary to the rather general belief that most masters used religious instruction to help their slaves adjust to and accept their status, many slaves were given no religious instruction at all. Their masters felt that the lash alone was sufficient to control their slaves, and as many owners themselves were not religious, they saw no need to make provisions for or allow religious instruction to their slaves.[36] Ex-slaves did much to perpetuate the myth of their great religiosity with oft-repeated tales of mid-week prayer meetings held in the woods or in the cabins with pots turned down to keep the noise in, and their boasting about the validity of the "old-timed" religion. Romantically-minded southern whites bent on justifying and glorifying the Old South also did much to launch and perpetuate the myth of slave religiosity. Thus Miles Mark Fisher is correct in his conclusion that most slaves were not basically, essentially, or seriously Christian. One ex-slave said: "White people were very hard on colored for being religious. They liked to see you fiddlin and dancing all the time."[28] This reporter said that whites gave Negro preachers a hard time. Many freedmen became acquainted with religious instruction for the first time after they were grown. Although there were many Negro preachers, due to careful selection and control by planters, the monotonous theme of their sermons was the same as with white preachers, i.e., "Servants obey your masters." Slaves hated these one-sided sermons.[29] Slaves observed that planters who were ministers of the gospel were often just as cruel as those masters who did not wear the cloth.[30]

Although they often feigned regret and sorrow, many slaves were actually jubilant at the news of a master's or mistress' death. An ex-slave declared: "If I had my way with them all I would like to have is a chopping block and chop every one of their heads off. Of course I don't hate them that is good. There are some good white folks. Mighty few though."[31] Another ex-slave said: 'When I first embraced a hope in Christ I never have felt that way since. It just looked like to me I had more strength than four or five men had. It just looked like to me I could just pick up a house and tote it."[32] One ex-slave mentioned the inhuman treatment given his race during slavery in a manner reminiscent of Booker T. Washington. "I don't like to get mad because I will sin," he declared.[33] Slaves particularly resented that many of them were not given "decent Christian burials."[34] Perhaps this accounts for the rather common observation that few things have been more important to the freedman than a respectable funeral at the end of life's earthly sojourn.

In general, history to the Afro-American has been a theodicy. The heady humanism of the eighteenth century, and the materialism and Godlessness of the nineteenth and twentieth centuries have little touched the Negro masses. Preaching in Trinity Church, Monrovia, Liberia in 1863, the Rev. Alexander Crummell stated: "We see everywhere God's hand in history; we feel that its anointing spirit is the breath of God. In all the movements of society we see the clear, distinct, 'finger of God,' ordering, controlling, directing the footsteps of men, of families, and of races."[35] But the tendency of slavery to produce polarization of thought and behavior is revealed in the abundant evidence of a contrary view. Here God's law taught disobedience to earthly masters and encouraged overt rebellion. It was this attitude toward law which inspired Nat Turner, Denmark Vesey, and Frederick Douglass no less than Garrison Seward, the Tappan Brothers, and John Brown.

David, who slew the giant Goliath with his small slingshot weapon, was a great hero of the slaves. In their oppressed circumstance, bondsmen often dreamed of and longed for a

'Moses" who would "Tell Old Pharoah to let My People Go."
They variously thought of God as patient and long-suffering
and as an angry, impatient, warrior God, and of Joshua who "Fit
de Battle of Jericho." Still, the overwhelming preponderance
of power held by the master class dictated and advised a general attitude of non-violence.

Afro-Americans sometimes have held steretyped notions of
themselves as a superior race. These ideas have varied from the
belief that they were a chosen and favored race collectively to
notions that Negroes are generally better Christians, singers,
orators, lovers, and athletes than Caucasians. At least one slave
believed that white people were not gifted by nature with the
slaves' ability to see ghosts. [36]   Mays and Nicholson, in *The
Negro's Church,* quote from a chauvinistic sermon which has
been often used in Negro churches. The text listed is: "Princes
shall come out of Egypt; Ethiopia shall soon stretch out her
hands unto God." Here the clear implication is that Negroes
constitute a chosen race.[37] These same authors found that in
most modern sermons by Negroes, the Kingdom of God is
placed on earth. It will be a kingdom of social justice, brotherhood, and equality.[38]

As with the nation generally, the earliest preoccupation of
the Negro with the concept of law centered around divine law,
and God's Will. This attitude was inextricably and unavoidably
tied in with the shifting concept of God which the thought of
the race manifests. At times, God's "law" dictated obedience
on this earth to the master's will, and the ultimate aim of this
law was to test the patience and endurance of the slave. Heaven
certainly would be the reward for obedience, docility, and
meekness. God could not err nor injustice endure after death.
Since the slaves made no sustained effort to overthrow the system, and since this note is so often struck in the spirituals and
other utterances, one must conclude that it was a dominant
view of law which they held. Even the spirituals, Mays observes, did not necessarily motivate them to"strive to eliminate
the source of the ills they suffered."[39]

As already has been indicated, Afro-Americans have been
greatly inspired and directed in their behavior by the life of
Christ. Especially have His suffering, death and resurrection

been significant in their thought—the suffering because they could identify it with their own, and the resurrection as a symbol of hope and victory, both in this world and the world to come. Next to Christ, perhaps no other biblical figure has so inspired the Negro as much as Moses. Few have been the leaders of the race who did not in some degree identify their actions with and draw inspiration from this man who led another enslaved race to the promised land, just as few have been the leaders and plotters of militant action for emancipation and equal citizenship rights who did not happily identify the perils which they were inviting upon their heads with the dangers and sufferings into which Christ willingly walked; and few have been the executed martyrs who did not, like John Brown himself, walk to their deaths drawing consolation from the knowledge that the Galilean carpenter bore His cross to an awful but triumphant Calvary. The event which finally convinced Nat Turner that he should seek to free Virginia's slaves was a vision in which he saw himself ordered by God to pick up the cross which Christ had laid down. Denmark Vesey was inspired by the Jewish epic, and believed that as God had delivered the Israelites out of Egypt and Babylonia, He would help Vesey's plot and insurrection to succeed.[40]

The Negro church has a record of considerable militancy, and has been a primary source of the race's optimism. As has been previously stated, the abolitionist movement was star-studded with the names of Negro ministers, and the various conferences of colored denominations held during ante-bellum days were seldom concluded without speeches and resolutions which demanded an end to slavery and racial bias. Typical is the resolution adopted at the 10th Annual Conference of the A.M.E. Church, September 5, 1850, which was presided over by Bishop Morris Brown. Here the Church voted to support education, temperance, moral improvement, and abolitionists "until every fetter shall be broken and all men enjoy the liberty which the gospel proclaims."[41] From his study of the Negro Church Carter Woodson concluded that this organization has been conservative. Yet, if by "conservative" is implied that it has been silent or non-militant against oppression and injustice, such a conclusion is false. Perhaps it would be better to state that this institution like the race and Americans in general, has been cautious and judicious.[42]

The southern reaction of the 1830-60 period wiped out almost every semblance of an independent Negro ministry in the South, and both slave and free Negro were often forced to hold worship service in the presence of whites. The beginnings which the African Methodist Episcopal Church had made in Charleston, South Carolina were eliminated as the Rev. Morris Brown yielded to unrelenting pressure and moved to the North. To protect slavery the white South accepted the greatest measure of integration in the churches which the section has ever known.

In anger at the 1850 Fugitive Slave Law Frederick Douglass said: "I take this law to be one of the grossest infringements of Christian Liberty, and, if the churches and ministers of our country were not stupidly blind, or most wickedly indifferent, they, too, would so regard it."[43] In his definition of true religion, Douglass said:

> I love the religion of our blessed Savior. I love that religion that comes from above, in the wisdom of God, which is first pure, then peaceable, gentle, and easy to be entreated, 'full of mercy and good fruits, without partiality and without hypocrisy.' I love that religion that sends its votaries to bind up the wounds of him that has fallen among thieves. I love that religion that makes it the duty of its disciples to visit the fatherless and the widow in their affliction. I love that religion that is based upon the glorious principles, of love to God and love to man; which makes its followers do unto others as they themselves would be done by. If you demand liberty to yourself, it says, grant it to your neighbors. If you claim a right to think for yourself, it says, allow your neighbors the same right. If you claim to act for yourself, it says allow your neighbors the same right. It is because I love this religion that I hate the slaveholding, the woman-whipping, the mind-darkening, the soul-destroying religion that exists in the southern states of America.[44]

Speaking in England May 12, 1846 Douglass declared that the treatment of the slave was not the worst thing about the U.S.A.

An even darker feature, he stated, was "that the religion of the southern states . . . is the great supporter, the great sanctioner" of these "bloody atrocities." The slave, he declared "is trampled under foot by the very churches of the land." "Slavery," he averred, had been made part of the religion of the land, and "Ministers of religion stand forth as the foremost, the strongest defenders of this institution."[45] "This I conceive," he continued, "to be the darkest feature of slavery, and the most difficult to attack, because it is identified with religion, and exposes those who denounce it to the charge of infidelity. Yes, those with whom I have been laboring, namely, the old organization anti-slavery society of America, have been again and again stigmatized as infidels, and for what reason? Why, solely in consequence of the faithfulness of their attacks upon the slaveholding of the southern states, and the northern religion that sympathizes with it." Again he opined:

> The fact that the church of our country (with fractional exceptions) does not esteem 'the Fugitive Slave Law' as a declaration of war against religious liberty, implies that the church regards religion simply as a form of worship, an empty ceremony, and not a vital principle requiring active benevolence, justice, love, and good will toward men. It esteems sacrifice above mercy; psalm-singing above right doing; solemn meetings above practical righteousness. A worship that can be conducted by persons who refuse to give shelter to the houseless, to give bread to the hungry, clothing to the naked, and who enjoin obedience to a law forbidding these acts of mercy is a curse, not a blessing to mankind.[46]

"In prosecuting the anti-slavery enterprise, we have been asked to spare the church, to spare the ministry; but how, we ask, could such a thing be done? We are met on the threshold of our efforts for the redemption of the slave, by the church and ministry of the country, in battle arrayed against us; and we are compelled to fight or flee. From what quarter, I beg to know, has proceeded a fire so deadly upon our ranks, during the last two years, as from the Northern pulpit?"

"The successors of Penn, Franklin, and Woolman," stated one observer in 1837, "have shown themselves the friends of the colored race. They have done more in this cause than any other church and they are still doing great things both in Europe and America. I was taught in childhood to remember the man of the broad-brimmed hat and drab-colored coat and venerate him." But this observer opined that even the Friends did not go far enough in their devotion to the colored man. With "but here and there a noble exception," he declared, "they go but halfway.—When they come to the grand doctrine, to lay the ax right down at the root of the tree, and destroy the very spirit of slavery—there they are defective. Their doctrine is to set the slave free, and let him take care of himself. Hence we hear nothing about their being brought into the Friends' Church, or of their being viewed and treated according to their moral worth."[47] In conclusion, stated this observer: "Let every man take his stand, burn out this prejudice, live it down, talk it down, everywhere consider the colored man as a man, in the church, the stage, the steamboat, the public house, in all places, and the death-blow to slavery will be struck." James McCune Smith once remarked: "It is a remarkable fact that the slaves of Catholics are better fed and better treated than those of Protestants."[48]

In addition to the appeal to be true to his professed Christianity and to the ideals and traditions upon which this nation was founded, one constant argument which the Afro-American has used in his appeal to the white man has been to the latter's sense of fair play and manliness. The Negro has questioned often the kind of courage which shows fear of a minority which started late in the race for education and economic goods. "Give us the opportunity of elevating ourselves:—It can do you no harm, and may do us much good," stated an 1856 address of Ohioans to that state's Senate and House of Representatives.[49] In this address was another persistent theme, that is, the malign consequences to the nation inherent in allowing Negroes to remain ignorant and degraded. "If we are deprived of education, of equal political privileges," commented these petitioners, "The natural consequences will follow; and the State, for her planting of injustice, will reap her harvest of sorrow and crime. She will contain within her limits a discontented population—dissatisfied, estranged—ready to welcome any revolution or invasion as a relief."[50] While he did not utilize the argument of possible treason, Booker Washington often mentioned that for the South to keep the Negro down it had to stay down with him.

One able observer points out that one light in which slaves saw planters and their mistresses was as crude, boisterous, gambling, uncouth braggarts who drank too heavily and were too often inexcusably and inordinately licentious and cruel. This same observer notes that "nearly all" ex-slaves who wrote accounts of their lives under the institution "refer to the cohabitation of masters and overseers with Negro women."[51] Like the Negro novelists of the 1865-1920 period, miscegenation was a subject of which both slaves and ex-slaves of the ante-bellum period were acutely conscious. Ignoring the agrarian-base of southern society and the impact of the ideal of medieval chivalry, Charles H. Nichols, Jr. concluded that: "Southern White Womanhood has long been glorified for the very obvious reason that her guilty [adulterous] men folk felt they owed it to her."[52] On this point Nichols quotes Harriet Martineau's statement that the plantation mistress was only "The chief slave of the Harem." Of the white American's religion, David Walker declared in his *Appeal*:

> Can anything be greater mockery of religion than the way in which it is conducted by the Americans? It appears as though they are bent only on daring God Almighty to do His best—they chain and handcuff us and our children and drive us around the country like brutes, and go into the house of the God of justice to return Him thanks for having aided them in their infernal cruelties inflicted upon us. Will the Lord suffer this people to go on much longer, taking His holy name in vain? Will He not stop them, preachers and all?

"God was against slavery," asserted one observer, "and in His own time and way He removed the foul blot from the national escutcheon. . . . God has wrought wonderfully among us. God is still opening the way for greater progress." Booker T. Washington declared: "From the time the first mutterings of rebellion were heard, and the war cloud no larger than a

man's hand appeared on our country's horizon, the Negro believed, with an unswerving faith, that slavery was the one
cause of the war; that God was now ready to punish the des-
poiler and let the oppressed go free."[53]   Bondsmen regarded
President Abraham Lincoln as the long-awaited Moses whom
God had promised would lead them out of bondage. Throughout the war they prayed for his success.

As in the days of slavery, for the freedman religion was
a chief source of inspiration, hope, and understanding of his
plight in the drama of history.

Often Afro-Americans have placed their preachers on a
pedestal and expected them to be not only saintly in their
thoughts and acts but solvers of all personal and social problems. When cracks and weaknesses have been revealed in the
minister's character or when his followers have realized that
the minister lacked the ability or desire to solve their social
problems, wrath born of disappointment has often been directed at him and his class. As recent as the 1920's a Negro
poet would write:

> That the Negro church possesses
> Extraordinary power
> That it is the greatest medium
> For influencing our people,
> That it long has slept and faltered,
> Failed to meet its obligations,
> Are, to honest and true thinkers,
> Facts which have to be admitted.
>
> For these reasons there are many
> Who would have the church awaken
> And adopt the modern methods
> Of all other institutions.
> Make us more enlightened Christians,
> Teach us courtesy and English,
> Racial pride and sanitation,
> Science, thrift and Negro history.[54]

Of the Negro church in the 1865-1900 period, Wilson
Record has noted:

> During this time the only organization that
> really reached down among the grass roots of the

race was the church. . . . It was conservative in the extreme; its appeals were emotional; its eyes were fixed on another world—after death. It held fast the values of Negro protest and piped the stream of revolt harmlessly into the clouds. It recognized the oppression of the Negro people, and spoke eloquently of their trials and tribulations. But it preached salvation after death and sang of the glories on the other side of Jordan.[55]

Record does not include here the facts that this was previous to the dominance of the social gospel, that white churches of the South also fitted this general picture, and that by 1900 a growing group of educated Afro-Americans were demanding that their churches de-emphasize this traditional conservatism, emotionalism, and extreme other-wordly outlook. This group demanded a more educated clergy to fit the growing literacy of the race, and an increased social consciousness and progressivism on the part of their churches. More and more Afro-Americans withdrew from their traditional Baptist and Methodist loyalties and affiliated with Catholic, Presbyterian, Episcopalian and other churches. Yet in the quarter century previous to 1900, Negro religious bodies were not dramatically affected by the controversy over Darwinism and the sometimes-ridiculous conflict between science and religion which was rending many white ecclesiastical bodies. Too, this period witnessed a growing interest in, and affiliation with the Young Men's Christian Association. Negro Y's date back to the 1850's, but it was not until 1888 that the organization had its first paid colored officer, in the person of William A. Hinton. A decade later Jesse E. Moorland became the second such person. In the first decade of the twentieth century, Julius Rosenwald and George Peabody extended their great philanthropy to education by contributing funds to erect YMCA buildings for the race. As the exoduses of World Wars I and II later increased the northern urban colored population, participation in the Y movement increased. With this organization, growing urbanization has had a similar result in the South.

Many Negroes took a moralistic attitude toward the lynchings, beatings, and other forms of brutality and oppression which were associated with the over-throw of Radical Reconstruction. Speaking on the subject, "Why is the Negro lynched," Frederick Douglass said:

> It should be remembered that, in the order of Divine Providence, the man, who puts one end of a chain around the ankle of his fellowman, will find the other end around his own neck. And it is the same with a nation. . . . As we sow we shall reap. . . . We tolerated slavery and it has cost us a million graves, and it may be that lawless murder now raging, if permitted to go on, may yet bring the red hand of vengeance, not only on the reverend head of age, and upon the helpless women, but upon even the innocent babes of the cradle.[56]

Douglass held the same Biblically-inspired moralistic conception of social affairs which permeated practically almost every avenue of Negro expression throughout the nineteenth and early twentieth century. This view held that there is a divine law which works to the end that we reap what we sow, that such a catastrophe as the Civil War was the result of the sin of slavery, and that hence the nation had best be careful in its treatment of the colored minority or God will send some other evil to punish the nation. Commenting on the later Spanish-American War, Booker Washington struck this same note. He observed:

> From the results of the war with Spain, let us leaern this, that God has been teaching the Spanish nation a terrible lesson. . . . God has been teaching Spain that for every one of her subjects that she has left in ignorance, poverty and crime the price must be paid; and, if it has not been paid with the very heart of the nation, it must be paid with the proudest and bluest blood of her sons and with treasure that is beyond computation. From this spectacle I pray God that America will learn a lesson in respect to the ten million Negroes in this country.[57]

Washington believed that God is just and will punish all unrighteousness eventually. He saw God behind every triumph of right and justice in the nation's history, and evil behind

every failure, and firmly believed that God answers prayer.
Daniel Alexander Payne declared that, "When God has a work
to be executed he also chooses the man to execute it and quali-
fies the workman for the work."[55] Kelly Miller gave this conviction a somewhat different slant, and used his ideas about God
to refute the doctrine of white supremacy. "In olden times,
when God communicated with man from burnish bush and on
mountain top," Miller declared, "He selected men of lowly,
loyal souls as the chosen channel of revelation. To believe that
those who breath out slaughter and hatred against their fel-
lowmen are now His chosen mouthpiece is to assume that Providence . . . has grown less particular than aforetime in the
choice of spokesmen."[59] Like Frederick Douglass, W. S. Scarborough, then Professor at Wilberforce University of Ohio,
hinted at the possible dire effects of continued oppression of the
colored man. "It is not a wise policy to continue alienating the
affections of the Negro," Scarborough wrote in 1891. "Whatever be the methods adopted by the blacks to ensure safety and
protection," he continued, "I'm justified in saying that no
radical measures will be taken until all other efforts fail."[60] In
one of his poems entitled "Resignation," Paul Lawerence Dunbar probably came closer to expressing the real mood of the
Negro. Dunbar wrote—

> Long had I grieved at what I deemed abuse,
> But now I am a grain within the mill;
> If so be thou must crush me for Thy use;
> Grind on, O potent God, and do Thy will.[61]

In his poem, "Fifty Years," written in 1913, James Weldon
Johnson erpressed the conviction that God has some large purpose in mind for the Negro. He believed, like so many other
members of his race, that the Heavenly Father had sent the
Abolitionists and the Civil War, and would in freedom always
send men competent and willing to do his work. In this poem,
Johnson wrote:

> Courage! Look out, beyond, and see
> The far horizon's beckoning span!
> Faith in your God-known destiny!
> We are a part of some great plan.

> That for which millions prayed and sighed,
> That for which tens of thousands fought
> For which so many freely died,
> God cannot let it come to naught.[62]

The intense fervor of the religiosity manifested by many freedmen was, even for the South, a unique and colorful phenomenon. Based largely on Old Testament precepts and fed by the dire circumstances of the benighted freedman's daily existence, these religious professions and manifestations impressed some persons as being a revival of ideal primitive Christianity. But as with many other Americans, with the freedmen there was often a big gap between the religion professed and that practiced.[63] Their religious faith and hope had all of the intensity and simplicity characteristic of mental children. Many believed that the wicked man, like the wicked nation, ultimately "never succeeded in life" in a material way.[64]

By 1900 there was considerable contempt one for the other among aged and young Negroes, as the old thought that the young were too irreligious, worldly-minded and soft, while the latter viewed the older generation as too old fashioned and uneducated. One ex-slave said of post-war youths . . . . "None of them ain't raised."[65]

Between 1900-1930 several new religious denominations of Negroes appeared on the national scenes, including the Apostolic Overcoming Holy Church of God, House of Lord, and the African Orthodox Church.

Princeton trained Rev. Francis J. Grimké believed that out of World War I would come "a higher type of Christianity than at present prevails—than the miserable apology that now goes under that name." Further, he opined in Dec., 1918:

> Things are as they are today in these great nations of the world, and it has fared with these weaker and darker races and nations as it has, because the so-called Church of God has been recreant to its high trust; has been dominated by such a cowardly and wordly spirit that it has always been willing to listen to the voice of man instead of the voice of God.[66]

This, of course, is the same criticism which Frederick Douglass levelled at the church during the days of slavery, and in the

1950's Benjamin Mays and other leading Negro spokesmen often through pen and forum would reiterate a similar charge. In the twenties Archibald Grimké penned *The Shame of America* or *The Negro's Case Against the Republic* in which he gave a ringing indictment of the nation's maltreatment of the black man. Here he declared:

> The North and the South are in substantial accord in respect to us and in respect to the position which we are to occupy in this land. We are to be forever exploited, forever treated as an alien race, allowed to live here in strict subordination and subjection to the white race. We are to hew for it wood, draw for it water, till for it the earth, drive for it coaches, wait for it at tables, black for it boots, run for it errands, receive from it crumbs and kicks, to be for it, in short, social mudsills on which shall rest the foundations of the vast fabric of its industrial democracy and civilization.
>
> No one can save us from such a fate but God, but ourselves.

Robert Kerling said of the Negro's protest of the twenties that it was "protest sometimes pathetic and prayerful, sometimes vehement and bitter."[68]

Race pride and racial unity were central themes of the thought of Negro leaders during the twenties. A new sophistication toward religion came into the thought of more Negroes than ever before; with some this sophistication inclined strongly toward agnosticism and atheism. Perhaps William Stanley Braithwaite typified the less radical sophistication. In his poem "Thanking God," Braithwaite describes the prayer of such a person.

During this period, "the first suggestion that God is probably useless in the Negro's struggle for decent existence comes from Countee Cullen."[39] Cullen wrote:

> A man was lynched last night;
> God, if He was, kept to His skies,
> And left us to our enemies.

In another place Cullen expresses faith that there must be reason in all events, that Gods plan is being worked out, but:

Inscrutable His ways are, and immune
To cathechism by a mind too strewn
With petty cares to slightly understand
What awful brain compels His awful hand.
Yet do I marvel at this curious thing:
To make a poet black, and bid him sing![70]

In *Darkwater,* W. E. B. Du Bois sounded a similar note when
he cried:

Keep not Thou Silent, O God!
Sit not longer blind, Lord God,
Deaf to our prayer
And dumb to our suffering.
Surely Thou, too are not white,
      a pale, bloodless,
Heartless thing.[71]

DuBois often identified humanity with God and held that injustice done to any member of the human race is done to God;
to exploit the darker races or to lynch their members is to exploit and lynch the Deity. This trend of thought is evident in
his "Prayers of God" found in *Darkwater.* Here is found again
the beautiful sensitiveness and hatred which DuBois had for all
war and killing. With him this feeling extended to dumb animals. Another outstanding writer of the period, Benjamin
Brawley, was less pessimistic and wrote:

Far above the strife and striving,
And the hate of man for man,
I can see the great contriving
Of a more than human plan.

And day by day more clearly
Do we see the great design,
And day by day more nearly
Do our footsteps fall in line.

For in spite of the winds repeating
The rule of the lash and rod,
The heart of the world is beating,
With the love that was born of God.[72]

Obviously referring to the Garvey movement, in an address delivered at the Harvard University Commencement,

June 22, 1922 Mordecai Johnson stated of his race that one "group among us believes in religion and believes in the principles of democracy, but not in the white man's religion and not in the white man's democracy. It believes that the creed of the former slave states is the tacit creed of the whole nation, and that the Negro may never expect to acquire economic, political, and spiritual liberty in America."[73] In one sense, the Negro Zionism to which Johnson was referring was a part of the rampant world-wide nationalism which contributed directly to the coming of World Wars I and II and to the great colonial unrest which have plagued the twentieth century.

Indicative of the de-emphasis on race which was one characteristic of Negro thought of the 1920's and 30's is the fact that the religious cult launched by "Father Divine" (George Baker) is inter-racial. This movement specifically forbids practice of race prejudice and does not allow use of the words "Negro," "Black," or "White" among its members. In its emphasis on providing economic security for its members, the Divine movement was a true child of the depression. In the penchant for purchasing expensive hotels and other properties, it is a child of the Great American Dream of material wealth, while, in the emphasis on Baker as a leader and a God, the movement reflects the traditional desire of Afro-Americans for a "Moses." In the ardent emotionalism of its practice of religion, the movement reflects the persistent tendency of lower-class people toward great emotionalism, and another twentieth century tendency of some Afro-American leaders to start "rackets" to exploit the credulity and emotionalism.

In the 1920's Kelly Miller had closely tied his race's fate and destiny to the plan of God.[74] "The Negro's cause is right," he declared "and right must finally win. The devils believe this, and tremble."[75] "Thinking of the experiences through which my ancestors passed along with thousands of other slaves, in their contact with the white people of America," opined R. R. Moton, "I have often felt that somehow in spite of the hardships and oppression which they suffered—that in the providence of God, the Negro has come through the ordeal with much to his credit, and with a great many advantages over his condition when he entered the relationship."[76] Moton believed that the nation had gained also. In a speech which he delivered in Washington, D. C. at the dedication of the Lincoln Monument, May 30, 1922, he said: "In the providence of God the black race in America was thrust across the path of the onward-marching white race to demonstrate not only for America, but for the World, whether the principles of freedom are of universal application, and ultimately to extend its blessings to all mankind."[77]

Many Afro-Americans have had a fatalistic conception of life that is derived from their view of history as a theodicy. When he could not draw faith and hope from his social environment, the Negro could turn to this teleological conception of history and life and find consolation. If this fatalism has been stultifying on the lives of some, it has not been so on the lives of many others. For the lives of Moton, James Weldon Johnson, Booker Washington, DuBois, and most other race leaders attest to their belief in helping fate along. Negroes have shared confidence in the Protestant gospel of work and idividualism.[78]

Carter Woodson said of the religious views of the masses of Negroes in the 1920s and '30s—

> They laugh at those who doubt the existence of an all-seeing Providence and question the divinity of His Son. The Lord has delivered these Negroes from too many trials and tribulations for them to doubt His power or His interest in mankind. God is not held responsible for the Negroes' being carried away captive to be the slaves of white men; but He is given credit for delivering them from bondage. God has nothing to do with their long persecution and the intolerant conditions under which they have to live, but great praise should be given Him for permitting them to exist under the circumstances.[79]

"The appeal of the Negro rural church, very much like that of the whites," concluded Woodson, "is based upon fear. God is not so much the loving Father who has provided many good things for His obedient children; He is rather Jehovah, Lord of Hosts, working the destruction of those who do not heed His com-

mands."[80] "The large majority of Negro preachers of today,"
Woodson opined, "are doing nothing more than to keep up the
medieval hell-fire scare which the whites have long since abandoned to emphasize the humanitarian trend in religion through
systematic education."[81] Of Woodson's own religious views,
Mays states: "In most of his writings where conceptions of religion and God are given, Woodson is an enemy to views of God
that lead the Negro to look for salvation in Heaven and to
ideas of God that blind the Negro so that he cannot see the
seriousness of the plight in which he finds himself."[82] Woodson,
like Walter White and others, had come to believe that too
often religion as then practiced was an opiate to many persons,
and that it made their thoughts too otherworldly. Further Mays
states:

> Woodson revolts against the white man's religion
> because it is a religion that has been used to justify
> slavery . . . Garveyites revolt against it because eco-
> nomic, political, and spiritual liberties are denied. It
> is a religion held by a people who still oppress and
> exploit the weak. Their idea of God is that of a God
> who opposes exploitation and who loves all mankind.[83]

Of the twentieth century religious views of Afro-American
writers, Mays has stated that, "in the development of the idea
of God in Negro Literature there is a tendency or threat to
abandon the idea of God as a useful instrument in social adjustment."[84] Obvious here is the considerable difference between
the ultra-modern religious views of the writers, or intelligentia,
and fundamentalist views referred to by Woodson. For the
class referred to by Mays, here again is further evidence that
with the twentieth century the faith, confidence, self-respect,
and secularistic outlook of the race were developing rapidly.
But that the rank and file of colored Americans were still largely of the older persuasions is to be seen in the 1930-31 analysis
by Mays and Nicholson of one hundred persons and fifty-one
prayers used in Negro churches. The study revealed that in the
thought of the masses:

> This life is almost completely denied and refuge
> is sought in Heaven. Even the fulfilling of the desire
> for intimate response in Jesus or God is a means of

endurance to the end, so that Heaven may be gained. It is not a response which sends one out buoyantly to achieve. God is to give complete security and adequate response but these are to be experienced in Heaven. Like the ideas of God expressed in the spirituals, *Gods Tronbones,* and in the other-wordly sermons, the ideas of God in the prayers adhere to traditional, compensatory patterns in that they support and sustain compensatory beliefs with respect to God.[55]

In this period Langston Hughes and a few other Negro intellectuals turned to Communist persuasions and repudiated many of the dominant elements of Western culture. Hughes wrote a poem entitled "Good-bye Christ," in which he accused Christianity of having become an organized racket and imperialist too of the white man.[56] Throughout its period of existence, *The Messenger* magazine severely attacked the fundamentalist tendencies of the Negro church. A Thanksgiving 1919 editorial of this journal stated: "Our Deity is the toiling masses of the world."[57] A few persons departed from the trend toward agnosticism and boasted of their atheism. Perhaps the best-known of them, George Schuyler, wrote:

It is well known, of course, that I am an atheist. I have said so time and time again and long before any of my literary contemporaries in Senegambia began to be assailed with doubts and said so in public. However, I am realist enough to agree with Voltaire that 'if there were no God, it would be necessary to create Him.' There is much that is noble and beautiful in religion and I would not take one iota of faith away from any human being who is comforted and can escape from harsh reality thereby. Much of the ranting against religion and the church is utterly devoid of sense. True, as religion comes to be highly institutionalized it develops into a racket and eventually suffers the fate of all rackets; that is, makes place for another racket. But what is here true of religion is likewise true of all the rest of man's activities.[58]

Here Schuyler's view of religion is similar to some of the ideas which were held by James Weldon Johnson. The statement or implication that much of organized religion is a racket is found in F. W. Bond, and in Woodson's writings, and the statement of a number of other educated Negroes. Mays has pointed out the manner in which religious doubts are evident in the writings of Nella Larsen,[89] and shows how Walter White, in his novel *Fire in the Flint,* "revolts against an other-wordly religion and the malignity of God as pictured by most ministers." The same tendency is evident in Jessie Remond Fauset's book, *Plum Bun* and in Richard Wright's novel, *The Outsider,*[90] all of which is evidence of a growing secularization of Negro thought. Gone was much of the romantic idealism found earlier, but rather than having changed to something less commendable, this idealism had matured and become more inhibited and objective. Throughout the Negro has remained a spearhead of Christian idealism in the United States and the Western World.

CHAPTER VII

ANTE-BELLUM CLASSES AND FAMILY LIFE
AMONG NEGROES

Although its true extent may have been exaggerated by abolitionists, sexual intimacy between planters and slave-women was doubtless more common than the Old South would ever admit. At times this intimacy was the result of force used by the master against his unwilling chattel, while at other times there was mutual consent. Southern cities saw women openly sold for the purpose of serving as mistresses, and long before the end of the slave era, thousands of mulattoes had been produced by these unions. They were a dominant element in the Free Negro class, and provided much of the leadership for the race during both the ante- and post-bellum eras. Recently the argument has been advanced that most mulattoes in the South were the result of illicit relations between Negroes and carpetbaggers during the days of Reconstruction, but, E. Franklin Frazier and other scholars have refuted this.[1]

Among factors which increased racial mixing were: (1) the fact that planters actually owned the bodies of their slaves, and the law took this to be literal even where sexual intercourse was concerned; (2) the economic value which mulattoes had over dark-skinned persons, (3) the existence of a chronic surplus of white males over white females in the South.

There is abundant evidence that mulattoes were keenly aware of their relationship to the dominant race in the South. Sometimes a kindly planter would manumit such of his offspring and send them to northern or foreign schools, or otherwise help them get started in life. At times he remained close to them, counselling and petting his illegitimate progeny along with his legitimate children. Doubtless this relationship accelerated considerably the Negro's acculturation in the United States.

"It is almost impossible for slaves to give a correct account of their male parentage . . . There is no legal marriage among the slaves of the South,"[2] Henry Bibb declared. Sometimes the

136

master chose each slave's marital partner, with no thought given to the feelings of the slaves. In such cases the breeding potential was usually the master's primary concern and the lash was used to persuade the dissident. One ex-slave declared—"Yes'm, the master would do all the courting for you."[3] There is some evidence that these forced unions produced in some female slaves a distaste for sexual cohabitation which lasted throughout their lives, and such forced unions did little to instill in the slaves an appreciation for the sex act as either an art or as an expression of gentle love. Here, as in so many other areas, slavery debased rather than elevated.

In their practically unanimous denunciation of miscegenation, Negroes have shown a streak of puritanism and respect for the women of their race that is reminiscent of the glorification of their women which southern white men have been given credit for. Looking back at this miscegenation of the slave era, Kelly Miller wrote in 1914:

> I see the haughty sons of a haughty race pouring
> out their lustful passion upon black womanhood,
> filling our land with a bronzed and tawny brood.[4]

Slaves usually accepted illegitimate children and their mothers the same as the legitimate. Some slaves had a song they sang:

> Ring a ring a rineo
> Ain't seen a nigger in a mile or more
> You take Sal and I take Sue,
> Ain't no difference 'tween the two.[5]

Still bondsmen longed to be married "right" like the whites. They felt that merely having their names "written in the book" or the widespread jumping over the broom was inadequate and discriminatory. Most of the time there was no marriage ceremony of any kind for slaves.[6] In the 1940's, one freedman reported of the slave-era marriages—"We were just like folks are now sometimes, just living together like cats and dogs."[7] William Wells Brown declared: "There is no such thing as slaves being lawfully married. There never yet was a case where a slave has been tried for bigamy. The man may have as many women as he wishes, and the women as many men."[8]

Like Booker Washington and many other slaves, Frederick Douglass never knew who his father was. Douglass scarcely ever saw his mother, and attested that most slaves did not even know their proper ages.[9] "Oh! Sir," Douglass wrote, "a slave-holder never appears to me so completely an agent of hell, as when I think of and look upon my dear children. It is then that my feelings rise above my control."[10]

According to the census of 1860, about twelve percent, or over 500,000 Negroes in the South were mulattoes. Not only census report figures, but statements given by former slaves reveal that miscegenation was far more widespread than is generally believed.[11] Kenneth Stampp states that the one-half million figure was certainly an underestimate.[12] Although it is well-known that slave women had sexual relations with members of the planter class, that a similar relationship between male slaves and female members of the dominant race sometime existed, is seldom mentioned. Helen Catteral reports cases where a number of white men sought to divorce their wives on grounds that the latter had been intimate with slaves.[13]

Stampp declares that "miscegenation . . . had a sharp psychological impact upon the slaves." On this he wrote:

> A devoted slave husband who was unable to protect his wife from the master or overseer, or whose wife willingly submitted to the advances of a white man faced a personal crisis of major proportions. Occasionally the husband ignored the consequences and retaliated violently against a white man for taking liberties with his wife. On the other hand, a male bondsman might incur the master's hostility if he won the affection of a female in whom the master also had an interest. Thus an Alabama slave found himself in trouble when the master 'became jealous' of him for 'running around after one of his women.'[14]

Stampp concludes his discussion of miscegenation thus: "When the effects of miscegenation upon all groups in southern society have been measured, one can hardly escape the conclusion that the principle victims were the colored females who were directly involved in it."[15] He points out that slaves resented and ostracized women who became regular and willing lovers of white men. These women were also often despised by the white wife on the plantation. "The veneration of white womanhood," he avers, "combined with the disrespect for Negro womanhood was a peculiarly cynical application of a double standard."[16]

Mulatto slaves who were field hands apparently had no preferential treatment,[17] and many were not proud of their white ancestry. One ex-slave reported "I hate to say it but I am just going to tell the truth, and that is that my old master was my father. . . .. I hate to say these things, but they often happened this way back in those days. The masters were often the fathers."[18]   One aged ex-slave reported: "Some of them thought it was an honor to have the marsa, but I didn't want no white man foolin' with me."[19]

During slavery, as in the early years of freedom, a light complexion often conferred privileges and opportunities upon the Negro. Mulattoes were preferred as domestic servants and as skilled artisans, but few planters would buy them for service as field hands, as they often resented the more menial tasks. Their kinship to the master class sometimes won manumission, and it often won kinder treatment. The same is true of the early days of freedom. So obvious were these advantages that dark-skinned persons sometimes consciously sought to marry into the mulatto class, both before and after emancipation.[20]

Among Negroes the attraction for light complexions has often taken the form of contempt for "dark" or "black" skins, and, with many persons the word "black" has been a synonym for "inferior," "debased," or "degraded." But the same words often have been symbols of pride, and at times the mulatto has been looked down upon as an inferior and contemptuous mixed breed. Writing in 1930, Langston Hughes has an old Negro character in his story, *Not Without Laughter*, reflect: "I ain't never seen a yaller dude yet that meant a dark woman no good." R. R. Moton stated in 1929: It "may sound strange to these accustomed to think that the Negro is ashamed of his race" to learn that "that is not true of the Negro everywhere."[21] Still Moton felt compelled to admit that, "A certain propaganda has pretty well succeeded in putting the stigma of inferiority on most things associated with the race, color, hair, speech." Moton contends that it is to escape prejudice and discrimination that some Afro-Americans take pains to conceal their racial identity. Yet, this defensive attitude does not explain why many colored Americans boast among themselves of their thin lips, pointed noses, light complexions, "straight" hair, and Caucasian ancestry.

There is evidence that slaves reverred the mulatto because a light skin sometimes brought favors from the master-parent. Henry Bibb states that the mother of the slave-girl whose hand he sought in marriage opposed him because she wanted her daughter to marry a mulatto slave who, because of his relationship to his master, might be manumitted.[22] As the post-bellum growth of Negro business began to presage the development of a bourgeois class, studies of this class revealed that its members often tended to marry light colored women.[23]

Because of the prejudice which many white Americans have held against Afro-Americans the latter has tended to be suspicious of all Caucasians who offer him friendship, and this fear and distrust of the white man has sometimes been extended to mulattoes. The truth would seem to be that most Negroes have long held both pride in and contempt for their race. Like the mind of the white South, the mind of the Negro is filled with paradoxes. Among other things, slavery, white supremacy, and the fiction that the Negro is not human, but a sub-species, have created these paradoxes for both races. Wilson Record has observed the tendency of many Afro-Americans to accept notions of their inferiority, and so to despise all characteristics and efforts thought of as peculiar to their race. "The phenomenon of self-hatred," he notes, is "not limited to Jews, Mexicans, or Indians."[24] Frances Kemble reported that slaves accepted and shared much of the contempt for their race which the planters held. The slaves, she wrote, "profess, and really seem to feel it [contempt] for themselves, and the . . . faintest admixture of white blood in their veins appears at once, by common consent of their own race, to raise them in the scale of humanity."[25]

In 1843[26] Henry Highland Garnett admonished the slaves to:

Look around you, and behold the bosoms of your
loving wives heaving with untold agonies! Hear the
cries of your poor children! Remember the stripes
your fathers bore. Think of the torture and disgrace
of your noble mothers. Think of your wretched
sisters, loving virtue and purity, as they are driven
to concubinage and are exposed to the unbridled lusts
of incarnate devils.[27]

Negro literature shows more bitterness about miscegenation after the Civil War than before. However, as stated, in
ante-bellum days slaves often looked down on women of their
group who willingly yielded to whites and black abolitionists
constantly showed resentment at the fact that slave women
were sometimes forced to serve as planter's mistresses. Probably
the typical position on miscegenation was well-stated by a colored man in 1834. "Abolitionists," he stated, "do not wish
'amalgamation:' I do not wish it, nor does any colored man or
woman of my acquaintance, nor can instances be adduced
where a desire was manifested by any colored person; but I
deny that 'inter-marriages' between 'white and blacks' are unnatural."[28] This remained throughout the characteristic position
of Afro-Americans, that is, while they were not seeking nor
did they desire intermarriage between the races, they defended
the *right* to this just as with all other rights. Here, on a sensitive subject, is proof that the colored American generally has
sought nothing short of full and complete civil, social, and
political equality.

There were only 400,000 town slaves in 1850, but in town
and on plantations were a great number of skilled slaves. The
number of highly skilled slaves working at trades in almost
every community made a lie of the argument that slaves were
too stupid to learn.

One ex-bondsman observed of domestic slaves: "They are
ever regarded as a privileged class; and are sometimes greatly
envied, . . . [imitated, and feared] while others are bitterly
hated."[29] An ex-domestic said: "We house slaves thought we
was bettern' the others what worked in the field . . . We was
raised; they, that is the field hands, wasn't."[30] Field hand slaves
were usually afraid to discuss many of their feelings, or hopes,

or plans before domestics and artisans, and the latter were often prohibited from talking or fraternizing with field slaves. Still, because they were uncomfortable around white persons, some slaves preferred field over domestic work.[31]

Domestics took pride in their uniforms and degree of responsibility, and they worked for the praise of their masters as to how efficiently the table was served or how well the food tasted. Skilled slaves often took great pride in their craftsmanship. "It was pride in craftsmanship, not monetary rewards which gave most carpenters, blacksmiths, coopers, cobblers and wheelrights their chief incentive," states a leading student of the institution.[32] Planters encouraged class thought and divisions among slaves as a means of controlling them.

There is evidence that field hands not only envied the domestics and artisans, but also felt at times that they were better off in some ways than these more privileged slaves. For example, when offered the opportunity of learning trades, some of the field hands refused on the grounds that while training would increase their value to the master, it scarcely meant that they would have any greater degree of real freedom. Frederick Law Olmsted was of the opinion that the field hands viewed "the close control and careful movements required of house-servants" as a mode of life less desirable than their own.[33] Too, field hands liked the manner in which their quarters constituted an isolated community existence in which all persons were intimate equals. Alone in their own groups they were free to give vent to their true feelings.

Frazier asserts that the cruelties inflicted on pregnant Negro women during the middle passage voyage from Africa, as well as during slave-trading within the United States, and on the plantation, sometimes caused these women to lose all maternal feeling for their own children. Often, he asserts, slave women felt more maternal feeling for the white children placed under their charge.[34] This he thinks, explains the celebrated devotion between black mammies or Grannies and the white children whom they nursed. In the latter case there was more intimacy and comfort associated with the relationship, hence a greater opportunity for the development of tender feelings.

Yet, it is clear that many slave mothers also developed a strong love for their own progeny. One ex-slave reported that while in bondage, her man died and left her an infant girl child orphan. The little child soon died, too, and the former said she was glad it died because then it was free of bondage.[35] Of her mother who had been sold away from her children, Sojourner Truth said:

> I can remember when I was a little, young girl, how my old mammy would sit out of doors in the evenings and look up at the stars and groan, and I would say 'Mammy, what makes you groan so?' And she would say, 'I am groaning to think of my poor children; they do not know where I be and I don't know where they be. I look up at the stars and they look up at the stars!'

In the intimate relationship which existed between the "Mammy" who was a foster-mother to white children of the plantation, and the concubinage which existed between planters and slave women, E. F. Frazier discerns "the fundamental paradox of the slave system."[36] This paradox he calls, "maximum intimacy existing in conjunction with the most rigid caste system." The image of the slave mammy has made a great impression on the mind of the Negro just as it has on the mind of white America.

When domestics married they were sometimes allowed ceremonies which included much of the traditional form and solemnity. For all of the slaves these weddings and the accompanying feasts were occasions of great joy.

Slave families were largely matriarchal. Since the husband lacked practically all of the legal, economic, and other supports which made the white father a dominating figure in the household, the slave husband often did not command the love, respect, obedience or faithfulness of his wife or children. Because of their weak authority, children of slaves were sometimes disrespectful of both parents. Married males could not wear the pants in their households, as those were worn by the planter who had the right to chastize all family members with the lash, break up the family through sale, or otherwise abuse it.[37] Kenneth Stampp points out that "the number of bastardy

cases in southern court records seems to confirm the conclusion
that women of the poor white class "carried about the same
reputation for easy virtue as their sable sisters."[38]   Although
there were numerous instances where slave families were stable
and ideal in spite of the great odds against them, there is much
evidence that throughout the period since emancipation, Negro
men have deserted their wives and children more often than
men belonging to other racial groups.[39]

A unique characteristic of Negro family life has been the
prevalence of matriarchal tendencies. This has been a heritage
from slavery. During the ante-bellum period both tradition
and economic necessity were lacking to instill in the slave wife
subordination to masculine authority. After emancipation, since
many mothers had to support themselves and their children,
female independence and self-reliance were further strengthened.[40] The census reports constantly have revealed proportionally
more female heads of families among Negroes than among
white Americans. In 1940 almost one-third of the families in
urban areas of the South had female heads. Also typical and
very important in this connection, has been the role of the
grandmother as tutor, adviser, and stabilizing element. Quite
often it has been "Granny" who took under her care and
guidance the deserted youths who were unfortunate products
of illegitimacy or the lack of stable family life. Also her role
as "midwife" has added to the esteem and veneration given
her by many communities. The independent and domineering
proclivities which some Negro women acquired is perhaps to
be seen in another connection. In the ante-bellum period, some
free persons purchased their wives from slavery and then refused to manumit them until a probationary period had been
passed. If the wife did not pass this period satisfactorily, her
husband sometimes sold her as a slave to another master.[41]

Just as urbanization and industrialization were primary
factors in causing the pre-Civil War North to become strongly
abolitionist in thought and action, these factors also militated
against slavery within the South. Bondsmen in areas near southern cities were sometimes utilized as parttime labor in southern
industries, and came to have less tolerance for slavery than
persons employed in agricultural occupations. A number of the

bondsmen were allowed to keep a portion of their earnings, and in this way bought their freedom. Some who lived in urban areas were literate skilled artisans, and held a higher estimation of their personal worth than the cotton, sugar cane, or rice field worker. Cities ever have been centers of the dynamic, cosmopolitan, and democratic life, and urban slaves were inevitably and unavoidably affected. Also, in the towns and cities were to be found more persons who felt themselves to be friends of the slave, either because of racial kinship as with the free Negroes, or because of ties of liberal thought, as was the case with a number of white southern abolitionists. Too, arms for insurrection could be more easily obtained and hidden in urban areas, and there was greater opportunity for absconding, or plotting rebellion. Planters knew these dangers to their slave property, and frequently commented that those employed in agricultural occupations were easier to manage.[42]

Slaves not only had systems for communicating with one another on the same plantation about the most forbidden topics, but they sometimes sent letters all over the South.[43] These might be passed on to bondsmen in urban areas, who would in turn pass them on to slaves working on boats, or those travelling with their masters. Because of these erstwhile committees of correspondence, insurrections were sometimes plotted which involved thousands of persons.[44]

It was among ante-bellum free persons that family life first became institutional among Afro-Americans.[45] At one time Baltimore alone had 25,647 free Negroes, while 18,647 were living in New Orleans. Almost one-half of the free population were listed as mulattoes.[46] There were over 32,-000 free Negroes in the South in 1790, and approximately 250,000 in 1860. Of Pennsylvania's 10,000 Negroes in 1790, one-third were free persons. By 1850 the northern free Negro population was about equal to that of the South. Before the Nat Turner revolt and the rise of militant abolitionism, free Negroes had a fairly large measure of freedom. By 1850, however, the South allowed free Negroes to hold no public meetings of any kind unless a white person was present; they could not visit or receive slaves in their homes, nor vote anywhere in the South after 1835, had limited job opportunities, and in many places they could not buy or sell spirited beverages.

In 1850 California had a Negro population of 962; by 1860, this figure had more than tripled, and there were 4,086 Negroes in the state. In the same decade, Michigan's Negro population had more than doubled to reach a figure slightly over six thousand. As after 1830 militant abolitionism was an unwelcome force everywhere, stirring up issues and consciences as it did, the Negro in the Old and New West was generally an unwanted personage, stoned, chased, beaten, legally proscribed, and lynched by individuals and mobs in western cities and states throughout the 1830-1860 period. If free Negroes, North and South, had been treated as equals of white persons, perhaps so many free Negroes would not have been such zealous abolitionists.

Like Americans in general, Negroes have been enthusiastic organizers of societies and associations. One of the first societies was formed in Philadelphia in 1787, through the leadership of Absalom Jones and Richard Allen. This society existed to bring together for mutual benefit, northern free persons of color of various religious denominations. Like many of the fraternal orders, this society set up a welfare service to provide financial aid to indigent members. Also evidencing the constant awareness which the Afro-American has shown that many members of his group do not always conduct themselves publicly in the most socially acceptable way, this organization provided that "no drunkard or disorderly person be admitted as a member."[47] In 1843 Peter Ogden and other Baltimore free Negroes founded the Grand United Order of Odd Fellows. Racial discrimination practiced by whites is the main reason that separate Negro churches, lodges, communities, schools, and other groups have come into existence. Between 1784-87 Barbados-born Rev. Prince Hall had launched in Boston the English-charted Negro masonic order which bears his name, and soon separate Negro churches and other institutions and organizations appeared. Evidence of the militant activity against slavery of Negro Masons is seen in the fact that the *Liberator* of March 17, 1843 reported that a Baltimore Grand Jury had ruled Negro Lodges as sources of danger to the institution of slavery.

Free persons sometimes participated in slave plots and rebellions. How often they fed and hid runaway slaves can never
be known, but they probably behaved much as slaves did when
the latter generally aided and refused to inform on fugitives.
That there were many persons of opposite calibre is sufficiently
evident. A slave exposed the Denmark Vesey plot, as well as
the hiding place of Nat Turner. Yet three free Negroes and
thirteen slaves were hanged immediately after the Turner revolt
was put down. Planters encouraged slaves to spy on one another
and to report all misdoings. While slaves often turned informer
because of a reward which stood to be gained, at times both
bondsmen and free persons informed because they were genuinely convinced that the plotted action was against the best
interests of Negroes.[48]

A few free persons of color rose to positions of considerable affluence. In the North, the almost steady growth in
property, education and culture of this class fitted it not only
for a prominent and vital role in the abolitionist crusade, but
also for roles of military leadership during the Civil War, and
for serving as the leader, prodder, and inspirer of the race on
all fronts in the post-bellum period. It should not be forgotten
that thousands of the North's free Negroes were fugitives
from the South. Even as early as 1830 the increase of free Negroes in the North, many by flight from the South, intensified
race riots, proscriptions, and prejudice in the North.

Free Negroes were nowhere contented with their lot, and
constantly petitioned governors and legislators for equal citizenship benefits.[49] Of proscriptions against the northern free
Negro, Rev. Theodore S. Wright stated in 1837:

> It is true that in these United States and in this
> state, there are men like myself, colored with the skin
> like my own, who are not subjected to the lash, who
> are not liable to have their wives and their infants
> torn from them; from whose hand the Bible is not
> taken. It is true that we may walk abroad; we may
> enjoy our domestic comforts, our families; retire to
> the closet; visit the sanctuary, . . . But sir, still we
> are slaves—everywhere we feel the chain galling us.
> It is by . . . prejudice . . ., the spirit of slavery,

> . . . by corrupt public sentiment, through the influ-
> ence of slavery . . . This spirit is withering all our
> hopes, and oftimes causes the colored parent as he
> looks upon his child, to wish he had never been born.
> Often is the heart of the colored mother, as she
> presses her child to her bosom, filled with sorrow to
> think that, by reason of this prejudice, it is cut off
> from all hopes of usefulness in this land. Sir, this
> prejudice is wicked.[50]

On the specific difficulties encountered, Rev. Wright mentioned
the difficulty which the northern free person of color had in
learning a trade, or in finding employment if he learned one,
due to the exclusion policies of the unions. He also mentioned
that while free Negroes could attend the public grade schools,
the colleges were barred against them. Seven years earlier another northern free Negro had declared:

> The freedom to which we have attained is de-
> fective. Freedom and equality have been 'put asunder.'
> The rights of men are decided by the colour of their
> skin; and there is as much difference made between
> the rights of a free white man and a free coloured
> man as there is between a free coloured man and a
> slave.[51]

While interested in improving their own lot, free Negroes
in the North were passionately concerned with the plight of
their enslaved brethren in the South. Frederick Douglass, William W. Brown, and other northern free Negroes were spear-
heads of the abolitionist movement. By unceasing word and
deed they revealed a deep love for, and interest in their race.
At a January, 1817 meeting in Philadelphia devoted to the
efforts of the American Colonization Society, a group of free
Negroes resolved: "That we never will separate ourselves vol-
untarily from the slave population in this country; they are our
brethren by the ties of consanguinity, of suffering, and of
wrong; and we feel that there is more virtue in suffering pri-
vations with them, than fancied advantages for a season." The
first Negro newspaper in the United States championed the
cause of "our brethren who are still in the iron fetters of
bondage," although the editors were not of the opinion that

their efforts would greatly affect the institution.[52] In his "Address to the Slaves of the United States," given at the 1843 National Negro Convention, Buffalo, New York, youthful Henry Highland Garnet echoed the sentiments of such men as Frederick Douglass, Charles L. Remond, William Wells Brown and Charles B. Ray. To the slaves he stated: "While you have been oppressed, we have also been partakers with you; nor can we be free while you are enslaved. Many of you are bound to us, not only by the ties of a common humanity, but we are connected by the more tender relations of parents, wives, husbands, children, brothers, sisters, and friends." The 1864 National Convention meeting at Syracuse, New York declared:

> We feel the terrible sting of this stupendous wrong, and that we cannot be free while our brothers are slaves. The enslavement of a vast majority of our people extends its baleful influence over every member of our race; and makes freedom, even to the free, a mockery and a delusion.

CHAPTER VIII

SOME SOURCES OF THE NEGRO'S FAITH IN HIMSELF AND IN AMERICAN DEMOCRACY

Neither slavery nor racial segregation and discrimination have been able to kill the Afro-American's faith in himself and in American democracy. Though in his trek along the road of American history there ever has been much to make him despair, many sources of faith and hope always have been present. In addition to drinking often from the same sources of faith as white Americans, the Negro has had a number of sources of faith and hope which were peculiar unto himself.

His long-time close identity in peace and war with the nation's central interests has been a source of the Negro's continuing faith in himself and in the nation. During the Reconstruction era Negro Congressman Richard H. Cain said of his race, "We have been identified with the interests of this country from its very foundation."

Like William Lloyd Garrison, Afro-Americans have based much of their faith on "the nature of man, the inherent wrongfulness of oppression, the power of truth, and the omnipotence of God." Faith in God, and in history as a theodicy rather than an odyssey, ever has been a source of the Negro's faith and optimism. On this, The Reverend Francis J. Grimké declared: "The ringing in of Jesus Christ holds the solution of all our problems, racial or otherwise."[1]

Each generation of Negroes in this country has been mindful that the "race problem" could not be completely solved in its day, and has been deeply concerned that they could leave their children improved circumstances. In order to do this, Negroes often have been willing to make great sacrifices. They have thought a great deal about the question of what type of social, economic, and political conditions they were going to bequeath to their children. Tomorrow, because of its promise of a better life, always has been a major source of the Negro's faith and hope. Paul Lawrence Dunbar avowed in his poem, "With the Lark,":

And though, like the rain-drops, I grieved through
    the dark,
I shall wake in the morning to sing with the lark.

On this, Frederick Douglass said to the nation in 1852:

> Three score years and ten is the allotted time
> for individual men; but nations number their years
> by thousands. According to this fact, you are, even
> now, only in the beginning of your national career,
> . . . I am glad this is so.   There is hope in the
> thought, and hope is much needed, under the dark
> clouds which lower above the horizon. The eye of the
> reformer is met with angry flashes, portending dis-
> astrous times; but his heart may well beat lighter at
> the thought that America is young, and that she is
> still in the impressible stage of her existence. . . .
> there is consolation in the thought that America is
> young. —Great streams are not easily turned from
> channels, worn deep in the course of ages. . . . As
> with rivers so with nations.[3]

and:

> While drawing encouragement from the 'Declaration
> of Independence,' the great principles it contains, and
> the genius of American Institutions, my spirit is also
> cheered by the obvious tendencies of the age. Nations
> do not now stand in the same relation to each other
> that they did ages ago. No nation can now shut itself
> up from the surrounding world and trot round in the
> same old path of its fathers without interference. The
> time was when such could be done. Long established
> customs of hurtful character could formerly fence
> themselves in, and do their evil work with social
> impunity. Knowledge was then confined and enjoyed
> by the privileged few, and the multitude walked on
> in mental darkness. But a change has now come. . . .
> Walled cities and empires have become unfashionable.
> The arm of commerce has borne away the gates of
> the strong city. Intelligence is penetrating the darkest
> corners of the globe. . . . Oceans no longer divide,
> but link nations together. . . . Space is comparatively
> annihilated.[4]

These sentiments and convictions are reminiscent of many

which would be heard emanating from Negro spokesmen over a century later.

Past achievements toward solving the race problem have been a constant source of faith that tomorrow would bring still more progress. Near the turn of the century J. C. Price reflected:

> In the memory of men now living, colored people were only allowed to ride on the outside of stages running between Boston and Cambridge. Prudence Crandall, whose house was burned to the ground because she dared, in Connecticut, to teach Negro boys and girls to read and write, died only a few months ago.[5]

Reflecting in 1914 on the ups and downs of his race and the periods of indifference which the nation-at-large too often, has had toward the Negro's plight, Kelly Miller could still be optimistic. On this, he wrote:

> I see that the great generous American heart, despite the temporary flutter, will finally beat true to the higher human impulse, and my soul abounds with reassurance and hope.[6]

The past achievements of individual Negroes have been a source of the race's faith in its future in America. R. R. Moton correctly observed that Booker T. Washington's life was a triumph of democracy itself. The lives of such men and women as Washington, Benjamin Banneker, Frederick Douglass, Mary M. Bethune, Marian Anderson, George Washington Carver, Charles C. Spaulding, Joseph S. Clark, Joe Louis, Sugar Ray Robinson, Jackie Robinson and Ralph Bunche have contributed greatly to the Negro's continuing faith in American democracy. This is a part of the rationale behind such celebrations as "Negro History Week" and the entire Negro History Movement, and the Negro Business League and its annual celebrations.

The collective achievement of the race in America always has been a source of the Negro's faith in himself and the nation. In 1913, Harvard Law graduate and Asst. Attorney General of the United States, William H. Lewis, asked:

> What of the Negro himself? Has he justified Emancipation? The statistics of his physical, intellec-

tual and material progress are known to all. He has
increased his numbers nearly threefold. . . . He has
reduced his illiteracy to 30 percent. He owns nearly
$700,000,000 worth of property including nearly
one million homes. He has shown that his tutelage
in American civilization has not been vain; that he
could live under the most trying and oppressive conditions.

Whatever be his present disadvantages and inequalities, one thing is absolutely certain, that nowhere else in the world does so large a number of
people of African descent enjoy so many rights and
privileges as here in America.[7]

And then:

I predict that within the next 50 years all these discriminations, disfranchisements, and segregation will
pass away. Antipathy to color is not natural, and the
fear of ten by eighty million of people is only a
spook of politics, a ghost summoned to the banquet
to frighten the timid and foolish.[8]

In 1905 Bishop W. T. Vernon stated:

Though weighted with the frailties as a necessary
consequence of the past, though far from what we
desire, we point to some things accomplished since
freedom.

From nothing we could call our own, in forty
years we own eight hundred and fifty thousand
farms, nine banks, two street railways, and pay taxes
on seven hundred million dollars in property.[9]

In his volume *Black Bourgeoisie*, E. Franklin Frazier would
show quite clearly that even in the 1940's and 50's Negroes
were still pointing often to their material achievements and
possessions as a source of faith. Also, the consciousness of and
boastfulness about the growth of his educational and business
institutions long have shown that faith in the power of education and of money have been persistent elements in Negro
thought. In 1905 Bishop Reverdy C. Ransom asked, "Do white
men believe that 10,000,000 blacks, after having imbibed the
spirit of American institutions, . . . will ever accept a place
of permanent inferiority in the Republic?"[10]

The Negro long has known that human progress is not a straight line from down to up, and this knowledge has given him hope whenever his path seemed to take a sudden dip. Reflecting on the ups and downs in the advance of his race toward citizenship and equality, Kelly Miller wrote:

> I see that the path of progress has never been a straight line, but has always been a zigzag course amid the conflicting forces of right and wrong, truth and error, justice and injustice, cruelty and mercy.[11]

In his poem, "Daybreak," George Marion McClellan said that:

> . In spite of all the Babel cries
> Of those who rage and shout,
> God's silent forces daily rise
> To bring His Will about.

Negroes have been inspired by the fight of people in other lands for freedom and equality. Beginning with the revolt of the thirteen colonies against Britain in the eighteenth century, reports of similar protest movements the world over have inspired and encouraged the Afro-American's fight for freedom and equality. These movements have given him the feeling that he was not alone in his sufferings, that his militant actions were part of a great tradition and movement which goes back at least to the fight of the ancient Hebrews against the Egyptian and Babylonian persecutions. These movements have been a source of faith to the Afro-American, strengthening his belief that ultimately right makes might. The speeches and literature of the Negro are full of allusions to history's democratic plots, revolts, and crusades. Although the Afro-American, true to his larger American cultural heritage, generally has shied away from advocacy and practice of violence, he has felt always that, considering his degraded status, not to protest is unmanly.

When the British and French carried out their emancipation of slaves—the British, with a gradual method (1833-38), followed closely on the 1808 U.S.A. end of the slave trade—Negroes in the U.S.A. were made glad and hopeful. The free Negroes especially praised the voluntary nature of the British and French emancipation, and Negro Anglophobia was considerably tempered by Britain's early abolition of the slave trade and slavery.

Throughout his struggle for freedom and first-class citizenship the Negro has known both moments of great optimism and despair. In 1832, Peter Osborne, a Connecticut Negro, addressed a meeting of members of his race with hope and optimism. "The signs in the North, the signs in the South, in the East and West, are all favorable to our cause," he averred.[12] But this did not cause him to feel that his race should just sit and wait. "What man of rational feeling would slumber in content under the yoke of slavery and oppression, in his own country?" he asked; and answered, "Not the most degraded barbarian in the interior of Africa!" The same year Charles Lenox Remond, agent of the American Anti-Slavery Society, said: "We have everything . . . to encourage us. Slavery is trembling, prejudice is falling, and I hope will soon be buried."[13] As early as 1827, Nathaniel Paul stated: "I declare that slavery will be extinct; a universal and not a partial emancipation must take place; nor is the period far distant." His reading of the signs of the times gave as evidence for this assertion—"The indefatigable exertions of the philanthropists in England to have it [slavery] abolished in their West India Islands, the recent revolutions in South America, the catastrophe and exchange of power in the Isle of Hayti, the restless disposition of both master and slave in the southern states, the constitution of our government, the effects of literary and moral instruction, the generous feelings of the pious and benevolent, the influence and spread of the holy religion of the cross of Christ, and the irrevocable decrees of Almighty God."[14] It is difficult to imagine a more realistic, objective, and thorough summary of the forces which were then militating against the institution. The Industrial Revolution would seem to be the only item not directly mentioned. In the statements by Negroes examples of allusion to the forces which were arraigned against the institution of slavery are legion.

Quakers were among the first abolitionists in the United States. Because of their championing of the cause of equality and freedom, many were beaten and driven from northern and southern communities. They sometimes bought and manumitted slaves, and among the plans laid by slave plotters-at-revolt was sometimes a stipulation that the lives of all Quakers in the area would be spared. Benjamin Banneker received much help in securing his education from a Quaker named George Ellicott, and William Wells Brown took on the name of a Quaker who befriended him as he was making good his escape from slavery.

The Negro American never has had to wage his battle in behalf of a greater democracy alone. Almost from the beginning of slavery in this country, there have been liberal reform movements, domestic or foreign, which included the Negro's objectives. There have been the Quaker and Jeffersonian brands of liberalism in the 18th century, the first half of the 19th century age of reform, then Grangerism and Populism, Progressivism, Socialism, New and Fair Deals, and the mid-20th century internationalism-rooted liberalism. In 1876, while dedicating the freedmen's monument in Washington, D. C., Frederick declared of his race: "That we are here today is a compliment and a credit to American civilization, and a prophecy of still greater national enlightenment and progress in the future."[15] A generation later Bishop W. T. Vernon stated— "In the darkest hours we hear the voice of the best of that which makes American life glorious, saying, 'Onward, freedmen' Onward, struggling race, we are with you!"[16] And near the turn of the century, J. C. Price averred:

> I have confidence not only in the better element . . . of the South; but I have also an unswerving faith in the appearance of a better, brighter day in that section,—a day filled with the gladdening light of freedom, prosperity and peace.
>
> Not to believe in such an era is to doubt the ultimate triumph of truth over error, of right over wrong, and to question the victories of the onward sweep and universal conquest of the subduing, humanizing and eternal principles of the enlightened Christian civilization of the nineteenth century.[17]

Travels abroad, as well as news from overseas always have done much to mould Negro thought. For example, when refugees in London, Ontario, having settled a community which they named Wilberforce, sent the Rev. Nathaniel Paul to England to raise money, he wrote William Lloyd Garrison of the contrast between treatment accorded a colored man in England

with that received in America. The treatment accorded by the
latter was such as to fill his soul with "sorrow and indignation."[18] Overseas experiences of Negro troops during World
Wars I and II and the Korean War have had a similar impact
on Negro thought.

The sense of group solidarity provided by national, state
and local Negro conventions has been an important source of
the race's optimism. At such meetings, the various evidence and
data which revealed race progress have been given emphasis, and
plans have been laid for quickening the pace of this progress.
At the Fourth Annual National Convention, 1834, held in
New York City, there were fifty delegates, including two
visitors from Canada and Haiti. The leaders often mentioned
the commendable condition of the Negro in those two countries
compared with his treatment in the U.S.A.

The successful revolt against the French led by Toussaint L'Ouverture provided a great source of hope and optimism for Negroes. After this episode slaveholders frequently
shunned the purchase of slaves from the West Indies because
of their recalcitrancy and unwavering determination not to
live in bondage. The spirit of Toussaint L'Ouverture weighed
heavily on these Negroes and on the southern planters, and
time and again slaves or free persons of color from the Caribbean were blamed for slave insurrections within the U.S.A. At
the 1834 Fourth Annual National Negro Convention, bondsmen were admonished to "Cheer up!" because

> Already a right feeling begins to prevail. The friends
> of justice, of humanity, and the rights of man are
> drawing rapidly together, and are forming a moral
> phalanx in your defense . . . From present appear-
> ances the prospect is cheering, in a high degree. Anti-
> Slavery Societies are forming in every direction. Next
> August proclaims the British dominions free from
> slaves. These United States are her children, they will
> soon follow so good an example. Slavery . . . shall
> be chained and cast down into blackness and dark-
> ness forever."

On his 1840 trip to the London World Anti-Slavery Conference, Charles L. Remond pointed out that he had the op-

portunity to listen to an address in Exeter Hall, on the 24th
of June by Daniel O'Connell. This Irish patriot "alluded to the
American declaration, and contrasted the theory with the practice; then," states Remond, "was I moved to think and feel,
and speak; and from his soul-stirring eloquence and burning
sarcasm would every fibre of my heart contract in abominating
the worse than Spanish Inquisition system in my own [coun-
try]."[19] Remond also contrasted the lack of race prejudice in
England with the prevalence which it enjoyed in the U.S.A.
"If you would rouse the honest indignation of the intelligent
Englishman," he wrote, "tell him of our school and academy
exclusions. If you would enlist the sympathies of the pious,
refer him to our Negro pews in the house of worship, and when
you tell him of . . . Jim Crow . . ., He at once, turning pale
then red, requires if this is American republicanism." On this
same trip a West Indian is quoted as having remarked to Remond that "liberty in the U.S.A." was, "in its best estate, but
the grossest licentiousness."

An October, 1843 Michigan convention of colored Americans, held in Detroit, urged Negroes to "come up, and, like
the oppressed people of England, Ireland, and Scotland, band
ourselves together and wage unceasing war against the high-
handed wrongs of the hideous monster Tyranny." In 1849, writing from London to his friend Wendell Phillips, William Wells
Brown stated:

    Dear Friend,—I observed in the American papers
    an elaborate discussion upon the subject of passports
    for colored men. What must . . . the countries think
    of the people of the United States, when they read, as
    they do, the editorials of some of the Southern papers
    against recognizing colored Americans as citizens? In
    looking over some of these articles, I have felt asham-
    ed that I had the misfortune to be born in such a
    country. We may search history in vain to find a
    people who have sunk themselves as low, and made
    themselves appear as infamous by their treatment of
    their fellow men, as have the people of the United
    States.[20]

Brown praised the unprejudiced treatment which he received
during anti-slavery lectures in England, and charged that his

own country was hypocritical in its interest in the underdogs and oppressed of the world.[21] "If the atrocities recently practiced upon defenseless women in Austria make the blood run cold through the veins of the human and good throughout the civilized world," he asserted, "the acts committed daily upon the slave women of America should not only cause the blood to chill,, but to stop its circulation." "With this gigantic evil in the land [slavery]," added Frederick Douglass, "we are constantly told to look at home; if we say aught against crowned heads, we are pointed to our enslaved millions now lying in worse than heathen darkness; if we express a word of sympathy for Kossuth and his Hungarian fugitive brethren, we are pointed to that horrible and hell-black enactment '*The Fugitive Slave Bill*'."[22] Further evidence of European influence on Negro thought is seen in the modeling of the Colored National League, organized during the 1880's, after the pattern of the Irish Land League, as well as in the impact of Socialism and Communism.[23]

Colored Americans have drawn comfort from the fact that they have long been numerous in this country. This, they have known, made them significant as laborers and potential purchasers and voters, made it impossible for them, ever to be successfully colonized outside the U.S.A., and made it improbable that persecutions and discrimination could ever exterminate them. That they long have comprised at least one-tenth of the nation's population, and an average of one-third of that of the South, has caused Afro-Americans to know that the "Negro Problem" was something that could not be hidden from the world's view, but always would be, until solved, there to embarrass the nation before the world. In a similar vein, Booker T. Washington said in his famed 1895 Atlanta address:

> One-third of the population of the South is of the Negro race. No enterprise seeking the material, civil or moral welfare of this section can disregard this element of our population and reach the highest success.

Some Afro-Americans even thought in ante-bellum times that their rapid increase would cause them soon to outnumber southern whites, thus by this means sound the death knell of slavery. One writer thought that by 1900 there would be in the slave states ten million white persons, and fifteen million slaves, and that for the nation-at-large the racial ratio would be fifty-fifty. When that happened, he stated, the "two great safety-valves for the restless and energetic among the slaves,—Christianity and the Underground Railroad"—would be ineffective in preventing the Negro from rising and overthrowing the institution by force.[24] Of the significance of population, P. B. S. Pinchback declared in 1875:

> The black people of this country can furnish in time of need, for its defense, over 800,000 soldiers to march under the glorious banner of universal liberty. With this force as a political element, and as laborers, producers and consumers, we are an element of strength and wealth too powerful to be ignored by the American people. All we need is a just appreciation of our own power and our own manhood. This rolling in the dust—this truckling to power, whether wrapped up in an individual or a party, I have long since abandoned . . . I am groping about through this American forest of prejudice and proscription, determined to find some form of civilization where all men will be accepted for what they are worth.[25]

In the 1880's and 90's several Negro spokesmen were still of the opinion that the rapid rate of increase of their group would be a solution to the race problem. J. C. Price, for example, often mentioned the Negro's "marvelous fecundity" and pointed out that in the United States his racial group had in less than twenty-five years increased from four to eight million persons.[26]

While both bondsmen and ex-bondsmen found some consolation and hope in their large numbers in the U.S.A., they would have had their pride and hope stimulated to even greater heights had they known generally that in 1850 Negroes comprised one-half of the population of Brazil, that over 200,000 Negroes had been taken into Mexico, over a half million into Venezuela, and that throughout Latin America there were large numbers of persons of African descent. This consolation and hope would have been increased still further if they had known better of the splendid record of Latin America's Catho-

lic Church in mitigating the evils of slavery and bringing about
its demise, and that the attitude toward race held by whites
"south of the border" was a far cry more modern and humane
than that which prevailed in the U.S.A.

To many slaves the colonization movement provided a
source of hope that they might be freed and sent to Africa.
The very existence of Africa and the conception of that continent as the Negro's "homeland" has been a source of hope to
Afro-Americans. The same is true of the existence within the
United States of a North and West which ever have been to
many Negro's both symbol and actuality of hope as an escape
from their plight in the South. Too, the slow improvement
of race relations, and efforts being made to effect this end, long
have been sources of the Negro's faith not only in himself and
the nation, but in the Southland with which he has been so
intimately connected. Although the topic "North and South
in Negro Thought" is given separate treatment herein, it is
a fact perhaps worthy of repetition that the Negro has been
mindful that within the South he long has had genuine friends
in the majority group, and he ever has hoped and believed that
their number would expand into that mighty chorus attuned
to mutual respect and esteem which is needed for wholesome
and happy human relationships.

Panaceas, Myths, and the Race Problem

The optimism of the Negro, as well as the sometimes des-
perateness of his plight, has led him to project several proposals
for solution of the "race problem" in such a form that they
may be termed "mythical." All proposals that were conceived
of and projected as solutions in and of themselves may be termed
myths. This is because it seriously may be doubted that in and
of themselves they could have effected the ends claimed for
them. The Negro's pursuit of myths usually has been due to
his impatience with the slowness of the democratic process and
his optimism about and faith in the American ideals of equality
and the good life for all, for had he not believed in American
democracy, he would not have devised and had faith in schemes
to bring it in its fullness to his racial group.

Before 1876 the Negro often appealed to white America, through its Christian conscience and highest political ideals, *to provide freedom and equality* for all of the populace. Since this date, most of the proposed solutions *have had self-help as their basis,* thereby reflecting the conviction between 1876 and 1933 that too often white America was either too indifferent to his plight or interested only in exploiting him.

Some of the myths accepted and propagated by Negroes have been:

(1) The "Revolt Myth" of Nat Turner, Denmark Vesey, Gabriel Prosser, and others. Here members of the race have believed that by leading or participating in revolutionary acts of violence, they could bring about freedom and equality of rights and opportunities. Some Negroes have believed that in history there is no real advance of any people without the shedding of blood.

(2) The "Character and Hard Work Myth."—Here the thought has been that, in the very nature of things, virtuous and exemplary living must be rewarded. The slave had it constantly drilled into him that rewards, even if only in Heaven, would be his if he caused no trouble. Since emancipation southern whites have continued to flatter and praise the "good darky," and many Negroes have believed that the only way to bring a solution to the race problem was for them to stay out of court, off public relief, go to church every Sunday, and otherwise lead "exemplary moral" lives. In a 1923 Commencement adrdress at Paine College, Bishop R. A. Carter sounded this note. The Bishop urged the graduating class to "Deport yourselves in such a gentle and quiet and confident and unassuming manner that you will make those ashamed who practice race prejudice."[31]

(3) The "Leave the race problem to God myth."—Here the thought has been that the less said or done about the race problem, the better; that God alone, in His own good time, will effect a solution.

(4)3 The "Emigrate to the North or West Myth."—Here the thought has been that to leave the South is to get away from prejudice and discrimination based on race or color, and that since emigration will lessen the threat of numbers to southern whites, the latter will treat the remaining Negroes better.

(5) The "Buy Land and stay on the farm myth."—This was particularly pushed by Booker T. Washington who felt that the southern Negro had a monopoly in the field of agricultural labor which he should not give up.

(6) The "Industrial Education Myth."—Booker Washington was also the leading proponent of this idea, which urged that by becoming artisans, Negroes would make themselves even more essential to the southern economy, and thereby insure an increasing measure of respect and justice. Here Washington failed to see that many of the trades which he taught at Tuskegee were fast becoming obsolete in the machine age, just as he failed to see that the trends in agricultural production were away from the small farm—many laborers type of farming.

(7) The "Good White Folks Myth."—This myth, of which Booker Washington was also the chief exponent, held that only the poor white held strong prejudices against the Negro and wanted to keep him down.

(8) The "Negro History Myth."—Here the belief has been that if whites can be shown that in the past Negroes have made outstanding achievements they will respect the race and treat it right accordingly, and that if Negroes themselves can be made aware of this, their true history, they will respect themselves more and demand better treatment.

(9) The "Communism Myth." — That only through changing the free enterprise capitalistic system for a communist one can the Negro achieve equality of rights and opportunities.

(10) The "Emigrate to Africa or Set up a Separate Negro State or cities in America Myth."—Here getting way from the white man is seen as the only solution to the "race problem." This is, of course, closely related to the "Emigrate to the North or West" myth.

(11) The "Talented Tenth Myth."—Here the emphasis has been on developing an elite whose manifestation of high training, ability, and genius would prove the validity of the race's claim to equality. In connection with the Talented Tenth idea, and in addition to the Negro Academy, Afro-Americans

founded in Philadelphia in 1904, the professional fraternity, Sigma Pi Phi. Like the Negro college fraternities, this organization grew in membership and has been a significant positive force in the upward push of the race.

(12) The "Myth of Negro Business."—Here the thought has been that the founding and cultivating of Negro businesses would supply the members of the race with adequate jobs and salaries and build wealth within the race, which automatically would command respect from whites. To establish economic autarky for the Negro in the United States has been one goal of proponents of this myth.

There are also persons who feel that the legalistic emphasis of the NAACP is mythical, also the "register and vote" impulse, as well as other programs pushed at various times by Negro leaders. The Negro has followed none of these proposals consistently, has been opportunistic, and, at times, has followed several of them simultaneously. While singly none of these programs was sound, taken together most of them had merit and reveal not only the complexity of the race problem, but also that the critical thinking which their cultural economic and social plight forced Negroes to do was by and large sound, if not always so.

Chapter IX

ELEMENTS OF THE THOUGHT OF FREE NEGROES DURING THE 1850's

During the so-called "fitful fifties," Afro-Americans were more pessimistic about their freedom than at any time during the previous two-decade history of radical abolitionism. The Democratic party held the nation's highest political office, and the Slavocracy appeared to hold firm control of the Democratic party. In this hour before the dawn, events of the decade sometimes kept Afro-Americans from seeing clearly the subtle forces which were slowly but surely working to unlock the slaves fetters.

Free Negroes were frightened by the immigration to the United States which followed the failure of the European revolution of 1848. Frederick Douglass averred in 1853:

> The old employments by which we have heretofore gained our livelihood are gradually, and it may be inevitably, passing into other hands. Every hour sees us elbowed out of some employment to make room perhaps for some newly-arrived immigrants, whose hunger and color are thought to give them a title to especial favor.
>
> White men are becoming house-servants, cooks and stewards, common laborers, and flunkeys to our gentry, and, for aught I see, they adjust themselves to their stations with all becoming obsequiousness. This fact proves that if we cannot rise to the whites, the whites can fall on us. . . . While the colored people are thus elbowed out of employment; while the enmity of emigrants is being excited against us; while state after state enacts laws against us; while we are hunted down, like wild game, the colonization society renews its fight in our behalf.[1]

Again Douglass opined:

> The Irish people, warm-hearted, generous, and sympathizing with the oppressed everywhere, when they stand upon their own green island, are instantly taught, on arriving in this Christian country, to hate

165

and despise the colored people. They are taught to
believe that we eat the bread which of right belongs
to them. The cruel lie is told the Irish, that our ad-
versity is essential to their prosperity. Sir, the Irish-
American will find out his mistake one day. He will
find that in assuming our avocation he also has assumed our degradation.[2]

Later, in the post-Civil War period some freedmen, fearing
that the influx of immigrants from abroad would undermine
their already precarious position in the American economy,
would adopt the ugly attitudes symbolized in such epitaphs as
"Dago," "Kike,' and "Pollock," while other freedmen would
see that these often-despised and harassed minorities from abroad
were allies in their pursuit of the great American dream.

The 1850 Fugitive Slave Act, which was passed as a part
of the famed Compromise of that year, greatly angered and
disturbed Afro-Americans. Because of the manner in which
the law was designed to make capture and return of fugitives
possible, many free persons were endangered by the possibility
that some slaveholders would abuse the law. A master's affidavit of ownership was all that was required to secure a "fugitive," and not only were northern residents required by law
to aid in their capture but the captured persons were denied
trial by jury, and the United States judge or Commissioner who
received the affidavit was to be paid doubly if he ruled the
Negroes to be fugitives. In petition and mass meeting, this law
was fought. The fight was aided by personal liberty laws which
were passed by northern states. Before an Ohio Convention of
Negroes, held in Columbus, in 1851, H. Ford Douglass called
the fugitive slave act, "a law unequaled in the worst days of
Roman despotism, and unparalleled in the annals of heathen
jurisprudence, and the compound of all villainies!"[3] In response
to the act, a New York convention of fugitives, which met in
September, 1850, admonished bondsmen who might escape in
the future not to join political parties that were not openly
against slavery, not to vote for any candidate for office who
held color to be a badge of inferiority, and not to join churches
which had a Negro pew. This advice continued: "Better die
than insult yourself, and insult every person of African blood,

and insult your Maker by contributing to elevate to civil rule, the man who refuses to eat with you, to sit by your side in the House of Worship, or to let his children sit in the school by the side of your children." Parents were advised not to send their children to any segregated school started for Negroes by whites. "Valuable as learning is," the advice ran, "it is too costly if it is acquired at the expense of such self-degradation."[4] A number of Negroes have continued with this conviction and will walk long distances where the only alternative is to ride jim-crow buses, or see no movies at all if none but jim-crow ones are available.

Negro abolitionists hated the Fugitive Slave Act of 1793 just as they did the one of 1850. Even before 1850, a planter could remove a Negro from several northern states on affidavit or oath before a single judge and without trial by jury, but passage of the 1850 Fugitive Slave Act caused the hope of many Negroes to reach a new low, and such leaders as James Theodore Holly and Martin R. Delaney began to urge that free Negroes leave the United States and settle in the Carribean or Canada. Frederick Douglass, Samuel Ringgold Ward, Charles Lenox Remond and other spokesmen were not pushed to such ends of despair, however, and they led in urging Negroes openly to defy the Fugitive Slave Act. Martin Delaney said:

> All the ideas I have of liberty and independence I obtained from reading the History of the Revolutionary Fathers. From them I learned a man has a right to defend his castle, even to the taking of life. My cottage is my castle; my wife and children are its inmates. If any man enters that castle to look for a fugitive slave—I care not if it be he who signed his name to that ignominious law; if he come with the Declaration of Independence flying in the air as a banner, and the Constitution of the United States upon his bosom as a breastplate—if he enters my house to search for a fugitive slave, and I do not strike him down dead, may the grave refuse my body a resting place, and righteous heaven deny my spirit admission.[5]

"Such crises as these," declared Samuel Ringgold Ward, "leave us to the right of Revolution, and if need be, that right we

will, at whatever cost, most sacredly maintain."[6] July 5, 1852
Frederick Douglass thundered:

> Americans! your republican politics, not less than
> your republican religion, are flagrantly inconsistent.
> You boast of your love of liberty . . . while the
> whole political power of the nation (as embodied in
> the two great political parties) is solemnly pledged to
> support and perpetuate the enslavement of three mil-
> lions of your countrymen. You hurl your anathemas
> at the crowned . . . tyrants of Russia and Austria
> . . . while you yourselves consent to be the mere
> *tools* and *body-guards* of the tyrants of Virginia and
> Carolina. You invite to your shores fugitives of op-
> pression from abroad, . . . but the fugitives from
> your own land you advertise, hunt, arrest, shoot, and
> kill.
>
> You are all on fire at the mention of liberty for
> France or for Ireland; but are as cold as an iceberg
> at the thought of liberty for the enslaved of America.
> You discourse eloquently on the dignity of labor; yet,
> you sustain a system which, in its very essence, casts
> a stigma upon labor. You can bare your bosom to the
> storm of British artillery to throw off a three-penny
> tax on tea; and yet wring the last hard-earned
> farthing from the grasp of the black laborers of
> your country.[7]

At an 1851 State Convention, Ohio Negroes debated the
often used topic of whether the United States Constitution
was pro-slavery or not, and if so, what should be the response of the race to this. At this meeting, H. Ford Douglass
said: "I hold . . . that the Constitution of the United States
is pro-slavery, considered so by those who framed it, and construed to that end ever since its adoption."[8] At the same meeting, William Howard Day of Lorain, Ohio, stated: "Coming
up as I do, in the midst of three millions of men in chains, and
five hundred thousand only half free, I consider every instrument precious which guarantees to me liberty. I consider the
Constitution the foundation of American liberties, and wrap-
ping myself in the flag of the nation, I would plant myself
upon that Constitution, and using the weapons they have given
me, I would appeal to the American people for the rights thus

guaranteed."⁹ He stated that those who felt that the Constitution was a pro-slavery document were mistaking the construction which pro-slavery people put on the document for the Constitution itself. At this same Ohio meeting Charles H. Langston agreed with H. Ford Douglass that the Constitution was a pro-slavery document. Despite this, however, Langston stated that as a matter of expediency he would vote under the United States Constitution on the same principle, he stated, "that I would call on every slave, from Maryland to Texas, to arise and assert their Liberties, and cut their masters' throats if they attempt again to reduce them to slavery."[10] It would seem that, like most Americans, Negroes in this country have adhered to William Day's poosition that the Constitution is the fountain-head of freedom and democracy for all citizens. True it is that a goodly number in the ante-bellum period accepted the doctrine that they were not citizens of this republic, but the majority never stopped contending that by virtue of birth and service and devotion to the United States, as well as often by statute, they were bonafide citizens. Infringements on their civil rights they regarded as unconstitutional acts.

While he was in this country in 1851, Lajos Kossuth, famed leader of the 1848 rebellion in Hungary, was addressed by George T. Downing on behalf of a reception committee of New York Negroes. Kossuth, at first popular with the race, was later denounced by Negro leaders because he refused to take a stand on American slavery.[11]

Speaking in 1852 on what was needed to rid the nation of slavery, Frederick Douglass in a Fourth of July address said:

> At a time like this, scorching irony, not convincing argument, is needed. It is not light that is needed, but fire; it is not the gentle shower, but thunder. We need the storm, the whirlwind, and the earthquake.[12]

Little could he have known that within a brief decade he would get all, and more, than he was calling for.

In a December 1852 letter to W. L. Garrison, William C. Nell asked that there be published in the *Liberator*, the state-

ment as coming from a recent meeting of Massachusetts Ne_
groes:—

> Resolved, That as the Whig and so-called Demo-
> cratic parties of this country are endeavoring to
> crush, debase and dehumanize us as a people, any
> man among us voting for their respective candidates
> . . . shall be held up to public reprobation as a
> traitor, a hissing and a by-word, a pest and a nui-
> sance, the off-scouring of the earth.

> Resolved, that the candidates of the Free De-
> mocracy need no eulogy—they stand out in bold
> relief, as the representatives of principles which com-
> mand the admiration and support of every lover of
> Truth, Justice and Humanity. Our hands, our hearts
> and our votes are theirs.[13]

Just as the 1850's saw a proliferation of southern conventions, free Negroes in the North held more "National Negro
Conventions" than ever before, and despair caused some black
abolitionists to advocate with William Lloyd Garrison that the
North should secede from the union. These men felt that the
1850 Fugitive Slave Law nationalized the institution of slavery.
Although northern secession probably would have meant abandoning the slave, Charles Remond and others advocated this
course. Remond, however, did not think this course would
mean abandoning the slave. He always believed that the slaves
would strike for their own freedom if such secession came.
Earlier, Henry Highland Garnet had sounded a similar note.

Reminiscent of the 1848 *Communist Manifesto,* in 1843
Henry Highland Garnet exhorted the slaves: "Brethren, arise,
arise! Strike for your lives and liberties. Now is the day and
the hour. Let every slave throughout the land do this, and the
days of slavery are numbered. You cannot be more oppressed
than you have been—you cannot suffer greater cruelties than
you have already. *Rather die freemen than to live to be slaves.*
Remember that you are *four millions!*"[14] This advice, in "An
Address to the Slaves of the United States of America," was
so radical that the National Convention of Colored Citizens,
Buffalo, New York would not adopt it. However, John Brown
did not regard it as too radical and financed its publication.
In the address Garnet had begun on a note of hope. "Mankind

are becoming wiser, and better," he opined, "the oppressor's power is fading, and you, every day, are becoming better informed and more numerous." But Garnet did not long continue in this vein, as he said of the institution of slavery—"Its throne is established, and . . . it reigns triumphant." As planters used the Bible to justify the enslavement of the black man, Garnet used this same book to justify the latter's revolt against his bondage. "The diabolical injustice by which your liberties are cloven down," he declared, "neither God nor angels, or just men, command you to suffer for a single moment. Therefore, it is your solemn and imperative duty to use every means, both moral, intellectual, and physical, that promises success." He urged resistance, "even to death." With most of the other abolitionists, Garnet indicated his belief that the wrong of slavery in his day was a link in a chain of wrongs which began with the "stealing" of the Negro in Africa, which he here termed "our fatherland." In his impatience, Garnet made several very impractical suggestions. To the slaves he declared: "Brethren, the time has come when you must act for yourselves. . . . You can plead your own cause, and do the work of emancipation better than any other." He counselled the bondsmen:

> Go to your lordly enslavers and tell them plainly, that you *are determined to be free.* Appeal to their sense of justice, and tell them that they have no more right to oppress you than you have to enslave them. Entreat them to remove the grievous burdens which they have imposed upon you, and to remunerate you for your labor. Promise them renewed diligence in the cultivation of the soil, if they will render to you an equivalent for your services. Point them to the increase of happiness and prosperity in the British West Indies since the Act of Emancipation. Tell them in language which they cannot misunderstand of the exceeding sinfulness of slavery, and of a future judgment, and of the righteous retribution of an indignant God. Inform them that all you desire is *freedom,* and that nothing else will suffice. Do this, and forever after cease to toil for the heartless tyrants, . . . If they then commence work of death, they, and not

you, will be responsible for the consequences. You
had far better all die—*die immediately*, than live
slaves, and entail your wretchedness upon your posterity. If you would be free in this generation, here
is your only hope.

Garnet could not know that in exactly twenty years the Emancipation Proclamation would come! It is of interest to note that
Garnet ended this exhortation to the slaves with the words:
"Brethren, adieu! Trust in the living God. Labor for the peace
of the human race, and remember that you are *four millions!*"

The most representative of the pre-Civil War National
Negro Conventions was that held in 1853. Attended by one
hundred and fourteen delegates it met in Rochester, New York.
Officers were: President, James W. C. Pennington of New
York; Vice-President, William F. Day of Ohio, Amos G. Beman
of Connecticut, William C. Nell of Massachusetts, Frederick
Douglass of New York, James C. McCrummell and John B.
Vashon of Pennsylvania, and John Jones of Illinois; Secre-
taries, Peter H. Clarke of Ohio, Charles B. Ray and Henry M.
Wilson of New York, and Charles Reason of Pennsylvania.
This group issued another address to the American people which
Douglass helped draft, planned for a National Negro Council,
and a manual labor school. The latter project was backed by
Charles Reason, George B. Vashon and Dr. Charles H. Langston. The Convention stated that Harriet Beecher Stowe's recently published book, *Uncle Tom's Cabin,* had led to "the
propitious awakening to the fact of our condition at home and
abroad."

In May and June, 1854, the fugitive slave case of Anthony
Burns held Boston in great excitement. Burns' own account of
his return to and rendition from slavery are given in the
Liberator, March 9, 1855. Of the arrest of Burns C. L. Remond
thundered:—

Can any man deny that, if John Adams, and Samuel
Adams, and John Hancock, were alive to-day, they
would, in view of the transactions in the city of
Boston, demand the immediate dissolution of the
Union? I believe in my soul they would. And why?
Because they would hold in too high estimation their
own liberties to submit to such outrages. . . . I would

rather be ten thousand times blacker than I am than
to be the proudest pale face that walks State Street
today, doing the bidding of the slaveholder.[15]

In this speech Remond asked that a mob go to the courthouse
and forcibly "rescue" Anthony Burns. He asked that the North
secede from the Union, and said that if this should happen the
slaves would free themselves. "It is the North that practically
keeps them in slavery," he declared. Remond ended with the
statement:

> I am irritable, excitable, quarrelsome— . . .
> and my prayer to God is, that I may never cease to
> be irritable, that I may never cease to be excitable,
> that I may never cease to be quarrelsome, until the
> last slave shall be made free in our country, and the
> colored man's manhood acknowledged.

The first state convention of California's approximately
6,000 Negroes was held in Sacramento from November 20th
to 22nd, 1855. Present were forty-nine delegates from ten
counties. Although only lukewarm toward the abolitionist
movement, this group too was contending for their rights as
citizens and protesting against discriminatory legislation.[16]

If it can be believed, the story of a decade of activity
against slavery told by Moses Dickson is one of the most interesting of the abolitionist period. Dickson was born in Ohio
in 1824. According to his testimony, he and eleven other Negroes from eight states formed the Twelve Knights of Tabor in
St. Louis, Missouri. This organization was active in the Underground Railroad. Dickson himself was a minister from 1867
until his death in 1901. A militant Missouri Republican, he
was also a founder of that states Lincoln Institute, now Lincoln
University. According to Dickson, the founders of this organization caused it to grow to a membership of 47,000 Knights of
Liberty, "for the historic purpose of aiding in breaking the
bonds of our slavery." The name was taken from the history
of the Israelites and, states Dickson, the name "gave the members Courage." The organization was highly secretive and mili-
taristic, with headquarters at Atlanta, Georgia. Eighteen fifty-
seven was the year in which they expected to march on Atlanta
with around 150,000 well-armed men from their earlier drill-

ing and hidden arms, and fight all over the South to end slavery.
"The Chief was almost ready to give the command to move
forward in July, 1857," he states, "but he paused and scanned
the signs that were gathering over the Union," and decided
that "a higher power" showed signs of being ready to end
slavery.[17]

The Supreme Court's Dred Scott decision of March, 1857,
read by Maryland's Roger B. Taney, opened all federal territory
to slavery and denied citizenship to Negroes. Together with
white Americans, northern persons of color bitterly assailed
this ruling. At an April protest meeting, Robert Purvis said:

> RESOLVED, That this atrocious decision furnishes
> final confirmation of the already well-known fact
> that under the Constitution and Government of the
> United States, the colored people are nothing, and
> can be nothing but an alien, disfranchised and de-
> graded class.
>
> RESOLVED, That to persist in supporting a Gov-
> ernment which holds and exercises the power to
> trample a class under foot as an inferior and de-
> graded race, is on the part of the colored man at once
> the height of folly and the depth of pulsillanimity.
>
> RESOLVED, That no allegiance is due from any
> man, or any class of men, to a Government founded
> and administered in iniquity, and that the only duty
> the colored man owes to a Constitution under which
> he is declared to be an inferior and degraded being,
> having no rights which white men are bound to re-
> spect, is to denounce and repudiate it.[18]

In a less bitter spirit of agreement, C. L. Remond of Salem,
Massachusetts spoke following Purvis. Remond agreed that,
although free Negroes had been held to be citizens of individual
states, and indeed treated as citizens on the national level, the
Supreme Court was acting within its powers by stripping the
race of this citizenship. Unlike Purvis, Remond saw cause for
optimism. He stated:

> RESOLVED, That we reject that slave holding des-
> potism which lays its ruthless hand not only on the
> humble black man, but on the proud Northern
> white man; and our hope is, that when our white

fellow slaves in these so-called free States see that
they are alike subject with us to the slave oligarchy,
the difference in our servitude being only in degree,
they will make common cause with us, and that
throwing off the yoke and striking for impartial
liberty, they will join with us in our efforts to re-
cover the long lost boon of freedom.[19]

Remond did agree with Purvis that, "after this, to persist in
claiming citizenship under the United States Constitution would
be mean-spirited and craven" of the Negro, and Remond too
denounced his patriotism. After considerable debate, the above
resolutions by Purvis and Remond were approved by the body.

In the celebration of the twenty-seventh anniversary of
the American Anti-Slavery Society, Purvis gave a ringing indictment of the United States for its treatment of his race.
In this speech Purvis stated that the "bloody code of Draco"
of antiquity was "mild . . . a law of love, compared with the
hellish laws and precedents that disgrace the statute books of
this modern Democratic Christian Republic!" He called American democracy "piebald and rotten" and alluded directly to
the Dred Scott decision.[20] Frederick Douglass declared of this
decision:

> The Supreme Court is not the only power in this
> world. We, . . . should meet this decision, unlooked
> for and monstrous as it appears, in a cheerful spirit.
> This very attempt to blot out forever the hopes of
> an enslaved people may be one necessary link in the
> chain of events preparatory to the complete overthrow
> of the whole slave system.

Douglass called the decision "an open, glaring, and scandalous
tissue of lies."[21]

So embittered was Charles Remond over the decision that
he advocated that the North secede from the Union. In his
bitterness at the arrest of Burns, Remond exhorted:

> Talk to me of Bunker Hill, and tell me that a
> fugitive passed through Boston today! Talk about
> Lexington, and tell me a slave mother must be kept
> secreted in Boston! Talk to me of commemorating
> the memory of Joseph Warren, while thirty thou-
> sand fugitive slaves are in Canada! I will scout the

memory of the Revolution, the memory of Washington, and Adams, and Hancock, until the soil of
Massachusetts shall be as free to every fugitive, and as
free to me, as it is to the descendants of any of them.
And until we shall do this, we talk in vain, and cele-
brate in vain.[22]

So bitter was Remond that he regretted that Negroes had
served in the Revolutionary War. "Better that any such man,"
he declared, "had folded his hands and crossed his knees, during the American Revolution, if this is the reward we are to
derive from such hypocrites, such cowards, such panders to
American slavery, as Judge Taney and his co-operators."[23]

One group of New England free Negroes, meeting to
protest the Dred Scott decision, termed it "a palpably vain,
arrogant assumption, unsustained by history, justice, reason or
common sense."[24] While they were hurt and further insulted
by the decision, free Negroes were not particularly surprised at
the ruling. Still, in the second decade of the twentieth century,
a Harvard trained Negro lawyer, Archibald Grimké would
give eloquent testimony of his race's estimation of Taney's epic
decision. On it Grimké wrote:

The fell apparition of American inhumanity,
which those words conjured up from the depths of an
abominable past and from that of a no less abominable
present, was indeed black, but it was no blacker than
the truth. The dark soul of the nation was embodied
in them, all of its savage selfishness, greed and iniquity. There they glared, large and lifelike, a
devil's face among the nations, seamed and inter-
sected with the sinister lines of a century of cruelty
and race hatred and oppression. Of course the fair
idealism of the Declaration of Independence was
wanting in the photographic naturalism of the picture, and so was the fictive beauty of the Preamble
of the Constitution, because they were wanting in
the terrible original, in the malignant, merciless, and
murderous spirit of a democracy which the dark
words of the dark judge had limned to the life.[25]

In an 1858 address in Boston, Dr. John S. Rock, Negro
physician, lawyer and abolitionist anticipated the views which

Booker T. Washington later popularized, that as the Afro-American acquired money and property race prejudice would disappear. Dr. Rock asserted:

> In this country, where money is the great sympathetic nerve which ramifies Society, and has ganglia in every man's pocket, a man is respected in proportion to his success in business. When the avenues to wealth are opened to us, we will then become educated and wealthy, and then the roughest looking colored man that you ever saw, or ever will see, will be pleasanter than the harmonies of Orpheus, and black will be a very pretty color . . . flattery will then take the place of slander . . . Then, and not till then, will the lip of prejudice be sealed.[26]

A segment among professional and middle-class Negroes have been attracted to the idea that their own salvation—if not that all members of their race—lies in accepting the tenets and mores of the monetarily rich. An early argument against this came from the pen of Frances Ellen Watkins, who said: "The important lesson we should learn and be able to teach, is how to make every gift, whether gold or talent, fortune or genius, subserve the cause of crushed humanity and carry out the greatest idea of the present age, the glorious idea of human brotherhood."[27]

Reporting on an August, 1858 Massachusetts meeting of free Negroes in New Bedford, the *Liberator* of August 13, of that year quoted C. L. Remond as stating that both the Free Soil and Republican parties had been false to the Negro. So disheartened was Remond that he was reported as saying again: "We must depend upon our own self-reliance." He recommended slave insurrections as proper action, and "boldly proclaimed himself a traitor to the government and the Union, so long as his rights were denied him for no fault of his own. . . . Were there a thunderbolt of God which he could invoke to bring destruction upon this nation, he would gladly do it," the *Liberator* reported. Another person present at this same meeting, doubted, as indeed did Remond, that insurrections would succeed. "The slaves," he said, "had no weapons or education." "When I fight," he stated, "I want to whip somebody."

The Afro-American constantly has been aware of the noblest of American traditions and principles, and of the danger to the nation of too-often compromising and proscribing principles and traditions. While his presence has without doubt unleashed much of the worst behavior of which mankind is capable, the colored man's constant appeal for justice and fair play and Christian treatment, has sharpened the nation's conscience on these matters. While pondering today the shrinking size of the planet in the twentieth century, and of the rise of the colored Asian and African, it is possible to see a blessing in disguise in the problems and solutions which have derived from the Negro's presence in the United States, for in learning to live with the colored man at home, the white American may be learning to live with the vast colored majority which comprises the world's population.[28]

THE ABOLITIONIST—CIVIL WAR ERAS

The Negro of the first half of the nineteenth century was not only more militant, he was much more articulate than the eighteenth century Negro had been. For example, Negro historiography was born in 1800-1860 period. Also, a considerable number of slave narratives and autobiographies appeared, and Negro journalism was born. After Phyllis Wheatley and Jupiter Hammon, Negro poetry had its beginning in this period with George Moses Horton's volume entitled *The Hope of Liberty* (1829), Daniel A. Payne's, *Pleasures and Other Miscellaneous Poems* (1850), Frances Harper's *Poems on Miscellaneous Subjects* (1854), and Armand Lanusse, ed., *Les Cenelles*, a book of poems by seventeen New Orleans, Louisiana Negro Creoles. Dramatic writing by Negroes was also born in this period with William Wells Brown's play, *The Escape; or a Leap to Freedom* (1858). The same is true of the novel which had its beginnings with Martin R. Delany's *Blake; or The Huts of America* (1859) and Wlliam Wells Brown's *Clotel.* The Negro scholar appeared in this period. While some persons may object to calling such members of the beginning group of Negro historians as William C. Nell, James W. C. Pennington, and

William Wells Brown "scholars," none could seriously object
to giving this appellation to Glascow University graduate Dr.
James McCune Smith who in 1846 published an article entitled, "Influence of Climate on Longevity, with Special Reference to Life Insurance."

Richard Bardolph has stated that, "The opening of the
1830's marks a watershed in Negro Social History."[1] In 1831
Garrison's *Liberator* was founded and Nat Turner's bloody
revolt took place in Virginia. Of the thirty-seven Negroes listed
by Bardolph as having reached prominence during the succeeding generation, twenty-eight achieved their renown as abolitionists, approximately one-half of whom were ministers of the
Gospel.[2] Carter Woodson, Herbert Aptheker, and other scholars
have pointed out that in the U.S.A. the first abolitionists, singly
or organized, were Negroes themselves.

The period from 1830-1860 is one of the most stirring in
the history of Negro thought and action. Through the black
abolitionists, this era also saw the underground railroad shift
into high gear and spread, the emergence of Negro oratory,
journalism, and organized protest. The mass meeting, used so
fittingly in this period by the black abolitionists, has been a
constant weapon used by the Negro in his fight for equality of
citizenship. At many of the Negro conventions of the 1830's,
40's, and 50's, a number of prominent whites were present to
lend their support. Here, as always during his fight for full
citizenship in this country, there always have been American
whites lending support to his cause.

The 1830 Philadelphia meeting of free Negroes was called
to seek means of elevating their group in the U.S.A. Samuel
Cornish, James Forten, and John B. Vashon were among the
outstanding Negroes present. Migration to Canada and the
establishment of a Negro college were among the schemes which
this convention supported, although by no means unanimously.
At the 1853 Rochester, New York convention, Negroes formed
the National Council of Colored People. Doubtless, Charles
Lenox Remond spoke for most abolitionists of his race when
he said:

> Some there are who are prevented from joining in
> the great struggle wherein we are engaged from a

false and corrupt pride, for they consider (or feign to consider) that the vindication of the slave's rights is an undignified employment; but I tell them it is an employment more dignified, more noble, more exalted than any other whatsoever in which man can be engaged.[3]

Of his own efforts, Frederick Douglass declared:

I expose slavery in this country, because to expose it is to kill it. Slavery is one of those monsters of darkness to whom the light of truth is death. Expose slavery, and it dies. Light is to slavery what the heat of the sun is to the root of a tree; it must die under it. All the slaveholder asks of me is silence.[4]

And though many would disagree with him on other particulars, doubtless Robert Purvis spoke for his fellow-fighters when he thundered:

We take our stand upon that solemn declaration, that to protect inalienable rights 'governments are instituted among men, deriving their *just powers* from the *consent* of the governed,' and proclaim that a government which tears away from us and our posterity the very power of *consent* is a tyrannical usurpation which we will never cease to oppose.[5]

In politics the colored abolitionists were pragmatists. In an 1850 speech against the fugitive slave bill of that year, Samuel Ringgold Ward said: "I agree not with Senator Seward in politics, but when an individual stands up for the rights of men against slaveholders, I care not for party distinctions."[6]

CHAPTER X

THE NEGRO AND AMERICAN WARS

The attitudes held toward war by Negro Americans generally have coincided with those exhibited by the majority group. Anti-militarism long has been a strong fabric in the cloth from which the American is cut.

Colored Americans always have rallied to the colors when the nation was in danger. Yet, feeling that they were not *bona fide* citizens, at times a few persons have contemplated refusing any military call for their services. Following the 1841 *Creole* affair, some Americans talked of going to war with Britain to force return of slaves who mutinied and sailed into a British port. During the talk of war, a Negro newspaper wrote the following:

> There is no law in existence which can compel us to fight, and any fighting on our part, must be a *voluntary act*. The states in which we dwell have twice availed themselves of our *voluntary services*, and have repaid us with chains and slavery. Shall we a third time kiss the foot that crushes us? If so, we deserve our chains. No! let us maintain an organized neutrality, until the laws of the Union and of all the states have made us free and equal citizens.[1]

That for over two centuries force was used to keep them in a degraded status may have given Negroes a somewhat greater abhorrence of force than is usually the case with many other Americans. As the majority group long ago produced Henry David Thoreau and other pacifists, the Negro American could point to advocates of non-violent resistance in his group long before the mid-twentieth century strictures of Reverend Martin Luther King. In the colonial period Benjamin Banneker gave serious thought to the problem of war and urged that a Secretary of Peace be added to the federal government and that all military titles, uniforms, and drills should be abolished. In 1837 William Whipple opined:

> I would not, for a single moment, sanction the often made assertion that the doctrines of the holy scrip-

tures justify war—for they are in my humble opinion its greatest enemy. And I further believe that as
soon as they become fully understood and practically
adopted, wars and strifes will cease. I believe that
every argument urged in favor of what is termed a
'just and necessary war,' of physical self-defense, is
at enmity with the letter and spirit of the scriptures,
and . . . should be repudiated, as inimical to the
principles they profess, and a reproach to Christianity
itself.[2]

Whipple was a pacifist and an early apostle of non-violent
moral resistance, and in this speech he gives about all of the
arguments that Gandhi and Martin Luther King later gave.
Whipple praised the abolitionists for not advocating or prac-
ticing violence even when they were its objects, and he vowed
that a soft answer turneth away wrath. Yet he praised the
abolitionists for using the slogan "Liberty or Death." Whipple
believed that Negroes had learned the principles of non-violence from the white abolitionists. Of mob violence he declared:

The enemies of the abolitionists are exhibiting a regard for the power of their principles that they are
unwilling to acknowledge. Although it is everywhere
known over the country that abolitionists will not
fight, yet they distrust their own strength so much
that they frequently muster a whole neighborhood
of from 50 to 300 men, with sticks, stones, rotten
eggs and bowie knives, to mob and beat a single individual, probably in his teens whose hearts law is
non resistance. There is another way in which they
do us honor—they admit the right of all people to
fight for their liberty but colored people and abolitionists—plainly inferring that they are too good for
the performance of such un-Christian acts.[3]

Shocked by the outbreak and course of World War I, in
December, 1918 South Carolina-born and Harvard-educated
Francis J. Grimké offered the sentiments of many Negroes and
white Americans. Grimké declared:

War means lying days and nights wounded and alone
in no-man's land; it means men with jaws gone, limbs
gone, minds gone; it means countless bodies of boys
tossed into the incenerators that follow in the train

of every battle; it means untended wounds and gan-
grene and the long time it takes to die; it means
mothers who look for letters they will never see and
wives who wait for voices they will never hear, and
children who listen for footsteps that will never
come. This is war—It's heroisms are but the glancing
sunlight on a sea of blood and tears. And through
all these physical horrors runs a horror more appalling
still, the persistent debauching and brutalizing of
men's souls.   One who uses his knowledge and his
imagination to perceive in its abominations what war
really is, while he might never dream of using Walt
Whitman's language, finds it hard to be sorry that
the language has been used. 'Wars,' he said, 'are hellish
business—all wars. Any honest man says so—hates
war, fighting, blood letting. I was in the midst of it
all—saw war where war was worst; there I mixed
with it, and now I say God damn the wars—all
wars; God damn every war; God damn 'em!'⁴

Despite their aversions to the military life and war, when
the nation has been imperilled, with their fellow Americans
Negroes have risen unhesitantly to the colors. This tradition
of reaction dates back to the War for Independence.

The Revolutionary War

Carter G. Woodson said—"One cause of the Boston Massacre was that a slave, out of love of country, insulted a British
officer. Negroes were in the front rank of those openly protesting against the quartering and billeting of British soldiers in
Boston to enforce the laws authorizing taxation in the colonies."⁵

At the time of the Revolution there were approximately
one-half million slaves in the English colonies, and it has been
estimated that approximately 5,000 Negroes served in the Continental forces.   At first only free Negroes were used in the
Revolutionary army. Although the promise of freedom was a
great factor, there is considerable evidence that strong patriotism was one of the forces which led Negro soldiers to serve so
ably in the Continental army. So many of the Virginia slaves
joined the Continental army that the state had to take drastic

action to prevent this exodus from slavery into military service. Except as substitutes for freemen, after 1777 Virginia allowed only free Negroes to enlist.

In their dire plight, the colonists could not afford to refuse the services of Negroes, who, at the time, constituted approximately one-sixth of the total population. One focal point of the fear that Negroes would fight with the British in the war was the fact that through the promise of fredom, beginning Nov. 7, 1775, Lord Dunmore had actually enlisted several hundred in his effort to maintain himself in Virginia. This and subsequent enlistment of Negroes by various British officers early in the war forced the colonists' hand on the matter. Still it has been estimated that during the war, over one-half of Georgia's adult male slave population fought with the British, while South Carolina lost Negroes to the British by the thousands.

While the colonies debated use of Negro troops, Georgia's delegates to the Continental Congress expressed fears that any British Commander who effected an occupation of the South might win the whole region by promising freedom to the slaves and enlisting them. Throughout the war, the number of runaway slaves mounted to vast proportions. Some were going to join the British Army, while others were just going. Events moved so fast that General George Washington's order prohibiting the enlistment of Negroes lasted only a few weeks.

Afro-Americans have shown great pride in the colored heroes of the war. They have been especially proud that Crispus Attucks was the first to die in the "Boston Massacre." George Washington Williams, in his history of the race, devotes four pages to Attuck's part in this incident.[6] In the decade before the Civil War free Negroes formed a military company and named it *Attucks Guards,* and in the twentieth century, along with numerous others, the poet Edward Smythe Jones, mentions Attucks in several of his poems. Two other Negro heroes of the Revolution whose praises have been sung with especial praise are Peter Salem, killer of Major Pitcairn, whom William calls "The intrepid Black Soldier," and Salem Poor, both heroes of the fighting at Bunker Hill. The valor of Salem Poor was commended in a report and recommendation to the Continental Congress.

So conscious are they of the charge of cowardice which biased persons have given as a Negro trait, in writing of the Revolutionary War Negro historians almost invariably devote several paragraphs or pages to evidence of the valor and bravery of Negro troops.[7] Their general estimation of the service of Negro troops in the Revolutionary War may be evidenced in the words of George Washington Williams:

> From the opening to the closing scene of the Revolutionary War; from the death of Pitcairn to the surrender of Cornwallis; on many fields of strife and triumph, of splendid valor and republican glory; from the hazy dawn of unequal and uncertain conflict, to the bright morn of profound peace; through and out of the fires of a great war that gave birth to a new, a grand republic,—the Negro soldier fought his way to undimmed glory, and made for himself a magnificent record in the annals of American History.[8]

War of 1812

The agricultural imperialism which was a great factor in bringing on the War of 1812 fitted into that larger American ethos which has been labelled "Manifest Destiny." John Hope Franklin has pointed to a strange incongruity between slave holders giving as a central aim of manifest destiny the desire to expand the geographical limits of the nation so as to carry the blessings of liberty to more and more people.[9]

Again in the War of 1812, Negro soldiers served integrated in predominantly white units. Barred from service in peacetime, these were largely free volunteers, often prompted to serve largely by love of country. Some slaves served on the promise of manumission at the end of the war. Led by Bishop Richard Allen and the wealthy James Forten, Philadelphia's free Negro population particularly performed outstanding defense services during the war. Negro soldiers have shown considerable pride in the commendations which Capt. Oliver H. Perry, Gen. Andrew Jackson, and other commanders gave to the Negro sailors and soldiers who served under them. The main action of ground forces in which Negroes participated was the famed Battle of New Orleans. In his proclamation "to the Free Colored Inhabitants of Louisiana," Andrew Jackson appealed directly to their patriotic sentiments to get them to enlist. Yet, that their service failed to alter the existence of slavery in Louisiana caused George Washington Williams to say: "The efficient service of the Louisiana Negro troops in the War of 1812 was applauded on two continents at the time but the noise of the slave marts soon silenced the praise of the Black heroes of the Battle of New Orleans."[10]

As had been the case with the Revolutionary War, the democratic ideals and freedom which the nation enunciated during the War of 1812 charged even the air that the nations bondsmen breathed, and they became restive in their chains. This, plus the general democratic upheaval symbolized by the triumphs of Jeffersonian-Jacksonianism stimulated an increase in slave abscondings, the awesome plots and rebellions of Nat Turner, Denmark Vesey and others, as well as the mighty protest of David Walker, Robert A. Young, Frederick Douglass, William Wells Brown, Samuel Cornish, Charles Lenox Remond, Henry Highland Garnet, Sojourner Truth, Harriet Tubman and others. And as had been the case with the Revolutionary War, during the War of 1812 the British-promise of freedom caused a number of Negro slaves to run away from their masters and to fight for the British.

Between the War of 1812 and the Civil War, the United States Army refused to accept Negroes as soldiers. Unwilling to acquiesce in this affront to the race, northern Negroes formed private militia groups and repeatedly sought admission into state militias.[11] Still, in presenting to the public his book entitled *Services of Colored Americans in the Wars of 1776 and 1812*,[12] William C. Nell stated in the Preface: "My predilections are *least* and *last* for what constitutes the pomp and circumstance of War." His excuse for writing the volume ran: "A combination of circumstances have veiled from the public eye a narration of those military services which are generally conceived as passports to honorable and lasting notice of Americans."

Like Henry David Thoreau, Abraham Lincoln, and others, many Afro-Americans opposed the 1846-48 war against Mexico as unwarranted imperialism for the extension of slavery. Frederick Douglass said:

In our judgement, those who have all along been loudly in favor of a vigorous prosecution of the war, and heralding its bloody triumph with apparent rapture, and glorifying the atrocious deeds of barbarous heroism on the part of wicked men engaged in it, have no sincere love of peace, and are not now rejoicing over peace, but plunder. They have succeeded in robbing Mexico of her territory, and are rejoicing over their success under the hypocritical pretence of a regard for peace. Had they not succeeded in robbing Mexico of the most important and most valuable part of her territory, many of those now loudest in their professions of favor for peace, would be loudest and wildest for war—to the knife. Our soul is sick of such hypocrisy.[13]

The Civil War

The Civil War ranks among the most momentous events in the history of the nation. It was the most momentous event in the history of slavery. Years later ex-bondsmen referred to it as the time of "the breaking up" and many used it as an *Anno Domini* from which they computed their ages.

While President Lincoln and most northern whites regarded the war as an hour of darkness, hardship, and sore travail, Negroes everywhere saw it almost immediately as the dawn of their day of jubilee. One of the main attitudes which they manifested throughout the war is joy mixed with grim determination not to let this glorious opportunity at emancipation pass. As Frederick Douglass said: "The day dawns: the morning star is bright upon the horizon! The iron gate of our prison stands half open." There is no time for hesitation, stated Douglass. "Action! Action! not criticism, is the plain duty of the hour, words are now useful only as they stimulate to blows."[14]

Together with the rest of the nation, most slaves knew that war was imminent long before the outbreak of actual hostilities. "I think I see the finger of God in all this," opined Dr. John S. Rock,[15] while Frederick Douglass called it, "A war undertaken and brazenly carried on for the perpetual enslavement of colored men."[13] At the outbreak of war, slaves sang: "Fier, my savior, fier, Satan's camp a-fire, Fier, believer, Fier, Satan's camp a-fire." One old slave looked hopefully to the coming of the Yankees. "Child," she declared, "we are going to have such a good time a-setting at the white folks' table, a-eating off the white folks' table, and a-rocking in the big rocking chair."[17]

Almost immediately upon the outbreak of civil war, many Negroes saw this as the death knell of slavery. There was little question in their minds that the long awaited day of emancipation was at hand. Richard H. Cain said, "I was a student at Wilberforce University, in Ohio, when the tocsin of war was sounded, when Fort Sumter was fired upon, and I never shall forget the thrill that ran through my soul when I thought of the coming consequences of that shot."[18] Addressing a Boston audience, in January, 1862, John S. Rock noted physician, lawyer, and abolitionist declared: "This rebellion," he opined, "means something! Out of it emancipation must spring."[19] At another point, Dr. Rock declared:

> The abolitionists saw this day of tribulation [Civil War] and reign of terror long ago, and warned you of it; but you would not hear! You now say that it is their agitation, which has brought about this terrible civil war. That is to say, your friend sees a slow match set near a keg of gun powder in your house and timely warns you of the danger which he sees is inevitable; you despise his warnings, and, after the explosion, say, if he had not told you of it, it would not have happened.[20]

One ex-slave commented on the buying and selling of slaves which continued during the war. "We hears some of 'em say they's gwine to throw a long war, and us all think what they buy us for if we's gwine to be free. Some was still buying niggers every Fall, and us think it too funny they kept on filling up when they gwine to be emptying out soon."[21] One ex-slave declared of the war: "niggers had no say in it. Niggers didn't know what the fight was 'bout."[22] Another said of one of the Confederacy's top military leaders: "Old General Jackson said before he would see niggers free he would build a house nine miles long and put them in it, and burn everyone of them up. A dirty old rascal; now he is dead and gone."[23] One ex-slave reported that when the war came the slaves on his plantation "thought the world was come to the end."[24] "The unanimous testimony of old slaves," states one scholar, "is that their secret prayers were for the success of the Union cause."[25] Booker T. Washington reports that during the last days of the war, when slaves were fairly certain that the downfall of the Confederacy was imminent, slaves almost abandoned the secrecy with which they had cloaked their hopes and prayers for a Union victory. Slaves were heard singing more often than ever and the old, almost hushed note of freedom, rang out clearer than ever.

Before the conflict one Negro had opined that when war came the South would lose because it would have to fight "with one hand while holding slaves and discontented poor whites down with the other."[26] That many slaves did not revolt during the war may be explained, not by their docility and happiness, as is so often said, but by the facts that: (1) Many of the slaves absconded to join the Union army; (2) those remaining on their jobs in the South had many reasons to be patient and wait for the success of the Union army; (3) it is highly doubtful that a general uprising during the war would have brought the slaves anything except near extermination; (4) No general uprising could have been planned due to lack of communication facilities and the fact that the Confederate armies were camped all over the South; (5) The habit of obedience and subservience was deeply ingrained.

No doubt overdrawn is the picture which Hebert Aptheker paints of slave militancy during this war. Aptheker, like his fellow Marxist W. E. B. DuBois, is high in praise of the militant role of the slave.[27] Although there is some truth in this picture, it fails to take into account the obvious fact that had the more than three million slaves been very militant, the Confederacy could not possibly have fought its northern foe for four years. In the end it was northern industry, manpower, and the blockade which brought the South to its knees, not slave militancy. It is quite easy to go to the extreme in the controversy which has raged over slave militancy and docility. Doubtless the truth about slave behavior lies somewhere between the extreme painted by southern apologists for the institution, and such attackers of these apologists as Aptheker and DuBois. DuBois and Aptheker are together on their effort to show a commonality of interest, against a common northern capitalist and southern planter foe, between southern Negroes and poor whites both during the war and the Reconstruction period.[28]

Many white Americans were prone to term this a "nigger war," and to turn their backs on the call to arms. Well known is the manner in which this attitude caused Andrew Johnson to become the only Southern senator who remained loyal to the Union, and how this sentiment produced the infamous "Draft Riots" which gripped New York and other areas during July 1863. The Afro-American accepted the idea whole-heartedly and unreluctantly that in many respects this was indeed his war. Individual leaders pointed out repeatedly that the stakes were emancipation and citizenship, and that the race should not play a passive role in the realizing of these ends. Colored volunteers to the Union cause came in such large proportion and so rapidly that the Union found great difficulty in shaping policy and machinery to handle them.

Black abolitionists now realized that their old program of speech-making and propaganda was completely outmoded, and that the needs of the hour were: (1) to get the federal government to accept colored troops, and (2) to recruit as many Afro-Americans into military service as possible.

The outbreak of Civil War found the Negroes eager to fight. Well-known is the fact that their offers to fight were not accepted until mid-1862. Military necessity may be listed as a prime factor which moved the federal government to enlist colored troops. In demanding the right to fight Negroes gave numerous reasons why they should volunteer. Many pointed out that it would be unmanly to acquire, and the race would not value as much, freedom won solely through the efforts of others; that being natives of the South, they knew the terrain and the enemy well and could thereby greatly aid the northern cause; that since they had more at stake than northern whites, Afro-Americans would probably make the better soldiers. Too, there is the likelihood that they wanted to be directly in the fray also because they wanted to square an account with the slave holders—in brief, the revenge motive.

The race saw in the hot war, what it had seen in the 1830-1860 cold war between North and South. This was to the Afro-American clearly a struggle of Liberty versus Despotism. In mid-twentieth century parlance, the North was the Free World, representative of the eternal struggle between right and wrong, civilization versus barbarism, God against the devil. As Dr. John S. Rock said: "It seems to me that a blind man can see that the present war is an effort to nationalize, perpetuate and extend slavery in this country. In short, slavery is the cause of the war itself."[29] In the face of persistent claims to the contrary by post-Civil War southerners and a number of historical scholars, the freedman persistently has maintained that slavery was the basic cause of the Civil War. Generally, Afro-Americans have adhered to the position of President Lincoln and the United States Supreme Court that during 1861-1865 the South was in rebellion against federal authority. The Negro has not recognized the right of any state to secede from the Union, or effectively to thwart federal power through such devices as secession, nullification, or interposition.

Most colored Americans have held the view that slavery was the almost sole cause of the Civil War. R. R. Moton held this view.[30] In a congressional speech in defense of the Civil Rights bill, James T. Rapier called the war "an appeal . . . from the forum to the sword, the highest tribunal known to man," and said that the war decided "that national rights are paramount to state-rights, and that liberty and equality before the law should be coextensive with the jurisdiction of the stars and stripes."[31] The Civil Rights bill, he declared, was "simply to give practical effect to that decision." Frederick Douglass said:

> The case presented in the present war, and the light in which every colored man is bound to view it, may be stated thus. There are two governments struggling now for the possession of and endeavoring to bear rule over the United States . . . One has its capital in Richmond, and is represented by Mr. Jefferson Davis, and the other has its capitol at Washington, and is represented by honest Old Abe. . . . Now the question for every colored man is, or ought to be, what attitude is assumed by these respective governments,

and armies toward the rights and liberties of the colored race in this country; which is for us, and which against us.[32]

Negroes had believed in the Higher Law Doctrine long before Seward's famed utterances. In 1838 James McCune Smith opined:

> Christians are governed by the laws peculiar to the commonwealth of Christ, and which are independent of mere human laws imposed by human communities; the citizens of the Church Catholic of the Redeemer may be spread through many climes and subject to various forms of political government, but no difference in clime, no diversity in form of political creed can break the links which makes them fellow-citizens in Christ, or free them from obedience to the precepts of the Saviour.[33]

In 1841, Charles Lenox Remond had said

> Very many good and well intentioned men in American would have lent us their assistance, long ago, were it not for this threat, that the slaveholders would dissolve the American Union. Now, if in this assertion there was or could be one iota of truth— the smallest particle of rationality—I would grant that the objection should have some weight; but the thing is preposterous; beyond all parallel. Why, the very thought is absurdity. . . . [in secession] would it be possible for the holders to retain their slaves greater in number than themselves? To whom should the slaveholders look for sympathy, cooperation, and support, in their endeavors to keep these wretches in bondage? . . . believe me, the moment when the American Union is dissolved that instant the power of the slaveholder is prostrated in the dust.[34]

Remond did not then believe that the South would ever carry out its threat to secede. Again Frederick Douglass said:

> Jefferson Davis and his government make no secret as to the cause of this war, and they do not conceal the purpose of the war. That purpose is nothing more or less than to make the slavery of the African race universal and perpetual on this continent. It is not only evident from the history and

logic of events, but the declared purpose of the atrocious war now being waged against this country. Some, indeed, have denied that slavery has anything to do with the war, but the very slave men who do this affirm it in the same breath in which they deny it, for they tell you that the abolitionists are the cause of the war. Now if the abolitionists are the cause of the war, they are the cause of it only because they have sought the abolition of slavery. View it in any way you please, therefore, the rebels are fighting for the existence of slavery.[35]

James T. Rapier said that secession was simply "following to its legitimate conclusion the doctrine of state-rights (which of itself is secession)."[36]

Negroes generally have taken Lincoln's position that this was a rebellion.[37] Harvard Law graduate William H. Lewis stated in 1913 that the Civil War was the "culmination of a moral revolution, such as the world has never seen. . . . Thirty years of fierce agitation and fierce politics made an appeal to arms absolutely certain."[38]

God's wrath at the sinfulness of the planters, whose chief sin was slaveholding, is the central cause which Afro-Americans have assigned to the Civil War. In support of their thesis, post-Civil War Afro-American authors frequently have referred to that part of Abraham Lincoln's Second Inaugural address which stated:

Fondly do we hope, fervently do we pray, that this mighty scourge of war may speedily pass away, but if God will that it continue till all the wealth piled up by the bondman's 250 years of unrequitted toil shall be sunk and till every drop of blood drawn with a lash shall be paid with another drawn with a sword, as was said . . . 'The judgements of the Lord are true and righteous altogether,[39]

M. C. B. Mason blamed the war on "the slave oligarchy being crazed by its power." Of the sectional compromises, Mason declared that all of them had been "broken by the South and her friends," with the Kansas-Nebraska Act as the final burden which changed the North's mood from "quiescent" to "aggressive."[40] Speaking at Harvard University in 1905 Roscoe

Conkling Bruce said: "In the interest of social justice, national economy, free institutions, human nature itself, your heroes fought to set my people free."[41] A few years later Archibald Grimké declared:

> As in Egypt more than three thousand years ago, the Eternal spoke to the master-race at diverse times and with diverse signs, saying, 'let my people go,' so he spoke to the master-race in this land through divers omens and events, saying likewise, 'let my people go.' Those with ears to hear might have heard that voice in the Hartford Convention and the causes which led to its call; in the successive sectional conflicts over Missouri, the Tariff, and Texas; in the storm winds of the Mexican Wars, as in the wild uproar which followed the annexation of New National territory at its close; in the political rage and explosions of 1850 and 1854, and in the fierce patter of blood-drops over Kansas. They might have surely heard that commanding voice from the appointed lips of holy men and prophets, from the mouth of Garrison and Sumner, and Phillips, and Douglass, from the sacred gallows John Brown heard and repeated it while his soul went marching on from city to city, and state to state.[42]

Following the Emancipation Proclamation and acceptance of colored troops by the Federal government, Frederick Douglass wrote an editorial in the *North Star,* March 3, 1863, entitled, "Men of Color, To Arms!" "The tide is at its flood that leads on to fortune," he exclaimed: "From East to West, from North and South, the sky is written all over 'Now or Never!' Liberty won by white men would lose half its luster! Who would be free themselves must strike the blow!" Through pen and forum he and other leaders hammered away at this theme.

The colored soldier fought not only for the emancipation of his race and to strike down the slave-holder. He fought also because he felt within his heart that right, justice, Christianity, and the interest of the nation-at-large lay on the side of the Union. The letters and speeches produced by Afro-Americans during the conflict are filled with expressions which reveal this larger motivation.[43] As the instigators of the 1864 National

Negro Convention said: "The nation and the age have adjudged
that the extinction of slavery is necessary to the preservation
of liberty and republicanism, and that the existence of the
Government itself is contingent upon the total overthrow of
the slaveholders' oligarchy and the annihilation of the despotism which is inseparably connected with it."[14] Over 200,000
Negroes enlisted in the Union Army and 30,000 in the Navy,
and about 250,000 more served in various capacities directly
related to the military actions.

In a speech in defense of the Civil Rights bill, Congressman James T. Rapier of Alabama described the atmosphere in
which the federal government made its decision to use Negro
troops. Rapier declared that it was only when white enlistments
were inadequate and disease and battle casualties were deci-
mating the ranks of the Union army, and—

> when grave doubt as to the success of the Union arms
> had seized upon the minds of some of the most san-
> guine friends of the government; when strong men
> took counsel of their fears; when those who had all
> their lives received the fostering care of the nation
> were hesitating as to their duty in that trying hour,
> and others questioning if it were not better to allow
> the star of this Republic to go down and thus be
> blotted out from the great map of nations than to
> continue the bloodshed; when gloom and despair
> were widespread; when the last ray of hope had
> nearly sunk below our political horizon, how the
> Negro then came forward and offered himself as a
> sacrifice in the place of the nation, made bare his
> breast to the steel, and in it received the thrust of the
> bayonets that were aimed at the life of the nation.[45]

Archibald Grimké said: "Not until bleeding at every pore,
sickened at the loss of its sordid dollar, and in despair at the
threatened destruction of that to which it ascribed, as to the
almighty, all of its sectional progress, prosperity and power
viz.; the dear Union, did the North turn for help to the Negro,
whom it had despised and wronged, and whom it even then,
in its heart of hearts, despised and intended, upon occasion, to
wrong anew."[46]

Douglass urged free Negroes to forget that "two years ago, . . . McClellan shamelessly gave out that in a war between loyal slaves and disloyal masters he would take the side of the masters against the slaves," that McClellan then had "openly proclaimed his purpose to put down slave insurrections with an iron hand," and similar indignities. Douglass continued:

> I do not ask you about the dead past. I bring you to the living present. Events more mighty than men, eternal Providence, all-wise and all-controlling, have placed us in new relations to the government and the government to us. What that government is to us today, and what it will be tomorrow is made evident by a very few facts. . . . Slavery in the District of Columbia is abolished forever; slavery in all the territories of the United States is abolished forever; the foreign slave trade . . . is rendered impossible; slavery in ten states of the Union is abolished forever; slavery in the five remaining states is as certain to follow the same fate as the night is to follow the day. The independence of Haiti is recognized.[47]

In his enthusiasm and zeal, Douglass made at least one statement which we now know was an exaggeration. "Once let the black man get upon his person the brass letter U. S.; let him get an eagle on his button, and a musket on his shoulder, and bullets in his pocket, and there is no power on the earth or under the earth which can deny that he has earned the right of citizenship in the United States."[48] At another point, Douglass averred:

> I hold that if the government of the United States offered nothing more, as an inducement to colored men to enlist, than bare subsistence and arms, considering the moral effect of compliance upon ourselves, it would be the wisest and best thing for us to enlist. There is something ennobling in the possession of arms, and we of all other people in the world stand in need of their ennobling influence.[49]

In his "Men of Color, To Arms!" Douglass had declared:

> The day dawns; the morning star is bright upon the horizon! The iron gate of our prison stands half open. One gallant rush from the North will fling it

wide open, while four millions of our brothers and
sisters shall march out into liberty. The chance is now
given to end in a day the bondage of centuries and
to rise in one bound from social degradation to the
place of common equality with all other varieties of
men. Remember Denmark Vesey . . .; remember
Nathaniel Turner . . .; remember Shields Green and
Copeland, who followed noble John Brown, and fell
as glorious martyrs for the cause of the slave . . .
This is our golden opportunity.[50]
Negro soldiers saw action in almost every battle of the
war, a number totaling over 250 battles in all. Over 38,000
Negro soldiers lost their lives during the war. Approximately
one-half of the Negroes who fought in the Union Army came
from the seceded states. Throughout the war Negro soldiers
complained that they were being required to do too much
fatigue duty and too little actual fighting.

During the war Negroes were sometimes treated badly in
Northern communities because whites there blamed the race
for being the cause of the war which had taken their sons and
husbands away to face possibly being maimed or killed. Also,
northern workers feared the freedman's job competition after
the war. That during the war Negroes were used in some places
as strike breakers added to the animosity.

Like almost all soldiers, the black troops revealed both
bravery and cowardice, with the former predominant. Indeed,
some had entered the service very much against their will.[51]
In neither the North or South was there unanimity among
Negroes regarding the necessity for their taking up arms.[52]
Doubtless some of the reluctance to fight may be attributed
to such things as the lack of clarity about federal war aims
which long existed, Negro troops being often assigned to onerous work details, and for a time being paid less than white
soldiers. The reluctance which some persons showed toward
fighting can be more than matched by the zeal of the many
who were eager to risk their all in defense of freedom. Many
competent persons have testified to this zeal, and perhaps there
is significance in the fact that of the total number of Negro
troops at least seventy per cent were slaves or former slaves
when they took up arms.

One veteran said: "Heap of slaves was afraid to go to the army."[53] Another ex-slave who served reported:

I sure wished lots of times I never run off from the plantation. I begs the General not to send me on any more battles, and he says I's the coward and sympathizes with the South. But I tells him I just couldn't stand to see all them men laying there dying and hollering and begging for help and a drink of water and blood everywhere you looks. Killing hogs back on the plantation didn't bother me none, but this am different.[54]

One ex-slave reported of his fellow sufferers—"They could enlist in the Union army and get good wages, more food than they ever had, and have all the little gals waving at 'em when they passed. Them blue uniforms was a nice change, too."[55] Bell I. Wiley has stated that in such matters as rank and work assigned the black troops "were dealt with in a manner more becoming to slaves than to freedmen."[56] Negroes showed a childish zeal for uniforms and guns and for marching and drilling to drums and music. The impact of their cultural attainments is seen in the fact that, despite their faults, they were generally better behaved than the white troops, and their favorite marching songs were religious.[57]

Early during the Civil War a number of free Negroes volunteered for military service with the Confederacy, and entire companies of them were formed in Richmond and New Orleans. The labor shortage in the South led most states by 1862 to vote for impressment of slaves into military service as laborers, and in 1863 the Confederate Congress passed a general impressment law, which not only increased the number of runways among slaves but heightened the Negro's sense of importance.

Many of the slaves helped to carry the South's burdens during the war, laboring with the Confederate soldiers or at the plantation house and in the fields. Many of them shared the sorrow which southern plantations felt when the news came that "Ole Marster" or one of his sons had fallen in battle. They felt the physical deprivations which the South came to know, and though freedom lifted their hearts and gave them a new conception of themselves, they shared with white southerners the want and suffering of the reconstruction years. Although bondage had inured many of them to hardships, nonetheless they suffered and worked with the white South through the long dark years of want and misery on which the new South was built.

Together with the whites on the home front during the war slaves shared the hardships caused by the scarcity of foodstuffs, clothing, and other items. Yet the bondsmen were happier probably because now the deprivation was not theirs alone, and because of the hope which charged the air. Too, the lack of white males around the plantations meant a greater opportunity to slacken work and some freedom from lashings. Most slaves felt that their freedom was the central issue in the war, and that God would not allow Lincoln and his forces to lose.

One proof that Negroes were not "perfectly happy" in bondage is that, during the war, whenever federal troops came near, soon almost all of the slaves in the vicinity had absconded.[58] Similarly, while the slaves did not go on a sit-down strike as W. E. B. DuBois contends in *Black Reconstruction*,[59] the lack of adequate supervision did cause their work efficiency to fall off noticeably. Some worked only when they felt like it and arrogance, insolence and assaults on whites saw a sharp increase. Bell Wiley reports that "one of the chief objections offered by planters in the interior to sending their slaves to work on fortifications was that such slaves brought dangerous ideas back to the plantations, creating dissatisfaction and unrest."[60] After reviewing the literature of this period Wiley came to a similar conclusion as that reached by Herbert Aptheker for the pre-1861 period. "A survey of the evidence," Wiley states, "makes inescapable the conclusion that disorder and unruliness on the part of the Negroes were far more common than post war commentators have usually admitted."[61]

Personal attachment to whites was a strong factor in slave behavior during the war. Field hands gave the most trouble and absconded most. Of the class of body servants, Bell Wiley states: "No class of slaves had as good opportunities for desertion and disloyalty as the body servants but none was more faithful."[62] On slaves serving as "soldiers" for southern whites one Kentucky slave reported of his father—"His young master

was to go to war, but he didn't want to go so they put my
father in his place."[63] White children of planters sometimes
loved their black mammy so much that they offered to run
away to the Yankees with the mammy rather than let her leave
alone.[64]

During the war slaves were employed by the Confederacy
as teamsters, cooks, body servants, railroad and dock workers,
medical workers, for the erection of ground works and forts,
in factories and mines of various types, and in other capacities.
Evidence seems to indicate that, other than body servants, in
preference to this military service, most bondsmen desired to
remain in their old duties on the plantation where slave-life
had taken a decided turn for the better, and they used many
ingenius devices to avoid impressment as military laborers.[65]
One ex-slave said—"When the war came on we stayed, scared
—what else could we do?" Another ex-slave said of her master
that "after war come up he got just as good."[66]

When federal troops reached them, many slaves were over-
come with joy. To some bondsmen these troops were God's
angels sent to effect their long promised deliverance, and in
many instances "massa Linkum" was the God. One ex-slave
reported: "I tell you, honey, some of the colored people sure
been speak praise to them yankees. I don't know how come,
but they never know no better. I say, they know and they
never know. One old man been riding one of these stick horses
and he been so glad, he say, 'thank God! Thank God!'"[67] Another reported on the coming of the soldiers and freedom:

> Everybody went wild. We all felt like heroes, and
> nobody had made us that way but ourselves. We was
> free. Just like that, we was free. It didn't seem to
> make the whites mad, either. They went right on
> giving us food just the same. Nobody took our homes
> away, but right off colored folks started on the move.
> They seemed to want to get closer to freedom, so
> they'd know what it was—like it was a place or a
> city.[78]

Slaves coined many songs during the war. One song had
the words: "Look up the road and seen the cloud arising; And
look like we're gonna have a storm, Oh, no, you're mistaken;

It is only the darkies' bayonets and buttons on uniform." Another went: "Old Master's gone away and the darkies stayed at home; Must be now that the kingdom's come and the year for jubilee." "Old Master, he drilled so hard they called him captain; He got so dreadful tanned he said he's going down yonder amongst the Yankees to pass for a counterbrand." And:

> Darkies, did you see old master
> with the mustache on his face?
> Left here early soon this morning
> Says he's going for to leave this place.[69]

And:

> Oh! fader Abraham,
> Go down into dixie's land;
> Tell Jeff Davis
> To let my people go,
> Down in the house of bondage
> Dey have watched and waited long,
> De oppressor's heel is heavy
> De oppressor's arm is strong.[70]

Federal troops in the South found some slaves willing spies and helpers in their cause. Yet, many slaves were afraid of the blue-coated strangers from the North, a fear induced in part by southern whites who told the bondsmen that Yankees had horns, only one eye, and were heartless fiends. Too, the bondsmen sometimes resented the manner in which northern troops entered plantations and insulted master and mistress while taking off horses, foodstuffs, and other valuables.

Whenever Yankee troops got close to their plantations many masters moved their slaves to places of safety. Some slaves were thus moved several times and although these trips involved considerable hardships, for the first time, perhaps, slaves now saw their masters frightened and running. Together with much heroism and sacrifice, bondsmen also saw southern white males of military age hiding or feigning illness in order to avoid risking life and limb in battle. These things must have contrbuted to a conviction that members of the master class were scarcely much more human than their human chattel.[71]

The Spanish American War

With the imminence of war between the United States and Spain which existed in March, 1898, the American Negro, for the first time since emancipation, was faced with the possibility of having to fight and die to defend a nation in which his citizenship rights were often flagrantly violated. As has been, customary with him, however, there was no doubt of what he should do when the national defense was at stake. An editorial in the *Cleveland Gazette* of March 26, 1898 stated: "This is our opportunity. Let us not stand upon the asking, but show ourselves ready to maintain intact the government from which we derive our hopes for life, liberty and happiness." Representative J. T. Walls of Florida had early made an effort to get the United States government to grant the revolting Cubans belligerent rights. He was very sympathetic toward the revolt and argued that in Cuba a half million Negroes were still virtually enslaved by Spain.[72] Representative George H. White of North Carolina, only member of his race in Congress at the time, was an avid supporter of the war. Still some Negroes, as did some white American supporters of such an anti-imperialist symbol as the Teller Amendment, had misgivings about the purpose and need for the Spanish-American War. One wrote of what "a glorious dilemma that will be for the Cuban Negro, to usher him into the condition of the American Negro,"[73] while another viewed American participation in the Cuban revolt as a reactionary counter-crusade against the "socialistic aspects" of the revolution. This writer, too, deplored the migration of this country's white supremacy doctrine and practice to the colored Cubans which he saw coming as a result of the war.[74] The New York *Tribune* of July 17, 1899 carried a report which stated that: "During the war with Spain a proportion of . . . colored people of New England and of some of the Middle and Southwestern States were ready to make an armed revolt against the United States and to espouse the cause of Spain." This report went on to state that the same sympathy of colored Americans existed where the then current war to suppress the Philippines was concerned. "Were it possible to render the fighting Fillipinos armed assistance," said this commentary on the Negro's attitude, "it would be done." It is just as obvious that this observer was exaggerating as it is obvious that colored Americans did have some misgivings about the nation's designs on Cuba and the Philippines. On this, Lewis H. Douglass, son of the celebrated abolitionist, wrote:

It is a sorry, though true, fact that whatever this government controls, injustice to dark races prevails. The people of Cuba, Porto Rico, Hawaii and Manila know it well as do the wronged Indian and outraged black man in the United States.

.   .   ..

It is hypocrisy of the most sickening kind to try to make us believe that the killing of Filippinos is for the purpose of good government and to give protection to life and liberty and the pursuit of happiness.[75]

Afro-Americans took great pride in the fighting and other service of the four Negro regiments which saw action in the Spanish-American War. These, the Twenty-fourth and Twenty-fifth Infantry Regiments, and the Ninth and Tenth Cavalry units, long remained strong sources of pride to Afro-Americans. At the onset of the war, the Civil War drama had been reinacted in many particulars, for again colored Americans had to wage a vigorous campaign to get the Government and the army to accept them as soldiers and as officers. Slowly the prejudice against arming them, and the argument that they lacked the native ability and courage to fight were over-come enough to get the above-mentioned regiments activated.

Only a few colored troops saw actual combat action in this very brief war, but their bravery and gallantry received high praises. There were those in both races who claimed that the Ninth and Tenth Cavalry units saved the famed Rough Riders from certain defeat at Las Guasimas. Even Theodore Roosevelt voiced high praise for these units. However, in the April, 1899 issue of *Scribner's Magazine* Roosevelt declared that without white officers, Negroes were poor soldiers. This remark angered many persons.

At the beginning of his term, President McKinley had voiced the sentiment of most Presidents of the 1876-1914 period. McKinley stated:

It will be my constant aim to do nothing, and
permit nothing to be done, that will arrest or disturb
this growing sentiment of unity and cooperation [be-
tween the sections], this revival of esteem and affiliation which now animates so many thousands in both
the old antagonistic sections, but I shall cheerfully
do everything possible to promote and increase it.[76]

Massachusetts Negroes spoke out in petition in 1899 on Mc-
Kinley's failure to take a stand in defense of the rights of
colored Americans.[77] This petition also condemned the imperi-
alistic policies of the administration. Colored Americans nowhere were impressed by the humanitarian preachments which
were used to gloss over, excuse, and inspire the wave of late
nineteenth century imperialism. Kipling's plea that Occidental's
were merely taking up "the white man's burden" was, to the
colored American, but another of the white man's rationaliza-
tions. Time and again the Negro warned white America of the
adage that charity begins at home, and that within the United
States the colored man, under the guise of citizenship, was the
object of a shocking exploitation which could match colonial
exploitation in any part of the globe.

Despite the general feeling that President McKinley was
heartless where the plight of the race was concerned, during
1899 and 1900 he appointed twice as many Negroes to federal
offices as any of his predecessors had done. Still, coming before
the age of all-out total war, the brief Spanish-American conflict
failed to open new and broad economic, political, and social
opportunities for the Negro such as those which World Wars
I and II wrought.

World War I

Like the Spanish American war and the later World War
II, World War I sharply focused attention on the plight of
colored colonials, and quickened the desire for freedom and a
better material life in India, the Indies, Africa, and the world
over. Thus, more Americans, brown and white, came to view
the native race problem as part and parcel of an international
one. As the Afro-American saw millions of humankind elsewhere segregated, discriminated against, and lynched, he felt less

lonely in his degradation and more hopeful for an early end
to practice of the white-supremacy doctrine. One reason why
Negroes have fought for the exemplification of the highest
ideals of Americanism is this realization that their destinies
were "interwoven and linked with those of the whole American
people." Thus slavery was not bad for the black man alone,
but was a degradation and a threat to the welfare of the entire
nation. The same attitude has been taken toward post-bellum
discrimination and segregation. Thus it is that, despite these
short-comings in democracy, the colored American always has
answered readily the call to colors when the nation was im-
periled. He has agreed with Lincoln that this nation is "the last
best hope of mankind." But casting these practical considerations aside, there is abundant evidence that the Negro readily
fights for this country because he loves it. To him, "be it ever
so humble, there's no place like home," has had special significance. The 1864 National Negro Convention, meeting at Syracuse, New York had said to the Southern white man: "We
would address you—not as Rebels and enemies, but as friends
and fellow countrymen who desire to dwell among you in
peace, and whose destinies are interwoven and linked with those
of the whole American people, and hence must be fulfilled in
this country . . . We ask for no special privileges, or peculiar
favors, we ask only for even-handed justice."[18]

The Christian Index, official organ of the C. M. E. Church,
stated in its issue of March 19, 1908, that the Negro wanted
"justice, . . . equality, . . . freedom of action and opportunity . . ., North and South alike." It also reiterated a main thesis
of colored Americans where the ballot is concerned. "A labor
class in an industrial Republic like ours," it was asserted, "which
is deprived of the ballot, is at the mercy of those that possess
it." Race prejudice, mob violence, and the convict lease system,
were herein attacked.

How much of the Afro-American's pacifist leaning has
been stimulated by the fact that until recently the United
States Army generally has treated him as though he was not
wanted in the service is a debatable point. Even in time of war,
generally Negroes were excluded from high offices and the
more desirable jobs, and positions and the best colored regi-

ments, such as the Tenth Cavalry and the Twenty-fourth Infantry were often given "insulting assignments."

Of Negroes and World War I, Mordecai Johnson observed:
"For the first time since emancipation, they found themselves
comparatively free to sell their labor on the open market for
a living wage, found themselves launched on a great world
enterprise with a chance to vote in a real and decisive way, and,
best of all, in the heat of the struggle they found themselves
bound with other Americans in the spiritual fellowship of a
common cause."[80] Of the causes of the war Francis J. Grimké
noted:

> So far as making the world safe for white su-
> premacy, there is no difference, or very little, between
> the Central Powers and the Allies. . . . this war
> would never have been brought on had Germany been
> content with the status quo—with the supremacy of
> the white races over all the darker and weaker race.
> But Germany got into her head the idea of a super-
> man, and of super nation, and the super-man and
> nation, the military Caste in Germany, felt itself to
> be the German nation; and, that it was the preroga-
> tive, the divinely appointed prerogative, of this nation
> of super-men not only to be supreme over all darker
> and weaker races, but also over all the other white
> races as well.   And there is where the rub came,
> where the trouble began, and that is why the war
> came on.[81]

Of the Negro's service, Archibald Grimké observed: "The
condition of the Negro was at its worse and his outlook in
America at its darkest when the Government declared war
against Germany. Then was revived the Republic's program
of false promises and hypocritical professions in order to bring
this black man with his brawn and brains, with his horny hands
and lion heart, with his unquenchable loyalty and enthusiasm
to its aid."[82]

The Afro-American has viewed his participation in all of
this nation's wars not only as a privilege and an opportunity
to serve in the cause of democracy and human freedom, but as
an opportunity to vindicate and further his own claims to the
right of equality of treatment.   During the war Francis J.

Grimké uttered the traditional attitude of Negroes toward their peculiar grievances and war emergencies. "The time to voice our dissatisfaction is now while the war is going on; while we are going across the sea to lay our lives down in order to make the world safe for democracy," Grimké declared. William Pickens, said:

> For real democracy the American Negro will live and die. His loyalty is always above suspicion, but his extraordinary spirit in the present war is born of his faith that on the side of his country and her allies is the best hope for such democracy. And he welcomes, too, the opportunity to lift the 'Negro question' out of the narrow confines of the Southern United States and make it a world question. Like many other questions our domestic race question, instead of being settled by Mississippi and South Carolina, will now seek its settlement largely on the battlefields of Europe.

At first W. E. B. DuBois and others opposed the establishment of a separate officer training school at Des Moines, Iowa for Negroes, but after a brief period of opposition DuBois supported the effort and before the war ended he was to consider the acceptance of a commission.

Approximately 350,000 Negro soldiers served in World War I, of whom 100,000 saw service overseas. Insults directed at colored troops at camps in the South were particularly irritating to soldiers from northern cities, and when white and colored Americans were sent to France, the "race problem" was evident both in bad relations aboard ship and in France.

Negro soldiers won hundreds of medals and citations for their service in the war. That many of these citations were won by troops commanded under fire by Negro officers was considered ammunition against the then often-heard argument that Negroes would fight well only if commanded by white officers. In late 1917, the United States Supreme Court again lifted the Negro's faith in American democracy when it declared the unconstitutionality of laws providing for residential segregation.

On October 5, 1917 the federal government took a step, similar to one which it was to repeat during World War II.

On that date it appointed the first advisor on Negro affairs in
the person of Emmett J. Scott, long-time secretary to Booker
T. Washington. Not only was Scott's appointment a source of
pride to the race, but he served as a sort of safety-valve
through which complaints and grievances could be channeled
during the war. The Federal Council of Churches took a similar step and set up a committee on the welfare of Negro troops
which was composed of distinguished colored leaders.

A month previous to the appointment of Scott, the 1906
Brownsville Riot seemed to be repeated, this time with white
citizens of Houston, Texas. Here race friction led to a blood-
letting in which soldiers of the 24th Infantry Regiment killed
seventeen white persons. Many Afro-Americans felt that the
thirteen bronze soldiers who were hanged and the forty-one
given life sentences as a result of the Houston riot did not
receive fair trials and justice. Repeated incidents of racial strife
kept Emmett Scott and the War Department quite busy as they
sought to keep the nation's troubled racial waters from further
impeding the war effort. As they were later to be during World
War II, Negroes were enthusiastic in their purchase of government bonds.

During the War Afro-Americans were not allowed to
serve in the Marine Corps and the Navy, and the Army often
restricted them to menial jobs. Colored troops generally have
desired that officers immediately over them should be of their
own race. Perhaps no better statement of the rationale behind
this desire can be found than that given by an anonymous
colored Sergeant during the Civil War, who wrote:

> We want black commissioned officers; and only
> because we want men we can understand and who can
> understand us. We want men whose hearts are truly
> loyal to the rights of man. We want men to be rep-
> resented in courts martial, where so many of us are
> liable to be tried and sentenced. We want to demon-
> strate our ability to rule, as we have demonstrated our
> willingness to obey. In short, we want simple justice.[53]

In the period immediately preceding World War I, Afro-
Americans had been proud of the accomplishments of Col.
Charles Young, the highest ranking Negro officer in the Army,

but when war came they were equally disillusioned when Col. Young was not made a General. When he was retired by the army for "reasons of health," many persons were convinced that the real reason for this retirement was to prevent promoting him to the next highest rank.

The war period saw about one-half million Negroes migrate from the South to the North, and the movement continued at an amazing pace throughout the twenties. The number of Afro-Americans who were residents of urban areas increased from 27.4 per cent of the total to 34.0 per cent between 1910 and 1920. The shortage of labor in northern industries served as a magnet to draw large numbers from the South. Indeed, these industries actively and consciously sought to pull this black labor, of which the section had a superfluity, into northern industries.

Although considerable attention has been given to the impact of the 1900-1920 Negro migration from rural areas of the South to southern and northern cities, little has been said of the very important impact of this period's Negro migrations from the Carribean islands to the United States. The latter migration was to add greatly to the militant and egalitarian aspect of the northern Negro's outlook, and hence indirectly to the thought of the southern Negro. These island-bred Negroes had a longer tradition of protest and freedom, and they contributed to Afro-American thought and history such luminaries as A. A. Schomburg, Marcus Garvey, Claude McKay, and J. A. Rogers.

The urban trek created a significantly large Negro economic market, as well as a large number of voters in several northern cities. Both conditions became levers which have been used to bring about greater integration of Negroes into the economical and political life of such states as Illinois, Pennsylvania, New Jersey, Ohio, and New York. The acute needs of the labor market, the need for large numbers of soldiers, and the widespread democratic ideology of the war period gave the Afro-American an enviable position from which to bargain for his rights, as both the South and North came to realize more fully his true significance to the nation, and this, in turn, brought about many advances for the race during the War, many of which were of a permanent character. Previous to this period the migration of Negroes had been largely to the West and within the South. For the new movement, however, Philadelphia, Detroit, Chicago, and Harlem were the main points of attraction. Not only labor demands, but southern reactionism and terrorism following the late nineteenth and early twentieth century disfranchisement movement were also forces behind this exodus. The southern peasant was looking for better economic and cultural opportunities in a region where "a man was a man" regardless of race, creed, or color.[84] He often entered the northern cities with exaggerated expectations and many were disillusioned at the existence of prejudice and squalor north of Mason-Dixon. Some of the disillusioned returned to the South, and some began to move from one northern city to another. Most settled down and eventually adjusted to the more dynamic and demanding environment. However, as the peasant of the South brought with him his labor, hopes, and ambitions, he also bequeathed to northern cities a lions share of their burdens of juvenile delinquency, illegitimacy, deserted wives and children, and intensified housing problems.

On the migration and Negro leadership, Alain Locke opined:

It is the 'man farthest down' who is most active in getting up. One of the most characteristic symptoms of this is the professional man, himself migrating to recapture his constituency after a vain effort to maintain in some southern corner what for years back seemed an established living and clientele. The clergyman following his errant flock, the physician or lawyer trailing his clients, supply the true clues. In a real sense it is the rank and file who are leading, and the leaders who are following. A transformed and transforming psychology permeates the masses.[85]

The World War I exodus created a dilemma for labor unions. Apart from the Knights of Labor, and the Industrial Workers of the World, unions had tended to ignore the black laborer. In part this was because Negro labor was mostly of the unskilled variety, while the dominant A. F. of L. was built around skilled workers. The strikes of the 1920s saw some

Negroes serving as strike breakers, and happy to work for lower wages than the unions were demanding, and the unions came to see that either they had to assimilate this large mass, or forever contend with its presence as a menace to labor's efforts to win higher wages and better working conditions. The former course would soon seem more attractive to the unions. R. R. Wright, eminent minister of the gospel and scholar, pointed out that there was considerable exaggeration of the extent to which Negroes participated in strikebreaking. Reasons given by him as to why some participated in this practice include: (1) many industries refused to hire colored persons except during times of labor troubles, and (2) attractively high wages were paid during strikes. Wright also criticised the unions, which suffered most from strikebreaking, for their policies of racial exclusiveness. The solution of strikebreaking he saw as the inclusion of colored workers as full members of the unions.[86]

As World War I drew to a close, R. R. Moton, sent to France by the federal government to investigate rumors of malbehavior among colored troops, reported that he found practically no evidence of such. He angered these troops, however, by advising them not to expect much change in America's pre-war treatment of their race when they returned home.[57] Writing of the returning Negro soldiers, Raymond G. Dandridge asked, "If you are still to be the herder's cattle?" and added—

> Democracy means more than empty letters, And liberty far more than partly free; yet both are void as long as men in fetters Are at eclipse with Opportunity.[88]

Upon their return to the States in the Spring of 1919, Negro troops received a tremendous welcome throughout the North. Individual heroes the race had had before, but nothing to match the pride which was felt as they viewed directly or by news photograph the G. I.'s marching in New York City's great welcoming parades.

The fear which some white Americans had that a newly belligerent and bellicose Negro would return from the battle fields of Europe was based more on the pronouncement of leaders at home than on any statements emanating from the soldiers abroad. In December, 1918 the Rev. Francis J. Grimké declared that the Negro troops in France had sniffed that country's "free, invigorating, liberty-loving air," and that when they returned home,

> There has got to be a change here. These boys will bring back that spirit with them, and it will have to be reckoned with. They know now what it is to be a man, and to be treated as a man. And that spirit will remain with them. It cannot be quenched. It will rather be sure to communicate itself to others.[59]

In May, 1919, W. E. B. DuBois wrote in the *Crisis*: "We return from the slavery of uniform which the world's madness demanded us to don to the freedom of civil garb." And:

> We stand again to look America squarely in the face and call a spade a spade. The U. S. A. .. is yet a shameful land. It lynches . . . It disfranchises its own citizens. .. . . It encourages ignorance. . . . It steals from us. . .. . We return. We return from fighting. We return fighting. Make our way for Democracy! We saved it in France, and by the Great Jehovah, we will save it in the U. S. A., or know the reason why.

Numerous Afro-Americans not only saw the deep and broad revolutionary nature of the struggle, but, with President Wilson, voiced hopes that this was a war to end all wars. In December, 1919, the Rev. Francis J. Grimké declared:

> We can't begin, as yet, to realize fully what a terrible, awful tragedy of blood, of suffering, or sorrow and woe, through which the world has been passing within the past quadrennium! And now, at last, the whole horrible business is over, and over, we trust never again to be repeated until time shall be no more. One such war is enough for all the generations that are to come.[90]

Grimké stated that when President Wilson announced the end of hostilities, "in every possible way the people sought to express their joy—white and black, . . . For once there was no division or separation, but all seemed to be moved by one common sentiment, as all ought to be, in all matters of public interest." Reminiscing on the war in his poem "The Heart of the World,," Joshua Henry Jones, Jr. declared:

In the heart of the world is the call for love;
White heart . . Red . . . Yellow . . and black.
Love in weak people; love in the strong;
Love that will banish all hatred and wrong.

Archibald Grimké declared that because of the Negro veteran's experience in fighting for democracy on the battlefield, and because of the democratic treatment which he received in France, he had come home "not as he went but a new Negro."[91] "The war over there is over; but the war over here for our manhood and citizenship rights is not over; and will not be over until they are all accorded to us as to other citizens of the Republic," another spokesman stated.[92] This same observer opined: "After these four years of unparalleled suffering there is every reason to believe that there is going to be a great change in the policy of nations toward each other. In their relations, one with the other, the principle of right, instead of might is going to have a larger place than it has ever had before."[93] And:

As a result of this great struggle, through which we have been passing, I believe, it is going to be better for all the darker and weaker races of the world. It is going to be better for them because in the dominant nations a higher sense of justice, of right, of fair play, is going to be developed; better for them because I believe there is going to be developed a higher type of Christianity than at present prevails—then the miserable apology that now goes under that name.[95]

One of the effects which World War I had on Afro-Americans was to make more of them impatient with the philosophy of gradualism which, for many, had been the order of the day in race relations since 1876. From an attitude of "make haste slowly" more persons were to be converted to the W. E. B. DuBois—Monroe Trotter philosophy of make haste hastily. Since in the war effort Afro-Americans had seared into their souls the powder burns of freedom's fight against autocracy and oppression, not even the riot of Ku Klux Klanism and other opposition which they encountered in the twenties could kill this impatience.

One competent observer has recorded the manner in which some white southerners expected the colored veteran of World War I to return home ready to use violence to elevate his position in the social, economic, and political life of the South. In a number of communities white authorities increased the store of weapons and enlarged the police force in order to meet this expected outbreak of violence. But there was no such violence emanating from the colored veteran, although he was sometimes beaten and murdered by overly anxious white authorities. Of the Negro, states this observer:

> Those who remained at home, both men and women, were more sensible than ever of their wrongs. But their indignation took the form of stern resolve to wield the moral weapons of their incongruous position to their utmost effect in securing what in the fervour of war was their admitted right as American Citizens. This was the attitude of the Negro then and is his attitude now, and has been his attitude throughout his long contact with the white man in America.[96]

In his poem "The New Day," Fenton Johnson told American whites—

> For we have been with thee in No man's Land;
> Through lake of fire and down to Hell itself;
> And now we ask of thee our liberty,
> Our freedom in the land of Stars and Stripes.

With the rest of the South Negroes favored the prohibition experiment. Blanche K. Bruce had sought a constitutional Amendment to this effect in the early years following the Civil War.[97]

A wave of gangsterism, political immorality, anti-communism, lynchings, and race riots swept the nation during the twenties. Writing in 1928 R. R. Moton played down the revival of Klu Kluxism. "The least important of its activities," he asserted, "were those directed against Negroes; and in turn Negroes were least disturbed over its existence."[98] In the light of the concern which more militant persons such as W. E. B. DuBois and Monroe Trotter had over this matter, it may be reasoned that Moton was not in this instance speaking for all members of the race.

Throughout much of the South, the life of the Negro was little changed during the twenties. Cotton remained dominant. The 1942 *National Survey of the Higher Education of Negroes* revealed that over one-half of the South's farmers, of both races, were still producing cotton as practically their sole crop and that their average annual cash income was pitifully low. The freedman's relationship to this agriculture was overwhelmingly in the status of share-cropper; his sustenance for the entire year usually coming from the white owner's credit. The cropper almost never got out of debt and his life was bare existence. His housing, clothing, and food, usually were wretched, and unless his children migrated to southern or northern cities, their lives, too, were largely void of hope. Here indeed appeared to be the "timeless peasant" so aptly described by Oswald Spengler. From this wretched creature could come little hope for the future of the race, and, as has been characteristic throughout history, the hope of the Afro-American lay in the cities and towns. To their already considerable black populations, a constant stream of the more ambitious, curious, or more defeated contributed new numbers, and the urban Negro continued to move forward, to demand, to challenge, to grow. As no poet of his race had done before, in the twenties, Leon R. Harris would tell in verse the plight of both the black rural and urban proletariat from southern share-cropper to northern steel workers. Himself the product of an orphanage who sent himself to Berea College and Tuskegee Institute, Harris was well qualified by personal experience to put into musical words the story of these people. Yet, describing the South in the Post-World War II period, Carl Rowan came to the same conclusion in his volume entitled, *South of Freedom* that Richard Wright had reached several decades earlier. Because the pattern of race relations was still pretty much what it had always been, Rowan concluded, he was leaving the South never to return again.

Lynching

Over five thousand Negroes have been lynched in the United States since emancipation. Between 1882 and 1900 lynchings were almost weekly occurences. Many explanations have been given for the prevalence of such a practice, all of which point up the fact that respect for law and order often has broken down in areas where the interests of the two races crossed. Booker T. Washington, R. R. Moton and some other persons became convinced that lynching was a major problem of the lower class Negro alone. In his novel *Fire in the Flint,* Walter White had the Caucasiam Roy Ewing express this sentiment for the Negro Medic Kenneth Harper. "Lynching never bothers folks like you," Ewing averred. White knew, however, that no class was immune from this threat.

The most popular reason given for lynchings has been that a Negro had raped a white woman. Frederick Douglass and other leaders early pointed out that in the South the enormity of the crime of rape was usually dependent on who committed the crime against whom. "For two hundred years or more," Douglass wrote, "white men have in the South committed this offense against black women, and the fact has excited little attention."[99] He also pointed out that the South was not alone in committing lynchings. The greatest campaigner against this evil, however, was Ida Wells Barnett, editor, lecturer, and ardent champion of justice who, because of her militancy, was forced to flee from Memphis, Tennessee in 1892. She served as Chairman of the Anti-lynching Bureau of the National Afro-American Council, and lectured throughout the United States and Europe against the evil. In 1898 she produced statistics to show that since the end of Radical Reconstruction on an average no more than twenty percent of Negroes lynched were charged with rape.

To Afro-Americans a newly disturbing feature during the 1920's was the increased boldness of the lynchers who now even used newspapers to advertise a lynching and welcome participants and onlookers to come view the show. Race riots, beatings, and killings and racial strife were so rampant during the first year when Negro troops returned home that James Weldon Johnson labelled the middle of 1919 "The Red Summer." It has been estimated that over twenty-five race riots occurred the year of 1919, and no section east of the Plains region seemed to be spared. Mordecai W. Johnson called for the establishment of a federal civil rights agency, and in 1921, many

Negroes were hopeful that the NAACP backed Dyer Anti-Lynching bill would be enacted into law. In his poem "Brothers," Joshua Henry Jones, Jr., joined others in pointing to the paradox of lynching in a Christian land. After describing in verse the lynch-burning of a Negro whose charred remains still 'hung pitifully o'er the swinging char," Claude McKay indicated the seeming lack of hope in it all—

And little lads, lynchers that were to be,
Danced round the dreadful thing in fiendish glee.[100]

R. W. Logan has indicated that the riots and lynchings of the twenties might have gone further than they did had whites been less afraid of Negro retaliation.[101] Certain it is that in the face of these assaults, Negroes were not as submissive as they had been in the 1870's, '80's and 90's. One reason is that unlike the 1870's, during the twenties Northern Negroes, ever more militant, were main objects of attack. Perhaps some persons feared a general race war. The militant Claude McKay urged his race to fight back, meet violence with violence, for—

If we must die, let it not be like hogs,
    Hunted and penned in an inglorious spot;
If we must die, O let us nobly die,
    So that our precious blood may not be shed in vain.

In the same vein, Lucius B. Watkins wrote:

We would be peaceful! Father—but, when we must,
Help us to thunder hard the blow that's just,
We would be prayerful: Lord, when we have prayed,
Let us arise courageous—unafraid!
We would be manly—proving well our worth,
Then would not cringe to any god on earth!

World War II

When Pearl Harbor was attacked on December 7, 1941, the colored American felt the righteous indignation and determination to defend the flag which swept the nation. While a few Marxist intellectuals saw in this war the doom of a capitalist system in the West which, irrevocably bound by its own inner contradictions, was in the final stage of death by suicide, the masses of Negroes did not stop to spin such fine theories.

Wilson Record has opined that well after Pearl Harbor, Afro-Americans had little enthusiasm for the War,[102] yet this cannot be construed to mean that they ever doubted on which side their loyalty lay. On this there never has been any serious doubt, and where doubt existed, it was sometimes due to pessimism springing from World War I memories as to whether war would substantially better the plight of the race. Too, this doubt was in part the larger feeling of a nation which could no longer feel enthusiasm for such World War I slogans as "making the world safe for democracy" or a "war to end all wars." Doubt as to what the nation should have done has been well demonstrated by that fairly large body of scholars who contend that President Franklin D. Roosevelt connived through Pearl Harbor to push a reluctant nation into war.[103]

Once the Japanese blow was struck, and the nation openly committed itself, there is little doubt that the Negro was ardent and enthusiastic in his support of the war effort. When the German invasion of Russia brought about another jolting switch in the party line, even Negro Communists became arch "patriots."

As America geared itself for the struggle against totalitarianism, Negroes demanded a larger share of jobs in the defense program. Early in 1940 Afro-Americans organized The Committee for Participation of Negroes in the National Defense Program in order to push for greater acceptance of their brains and brawn in both civilian and military capacities. The Negro press, Urban League, NAACP, and other groups pushed relentlessly and successfully toward these ends. Among the encouraging victories which they won were: (1) Opening of a training center for Negro pilots at Tuskegee Institute; (2) acceptance of officers trained on a racially integrated basis; (3) acceptance by the Marine Corps, (4) greater and wider use by army and navy, (5) William H. Hastie appointed civilian aide to the Secretary of War, and Major Campbell C. Johnson appointed Executive Assistant to the Director of Selective Service; and, (6) More Negroes appointed to West Point and Annapolis. In late 1940, A. Philip Randolph had laid plans for a 1941 nationwide March-on-Washington to dramatize these and other demands. The embarrassed White House, unable to forestall the March by persuasion, yielded and issued Executive Order 8802, which launched the Fair Employment Practices

Commission. Randolph had consciously steered clear of the Communist-dominated National Negro Congress, but whether he was indebted for the idea of the "March" to Communist handling of the Scottsboro case and their techniques in general, to "Coxey's Army," or similar precedents is an interesting conjecture.

World War II liberalism and increased political activity of the race combined with other factors to more than double the number of Negro clerical workers between 1940 and 1958, and during the war the number of skilled workers in industry doubled in what has been a veritable revolution in the pattern of Negro employment in the United States. During the war the *Pittsburgh Courier* carried on a "Double V" campaign which was aimed at winning the war on the foreign battlefield as well as winning the fight for racial equality at home. Most other Negro newspapers were equally arduous and enthusiastic in support of the war effort.

On October 25, 1940, Benjamin O. Davis, Sr., became the first American Negro to hold the rank of General in the U. S. Army. That this promotion came on the eve of a presidential election caused some persons to view it as a political move.[104] The Negro soldier who stood up for his rights on the home-front became a sort of folk hero. "Well, if I am going to die for democracy," he said, "I might as well die for some of it down here in Georgia." Oft-repeated was the quotation: "Here lies a black man, killed by a yellow man, while fighting to save democracy for the white man."[105]

In this war almost 1,200,000 Negroes saw active military service, of whom approximately 500,000 served overseas, and the stimulus to cultural growth and social protest was greater in this war than had been the case in any previous military effort. These results were due to such factors as the greater effort put forth by the federal government through such programs as U.S.A.F.I., A.S.T.P., and The Army University Extension Program. Also, during World War II Afro-Americans served in a world-wide theater, whereas during World War I service had been largely confined to France. The G. I. Bill which provided government sponsored educational opportunities was eagerly grasped by Afro-Americans, many of whom had never dreamed that they would be able to afford the up-to-then luxury of graduate and professional training. Similarly, the G. I. home loan legislation encouraged and made it possible for many persons to become home owners who otherwise might not have done so.

Soon after the United States entered the war the all-colored 99th Pursuit Squadron, headed by B. O. Davis, Jr., was created. Again the military policy was one of segregation, but the race was especially proud of its fighter pilots and of the all-Negro 92nd and 93rd Infantry Divisions. The 92nd was the only colored combat division in Europe, and its vicissitudes were followed closely by the home-front. When Senator Bilbo of Mississippi attacked the fighting prowess of the colored soldiers, criticism was directed at him from all quarters of Negro life. The race was proud, too, because President Roosevelt, while making no major governmental appointments among them, consulted Negro leaders on major policy matters which directly concerned the race's welfare.

While most Afro-Americans dearly loved him and supported Roosevelt's wartime bids for third and fourth terms, the *Pittsburgh Courier* was especially opposed to the fourth term. With bold headlines stating that "Power Leads to Tyranny," the September 30, 1944 issue carried a page-one protest against Roosevelt's bid for another term. "Whatever tends to destroy the two-party system in this country," the paper averred, "is dangerous for the Negro." By this date, the *Courier* was highly critical of the New Deal and claimed that many of Roosevelt's policies had led "directly to racial conflict."[106] The paper advised its readers that a "straight Republican ticket is the strongest and the most intelligent protest against racial discrimination and indignites."[107] Joining this protest against Roosevelt and the New Deal were the St. Louis *American, Amsterdam News, Afro - American, Philadelphia Tribune,* and several other papers. One author hinted rather strongly that some elements of the Negro press had been "bought" by the Republicans.[108] Such criticism must be viewed, however, in the light of the fact that the nation later amended the federal Constitution to make it impossible for any future president to be elected to four consecutive terms.

One result of the war was an increase in the number of inter-racial marriages and the lack of excitement which colored Americans in general showed toward them. Several such marriages were between tan G.I.'s or veterans and European, Japanese, or Hawaiian girls, while a number of others involved white and colored Americans. Only in the case of Walter White was any considerable resentment shown toward these matches. His case was complicated because, as Executive Secretary of the NAACP, White occupied a sensitive position. He had come to be thought of as "Mr. Negro," and "Mr. Civil Rights," and his marriage seemed to many to be traitorous to the racial cause. In his post-war novel, *Last of the Conquerors,* William Gardner Smith championed social equality even to the point of inter-marriage.[109] There is evidence that their overseas experiences during World War II and the Korean conflict left many Negro men with a heightened sensitivity to the characteristic independence of American females. Malcolm Cowley has observed that the G.I.'s portrayed in *The Last of the Conquerors,* voiced dissatisfaction with the self-centered American female. Cowley notes that this theme is "almost a constant refrain in almost all of the books by veterans of foreign service."[110]

During and following World War II, there was another exodus of Negroes to southern and northern cities, and approximately 250,000 moved to Western cities during this period. As California, to which many moved, has been for sometime the fastest growing state in the Union, here again the race was following a national trend.

CHAPTER XI

THE DAY FREEDOM CAME

In the history of nations, institutions, and racial or other groups there is usually one day the significance of which causes it to stand out in bold relief.[1] To Americans, for example, Independence Day stands perhaps unrivalled in significance. Yet, because of the institution of slavery, for almost one hundred years this day had little significance to a very large segment of the nation's populace. Although some slaves were granted respite from labor on each Fourth of July, they could scarcely enter into the real joy and meaning of the day. Addressing a group of citizens of Rochester, New York for the Fourth of July celebration in 1852, Frederick Douglass used the topic: "What to the Slave is the Fourth of July?" To whites, he concluded: "This Fourth of July is *yours*, not *mine*. You may rejoice, I must mourn. To drag a man in fetters into the grand illuminated temple of liberty, and call upon him to join you in joyous anthems, were inhuman mockery and sacrilegious irony."[2] Douglass stated that the character and conduct of the nation never looked blacker to him than on the Fourth of July. "America is false to the past, false to the present, and solemnly binds herself to be false to the future," he said. Slavery he called "The great sin and shame of America!"

In the species of knowledge termed Afro-American history there is probably no day more significant than that on which the bondsman became aware of the elevation of his status from slave to free person. Today the words "slave" and "free" lack ability to reveal the tremendous meaning and magnitude which this change meant to nineteenth century persons, black and white, North and South. Now the advantage of hindsight which lets us know that the ex-bondsman's new freedom was to be far from ideal also makes it unlikely that we can appreciate fully what this day originally meant. Thus it may be well in the mid-twentieth century to attempt to see this day through the eyes and hearts of some of the persons who were directly

222

affected by the transformation. The reader doubtless will quickly perceive that for Afro-Americans in general there was no one day on which freedom came, and that for this reason, what we are discussing is more accurately "The Days that Freedom Came."

Individual Negroes were to experience a great day of freedom when as fugitives they fled to the North from the South. It may be forever impossible to know fully whether these thousands of persons were more pushed into their daring escapes by the horrors of slavery or pulled by the bright promise of freedom. Evidence would seem to indicate that the former was the case. Despite the existence of compelling motivations on both sides, almost always the decision to flee bondage was made with painful apprehensiveness and fear. For always countering freedom's gentle tug was the fear of dreadful reprisal if the break was unsuccessful, unhappiness at leaving relatives and friends, and perhaps even fear of freedom itself— a state of mind largely atrributable to the bondsman never having known freedom directly. Frederick Douglass has given a poignant account of this feeling.

> The hopes which I had treasured up for weeks of a safe and successful escape . . . were powerfully confronted at this last hour by dark clouds of doubt and fear, making my person shake and my bosom to heave with the heavy contest between hope and fear. I have no words to describe . . . the deep agony of soul which I experienced on that never to be forgotten morning. . . . I was making a leap in the dark. The probabilities, so far as I could by reason determine them, were stoutly against the undertaking. . . . I was like one going to war without weapons—ten chances of defeat to one of victory.[3]

Yet to the thousands who, like Douglass, successfully fled the institution, the joy of the day freedom came more than matched the apprehension and fear. None ever chose to return to bondage and so sweet did they find the joys of freedom that many became zealous crusaders in the abolitionist movement, sometimes even risking their very lives by daring trips into the South to urge and help others escape.

The next great day of freedom to Afro-Americans was January 1, 1863. The occasion was Abraham Lincoln's signing of the Emancipation Proclamation. Free Negroes of the North had long exerted pressure to get the President to issue such a declaration and were to feel when the order came that they had gained a hard-earned victory. When after the battle of Antietam Lincoln announced on September 22, 1862 that on January 1 of the ensuing year he would declare bondsmen in states still in rebellion "henceforth and forever free," northern Negroes began to rejoice. But the exultation was qualified by a fear that the President might change his mind. Again Douglass has given what is perhaps the most vivid description of the fullness of joy which swept over northern Negroes when the Proclamation finally came. In Boston, Massachusetts a large crowd gathered in Tremont Temple to await the news. "We were waiting and listening as for a bolt from the sky, which would rend the fetters of four millions of slaves," Douglass stated. "We were watching as it were, by the dim light of the stars for the dawn of a new day." Near midnight, after several hours of tense expectation, the glad tidings started coming through from the nation's capital. Douglass continues:

> At last when patience was well-nigh exhausted, and suspense was becoming agony, a man . . . with hasty step advanced through the crowd and with a face fairly illumined with the news he bore, exclaimed in tones that thrilled all hearts, 'It is coming!' 'It is on the wires!'
>
> The effect of this announcement was startling beyond description, and the scene was wild and grand. Joy and gladness exhausted all forms of expression, from shouts of praise to sobs and tears. My old friend Rue, a Negro preacher, . . . expressed the heartfelt emotion of the hour, when he led all voices in the anthem, 'Sound the Loud Timbrel o'er Egypt's Dark Sea, Jehovah Hath Triumphed, his people are free!'[4]

For years after 1865, January 1, as Emancipation Day, was celebrated by Afro-Americans with parades, speeches, and great festivity. Although now more toned down and dignified, each year still sees Emancipation Day celebrations in many of the leading colored churches throughout the nation.

The majority of Afro-Americans had to wait until 1865 for their "Day of Jubilee." If the greatest joys are those which come suddenly and unexpected, perhaps a little of the significance of this day was diminished by the fact that, with the rest of the nation, the majority of bondsmen knew for months in advance of actual surrender that the Confederacy was in its death-throes and that freedom was a probability for them.

When the war ended agents of the federal government went from farm to farm checking on the status of the ex-slaves. A number of masters either had failed to inform their Negroes that they were free or else had compelled them to continue working in a state of servitude.[5] Thus it was that some persons did not learn of their legal emancipation for a year or two, and often they heard the news from these federal agents whom they called "freedom men." Some slaves found out they were free from sympathetic poor whites who had owned no slaves,[6] and often the Yankee soldier in blue brought the first news of freedom. An ex-slave reported:

I don't remember how the slaves found it out. I remember them saying, 'Well, they's all free.' . . . And I remember someone saying—asking a question—'You got to say 'Master'? And somebody answered and said, 'Naw.' But they said it all the same. They said it for a long time.[7]

Another remembered: "One day Mr. Mose came and told us that the war was over and that we would have to root for ourselves after that."[8] Planters often referred to their own status when informing slaves that they were emancipated. One ex-slave said his master stated: "Well, you all is just as free as I is this morning."[9]

At emancipation Negroes were told, "You are now free." Practically no provision had been made for their easy adjustment from slavery to freedom. They had almost no money, clothes, food, home, or education and were in the midst of an indifferent or hostile environment. It is not easy to imagine more difficult circumstances under which a people ever set out to make their way in the world, and there can be little wonder that some took to idleness, vice, and wandering. Many felt that this vagabondage was necessary to prove that they were really free or that they would not be reenslaved. But despite these most unfavorable circumstances under which freedom came, nothing could dampen the initial ardour with which it was received.

When the glad tidings actually came, indescribable joy leapt from the souls of these long oppressed people. John Greenleaf Whittier, writing for newly emancipated brown and black school children on St. Helena Island, South Carolina, caught the spirit which charged the air. Whittier wrote:

> The very oaks are greener clad,
>   The waters brightly smile;
> Oh, never shone a day so glad,
>   On sweet St. Helena's Isle!
> For none in all the world before
>   Were ever glad as we,
> We're free on Carolina's shore,
>   We're all at home and free![10]

Booker T. Washington stated that on the plantation where he had been a slave the news of emancipation was greeted with an all-night revelry of rejoicing and "wild scenes of ecstasy." While pondering the news, one ex-slave female got "happy" and pierced the night with a blood-curdling "Thank Gawd! Thank Gawd A' Mighty!"[12] Another ex-slave remembered that "When freedom come, folks left home, out in the streets, crying, praying, singing, shouting, yelling, and knocking down everything. Some shot off big guns."[13] "When news of the surrender come," stated another, "lots of colored folks seem to be rejoicing and sing, 'I's free, I's free as a frog,' 'cause a frog had freedom to git on a log and jump off when he please."[14] Still another group of ex-slaves sang jubilantly:

> Mammy, don't you cook no more,
> You are free, you are free!
> Rooster, don't you crow no more,
> You are free, you are free!
> Old hen, don't you lay no more eggs,
> You free, you free![15]

Another composed a ditty which went:

> I free, I free,
>   I free as a frog
> I free till I fool
>   Glory Alleluia![16]

One ex-slave reported that on his plantation all bondsmen were called together and told they were free. Then, he said, "Old colored folks, old as I am now, that was on sticks, throwed them sticks away and shouted."[17] Another declared:

> When the war ended, white man come to the field and tell my mother-in-law she free as he is. She dropped her hoe and danced up to the turn road and danced right up into Old Master's parlor. She went so fast a bird coulda sot on her dress tail. . . . That night she sent and got all the neighbors, and they danced all night long.[18]

Most Negroes left their masters as soon as they found out they were free and could get away.[19]

At the very moment that the ex-bondsman's spirits were vibrantly soaring from the mountain tops and into the heavens, those of his former master were in the lowest depths of despair. The white South was shocked, stunned, humiliated, aggrieved and dismayed. Not only had a war and a way of life been lost, but the bulk of southern wealth, represented by the investment in slave property, was at once forever lost to the planters. Here stood the ex-slave overwhelmed by and blissfully lost in what the present moment meant, and the planter completely despondent because of concern over a future which looked bleak indeed. Here stood the two great segments of the southern populace diametrically opposed in their attitudes and feelings about this day, one convinced that it was emerging into the light while the other was equally convinced that it was entering into the blackest darkness. This day's gap in the feelings and emotions of the two population groups is poignant testament to the yawning gap which had so long existed in their efforts at survival and life.

Years later there would be those to erect the myth that Negroes as slaves had been idyllically happy. Such a conviction is entirely contrary to the almost unanimous testimony of the persons who were in the best position to know the truth, the ex-slaves themselves. Their practically unvarying testimony repeats sentiments and convictions such as the following.

> What I likes best, to be slave or free? Well, it's this way. In slavery I owns nothing and never owns nothing. In freedom I's own the home and raise the

family. All that cause me worriment, and in slavery
I has no worriment, but I takes the freedom.[20]

.   .   .   .

A man has got more his own say now than he did
have. We can do more what we want to and don't
have to go to the other fellow. Slavery mighta done
the other fellow some good, but I don't think it ever
done the colored people no good. Some of them after
freedom didn't know how to go out and work for
themselves. . . . Depending on somebody else is poor
business. Look at the Indians! They're all living. I's
always been able to eat and sleep.[21]

Another proof of the contempt and revulsion which they felt
toward slavery as against their love of freedom is found in the
following. The spirituals, escapes, revolts, plots to revolt, lashings, patrols, and mass of repressive legislation stand as starkly
vivid testimony that the slave was not generally contented and
happy. Too, while there is no record that the ex-bondsmen
ever formed organizations and petitioned and fought to be
returned to bondage, the record is replete with instances where
they continuously have organized, petitioned, entered litigation,
and in other ways fought to protect and extend their freedom.

After 1865-66 Afro-Americans were to have other days
of freedom. In the 1870's and 80's, and again in the eras of
World Wars I and II, many would once again relive the experience of "escaping" from South to North. Although Roi
Ottley would declare that there was no day of triumph[22] and
others would write of no green pastures, in the 1940's and 50's
Richard Wright would end Black Boy[23] on a contrary note,
Carl Rowan would declare that Dixie was still south of freedom,[24] and the United States Supreme Court would make May
17, 1954 a day to remember. In the mid-twentieth century,
his belief that the promised land of genuine and full freedom
is near, coupled with the distantness of the long night of slavery makes it highly doubtful that the Afro-American ever
again will have another day of freedom comparable to those
which he already has known. Probably no other statement
could better illustrate the fact that criticism which long has
been directed at America because of the tragic gap between
national ideals and reality may soon be completely invalid.

CHAPTER XII

THE AFRO-AMERICAN AND SOME OF HIS BENEFACTORS

As might be expected, Negro historians, orators, and poets have led in extolling the praises of their race's benefactors. So much is this the case with the historians that at times their writings appear to be a long song of praise to those who fought to make Negro freedom and citizenship possible, and to the members of their race whose noteworthy achievements are held up as justifications for this freedom and citizenship. While Negroes have written little in the area of biography, largely through their poets and orators they have not failed to eulogize the outstanding members of their race. Thus it is largely to their verse, and oratory that one must turn to find evidence of this race's pride in and gratitude for the achievements and contributions of such personages as Phillis Wheatley, Benjamin Banneker, Frederick Douglass, Joe Louis, and others.

Discussed herein are only a few of the more prominent nineteenth century benefactors of the race. From the majority group, attitudes toward the most prominent benefactor of all, Lincoln the Great Emancipator, are discussed elsewhere in this volume.

Of the nineteenth century Negro fighters for Civil rights, Frederick Douglass is easily the most outstanding. So well has he been remembered and honored that practically every colored high school or college boy and girl long has known his name, although often they cannot be specific about any of his achievements.

Leaders of Slave Plots and Revolts

Negro writers appear to have shown greater interest in the plot to revolt led by Denmark Vesey than in the bloody insurrection led by the enigmatic Nathaniel Turner. Not long after the Vesey plot, Henry Highland Garnet informed the nation's bondsmen that Vesey "was betrayed by the treachery of his own people, and died a martyr to freedom. . . . but history, faithful to her high trust, will transcribe his name on the same monument with Moses, Hampden, Tell, Bruce, and Wallace, Toussaint L'Ouverture, Lafayette, and Washington. Vesey's tremendous plot shook the whole empire of slavery. The guilty soul-thieves were overwhelmed with fear."[1]

George Washington Williams spoke highly of Nat Turner, and called him the "Black John Brown." Williams concluded in 1882:

> The image of Nat. Turner is carved on the fleshy tablets of four million hearts. His history has been kept from the Colored people at the South, but the women have handed the tradition to their children, and the 'Prophet Nat.' is still marching on.[2]

The heroes closest to the slaves probably were not such radical leaders of the resistance as Gabriel Prosser, Denmark Vesey, and Nat Turner. Probably more than anything else such radicalism frightened the slaves. However much they may have admired these or Toussaint L'Ouverture and the people of Santo Domingo, the majority of bondsmen in America were confident that open revolt on their part could not be effective. Years later there would be persons who would call this attitude and conviction timidity or cowardice or natural docility, but contrary to the popular stereotype, the Negro in America has been primarily a realist, not a romanticist, and it is his realism which helped to save him from extinction. In addition to those bondsmen who could plow the straightest row, chop the most cotton, or outdo all others in wrestling, foot racing, or some similar feat, heroes also were those cautiously bold persons who "outwitted" the whites in the little things—successfully feigned sickness, or shirked hard work without getting the lash, stole a chicken or a ham, with tongue in cheek told an overseer or owner a straight-faced lie about how handsome a figure he cut in his clothes. Such heroism drew praise in the form of laughter from fellow slaves to whom the tales were told. By their choice of heroes, the slaves reveal the great role which fear, caution and conservatism played in their lives and thought.

Elijah P. Lovejoy

In late 1837, Elijah P. Lovejoy was killed by a pro-slavery mob as he attempted to defend the press of the Alton, Illinois

Observer. In editorials and mass meetings, Negroes denounced Lovejoy's murderers and raised funds for his bereaved family. Lamenting the murder, a New York group stated: "Who are guilty in this matter? Is it the poor, ignorant, sunken and abandoned wretches who consummate the work planned out by 'gentlemen of property and standing'? No! They know not what they do. But the Press, which from the commencement of the Anti-Slavery controversy, has kept alive by base misrepresentations, the worse passions of the human heart, and pointed at Abolitionists as fit subjects for the assassin's dagger . . . is guilty of this crime."[3] A number of Afro-Americans constantly have voiced the opinion that the nation's press generally has sided with "gentlemen of property and standing." Still, like most Americans, Negroes generally have kept their faith in the fourth estate, and have continued to demand a free and untrammeled press. In protest against Lovejoy's murder, the above-mentioned group also stated: "The Pulpit, . . . standing aloof from the contest and the efforts for emancipation, by putting forth its bulls of condemnation, against the efforts making for Emancipation, is guilty."[4] Here also, the failure of the white pulpit to rise up in a body against the institution of slavery, and its often seeming acquiescence in post-bellum discrimination and segregation, plus evidences of un-Christian behavior in their own segregated churches, have all combined with the general secularstic outlook of the modern age to make a number of Afro-Americans severe critics of organized religion.

William Lloyd Garrison

Little known is the fact that without Negro aid, William Lloyd Garrison's *Liberator* would not have succeeded. During its first year, this paper had approximately four hundred and fifty subscribers, of whom all but about fifty were Afro-Americans. Leaders of the race, appreciating this effort, and sensing its importance, were active in soliciting colored subscribers for Garrison, and not only did they assist him financially, but encouraged him greatly by letter and in other ways.

When, in 1839, the Abolitionist movement split because of differing opinions regarding the suffragette movement, whether to act through political channels, and Garrison's extreme criticism of organized religion, Afro-American members of the movement became divided on the same issues. James Barbadoes, William C. Nell, and William Powell were prominent among those who remained loyal to the views and methods of Garrison, while Frederick Douglass, Charles B. Ray, Christopher Rush, and Samuel Cornish seceded and formed a new abolitionist society. In 1954, Jack Abramowitz would write of "the patronizing attitude" which "many abolitionists" had held toward Negroes.[5]

Partly because he believed that the race could and should plead its own cause, Frederick Douglass started his paper *The North Star,* in Rochester, New York on December 3, 1847. In the first issue, Douglass editorialized: "We solemnly dedicate the "North Star" to the cause of our long oppressed and plundered fellow countrymen. Giving no quarter to slavery at the South, it will hold no truce with oppressors at the North."[5] Co-editor of the paper was Martin R. Delany. For thus dividing abolitionist efforts, Douglass was criticized by Garrison and others. To the criticism from his anti-slavery cohorts, Douglass stated: "It is neither a reflection on the fidelity, nor a disparagement of the ability of our friends and fellow-laborers, to assert what 'common sense affirms and only folly denies,' that the man who has *suffered the wrong* is the man to *demand redress,* the man *struck* is the man to *cry out* and that he who has *endured the cruel pangs of slavery* is the man to *advocate liberty.*"[7] Along with numerous other colored abolitionists, Douglass' life is proof that the charge that the Negro did not fight for his own freedom is wholly incorrect. Speaking before the New York anti-slavery society, September 20, 1837, the Rev. Theodore S. Wright stated: "Were it not for the fact that none can feel the lash but those who have it upon them, that none know where the chain galls but those who wear it, I would not address you."[8]

Speaking in Faneuil Hall, Boston in 1905 and taking jibes at the Booker T. Washington philosophy of compromise, Bishop Reverdy C. Ransom had nothing but praise for William Lloyd Garrison's uncompromising fight and zealous devotion to the cause of human freedom. Here Bishop Ransom assailed the compromise philosophy and told colored Americans that it was not their right but their duty to fight to eliminate all bars to equality of citizenship and opportunity, and to emancipate the nation 'from un-Christlike feelings of race hatred and the . . . bondage of prejudice." Of Garrison, Ransom said: "He put manhood above money, humanity above race, the justice of God above the justices of the Supreme Court, and conscience above the Constitution."[9]

Concerning the schism among Abolitionists, David Ruggles lamented the division within the Negro group. At a meeting of free persons in New York, September 8, 1841, he stated:

> While every man's hand is against us, our every hand is against each other. I speak plainly, because the truth will set us free. Are we not guilty of cherishing to an alarming extent, the sin of sectarian, geographical, and complexional proscription? The spirit abroad is this: Is that brother a Methodist? He is not one of us. A Baptist? He is not one of us. A Presbyterian? He is not one of us. An Episcopalian? He is not one of us. A Roman Catholic? He is not one of us. Does he live above human creeds, and enjoy the religion of the heart? He is of Beelzebub.
>
> Again, is that brother from the East? He is not of us. From the West? He is not of us. From the North? He is not one of us. From the South? He is not of us. From the Middle States? He is not of us. Is he a Foreigner? He can never be of us. But, forsooth, is that brother of a dark complexion? He is of no worth. Is he of light complexion? He is of no nation. Such, sir, are the visible lines of distinction marked by slavery for us to follow. If we hope for redemption from our present condition, we must repent, turn, and *unite* in the hallowed cause of reform.[10]

In 1840 a group of Boston Negroes wrote of the maligned Garrison: "We doubt not that the day will come, when many an emancipated slave will say of him, while weeping over his monument, 'This was my best friend and benefactor. I here bathe his tomb with the tears of that liberty, which his services and sufferings achieved for me'."[11] Even after the 1839-40 schism, those who broke with Garrison to help form the American and Foreign Anti-Slavery Society remained admirers of the man and his work. Still, his reading of the documents of Negro thought causes the present writer to feel that Afro-Americans generally have not shown the enthusiastic appreciation for the work of such men as Garrison, John Brown, Charles Sumner, and Thaddeus Stevens which one might expect.

John Brown

Five Negroes were direct participants in John Brown's famed "raid" at Harper's Ferry, Virginia. They were Shields Green, Dangerfield Newby, Sherrard Lewis Leary, Osborne P. Anderson, and John A. Copeland. Copeland escaped and later published the story of the "raid."[12] Copeland emphatically denied the charge that the slaves had not been in sympathy with Brown's effort, reported that the Afro-Americans who fell during the siege died with commendable bravery and that Brown himself stated that he was agreeably surprised at the loyalty and bravery which the slaves showed. Replying to an implication that he was involved in the conspiracy, Frederick Douglass denied any participation, but praised "the noble old hero" John Brown. Douglass denied that the fact that he was not present at the time of the raid showed him to be a coward. He never promised to be there as some charged, he stated. He gave evidence that he thought the venture "rash and wild."[13] Nonetheless, as Superintendent of the Rochester, New York Underground Railroad Station, Frederick Douglass directly aided approximately four hundred fugitives per year in their break for freedom, and there is little doubt that he was an accessory before the fact in John Brown's raid on Harper's Ferry.[14] Throughout the Civil war, a number of slaves reckoned time from the year of Brown's death.[15] One Virginia slave, who "happily" witnessed Brown's death because he had never seen a hanging before, years later did not understand what the martyr had in mind.[16] George Washington Williams said that Brown was "greater than Peter the Hermit, . . . Ignatius Loyola, . . . Oliver Cromwell,"[17] and Williams reports that by coincidence the first Negro killed in the Civil War was named John Brown.[18] Negroes showed their feelings about the "raid" through mass meetings, letters to Brown, letters to friends and newspapers, and in other ways.[19] The *Liberator* of December 16, 1859 reported that at a Massachusetts meeting one group voted endorsement and hearty approval of the spirit shown by Brown, and their regrets that he did not succeed. This group stated: "That act will do more to hasten the down-fall of slavery than the liberation of a thousand slaves," and "the memory of John Brown shall be indelibly written upon the tablets of our hearts, and . . . we will teach our children to revere his name . . . as being the greatest man in the 19th century." In the dawn of August, 1906, W. E. B. DuBois, John Hope, and other intellectuals, in organization designated as the Niagara Movement and marching in solemn procession at Harper's Ferry, found in Brown's martydom inspiration for their fight for equality of citizenship. They viewed themselves as legatees of Brown who owed him an obligation to carry the torch which he had so dramatically sustained.

Charles Sumner

Between Thaddeus Stevens and Charles Sumner, the latter has been much more honored by Afro-Americans of the late nineteenth and twentieth centuries. The 1864 National Negro Convention, held at Syracuse, New York, voted its thanks to Senator Sumner for his efforts to win political and civil equality for the race, and declared:

> The Democratic Party belongs to slavery; and the Republican Party is largely under the power of prejudice against color. While gratefully recognizing a vast difference in our favor in the character and composition of the Republican Party, and regarding the accession to power of the Democratic Party, as the heaviest calamity that could befall us in the present juncture of affairs, it cannot be disguised, that, while that party is our bitterest enemy, and is positively and actively reactionary, the Republican Party is negatively and passively so in its tendency.

At Sumner's death James Hayne Rainey of South Carolina delivered an able eulogy in the House of Representatives of the United States Congress.[20] Castigating the deceased Congressman Brooks for his celebrated assault on Sumner, R. B. Elliot said in Boston's Faneuil Hall in 1874: "My heart bows in gratitude to every man who struck a blow for the liberty of my race. But how can I fail to remember that alone, alone, of all the great leaders of our cause at Washington, Charles Sumner kept his faith to freedom, stern and true."[21] Elliot felt that Sumner saved the nation from "the fatal mistake of Mr. Lincoln's Louisiana scheme of reconstruction," and called Sumner, "the fair consummate flower of humanity, the fruit of the ages." Elliott declared that "to the colored race, he is and ever will be the great leader in political life, whose ponderous and incessant blows battered down the walls of our prison house."[22] "If others forget," Elliot declared, "thy fame shall be granted by the millions of that emancipated race whose gratitude shall be more enduring than monumental marble or brass." Elliott said: "He was a man of absolute rectitude of purpose and of life. His personal purity was perfect . . . He carried morals into politics."[23]

Since Sumner's death many Afro-Americans have not known of his mighty efforts in their behalf. It seems that the opprobrium and neglect which the condemnation of many white Americans has brought upon such men as Garrison, Brown and Sumner because of their "radicalism," has tarnished also the respect and esteem which Afro-Americans have held for them. Few, indeed, have been the biographies, novels, plays, poems, paintings, and other expressions which Americans of color have centered around these often-despised benefactors of the colored man.

CHAPTER XIII

SHADOW OF THE PLANTATION, 1865-1900

Some persons interested in the bondsmen wondered whether they could take care of themselves if emancipated. In some quarters there were doubts about the race's capacity to survive competition with other groups in a free society. As the day of emancipation drew nearer, colored abolitionists spoke repeatedly to this theme, and they berated and belittled the fear.[1] Especially did Dr. John S. Rock and Frederick Douglass point out that for years the Negro's labor often had been taking care of both himself and many southern white men.[2] Writing from St. Helena's Island, South Carolina, November 20, 1862 Charlotte Forten said of the Negroes there:

> They are eager to learn; they rejoice in their newfound freedom. It does one good to see how jubilant they are; . . . There is not a man, woman, or even child that is old enough to be sensible, that would submit to being a slave again. There is evidently a deep determination in their souls, *that* shall never be. Their hearts are full of gratitude to the Government and to the 'Yankeees.'[3]

As anyone would expect, behavior of many of the freedmen markedly revealed the effectiveness of the long years of conditioning which they had undergone, and for decades a majority of the race were fated to live in the shadow of the plantation. Some of the least desirable heritages were docility, disparagement of their race and its history, color consciousness, suspiciousness and distrust, two-facedness, lack of initiative and self-reliance, lack of foresight and industry; lack of appreciation of value of time, person, property, marital obligations, or written contracts; excessive love of titles, positions, and membership in organizations; and love of ostentation, noise, and display.[4] Of one deficiency an ex-slave said: "You now our folks just won't hang together, they won't be in no union or nothing. It's a shame."[5] The freedmen developed manias to hold the positions and to own the material goods which white Americans cherished and which had been denied them during

237

slavery. To be sure, they did not always understand either the nature or purpose of many of the things which, at a distance, they had observed whites cherishing, and the freedmen's misconception of the "right" thing to own, wear, or do sometimes made them objects of jokes and laughter. In addition to the general national culture as a source, their bondage sometimes gave an added impulse and dimension to the freedmen's desire to wear fine clothes (especially shoes and hats) and jewelry, own land, get "educated," hold a white collar job, be a homeowner, vote, hold public office, own and operate a business; given parties, banquets, dances, and dinners; hold a position at the head of some institution or organization, live in the city, spend money, have a wife and children of light complexions, aquiline noses, thin lips, and "good" hair, and similar behavior patterns which certain segments of the Negro populace have manifested.

Their experiences in slavery left ingrained in many freedmen some other attitudes and proclivities which, together with forces operating on the general populace, have been major factors in shaping their thoughts and actions. Among these are:

1. Although the lack of physical cleanliness, neatness, and orderliness to which bondage had doomed most of them caused some freedmen to revel in dirt, others were led to an especial abhorrence of all forms of untidiness. Since emancipation, great stress on cleanliness, orderliness, and neatness has been a unique characteristic of the thought pattern of many Negro teachers and parents.

2. Some Negroes accepted the negative picture of their race which had been used to justify slavery, and hence entered freedom with a strong sense of shame and a weak group and personal ego. Wanting to forget their history and race, as evidenced in such things as not "liking" chicken, watermelon, beans, grits, hominy or similar "hallmarks" of the race, and not wanting to read or see anything with a "Negro" label on it, is a form of psychological repression. Too many Negroes have shown a strong sense of personal unworthiness, which also at times has caused them to care little about their own lives, time, ballot, or rights. To rectify this attitude Negro leaders constantly have pointed to and sometimes exaggerated

the achievements of individual members of their race as well as of the group collectively.

If at one extreme race has deprived the Negro of drive, at the other it has added to the Negro's drive. When Booker Washington, Jackie Robinson, Joe Lewis, Marion Anderson, Jessie Owens, John Thomas, Oscar Robertson, or Wilt Chamberlin perform they are not just artists or athletes, and doubtless most derive a little extra ambition, drive, and determination from the fact of race. Individuals with outstanding family backgrounds often get this extra drive, ambition, and determination from their family name, but lacking family names of distinction, the factor of race often has filled this role for Negroes.

Because of the brevity, hence poverty, of their history as freemen, in their effort to unearth history of which they can be proud, some Negroes have had a tendency to make veritable mountains out of mole-hills. Irwin D. Rinder noted this in a recent study of the Negro pictorial,[6] and in his *Black Bourgeoisie*[7] E. Franklin Frazier described this as a characteristic of Negro newspapers. Other examples are numerous. One ex-slave reported that in 1872 there was a fire in which all of Clarksville, Tennessee "liked to have burned down," and "all the fire departments from Nashville came . . . only the colored fire department putt it out."[8] Both George Washington Williams and John Hope Franklin thought it worth mentioning in their histories of the race that by butting in a door with his head the Negro, Tack Sisson, became a "hero" when George Washington's colonial forces captured the English General Prescott at Newport, Rhode Island in 1777. In his discussion of the troops in World War I Franklin found it noteworthy that the overseas service of Negro stevedores "amazed" Frenchmen by the rapidity with which they could unload flour from boats. In his discussion of the services of his race on the home-front during the war, this same scholar found it noteworthy that a Negro helping to build ships broke the world's record for driving rivets.[9]

3.   Both his bondage and segregation instilled in the freedman a sense of being an outsider, which had provided impetus

to his desire to be integrated into the mainstream in all areas of human activity.

4. Not being able to strike or talk back to whites who abused them under the slave regime left many freedmen with a sense of cowardice for which they often have over-compensated by becoming bullies with an extraordinary readiness, willingness, and eagerness to do personal combat with one another.

5. Many Negroes entered freedom with a strong sense of rootlessness which has manifested itself in an unusual desire to belong. Thus Negroes have been great "joiners." Yet, partly because bondage instilled in them a strong distrust for the advantaged slave, who in freedom often became the "leader," a sizeable number of freedmen would be reluctant to join anything which was promoted and led by members of their own race.

6. In sexual promiscuity, both male and female slave found compensation for other pleasures denied them. They did not have the baffling, oppressive, and frustrating restrictions imposed on their natural sex urges with which society imprisons the cultured and sophisticated. During slavery and freedom some persons revelled in this promiscuity and others reacted strongly against it.

Although some Negroes came to share the low attitude held by some whites toward their women, many Negroes have exalted the female members of their group. As would be the case with Negro novelists of the 1865-1920 period, miscegenation was a subject of which both slaves and ex-slaves of the ante-bellum period were acutely conscious. In his 1843 exhortation to the slaves, Henry Highland Garnet several times referred to the abused treatment of slave women. At one point he thundered: "Think of the torture and disgrace of your noble mothers. Think of your wretched sisters, loving virtue and purity, as they are driven into concubinage and are exposed to the unbridled lusts of incarnate devils." Later he added: "Seq your sons murdered, and your wives, mothers and sisters doomed to prostitution. In the name of the merciful God, and by all that life is worth, let it no longer be a debatable question, whether it is better to choose liberty or death."[10] Criticizing slave patience, he added: "And worse than all, you tamely

submit while your lords tear your wives from your embraces
and defile them before your eyes. In the name of God, we ask,
are you men?" In 1849, writing from London, England to his
friend Wendell Phillips, Williams Wells Brown stated: "If the
atrocities recently practiced upon defenseless women in Austria
make the blood run cold through the veins of the human and
good throughout the civilized world, the acts committed daily
upon the slave women of America should not only cause the
blood to chill, but to stop its circulation."[11] In the 1920's the
Negro poet Andrea Razafkeriefo would say in a poem entitled
"The Negro Women":

> Were it mine to select a woman
>> As queen of the hall of fame;
> One who has fought the gamest fight
>> And climbed from the depths of shame;
> I would have to give the sceptre
>> To the lowliest of them all;
> She, who has struggled through the years,
>> With her back against the wall.
> Wronged by the men of an alien race,
>> Deserted by those of her own;
> With a prayer in her heart, a song on her lips
>> She carried the fight alone.

A number of Afro-Americans have glorified in the myth
of their perfect bodies and physiques and have believed that
their women were especially beautiful examples of these unexcelled physiques.[12]

As ever has been the case between the sexes, the female
among slaves was usually, but by no means always, more conservative than the male, ever cautioning him to mind his sassy
tongue, to work hard, believe in God, don't run away, or even
think of such things. A major reason why planters loved the
black "Auntie" or "Granny" was her loyalty and devotion,
and it is highly probable that but for her the number of plots,
revolts, and runaways among slaves would have been considerably increased. The female slaves' greater "loyalty" to the
planter implied no rejection of her own race, rather great concern for its preservation and well-being was the mainspring of
her "loyalty and devotion" to the planter class. Respecting the

odds, she urged caution and patience. Giving and preserving, healing and sustaining, ever have been the central roles of women, and it well may be that in controlling bondsmen, the female slave was as potent a force as the overseer's lash. It is she who probably first sang: "O' Stand the Storm, it won't be long, we'll anchor by and by." Woman has ever been more receptive, patient, adaptive, more psychologically elastic, and it is precisely these qualities which enabled the Negro race to survive slavery in America.

7.   Because during slavery food given them was poor in terms of quantity and quality, while such things as cakes, candies, and ham were generally denied them, many Negroes entered freedom with an unusual ambition and determination to "eat well" or "high on the hog."

8.   Some persons entered freedom with a strong impulse toward playfulness. The clowning, joking antics of the slave were an absolute necessity for his physical and spiritual survival. There is a cruel element in the fact that urbane, sophisticated jokers have made light of this playfulness which was born of one of the greatest human tragedy's short of death, chattel slavery. One of the world's leading psychiatrists, in a chapter on "Play," has indicated this great human need, particularly for the oppressed. Of play, this psychologist, Karl Menninger, writes: "play permits the opportunity for many miniature victories in compensation for the injuries inflicted by the daily wear and tear of life. This is a comfort which some egos sorely need." And:

> The most important value of this unrealistic nature of play is the opportunities that it affords for the relief of repressed aggressions. It enables us to express aggression without reality consequences; we can hurt people without really hurting them; . . . 'It is all in play.' We say that we do not really mean it, although this is not quite true. We do mean it, but we know and our victim knows that it has no dangerous consequences and he can therefore tolerate it and [usually] forgive us.[13]

The Nature of Freedom

Years after their emancipation ex-bondsmen were lamenting that they were not given clothing, food, money, or land along with their freedom. One declared: "They makes us git right off the place just like you take a old hoss and turn it loose, No money, no nothing."[14] Another said: "I don't know as I 'spected nothing from freedom, but they turned us out like a bunch of stray dogs, no homes, no clothing, no nothing, not 'nough food to last us one meal."[15] One ex-slave reported that she and her sister learned they were free one year after the Civil War, and that when they left the plantation on which they had been slaves they were completely nude. The angry mistress had hid their clothes.[16]

Freedom wrought few discernible changes in the lives of many persons. Some of those who had been well treated under bondage, or who were especially deficient in initiative and self-reliance, revealed few signs of elation and upon being notified of their freedom remained on the plantation quite content with whatever adjustment the former master contrived.[17] Bondage had robbed a sizeable number of Negroes of the courage, self-reliance, and hope which freedom demanded, and some ex-slaves doubted that they could live without the direct supervision of the former ruling class. One ex-slave reported that when bondsmen were told they were free, "some rejoiced so they shouted, but some didn't, they were sorry."[18] Another remembered:

> When freedom come, folks left home, out in the streets, crying, praying, singing, shouting, yelling, and knocking down everything. Some shot off big guns. Then come the calm. It was sad then. So many folks done dead, things tore up, and nowheres to go and nothing to eat, nothing to do. It got squally. Folks got sick, so hungry. Some folks starved nearly to death. Times got hard.[19]

Although Afro-Americans still were celebrating Emancipation Day over ninety years after the end of the great war, the latter celebrations generally lacked the fervor and enthusiasm of the first few celebrations. While the speech-making remained, the earlier parades and feasts are lacking in the celebrations of the twentieth century. One ex-slave quickly wanted to forget the race's dark past. He exclaimed—"I think it is against the race to tell about how the white people done us back in slavery. I don't want to do anything to tear down; I want to build up."[20]

In, the words of R. R. Moton emancipation, "released the Negroes' energies for self-improvement, and ambitions repressed by slavery found immediate expression in efforts toward education, the acquisition of property, and the cultivation of religion."[21] William H. Lewis declared:

Emancipation redeemed the precious promises of the Declaration of Independence. It rid the Republic of its one great inconsistency, a government of the people resting upon despotism; it rescued the ship of state from the rocks of slavery and sectionalism, and set her with sails full and chart and compass true once more upon the broad, ocean of humanity to lead the world to the haven of true human brotherhood.[22]

J. C. Price said—"The Confederacy surrendered its sword at Appomattox, but did not there surrender its convictions."[23] Of emancipation, Frederick Douglass lamented that the bondsman was set free "Without food, without shelter, without land, without money or friends."[24]

"Indeed, two nations have been born in a day," said John Mercer Langston of Emancipation, "for in the death of slavery . . . the colored American has been spoken into the new life of liberty and law; while new, other and better purposes, aspirations and feelings, have possessed and moved the soul of his fellow countrymen."[25]

In 1867 John Sella Martin said that during the Civil War the Negro "proved that he will fight, though for one I have no high eulogy to pass upon him for doing that which is the last resort of a cur that cannot run away."[26] John Mercer Langston thought that the war settled the matter of a homeland for the Negro, and that no longer would Negroes be persuaded to become expatriates as the Colonization Society had done with some. For the Negro, the war decided "that the country of his birth . . . is his country . . . With emancipation . . . comes . . . that which is dearer to the true patriot than life itself: country and home."[27] Another Negro opined before the Forty-Second congress:

The decision of the sword is conceded to be the most arbitrary of all decisions which we have on record,

and it might be added that they are written in blood
and will assuredly withstand, all corrosive arguments
to the contrary notwithstanding. The results of the
rebellion have decided some things, and, in my judgment, defined the boundaries of State rights.   Sir,
speaking of centralization, all powerful Governments
have a tendency in that direction, and those who have
not are showing this day their sad want of power to
control their internal affairs, and at the same time
exercise a salutary influence on the actions and affairs
of other nations.[28]

Emancipation ended the long-standing *modus vivendi* between
the two races which slavery had afforded, and there was now
desperate need for a new relationship to be fashioned which
would be reasonably tolerable for both. During Reconstruction,
the federal government attempted to impose a pattern of racial
equality, but for the white South this proved wholly too radical
a departure from the slave-master relationship. In a section
experiencing the abounding economic prosperity such as the
North had after the Civil War, the effort to establish equality
before the law might have had a chance, but not in the economically ruined and prostrate South. Both races long have
been criticized for their ignorance, shiftlessness, prejudices, and
superstition, but poverty has been the real nemesis of the post-
bellum South.   Race relations tend to be worse and illiteracy
and ignorance greatest in those southern states and sections
where per capita income is lowest.

Reconstruction was not only a continuation of the Civil
War, usually in cold-war form, but it saw a continuation of
the fight over the same basic issues of the status of the Negro
and state or local versus federal authority which had vexed the
nation so sorely in the eighteen thirties, forties, and fifties. To
the whites of the North and South, and to the Negro, at bottom
all of the issues were related to the question of the democratic
rights of the individual. It was their democratic rights that
white Southerners held were being violated by abolitionists and
radical Republicans, but on practically every issue the Abolitionists and radical Republicans held that not they, but the
slave-holders and segregationists were the real negators of
democracy, and throughout it all the Negro held that the white

South was indeed the enemy rather than the friend of democracy. To assume that the white South was insincere in its beliefs is to fly in the face of the bravery, tenacity, and sacrifice which it long made in defense of its beliefs. It may be doubted if anywhere a clearer example of the essential and basic problem of all democratic societies can be found, that is, the problem of reconciling equally sincere rival, and sometimes contradictory, feelings, convictions, claims, and rights. In such instances it is obvious that either compromise is effected or someone's claim to democratic treatment must be entirely ignored. Those who cannot compromise are not democrats, and in this sense democratic decisions are usually imperfect from the standpoint of all groups involved in a conflict. The, New South was in part a creature compelled to take on a certain posture. The bourgeois ideals of pragmatism and racial and political democracy were forced down the South's throat, and as is common in such matters, a part of this forced meal was regurgitated, and a part of that which remained down was not digested.

During the maelstrom of events which was the year 1865 Negroes North and South met to consider their condition and push for means to improve it. Few large cities of either section were without such meetings by Negroes. Of the key political events of the year, perhaps R. B. Elliott voiced the sentiment of most Negroes when he called Andrew Johnson's efforts "ill-advised."[29] Bishop W. T. Vernon felt in 1905 that Radical Reconstruction was necessary if the Negro was not to lose his freedom by being thrown on the "mercy of his oppressors."[30]

In the second decade of the 20th century Harvard-trained Negro lawyer Archibald Grimké would view the passage of the 13th, 14th, and 15th amendments as acts inspired by the North's desire to erect "a solid wall of Negro votes" between itself and the danger of a return of the South to political power.[31] Grimké declared that during Reconstruction the North "considering mainly it's own and not the Negro's necessities at this crisis, . . . gave the peculiar wants of the Negro beyond that of the ballot but scant attention." Deploring that more was not done by the federal government for his race, Grimké said that in addition to the ballot the freedmen needed the "unfaltering care and guardianship," of the federal government during "the whole of their transition from slavery to citizenship."[32] Retrospecting on the amendments, Kelly Miller said—"I watch the Congress as it adds to the Constitution new words, which make the document a character of liberty indeed."[33]

Some ex-bondsmen felt that emancipation meant freedom from certain types of work. Some refused to perform domestic services in the belief that to do such was a stigma reminiscent of their former status. "Some would work for one man and not another."[34] Although federal troops and officials in the South were to some degree responsible for the freedman's attitude that he was a privileged person, it required no great degree of intelligence for all freedmen to see that they were the central theme of the war and Reconstruction, or that against the federal might aligned on their side white Southerners had little immediate chance. This realization accounts for much of the arrogance, pride and conceit which some freedmen manifested. There is evidence that some freedmen did not properly understand the tentative and limited nature of aid provided by the Freedmen's Bureau. Often these persons actually expected to receive forty acres and a mule, and some expected free rations to be provided *ad infinitum*. Some whites felt that the aid provided by the Freedmen's Bureau was the main reason why some Negroes were reluctant to enter into work agreements.[35] Especially were towns and cities centers of idleness, vice, disease and death.

Most of the freedmen remained in the economic pursuits which had been their lot under slavery. The comparative few who were skilled craftsmen continued to ply their trades while the vast majority remained in agriculture. So strong was the hold of agriculture on the freedmen that many were long convinced that their best future lay in eternally husbanding the soil. There were those, however, who were convinced that any type of work with the hands was degrading, and these persons often spared no sacrifice that their children might gain enough education to enter one of the professions.

While most freedmen readily acquired that love of money which has been such a pronounced characteristic of American society, many had little idea as to the best ways of spending the money which they acquired. Long deprivation had given them an inordinate love of frills and genuine necessities were sometimes slighted in order that needless gloves, hats, kerchiefs, spats, watches, rings, canned meats, candies, alcohol, and similar items might be purchased. While some were short-sighted, and this was why they failed to save for a rainy day, because of their small earnings many believed that to attempt to save would not be worth the effort.

Freedmen preferred wages over the share-crop system but the cash shortage in the South soon forced most of them into the latter. Because many knew that the end of the year would find them still in debt, the share cropping system deprived them of initiative and hope. Some consciously over-purchased on their accounts at the general store with the conviction that, if they could not get ahead, at least they might as well live in as satisfying a manner as possible. Roscoe Conkling Bruce's description of share-cropping in 1905 was true from the beginning. Bruce declared:

> Idle a large part of the year, burdened with no particular responsibility, a member of no particular community with position and reputation to make or sustain, without a home or even a fixed abode, accessible to few of the incentives to probity and thrift and progress that wholesome family life exerts, exposed to the myriad temptations of careless roving—— the black farm hand presents a very grave problem.[36]

A portion, but by no means all, of the share-croppers conviction that he was always cheated when "reckoning time" came was due to the suspiciousness engendered by his own illiteracy.

Freedmen often refused to work on plantations which kept the overseer and gang system of work. Some planters found it necessary to change the title of the overseer to superintendent or to break up their estates into several small farms. The antipathy held by freedmen toward working in large groups was a factor in the spread of share-cropping. For some time after emancipation some freedmen had an aversion to the cultivation of cotton. In some sections they destroyed gins in an effort to make certain that cotton cultivation would not be resumed.[37] Many had so much of forced labor under bondage until they never again wanted to perform the same tasks, and this aversion was sometimes applied to the foods or some items of clothing which had been their common fare under slavery.[38] Some freedmen had little respect for the work contracts they signed. Used to a regime under which all of their serious and important obligations were fixed by oral expressions, they were poorly equipped for life in a society of written laws.

When Congress in 1866 placed the public lands of Alabama, Arkansas, Florida, Mississippi and Missouri on sale, several thousand families of freedmen found it possible to make purchases. Some of the freedmen early realized the value of cooperative efforts and in a few urban areas this attitude manifested itself in the establishment of building and loan associations.[39] In conformity with the trend evident in efforts of the Granger Movement and the Patrons of Husbandry some freedmen launched cooperative stores, brickyards, farms, and other enterprises.

Reminiscences

Some freedmen looked back at the days of slavery with deep nostalgia. One freedman said—"Yes, the South is a beautiful place; it's so pretty."[40] Another reported: "Where I was born, it is a mighty fine country, and they was awful mean to the colored people in that country."[41] Significant in the life of the slave was ringing bells and resounding horns. One ex-slave reported the beginning of a typical day on the plantation with eloquent nostalgia. He stated:

> When the day begin to crack, the whole plantation break out with all kinds of noise you hear.
>
> Come the daybreak you hear the guinea fowls potracking down at the edge of the woods lot, and then the roosters all start up round the barn, and the ducks finally wake up and jine. You can smell the sowbelly frying down at the cabins in the row, to go with the hoecake and the buttermilk.
>
> Then pretty soon the wind rise a little, and you can hear a bell donging way on some plantation a mile or two off, and then more bells at other places and maybe a horn, and pretty soon yonder go Old Master's old ram horn with a long toot and then some short toots, and here come the overseer down the row of cabins, hollering right and left, and pick-

ing the ham out of his teeth with a long shiny goose-
quill pick.[42]

Other ex-slaves had similar memories. One remembered:

> It wasn't very fancy at the big house, but it was
> mighty pretty just the same, with the gray moss hang-
> ing from the big trees, and the cool green grass all
> over the yard, and I can shut my old eyes and see it
> just like it was before the war come along and bust
> it up.

> I can see Old Master setting out under a big tree,
> smoking one of his long cheroots his tobacco nigger
> made by hand, and fanning hisself with his big wide
> hat another nigger platted outen young inside corn
> shucks for him, and I can hear him holler at a big
> bunch of white geese what's gitting in his flower
> beds and see em string off behind the old gander
> toward the big road.[43]

Contrasting slavery with freedom one aged ex-bondsman reported in the 1940's—"We ain't got a bit more show now than
we has then. Let me tell you, child, black folks, black men
ain't got a bit more show with white folks than a rabbit sitting
before a gun. Just to see how they treat us—we ain't got no
law; we ain't got a chance."[44] Another said: "Sometimes I
think we was a little better off than now. Then we didn't have
to worry about nothing to eat and wear."[45] Still another opined
of such things as corn-shuckings and slave dances, "Sometimes
I think a nigger was happier then than he is now."[46] Some ex-
bondsmen felt that Negroes "stuck together" better as slaves,
than they did in freedom.[47] Some felt that because they had
such hard times together in bondage, "colored people oughtn't
be so mean to one another."[48] Yet some Negro leaders felt
it necessary to inveigh against the fact that during reconstruction pride in their new-found status and seeming importance in national and local affairs sometimes carried the attitudes and behavior of freedmen to unseemly heights of arrogance. They also cautioned against taking excessive pride in
one's skin-color, appearance, or education.[49] At emancipation
approximately ninety per cent of the race was illiterate, and
by the turn of the century, approximately one-half were still
adjudged illiterate. Nineteen hundred thirty saw this figure

reduced to three-eighths.[50] By 1900 the nation's colored population had doubled.

At emancipation, by the thousands Negroes left their plantation quarters to find a new job or lost relatives, visit the nearest town or army camp, or sometimes just to travel, more or less aimlessly. Problems of morality, health, food supply, housing, and medical care were created by this sudden and unplanned emancipation of over three million persons. It cannot be said with complete truthfulness that these were largely aimless, childish vagrants who needed the restraints which the post-war Black Codes attempted to provide. Often they had very legitimate reasons for being on the move. If hundreds of freedmen remained on the plantations, it was not always out of love for the former master. Oftentimes this seemed to be the only way to assure the necessities of life. Much, though by no means all, of the old paternal relationship between black and white was gone. One observer wrote of the planter in this period that, "He [the planter] finds it impossible to come near enough to them [freedmen] to win and hold their attention, for child and parent alike shrink from association with him. His advances are not cordially met."[51]

Land Hunger and Family Life

Negroes had long shown considerable interest in acquiring western lands. Before 1865, on the basis of their lack of citizenship, efforts were made to deny their land claims. The 1864 National Negro Convention, meeting in Syracuse, New York had declared: "We claim the right to be heard in the halls of Congress; and we claim our fair share of the public domain, whether acquired by purchase, by treaty, confiscation, or military conquest."[52] After emancipation this agitation for land continued. In an 1869 petition to Congress the Negro National Labor Union stated that the dire economic plight of the freedman left him in no position to fight to protect his political and civil rights. "The freedom of the ballot is thus sought to be subdued by the necessity for bread," it was averred. "The true and immediately practicable remedy," which they saw for this defenseless position was "in making a fair proportion of the laborers themselves landowners. [For] this will place colored agricultural labor beyond the absolute control of artificial or political cause, by lessening the amount of labor *for hire,* and increasing at the same time the demand for that class of laborers."[55] The *AME Church Review* declared in July, 1887:

> Life at best is a serious problem with the Negro. Throughout the land he is the football of caste, the servant of mercenary capital. Whatever therefore, lifts him above his present level is to be eagerly embraced and fostered. Every true man in the race should bestir himself and organize land purchase associations; the cry should be heard from one end of the country to the other, 'Land for the landless Negroes.'

The ideal of thrift taught freedmen, especially by the New England missionaries, sometimes bore commendable fruit. At the same time the puritanical outlook which many Negroes had earlier absorbed from Christian teachings was enforced by the puritanical bent of many of these missionaries. As slaves, with quarters devoid of floors, windows, or beds, and usually living overcrowded, often with an average of five persons per cabin, it is not difficult to see the effect on health, or the later strong desire to become homeowners which some freedmen manifested.

Proof that some Afro-Americans were able to view the plight of their race in a larger setting is found in the views of Pennsylvania-born Richard T. Greener, educator, lawyer, and first Negro graduate of Harvard University. In 1874 Greener declared before the American Social Science Association:

> The land question is no new one, at the present time there are difficulties in England, Ireland, Scotland, and India with regard to this tenure of land; and when we come to study them, we find many cases analogous to those in America. There are remarkable coincidences . . . which show conclusions that injustice and wrong, and disregard of rights and abuses of privilege are not confined to any one country, race or class. As a rule, capital takes advantage of the needs of labor.[54]

Some colored Americans have felt since emancipation that once northern and southern whites realize the true economic potential of their race, both as producer and consumer, they could not persist in their prejudice and discrimination. Legislation and other efforts to keep them down they have felt, also keeps the white man down. Especially did Booker Washington repeat this theme over and over again. Writing in July, 1887, William H. Thomas said: "The financial world has no conception of the wealth which would grow out of the acquisition of land by Negroes." Even in the ante-bellum period colored abolitionists often were wont to speak of the economic benefits which would come to the nation as a result of emancipation and the elevation of the slave.

In his 1913 novel, *The Conquest's: The Story of a Negro Pioneer,* Oscar Micheaux proposed migration of freedmen to the West as a means of improving race relations in the South. Micheaux also believed that colored Americans were over-looking great economic opportunities in the West.

As the period since 1865 has found the Afro-American trying to establish himself as a businessman and citizen, it also has found him struggling to establish a stable family. His problems in this regard, like those of all Americans, have been further compounded by the rapid urbanization, industrialization, and individualization of Occidental society, but the colored American has had the added disadvantage that the slave family was largely a matriarchiate and was highly unstable.[55]

To some married ex-bondsmen freedom meant release from family obligations. The weak marital bonds which slavery had allowed the Negro all too often broke when freedom came and in their new-found mobility a number of males deserted their wives and children. For a long time common-law marriages, desertions, bigamy, and bastardy would be sins peculiarly prevalent among Negroes. Yet there were exceptions aplenty, and many freedmen took unusual pride in contracting legal marriages and supporting their families. Too, some took especial pride in exercising the domestic authority which often had been denied them under slavery. With the less sensitive or maladjusted males this delight too often took the form of violent beatings inflicted on both wives and children, and the latter too frequently left home in early adolescence to lead independent lives. This tendency was aggravated by the fact that the little formal education acquired by the young sometimes caused them to be contemptuous of their usually illiterate parents.

That not all freedmen were childish spend-thrifts is attested by the fact that by 1900 many had become property owners. When the Freedmen's Savings Bank and Trust Company failed, its 61,131 depositors—almost all of whom were Negroes, had deposited over three million dollars in savings in the bank. The Panic of 1873, and the conditions which produced it, wiped out the Freedmen's Bank which closed during the summer of 1874. Repr. J. H. Rainey of S. C., declared that business conditions and not fraud or mismanagement caused the failure of the Bank.[56] Although the failure of this bank, plus too frequent failures of banks operated by white Americans, shook the faith of many freedmen in "money houses." Yet Negro banks continued to appear in the last decade of the century and after, and by 1948 fourteen Negro banks in the United States had total assets of over thirty-one millions of dollars.[57] During the post-bellum period fraternal associations continued to grow among Negroes. Like those formed during the pre-war period, their growth was rooted in the abject poverty of the race. In addition to the factors which have made secret and fraternal societies everywhere attractive to all people, the loneliness, isolation and frustration of Negro life were contributors to this phenomenon. Especially attractive were the burial insurance features of these organizations. Because they had been buried "like dogs" during slavery, having a "big" funeral is said to have been a peculiar desire of the freedmen.

Reconstruction, Political and Social

Despite the existence of the Thirteenth Amendment, in 1865 Frederick Douglass fought to keep the American Anti-Slavery Society from disbanding. "What advantage is a provision like this Amendment to the black man," he asked, "if the legislature of any State can tomorrow declare that no black man's testimony shall be received in a court of law?"[58] In this speech, delivered before the 32nd Annual Convention of the Society, Douglass asserted: "While the Legislatures of the South retain the right to pass laws making any discrimination between black and white, slavery still lives there." Thus he wanted the Society to maintain an active organization until the civil and political equality of his race was assured. He asked the members, before voting to disband, to "wait and see what new form the old monster will assume, and in what new skin this old snake will come forth." "Where shall the black man look for support, my friends, if the American Anti-Slavery Society fails him?" he asked.[59] Beginning as early as the so-called "Bargain of 1877," events of practically every year made it clearer to Afro-Americans that many white liberals had tired of the race issue.

That Radical Reconstruction represented no period of Negro domination in the South is rapidly gaining acceptance today. For a long time, however, this propaganda was chanted as an excuse for the fraud, violence, and intimidation which was inflicted on the Negro people. Even the view that the Radical Reconstruction legislators were generally ignorant, incompetent, and crooked is losing ground. The contemporary accounts by critics who can be considered in any way objective reveal that most of the participants were intelligent and well-mannered. Much of the increase of governmental expense which the southern states saw has been traced to the provision of new and necessary social services. For the first time the South acquired a state supported public school system, modern criminal code, universal manhood suffrage, internal improvements, ended Jim Crow legislation, and acquired eleemosynary institutions. Numerous large estates were broken up and came into the hands of the poor. Of the graft and corruption which existed, it is generally agreed today that the colored man was neither the primary instigator nor benefactor, nor did the South suffer from these evils during this period much more than New York did from the Tweed Ring, St. Louis the Whiskey Ring, or many other cities and states as well as the federal government. Immigration, the newness of industry and urbanization, as well as the malign effects of four years of fratricidal warfare brought corrupt machine government to practically every section of the nation. Through Credit Mobilier, the Jay Gould instituted "Black Friday," and similar episodes, the evils of corruption reached right up to the cabinet of President Grant.

From 1869-1877 a total of 14 Negroes served as members of the House of Representatives.[60] Two, Hiram R. Revels and

Blanche K. Bruce, both of Mississippi, served as members of the Senate. The longest period served in Congress was from 1875 to 1887 by Robert B. Smalls of South Carolina. Little but praise has been said of the service of these men.

In addition to the American tradition and the temper of the times, a major factor in the equalitarian drive of freedmen during the immediate post-Civil War period was that a goodly number of Negro spokesmen in the South were highly sensitive mullatoes or else were either born in the North or had spent considerable time there. The latter was the case with such men as P. B. S. Pinchback of Louisiana and Representative James Thomas Rapier of Alabama.

The political leaders of the race stood practically unanimous in their support of universal suffrage. Samuel D. Smith says that in Alabama during the Radical Reconstruction era Negroes "furnished 90,000 votes in the Republican party, but the whites with only 10,000 votes, held all major offices."[61] A very similar situation existed in Georgia and other states, with the exception of South Carolina. Defending his race against the charge of "Negro domination," Rep. Joseph H. Rainey of South Carolina said:

> I ask this House, I ask the country . . . I ask Democrats, I ask Republicans whether the Negroes have presumed to take improper advantage of the majority they hold in that State by disregarding the interest of the minority? They have not. Our convention which met in 1868, and in which the Negroes were in a large majority, did not pass any proscriptive or disfranchising acts, but adopted a liberal constitution, securing alike equal rights to all citizens, white and black, male and female, as far as possible: Mark you, we did not discriminate, although we had a majority.[62]

The freedmen showed a commendable realism in yielding the political initiative to the whites who were more experienced in such matters, yet, in some instances their trust was betrayed by unscrupulous men. J. C. Price denied that complete enfranchisement of freedmen would lead to control of political affairs by the most ignorant and base persons. Price pointed out that although the majority of southern whites had full enfranchisement in the 80's and 90's, control of political affairs was still in the hands of the most enlightened whites. "The Negroes believed in an intelligent administration of govern_ment as much as anybody else," he declared. "The Negroes enter protest—to the presumption that all the intelligence or capability is in one party, or one race."[63] Price continued:

> The Negro is not seeking supremacy through the ballot, he is not after power, but protection—not con_trol, but right. He has no desire to rule the whites, but he does insist that the whites shall rule him only on the principle of humanity and justice. The Negro is after friends, more than supremacy. If he does not find them in one set of men, he seeks them in another, if not in one section of the country, he looks to another.[64]

If intelligent, forceful, and sound presentation of one's case before Congress were all that was needed, the Negro would have been granted full civil rights during Reconstruction, never again to lose them. The greatest concern of Negro politicians during Reconstruction was with education, civil rights, and promoting racial and sectional concord. Some backed legisla_tion to benefit directly the cities or states from which they came. While in general Negro congressmen were regarded as race heroes, this opinion was by no means unanimous. Northern Negroes especially were sometimes critical of the ineffectiveness of the congressmen and sometimes implied that they were quasi-ignorant men. Even among southern Negroes they had opposi_tion and critics, sometimes on charges that they were selfish and corrupt, sometimes that they were too friendly with whites, and sometimes on the ground that they were mulattoes.

Afro-Americans have tended to believe that, in the long run, federal legislation improves race relations. They have never believed that legislation guaranteeing civil rights leads to social equality and inter-marriage. They have felt that the cause of justice and the national ideals demand that there be only one legal class of citizenship, and that social equality is an indi_vidual, not a group matter.

A major source of the myth that Negro politicians of the Reconstruction era were mostly corrupt is to be found in the investigation weapons used by the Democracy to justify the

Klu Kluxism, fraud, bribery, anti-democratic legislation, and other ugly aspects of its program. While not all charges were fabricated, exaggeration was rampant. Too, Samuel D. Smith in his assertion that every Negro Congressman of the 1869-1901 era "was a Negro first, and a Republican next," appears to be incorrect.[65]

Negroes generally approved of the use of federal troops in the South, but there were those opposed to this. Jeremiah Haralson of Alabama opposed the use of troops in 1876. "Every blue jacket sent to the South," he declared, "makes Democratic votes." Like William H. Councill and Booker T. Washington of the same state, Haralson was intensely devoted to racial peace in the South.

Negro Congressmen of this period were stout in defense of all civil rights for their race but they usually took pains to point out that social equality was not their object. J. H. R. Rainey declared that "social equality consists in congeniality of feeling, a reciprocity of sentiment and mutual social recognition among men which is graded according to desire and taste and not by any known or possible law."[66]

When Congress was debating its first Civil Rights bill, several southern states already had in their own constitutions and laws similar provisions as those set forth in the proposed federal legislation, but the state constitutions and laws had been enacted when Republicans were in power in southern states, and often were not being sustained. Debate over this civil rights bill was long and acrimonious. Speaking to the 43rd Congress in defense of the Civil Rights Bill, John R. Lynch stated that he did not feel that either the state-supremacy or central-government supremacy argument had been settled by the war. He hoped, however, that the war resulted in "acceptance of what may be called a medium between these two extremes."[67]

The question of social equality between the races became a big issue for the first time during the debates over the civil rights laws. Lynch gave the charactristic attitude of Afro-Americans on this topic, "I have never believed for a moment," he declared, "that social equality could be brought about even between persons of the same race. I have always believed that social distinctions existed among white persons the same as among colored people."[68]

J. C. Price declared:

> The Negro does not desire and does not seek social equality with the whites. Such an equality does not obtain among the Negroes themselves . . . The Negro in his own race has the rare privilege of choosing any color, from the snowy white to the ebony black.
>
> The colored man . . . does not seek a seat in a car free from tobacco smoke and juice, or profanity and obscenity, or ask for a meal in a decent dining room because he desires to be in the society of whites, but because he desires comfort, protection, and nourishment.[69]

Lynch tore into a North Carolina Congressman for his manifestations of race prejudice, and praised the state of Mississippi for its "better" race relations. In the next Congress, Lynch stated:

> I deny that race prejudice has anything to do with fraud and violence at elections in the Southern States. There is not half as much race feeling at the South as many of the Bourbon leaders in that section would have the country believe. The antagonisms that exist there today are not based on antipathies of race, but they are based on antipathies of parties. The race feeling was strong shortly after the war, but it has now very nearly died out. Colored men are not now persecuted in the section from which I come on account of their color, but Republicans, white and colored, are persecuted in many localities on account of their politics. More colored than white men are thus persecuted, simply because they constitute in larger numbers the opposition to the Democratic party.

Richard H. Cain declared of his race:

> We do not want any discriminations. I do not ask legislation for the colored people of this country that is not applied to the white people. All that we ask is equal laws, equal legislation, and equal rights throughout the length and breadth of this land.[70]

Lynch referred to the 14th and 15th amendments and said that those who argued the unconstitutionality of the bill "seem to forget that the Constitution . . . is not in every respect the Constitution it was" before the War.[71] He denied that the recent supreme court decision in the Slaughterhouse cases ruled out federal action on civil rights.[72] In the 1950s the United States Supreme Court would vindicate his argument. Lynch ended his lengthy speech on this bill thus:

The duty of the law-maker is to know no race, no color, no religion, no nationality, except to prevent distinctions on any of these grounds, so far as the law is concerned.

Mr. Speaker, if this unjust discrimination is to be longer tolerated by the American people, which I do not, cannot, and will not believe until I am forced to do so, then I can only say with sorrow and regret that our boasted civilization is a fraud; our republican institutions a failure; our social system a disgrace; and our religion a complete hypocrisy. . . . but still I have an abiding confidence in the patriotism of this people, . . . I hope that I will not be deceived. I love the land that gave me birth; I love the Stars and Stripes. This country is where I intend to live, where I expect to die. To preserve the honor of the national flag and to maintain perpetually the Union of the States hundreds, and I may say thousands, of noble, brave, and true-hearted colored men have fought, bled, and died. And now, Mr. Speaker, I ask, can it be possible that the flag under which they fought is to be a shield and a protection to all races and classes of persons except the colored race? God forbid!

My honest opinion is that the passage of this bill will have a tendency to harmonize the apparently conflicting interests between the two races. It will have a tendency to bring them more closely together in all matters pertaining to their public and political duties. It will cause them to know, appreciate and respect the rights and privileges of each other more than ever before.[73]

With every advance in civil rights, Afro-American spokesmen or leaders have been concerned that the race would exercise their new won freedoms with dignity and proper humility. In his defense of the Civil Rights bill, John R. Lynch had said: "Let us confer upon the colored citizens equal rights, and . . . they will exercise their rights with moderation and with wise discretion."[74] Almost a century later, when Negroes of Mont_ gomery, Alabama won the right to sit in any vacant seat on city busses, the Reverend Martin Luther King challenged the Negroes to exercise this newly won right with discretion and dignity. Freedmen often told white southerners how, as slaves during the Civil War, they had faithfully cared for the sections' white wives and children. In the minds of many freedmen this left the white South obligated to treat their race with fairness and justice. Richard H. Cain said:

> I have voted in this House with a free heart to declare Universal amnesty. Inasmuch as general amnesty has been proclaimed, I would hardly have expected there would be any objection on this floor to the civil-rights bill, giving to all men the equal rights of citizens. There should be no more contest. Amnesty and civil rights should be together. Gentlemen on the other side will admit that we have been faithful; and now, when we propose to bury the hatchet, let's shake hands upon this measure of justice; and if heretofore we have been enemies, let us be friends now and forever.[75]

Speaking in defense of the Civil Rights bill before the 44th Congress, Canadian - educated Congressman James T. Rapier of Alabama declared:

> I am told that I must respect the prejudices of others . . . no one respects reasonable and intelligent prejudice more than I . . . But how can I have respect for the prejudices that prompt a man to turn up his nose at the males of a certain race, while at the same time he has a fondness for the females of the same race to the extent of cohabitation?

Of the contradictions in American thought, Rapier further stated—"Here a drunken white man is not equal to a drunken Negro . . ., but superior to the most sober and orderly one; here an ignorant white man is not only the equal of an un-lettered Negro, but is superior to the most cultivated." Rapier continued:

Mr. Speaker, nothing short of a complete ac-
knowledgement of my manhood will satisfy me. I
have no compromises to make and shall unwillingly
accept any . . . I cannot willingly accept anything
less than my full measure of rights as a man, because
I am unwilling to present myself as a candidate for
the brand of inferiority, which will be as plain and
lasting as the mark of Cain. If I am to be thus
branded, the country must do it against my solemn
protest.[76]

Of Southern whites Rapier said: "They question the constitutionality of every measure that is advanced to ameliorate the
condition of the colored man," and Rapier continued:

Just think that the law recognizes my right to secure
to me any accommodations whatever while traveling
here to discharge my duties as a Representative of a
large and wealthy constituency. Here I am the peer
of the proudest, but on a steamboat or car I am not
equal to the most degraded. Is not this most anomalous and ridiculous?

And: "I affirm, without fear of contradiction, that any white
ex-convict . . . may start with me today to Montgomery,
that all the way down he will be treated as a gentleman, while
I will be treated as the convict. He will be allowed a berth in
a sleeping-car with all its comforts, while I will be forced into
a dirty, rough box with the drunkards, apple-sellers, railroad
hands, and next to any dead that may be in transit, regardless
of how far decomposition may have progressed. Tender, pure,
intelligent young ladies are forced to travel in this way if
they are guilty of the crime of color, the only unpardonably
sin known in our Christian and Bible land . . ." "Now . . .
is there a man upon this floor who is so heartless, whose breast
is so void of the better feelings, as to say that this brutal custom
needs no regulation? I hold that it does and that Congress is
the body to regulate it. Authority for its action is found not
only in the fourteenth amendment to the Constitution, but by
virtue of that amendment . . . authority is found in Article
4, section 2, of the Federal Constitution, which declares in
positive language 'that the citizens of each state shall have the
same right as the citizens of the several States." "Congress,"

Rapier said, "is the law-making power of the General Government, whose duty is to see that there be no unjust and odious discriminations made between its citizens." This, he said, is why "I come to the national, instead of going to the local Legislatures for relief."[77] Richard H. Cain also asked for equality of rights for Negroes in all public places and on public conveyances.[78]

In an age of strict party loyalty Negro Congressmen generally voted with their party. Owing perhaps to their staunch party loyalty Representatives Benjaim S. Turner of Alabama and R. H. Smalls of South Carolina both opposed civil service reform. Although throughout his career he remained a party regular, Blanche K. Bruce denounced both Grant and the Republican party because of their refusal to seat P. B. S. Pinchback.

Frederick Douglass and John Mercer Langston were political enemies. Langston, sometimes able lawyer, Vice-President of Howard University, and President of Virginia State College, was born of an ex-slave mother and her white owner. The latter had him educated in Ohio. Langston became an outstanding abolitionist and also held the office of Inspector-General of the Freedmen's Bureau. Douglass and Langston became rivals for primacy in Negro leadership. When Langston won a congressional seat from Virginia in late 1890, he predicted that soon Negroes would sit in the United States Senate again and ultimately would hold the Presidency of the nation.[79]

The End of Reconstruction

Some colored Americans have believed that Radical Reconstruction was unfair to the South, but probably most have believed that the section deserved the disfranchisement and military rule which was imposed on it by the Act of March, 1867. Too, Negro writers have tended to minimize the corruption and other evils which then plagued the section. "It is significant," R. R. Moton has observed, "that during the reconstruction period, when the Negro was represented both in the state legislatures and the national congress, there were no disabling laws passed against the white men and no legislation enacted specially favoring the Negro."[80] This is a point of which Negroes have been especially proud.

As the "Carpetbag"—Negro—"Scalawag" coalition began to assert its influence, the white South turned to thoughts and deeds of violence. Rioting was particularly vicious in Memphis, Tennessee, in early May of 1866 and in New Orleans, Louisiana, on July 30 of the same year. In the majority of these and similar assaults on the person and property of the freedmen, there was surprisingly little meeting of force with force. To be sure whites were wounded and killed in almost every major outbreak, but the preponderance of casualities was almost always on the side of the colored man. When it is considered that the lynching and pillage usually represented an invasion of a colored community, this failure of the freedmen to organize and effectively meet this violence is all the more interesting. Perhaps their acceptance of the American creed plus the long years of indoctrination to the effect that no Negro should do violence to the person of any white man, whatever the circumstances, and that all violence is sinful, caused this reaction. During the Reconstruction period there were a few instances in which Negroes lynched whites, of less serious instances of mob action by Negroes, and on occasions Negroes carried arms to the polls.[81] Doubtless another reason why freedmen failed to fight violence with violence is the fact that many of them were without guns. A major objective of the Klan was to seize and confiscate all guns found in the possession of Negroes.

As Reconstruction was a great traumatic experience for southern whites, its overthrow was no less of a trauma for the Negro. On one aspect of the end of Reconstruction, Boston-born and England-educated Robert Brown Elliott, who served in the 42nd Congress admitted the soundness of the dual citizenship annunciation by the Supreme Court, yet he claimed that for a state to deny him "the right to enjoy the common public conveniences of travel on public highways, of rest and refreshment at public inns, of education in public schools, of burial in public cemeteries" is "a denial to me of the equal protection of the laws." "No matter, therefore," Elliot continued, "whether his rights are held under the United States or under his particular State, [the Negro] is equally protected by this Fourteenth Amendment. He is always and everywhere entitled to the equal protection of the laws. All discrimination is forbidden; and while the rights of citizens of a State as such are not defined or conferred by the Constitution of the United States, yet all discrimination, all denial of equality before the law, all denial of the equal protection of the laws, whether State or before national laws, is forbidden."[82]

John Mercer Langston declared in 1877 that Radical Reconstruction was "a failure" and must end, and "some new and, if possible, better method . . . tried. This, the welfare of those immediately concerned, as well as the general good of the country in all its material and moral interests, requires."[83] Here almost twenty years before Booker T. Washington's famed "Atlanta Compromise" speech, is the same note and spirit of retreat and compromise for which Washington was to be so vehemently denunciated during the opening years of the twentieth century. Langston regretted the use of troops in the South and asked that this means not be used again to settle disputes. The use of troops, he declared, was "exciting, irritating, and exasperating" to white Southerners. Langson denounced Radical Reconstruction and gave a number of reasons for its demise. Among these were: "The unhandsome and obnoxious conduct of political adventurers; the unnecessary and too constant political excitement and agitation of the people, the injudicious and oppressive acts of Republican legislatures and officials, the former composed, frequently, largely of ignorant, unqualified, and impecunious persons, white and black, and the latter frequently not only incompetent but offensive and exasperating in their conduct; the too frequent interference by the National Government in State affairs with the Army, seemingly for party purposes; the general bad temper and purpose of the native dominant white class."[84]Langston was eager to see the South returned to local control, and he apparently believed and hoped that somehow this could be done and Negro equality made a reality at the same time.

Although at the time few Negroes expressed lament at the Bargain of 1877, in the twentieth century Archibald Grimké, W. E. B. DuBois, Rayford W. Logan and others would scathingly denounce the laissez-faire attitude toward the race problem which the Bargain signaled. Giving his estimation of how and why this turn of events ensued, Grimké declared of the North:

> The clamor of all its million-wheeled industry and prosperity was for peace. 'Let us have peace,' said Grant, and 'let us have peace' blew forthwith and in deafening union, all the big and little whistles of all the big and little factories and locomotives, and steamships from Maine to California. Every pen of merchant and editor scratched paper to the same mad tune. The pulpit and the platform of the land cooed their Cuckoo-song in honor of those piping times of peace. The loud noise of chinking coin pouring into vaults like coal into bins, drowned the agonizing cry of the forgotten and long-suffering Negro. Deserting him in 1876, the North, stretching across the bloody chasm its two greedy, commercial hands, grasped the ensanguined ones of the South, and repeated, 'let us have peace.' Little did the Northern people and the government reck then or now that at the bottom of that bloody chasm lay their faithful black friends.[35]

Retrospecting about the Negro and the end of Radical Reconstruction, Kelly Miller later wrote: "I see him thrust down from the high seat of political power, by fraud and force, while the nation looks on in sinister silence and acquiescent guilt."[36]

As Sojourner Truth and Harriet Tubman had been active in the fight against slavery, so Negro women were often quite active in arousing their husbands and relatives to oppose the discrimination and oppression which followed the overthrow of Radical Reconstruction. Failing in efforts to secure equality of treatment within the South, many women urged their families to emigrate. The high incidence of violence and threats of violence attendant upon the effort has caused a number of Negroes to feel that the fight to exercise their political and civil rights is not worth the price. During the early years of Radical Reconstruction the number of persons who held this conviction was small, but as violence and opposition increased to a point constituting an undeclared civil war against the legally constituted authority, and as the federal government slowly retreated from its militant support of Negro rights, "Uncle Tomism" in the race increased. For this and other reasons, a number of colored southerners became supporters of the Democratic party.

Emigration and Immigration

The first great Negro exodus from the South ·was Free Negroes of the early 19th century who fled the section after cotton became King and Garrisonianism and the Nat Turner and Vesey acts evoked strong repressive measures in the South. This exodus helped to make the "Negro problem" national instead of sectional.

The exodus of freedmen from the South which started in the 1870's, and had Kansas, Oklahoma, and such northern cities as Chicago, Philadelphia, and New York as primary targets, was due to such factors as the overthrow of Radical Reconstruction, lack of civil, educational, and political opportunities, peonage, and crop failure. Too, the post-Civil War wanderlust was doubtless one cause of the exodus of 1879. Here were colored 49'ers, or the Africaander Trekkers, or the thousands of Conestoga-wagoned white Americans who crossed or conquered the plains. In some aspects the Negroes who went West were drawn by the same forces which lured American whites. Among the causes of the exodus was a speech made in the Senate during the winter of the previous year by Senator Windom. Frederick Douglass called this speech "a powerful stimulus to this emigration."[87] Evils in, and blind-alley nature of share-cropping, the crop lien system, poor educational facilities, violence and intimidation, unequal application of the criminal code, fear that the return to power of the "Slavocracy" meant the virtual reenslavement of the Negro, the low price of cotton, charging of excessive rent and prices for credit, food, clothing, and land, and the insecurity of life and property, appear again and again as factors generally recognized by Douglass, Richard Greener and other Negro spokesmen as contributing heavily to the migrations. Particularly onerous to Negroes was the manner in which whites invaded their homes to search or arrest without warrants or to pillage and abuse without punishment.

During the first eight months of 1874 approximately 15,-000 southern Negroes moved to the West. The exodus started in Mississippi, but soon all of the lower South was involved.

Another mass movement started in early 1879, beginning
with the state of Louisiana, and during 1889, the same happened to Alabama. So large were these migrations that the
United States Senate was moved to investigate the causes. In
the migration to Kansas and other western states which started
in 1879 approximately 40,000 Negroes went West. The census
of 1910 revealed that almost two million Negroes were living
in places other than the state of their birth. The significance
of this exodus can hardly be exaggerated. To the freedmen who
left the South to go West, to those who remained in the South,
and to those of the North as well, the exodus was in part a
protest, and although few saw it as a solution of the "race
problem," Negroes everywhere took pride in it.

Frederick Douglass thought that the rigors of northern
and western climates and the speedy tempo of life in these
sections were too much for most "South-adjusted" Negroes to
take, but he, too, praised the protest element in the exodus.
Some Negroes opposed the exodus of 1879, as well as those of
the World War eras, because their race stood "to lose" politically, economically, or otherwise by the loss of population to the
North or West. Throughout the history of the nation there
always have been Negroes who were acutely conscious of their
vested interest in the status quo. Segregation, discrimination,
and the amassed colored population in the South have been
conditions out of which some Negroes have made capital, and
thus some have not wanted these conditions changed.

A major reason for the western migration of Negroes was
the propaganda which helped pull whites into the West. Horace
Greeley was urging, "Go West Young Man," and the railroad
companies were advertising as far away as Europe. Speaking
before the American Social Science Association in September
12, 1874, Richard T. Greener declared that over the previous
ten years southern Negroes "had heard" and "read . . . much"
of the "great West."[88] In part, these migrants were attracted
by the growing labor demands of the industrial North and the
expanding West. Some freedmen who left the Southeast to go
West did so because they had heard tall tales of easy livelihoods
to be made in Arkansas, Texas, or Oklahoma, where it was
reputed that cotton and corn required no tending, white pota-

toes grew as big as watermelons, and cotton grew as tall as a man. Blanche K. Bruce thought that many Negroes might improve their lot through emigration to Liberia.

The migrations not infrequently had dramatic leadership. Edwin P. McCabe performed almost unbelievable services in getting Afro-Americans out of the South. A former state auditor of Kansas, he is generally credited with having been directly responsible for over eight hundred families from the Carolinas leaving those two states. His plan to settle 5,000 families in Oklahoma had the backing of several congressmen, but not enough to get federal aid for the ill-fated project.[89] That southern whites in Congress, in both the ante- and post-bellum periods, opposed and blocked any substantial federal aid in support of schemes which would drain off their labor is understandable. Still, had the South supported these colonization efforts more, the section might today have a less acute racial situation. The move to Kansas had some leadership in Benjamin Singleton. Henry Adams, Georgia born ex-slave, was prominent also in the 1879 migrations. Adams reported that he was a leader of a South-wide colored committee of up to five hundred members. This committee, he stated, was started in 1869 for the purpose of investigating opportunities for the race in the South. Its members reported that conditions were best in the upper South, but far from ideal even there. After the overthrow of Radical Reconstruction, this committee appealed to the federal government for permission to colonize the Negro within the boundaries of the United States. This failing, the group decided on emigration from the South. Adams summed up the reasons for the exodus as follows:

> It is because the largest majority of the people, of the white people, that held us as slaves treats our people so bad . . . that it is impossible for them to stand it . . . Our people most as well be slaves as to be free; because in times of politics, if they have any idea that the Republicans will carry a parish or ward . . . why, they would do anything on God's earth. There ain't nothing too mean for them to do to prevent it.[90]

Some white southerners became alarmed at this drain on the section's cheap labor supply. In numerous areas cotton was left standing in the fields with no one to pick it, and to halt the movement, in some areas local debts were held over the heads of tenant-farmers to prevent their leaving, and at times ticket agents at railroad stations refused to sell tickets to Negroes.

Frederick Douglass was in favor of the exodus because it indicated to southern whites the limits to which the race would allow itself to be pushed and exploited, and "revealed to southern men the humiliating fact that the prosperity and civilization of the South are at the mercy of the despised and hated Negro."[91] Accepting some of the current stereotypes about his race, Douglass felt that only the Negro could perform the agricultural labors of the South. Accepting also the stereotype of the lazy southern white, he felt that the Negro was the only person in the South who would work. The South had to depend on Negro labor or starve. Of southern whites, Douglass averred:

> There is only one mode of escape for them, and that mode they will certainly not adopt. It is to take off their own coats, cease to whittle sticks and talk politics at the cross-roads, and go themselves to work in their broad and sunny fields of cotton and sugar. An invitation to do this is about as harsh and distasteful to all their inclinations as would be an invitation to step down into their graves. With the Negro, all this is different. Neither natural, artificial nor traditional causes stand in the way of the freedman to such labor in the South. Neither heat, nor the fever demon . . . affrights him, and he stands today the admitted author of whatever prosperity, beauty, and civilization are now possessed by the South. He is the arbiter of her destiny.
>
> This, then, is the high vantage ground of the Negro; he has labor, the South wants it, and must have it or perish. Since he is free he can now give it, or withhold it; use it where he is, or take it elsewhere, as he pleases. His labor . . . is more to him than either fire, sword, ballot-boxes, or bayonet. It touches the heart of the South through its pocket.[92]

Clearly Douglass overlooked or minimized the difficulties which the oftentimes benighted impoverished Negro would have in using his labor as such a weapon, and he exaggerated the extent of the white man's contempt for labor. Here Douglass probably generalized from the image of the southern planter class as not being willing to soil their hands with manual labor. Along with many abolitionists, Douglass overlooked the fact that most southern whites had never owned a single slave a day in their lives. Because of this reasoning and the "monopoly of the labor market" which he thought the race had in the South and because of the "careless and improvident habits" which he thought slavery had inculcated in the Negro, and the rigorous northern and western climates, Douglass' final advice on the exodus coincided with that of Booker Washington—Negroes should remain in the South. However, the success of these and subsequent migrations have proved that Douglass, like so many of his contemporaries among colored leaders, was wrong in accepting some of the stereotyped and mistaken notions about the race.[93] In opposing the exodus Douglass penned resolutions and made numerous speeches before important groups, and he gave still another reason why most Negroes should remain in the South:

> By staying where they are they may be able to send abler, better, and more effective representatives of their race to Congress. In the South the Negro has at least the possibility of power; in the North he has no such possibility, and it is for him to say how well he can afford to part with this possible power.

Douglass continued realistically:

> Go where they will, they must, for a time, inevitably carry with them poverty, ignorance and other repulsive incidents inherited from their former conditions as slaves; a circumstance which is about as likely to make votes for Democrats as for Republicans, and to raise up bitter prejudices against them as to raise up friends for them.[94]

Douglass feared that the Republican party would lose Negro voters by the exodus, and that by giving up concentration for dispersal Negroes would lose the ability to elect members of their own race to high public office. "No people can be much respected in this country . . . that cannot point to any one of their class in an honorable, responsible position," he declared. Douglass opposed the exodus also because of, (1) his optimism that the plight of the southern Negro was improving, and (2) his belief that it is un-manly to run from a fight or hard conditions. To run, he said, "is necessarily an abandonment of the great and paramount principle of protection to person and property in every State of the Union. It is an evasion of a solemn obligation and duty. The business of this nation is to protect its citizens where they are, not to transport them where they will not need protection." "A rolling stone gathers no moss," he declared. "The colored people of the South," he averred, "just beginning to accumulate a little properety, and to lay the foundation of families, should not be in haste to sell that littld and be off to the banks of the Mississippi."

Douglass felt that Negroes would do better if most remained on farms. In towns and cities, he said, they would come into competition with white labor. Too, he believed that Negroes were slow mentally and physically, and by temperament best suited to the rural South. It seems that by the end of the Civil War, and even before, Douglass had risen from slavery to a middle class outlook which, among other things, carried an attitude of both contempt and love for the masses of his own race. Booker T. Washington appears to have gone through a similar metamorphosis. Although he opposed the exodus, Douglass stated:

> In no case must thq Negro be 'bottled up' or 'caged up.' He must be left free like every other American citizen, to choose his own local habitation and to go where he shall like. Though it may not be for his interest to leave the South, his right and power to leave it may be his best means of making it possible for him to stay there in peace. Woe to the oppressed and destitute of all countries and races if the rich and powerful are to decide when and where they shall go or stay. The deserving hired man gets his wages increased when he can tell his employer that he can get better wages elsewhere. And when all hope is gone from the hearts of the laboring classes of the old world, they can come across the sea to the new.

Richard T. Greener advocated the formation of a national Negro organization to aid the freedmen who wished to go West. Greener thought the movement "came from God." "That the departure of the few will benefit the many," he declared, "might be abundantly illustrated by the condition of Ireland after the famine of 1848, or England after the Lancashire distress, when Canon Girdlestone, Mr. Froude and Goldwin Smith counseled emigration." Later to be a close associate of Booker Washington, where the exodus was concerned, in 1874 Greener differed with Douglass on practically all counts. For those who remained in the South Greener thought the emigration would lead to higher wages, while the emigrants would be stimulated to unlearn the lack of thrift, excessive drinking, and other bad habits and qualities which he felt were characteristic of southerners of both races. Douglass had drawn an analogy between the emigration to the West of the 1870s and the earlier despised schemes of colonization in Africa. Greener denied the validity of this analogy, pointing out that the Westward migration did not involve leaving the land of the Afro-American's nativity. Where Douglass saw a great difference between the climates of the South and Kansas, Greener minimized the difference. To Douglass' argument relative to the "potential" power of the Negro vote in the South, Greener countered with the observation that the vote was presently impotent, and that as Negro legislators had appeared already in such states as Massachusetts and Ohio, even in the West they would appear. Greener was firm in his conviction that Greeley's advice, "Go West, young man" was good for colored as well as white Americans.[35]

Study of the rising economic wealth possessed by the race, of the establishment on a firm foundation of its churches, colleges and normal schools, of the growing number of college graduates and the battles against illiteracy, of the shifting of population to urban areas of the North, South, and West; of participation in the Populist Revolt and the labor movement, and of the developing race pride, reveals that despite the defeats suffered on the political front, for Negroes the period from 1877-1900 was not a static era.

By the 1880's Carl Schurz, Thomas Wentworth Higginson, and a number of former abolitionists had joined the ranks of Liberal Republicans. They became highly critical of Negroes, and sympathetic to the views and program of the white South.

Seemingly abandoned by the North and its party, Negroes were at first shocked and dismayed at the retreat of many of their former supporters. For the first time in their history in the United States, Afro-Americans found themselves to a considerable extent without paternalistic sponsorship. Now the race had to "call its own plays" and justify them, and despite the substantial financial aid received from white philanthropy, many Negroes knew that financial aid was increasingly both more difficult to get and inadequate for their needs. Through pen and forum some spokesmen unleashed their anger and·resentment at their "former friends" for abandoning their cause. But they did not stop with anger. They began to grope for new solutions to their problems.

Some sought an answer in emigration. In both West and South one solution tried was that of segregated Negro towns. Some persons proposed emigration to Africa, while others sought a solution through the launching of a national Afro-American political party and labor union. To some, acquiescence in the social and political status quo was the key to advancement of the race, while there were others who were equally certain that the panacea was the acquisition of culture and character. Many others felt that most important were frugality and the acquisition of property and wealth. At times several of these views, even where they were contradictory, were held by the same person, and for every proponent of most of them, there were numerous opponents. In brief, with the more thoughtful Negroes, among other things this was an age of confusion. As much as anything else, their dire plight and frustration caused some Afro-American leaders with divergent views to be suspicious of and to quarrel with not only white persons of both sections, but with one another. One individual or group impugned the motives, character, and sincerity of the other. The well-known quarrel between Booker Washington and W. E. B. DuBois was not the only instance of this. Yet it is clear that most spokesmen sincerely had their racial group at heart, and it is highly probable that the masses of Negroes, not given to or able to base their actions on finely-spun theoretical beliefs, plodded on scarcely mindful of the conflicting views, eyes fixed on obtaining the humble necessities of life.

Despite the often confused counsels which emanated from without and within Negro ranks, during this period the basic Americanization of the Negro dictated the central trend of his actions. Most Negroes simply thought and acted like most Americans—particularly southern Americans—of the age. Indeed, it always has been easy to exaggerate the extent to which the colored American and his problems were different from those of other Americans. While his problems without doubt had their unique aspects, they had even more in common with those of the nation-at-large, and despite the noise and raised blood pressures which the "race question" caused, the problems of the South were not at bottom racial, but largely cultural and economical.

Especially did Negro conventions of the 1880's and 90's urge financial support for the migrants from the South, federal aid to education, and anti-lynching legislation. During this period not only did northern Negroes continue the national conventions which the colored abolitionists had begun, but the freedmen of the South adopted this method of group protest and progress. North and South, the race made considerable progress, evidences of which are to be seen not only in such economical areas as the growth of Negro business and expansion of land and home ownership, but in cultural growth as well. For example. In 1892 the Colored Women's League was organized in Washington, D. C. Within three years the National Federation of Afro-American women was organized, and a year later these two organizations merged into the National Association of Colored Women. In addition to their support of anti-lynching legislation and federal aid to education, industrial and college training for Negroes, these groups supported civil rights, temperance, and women's rights and attacked the delinquent behavior of members of their race. By the 1950s this organization could boast of a membership of over 40,000 and a long record of outstanding service. Its annual conventions, plus its journal *Woman's Era,* have been effective media for evaluating the progress of the race, attracting attention to its plight, and planning courses of action. One of the founders of this organization, Mrs. Mary Church Terrell, was for over a half century a most ardent spokesman and agitator for equality. The same is true of Mrs. Daisy Lampkin, Mrs. Mary McCloud Bethune, and other women who have been identified with this organization. Charles Chestnutt, the first outstanding Negro novelist, was writing in this period, which saw also George Washington Williams begin the serious study of Negro history. In addition, Henry Ossawa Tanner's "Resurrection of Lazarus" was received with great praise at the Paris Exhibition of 1897. Similar examples of social and cultural growth are numerous.

Before the year 1900 the more able southern Negroes had been caught up in the great American dream of becoming millionnaires. As many whites had done two or three decades earlier, the more able Negroes frequently turned their backs on politics and viewed education, religion, and business as the more roseate fields of personal endeavor. Negroes were not all pushed out of politics by the proscriptions which southern states placed on Negro voting, but rather many were pulled away by new and dynamic economic and social forces. Indeed, the ease with which southern states got away with the proscriptions of Negro voting was due not only to the acquiescence of northern whites, but to a comparable acquiescence by many Negroes.

Rayford W. Logan believes that the presidents of the United States between 1877 and 1901 were "weak," and that having such men in the White House facilitated the overthrow of the Reconstruction efforts.[96] So far as the racial situation in the South was concerned, Logan, like Frederick Douglass and numerous other Negro spokesmen, does not seem to have much respect for the leadership of Rutherford B. Hayes, Chester A. Arthur, Benjamin Harrison, Grover Cleveland, or William McKinley. The same is true of the race's general attitude toward Presidents Harding, Coolidge, and Hoover. The failure of the nineteenth century presidents vigorously to enforce the Fourteenth and Fifteenth Amendments or to offer much political patronage to Negroes helped bring about a steady drift of the race away from the Republican Party, and led in the late nineteenth century to their demand for a third party. Especially notable was this alienation after the Supreme Court decision of 1883 which declared the Civil Rights Act of 1875 to be unconstitutional. How much this disaffection had to do with Grover Cleveland's two presidential victories is a moot question.

It was not the twentieth century which discovered, through the researches of Carter Woodson, W. E. B. DuBois, Herbert Aptheker and other scholars, the true record of Negro militancy in this country. In 1882 John R. Lynch stated in the House of Representatives: "The impartial historian will record the fact that the colored people of the South have contended for their rights with a bravery and a gallantry that is worthy of the highest commendation."[97] Despite the compromise which the race was forced to make in this period, Lynch was right. The compromise was one of expediency rather than principle. Furthermore, as indicated, the de-emphasis on political action coincided with the national trend which saw most American boys become more interested in becoming financial magnates and millionaires rather than senators or presidents.

Hundreds of thousands of Post-Civil War immigrants from Europe, approximately 4,000,000 freedmen, and the move to the cities of rural people created new political, economic, and social problems for the nation. In his 1895 Atlanta Exposition Address Booker T. Washington urged the White South not to "look to the incoming of those of foreign birth and strange tongue and habits for the prosperity of the South,' but instead to depend on and utilize the labors of the "8,000,000 Negroes whose habits you know, whose fidelity and love you have tested in days when to have proved treacherous meant the ruin of your fire sides." The Negro's labor, he declared, "without strikes and labor wars," had been a great boon to the South and the nation. To the White South, Washington said of his race—"we shall stand by you with a devotion that no foreigner can approach, ready to lay down our lives if need be, in defense of yours." Throughout the period of 1880-1924 Afro-Americans showed considerable fear that the influx of immigration from Europe and Asia would displace them in the labor market, particularly if these immigrants were to come into the South in considerable numbers. Too, colored Americans were sensitive to the fact that in the land of their birth they were often treated as pariahs while the country served as an asylum for the oppressed of Europe.[88] Despite the popularity of proposals to stop Chinese immigration into the United States, in 1879 Blanche E. Bruce placed his political career in jeopardy and voted against exclusion.[99] In this same period Representative Rainey sought to bring about better treatment of the Chinese on the West Coast.[100]

Bishop Reverdy C. Ransom voiced the opinion that immigation of millions of white Europeans to this country kept white Americans from properly appreciating and accepting the Afro-American citizenry. "Once the tides of immigration have ceased to flow to our shores," he said in 1905, "this nation will evolve a people who shall be òne in purpose, one in spirit, one in destiny—a composite American by the co-mingling of blood."[101]

In addition to the race riot which Fayetteville, North Carolina witnessed during the waning months of the nineteenth century, and riots in Atlanta, Georgia and Brownsville, Texas in 1906, the disfranchisement period which followed the fusionist threat saw many other riots and lynchings, both North and South of the Mason-Dixon Line. Neither New York, Pennsylvania, Illinois, Ohio, or Indiana were spared. Springfield, Ohio had a particularly protracted riot in 1904, while in August, 1908 one in Springfield, Illinois so disgusted thinking Americans until it led directly to the formation of the National Association for the Advancement of Colored People.

Rayford Logan stated in 1954 that during the late nineteenth and early twentieth centuries—"Negroes were subjected to villification in Congress the like of which has rarely been equalled except in the early days of Nazi struggle for power in Germany and some recent attacks upon eminent Americans by an irresponsible senator."[102] One of the stereotypes which crystallized in some sectors after 1865 was the notion that Afro-Americans are innately lazy. Like practically all stereotypes of racial groups, this one, too, had origin in fact and fancy. On the factual side are the obvious truths of prevalent conditions such as hook worm, tuberculosis, and malnutrition, and that as slaves and share-croppers Negroes often had no inner incentives for hard work and ambition. The profit motive scarcely existed in their world. Then there is the observation that contempt for manual labor and an easy-going nonchalance in speech, thought, and action has been ascribed to the majority of white southerners, doubtless behavior patterns to which hot summers and the section's agrarianism, poverty, and frontier nature contributed. When freedom came to Negroes, many aped the planters in habits and thought. Whether with fairness or not, most of the stereotypes which have been listed as peculiarly Negroid, also at one time or another have been ascribed to southern whites. Still, this "laziness," where it existed, was not innate, and many freedmen were soon caught up in the great American effort to go from rags to riches. While a number of the unlettered long hoped through such devices as rabbits feet, "mojos," horse shoes, gambling, and "playing the numbers" suddenly and effortlessly to strike it rich, most knew well what such leaders as Booker Washington and Frederick Douglass preached, that hard labor, thrift, and character were the surest roads to success.

The early decades after Reconstruction, as a part of the Romanticist penchant of the southern writers of the period, saw Uncle Remus and Uncle Tom made into the "typical" Negro folk characters. Their amiable docility and picturesqueness fitted well into the idolization of the Old South. Since Afro-Americans were often ashamed of their slave heritage, as well as of slave songs and spirituals, they long neglected their folk tales and aphorisms. By the early years of the twentieth century, however, the growing spiritual and intellectual emancipation of the race, plus resentment at the interpretations which white collectors were placing on these materials, caused Negroes themselves to begin an objective and scholarly interest in the various manifestations of their folk heritage. This interest revealed, "Both Uncle Remus and Leadbelly" to be portrayers of "sides of the Negro folk, but to round out the portraiture Bessie Smith, Josh White, the Gospel Singing Two Keys, and such big old liars as those heard by E. C. L. Adams in the Congaree swamps and by Zora Neale Hurston in central Florida" were needed also.[103] During this period, folk expression depicted nearly all aspects of the hard lot of the near illiterate lower class Negro. Whether on the sharecropper farm, in a sawmill gang, on the chain-gang, working on the railroad or construction crew, the theme is the same—too much work and too

little pay, no future in sight, and ever the object of race prejudice and oppression. But also ever present was the humorous
twist, and the optimism-blended-with-pessimism which these
persons gave to even the harshest and most ironic of experiences.
The Negro novelist, unlike the unlettered authors of blues,
spirituals, and tunes, has seldom been able to mix the "saving
grace" of humor with his dark portraiture of life. But humor,
if often the Pagliacci type, has been a dominant aspect of the
mind of the Negro masses.

Of this period James Weldon Johnson wrote—"The Negro
was to have a new day in drama. Ambitious playwrights of the
race had long been anxious to bring a higher degree of artistry
to Negro songs, with an idea of displacing the 'coon songs'
which had as their themes jamborees, razors with the gastrono-
mical delights of chicken, pork chops and watermelons, and
the experiences of their red-hot 'mamas' and their never too
faithful 'papas'."[104] William Stanley Braithwaite has given an
excellent evaluation of the treatment which the race received
in the serious literature of the 1865-1900 period. In 1925 he
noted:

> In literature, it was a period when Negro life
> was a shuttle cock between the two extremes of humor
> and pathos. The Negro was free, and was not free.
> The writers who dealt with him for the most part
> refused to see more than skin-deep—the grin, the
> grimaces and the picturesque externalities. . . . [For]
> to see more than the humble happy peasant would
> have been to flout the fixed ideas and conventions of
> an entire generation. For more than artistic reasons,
> indeed against them, these writers refused to see the
> Tragedy of the Negro and capitalized his comedy.
> *The social conscience had as much need for this comic*
> *mask as the Negro.*[105]

The birth of minstrel shows added color to the American
scene as they went from town to town caricaturing the lighter
side of the life of the Negro masses. Minstrelsy in organized
form has been traced to the year 1865 when Charles Hick's
famed Georgia Minstrels was started. From that company to the
celebrated "Silas Green from New Orleans," minstrel companies
appeared one after another, leaving a long line of individual

stars among whom were Lew Johnson, Wallace King, Primrose and West, Billy Windom and William Kersands. These were the fore-runners of such nationally acclaimed individuals as Bill "Bojangles" Robinson, Steppin' Fetchit, Eddie "Rochester" Anderson, Mantan Moreland, Hattie MacDaniels, and Louise Beavers, persons who operated through the different media of legitimate stage, screen, and radio. The more educated Negro usually has resented the stereotyped roles depicted by these persons. The Great Depression and changed attitudes killed most minstrel companies; by the 1940's this type of entertainment had all but disappeared, and southern whites had come to present the only group still putting on the black-faced comic show to any noticeable extent. Still the contempt and disrespect for the race which the stereotypes showed sometimes became a part of the Negro's own attitude, but this racial disparagement always was mixed with race pride. George H. White, last colored Congressman from North Carolina, answered attacks on his race in Congress with a reply similar to that long used by Afro-Americans. Speaking in February, 1900, White declared:

> It is easy for these gentlemen to taunt us with our inferiority, at the same time not mentioning the cause of this inferiority. It is rather hard to be accused of shiftlessness and idleness when the accuser closes the avenue of labor and industrial pursuits to us. It is hardly fair to accuse us of ignorance when it was made a crime under the former code of things to learn enough about letters to even read the Word of God.[106]

Still another source put its finger on a central point in the "race problem." "Much of the opposition to the Negro today," this source averred, "is not based as formerly on the ground of the Negro's fundamental incapacity, but is publicly stated and stoutly defended on the theory that the superior race must be protected from the Negro's physical prowess, his enthusiasm and acknowledged capacity, [which is] a plain confession that the prevailing secret opinion of the Negro of 1895-96 is that he is not an inferior but a formidable competitor."[107]

CHAPTER XIV

ELEMENTS OF NEGRO THOUGHT ON EDUCATION AND SEGREGATION

The interest of the Afro-American in education always has been keen. Inasmuch as the English Colonies were from the very first education-minded, one would expect that colored persons brought into North America would share this desire for learning. In addition to drawing impetus and stimulation from the culture at large, many Afro-Americans have shown awareness that in the quest for knowledge their group started behind and hence must "run faster" than others or remain forever behind.[1] Too, Negroes often have conceived of the tools of knowledge as very useful weapons in the fight to help lift themselves to freedom and equality of citizenship. "It is perfectly well understood at the South," Frederick Douglass once wrote, "that to educate a slave is to make him discontented with slavery, and to invest him with power which shall open to him the treasures of freedom."[2]

Negroes have believed that not only is the race prejudice directed at them due to the miseducation of many white men, but that members of their own race were too often poorly informed. The race often has been quite objective about its shortcomings and constantly has sought to remedy them.[3] For example, in 1818 free persons of color founded the Augustine Society for the propagation of education within their group, and in the first issue of the first colored newspaper the editors expressed an interest in education as a means of elevating the race.[4] In his classic militancy, David Walker stated that he would make every exertion to throw off the ignorant condition which then beset members of his race. "I would crawl on my hands and knees through mud and mire," he wrote, "to the feet of a learned man where I would sit and humbly supplicate him to instil into me, that which neither devils nor tyrants could remove . . . for colored people to acquire learning in this country, makes tyrants quake and tremble on their sandy foundation." Nat Turner, famed leader of the 1831 insurrection in Southhampton, Virginia reported that the slaves looked up to him because of his learning and intelligence, and wondered why he did not run away. "If they had my sense," he reports them as saying, "they would not serve any master in the world."[5] In 1834 Negroes in Cincinnati opened their first school. Within a year three more were opened. In Pennsylvania in 1838 there were among the Negroes of Philadelphia, Pittsburg, York, West Chester, and Columbia, 22 churches, 48 clergymen, 26 day schools, 20 Sabbath schools, 125 Sabbath school teachers, 4 literary societies, 2 public libraries, with a total of around 800 volumes and ten times that number of volumes in private libraries, 2 Bible societies, and 7 temperance societies.[6] At a Troy, New York meeting in 1847 William C. Nell pushed a scheme whereby Negro students would begin to enlist in the colleges of the North, which had up to this time almost completely excluded them from their student bodies. Since, there was at this time not a single Negro college in the nation to match the fairly numerous Negro grade schools, the push of free persons to establish a college or fight for admission to the white ones is indication of the growing maturity of the free Negro population. On December 28, 1857 the New York Society for the Promotion of Education Among Colored Children, led by Charles B. Ray and Philip A. White, presented a request for improved educational facilities to a state education commission. As early as 1853 Afro-Americans were advocating industrial education as a prime need of their group. The 1853 National Negro Convention heard arguments in favor of its founding a manual labor school. One advocate of this idea said: "Every person is here not merely to enjoy, but to work; and schools are only valuable in their teachings, as they assist in making both thinker and worker. They may saturate men with the learning of every age and yet, except they strive to make them something more than literary flowers, they sin greatly against the individual and humanity also."[7] This same advocate declared: "Literature has too long kept itself aloof from the furrowed field, and from the dust and bustle of the workshop. The pale, sickly brow and emaciated form have been falsely shown to the world as the ripeness of mental discipline." The entire statement was strongly in favor of agricultural and mechanical training as the most intensive need of the Afro-American. This anticipated by several decades later thought along these lines popularized by William Hooper Councill, Booker Washington, and others. Here is good evidence that the economic and educational thought of the Negro was in step with the rising industrialism and scientific advance. Charles Reason was one of the leading champions of industrial education. Reason gave serious thought to preparation for the emancipation which all expected. He wrote:

> Whenever emancipation shall take place, immediate though it be, the subjects of it, like many who now make up the so-called free population, will be in what geologists call, the 'Transition State.' The prejudice now felt against them for bearing on their persons the brand of slaves, cannot die out immediately. Severe trials will still be their portion and the curse of a 'tainted race' must be expiated by almost miraculous proofs of advancement; and some of the miracles must be antecedent to the great day of Jubilee.[5]

He felt that preparation for a worthy vocational contribution to the nation was the immediate need.

Few facts belie the claim of the Slavocracy that the bondsman was mentally inferior and always happy than the zeal with which the freedmen sought formal education. After emancipation, schools sprang up everywhere, in churches, homes, tents, or old abandoned buildings and were taught by any and all who knew or thought they knew the barest rudiments of spelling and ciphering. The race seems to have hungered for generations for the opportunity to know. Well-known is the manner in which Booker Washington left the coal fields of West Virginia to hike penniless to Hampton Institute, and his case is duplicated many-fold.[6] Slavery and repression seem sometimes to have given the race added zeal for knowledge, and song, eternal expressions which symbolize freedom. His childlike curiosity, laughter, song, boisterousness, and activism have been called qualities inherent in the race, but they may more properly be explained as the result of living in a society where he is often repressed.

˙ While the freedman deserves great credit for what he did for himself during the early days of freedom, from 1861-65 and after, white America rendered aid to the freedman in a magnitude and manner which has not yet been properly told. The real story of the freedmen's aid societies belongs to one of the noblest chapters of the American spirit. Perhaps the American Missionary Society led all of the organizations that were active in founding schools for the freedmen. Northern whites instituted much philanthropy aimed at aiding Negroes without being asked and as early as 1863. General Sherman was one of the first to take initiative as he saw the needs of freedmen his army encountered. In the major cities of the North, freedmen's aid societies sprang up as if by magic, and when the Freedmen's Bureau was founded by Congress, this was but the institutionalization at the federal level of a process already well under way. After 1865, the problem of providing formal education for the race was especially crucial. Before the Civil War, in 1856, the Methodist Episcopal Church had founded Wilberforce University in Ohio. After the war this denomination started Morris Brown, Paul Quinn, Allen, and Kittrell colleges.[9] D. O. W. Holmes pointed out that Negro "Colleges and Universities" of the period 1861-1885 represented in their titles "The expression of distant hopes rather than actual descriptions."[10] The primary concern of the Freedmen's Bureau was educating the freedman, and in this effort the bureau founded over four thousand schools, among which were not only grade schools, but Howard, Atlanta, and Fisk Universities. These and other universities were established with an eye toward fitting Negro teachers to man the classrooms which their race increasingly would have to fill before it could meet the demands of the equality for which it yearned. Among the other colleges that the bureau either founded or aided were Hampton Institute, Johnson C. Smith University, and St. Agustine College. At the same time that the bureau was working in the field of education, so were the churches of both races, through their missionary societies, and when the bureau ceased operations in 1870, almost a quarter million Negroes were enrolled in almost five thousand schools in the South.

During Reconstruction and since, Afro-Americans have had only deep gratitude for the work of the Freedman's Bureau. Like the later WPA and similar New Deal agencies of the depression era, the Freedmen's Bureau was a friend in time of dire need. It is not that Negro scholars have not been aware of the faults and evils which went with the operation of this agency, but they have been aware that, as ever with the nation's wartime agencies, and with the New Deal attempts at relief, recovery, and reform, these faults and evils have been traditional, not just peculiar to the Freedmen's Bureau. In 1903, W. E. B. DuBois expressed a wish that the federal government had set up a permanent Freedmen's Bureau. Doubtless through its many programs the Freedmen's Bureau contributed much to teach many freedmen not only the three R's but a new respect for manual labor, education, maintenance of good health, and respect for contractual obligations and the ballot.

The so-called mania for classical education which the freedmen supposedly possessed was simply an imitation of white scholars of the era. That the classical pattern often seemed predominant was due in part to the fact that the white northern teachers who emigrated Southward as humanitarian educators of freedmen, were themselves educated in the classical mode and "had known no other kind of schools and felt that what had been good for them was best for . . . their lately liberated pupil."[11] In a number of instances white state educational officials chose the classical curriculum and carried it out over protests of the freedmen. Such was the case with the curriculum of Southern University in New Orleans, Louisiana.

How much of Negro "disinterest" in education can be laid at the feet of southern whites who openly opposed "nigger education" is open to question. Still, it is a fact that in numerous instances, white southerners stoned and beat both colored students and teachers as well as the northern whites who sought to teach Negroes.[12]

The contribution of Negro colleges to the race's social and cultural growth is of tremendous significance. Beginning essentially as grade schools, only since the end of World War II did most of them come to justify the titles college or university. Yet from their early beginnings, they have been oases of culture, and even when practically no one regarded Negro college students as "scholars," most persons recognized that they were relatively refined. As such, to both friendly whites and the Negro masses, these colleges and their students long have constituted a central hope of the race.

By the opening of World War I, a few of the faculties of such schools as Wilberforce, Howard and Fisk Universities, and Morehouse College, had made them recognized centers not only of Negro culture but of scholarship as well, while other institutions, such as Spellman and Bennett College for girls, Talladega in Alabama, Xavier in New Orleans, Wiley in Texas, Payne in Georgia, Bethune-Cookman in Florida, were especially noted as centers of cultural training. By 1905, most teachers of Negro pupils in the South were of their own race. Yet, by this date only about fifty percent of Negro children of school age were in school, and of these, fewer than one-third attended school as many as six months per year. At this time southern states were spending less than one-fifth of school expenditures on Negro schools and teachers. Perhaps for most freedmen, the word education meant only an elementary knowledge of reading, writing, and arithmetic. Many who aspired for more learning had in mind entering the ministry, teaching or perhaps politics. To most, education was a badge of freedom and key to distinctiveness, and sometimes was expressed as a love for "big" words and Latin phrases. Too few conceived of knowledge as having intrinsic as well as extrinsic values and it was not long before with some the initial intense interest in education would give way in some to indifference and even hostility, and teachers throughout the South would be complaining of parents who kept their children out of school at the slightest pretense.[13]

Although the Afro-American has absorbed much of his conservatism from the same sources which have bred this attitude in American whites, the conservative character of Negro education has been due in no small degree to control exercised, albeit ever so indirectly, by those who granted the money to make the schools possible. The most notable sources of funds have been appropriations by Negro religious bodies, southern state legislatures, and the philanthropy of northern capitalists. Because so many were sponsored by religious societies, the freedmen's schools represented a close marriage of religion and education, and in time, some critics came to feel that in a number of these schools too often there was such an emphasis on religion that education in other things was slighted.

Representative Josiah T. Walls of Florida declared: "Education is the panacea for all our social evils, injustices, and oppressions."[14] Believing that southern states could not be trusted to give the Negro ample educational opportunities, Walls sought to get Congress to establish a national education fund.

At the national level the debate over Negro education may be said to have begun in earnest when the 43rd Congress was debating the Civil Rights bill which contained an education clause. John R. Lynch took a moderate stand:

> The colored people in asking the passage of this bill . . . do not thereby admit that their children can be better educated in white than in colored schools, nor that white teachers because they are white are better qualified to teach than colored ones. But they recognize the fact that the distinction when made and tolerated by law is an unjust and odious proscription . . . Let us confer upon all citizens, then, the rights to which they are entitled under the Constitution; and then if they choose to have their children educated in separate schools, as they do in my own State, then both races will be satisfied, because they will know that the separation is their own voluntary act and not legislative compulsion.[15]

Again Lynch said:

> Another reason why the school clause ought to be retained is because the Negro question ought to be removed from the politics of the country. It has been a disturbing element in the country ever since the Declaration of Independence, and it will continue to be so long as the colored man is denied any right or privilege that is enjoyed by the white man. Pass this bill as it passed the Senate, and there will be nothing more for the colored people to ask or expect in the way of civil rights. . . . Let us confer upon the colored citizens equal rights, and . . . they will exercise their rights with moderation and with wise discretion.[16]

Time after time in these debates, Negro spokesmen indicated that they were tired of the fight for equal rights and wanted it ended through the granting of equality before the law.

Congressman Joseph H. Rainey declared: "What we want is schools, and more of them. We want them strung along the highways and by-ways of this country."[17] In defence of a bill to provide federal aid to education which was being debated before the 42nd Congress, Rainey declared that the recent military victory of the Germans over the French was due to the superior educational system of Germany. Further, he felt that federal aid to education "will materially assist and eventually succeed in obliterating sectional feeling" and thus contribute to "harmony, concord and perpetual peace; thereby aiding the industries of our country and developing our vast national resources."[18] Bishop W. T. Vernon stated:

> He who denies education to any class of citizens, in such measure inveighs against public safety, gives us a dangerous element, places a millstone around the neck of all, and jeopardize the welfare of our common country.[19]

Since emancipation this has been a favorite argument of Afro-Americans as to why they should be granted educational opportunities. They have emphasized the benefits to be gained by the South from its investment in Negro education and have thought little of the conviction held by some southerners that to educate the Negro might create more problems for the majority group than it might solve. On this another Negro opined:

> There can be no real democracy between two natural groups if one represents the extreme of ignorance and the other the best intelligence. The common public school and the state university should be the foundation stones of democracy.[20]

Another stated: "The free play of each individual's best powers can be secured only through education,"[21] while still another declared, "It does not become southern white men . . . to boast about the ignorance of the colored people, when you know that their ignorance is the result of the enforcement of your unjust laws."[22]

Evidence that Negroes were not just interested in education for their race alone, but that they felt that more and better

education was a great need of many American whites is to be
seen in their support of the education clauses of the post-Civil
War southern constitutions and of federal aid to education
proposals. Joseph H. Rainey averred that "educational facilities
are needed alike by all classes, both white and black." "There is
an appalling array of the illiterate in America," he stated,
"surely this ought to be sufficient to disarm all hostility to this
laudable and much-needed measure."[23]

To the charge that federal aid to education would lead to
racial integration in the schools, Rainey replied:

> What of that? Suppose it should be so, what harm
> would result therefrom? Why this fear of the Negro
> since he has been a freedman, when in the past he
> was almost a household god, gamboling and playing
> with the children of his old master? And occasionally
> it was plain to be seen that there was a strong family
> resemblance between them. . . . Schools have been
> mixed in Massachusetts, Rhode Island, and other
> States, and no detriment has occurred.[24]

John Mercer Langston said:

> Schools which tend to separate the children of
> the country in their feelings, aspirations and purposes,
> which foster and perpetuate sentiments of caste, ha-
> tred, and ill-will, which breed a sense of degradation
> on the one part and of superiority on the other,
> which beget clannish notions rather than teach and
> impress an omnipresent and living principle and faith
> that we are all Americans, in no wise realize our ideal
> of common schools, while they are contrary to the
> spirit of our laws and institutions.
>
> Two separate school systems, tolerating discrimi-
> nations in favor of one class against another, inflating
> on the one part, degrading on the other . . . cannot
> educate these classes to live harmoniously together,
> meeting the responsibilities and discharging the duties
> imposed by a common government in the interest of
> a common country.[25]

Thus it can be seen that although they disclaimed desire for
social equality, a number of Negro spokesmen fought for integrated education,[26] and Representative John R. Lynch and

others championed federal aid to education, while Representative R. H. Cain of South Carolina and others proposed that the
nation's surplus of public lands be used for educational purposes.[27]

It has been often charged that after emancipation, too
many Negroes wanted an education which would lead to a
white collar job. If in education many were copying the dominant curriculum of the era, in the latter they were, to a large
extent, but imitating the national trend evoked by the industrial revolution and urbanization.

Americans of color generally have felt that prejudice and
false notions on race stemmed largely from an educational and
propaganda campaign aimed at them. "Do children feel and
exercise that prejudice toward colored persons? Do not colored
and white children play together promiscuously until the white
is taught to despise the colored?" asked David Ruggles in 1834.[28]
This conviction was a vital force in producing the Negro History Movement of the 1850-1900 period, and of the later more
scientific movement launched by Carter Woodson, W. E. B.
DuBois, and others. The Afro-American has wanted to bring
about a re-education of the white American on race so as to
overthrow the stereotypes and race sociology concocted by both
the old and new imperialisms to justify degradation of the
Negro.

[A significant index of the growing protest and rising educational level of the Negro was the emergence of Negro college
fraternities] around the turn of the century. Interestingly
enough, the first such organization to be formed, Alpha Phi
Alpha, was begun in 1906 by Negro students attending Cornell
University, who had experienced a good deal of social ostracism. Within two years a chapter of this fraternity, along with
its female counterpart, was established on the Howard University campus in Washington, D. C., and within a decade at
least three other Negro college fraternities, and female counter-
parts, had been organized. All have continued to have a thriving existence and, in addition to their social activities, they have
devoted considerable attention and effort to the end of bringing
about full citizenship rights for Negroes. ((—)

The economic boost which the World War I era gave the
nation's economy, together with the new critical awakening,
produced commendable growth in Negro education, one aspect
of which was the effort made to up-grade higher education to
a level where it could more nearly merit this long-abused designation. Significant improvement in organization and financ-
ing were made with Howard University, by organization of
the Atlanta University system, and the mergers in New Orleans, Louisiana which produced Dillard University. W. E.
B. DuBois and others led in a successful campaign to get both
faculty and administrators of Negro colleges members of their
own race. There was evident in these and other changes a revolt
against the old educational and social order and its ideals.

In 1917 the Phelps-Stokes Fund had published through
the United States Bureau of Education the results of an exten-
sive survey of Negro education which revealed the existence of
serious inadequacies, and which stimulated members of both
races toward greater appropriations for better facilities and
curricula at all levels. This study had given conclusive proof
that the seventeen state-supported Negro land-grant "colleges"
were, in terms of faculties and instruction being offered, scarcely more than secondary schools. Indeed, showed this study, in
all 17 of these institutions, only twelve students were enrolled
as college students. Furthermore, in 1915 there were in all
southern states combined just sixty-four state-supported high
schools for colored Americans.[29]   In 1928 the United States
Bureau of Education published its *Survey of Negro Colleges,*
a study which again stimulated much criticism and improvement of these institutions. The effort which most southern
states were making in the area of Negro education was confined
primarily to the grammar grades and to the so-called colleges.
To fill this gap between the grammar grades and college, numerous private and church schools had been started. Many colored
Americans have been well aware of the manner in which the
poverty of southern states limited what they could do for
public education, but they often have pointed out that at
least seventy percent of available funds were long used to
educate white youth. Negroes have been very grateful to such
altruistic contributions as the Peabody, Carnegie, and Rosen-

wald Funds, as well as the host of wealthy northerners and southerners who have made contributions to their schools.

In their writings, George Schuyler, Nella Larson, J. saunders Redding, and a number of other Afro-American authors are highly critical of southern Negro colleges. No doubt much of this criticism stems from a comparison of these schools with the outstanding northern universities. Perhaps also, some of the criticism stems from the fact that presidents and staffs of southern colleges long have been thought of by some Negroes as being unqualified submissive "Uncle Toms." *Greater Need Below,* published by O'Wendell Shaw in 1936 is perhaps the most denunciatory treatment of these colleges. Like most novelists of his race who have touched upon this theme, Shaw's criticism is directed primarily at the "Uncle Tom" demeanor of the presidents of some of these institutions, as well as the autocratic government of their administration, and poor facilities and inadequate training and courage of the teaching staffs. J. Saunders Redding's *Stranger and Alone* (1950) is a work of similar vein.

Northern universities have provided most of the graduate training which Afro-Americans have received. Since the North usually has been ahead of the South in its liberalism and social dynamism, no doubt this has had important implications for the Negro mind. Daniel A. Payne, J. C. Gibbs, John B. Russwurm, Henry Highland Garnet, and a number of other abolitionists were graduates of northern colleges, and in the postbellum period many outstanding race leaders have received their graduate training in northern universities. More than any single institution, Harvard has provided perhaps the largest share of the top scholars of the race. In retrospect, it would seem that the South might have succeeded better in its object of "controlling" the colored man if the section had opened its graduate and professional schools to him from the beginning, for then the section could have controlled the education of future leaders of the race. For example, there can be little doubt that the liberalism and equalitarianism of Harvard University and New England played a considerable role in shaping the lives of such leaders as Carter Woodson and W. E. B. DuBois.

Though Afro-Americans comprise about one-third of the South's population, in 1941-42 there were only 417 colored medical students in the South, all at Howard University and Meharry Medical College, the race's only two medical schools, while at the same time there were 6,580 white southerners in the section's own medical schools. Almost all Afro-Americans who have earned the Ph.D. degree have done so since 1914. From 1876 to 1936, 132 persons were awarded this degree.[30]

Near the turn of the century there was held at Atlanta University, under the inspiration and guidance of W. E. B. DuBois, twelve annual conferences devoted to a collection of scientific information on the race. These conferences studied and reported on such things as mortality, family life, efforts at group betterment and self-help, business, schools, churches, and crime; and also published bibliographical information on the race. The studies grew out of the conviction that too much confused thinking about the Negro existed, and that an initial need in solving the race problem was the collection of sound and reliable facts. This idea was also prominent in the activities of the Association for the study of Negro life and History, which was started in Chicago by Carter G. Woodson in 1915. To attain a more adequate financial structure, in 1944 the United Negro College Fund was started in an effort to put the fund-soliciting of about thirty-two Negro colleges on a basis similar to that of the Red Feather or United Givers and similar drives.

Racial Discrimination

The animosity which many Negroes have felt because of racial segregation and discrimination in education and other areas is evident in their earliest commentaries on the American scene. Chattel slavery was not the only condition against which they protested previous to 1865; Negro abolitionists constantly protested against all manifestations of color prejudice. Speaking at Oberlin University in 1874 John M. Langston summarized several aspects of the race's reasoning in protesting against discrimination on public conveyances and at inns. Langston said:

> The obligations and liabilities of the common carrier of passengers can, in no sense, be made dependent upon the nationality or color of those with

whom he deals. He may not, according to law, answer his engagements to one class and justify non-performance or neglect as to another by consideration drawn from race. His contract is originally and fundamentally with the entire community, and with all its members he is held to equal and impartial obligation.[31] . . . these are doctrines as old as the common law itself; indeed, older, for they come down to us from Gaius and Papinian. .. . . It is strange, indeed, that the colored American may find place in the Senate, but is denied access and welcome to the public place of learning, the theater, the church and the graveyard, upon terms accorded to all others.[32]

In the 1920's Robert Russa Moton stated:

No phase of discrimination against the Negro touches the race more widely or intimately than segregation. In its application no measure operates so effectively to retard the general progress of the race, not even disfranchisement. Its defenders urged it originally to reduce friction between the two races, which it probably has done on the face of it; but it acts daily and hourly to excite the resentment of all Negroes against the continuous injustices perpetrated under the cover and protection of segregation policies.[33]

And in the same general period another Negro opined:

Discrimination laws are the mother of the mob spirit. The political philosopher in Washington, after publishing his opinion that a Negro by the fault of being a Negro is unfit to be a member of Congress, cannot expect an ignorant white man in Tennessee to believe that the same Negro is, nevertheless, fit to have a fair and impartial trial in a Tennessee court. Ignorance is too logical for that.[34]

The origins of the recent success which Negroes have had in their legal battle against racial segregation and discrimination date back at least to the founding of the NAACP. Although the organization was less than five years old when its first significant legal victory was attained, a victory against the "Grandfather Clause," the organization and the nation would have to wait until the World War II era before achievement of the goal of total citizenship equality would seem to be within sight. The 1941 Supreme Court decision in *U. S. vs. Classic*, in which the court upheld the conviction of election officials guilty of fraud committed in the course of holding federal elections was held as a great step forward. In the Mitchell decision of the same year the court used the Interstate Commerce Act to keep railroads from barring Negroes from unrestricted use of pullman cars. In 1944, the fighters for racial equality were greatly encouraged by the decision in *Smith vs. Allwright*, in which the court ruled that discriminatory acts against Negroes committed by the state Democratic party were tantamount to discrimination by the state itself. This decision, dealing specifically with the white or closed primary, opened many local elections to Afro-Americans. The 1946 decision in the case of *Morgan vs. Virginia*, in which the court ruled that interstate bus passengers cannot be discriminated against on account of race or color led to emboldened action by Negroes in this area, and a number of test actions and resulting litigations in several states followed. Since many colored interstate bus and train passengers were northerners visiting the South or college students traveling between home and school, these persons were more likely to resent and oppose segregation than many others. Encouragement to militancy in this area was brought about by the 1950 ruling in *Henderson vs U. S.* which forbade discrimination in dining cars and the 1955 ICC ruling against passengers being discriminated against in waiting rooms of bus and train stations. The growing interest by the federal government in the Negro's quest for equality of treatment was reflected also in the late 1946 establishment of the President's Committee on Civil Rights. This step by President Harry S. Truman was one of several which endeared him to Negro voters, and doubtless aided considerably in his election in 1948. The 1947 committee's publication, *To Secure These Rights*, was in part a propaganda device which probably did much to commit Negroes, as well as whites, more firmly to the object reflected in the establishment of the committee and title of the report. The recommendations of the committee were largely the whole body of proposed legislation which W. E. B. DuBois and other uncompromising Negro spokesmen had been championing for at least a half century, and if effected would eliminate all legal discriminations based on race or color.

Integration in the armed forces, begun during the closing months of World War II, proceeded with such smoothness that most Afro-Americans paid scant attention to President Truman's organization in 1948 of a committee whose job it was to study and recommend ways to augment this integration. The report of this committee, which appeared two summers later under the title, *Freedom to Serve,* was accepted in similar manner by Afro-Americans, who, by this time were more likely to get excited about the feats on the baseball diamond of tan players than by unspectacular steps forward in the fight for equality. Still Congressman Adam Clayton Powell kept the initiative in pointing out to the American public that vestiges of segregation and discrimination remained here and there among the military establishments.

In the battle against segregation the District of Columbia has been a focal point of Negro interest and protest the same as it was in the 1800-1861 battle against slavery. As the center from which radiates the spirit of such things as the Presidency, the Supreme Court, and the nation's most outstanding Negro University, violations of democracy in the District of Columbia ever have been of major concern to Negroes. Thus it is that the 1953 Supreme Court decision in *District of Columbia vs. John R. Thompson Company,* which opened the District's theaters, hotels, and restaurants to Negroes was hailed as a significant omen of similar victories to be won in other parts of the country. Afro-Americans repeatedly have voiced their belief that segregation has served, probably more than any other single factor, to keep alive the myth that they are "different" and "inferior." They have declared that one needs no verbal arguments to convince a white child that a group which is forced to live in the least desirable parts of town, perform the most menial jobs, use the smallest and worst public facilities, and to ride in the back of public conveyances or in the worst train coaches is "beneath" white people.

Perhaps Negroes generally have felt that all racial segregation was originally imposed on the race, while in actual fact some of it was sought and created by themselves. Such was the case with the first race churches. Rather than remain in white churches and be discriminated against, they organized their own. The same has been true in a number of other endeavors. Many of the first schools which sprang up after emancipation were of necessity segregated, but not so by law. This voluntary segregation, regardless of which side initiates it, has not been resented. It is largely when legal sanction and coercion is used that the Afro-American has complained.

Afro-Americans have been well aware that segregation has carried some benefits for the race. The main benefit of segregated education, R. R. Moton saw as being the "opportunity for employment which these separate schools provide for Negro men and women as teachers."[36] He pointed out that in 1928 some 50,000 were employed as teachers, almost exclusively in segregated schools, with an aggregate annual income of $15,-000,000. When in 1951 the Negro municipal college at Louisville, Kentucky was closed and the students taken into the University of Louisville, Negro teachers were alarmed because only one faculty member of the closed school was retained at the white university. A similar reaction later occurred when schools were integrated in West Virginia and other states. To some, this presaged a trend which would see the end of the class of Negro teachers along with the demise of segregated education. Some fear that although the nation generally may agree to allow its colored and white children to attend the same schools as pupils, in most places public opinion and group economic selfishness will not allow all colored teachers to be absorbed into integrated systems. However, so strong is their antipathy toward compulsory segregation and their faith in the ultimate triumph of democracy, until by far the majority of Negroes seem willing to take the risk. These are not blind to the fact that the nation has a serious shortage of teachers at the grade school levels.

Along with other spokesmen, Rufus Clement, President of Atlanta University, has pointed out that when southern states completely abandon their segregation practices in higher education, the major reason for the existence of colleges exclusively for Negroes will no longer exist. The best of these he believes, along with Benjamin Mays and others, should then become integrated institutions. These spokesmen believe that, among other factors, the poverty of southern states leaves them where they could ill afford to do away with Negro teachers and their facilities. Also, with a growing number of Americans, Dr. Clement believes that with their characteristically greater academic freedom and oftentimes richer tradition, and greater emphasis on high scholarship, private colleges are a vital and necessary part of the nation's educational pattern.[37]

Segregation has been defended often on the grounds that it reduces friction between the races, but many Negroes feel that it also perpetuates a condition where friction is inevitable. The modern Negro declares that two groups kept as far apart as white and colored are in the South cannot but distrust, and remain generally ignorant of each other. The colored American always has "pooh-poohed" the idea that what he ultimately and really wants is racial intermarriage. He has pointed out repeatedly that in those sections of the country where intermarriage is not forbidden, it still remains rare and unusual, and the Negro still often looks down on members of his group who marry into the majority race.

Perhaps more than any other factors, segregation and discrimination have prevented the Negro intelligentsia from seceding from their race. It is likely that had Negroes not all been treated alike before the law, the upper class would have been less wedded to the cause of the race. Evidence of this is found in the fact that in the ante-bellum South domestic slaves and members of the free class sometimes betrayed the cause of the slave. The free Negro populace of New Orleans, Louisiana offered over a regiment of mulatto troops to the cause of the Confederacy. But even New Orleans, by prejudice and discrimination, drove her mulattos closer and closer to the slave population. Many of the former sought to settle in France in order to escape this prejudice against their class.

Where life work is concerned, millions of Afro-Americans have been discouraged by race prejudice. Often the colored man has had to begin at the bottom, generally with no hope of rising to the top as the American success story promises. Except in Negro-owned enterprises, managerial and supervisory positions almost all of the time have been closed to him. In both northern and southern schools and colleges, at times he has been trained in vocations where there was very little opportunity of his finding employment. Afro-Americans have been either excluded or frozen at the bottom, in the menial low-paying occupations. This fact has caused large numbers of northern youth to lose interest in school even before the grammar grades were completed. It has discouraged many others from attending the colleges and universities.

R. R. Moton, following Booker Washington's views, was willing to accept segregation provided that it was "equitable and voluntary" and "following the natural lines of social cleavage."[38] In his book entitled *What the Negro Thinks,* Moton revealed that there is a class aspect where attitudes toward some forms of discrimination are concerned. When he discusses segregation and discrimination on trains and other common carriers, Moton showed that segregation on trains was especially chaffing to him. He devoted twelve pages to this type of segregation, while alloting only four to discrimination on streetcars. Obviously, since many Negroes seldom or never had been on a train previous to 1929 when this book appeared, it was the latter type of discrimination that was most general. Moton observed that it was not necessarily segregation *per se* that the Negro always resented, but the fact that the race always got the worst of segregated facilities.[39] Since the colored American is forced to pay the same price for schools, tickets on trains, busses, or trolleys, he feels that it is unfair to give him inferior services. The same applies to public parks, playgrounds, and similar facilities for which the race has been taxed but excluded from their enjoyment. Thus the Negro feels that he is being cheated. This conviction, observed Moton, "rankles deep in his [the Negro's] bosom, producing inevitably an ever-increasing contempt for the white man's standards of honour and justice and simple honesty."[40] On this point, in a vein reminiscent of the Black Abolitionists, Moton continued:

> When he [the Negro] has outgrown his resentments the thinking Negro comes at length to pity the white man who is the victim of this conception, and this system of establishing 'superiority.' When a man must crucify his own finer impulses toward justice and

honesty and even courtesy in order to establish his superiority over another individual or another race he is in reality degrading himself rather than the other, and of the two is the more to be pitied. . . . For the man who is kept down may still preserve his ideals and his character intact; but he who keeps him down cannot do so without deadening his own sensibilities and searing his own soul.[41]

The colored American has viewed segregation and discrimination as being motivated not only by the desire to quarantine the worst aspects of his behavior, but that often discriminatory laws were aimed at insuring "an advantage to the white man and a degree of ignorance and incompetence in the Negro that will avoid the individual hazards of a too keen competition."[42] "The real animus" behind segregation, many Negroes have felt, is not the concern of southern whites with their own comfort, but their "morbid repugnance to seeing coloured people amid scenes and circumstances with which they are unaccustomed to associate them."[43] Colored Americans often have observed that there is no place frequented by southern whites where a Negro cannot go so long as he or she is a butler or maid, or otherwise cast in a servile role. Moton writes that in America the race's lot has been living among "uncertainties, perplexities, and inconsistencies."[44] He went on to describe some of these inconsistencies:

> There is no one word to describe the complex of his [the Negro's] emotions when a Pullman ticket agent tells him he has no space, and he then, going around the corner and calling the agent over the 'phone, is told that there is plenty of space. Only the word 'contempt' describes his emotional reaction when, after reading of a 'black brute' done to death by a quiet, orderly mob' accompanied by women and children, on the next day he reads of young colored girls ravaged by a member of one of the 'best white families' who is later declared 'insane'; and then recalls that a short while before a Negro already adjudged insane and confined in a state asylum for his malady is dragged out of his bed and lynched for the irresponsible killing of a white nurse.[45]

Benjamin Mays stated in 1955 that of all sins, discrimination on account of race is the greatest because it says: "You made a mistake, God, when you made people of different races and colors."[4c] Drake and Cayton contend that Negroes, "feel most resentful about the Job Ceiling, are ambivalent about residential segregation, and are generally indifferent to the taboo on intermarriage."[47] Although it is true, as these writers contend, that "in the matter of 'social segregation' . . . . [Negroes] are seldom articulate," the concern which novelists of the race have shown for intermarriage and passing, plus the resentment which colored Americans have sometimes shown toward marriages across race lines, would seem to belie the contention that Negroes are "generally indifferent to the taboo on intermarriage." Then, too, recent experience with the compulsory school segregation laws would seem to indicate that colored Americans resent *all* legal restrictions on their freedom which are not equally applied to white persons.

The Afro-American often has deplored the need which he has had to form segregated racial organizations. He has felt that such self-segregation should not be necessary in a democratic republic, but like most Americans, he has believed profoundly in the merits of organization and group action as often the best means of securing results in a democratic society. Finding himself ignored and excluded from many institutions, he has been forced to organize his own. Churches, schools, fraternal orders, political and economic associations, and almost every other conceivable type of organization have arisen among colored Americans. Often colored Americans have indicated their qualms about segregated organizations through a keen awareness of the word "Negro" in the name of the various groups. They have pointed out that their churches, schools, and other institutions were not closed to white Americans and a number of groups recently have ceased altogether to use the word "Negro" in their title. The post-World War II scene at Durham, N. C., where students at the North Carolina College for Negroes celebrated the change of their school's name to "North Carolina College at Durham," has been repeated by numerous institutions and organizations, and in this period there has been acute concern as to whether certain organizations should not be abandoned altogether. At times this movement takes on illogical proportions and seems to be a flight from racial identity. Especially does this become clear when members of such an organization as the Association for the Study of Negro Life and History holds serious debates, as happened at the 1954 meeting in St. Louis, Missouri, as to whether their efforts should be continued. The debate revealed that this Association has not been devoted to scientific scholarship alone, but that it has had a persistent and strong propagandist design and orientation. The Negro ever has been aware that Irish, German, Jewish, Polish and other minority groups in this country have formed their restricted associations and activities to further their own efforts at fullness of citizenship and expression.

A prominent feature of the 1950's was one climax to the fight of colored Americans to end compulsory segregation in the public schools. The immediate story which led to this climax, coming in the May 17, 1954 Supreme Court decision of current interest, has a lengthy history. In 1938 came the United States Supreme Court rendering the decision in the case of *Gaines vs. Missouri,* in essence ultimately "compelling" states to make available to Negroes the same educational offerings being given whites. From press and platform, optimistic spokesmen saw in this decision the beginning of the end for compulsory segregated public education. These spokesmen knew that most southern states either could not or would not provide the equal facilities which the court declared had to exist to meet the demands of the law, hence the only legal alternative ultimately would be use by Negroes of integrated educational facilities. In 1949, Ada Sipuel gained admittance to the Oklahoma University law school. She had refused to attend a segregated school launched by Oklahoma after a 1946 court order ruled that the state had to provide her with opportunities for a legal education. The demand of several persons for graduate and professional training caused several states to come forward by 1946 with the idea of regional schools for Negroes. When Oklahoma, rather than organize an expensive graduate school for G. W. McLaurin, admitted him, under a strict caste arrangement, to the white university, McLaurin sued. In June, 1950, the Supreme Court held that he had been denied the equal protection of the laws. Some southern states started setting up Negro graduate schools, while others opened doors of the white schools, and some did nothing about this particular problem. Another case, Sweatt vs. Painter, coming out of Texas, was decided in 1950. The state of Texas had set up a segregated law school which Sweatt did not like because of its obvious inferiority. The Supreme Court found in his favor. In this case, Chief Justice Fred Vinson mentioned the intangible qualities of a school which physical facilities alone cannot give. This viewpoint prompted the NAACP to begin a fight to get all compulsory segregated education declared unconstitutional, not on grounds of inferior physical facilities, but on the fact of segregation itself. Thus it can be seen that, in a number of decisions, while refusing to overthrow the 1896 established "separate but equal" doctrine, the court had been gradually emasculating it; first, by insisting on what for at least three decades had been largely ignored, that is, that the separate facilities shall actually exist and be "substantially equal," then by showing that separate facilities cannot be equal.

Indicative of the widespread nature of the Afro-Americans protest against segregation is the fact that the four cases ruled on together in the epochal May 17, 1954 decision came from widely separated Delaware, Kansas, South Carolina. Too, top NAACP spokesmen have stated that in this and similar instances of court action against segregation, the initiative came from local communities which acted first and later sought NAACP assistance in their legal efforts. When on May 31, 1955 the Court indicated more clearly the *modus operandi* of its 1954 ruling, Afro-Americans found no major quarrel with the courts doctrine. Supremely realistic by now, they knew that "all deliberate speed" was as close as a democratic body could come in ordering integration, and they appreciated that federal courts were given the responsibility of supervising integration. Many Negroes agreed that in each community they had a new responsibility constantly to prod their school boards into quickened action.

In the realm of education, from 1865 to May 17, 1954 there usually was contact between Negroes and whites only at the summit, that is, between the leaders of both races. This contact often took place between "safe' or conservative Negroes and state or local education officials. After the Supreme Court decision that the schools must de-segregate, a prominent white educational leader declared that the contact "must now be at the crossroads in every hamlet in this country." "In many respects," comments this observer, "it is at the local level . . . that we shall [now] hammer out our future and chart our destiny."[48]

In an address to the forty-second annual convention of the NAACP, held in Atlanta, Georgia, July 1, 1951, Ralph Bunche probably voiced the general sentiment of his race on social aims of the mid-twentieth century. The Negro demands, Bunche asserted, "complete integration as an American citizen." Bunche continued: "That means simply that he insists upon his Constitutional heritage, without let or hinderance; equally, without qualification of race or color; an end to discrimination and segregation, for segregation itself, in any form, is discrimination. To speak of 'segregated equality' among American citizens is to engage in wanton sophistry."[49]

In the South repressive measures followed the famed May 17, 1954 Supreme Court rulings. As Georgia, Mississippi, Louisiana, and South Carolina passed legislation to the effect that any teacher caught championing racial integration would be immediately fired, and to ban from the schools members of the NAACP, Negroes saw these as blows at freedom of thought and expression.[50] When the state of Georgia set September 15, 1955 as the deadline for its teachers to resign from the NAACP, the colored head of the Protestant Episcopal Church in North Georgia accused the state of attempting to bring about state control of thought, and charged that the Georgia State Board of Education was "taking its place in line with those subversive organizations that seek to change our Government by force."[51]

Speaking to the forty-second annual convention of the NAACP at Atlanta, Ralph Bunche had voiced a theme that has been prominent in the post World War II utterances of colored Americans. That theme is the urgency which America's race problem assumes *vis-a-vis* the Communist threat to the United States and the entire Western world. This threat, stated Bunche, leaves the nation precious little time to solve a problem which is robbing it of "strength, unity, moral position and prestige."[52] "Indeed," Bunche continued,"it might well be said that rapid progress toward the full integration of the Negro in the society is of even greater urgency for the nation today than for the Negro."[53]

The post-May 17, 1954 period saw an especial stiffening of southern opposition to the growing integration movement. While opposition has largely operated through White Citizens Councils and legislative enactments aimed at silencing protest and killing the NAACP in the section, this movement has included economic reprisal, beatings, bombings, and murders. The 1955 murder of young Emmett Till and subsequent shootings of others, including a prominent Mississippi preacher and a South Carolina physician, plus the threats to the life of Autherine Lucy at Tuscaloosa, Alabama stirred some members of both races to raise the cry that the Negro had better slow down his relentless push toward integration and equality. A colored North Carolina editor probably voiced the convictions of the majority of his race when he said that to accept this "slow down" advice would only give whites the opportunity to wipe out gains made by the Negro. "Why is it that the Negro [alone] is always asked to 'go slow'," he asked.[54]

There were several new elements in the Negro's position by 1955. One condition which had given rise to such essential legal-action organizations as the NAACP was the inability of individual Negroes to carry expensive litigation to federal courts when justice was denied them. By 1955 such litigation was often no longer prohibitively expensive for the reason that, so clear was the Supreme Court's position, one needed only to introduce a complaint into any federal district court. Furthermore, the fear and timidity of many southern Negroes had clearly disappeared. If school teachers often could be easily silenced because they were on the public payroll, ministers, physicians, dentists, businessmen and college students had a new and unyielding militancy. And unlike a generation previously, when Negro lawyers were very scarce in southern states, by 1955 they were more plentiful and eager to obtain civil rights cases.

By 1955 many Negroes had concluded that after the *sine qua non* of getting the law and federal courts committed to their fight for equal rights and opportunities, the rest must be up to both races at the local level; that with emotionally charged issues, there comes a point beyond which laws and courts are ineffective. They were convinced that ultimately only law-respecting local leaders and civic groups can make progress and bring a final solution to America's color problem. On the racial "front," almost always leaders of both racial groups have acted, talked, and written of "the fight." There was a growing conviction among both groups that where this is the dominant attitude and approach, ideal race relations are impossible, for a fight or contest implies competition, winner—vanquished, superior—inferior, and the possibility where feelings are high that Marquis of Queensbury rules may not be adhered to. Instead of competition, conflict, and different goals, these persons felt, harmonious cooperation toward common sectional goals must be more than ever the preeminent consideration.

In 1959 on the television program *Outlook,* the noted news analyst Chet Huntley suggested that Afro-Americans and the NAACP might well consider easing up the pressure of their fight for integration, as a tactic which would allow passions to cool and further their aims better than a continuing policy of pressure. Through the Negro press, a storm of "No's" came back at Huntley as Afro-Americans repeatedly voiced the conviction that they had followed a policy of gradualism and waiting long enough. Their answer to Huntley was reminiscent of the statement made by the Rev. Francis J. Grimké when the suggestion was made in the immediate post-World War I period that Negroes might best not press right away for a fuller measure of rights and opportunities. To this Grimké replied:

> Should we be less insistent, less persistent, less determined, less alive, less wide awake to the things that pertain to our rights, than the people who are sleeplessly vigilant in their efforts and determination to filch them from us to keep us in, what they call, our proper place . . .? It is astounding, almost incredible, that any colored man, even to the stupidest of them, should be led into such utter folly as to counsel the cessation of the struggle for our rights, even for a

moment, when nothing is ever accomplished except
by a struggle, by earnest, persistent effort.

When in August, 1959, the Little Rock, Arkansas Board of
Education voted acceptance of token integration of the city's
Central High School, the NAACP protested that the city's
plan whereby only five Negro students were enrolled was inadequate and would be fought in the courts. However, the
Rev. Joseph Jackson, then president of the National Baptist
Convention, wired the NAACP that its continuing pressure
was unrealistic and that the small victory should be accepted
as adequate for the time being. As further token integration
was achieved in the schools of several southern cities, Negroes
seemed at least temporarily willing to settle for it, but the student 'sit-in" assaults on segregated lunch counters, beaches,
and churches, plus a stepped up boycotting of business firms
which discriminated racially in their hiring practices, clearly
revealed a growing impatience with the existence of caste in
America.

Recent evidences of the militant turn of the Negro mind
was the wave of lunch-counter or "sit-in" demonstrations by
college students which swept the South during 1960. At least
two years earlier, with their Youth Marches on the nation's
capital, Negroes had given warning that enlistment of teen-
agers and young adults was a new-found weapon in their battle
for equality. An equally significant aspect of these protests
against second-class citizenship status was the manner in which,
unlike the characteristic behavior of their predecessors of the
previous generation, most Negro college presidents and parents
of the students refused to take direct responsibility for sup-
pressing the demonstrations. Those southern whites who did
not want to accept the New Negro found this radically new
and effective type of leadership and militancy particuarly dis-
tressing, and some southern governors began to take a new look
at Negro colleges and to wonder what could be done to get
the students to stick to their books and to refrain from attacking the status quo. A few governors spoke of Communist
influence and apparently could see no relationship between student protest movements in such places as Korea and Turkey
and those in their own states, and seemed to feel that the

teachers of the students might be to blame. Writing in the Spring, 1960 issue of *Harpers*, Louis Lomax expressed the opinion that in their militancy Negro youth was repudiating the traditionally conservative leadership of such organizations as the NAACP and Urban League.

Among Negroes per capita income had risen from approximately $365.00 in 1939 to approximately $1,300.00 in 1950. Although these figures represented scarcely one-half of the national average, they reflected some progress and indicated one main source of the constant drive to accelerate it. Speaking in Boston in 1905 Bishop Reverdy C. Ransom had evinced a belief that the Negro, by his "steadfast devotion to the flag [and emphasis on] constitutional rights" may some day be the salvation of the nation when the majority of its citizenry may be "surfeited with wealth, haughty with the boasting pride of race superiority, morally corrupt in the high places of honor and trust, enervated through the pursuit of pleasure, or the political bondmen of some strong man plotting to seize the reigns of power."[55] During the 1950's a number of Negroes would be heard voicing opinions that the nation had reached some such condition and that their race was indeed performing such a work of salvation. This judgment would derive in no small degree from such incidents as the corruption being revealed at home and the contrast between the mobbing of American embassies or then Vice-President Richard Nixon's unpopular reception in Latin America and the acclaim recently given to Marian Anderson in Asia and Louis Armstrong and other Negro artists in Europe.

CHAPTER XV

THE WASHINGTON - DU BOIS CONTROVERSY

The 1895 Atlanta Exposition address of Booker T. Washington is the focal point around which much controversy as to the man's personality, character, and philosophy has revolved. That an able and eminent scholar could in 1954 make Washington the *"bete noir* and most evil genius" of a historical volume reveals that this controversy is far from settled.[1]

The Atlanta speech catapulted Washington into the national limelight. Here in a brief but memorable message that is sometimes compared with Abraham Lincoln's Gettysburg Address, he struck a conciliatory note on race relations which was attuned to the thought of most white southerners and northerners alike. Although he states that "there was practically nothing new in the address," Rayford W. Logan believes that this speech "was one of the most effective pieces of political oratory in the history of the United States."[2] Logan thinks that it "deserves a place" alongside the earlier epic utterances of Patrick Henry and William Jennings Bryan.[3] At the conclusion of the Atlanta address, most of the platform speakers, including an ex-governor of Georgia, enthusiastically shook Washington's hand, and the next day telegrams containing congratulations and offers of lecture engagements began to pour into his office from all over the nation. One telegram came from President Grover Cleveland, and the next year Harvard University conferred on Washington the first honorary degree which any New England school ever granted a Negro.

In this speech Washington expressed a faith in economic determinism. He said:

> The wisest among my race understand that the agitation of questions of social equality is the extremest folly, and that progress in the enjoyment of all the privileges that will come to us must be the result of severe and constant struggle, rather than of artificial forcing. No race that has anything to contribute to the markets of the world is long in any degree ostracized.[4]

While one may quarrel with this doctrine, there is no doubting the soundness of the statement which followed it. "The opportunity to earn a dollar in a factory just now," he said of his race, "is worth infinitely more than the opportunity to spend a dollar in an opera house."[5] Sheer wisdom stood out also when, to the white South, he declared—"There is no defense or security for any of us except in the highest intelligence and development of all."[6]

Washington probably spoke for the majority of the race in the South when he renounced "agitation of questions" of equality of citizenship until such a time as more white people would feel differently toward the colored man. While temporarily "accepting" this *modus vivendi* between the two races, Washington asked for the *quid pro quo* of a good neighbor policy. Unharmonious race relations, he believed, would serve to the detriment of all. "In all things that are purely social," he declared, "we can be as separate as the fingers, yet one as the hand in all things essential to mutual progress." Washington apologized to southern whites because the freedmen, in his belief, had put interest in politics before such interests as learning a trade or building character, and he indicated his belief that the race had thus put the cart before the horse, and that the Negro was now ready to reverse the situation and by so doing slowly *earn* the political and civil rights which had been held briefly as the result of "artificial forcing." With Abraham Lincoln, Andrew Johnson, and others, Washington believed that only the most literate and cultured Negroes, like himself, were fit and had a right to exercise the franchise. Again reflecting his economic determinism, realism, and optimism, Washington said:

> Our greatest danger is, that, in the great leap from slavery to freedom, we may overlook the fact that the masses of us are to live by the productions of our hands, and fail to keep in mind that we shall prosper in the proportion as we learn to dignify and glorify common labor and put brains and skill into the common occupations of life; shall prosper in proportion as we learn to draw the line between the superficial and the substantial. . . . It is at the bottom of life

we must begin and not the top. Nor should we permit
our grievances to overshadow our opportunities.

He urged the South to view the Negro as a friend, because the latter had made a great contribution in labor to the
building of the nation. Playing up to the anti-labor sentiment
of the times, Washington stated that the Negro had made his
contribution in labor "without strikes and labor wars." Of the
South, Washington averred: "To those of my race who depend
on bettering their condition in a foreign land, or who underestimate the importance of cultivating friendly relations with
the Southern white man who is their next door neighbor, I
would say, cast down your bucket where you are. . . . And
in this connection it is well to bear in mind that, whatever
other sins the South may be called upon to bear, when it comes
to business pure and simple it is in the South that the Negro
is given a man's chance in the commercial world." In this
speech Washington spoke of "our beloved South." No doubt
he shared much of the faith in the section which Henry W.
Grady and others were then revealing, but here Washington also
was reflecting the views of many Afro-Americans on their
native Southland. The sentiment which provoked such songs
as "Carry Me Back to Old Virginny," and "My Old Kentucky
Home," caused Frederick Douglass to express similar feelings
in a letter to his former slave master. On this, Douglass wrote
in 1848:

> The fact is, there are few [fugitive slaves] here who
> would not return to the South in the event of eman-
> cipation. We want to live in the land of our birth,
> and to lay our bones by the side of our fathers; and
> nothing short of an intense love of personal freedom
> keeps us from the South.[7]

Still another Afro-American had opined in 1884:
> The colored man is in the South to stay there. He
> will not leave it voluntarily and he cannot be driven
> out. He had no voice in being carried into the South,
> but he will have a very loud voice in any attempt to
> put him out.[8]

The Industrial Education Issue

Washington believed that education could work wonders
in eliminating the race problem. On this, he wrote: "The proper

education of all the whites will benefit the Negro as much as the education of the Negro will benefit the whites. The Governor of Alabama would probably count it no disgrace to ride in the same railroad coach with a colored man, but the ignorant white man who curries the Governor's horse would turn up his nose in disgust."[9] Washington believed that there is "an indescribable something about work with the hands that tends to develop a student's mind."[10] Having been exposed to General Armstrong and Hampton Institute, this was the only type of education that Washington knew well. There is an adage in education which states that people teach as they were taught. In view, however, of Washington's very strong emphasis on maintaining at least the semblance of amicable relations between the races in the South, there can be little doubt that one of his major reasons for championing so-called industrial education was that southern whites favored this type for his race. Then, too, his close friendship with the nation's top industrialists undoubtedly helped mould his views. He came to share practically every article of their faith, from the laissez-faire emphasis and Horatio Alger rags-to-riches dream to their antipathy toward labor unions. Also through the temper of the times and General Armstrong Washington was a staunch champion of the Gospel of Work.

Washington stated in many places his preference for manual or industrial training rather than general education or the liberal arts. Like so many Americans of his period, he believed that acquisition of wealth was the panacea for practically all of an individual's or nation's needs. Washington knew that, while the white South tended to fear liberally educated Negroes, it did not fear the person who was supposedly educated to work only with his hands. Washington never believed that he was compromising or retreating from his own principles or the principles and ultimate goals of his race. To him it was largely a matter of method and of expediency. His educational convictions were expressed as early as 1884, just three years after Tuskegee Institute was founded. Speaking on the subject, "The Educational Outlook in the South," before the National Association meeting in Madison, Wisconsin, he stated: "A certain class of whites in the South object to the general education of the colored man on the ground that when he is educated he ceases to do manual labor, and there is no evading the fact that much aid is withheld from Negro education in the South by the states on these grounds. Just here the great mission of *Industrial Education* coupled with the mental comes in. It 'kills two birds with one stone,' viz.: secures the cooperation of the whites, and does the best possible thing for the black man.'"[11] "God for two hundred and fifty years, in my opinion," Washington declared, "prepared the way for the redemption of the Negro through industrial development."[12]

Long before Washington, industrial education had been an especial interest of Afro-Americans. Beginning in 1831, most of the annual Negro conventions championed this type of education.[13] Frederick Douglass was a very active leader in most of these conventions. The first such convention had met in Philadelphia, Pennsylvania. Fifteen delegates from five states attended. This Convention voted to institutionalize a vocational training program for Negroes which had been proposed as early as 1827 by Samuel Cornish, and which had the support of such outstanding abolitionists as William Lloyd Garrison, Benjamin Lundy, and Arthur Tappan. It was proposed that this school should be located in New Haven, Connecticut, but opposition from this city and from persons elsewhere kept this project from being realized. As early as 1853, Frederick Douglass had advised members of his race to "learn trades or starve." "If the alternative were presented to us of learning a trade or getting an education," Douglass had said, "we should learn the trade, for the reason that with the trade we could get the education while with the education we could not get a trade."[14] Later, continuing the industrial school trend, Hampton and Tuskegee graduates founded in Alabama the Snow Hill and Mount Meigs institutes; Voorhees Industrial School of South Carolina; in Virginia the St. Paul Industrial School, Christiansburgh Institute, the Franklin Normal and Industrial Institute, and the Glouchester Agricultural and Industrial School; and other institutions. In 1900 and thereafter Tuskegee students went to Africa to introduce cotton growing into German, British, and Belgian colonies, and the Tuskegee idea even spread to China.

Washington, ever a pragmatist of sorts, had little use for the "education-for-private-use" attitude. To him the benefits of education had to be clearly visible. On this, he stated:

> I would set no limits to the attainments of the Negro in arts, in letters or statesmanship, but I believe the surest way to reach those ends is by laying the foundation in the little things of life. . . . I plead for industrial education and development for the Negro not because I want to cramp him, but because I want to free him. I want to see him enter the all-powerful business and commercial world.

In 1905 Harvard trained former Tuskegee instructor, Roscoe Conkling Bruce attacked this Washington-propagated attitude. Bruce declared:

> The effects of education are really to be sought in the mind and character and growing power of the student; the process is . . .. essentially intangible, and to estimate the thoroughness of the process and its value for life in terms of the ponderable character of the apparatus is a fundamental error. Anything is practical that is of service to the community. Clear thinking and insight into human nature, certainly have as many practical uses as deftness with hammer and tongs.[15]

In his emphasis on industrial-type education, Washington was in step with a major trend of his times, and the opposition which was directed toward him was in many ways characteristic of the same critcism which was then being directed at white pedagogues who were calling for a deemphasis of the old aristocratic education and the giving of more attention to meeting the educational needs peculiar to an industrialized society.

Many Negro leaders saw that the classical curriculum did not properly fit the needs of the freedmen, but, they pointed out that by the '70s and '80s this curriculum no longer fitted the needs of most whites also, and the strong opposition which Horace Mann and other educational reformers encountered proved that the classical curriculum was a fetish to many whites as well as Negroes. Among the outstanding Negro educators who saw these things was Roscoe Conkling Bruce who was for fifteen years Assistant Superintendent in charge of Colored

Schools in the District of Columbia. In 1905 Bruce was championing an enriched curriculum for Negro colleges in the South, a curriculum which would see the addition of "thorough courses in natural science with its application to industry; in history and social science with special attention to the traditions and progress of Negro peoples in Africa and in America, and to the sociological problems in which Negro life in America is enmeshed today."[16]   Further, he added, "the Negro college should render its curriculum flexible and more widely serviceable through the introduction of an elective system by the provisions of which the dead languages might give way to the living languages and history and social science, and advanced mathematics to psychology and ethics and the principles and practices of education."[17] He also urged Negro colleges to have well-equipped schools of education, agriculture, engineering, and medicine. It was essentially the *idea* and principle implied in industrial education which was most repugnant to many Negroes. In truth, all such schools as Tuskegee or Hampton rapidly became primarily teacher training institutions. Since over sixty per cent of the graduates of almost all Negro colleges have entered the teaching profession, whether the institution was labeled a liberal arts college or an agricultural and mechanical one often has mattered little.

With many Afro-Americans, Washington believed that the race problem is essentially a moral issue. William Hooper Councill, an outstanding contemporary, who was also an Alabama educator, enunciated the same opinion. "Problems are born in the souls of men," Councill declared, "and if solved at all, must be solved there."[18]   In the same vein, Washington averred: "If you want to know how to solve the race problem, place your hands upon your heart and then, with a prayer to God, ask him how you . . ., were you placed in the position that the black man occupies, how you would desire the white man to treat you."[19]

One would make a grave error in concluding that Washington was an Uncle Tom type in the sense of a meek, frightened, and cowed individual. Quite the contrary is true. Especially in his speeches made in northern cities, he was outspoken in his contention that ultimate equality of the races was his desire. About the only justification one could have for calling Washington an "Uncle Tom" was his insistence that, in his day, the southern Negro should de-emphasize political action in favor of fighting on the economic and educational fronts. "Brains, property, and character for the Negro," he stated, "will settle the question of civil rights."[20] "Now, in regard to what I have said about the relations of the two races," he once said, "there should be no unmanly cowering or stooping to satisfy unreasonable whims of southern white men, but it is charity and wisdom to keep in mind the two hundred years' schooling in prejudice against the Negro which the ex-slave holders are called upon to conquer."[21] With reservations, Washington favored the founding of the NAACP. Washington's resentment at the color line in labor unions was very bitter.[22] While working in West Virginia's coal mines, he had belonged to the Knights of Labor for several years. Also, in his usual inoffensive way, he tried to arouse the best white people of the South against lynching. He reminded them constantly that if they were to maintain home-rule in the section free from federal interference, they would have to carry out their "sacred trust" of maintaining law and order.[23] Washington also sometimes planted "radical" letters in newspapers under pseudonyms, and quietly contributed money to test in court various disfranchisement laws.[24] Still Rayford W. Logan, writing in 1954, made Washington the *"bete noir* and most evil genius" of his historical volume on the period 1877-1901. In a review of Logan's study, G. W. Grimké observes that, "Washington was an ardent politician, but he has not yet been proved to have been an Uncle Tom."[25]

Washington believed htat the freedmen themselves had to complete the work of emancipation. He averred:

> This work must be completed in the public school, industrial school and college. The most of it must be completed in the effort of the Negro himself, in his effort to withstand temptation, to economize, to exercise thrift, to disregard the superficial for the real, the shadow for the substance, to be great and yet small, in his effort to be patient in the laying of a firm foundation, to grow so strong in skill and

knowledge that he shall place his service in demand
by reason of his intrinsic and superior worth.

Even before he achieved nation-wide fame, Washington expressed the belief that "reforms in the South are to come from
within." Indicative of the fact that he based his approach to
the race problem on cooperating with rather than clashing with
southern whites, he declared that these persons "don't like to
obey orders that come from Washington that they must lay
aside at once customs that they have followed for centuries."
In his agrarianism, deep love of the South, and respect for states
rights, Booker Washington is somewhat reminiscent of Thomas
Jefferson, while in his contrary views on these points and in
his faith in an elite (the "Talented Tenth"), W. E. B. DuBois
is somewhat reminiscent of Alexander Hamilton. Washington
seems to have understood the stubborn unreasoning nature of
human prejudice, yet, with great faith in the power of education and human reason, he always believed that more formal
education would lift both poor whites and Negroes to a level
where thought triumphs over emotions. Although he fought
for his race, typical of educated mulattoes of his day, he had
considerable contempt for the Negro masses. To Washington,
farm ownership was a sort of panacea which could eliminate
the evil crop lien system and also give Negroes pride in their
work and an incentive to work harder and make improvements.
He knew that his race needed a second emancipation which required attention to the economic and cultural spheres as much
or moreso than to the area of political and civil rights action.
He often spoke of his dream that both sectionalism and racism
would disappear from the nation. There was a strong strain of
puritanism in him, which was partly religious in origin, and
which fitted in with and was partially derived from the Vic-
torianism of his times. His puritanism and disdain of violence
are characteristics evident in many Negro leaders, even those
who may stand at variance with other aspects of his philosophy.
Washington was a disciple of the Liberal Republicanism which
Radical Reconstruction spawned. As was the case with such
politicians as Horace Greely and Carl Schurz, and the nation's
leading industrialists, Washington wanted the sections to "shake
hands across the bloody chasm," and like these he thought that

a quiescent race relations front was essential to the growth and development of business, hence of the nation. He urged that his race must learn to "mix with their religion some land, cotton, and corn, a house with two or three rooms, and a little bank account."[27] In his view that politics was the area of life Negro participation in which southern whites were most vehemently opposed, Washington had plenty of company among members of both races. The eminent educator J. C. Price stated on numerous occasions

> The great discordant element between the races, that which makes the so-called race problem, is Negro Citizenship and its consequent eligibility to office. If there is a race problem, here are its centripetal and centrifugal forces.[28]

Washington urged Negroes to be Republican in national politics, but Democratic at the state and local level.

Between 1866-1876 Booker Washington's program of accommodation would not have been acceptable to the leading white and colored politicians, who were then idealistically championing a program of uncompromising racial equality. Even in the heyday of Washington's dominance, the rising democratic fervor evident in the Populist revolt and Progressive movement led to a mounting protest against the view of black mankind which quiescence in the face of jim-crow implied. Washington's triumph and popularity is proof of the great need which the South and the nation had by 1895 for a respite from the long-drawn out strife over the status and rights of the colored man. Washington's triumph was the Thermidorean reaction which follows almost every intense and protracted attempt at social, economic, and political reform. Knowing that his race, starting late and handicapped, had greater obstacles to overcome, Washington asked it to glorify in this and to rise cheerfully to the challenge. During slavery most of the Negro's impetus to work was external in origin and symbolized by the lash. Washington wisely knew that, in order for it to survive and prosper, the race's impetus to work would have to be internalized. On this, he stated:

> We must not be afraid to pay the price for success—
> the price of sleepless nights, the price of toil when

others rest, the price of planning today for tomorrow, this year for next year. If someone else endures the hardships, someone else will reap the harvest and enjoy the reward.[29]

Again and again he declared that the greater one's difficulties, the greater should be his success.

Washington accepted the dictum that the masses of Negroes were not ready for equality of citizenship and opportunity, and he felt that they would not be ready for fifty or more years. At a Harvard alumni dinner in 1896, as he had at Atlanta the previous year, he laid down the conditions which his race must meet before it would be ready. At Harvard he declared—

> During the next half century and more, my race must continue passing through the severe American crucible. We are to be tested in our patience, our forbearance, our perseverance, our power to endure wrong, to withstand temptations, to economize, to acquire and use skill, and our ability to compete, to succeed in commerce. . . . This, this is the passport to all that is best in the life of our Republic, and the Negro must possess it, or be debarred.[30]

Washington's emphasis on "self-help, self discipline, self-salvation" were also in step with his times, for these emphases had their echoes in Horatio Alger, William Makepeace Thayer, Russell Conwell, Orison Swett Marden, and others. "It is important and right that all privileges of the law be ours," Washington wrote, "but it is vastly more important that we be prepared for the exercise of those privileges." And again: "With proper habits, intelligence and property, there is no power on earth that can permanently stay our progress."[31]

Negro novelists of the period 1895-1920 paid considerable attention to the controversy over whether their race should follow the Washington formula in race relations or take the more militant line which W. E. B. Du Bois was championing. Most of the writers sided with Du Bois, but how much their inclinations represented the rank and file of the race is a moot question. Quoting the views of numerous Tuskegee alumni who were polled by Washington in 1894 as to their views on solving the race problem, Jack Abramowitz shows that they were avid

in their support of the self-help-accommodation philosophy of
Washington. On this, Abramowitz comments:

> Such views by the men and women graduates from
> Tuskegee stemmed from the fact that the virtues of
> self-government, progress through economic success,
> and advancement within the framework of existing
> conditions rather than struggle against them, were
> an integral part of the curriculum of the institution.
> Day in, day out, in class and at chapel, in private
> conversations and in Sunday evening talks to the stu-
> dents, the point was made that the failure of any
> man stems from his own deficiencies. . . . Tuskegee
> students heard this from Booker T. Washington who
> had learned it from General Samuel Chapman Arm-
> strong at Hampton.[32]

Further, Abramowitz notes:

> Insistence upon ascribing the conditions of the Negro
> to personal deficiencies runs rampant in the Negro
> press of the 1890s, and it was particularly stressed in
> such institutions as Hampton and Tuskegee and the
> scores of lesser schools modeled after them.[33]

Numerous writers have pointed out that Washington did
not properly understand the changes which laissez-faire capitalism was undergoing in his day. In the antipathy which he
seems to have developed toward labor unions, he was unrealistic. The same is true of his insistence that Negroes remain
in rural areas, or even in the South while mechanization of
farms and the rising development of urban areas counselled
differently. Washington did not see that the growth of commercial and monopoly capitalism was fast killing the great
American illusion that by dint of hard work and ingenuity
any boy could become a millionaire, and where he genuinely
believed that liberal education was of little value, he did the
race a disservice.[34] Still, by "accepting" the harsh and cold facts
of their *fait accompli*, Washington performed the important
and needed service of allaying the fears of southern whites. In
the effort which Radical Reconstructionists made to force political and civil equality of the Negro on southern whites, the
latter saw this as a dire threat to practically every aspect of
their traditional way of life. Washington calmed these fears
somewhat by pointing out that his race would accept without

violence the subordinate role to which it was forcibly assigned in southern life. If he was wrong in that he misled some Negroes into the dangerous belief that political and civil rights are of secondary importance, he was very correct in the emphasis which he gave to the importance of industry, thrift, manners, morals, and character.

William Edward Burghardi Du Bois was the first person to raise effectively objection to the Washington philosophy. In his *The Souls of Black Folk,* Du Bois took Washington to task, accusing him of advocating a "gospel of Work and Money" which would make men carpenters but not carpenters men.[35] "Men we shall have," Du Bois wrote, "only as we make manhood the object of the work of the schools—intelligence, broad sympathy, knowledge of the world that was and is, and of the relation of men to it."[36] He dubbed Washington's 1895 speech the "Atlanta Compromise." On the racial formula which Washington had laid down, Du Bois said that the formula contained a "triple paradox." These were:

1. He [Washington] is striving nobly to make Negro artisans, business men and property-owners; but it is utterly impossible, under modern competitive methods, for workingmen and property-owners to defend their rights and exist without the right of suffrage.
2. He insists on thrift and self-respect, but at the same time counsels a silent submission to civic inferiority such as is bound to sap the manhood of any race in the long run.
3. He advocates common-school and industrial training, and deprecates institutions of higher learning; but neither the Negro common-schools, nor Tuskegee itself, could remain open a day were it not for teachers trained in Negro colleges, or trained by their graduates.[37]

Du Bois contended that Washington's protests against lynchings and disfranchisement were too mild, and that his insistence on self-help was placing on the Negro's back practically alone a burden which properly belonged to all of the South and the Nation as a whole. Du Bois charged that the price which the white South was demanding for Negro cooperation and friendship was excessive. While Washington constantly thought of the southern white man as a friend, Du Bois thought of him as a foe.

The *Boston Guardian,* founded by Monroe Trotter and George Forbes in 1901, was dedicated to a crusade against the leadership of Washington. Du Bois, friend and admirer of Trotter, led in founding the Niagara Movement in 1905-6, which also was dedicated to a denunciation of the Washington formula and to a more militant type of leadership. Nineteen hundred nine saw the founding of the National Association for the Advancement of Colored People as a prototype of the Niagara Movement, and the *Crisis,* founded and long edited by DuBois, and official organ of the NAACP, took the place which the *Guardian* had filled in championing an approach to the race problem which was practically the opposite of that which Washington was advocating. Thus it may be said that, due perhaps to the leadership of Du Bois more than to any other person, the radical-militant type of racial leadership of which Frederick Douglass was for so long one of the highest embodiments rose to prominence again.

One key to an understanding of the quarrel between Washington and Du Bois lies in the personalities of the two men. But their ultimate desires and goals were the same. Essentially Washington and Du Bois differed in method. The latter, throughout most of his life, was an uncompromising idealist, while the former, in line with the slave tradition to which he was a successor and the compromising spirit for which his age was so especially noted, was more of a pragmatist. To Washington, as with all good pragmatists, each thought and act was to be measured chiefly by its results. Pragmatism has been called a uniquely American philosophy, and Washington's contempt for higher education is also in the American tradition of contempt for the professor and the man of theory. Booker Washington was a gradualist, an evolutionist, and he was supremely patient. Having known first-hand the hopelessness and lack of opportunity which existed under chattel slavery, even the advance to third-class citizenship was to him cause for thankfulness and optimism, while Du Bois, having begun life in New England where race and color were not so much noticed, had not gone through the same conditioning. Ever conscious of his origins in slavery, Washington usually tended to look back at the distance the race had come, while Du Bois tended more to look forward at the long miles yet to be travelled, hence he was less optimistic, more bitter, and less patient. Washington never went before an audience to speak without "asking the blessing of God" upon what he wanted to say,[38] but, while he was employed as a teacher at Wilberforce University, Du Bois sharply refused to lead a student audience in prayer.[39] Du Bois approached action through philosophy and theory, while Washington was a man of action largely by faith and intuition, and while Du Bois was sophisticated, urbane, and cosmopitan, Washington was the rural type who loved his chickens and pigs, as well as horse-back riding, hunting, and fishing. Du Bois was much more of the artistic and intellectual bent. Although he was teaching in the heart of the South when he first took up the cudgel against the Washington philosophy and formula, Du Bois was voicing the traditional sentiments of the northern Negro. But just as this approach, philosophy, and adjustment was impossible for the *ante-bellum* bondsman in the South, so it was impossible for most of the *post-bellum* freedmen in that section. Later, Du Bois gave up classroom teaching and moved physically to the section for which his approach and philosophy were indigenous. Only in the post-World War II period has his approach won wide acceptance in the section where the type of philosophy held by Washington was so long dominant. Washington called Du Bois and his intellectual advocates of a "Talented Tenth" leadership "fighting windmills" who "know books, but . . . not . . . men," who "understand theories, but . . . not . . . things," who are "ignorant in regard to the actual needs of the masses of the coloured people in the South."[40]

One of the things which Du Bois resented most about Washington was the latter's personal power.[41] So great was Washington's prestige that he was regarded by American whites as the elder statesman of his race, and his approval or disapproval was often decisive in determining whether some philanthropists contributed to Negro institutions. In this way he sometimes could often "make" or "break" men. In 1905

Du Bois asserted that many of the most prominent Negro newspapers were being silenced in their opposition to Washington. Du Bois then wrote of the "Tuskegee Machine," and sought to expose and weaken it. Through Ralph W. Tyler, whom Washington aided in getting placed in the federal government, and the Colored Press Bureau of Washington, D. C., also launched by the Tuskegee President, newspapers in Chicago, Indianapolis, New York and other cities were influenced by Washington's efforts.[42] Not only did Washington use money to buy the support of several newspapers, he also secretly owned the influential *New York Age* during the five-year period from 1905-1910.[43] His firm control of northern philanthropy kept some Negro liberal arts colleges from getting financial aid from this source.[44] One of his latest and ablest biographers agrees that Tuskegee's founder was a "benevolent despot."[45] Although he warned Negroes not to be all for one political party, Washington supported William McKinley, Theodore Roosevelt, and William Howard Taft in almost complete devotion. In return, Washington had practically complete control over Negro patronage during their administrations.[46]

To Du Bois, the mere fact that one man possessed as much power as Washington did was objectionable in a democratic society. In the "Apologia" to the 1954 reprint of his volume on *The Suppression of the African Slave Trade to the United States of America*, Du Bois confesses to his moralistic judgments of men and issues, and regrets that previous to the early 1930s he did not have a thorough appreciation of Marxism and Freudianism.[47] This appreciation, he felt, would have altered his interpretation of and reaction to a number of things in his early life. It is of interest to note that this clash with Washington, in which Du Bois was by no means alone, came previous to his conversion to Marxism. It may be that had he then held the appreciation for Marx's philosophy that he later came to have, Du Bois would have paid less attention to Washington. Dr. Du Bois asserts that he became a convert to Marxism in the post-World War I period. From the discussion which he gives of this conversion in his autobiography, the impression is given that his conversion was rather sudden, and the result of a trip to Russia which was made at the expense and invitation of the

Soviet Union. He gives no hint of the fact that as early as 1904 his thinking was partially Marxist-oriented. His early faith in economic determinism seems to have sprung mainly from his observations of the growing political and social power of capitalists as they manipulated and controlled many facets of the national life, including, he thought, the Booker Washington "machine." Although previous to the Russian Revolution of 1917 there is evident in the writings and speeches of Du Bois a growing faith in economic determinism, there is no evidence that previous to this date he believed in the imminent downfall of capitalism and its displacement by socialism, or in the need for militant group action aimed directly at the downfall of monopoly capitalism. He was not yet a doctrinaire. Previous to his trip to Russia, he did not speak often of the Afro-American as being part of the "world proletariat" as he so often has done since the early 1930's. Until his complete conversion to Marxism, one finds little bitterness in his writings, and he seems to have had more patience with slow democratic processes. Previous to this conversion, Du Bois' writings seem less propagandistic, and he showed considerable contempt for dictatorial movements and individuals. Earlier he had felt that the race problem sprang either from ignorance or from a failure in the nation's morals, but his Marxist conversion caused him to feel that at last he really "understood" the American white man, the race problem and Western civilization for the first time. The real enemy and determinist factor was now viewed as being the capitalist system, for the nation was not being immoral if one considered that capitalism dictated "profits by any means and at all costs." To the new Du Bois, as with all Marxists, this eternal and infernal quest for profits was the source of the slave trade, the cruelties and fanaticism of slavery as well as of such phenomena as racial segregation, lynchings and the too-low wages of industrial and agricultural workers. Thus, instead of being immoral, the white American exploiter of the Negro was a good or amoral capitalist-Christian. What was immoral and wrong now was not so much the man as the economic system which bred him, and the race problem, as only one of a multiplicity of wrongs bred by this system, would disappear only through the triumph of socialism.

Although many Afro-Americans have long dreamed of a "Moses," who would lead the race into full integration in society, a significant fact is that most of the race's major movements have been without any one outstanding leader. Although Frederick Douglass gave voice to the highest aspirations of his race before 1895, he did not lead the race, the majority of whom were in the South and unfree to follow his militant efforts. Within the South, no individual was largely responsible for either the militancy against or resignation to slavery which the race showed. The Reconstruction period also saw no single outstanding leader in the South. Although after 1896 Washington was accepted by whites as the spokesman for his race, it may be doubted that Washington was ever as much a true leader of the masses of his race as is popularly imagined. That he, in his patience, gradualism, compromise, Social Darwinism and emphasis on industrial education did not speak for many northern Negroes is clear. The desire of most southern Negroes for equality of treatment and opportunity was dominant with them before Washington was born, and their acquiescence in third-class citizenship, and their temporary abandonment of political action and of the quest for equality was not done by choice. Long before Washington "accepted" this *modus vivendi,* it was a *fait accompli,* brought about by the federal government's laissez-faire policy after 1876, and other factors.[49]

"Washington was first and last an American, Du Bois first and last a Negro," one of Washington's latest biographers has declared.[49] This statement, however, makes the erroneous implication that there was in the period in which this controversy raged most heatedly a significant difference between being an American and being a Negro. Just as was true of their race in general, both of these men were thoroughly American. The primary difference between them, and a main historical source of their quarrels, was that they represented different sides of the coin. The thought and life of Dr. Du Bois are in the militant, protesting, even radical American tradition which is typified by Tom Paine, Samuel Adams, William Lloyd Garrison, Frederick Douglass, Populists, Muckrakers, and others, while Booker Washington's life and thought follow that more conservative tradition of compromise which is to be seen in the life and thought of Alexander Hamilton, Daniel Webster, Henry Clay, and others.

Great concern with the Hot War which existed between the sections from 1861-65 and the Cold War which they waged from 1865-75 has obscured the fact that when Washington spoke in 1895 there had been going on constantly in the South for over two hundred and seventy-five years a cold war between the black and white races.[49] For the brutal fact is that Cold War between the races was often inherent in slavery before 1865, just as it often has been inherent in segregation and discrimination since 1865. And just as Winston Churchill at Fulton, Missouri urged the United States to accept the realities of the cold war with Russia, some Negro spokesmen from David Walker, Nat Turner, Denmark Vesey, Frederick Douglass, and W. E. B. Du Bois to Robert Williams of Monroe, North Carolina in 1959 have urged Negroes to accept the existence of cold war as a reality between the races. At times this "cold war" has erupted into "hot war" in such forms as revolts, riots, beatings and lynchings, and southern whites ever have had their spokesmen who openly have proclaimed war as an inherent and essential reality of southern Negro—white relations. These spokesmen constantly have urged that the Negro be clearly recognized and plainly treated as a weak but dangerous enemy of the "white man's civilization."

During the 1850s Negro Abolitionists, together with Elijah Lovejoy, John Quincy Adams, William Lloyd Garrison, the Tappans, John Brown, and others succeeded in convincing many northerners that the more intense age-old cold war between the races in the South had spread and that in the interest of self-preservation the North should abandon its isolationist or quarantine "foreign policy" vis-a-vis the South in favor of a more open interventionist policy. Thus the North came to see that there could be no peace in the Nation until there was an end to the situation between the races in the South. This is what Abraham Lincoln gave voice to in his "House Divided" speech, and this is what the Civil War sought to effect. The reconstruction policy voted by the Radicals in March, 1867 fitted the realities of the existing situation much better than the Lincoln-Johnson plans which failed because of their unreality. The plundering and profiteering in the South, as well as the Ku Klux Klan and other southern groups based on the use of naked force are best understood in the light of a war theory applied to the post 1865 period, just as many of the pre-1861 incidents and utterances and acts are best understood in this light.

Although the long-vanquished Negro was in the role of victor roughly from 1867-76, by the latter date this short-lived position and role were over. Some vengeance was wreaked upon him, for his briefly successful revolt, but the watchful eye of his old northern ally helped to prevent his annihilation, and previous to the emergence of Washington, numerous southern leaders had decided that there might be merit and profit in changing the posture between the races and sections from one of war to something less exacting in terms of attention, time, energy, hatred and bloodshed. Perhaps there is no greater proof to be found that by 1895 a new South was emerging than the popularity of Washington's ideas. By 1895 the South, black and white, was tired of war between the sections and between the races. Although the white South wanted peace on the race relations front, the section was still too bound by the war-induced prejudices and convictions and the old desire to make capital out of class divisions to accept the obvious fact that a peace based on segregation and racial discrimination could not be deep and enduring. Midst these circumstances, Booker Washington stepped forth as a practical-minded "General" who saw that his weak and beleaguered forces sorely needed peace at almost any price. Never despairing of ultimate victory, and ever fighting on different ground, he hoped to build the strength of his forces and perhaps renew the old fight at some more propitious future date. Subsequently the American democratic creed itself was the source of the division and revolt which occurred as the more articulate minority within his ranks became more and more impatient with all approaches to battle which allowed the nation peacefully to renege even for a moment on its promise that all men are born and of right ought to be free and equal.

The Booker Washington philosophy and program were the first positive ones that the masses of Negroes in America ever

had. Previous to 1865 these masses had an externally imposed
life-program which, for them, may be called negative in nature;
almost nowhere in their lives had there been much opportunity
or room for initiative, advance, growth, or maturity. For most
bondsmen only death or insanity—and they are only slightly
different—provided an escape from that most awful plight of
being forced forever to remain a child. Here was the central
and great wrong of slavery to which the beatings and other
wrongs were subsidiary and symbolic. For most southern Negroes, and many whites, slavery made true adulthood impossible.
Limited though it was, Washington's philosophy and program
had enough elements of positive thought and action in them
for the Negro to attain a type of adulthood under them, and
in this sense, Washington offered an advance to his race and
not a retreat. Washington correctly saw that for most of the
freedmen even his philosophy-program was revolutionary, and
thus it is that despite his conservatism, he conceived of himself
as a revolutionary leader. He did not conceive of his quarrel
with Du Bois in the light of a conservative versus a militant
liberal, but rather in the light of a practical brand of militancy
versus an impractical type.

Many Negro leaders have been aware that so low was
their race's position on the scale of rights and opportunities,
that to bridge the gap between its position and that of the
majority group would of necessity constitute an achievement
of revolutionary proportions. Thus it is that, although having
racial uplift as their dominant theme, whether the programs
they espoused were popularly thought of as ultra-conservative
or radical, Negro leaders have tended to conceive of themselves
as social revolutionaries. Too, whether they worked in the religious, fraternal, political, educational, or business worlds, and
whether their positions were "big" or "little," these leaders often
have tended to conceive of their work as a holy mission and of
themselves as indispensable divinely-inspired emissaries. Because
of this, the tremendous obstacles which they have faced, and
their own group's long lack of education, culture, and wealth,
Negro leaders too often have been unusually suspicious and in-
secure, two results of which have been a deep intolerance toward differences of opinion emanating from within their group,

and unusual concern with the question of loyalty to the group. Although they frequently have claimed that as leaders, in the interest of "the cause," they were sacrificing themselves in a dangerous inhospitable work, Negroes have shown what is perhaps an unusual desire to attain and keep positions of leadership. Doubtless the fact that most high offices in the "white world" of industry, politics, and general culture long have been closed to Afro-Americans has helped give them an especial reverence and desire for the leadership positions which exist in the "Negro world," and has made competition for these positions unusually intense. This pattern of charismatic leadership was especially dominant during the 1877-1933 period. The uncompromising William Monroe Trotter and W. E. B. Du Bois were among the best-known prototypes of this pattern of leadership, but by no means the only examples of it. Before the overthrow of Reconstruction, the democratic leadership typified by Frederick Douglass was probably dominant among Negroes, a leadership which was typically American in its optimism and friendliness. During this period the Negro had white allies of significance in the North before 1865, and in both major sections from 1865-1895. By 1895, however, laissez-faire and Social Darwinist-thinking combined with other factors to change this situation, and Negro leadership felt more alone, threatened, desperate, and pessimistic than ever before. Too, the general weakening of religious faith in this period tended to rob this leadership of another strong source of its confidence, optimism, and patience. Since 1933, due to the federal government's abandonment of the laissez-faire philosophy, the ever-expanding world liberalism on race, and an awareness that its army of "followers" is better educated and possesses greater economic resources, Negro leadership probably has tended to return to the pre-1877 democratic pattern.

Some Aspects of the Thought of Frederick Douglass, Booker Washington and W. E. B. Du Bois Compared

A comparison of some aspects of the thought of three of the best known leaders of the Negro race in America is revealing. Although perhaps popularly Frederick Douglass, Booker Washington, and W. E. B. Du Bois are thought of as greatly diverse personalities and types of leaders, the similarities among them are greater than is commonly thought.

All three of these men started their adulthood with a highly moralistic outlook on men and society, and gradually changed to a rather thorough-going pragmatism. Influenced greatly by William Lloyd Garrison, Douglass began his career as an enthusiastic critic of organized religion, as an anarchist or no-government man, and as an opponent of political parties.[51] He felt that political parties were composed of venally selfish men and that abolitionism should be carried out through moral suasion alone. So strong was the religious influence on him that it moulded his thinking into the narrow cast for which Garrison is so often criticized. Douglass' conversion to a broader view of religion, politics, and government, first openly declared at an 1851 anti-slavery convention, was the beginning of his celebrated breach with Garrison.

Through Mrs. Viola Ruffner in the town of Malden, West Virginia, and later through General Samuel C. Armstrong of Hampton Institute and others, Booker Washington was greatly influenced by New England's Puritan tradition.[52] This was the same New England into which Du Bois was born and nurtured, and in his life and thought a similar strong strand of puritanism is evident. Practically all of his writings express a moral indignation for which he has been criticized, and which he himself came to deprecate.[53] There is little or no evidence that Washington ever harbored any strong feelings against organized religion, and he never seems to have shown the antipathies toward political activity which was at times evident in the thought of Douglass and Du Bois. Of the three men, idealism as opposed to pragmatism never seems to have had as firm a grip on Washington as was the case with Douglass and Du Bois, and of these latter two, Du Bois is the only one of whom it may be said that throughout his life the hold of idealism on him was firmer than that of pragmatism. Du Bois shared Douglass' antipathies toward organized religion and political parties. Although Douglass became an avid supporter of the Republican party, and Washington always remained such, Du Bois always tended toward political independence. As has been previously stated, during the 1930s Du Bois became a convert to

Marxism, the only one of the three to be so influenced.[54] After his conversion, like every true Marxist, Du Bois acted more in terms of what he conceived to be the practical and achievable.[55] His once thoroughly scholarly productions became more propagandistic, and he attempted to get the National Association for the Advancement of Colored People to align itself with and to work for what he was convinced was the inevitability of a socialist order.[56]

Douglass' and Washington's conversions to pragmatism seem to have been rooted in large part in their personalities. They were by nature opportunistic. Benjamin Quarles states that Douglass, essentially a reformer and compromiser, had a "resilient mind."[57] One example of this bent is the fact that after about ten years of supporting the futile Liberty Party, in 1856 Douglass suddenly switched to the Republican Party.[58] This change "betrayed his anxiety to be affiliated with a group that had a chance of success at the polls."[59] Even on the very eve of the Civil War—

> Douglass despaired as the new year got underway. To him the 'fifties had been a decade of unfulfillments. He had no new plans for hastening the good time coming. His feelings were so caught up in the day-to-day struggle that his perspective was distorted. . . . his gaze [was] endlessly on the immediate.[60]

Although Frederick Douglass was never involved in any great controversy which necessitated an elaboration of his educational views, it seems that they had more in common with those held by Booker Washington than those of W. E. B. Du Bois. How much Douglass' own lack of formal education had to do with his failure to say more on Negro education during the last twenty years of his life is a moot question. He was not alive when the Washington-Du Bois controversy was raging.

All three of these men believed in the American Gospel of Work and may loosely be termed economic determinists. The mere fact of Du Bois' admitted Marxist convictions suffice to place him under such a heading. Douglass, a man of considerable financial means during his last years, said: "Aristotle and

Pericles are all right; get all that, too; but get money besides, and plenty of it."[61] He once advised Negroes:

> The American Colonization Society tells you to go
> to Liberia. Mr. Bibb tells you to go to Canada. Others
> tell you to go to school. We tell you to go to work.[62]

"No race that has anything to contribute to the markets of the world," Washington declared, "is long in any degree ostracized."[63] His willingness to retreat from activity on the political and civil rights fronts, in favor of pushing on the economic and educational ones, sprang perhaps as much from his economic determinism as from his realization that southern whites were bitterly against the political activity of his race.

The ultimate desires and goals of Washington, as with Douglass and Du Bois, were equality of rights, opportunities, and privileges for their race. Although they differed in temperament and personality, essentially their difference was one of method.

CHAPTER XVI

NORTH AND SOUTH IN NEGRO THOUGHT

The South and Southern Whites

In 1843 Henry Hibhland Garnet gave his description of the initial contact of Africans with the white man. Speaking of his ancestors, he stated: "The first dealings they had with men calling themselves Christians, exhibited to them the worst features of corrupt and sordid hearts; and convinced them that no cruelty is too great, no villainy and no robbery too abhorrent for even enlightened men to perform, when influenced by avarice and lust."[1] Reverend Nathaniel Paul said in 1827 that the "pernicious tendency" of slavery was all pervasive. "Not only are its effects of the most disastrous character, in relation to the slave," he declared, "but it extends its influence to the slave-holder; and in many instances it is hard to say which is most wretched, the slave or the master."[2] The colored abolitionists often said that slavery made for a corrupting excess of power, idleness, and luxury for southern whites. Charles Lenox Remond declared in 1841:

> If I must take the alternative of being the oppressed slave or the oppressor, give me the condition of the former. Give me the chance . . . of being the poor slave, rather than the oppressor, when they shall meet at the bar of God, and there shall be no question of bank or antibank, tariff or antitariff. I trust that the day is not far distant when . . . mankind shall be considered great only as they are good.[3]

A constant strand in Negro thought is the strong denunciation of those "who deny a common brotherhood." Perhaps the young poet of the 1920's, Roscoe C. Jamison, put this as well as anyone, when in his "The Edict," he wrote:

All these must die before the morning break:
They who at God an angry finger shake,
Declaring that because he made them white,
Their race should rule the world by sacred right.
They who deny a common brotherhood—
Who cry aloud, and think no blackman good.

Another Negro opined:

> Of all the fools who have crawled to dusty death the most stupendous and bedeviled lot are those who strut their fools' feet and toss their fools' heads across their little stage of life, thanking their fools' selves that God made them different from other men—superior to other men—to rule over other men.[4]

Writing on slave attitudes toward whites, Kenneth Stampp asserts:

> Several points are clear: (1) slaves did not have one uniform attitude toward whites, but a whole range of attitudes; (2) they gave much attention to the problem of their relationship with whites; and (3) they found the 'management of whites' as complex a matter as their masters found the management of Negroes.[5]

Stampp describes some of the attitudes and feelings shown by slaves toward whites as being "coldly opportunistic," "deep suspicion," "hatred," "indifference," and "deep affection." When the latter feeling predominated, he points out that "a slave's love for the good white people he knew was not necessarily a love of servitude."[6] Stampp concluded that "the predominant and overpowering emotion that whites aroused in the majority of slaves was neither love nor hate but fear."[7]

Attitudes Toward Poor Whites and Their "Betters"

In the ante-bellum period bondsmen sometimes sang,

> I'd druther be a Nigger, an plow ole Beck,
> Dan a white Hill Billy wid his long neck.

And—

> I had a dog, his name was Dash
> I'd rather be a nigger, than poor white trash

Planters forbade fraternization of slaves with poor whites, often telling the former that the poor whites would teach them bad habits such as stealing and drinking.[8] Much of the superiority which slaves sometimes felt where poor whites were concerned, and vice versa, was cultivated by the planters, doubtless out of realization that as have-nots, poor whites constituted natural potential class allies of the slaves. In a number of the slave plots and rebellions poor whites were found to have aided the slaves.[9]

Yet, many Negroes have long believed that the upperclass white man was more of a friend to the black man than is the case with the poor white. This is partly because of (1) The "meanness" of some poor white overseers and "Pattyrollers." The slave system relied heavily on the lash as inducement to work, and often the overseer's job depended on his willingness to use the lash. (2) Negroes have seen that since both they and poor whites were largely unskilled, sometimes they were both natural competitors for the same jobs. This is the main burden of thought in H. R. Helper's *Impending Crisis*. (3) Poor whites often have manned the lynch mobs. In his book *Black Reconstruction*, which appeared in 1935, W. E. B. DuBois is highly critical of southern poor whites for not effecting an alliance with the freedmen to bring about a greater measure of political and economic democracy in the South.[10] In his poem, "Let America Be America Again," Langston Hughes wrote in the thirties—"I am the poor white, fooled and pushed apart." The note of this class being duped and exploited along with the Negro was also struck in this period by Frank Marshall Davis' poem "Snapshots of the Cotton South," and in the writings of Richard Wright and other persons and is in line with the sympathy and concern for this class which was then being shown by Erskine Caldwell, John Steinbeck and other white writers. In "Let America Be America Again" Langston Hughes depicted the plight of the Negro and white sharecropper as well as the urban white and colored workers who were, "Tangled in the ancient endless chain of profit, power, gain, and grab of land and gold." Here, with Hughes, as with many other Negro writers of this period, the previous almost exclusive concern with plight of race has grown to the larger concern of plight of class.

By no means have all Negroes denied the genteel tradition to which the Old South laid claim. Reflecting on this, Kelly Miller wrote in 1914:

> I see a chivalric civilization instinct with dignity, comity and grace rising upon pillars supported by the slave's strength and brawny arm.[11]

Many slaves and freedmen believed that "quality white folks" were always kind and in all ways exemplary of the highest conduct. They tended to blame the cruelty and degraded behavior of many slave traders and overseers on their poor - white origin.[62] "It is this class of the white race," writes Moton of "the best white people," "who have made the term\ 'white' the hall-mark of excellence so commonly used by Negroes, and appropriated by other whites for such advantages as it gives."[13] Moton points out another aspect of the Negro's high estimate of this class. He writes that "for a long time many of the race found it hard to believe that a Negro could be just as proficient as a white man in the same line, diplomas and licenses notwithstanding."[14] This attitude, though now disappearing, still may be found among numerous Negroes.

Commenting on whites who were cruel to their slaves, one freedman said: "I hear my children read about General Lee, and I know he was a good man. I didn't know nothing about him then, but I know now he wasn't fighting for that kind of white folk."[15] Some ex-slaves dreamed of spending eternity in heaven with the ex-master whom they had venerated.[16] Hard times, plus loss of friends and acquaintances, caused the aged slaves sometimes to look back at the days in bondage with some of the same nostalgia and longing that ex-planters did.

Some freedmen saw and sympathized with the difficult revolution in thought which was necessary before most southern whites could accept the Negro as a brother and fellow citizen. By the late nineteenth century, J. C. Price was mildly optimistic where the "race problem" was concerned, and thought that considerable progress had been made by southern whites in making the necessary "thought revolution."

Looking back at slavery, Kelly Miller said:

> I see . . . the patriarchal solicitude of the kindly-hearted owners of men, in whose breast not even an iniquitous system could sour the milk of human kindness.[17]

Booker T. Washington, J. C. Price, and other leaders constantly extolled the virtues of "the best white people," and declared that they were true friends of the Negro. Price averred: "The white man of the South has evolved into his present attitude by the environments which logically drove him to it; and he can only be effectually and permanent changed by a correspondent change, not of the portion, but of the character of the environment."[18]"Time and patience," Price continued, "will be large elements in the solution of the problem." As Booker Washington and others often had done, in a 1923 commencement address to Negro college students Bishop R. A. Carter said:

> Try to make friends with and command the respect of those with whom you live. Do not depend upon friends who are far away. Whatever the color of the people with whom you deal daily, they will respect refinement, modesty, integrity, scrupulous honesty, industry, and money.[19]

In this same period, in his poem "Daybreak," George McClellan said:

> Though wrongs there are, and wrongs have been
>   And wrongs we still must face,
> We have more friends than foes within
> The Anglo-Saxon race.

Love for the South

As the Negro has felt hatred for the South, he also has felt deep love for that section. It was the latter sentiment which inspired such songs as "Carry Me Back to Ole Virginny," "My Old Kentucky Home," and "Way Down upon the Swanee River," "Basin Street," "Beale Street Blues," "Southern Echoes," and "Tuxedo Junction." In a notable 1874 speech in defence of the Civil Right Bill, Congressman R. B. Elliot declared that the Negro would never leave the South. Of the section he declaimed:

> Entreat me not to leave thee, nor to depart from following after thee . . . The Lord do so to me and more also, if aught but death part thee and me.[20]

In 1895 and after, Booker T. Washington urged upon Negroes his conviction that their best hope lay in the South. Lamenting the violence and corruption attendant upon the 1875-76 Mississippi elections, John R. Lynch blamed the trouble on a small Democratic clique which was determined to rule at any cost. Yet he said of the state—"My home is there, my interests are there, my relatives are there, and I want to see the state happy and prosperous."[21] During the 1920's few persons of other races would match the lyric hymns of the southern scene found in the poetry of George Marion McClellan. His book, *The Path of Dreams*, is in many ways an ode to the natural beauty of the South which he never ceased to love. In the same period a southern-reared Brown University graduate and New England journalist would sing of the South in a manner which would do justice to the most avid native white. In his poem, "A Southern Love Song," this poet, Joshua Henry Jones, Jr. wrote:

> Dogwoods all a-bloom
> Perfume earth's big room
> White full moon is gliding o'er the sky serene.
> Quiet reigns about,
> In the house and out;
> Hoot owl in the hollow mopes with solemn mien.
> Birds have gone to rest
> In each tree-top nest;
> Cotton fields a-shimmer lash forth silver-green.
> O'er the wild cane brake,
> Whip-poor-wills awake,
> And they speak in tender voicings, heart, of you.

After asking the South if it had not heard "The mighty beat of onward feet," James Weldon Johnson wrote:

> O Southland, fair Southland!
> Then why do you still cling
> To an idle age and a musty page,
> To a dead and useless thing?
> 'Tis springtime.' 'Tis work-time'.
> The world is young again!
> And God's above, and God is love,
> And men are only men.
> O Southland! my Southland!
> O birthland! do not shirk
> The toilsome task, nor respite ask,
> But gird you for the work.
> Remember, remember
> That weakness stalks in pride;
> That he is strong who helps along
> The faint one at his side[22]

One evidence of the love of the Negro for the South is the manner in which he constantly has contended that the advancement of his own group means the advancement of the

South. Afro-Americans have viewed their progress in such things as land and home-ownership, business growth, and rising literacy as not only progress for themselves, but for their states and the entire southern region, and many have believed that material progress in the section automatically would bring progress in the area of race relations. Near the turn of the century, J. C. Price opined:

> The great need of the South today is industrial power, and the development of this power is imperative, not only for the speedy recovery of lost fortunes and the rapid strengthening of paralyzed energies, but as an unfailing agency in unifying the interests and making common the destiny of both races in the South, and in the nation as well.[23]

Many, perhaps most, of the Negroes who launched business enterprises in the South during the late nineteenth and early twentieth centuries were gripped by the notion that the existence of successful Negro businesses would bring independence and respectability to their race, and would serve as a means of furthering racial harmony. Price and these other economic determinists of his race failed to see what Wilbur Cash so ably has pointed out, that to the white South industrialization was viewed as a means of preserving and not destroying the old racial pattern.

Some Afro-Americans have prided themselves on 'understanding" and being able to manipulate whites in a fashion reminiscent of the claim of southern whites that they possess a unique understanding of the colored man. For example, one of Booker T. Washington's admirers declared that Washington "knew the southern white man better than he knew himself, and knew the sure road to his . . . heart."[24]

The North

Although they looked to the North as a haven of freedom, Negroes were from the beginning acutely aware of the racial prejudice and discrimination there. Speaking before the Pennsylvania Senate in opposition to an early-nineteenth century bill to exclude free Negroes from migrating to the state, James Forten said: . . . the passage of this bill "will only tend to show that the advocates of emancipation can enact laws more degrading to the free man, and more injurious to his feelings, than all the tyranny of slavery, or the shackles of infatuated despotism."[25] Although they were direct participants in the abolitionist movement, colored Americans often protested that the North, where this movement was concentrated, was also very prejudiced against their race, and that within the national abolitionist society itself, considerable race prejudice existed. This matter was disparaged at almost every one of the first five national Negro conventions which began in 1830. At the September 20, 1837 meeting of the New York Anti-Slavery Society, Reverend Theodore Wright scored this prejudice, and stated that many constitutions of anti-slavery societies, because of a desire to make the societies acceptable and popular, "have overlooked the giant sin of prejudice . . . which is at once the parent and off-spring of slavery." In the 1840's Frederick Douglass stated:

> The northern people have been long connected with slavery; they have been linked to a decaying corpse, which has destroyed the moral health. The union of the government, the union of the North, and the union of the South, in the political parties; the union in the religious organizations of the land, have all served to deepen the moral sense of the northern people, and to impregnate them with sentiments and ideas forever in conflict with what as a nation, we call *Genius of American Institutions*. . . In a moral sense, as well as in a national sense, the whole American people are responsible for slavery.[26]

Despite the advice of Frederick Douglass, Booker T. Washington, and others that they should stay in the South, since the late 1870's Negro Americans have migrated to the North by the hundreds of thousands. Throughout the twentieth century race riots have not been uncommon in the North, and segregation and discrimination, while often more subtle, in many communities have been constant. After the Atlanta Race Riot of 1906 W. E. B. Du Bois stated that he did not know in which direction the race should move. In his "A Litany at Atlanta," he said: "Whither? North is greed and South is blood —within the coward, and without the liar!" And in the 1920's, Archibald Grimké informed his race—

You think, I know, that the North is more friendly
to you than the South, that the Republican party does
more for the solution of this problem than the Democratic. Friends, you are mistaken. A white man is a
white man on this question, whether he lives in the
North or in the South.[27]

Still the Afro-American has regarded some northern cities and
states as meccas of freedom and opportunity. One of the first
formal Negro churches of record was formed by free Negroes
in Boston in 1805. The same city had seen the Negro Prince
Hall Masonic Lodge founded in 1784. Charles Lenox Remond
called Boston "the Athens of America."[28] Frederick Douglass
fought for the return to freedom of George Latimer, fugitive
captured in Boston and returned to slavery in the South. Of
this case, Douglass wrote: "Just look at it; here is George Latimer a man and a brother and a husband and a father, stamped
with the likeness of God, and redeemed by the blood of Jesus
Christ, out-lawed, hunted down like a wild beast, and fero-
ciusly dragged through the streets of Boston . . . all this is
done in Boston—in liberty-loving slavery-hating Boston and
intellectual, moral, and religious Boston . . . Boston has become the hunting ground of merciless men-hunters and men-
stealers."[29]

One of the nine Afro-Americans awarded the Congressional Medal of Honor for bravery during the Civil War, described his trek northward from Norfolk, Virginia. Accom-
panied by his father who was looking "for a place to live in
peace and freedom," he states that they first stopped in Pennsylvania. They did not remain there long because "the black man
was not secure on the soil where the Declaration of Independence was written."[30] They proceeded on to the state of New
York, but did not stay there because her "ambition seemed to
be for commerce and gold," and "she heard not the slave."
Of his father's subsequent arrival in Massachusetts, this spokesman said:

At last he set his weary feet upon the sterile rocks
of 'Old Massachusetts.' The very air he breathed put
enthusiasm into his spirit. He selected as his dwelling-
place the city of New Bedford where 'Liberty Hall'
is a sacred edifice. Like the Temple of Diana which

covered the Virgins from harm in olden times, so old Liberty Hall in New Bedford protects the oppressed slave of the nineteenth century. After stopping a short time, he sent for his family, and there they still dwell.

Samuel Ringgold Ward referred to Massachusetts as, "A State to which many of us are accustomed to look to as our fatherland, just as wa look back to England as our mother country."[31] In his 1863 appeal, "Men of Color, to Arms," Frederick Douglass pointed out that Massachusetts was accepting and training colored persons. Of this state, he asserted, "she was the first in the War of Independence; first to break the chains of her slaves; first to make black men equal before the law; first to admit colored children to her common schools, and she was first to answer with her blood the alarm cry of the nation, when its capital was menaced by rebels. You know her patriotic governor, you know Charles Sumner. I need not add more."[32] When an early nineteenth century Philadelphia Senate was debating a bill to bar free Negroes from migrating into the state, Negroes protested against this proposed action. In a speech before this body, James Forten declared:

> This is almost the only state in the union wherein the African race has justly boasted of rational liberty and the protection of the laws, and shall it now be said they have been deprived of that liberty. and publicly exposed for sale to the highest bidder? Shall colonial inhumanity that has marked many of us with shameful stripes, become the practice of the people of Philadelphia, while Mercy stands weeping at the miserable spectacle? People of Philadelphia, descendants of the immortal Penn, doom us not to the unhappy fate of thousands of our countrymen in the Southern States and the West Indies; despise the traffic in blood, and the blessing of the African will forever be around you.[33]

Afro-Americans have been especially concerned about the status of freedom and civil rights in the nation's capital. In 1846 Frederick Douglass stated:

> In the national District of Columbia, over which the star-spangled emblem is constantly waving, where orators are ever holding forth on the subject of Am-

erican liberty, American democracy, American Republicanism, there are two slave prisons.[34]
In 1876 after emancipation had been effected, Douglass called
Washington, D. C. "the most luminous point of American territory; a city recently transformed and made beautiful in its
body and its spirit."[35] Yet in the 1920's, another eminent
spokesman would say of the national capital:

> In this city where Christianity has back of it so much
> respectability, so much official dignity and power
> . . . a colored man, if he were down on Pennsylvania
> Avenue, never mind how hungry he might be,
> couldn't find a restaurant in which he could get a
> cup of tea, or a sandwich and a glass of milk; or
> however tired he might be, is there a rest room into
> which he could go and be received, and simply be-
> cause of the color of his skin, because of his race
> identity![36]

Afro-Americans have been especially proud of the great strides
made since World War II toward ending racial segregation and
discrimination in the national capital.

Urban Trends

Since emancipation, cities and towns have served as a
great magnet for Afro-Americans. As indicated, probably the
greatest feature of this attraction was the same expanding economic, cultural, and social opportunities which lured white
Americans in such large numbers. The city offered a richer
and more exciting life than could be found in rural ideas. For
the young, urban areas offered among other things, escape from
the tyranny of rural public opinion as night club, cabaret, or
private party offered unbridled liberty to an increasingly secularistic Negro. Jazz music typified this unreined freedom,
but earlier than jazz came the "Blues." From Beale Street in
Memphis, Fourth Avenue in Birmingham, or South Rampart
Street in New Orleans, these songs made their way to northern
cities. In 1918, W. C. Handy had published a blues anthology.
Like the modern cowboy and hillbilly ballads which rose to
popularity at about the same time, blues songs are folk music.
The dominant note is sadness and disappointment over a lost
lover, or nostalgic longing for the warmth and friendship
known "back home" in small town or on the farm, but not

present in the cold and impersonal city. This is much like the cowboy on the lonely prairie who yearns for the girl he left behind, for friendship, sympathy, and a more settled life. Frazier states that in blues songs one may find the beginnings of expressed romantic sentiments among Afro-Americans.[87] These sentiments, he found, had been conspicuously lacking in the sex and mating practices of the rural slave and peasant freedman.

Alain Locke has noted the prominence of singing and dancing as modes of expression for the Afro-American. Calling him a "master artist" in the plastic idioms of his original African culture, Locke declares:

> Slavery not only transplanted the Negro; it cut him off from all this. Stripped of all else, the Negro's own body became his prime and only artistic instrument, so that dance, pantomine and song became the only gateway for his creative expression. Thus was the American Negro forced away from the craft arts and the old ancestral skills to the emotional arts of song and dance, for which he is now so noted.[38]

In the cities, the transplanted Negro often continued in many of the attitudes and behavior patterns which had characterized him on the plantation. In speech, Saturday night revelries, and other ways, this was evident. Couples still frequently married and separated, and remarried without benefit of legal divorce, and illegitimate off-spring abounded. Loose habits and unfamiliarity with urban laws and customs brought many before the courts and welfare agencies. Yet, with the mass migrations to northern urban areas, and resultant conflicts and race riots over housing and job opportunities, the nation began to realize that the so-called "Negro problem" was national in scope rather than peculiarly southern, and northern liberalism, which had become silent on race relations after the storm of abolitionism had been followed by Civil War and radical reconstruction, was aroused to speak out again against racial prejudice and discrimination. This liberalism, the earliest and most ardent protagonist of racial equality, was again the ally of Brown America, and was to play a significant role in the NAACP, Urban League, and almost all other subsequent similar efforts of the race.

With the rest of the nation, beginning with the 1920's, Afro-Americans waxed enthusiastic over motion pictures. Although from the beginning, educated Negroes chafed at the menial and servile roles given their race in many of the pictures being produced, the masses of Negroes appear to have accepted the actors of these roles as stars, hence race heroes in their own right. In the post World War II period most Negro actors were refusing such roles and some criticism was even directed at the well-known boxer, Archie Moore, for accepting the role of Jim in "Huckleberry Finn."

The clubs or lodges established by Negro fraternal organizations provided a major source of recreation for many adult Negroes. The 1920's also brought the automobile to the fore on the American scene. In addition to such advantages and benefits as enabling one to live a good distance from his place of employment, and making it possible for rural people to enjoy the recreational benefits of urban areas, to the colored American the automobile has been an additional boon, for with it he has found it possible to travel long distances within the South and escape the discriminations long found on trains and busses and at restrooms. Until the advent of the automobile, many persons refrained from taking vacations rather than subject themselves to insult and injury on the common carriers, while others without cars always have walked rather than ride local segregated streetcars or busses.

Chicago, Illinois was a magnet which attracted many Negroes, who have taken pride in such things as the fact that a person of color, Baptiste Point de Saible, is given credit for founding the city,[39] and in their militant race paper located there, the *Chicago Defender*. Another mecca was New York's Harlem. Although colored occupancy of this area appears to have begun around 1903, it was the World War I period which saw Harlem become the capitol of the Negro world. Of the Harlem vogue in the 1920's, Langston Hughes has written that "thousands of whites came to Harlem night after night, thinking the Negroes loved to have them there and firmly believing that all Harlemites left their houses at sundown to sing and dance in cabarets."[40] Colored writers and other intellectuals poured into the area, and, for the first time, major New York publishers were eager for manuscripts on the Negro. Harlem was the headquarters for the Garvey movement, the NAACP, and the Urban League. *Crisis* and *Opportunity*, journals of the latter two organizations, respectively, published much of the material of these intellectuals.

The maze of southern segregation laws have been a source of no small confusion to the Negro, but one thing he has always "appreciated" about prejudice and segregation is the fact that usually it is open and unhidden. The bronze southerner has known that in public services, one was marked "White Only" and the other "Colored," and he has looked for the facilities and place for his group and has seldom been caught in humiliating surprise. He has known, however, that in the North prejudice is often subtle and hidden, but still there poised, ugly, and ready to strike when a dark face appears. This has been a source of bitterness and resentment to the southern migrant to northern cities. Of the freedom of the North during the 1920s, George Schuyler wrote that it was "pretty much a mockery."

The liberal spirit which was behind the Progressive Movement brought to the fore a growing number of inter-racial commissions in the South. In addition to the growing liberal spirit, the white South was increasingly concerned that the section, because of its too-often ugly racial situation and anti-democracy, had become the butt of criticism and jokes. The Negro exodus also had an effect, and a new objectivity toward the color problem was clearly evident in some circles. With many others, Alain Locke saw welcome signs in this new development. In 1925 he wrote: "It does not follow that if the Negro were better known, he would be better liked or better treated. But mutual understanding is basic for any subsequent cooperation and adjustment. [The races] have touched too closely at the unfavorable and too lightly at the favorable levels."[41]

In 1919, the Commission on Interracial Cooperation was founded. Although the Commission was very conservative, with white southern liberals setting the pattern of its efforts, still, to Negro intellectuals, this and similar commissions represented a significant step forward. Perhaps the best known of all southern interracial groups was the Southern Conference for Human Welfare, which was founded in November, 1938 in Birmingham, Alabama. With support from the federal government, the movement was launched by many of the South's top white and colored citizens, and aimed at raising the section from its position at the bottom of the social, cultural and economic scale. Among the Negro leaders were Dr. F. D. Patterson, then president of Tuskegee Institute, and John P. Davis, then Executive Secretary of the National Negro Congress.[42] By this time, the Tennessee Valley Authority and other large scale social and economic planning efforts had given a stimulus to thought and activity on the regional scale. Many Afro-Americans viewed these trends optimistically and the Southern Conference for Human Welfare got off to a good start, however, the coming of World War II, internal bickering, and other factors caused it to become less important.

The new lower class Negro, contrasting the freedom of the North with the lack of it in the deep South from which he had recently migrated, was less liable to be so aware of the North's "mockery" of freedom. To him, New York or Chicago, or other points North, were all "Nigger Heavens," and he would "rather be a lamp post in Chicago than mayor of New Orleans." This class has been sorely neglected in serious literature. Largely in jokes, cartoons, and in isolated cases of fiction only has he been dealt with. So much is this the case that the book to which Alain Locke appended the title, *The New Negro*, omits him entirely. Carl Van Vechten, who closely studied some aspects of the Negro mind, stated that: "Negroes are sensitive in regard to diction which attempts to picture the lower strata of the race."[43] What Van Vechten observed of fiction was long true in general.

The new lower class person, who began to emerge around the turn of the century and was clearly distinct by the 1920's, represented the sons and daughters of recent rural migrants to the towns and cities. To be sure, he had his counterpart in white America. Usually lacking all but the barest rudiments of formal education, he was distinct by speech, dress, walk, and general demeanor. He loved the bizarre and flashy, created the zoot-suit craze of the late thirties and early forties, and was often humorous in his imitation of high society. He worked hard, played hard, loved hard, and drank hard. Among colored Americans, he was especially noted for his love of fast flashy cars, brightly colored clothes, and "yaller gals." By the mid-twentieth century education and assimilation are causing this type to lose much of its distinctiveness and in outlook and behavior to merge into the middle class. The latter, whose members often have graduated from high school or beyond, can scarcely be distinguished in behavior from any other segment of the nation's populace.

There is much in the poetry and novels of Negro writers of the twenties which reveals that the "big times" which, according to the popular image, transplanted Negroes, were supposed to be having in the metropolitan centers of the North was often more form than reality. For even here, the ability which the slave had shown to laugh "like Pagliacci" was evident. In his poem about "Zalka Peetruza" who was christened Lucy Jane, Raymond Garfield Dandridge informs us that "her all was dancing—save her face." Claude McKay strikes a similar note in his "The Harlem Dancers," whose seeming ecstatic joy was much form and little substance.

Studies have shown that Negro boys and girls run afoul of the law in urban areas far more than juveniles of other groups. Due to poverty, broken homes, slum conditions and other factors, this has long been the case,[44] and an average of twelve percent of Negro births since emancipation have been illegitimate.[45] Frazier points out that much of this illegitimacy as it is reflected in urban areas was but a carry-over of behavior regarded as more-or-less normal on post-bellum southern plantations, and that strong family ties have been long in developing with many Negroes.[46] Also, much of this behavior can be traced to the same sources which, in the twentieth century, have produced such widespread juvenile delinquency among all elements of the population. Studies have shown that illegitimacy was highest with girls who were newcomers to northern cities.[47] The peasant from the South had to make many adjustments. The impersonal element in many of the large churches caused some to feel that they were veritably lost in the crowd,[48] and consequently, many of these lonely individuals organized small "store-front" churches. In order to attract attention, many of the younger persons resorted to boisterousness and flashy dress and automobiles. Many were extremely sensitive and race conscious, and the slightest sign of race prejudice aroused their fighting impulses.

At times the Negro has resorted to "passing" as a Hindu, Latin American, or some other group which was less an object of race prejudice. Of course "passing" was possible for only those persons who possessed considerable intelligence and features not readily typed as Negroid. Equally well known is that a number of mulattoes each year pass over into the white world, while others "pass" on their jobs and then return to a Negro community.

Booker T. Washington, his successor at Tuskegee, R. R. Moton, and some other Negro spokesmen, especially southern ones, appear to have believed that segregation, and discrimination "are attributable more to the activities of a vociferous minority [of whites who are] able to command the floor and give the semblance of a majority support to its unchallenged declarations."[49] As Moton stated: "a mob bent on lynching" does not represent "the charactristic sentiment of the whole community." Still bronze America paradoxically has idolized "white people" and "the white man." Writing in 1930, Langston Hughes has one of the characters in his story, *Not Without Laughter*, reflect this view. This character declared that "Colored people certainly need to come up in the world . . dress like white people, think like white people, talk like white people,—and then they would no longer be called 'niggers'." And Moton observed: "There was a time when a large element of the Negro race associated superiority almost invariably with a white skin. But this spell has been broken by two distinct developments—one of them the Negro's own excursions into fields of achievement previously occupied by the white man alone; and second, the failure of so many of the latter to manifest the superiority with which they would be credited."[50] Moton's statement that "This spell has been broken" is not yet true for many Afro-Americans, and always there have been many who never came under "the spell."

The Afro-American ever has been aware of the manner in which his presence in the United States has caused the Declaration of Independence, Constitution, state and federal legislation and judicial rulings, and all that is finest and most decent in the American tradition to be trammelled, abased, and and ashamed both at home and in the eyes of foreigners, and he knows that his presence has led an ever-impoverished South to keep itself impoverished by its attempt to maintain dual facilities for the two races. He long has believed that the discriminatory laws of the South aimed at keeping him down, also keep the South down, and that the only way for the section to rise is to let the dark-skinned one-third of its population rise; that the tremendous mental and physical energy expended to keep him down, if turned into channels of cooperative interracial activity could make the South a veritable Garden of Eden. Commenting in 1929 on progress made in relieving racial prejudice and discrimination, R. R. Moton had high praise for the role of southern white women. He stated that until they received the ballot, these were "silent concerning things they have seen with their own eyes and against which their hearts burned with indignation."[51] With the acquisition of political recognition and power, he observed, they were demanding for Negro womanhood every protection accorded their own honor, and a fairer treatment for all people. Moton praised also the role of southern white churches in bringing about better treatment of the section's colored population. The Negro's disadvantages are not, he wrote, "the result of malicious intent so much as of ignorance and indifference," and that "the inborn sense of fairness which in general characterizes American life, will, when the facts are revealed, assert itself in removing the inequalities and opening the way for the unhampered development of the race."[52]

During the late nineteenth and first two decades of the twentieth centuries, colored Americans were especially rankled by the stereotypes which were by-products of the minstrel vogue, the general race prejudice, and pseudo-scientific notions of the period. These stereotypes not only depicted the Afro-American as a mental and emotional child of a sub-human species, but invariably assigned to him a large mouth, big flat nose, ebony complexion, red eyes, and flat feet with protruding heels. Of this tendency to stereotype the race, the first Negro newspaper in the country said in its initial editorial—"though there are many in society who exercise toward us benevolent feelings; still . . . there are others who make it their business to enlarge upon the least trifle, which tends to the discredit of any person of colour; and pronounce anathemas and denounce our whole body for the misconduct of this guilty one."[53] "To a large extent," Moton declared in 1929, "the white people who do any thinking about the Negro today carry in their mind a picture of the black man such as is carried in the advertisements of commodities like Cream of Wheat, Swift Hams, Gold Dust Washing Powder, and the illustrations accompanying the stories of Octavius Roy Cohen."[54]

Since emancipation Afro-Americans have been especially sensitive about use of such titles as "Mr." and "Mrs." The educated Negro especially has resented being addressed by the first name, or by such stereotyped forms as "Boy," "Uncle," or "Auntie." Because of the custom which some white southerners have of addressing colored women by their first names, many have refused to allow bill collectors to come to their homes, and when opening accounts at downtown stores give only their initials or the names of their husbands. The word "nigger" has been an especial object of hatred. Here one observer has noted:

The word 'nigger' as employed in the American vernacular embodies every shade of discrimination, from good-natured tolerance to despicable contempt.

It reflects the same sentiment that has coined the words, 'Sheenie' for the Jew; 'Dago' for the Italian; 'Frog' for the Frenchman; 'Heinie' for the German; 'Hunkie' for the Hungarian; 'Chink' for the Chinese; and 'Wop' for the European group whom the American cannot distinguish ethnologically.

Only slightly less offensive are the terms 'darky,' 'shine' all of them expressions of contempt.[55]

Still it seems paradoxical that Afro-Americans at times have called one another "nigger" in a manner denoting half good-natured raillery and a half-friendly contempt for the other person. Also, when angry, they sometimes have used this expression in consigning the person addressed to the lowest depths of contempt and rascality. Here the reaction is similar to that, common among families and other close-knit groups, who as members of the in-group may criticize ane another and fight among themselves but resent any criticism or attack from a member of an out-group. "There was a time," this observer continues, "when the colored people of America were offended at the designation 'Negro.' The thinking Negro no longer finds opprobrium in the term but he would insist that it be spelled with a capital 'N' and not "n.""[56] It is not altogether true that "the thinking Negro no longer finds opprobrium in the term." Paradoxically, the slave heritage has left both pride and a definite distaste for the word "Negro," so that anything with it as a prefix is *per se* inferior to some colored Americans. For example, numerous colored social scientists have nothing but contempt for Negro History, and some persons, lay and scholarly, will not read anything emanating from the Afro-American press. To such persons usually any white physician or dentist is assumed to be automatically and unquestionably better than a Negro physician or dentist.[57]

Of one aspect of the Negro's sensitivities, a scholarly observer has noted:

> I am fully aware of the fact that there are many Negroes who do not like dialect plays. It has long been my opinion, however, that it is not the crude expressions of the peasant characters that contribute to this dislike; but rather the repelling atmosphere and the psychology of the inferior that somehow creep into the peasant plays of the most unbiased authors of other racial groups.[58]

In the open-closed society dichotomy, it has been held that the South is most often the closed type which is tradition bound and which reacts against new ideas and change. Rigid conformity to the prevailing mores is stressed by the closed society which also tends to be more concerned with the past than the future. If this is a good characterization of the prevailing aspect of the white southerner, it is not so for the colored populace. Because the prevailing southern mores have glorified the Caucasian while relegating the Negro to a position of inferiority and degradation, the Negro frequently has been up-in-arms against those mores. In his struggle, the Negro often has looked to the North for his ideal social system, and, where southern mores are concerned, has venerated change, progress, and non-conformity.

As Negroes in the 1950's took pride in and encouragement from the great progress which their race had made since 1865, progress which Margaret Just Butcher, Rayford Logan, and others boasted had no parallel in human history, far too, few were willing to give the southern white man much credit for this record. As was sadly true from the other side, far too many Negroes thought of the southern white man only as "the enemy" who should be despised and opposed. These persons too often were wont to discount with contempt Booker T. Washington's oft-preached dictum that in the South the colored and white man should studiously cultivate each others friendship in every area and manner possible. Just as too many southern whites could not see the great debt which the section's progress owed to the Negro, so too many Negroes had failed to see the debt which their progress owed to southern whites. Yet, their common survival and progress were in themselves proof that the two races had not been "enemies" only. Though the fact was affected by the noise and drama of conflict, headlines and politics, some Negroes knew that from the days of slavery to the present, their race constantly has had friends among southern whites, that the kindness extended by these friends not only have been eternal reminders of the genuineness in American democracy, but substantial material and spiritual aid throughout the course of their trek from slavery to freedom; that to extend on both sides recognition of this common heritage of neighborliness and friendship, and to help it to grow, is the debt which colored and white southerners owe each other, their section and their nation.

One can only hope that time, education, and experience have revealed to enough members of both groups that their common location, history, and destiny dictate that they should fear disharmony, hatred, prejudice, and untruth more than they should fear one another.

SOME SOURCES AND PATTERNS OF
PUBLIC BEHAVIOR

The central theme of Negro history is the quest for freedom and equality of citizenship, a motif which inevitably has been tied to the central theme of the nation's history, that is, the effort to achieve and maintain a democratic society. Though he often has been critical of the portion of freedom and democracy allotted him within this nation, the Negro's love for the United States always has been strong. He consistently has defended the nation in war and in peace, and has rejected all programs which would separate him from it, either physically or otherwise. At the first annual Negro Convention, meeting at Philadelphia, delegates called the United States "our own native land," and mentioned the customarily stated fact that this was the birthplace of their forebears, whose blood and sweat had hallowed it. They stated that the cause of general emancipation "is gaining powerful and able friends abroad," mentioning specifically Britain and Denmark, but remarked that when they looked at their own native land their Convention "had cause to hang its head and blush."[1] This was a period when abolitionism was rising in the North together with a concomitant wave of oppression in the South. "I will not yield to you in affection for America," wrote William Wells Brown from London, England, "but I hate her institution of slavery."[2] "With all her faults and all her follies," stated Charles Lenox Remond, "I cannot but regard my native land with feelings of the proudest affection."[3] And in the twentieth century, a noted Negro would say:

> I care nothing for the past; I look beyond the present;
> I see a great country . . . tenanted by untold millions of happy, healthy human beings, men of every race that God has made out of one blood to inherit the earth, a great human family, governed by righteousness and justice, not by greed and fear—in which peace and happiness shall reign supreme.[4]

Citizenship and the Ballot

Americans of color have regarded the ballot as a *Sine Qua Non* of true citizenship. Of the original thirteen states at the time of the adoption of the Federal Constitution eleven allowed free Negroes the right to vote; however, as cotton and the industrial revolution fastened slavery more firmly on the South, this right was curtailed and taken away, and pro-slavery men began to contend that neither the Declaration of Independence, Federal Constitution, nor state constitutions had ever conferred citizenship upon the colored man. Well known is the manner in which this position reached its zenith with the Dred Scott decision in which Chief Justice Roger B. Taney declared that the Negro never had been, and never could be, a citizen of the United States.

The fight for citizenship has forced the Afro-American to a keen consideration of the constitutionality of his claims to civil and political rights. During the ante-bellum period his basic argument was that the fact of his birth in this country conferred citizenship upon him. Next came the contention that the long toil of his forebears, both requited and unrequited, which went to build the nation, plus the blood which they shed in defense of it, are more than ample justifications. The American of color has pointed to the fact that the fourth article of the Articles of Confederation implied that free persons of color were citizens, and that the federal Constitution neither directly ordained slavery nor denied Negro citizenship. Various state judicial decisions and constitutions were quoted from time to time to point out that the Negro had been included among the citizenry. In a speech before the Massachusetts House of Representatives in 1842, Charles L. Remond said: "Our right to citizenship in this State has been acknowledged and secured by the allowance of the elective franchise and consequent taxation; and I know of no good reason if admitted in this instance, why it should be denied in any other."[5]

One source of the feeling that their treatment by the majority group at times has been grossly unfair is the fact that the African did not willingly emigrate into the United States of America, but was brought there by force. This was an almost omnipresent statement in the speeches of colored abolitionists.ᶜ William Wells Brown asserted: "This is emphatically an age of discoveries; but I will venture the assertion, that none but an American slaveholder could have discovered that a man born in a country was not a citizen of it. Their chosen motto, that 'all men are created equal' when compared with their treatment of the colored people of the country, sinks them lower and lower in the estimation of the good and wise of all lands."[7] The National Negro Convention of 1853, meeting in Rochester, New York, stated in its address to the People of the United States: "We would . . . be understood to range ourselves no lower among our fellow-countrymen than is implied in the high appellation of 'citizen'."[8] This claim was made, the statement said, "Notwithstanding the impositions and deprivations which have fettered us—notwithstanding the disabilities . . . pending and impending—notwithstanding the cunning, cruel and scandalous efforts to blot out that right, we declare that we are, and of right we ought to be American *citizens*. We claim this right, and we claim all the rights and privileges, and duties which, properly attach to it." Justification given for this claim ran: "By birth, we are American citizens; by the principles of the Declaration of Independence, we are American citizens; within the meaning of the United States Constitution, we are American citizens; by the facts of history, and the admissions of American statesmen, . . . by the hardships and trials endured; by the courage and fidelity displayed . . . We are American citizens."

Although in the post-bellum period Booker T. Washington and others were to contend that Negroes still had to earn the right to equality of citizenship by acquiring property, education and culture, many Negro spokesmen felt that their race already had earned this right. In a speech in defense of the Reconstruction era Civil Rights Bill, Congressman James T. Rapier declared that the Negro "has not been properly treated by this nation; he has purchased and paid for all, and for more, than he has yet received. Whatever liberty he enjoys has been paid for over and over again by more than two hundred years of forced toil; and for such citizenship as is allowed him, he paid the full measure of his blood, the dearest price required at the hands of any citizen."[9] Speaking in Boston in 1905, Bishop

Ransom declared that the Negro's "title to citizenship is without blemish or flaw."[10] One of the ablest arguments against the charge that the race was "not ready" for first-class citizenship was later given by William Pickens during the 1920's. He declared:

> The door of opportunity should not be closed to a man on any other ground than that of his individual unfitness. The cruelest and most undemocratic thing in the world is to require of the individual man that his whole race be fit before he can be regarded as fit for a certain privilege or responsibility. That rule, strictly applied, would exclude any man of any race from any position.[11]

Negroes based their right to use public inns and transportation on their citizenship claim and on the English common law and its antecedents in Roman civil law and the theory of natural rights. They almost always felt that the law and the Constitution were on their side, even when these, as they felt, were not being correctly applied due to racial prejudice. Speaking at Oberlin College, May 17, 1874, on occasion of the anniversary of the 15th amendment to the Federal Constitution, John Mercer Langston averred that the fact of equality is the soul of the American system. He cared little for what the written law might say, for this argument—

> is only to drive us back of the letter to the reasonableness, the soul of the law, in the name of which we would, as we do, demand the repeal of that enactment which is . . . not law, [and] contrary to its simplest requirements. It may be true that that which ought to be law is not always so written; but in this matter, that only ought to remain upon the statute book, to be enforced as to citizens and voters, which is law in the truest and best sense.[12]

Thus it can be seen that another persistent theme of the Negro has been reference to the high ideals on which this nation was founded in the eighteenth century. Commented an 1856 address of Ohions to their State Senate and House of Representative: "We are aware that it has been recently asserted by a high political personage that this is a government of white men. This we cannot admit. We submit that the . . . [Founding

Fathers] desired to found a government in which the doctrine of human equality would be reduced to practice." Seldom, if ever, has the American Negro been willing to accept disfranchisement and indirect representation through the white man. In their address to the Senate and House of Representatives of the State of Ohio, a January, 1856 Convention of Ohio Negroes said: "No class of the white population would be willing to concede to any class, however honest and enlightened, the custody of their rights. To demand such a thing, would be deemed monstrous; and the injustice is not lessened when the demand is made upon black instead of white men." In the first editorial of the first Negro newspaper, civil rights and the ballot were championed. Here, too, is found evidence of the traditional approach to politics for the securing of these rights. Like the nation's labor unions, the colored American has not sought to found his own political party, but rather has supported the major party which he thought promised to do most for him.

This editorial called for an independent use of the ballot and the author stated that he did not want the race "to become the tools of a party."[12] In 1833 New York Negroes organized what was known as the Phoenix Society to get members of their group to (1) attend Sunday School and Church, (2) subscribe to an abolitionist newspaper, (3) encourage their women to form Dorcas Societies, (4) help the poor and needy among them, (5) assist poor children in attending school, (6) establish circulating libraries and lyceum series, (7) assist members of their group in getting libraries and jobs, (8) and to improve their morals and behavior. Leaders of this group were the Reverend Christopher Rush, Reverend Theodore S. Wright, Benjamin Hughes, and Thomas Jinnings. Such organizations sprang up in practically every community in the United States and Canada where there were sizeable numbers of free persons of color. By 1840 Negroes had clearly shown that they had the ability and the desire to found model communities which, everything considered, equalled the best that the majority group was doing. In 1843 a group of young colored Americans, led by William H. Day, David Ruggles, and Henry Highland Garnet, formed an organization known as The Garrison Literary and Benevolent Association of New York. Thus one hundred and fifty colored youths, under twenty - nine years of age, met as an organization to work for the downfall of slavery, to promote religion, virtue, literature, and intellectual attainment.[14] In 1835, in Philadelphia, there met the last of the regular annual conventions. After this, frequent conventions were held annually by Afro-Americans at the city and state level. Outstanding members of the 1835 gathering included Robert Purvis and John F. Cook. Here is found one of the earliest instances of a movement among Negroes, to stop referring to themselves and their institutions as "Colored," "Negro," and "African." By the use of such prefixes, some members of the race have felt that they were segregating themselves and tacitly admitting difference and inferiority.[15] Since World War II there has been a great acceleration of the movement to blot out this prefix, but a counter movement of considerable proportions also has been evident.[16]

Negroes in Pennsylvania fought vigorously the efforts of that state's Constitutional Convention of 1837 to disfranchise them. By petition and mass meeting James Forten, Bishop Morris Brown, James Cornish, Robert Douglass, and others, representing 40,000 free colored, carried on to no avail, a fight against disfranchisement which was repeated in many of the states, both Northern and Southern, during the first three decades of the nineteenth century. "This is a question, fellow citizens," declared Robert Purvis of Pennsylvania's disfranchisement proposals, "in which we plead your cause as well as our own. It is the safeguard of the strongest that he lives under a government which is obliged to respect the voice of the weakest."[17] Purvis appealed to the patriotism of Pennsylvanians. Of the nation, he said: "We love our native country, much as it has wronged us." Of the state: "We are Pennsylvanians, and we hope to see the day when Pennsylvania will have reason to be proud of us, as we believe she has now none to be ashamed. Will you starve our patriotism? Will you cast our hearts out of the treasury of the commonwealth?"[16] At an 1840 state convention of New York Negroes, held in Albany, Afro-Americans spoke of the ballot as that which "sends life, vigor, and energy through the entire heart of a people," while the want of it "is the cause of carelessness, intellectual inertness and indolence." As to why Afro-Americans should be granted citizenship and the ballot, as was customary, the Declaration of Independence, nativity, and the colored man's contribution to the defense of the nation were cited. Finally given was: *"We are Americans.* We were born in no foreign clime. We have not been brought up under the influence of other strange, aristocratic, and uncongenial political relations. In this respect, we profess to be American and republican. With the nature, features, and operations of our government, we have been familiarized from youth; and its democratic character is accordant with the flow of our feelings, and the current of our thoughts." The 1853 national convention meeting at Rochester, New York, stated in an address to the people of the United States: "We ask that (inasmuch as we are, in common with other American citizens, supporters of the State, subject to its laws, interested in its welfare, liable to be called upon to defend it in time of war, contributors to its wealth in time of peace) the complete and unrestricted right of suffrage, which is essential to the dignity even of the white man, be extended to the Free Colored man also."[19]

Negro women have shared in practically every detail the interests and movements which have touched their sex in the United States, and there is no evidence that their thought on such matters as slavery, civil rights, love of country, devotion to education, culture, and family has been significantly different from that of their menfolk. Although, true to Occidental culture, they have not spoken out publicly as often as have the men, such silence betokens no conservatism or lack of interest. Often when they have spoken they have done so to prod the males on to greater militancy and action. One of the earliest demands of a Negro woman that her sex should have equal civil, education, and voting rights with men is found in the August 10, 1827 issue of *Freedom's Journal,* the first Afro-American newspaper. In December, 1852 in a letter to W. L. Garrison, William C. Nell reported on a Massachusetts meeting of Negroes in which Frederick Douglass participated. Reporting on one part of Douglass' address, Nell said:

> There were other ways of advancing the anti-slavery cause than at the ballot box; and he concurred

with other speakers in reference to the women, who he regretted were yet denied their right to vote, but stated that their means of appeal to husbands, fathers, brothers, intelligently directed, were various and all powerful. The emancipation of 800,000 slaves in the British West Indies was mostly attributable to the women's petition, two miles and a quarter long, which as declared by members of parliament, could no longer be resisted.[20]

Charles L. Remond, delegate to the London World Anti-Slavery Conference, excluded himself from this conference because it refused to seat women delegates. Female groups had been largely responsible for his being able to attend the conference.[21]

In August, 1840, there met in Albany, New York, a state convention of Negroes of over one hundred and thirty delegates, led by Charles B. Ray, Theodore Wright, Timothy Seaman, John J. Zuille, Charles L. Reason, and Alexander Crummell. The object of the meeting was to formulate and take action to secure political and civil rights. In August of 1841 almost one hundred and fifty persons of color met in Pittsburgh in a Pennsylvania State Convention. They gave as a justification of their meeting, their love of liberty, country, themselves, and their posterity, and, as usual the object to unite to secure equal rights. In general, Afro-Americans have ever respected the private rights of all individuals. In an 1842 speech before the Legislative Committee of the Massachusetts House of Representatives, Charles Lenox Remond recognized this fact. He asserted: "There is a marked difference between social and civil rights. It has been well and justly remarked that we all claim the privilege of selecting our society and association but, in civil rights, one man has not the prerogative to define rights for another."[22] After several southern legislatures passed laws aimed at keeping free Negroes from other areas from entering their states, colored residents of these states and of non-affected ones, protested against these encroachments on their rights as unconstitutional. Alabama, Georgia, Louisiana, Mississippi and South Carolina had such laws by 1842. Free Negroes pointed out that, "inasmuch as the Constitution declares that the citizens of each State, shall be entitled to all the rights and immunities of citizens of the several States," such laws were illegal.[23]

The Democratic and Republican Parties

Robert Purvis, fiery abolitionist from Philadelphia speaking in New York City on May 8, 1860, denounced the Republican party because it did not take an unequivocal stand against slavery and because of its discriminations against colored Americans. "How could I, a colored man, join a party that styles itself emphatically the 'white man's party'?" he demanded. "The Republicans may be, and doubtless are," he averred, "opposed to the extension of slavery, but they are sworn to support, and they will support, slavery where it already exists."[24] Little did he know that, though it did not oppose slavery as unqualifiedly as he wished, Republican opposition to slavery, in the face of southern fanaticism in favor of it, was to be sufficient for the ends which he desired.

The Afro-American usually has been objective about the two major parties. He long has been highly critical of the party which, previous to 1933—he supported most—the Republican Party. During the Reconstruction period, Negroes became aware that the Republican party too often used the race question for political purposes, and they more and more demanded that the party prove its sincerity to them. It appears that even in this period often the Negro would have voted for some other party which he felt had a chance of winning, had any other party stood unqualifiedly for protecting his citizenship rights. Sometimes the freedman sided with the Republican party so faithfully because to him it represented the lesser of two evils. The 1864 National Negro Convention proclaimed: "In the ranks of the Democratic Party, all the worst element of American society fraternize; and we need not expect a single voice from that quarter for justice, mercy, or even decency." Still another observer noted:

> We are not opposed to united action. We will gladly welcome union with all our Southern friends, but let them join the party which is true and has been tried, and then there will be united action. But if any advise you to leave that party whose principles are so clearly those of justice and right, depend upon it that

man is your enemy. If he is our friend let him act
with you. We bear no enmity to any but we are determined to secure our rights.[25]

With the advent of Radical Reconstruction, the attitude
of most Negroes toward the Republican Party became one of
complete support. Gone then was the wavering and misgivings
which had characterized their attitude toward this party during
the decade before 1867, because gone was the equivocal stand
on civil and political equality for the colored man which had
characterized the dominant wing of the party. Passage of the
Reconstruction Act of March, 1867 revealed that the party
was now dominated by the Summer-Stevens wing which had
been persistently the champion of equality. "The Democratic
Party may court us and try to get us to worship at their shrine,
but . . . we are Republicans by instinct, and we will be Republicans so long as God will allow our proper senses to hold
sway over us," declared Representative Joseph H. Rainey of
South Carolina.[26] In asking the 43rd Congress to pass the Civil
Rights Bill, John R. Lynch urged Republicans to vote for the
measure and by a policy of continued loyalty to the interests
of the Negro, ensure that the latter would never desert the
party in national elections. "Of course," Lynch added on his
race, "in matters pertaining to their local State affairs, they
will divide up to some extent, as they sometimes should, whenever they can be assured that their rights and privileges are not
involved in the contest."[27]

There long has been a popular misconception that at least
during their first decade of freedom *all* Negroes were adherents
of the Republican Party. Doubtless this idea was given impetus
by the propaganda which many Democrats later used in their
efforts to proscribe the Negro vote. From the beginning, however, a considerable number of freedmen chose, for a variety
of reasons, to exercise their political rights under the Democratic banner. In taking this course some were prompted by
the desire to follow the lead of their former masters, while
others were seeking some long-term political advantage or sincerely believed the Republican Party to be anti-South and dominated by corrupt whites who were "using" the Negro for their
own advantage. It must not be forgotten that a sizeable num-

ber of Afro-Americans have held the conviction that the South
has peculiar problems which only Southerners properly understand. Too, many Negroes were Democrats for the same base
reason that some others were Republicans; they were bought
with "hard cold cash." Some sincerely believed that in the long
run their race would be better off if they did not all adhere to
one party. They did not like the idea of a black man's party
and a white man's party any more than their progeny later
would care for a Negro labor union or a separate colored state.
These freedmen early sensed that extreme and one-sided political partisanship was a species of dangerous self-imposed segregation.[28] Freedmen who chose to cast their political fortunes
with the Democratic party sometimes found that the majority
of their race directed fearsome and sometimes ugly currents of
criticism at them. In such instances Negroes proved that they
could be as intolerant as they often thought southern whites
were. "Black Democrat" and "nigger Democrat" were epithets
of contempt, but these persons were not only objects of harsh
and bitter words. There were beatings, murders, ostracism, and
intimidation in a variety of forms.[29]

Corruption in the Republican ranks was a major reason
why some politicians went over to the Democracy.[30] In 1875
many Negro Republicans in Mississippi, including the venerable
Hiram Revels joined the Democratic ranks and helped defeat
their former party. Corruption in Republican ranks appears to
have been a dominant cause of this disaffection. Yet, no Negro
Democrat was elected to Congress before Oscar dePriest in
1928. He was also the first Negro Congressman from a northern state. While it is true that too many freedmen bartered
their votes for money or whiskey and were sometimes voted in
droves by and for unscrupulous members of their own and the
majority race, this is not the whole story. Many were serious
about voting and honestly sought through political action to
further not only their own race's interests, but those of their
state and the nation. Probably too much attention has been
given to those persons who were unprepared, and too little to
those whose records were models of ideal civic action, whatever
the motivation and limitations. A portion of the blame for
large-scale selling of votes on the part of freedmen can be at-

tributed to their extreme poverty and the feeling that voting was a right which should bring an immediate and tangible result. Political tutelage given by federal soldiers and officials was oftentimes indoctrination for the freedmen. That in this period Negroes did successfully elect their own candidates to office was never to be forgotten and would serve as stimulus to political action long after most of their political power had been destroyed.

The late nineteenth and early twentieth century preachment of Booker Washington and others that the colored man in the South should de-emphasize political activity was only the culmination of a long-growing conviction which many Negroes held. Such an acquiescence usually symbolized temporary acceptance of defeat on the civil and political front, and did not mean at all that the colored man had found and accepted his rightful "place" in southern society, nor that he was happy in this acquiescence, but rather that again, as in antebellum days, he found it expedient "common sense" temporarily to resign himself to less than first-class citizenship. After the over-throw of Radical Reconstruction many Afro-Americans came to fear and distrust all politicians and all political activity.[31] Many freedmen failed to perceive that one reason why the Republican party abandoned the race after 1876 was that disfranchisement measures had deprived the race of the ability to deliver electoral votes to the party; that, in politics, to him who can deliver the most votes usually goes the most attention and concern.

The new fronts on which the Afro-American resolved to battle after 1876 were largely the economic and educational. In choosing these areas for concentrated effort, the Negro again was revealing his basic Americanism, for the post-Civil War period saw the beginning of the public high school and the graduate education movement in the U.S.A. generally. This is the era of Barnard, White, Hopkins, Vanderbilt, and other luminaries and benefactors in the area of education. It is also the period when the brilliant successes and preachments of the "Robber Barons" created the great illusion that wealth was a door easily opened to everyone and the key to all other human wants. Of this retreat from politics, one freedman stated:

The only way for us to get along and do well is
to let politics alone and go to work to gather crops
that are now growing, and have something to live on.
Politics is a thing we know nothing about; and if we
did, it is a mighty unprofitable business. We are encouraged by a certain class of people to go ahead with
politics, because they want to use us to get our votes.
If we take part in politics, let us do it like men, and
not have so much parade and 'to do' about it. Let us
respect everybody's opinion, and those that have
known us since childhood till the present hour. They
are the ones that have helped and assisted us, and all
the money I have made since I have been free come
from them. We must continue to live together, and
unless there is good feeling between us, it is impossible for us to prosper, make money or a living.[32]

Here can be seen the many reasons which went into the thought
of the freedman who advocated either abandoning political
action entirely or else going about it in such a way as not to
offend the majority group. Here is revealed not only the desire
to refrain from action which might endanger person, property,
or the opportunity to earn a living, but also an expression of
what has been with some Negroes a genuine affection for the
southern white man. During the same period that some spokesmen were advising their race to abandon political action, a
Montgomery, Alabama group of Negroes resolved that "the
interests of white and colored people have been and are one
and in common."[33]

Evidence of one shift in Negro thought of this period is
seen in the fact that in 1874, Robert Smalls, William Still, and
numerous other Negroes bolted from the liberal Republicans to
support the "Peoples Party" candidate for mayor of Philadelphia. Still gave as their reasoning:

The slavery issues on which the two parties have
so long been contending are all, except Senator Sumner's Civil Rights Bill, settled, and the way is now
prepared for new issues; such as tariff, Currency,
Specie Payments, Railroads, Government bonds, the
United States Debt, the Granger movement, etc. It
needs but half an eye to see that these issues are soon
to bring about many political changes.[34]

Like the nation's labor unions to date, sensing the futility of minority parties in this country, Afro-Americans generally have sought to bargain with the two major parties. In state and local elections generally they have followed the practice of supporting those candidates who promise and do most for the race. This pragmatism has extended even to their relations with minority parties. One authority on Communism has pointed up the manner in which this practice has been followed. He observes that "in using the Communist Party when it could serve their immediate interests and in rejecting it when it tended to separate them from their friends, Negroes have displayed a rare political sharpness."[25]

Most Afro-Americans have known that in the securing of desired political ends, what often counts most is the number of votes that a group can deliver to those who will exercise power.[36] "In those places where race discrimination is practiced least," Moton points out, "there the Negro vote is less subject to control by a racial appeal."[37] He points out that until 1929 Harlem Negroes, although numerically able, had sent no members of their group to Congress, and to instances in St. Louis, Missouri, where white candidates were preferred by Negroes to colored ones. One of the most trenchant summaries of the Afro-American's counter-argument to the criticism that his interest in office-holding is excessive comes from the pen of Frederick Douglass. On this point, Douglass said during the late nineteenth century:

> We are as a people often reproached with ambition for political offices and honors. We are not ashamed of this alleged ambition. Our destitution of such ambition would be our real shame. . . .
>
> We are far from affirming that there may not be too much zeal among colored men in pursuit of political preferment; but the fault is not wholly theirs. They have young men among them noble and true, . . . who find themselves shut out from nearly all the avenues of wealth and respectability, and hence they turn their attention to politics. They do so because they can find nothing else. The best cure for the evil is to throw open other avenues and activities to them.[38]

Speaking in defense of the Civil Rights Bill before the 44th Congress, James T. Rapier of Alabama said: "Let this bill become law and not only will it do much toward giving rest to this weary country on this subject, completing the manhood of my race and perfecting his citizenship, but it will take him from the political arena as a topic of discussion, . . . and thus freed from anxiety respecting his political standing, hundreds of us will abandon the political fields who are there from necessity, and not from choice, and enter other and more pleasant ones."[39] So completely did both of the major parties come to ignore the Reconstruction Constitutional amendments and the plight of the colored American, until the latter became thoroughly convinced that, by and large, the platforms and promises of presidential candidates and political parties were all sound and fury, signifying nothing. Still all members of the race were not convinced that they should abstain from political action. In December, 1895 Bishop Henry M. Turner stated:

> Thousands of white people in this country are ever and anon advising the colored people to keep out of politics, but they do not advise themselves. If the Negro is a man . . . why should he be less concerned about politics than any one else? Strange, too, that a number of would-be colored leaders are ignorant and debased enough to proclaim the same foolish jargon. For the Negro to stay out of politics is to level himself with a horse or a cow . . . If the Negro is to be a man, full and complete, he must take part in everything that belongs to manhood. If he omits a single duty, responsibility or privilege, to that extent he is limited and incomplete.[40]

Obvious here is the manner in which Turner differs with the Booker T. Washington doctrine that the race should steer clear of those activities which were most liable to arouse opposition from white Southerners. Writing in 1903, Charles W. Chesnutt declared, "The direct remedy for the disfranchisement of the Negro lies through political action,"[41] but in his novel, The Quest of the Silver Fleece (1911), W. E. B. DuBois satirizes both white and colored politicians. Dark Princess, a novel published by DuBois in 1928, also goes to great lengths to satirize Negro political organizations, as well as the general politics of the period, and the 1896 call for another Tuskegee Conference, issued by that school, stated that the aim of these meetings was "to bring together for a quiet Conference, not the politicians, but the representatives of the common, hard-working farmers and mechanics—the bone and sinew of the Negro race—ministers and teachers."[42] The welcoming remarks of Booker T. Washington to this body, applauded the spread of the conference movement among Negroes. W. S. Scarborough, then Professor at Wilberforce, wrote in 1891: "He [the Negro] has seen so many broken pledges, violations of oaths, and disregard for platforms and public declarations on the part of political parties, that it is found no longer advisable for the colored people to have faith in them. This is the conclusion many have come to."[43] Though now in decline, this attitude is by no means yet dead with many Negroes. In combination with the fear of physical and economic reprisals, this attitude is one reason for the lack of interest in voting and other political activity which some Negroes have shown.

Expressive of the growing political independence of the Negro, the New York *Age* of April 11, 1907 championed the need for a third party. Also, in this period, on March, 1904, at St. Louis, Missouri, there was formed the National Liberty Party, one of the race parties which the colored American has launched, and the only national one. In 1904 this organization ran George Taylor, a free-born person from Arkansas, for the Presidency. Taylor had an interesting and varied political career in several midwestern states previous to 1904. Though the party wass short-lived, the foundation convention had delegates from over thirty-five states. In his acceptance speech to the convention Taylor said that his party was "struggling to revive the well-nigh deserted principles of the grand old Whig party (the mother of the Republican party)." His party, he said, was an outgrowth of the civil and personal liberty leagues which Negroes had sponsored at the state and local level for several years. He demanded the "full exercise" of citizenship rights and called for "a rebellion, a revolution, an uprising, not by physical force, but by the ballot."[44]

The Negro often has tended to side with the national government in the matter of state against federal powers. During

the Civil War Frederick Douglass sounded this note in urging
Negroes to volunteer their services as soldiers. Douglass declared:

> Do I hear you say you offered your services to
> Pennsylvania and were refused? I know it. But what
> of that? The State is not more than the nation. The
> greater includes the lesser. Because the State refuses
> you, you should all the more readily turn to the
> United States. . . . 'You came unto your own, and
> your own received you not.' But the broad gates of
> the United States stand open night and day. Citizen-
> ship in the United States will, in the end, secure your
> citizenship in the State.[45]

Defending the first federal civil rights bill, a Negro congressman declared:

> If the several states had secured to all classes within
> their borders the rights contemplated in this bill, we
> would have had no need to come here; but they hav-
> ing failed to do their duty, after having had ample
> opportunity, the general government is called upon
> to exercise its rights in the matter.[46]

Of the dire predictions being made by southern whites as consequences of proposed federal legislation to raise the Negro to
equality of citizenship, this congressman stated:

> I want someone to tell me of any measure that was
> intended to benefit the Negro that they have ap-
> proved of. Of which one did they fail to predict evil?
> They declared if the Negroes were emancipated that
> the country would be laid waste, and that in the end
> he would starve, because he could not take care of
> himself.

On the assertion of federal authority the Negro often has been
Hamiltonian because, in the "home" of states-rightism, the race
often could look only to the federal government for backing
of its claim to first-class citizenship. Too, it was through action
of the federal government that emancipation from slavery, the
Fourteenth and Fifteenth amendments, and most of the civil
rights legislation which was aimed at protecting the claim to
equality came, and in legal protests the colored American has
met success largely through appeals to the federal courts. Thus
in the Jeffersonian-Hamiltonian duality, the Negro usually has

been Jeffersonian only in terms of his love for and faith in education and in the common masses, and in the manner which Booker Washington and other persons have extolled the virtues of the agricultural way of life. However, R. R. Moton pointed out that the Negro would prefer that the southern states be the main defender of his civil and political rights. "One feels more secure," he wrote, "in the knowledge of the goodwill and support of his immediate neighbors than in the constructive protection of police headquarters fifteen blocks away when he lives in a hostile neighborhood."[47] The colored American has turned to the federal government, Moton continued, simply because too often he did not have the more desired protection in the South.

The census of 1880 showed seventy percent of the nation's nine million Negroes to be illiterate, but still the race continued the struggle against disfranchisement, discriminations, and lynchings, and for land and better educational opportunities. Examples of this are numerous. In January, 1881, a delegation representing six southern states, led by Robert B. Elliott of South Carolina, made a formal plea to President-elect James Garfield to foster legislation to improve the political and civil status of the southern Negro.[48] In April, 1882, forty-five delegates from over one dozen Kansas counties met and drafted a petition to Congress requesting public lands in Oklahoma be made available. The petition requested, "That Congress appropriate every third section of land in the Oklahoma territory for the occupancy of colored emigrants from the South, leaving the two intermediate sections open for settlement as may be thought best."[49] In late 1882 a Rhode Island State Convention, meeting in Newport, attacked the Republican party for its failure to "properly recognize the worthiness and faithful devotion of its colored adherents."[50] An 1883 state convention, held in Austin, Texas, was attended by over one hundred and twenty delegates. This body attacked discimination in education, selection of juries, and many other areas.[51] At the 1883 National Convention of Colored Men, held at Louisville, Kentucky, September 24, 1883, Frederick Douglass justified the convention on the ground that the social injustices of which the Negro was the object made the meeting necessary. In characteristic fashion, Douglass stated that protest was an absolute necessity. He continued:

> Men may combine to prevent cruelty to animals, for they are dumb and cannot speak for themselves; but we are men and must speak for ourselves, or we shall not be spoken for at all. We have conventions in America for Ireland, but we should have none if Ireland did not speak for herself. It is because she makes a noise and keeps her cause before the people that other people go to her help. It was the sword of Washington that gave Independence the sword of Lafayette.

One evidence of the growing political independence of the colored American was the 1885 published volume entitled *The Negro in Politics,* by T. Thomas Fortune. In this work, Fortune enthusiastically attacked the assertion by Frederick Douglass that—"The Republican Party is the ship, all else is the ocean." But Douglass, by that date, had modified his own earlier stand on the Republican party. At the 1883 National Convention of Colored Men, he deplored that some Republicans had opposed the meeting on the grounds that the race issue should be played down. Douglass declared: "The suggestion came from coward lips and misapprehended the character of that party. If the Republican party cannot stand a demand for justice and fair play, it ought to go down. We were men before that party was born, and our manhood is more sacred than any party can be. Parties were made for men, not men for parties." In 1871 Representative Alonzo J. Rapier of South Carolina had called for a rejuvenation and reformation of the Republican party from within, a reformation which would consist of the elimination of crooked politicians and the choosing of scrupulously honest men to be the party's standard bearers.[52] T. Thomas Fortune denounced the Republican party because, "in 1876, it abandoned all effort to enforce the provisions of the war amendments." The party, he wrote, had come to stand for "organized corruption, while its opponent stands for organized brigandage," and he advocated that henceforth Negroes should forget any debt of gratitude which they might have owed the Republicans and become independent voters.[53] As DuBois, Rayford Logan and other leaders were later to do, Fortune deplored the general attitude of the American press on race. "The great newspapers, which should plead the cause of the oppressed and downtrodden, which should be the palladiums of the people's rights," he declared, "are all on the side of the oppressor, or by silence preserve a dignified but ignominious neutrality."

In Chicago in 1890 there assembled one hundred and forty-seven delegates from over twenty states for the purpose of establishing an Afro-American National League. J. C. Price, noted North Carolina educator was chosen as first President of the organization. T. Thomas Fortune became the first Secretary. This organization thrived for nearly ten years. At the foundation meeting, prejudice and discrimination in nearly all of their forms were scathingly attacked. Proposed, but not accepted, was an Emigration Committee which would see that Afro-Americans emigrated from their concentration in the South, and the establishment of a national Negro bank. The Republican party was vigorously attacked for its "unfinished work" where the race and its rights were concerned, and political independence was advocated.[54] Still another source reflects the growing political independence, as another group of freedmen declared—"We feel that it is our duty to applaud the acts and endorse the utterances of our friends, it matters not where they are or to what party they may belong."[55]

Law and Government

By 1887 Afro-Americans had formed organizations specifically devoted to fighting in the courts to win equality of treatment. A counsel for one of these groups, the United Brotherhood of Liberty, said: "We have law enough. It remains for us to exact our rights and privileges from the law. Our difficulty is our individual inability to meet the expense of a legal contest."[56] This organization had grown out of the 1883 Supreme Court decision which invalidated the Civil Rights Bill. With the object of fighting on fronts other than, and in addition to the legal, a Georgia consultation convention, attended by over three hundred delegates meeting in Macon, voted to form a Union Brotherhood of Georgia. As indicated, the racial legal-aid societies grew out of the realization that, due to the great expense involved individually Negroes could not take their cases to the federal courts. This movement reached its acme with the NAACP. Those southerners who are prone to think that if they can kill this organization in the section protest will stop, overlook the well demonstrated ability of colored Americans to form new organizations. Their recent support of the Congress of Racial Equality would appear to bear this out. The past of the race would seem to indicate that Negroes will continue to organize for protest as long as they are objects of discrimination.

While the colored American generally has had great respect for law, always he has believed in the higher law doctrine. Still most Negroes have believed in using only moral and legal means to combat what they felt was illegal legislation.[57]

The extremes of the social injustice of which their race sometimes has been an object has caused several Negroes to countenance and advocate unethical and illegal forms of retribution. In the ante-bellum period, a number of abolitionists joined with the sentiment of David Walker's *Appeal* to the affect that whatever the cost in blood, life or property the bondsmen should rebel and overthrow the institution of slavery. It was this spirit which applauded the effort of John Brown at Harper's Ferry, and which welcomed the outbreak of the Civil War. In post-bellum days some colored newspapers, especially northern ones, have applauded instances where Negroes, in retaliation for injustices, killed or wounded whites or burned their property. In November of 1835, Afro-Americans in New York City formed a vigilante committee to foil the kidnapping of free Negroes or fugitives. Similar organizations later existed throughout the North.

Colored Americans have realized well that unless legislation is backed by public opinion, it is useless. Henry Highland Garnet wrote that "public opinion . . . in this country is stronger than law." In 1897 Booker Washington stated: "We are learning that neither the conqueror's bullet nor the fiat of law could make an ignorant voter an intelligent voter; could make a dependent man an independent man; could give one citizen respect for another, a bank account, nor a foot of land, nor an enlightened fireside."[58] A Negro Assistant Attorny

General declared in 1913: "Laws, customs, institutions are no_
thing unless behind them stands a vital, living, throbbing public
sentiment in favor of their enforcement in the spirit as well as
in the letter."[59] In the same period a noted Negro educator
stated: "Wherever there is lawlessness, or disorder, or mob violence of any kind, law is always in order to restrain and punish
the lawbreakers. . . . but legislatiton without a sentiment to
sustain it cannot solve the problem."[60] Still, while defending
the Civil Rights Bill before the 44th Congress, James T. Rapier
of Alabama said:

> I am told that I must wait for public opinion; that it
> is a m'atter that cannot be forced by law. While I ad-
> mit that public opinion is a power, and in many cases,
> is a law of itself, yet I cannot lose sight of the fact
> that both statute law, and the law of necessity manu-
> facture public opinion. I remember it was unpopular
> to enlist Negro soldiers in our late war and after they
> enlisted it was equally unpopular for them to fight
> in the same battles; but when it became a necessity
> in both cases, public opinion soon came around to that
> point.[61]

Moton wrote that where race relations are concerned, public
opinion is the paramount consideration. He opined:

> In the face of it honest hearts grow indignant
> at abuse and outrage, but they still remain silent;
> sensitive consciences protest, what is manifestly un-
> just and even dishonest, but the protest seldom
> crystalizes into action. This dread of what his neigh-
> bor may think more than anything else appears to
> paralyze the white man in America when it comes
> to public dealings with the Negro. This is true from
> the lowest circles to the highest, from the weakest
> to the strongest.[62]

Defending the Civil Rights bill before the Forty-Third Congress, John R. Lynch had said:

> You may ask why we do not institute civil suits
> in the State courts. What a farce! Talk about insti-
> tuting a civil rights suit in the State courts of Ken-
> tucky, for instance, where the decision of the judge
> is virtually rendered before he enters the courthouse,

and the verdict of the jury substantially rendered before it is impaneled.[63]

On this same note, *The Crisis* observed in 1917: "It is lynching, forced labor, and discrimination that is sending the Negro North. When he comes North he may find mobs and hostile labor unions, but he will also find the law and the law will be enforced."[64]

With further reference to the Negro *vis-a-vis* the law, it has been pointed out that until the family allotments paid World War II G.I.'s made many southern Negroes conscious of the need for birth and marriage certificates, many of them saw no need for legal divorce. While religious convictions and custom often dictated the need for a marriage ceremony, divorce by many was a simple matter of mutual consent. Re-marriage without legal divorce could take place as often as desired so long as the previous mate was residing in another county or state.[65] Statistics have shown that in the more recent decades Negroes have gained a greater appreciation for the need of securing a legal divorce before entering into a subsequent marriage. Publication of bigamy prosecutions by the courts, increased educational attainment, and other factors combined to bring about this change.

Since emancipation, Afro-Americans have been divided between two schools of thought as to whether prejudice and discrimination could best be ended through legislation and legal action or through more indirect means. Knowing the power of public opinion, some have felt that it was futile to concentrate efforts on the legislative and legal fronts. These persons feared that political and legal action would unnecessarily antagonize the white man, that the chances of success on these fronts were very small, and that even if successful in winning legislation and court action in favor of the race, these would be ineffectual unless white southerners realized a change of heart. So this latter group has preferred to concentrate on activities designed to bring about a changed attitude toward the Negro. This, they felt, could be done through the acquisition of property, education, and culture, and through leading exemplary Christian lives.

The opposing school of thought has been expressed characteristically by such a legal action group as the NAACP. Its members have urged militant action on *all* fronts. They have felt that the tremendous respect which Anglo-Saxons traditionally have held toward law and the courts dictate that the race work for legislation and court rulings against racial segregation and discrimination. These men have believed, in contradistinction to the first group, that ours is a government of laws primarily, not a government of men. A number of observers have pointed out, however, that both schools of thought are identical in their opposition to segregation and discrimination. They differ only in approach. Again Moton has reflected what is perhaps a dominant thought with Afro-Americans. He writes:

> Nowhere is the white man more overbearing than when, with the sanction of the law, which is to say with the organized support of society, his society, he is dealing with the person of a Negro. In many places an indignant retort from a Negro is sufficient occasion for an arrest for 'disorderly conduct'; the attempt to run from an officer is sufficient for killing the offender for 'resisting an officer of the law.' In prison the most palpable distinctions are made between white and Negro prisoners in food, clothing, bedding and facilities.[66]

The 1853 meeting of the National Negro Convention had stated in its address to the people of the United States: "We ask that (since the right of trial by jury is a safeguard of liberty, against the encroachments of power, only as it is a trial by impartial men, drawn indiscriminately from the country) colored men shall not, in every instance, be tried by white persons; and that colored men shall not be either by custom or enactment excluded from the jury-box."[67] This same sentiment was repeated years later when another observer noted: "An honored phrase in the procedure of the courts is 'A jury of his peers.' When a Negro is involved it is observed most in the breach, unless it be thought to pay an extra tribute to justice by selecting a jury regarded as his superiors."[68] Thus, he continued, "Negroes very generally feel that they have better chances for justice before a judge than before a jury." It sometimes has been charged that Negroes refuse to cooperate with the law in apprehending criminals, and that the race has little respect for laws where discriminatory practices against the race are concerned, Moton declares that often government appears to the colored man "not as an instrument of justice, but as an instrument of persecution; . . . simply white society organized to keep the Negro down," while officers of the law sometimes appear to be "agents authorized to wreak upon the helpless offender the contempt, the indignation, and the vengeance that outraged law and order feels when stimulated by prejudice."[69]

In Detroit there was founded in January, 1896, the National Association of Colored Men, led by R. T. Greener, Joseph Dickinson, and D. A. Straker. This organization deplored the violation of Negro citizenship which existed in many parts of the nation, and asserted the claim of the race to full and equal citizenship. In a memorial to Congress of that year, it was stated that the members of this Association did not "acquiesce in the dictum that we must trust in time and to the pleasure or disposition of our enemies to grant rights."[70] Unlike its women's counterpart, this organization had a very brief history.

Booker Washington's 1895 Atlanta speech was followed the next year by the Supreme Court decision of *Plessy vs. Ferguson*. Since the Slaughterhouse Case, the Court, reflecting the general trend of the period, had followed the line of allowing home-rule to the southern states where racial matters were concerned. Thus *Plessy vs. Ferguson* which legalized the "separate but equal" doctrine where public facilities were concerned, was but the recognition of a *fait accompli*. The decision had been preceded by the 1883 court ruling against the Civil Rights Act, and by three similar rulings by the Interstate Commerce Commission, and was soon to be followed by the "Insular Cases" rulings, in which the Court would state again and again that this nation could have more than one class of citizenship. Although numerous Afro-American writers have expressed bitterness at the abandonment by the Republican party of the cause of the freedman after 1876, R. R. Moton thought in 1924 that this might have been a good thing. "Thinking in the large," he observed, "it may be well to have let the public agi-

tation on this question subside while passions cooled, till thinking could again become clear and straight and sane."[71]

Populism and Reaction

The Populist movement of the 1880's and 90's was the
last great effort of American farmers to dominate the federal
government. This was also a partially successful effort of
Americans to create legislature machinery for mitigating some
of the worst evils of the nascent industrialism. Centering around
the Farmers' Mutual Benefit Association, the Southern Alliance, and the Colored Farmers' Alliance, the movement reached the apogee of its prominence with the 1896 campaign against
William McKinley and Republicanism.   Its greatest success,
however, was experienced on the state level, where Populist
candidates came to dominate some states and considerably to
influence the course of government in others. Well-known is
the manner in which poor whites of the South, and Negroes,
formerly staunch Democrats and Republicans respectively, effected a temporary union known as Fusionism. This political
cooperation resulted in considerable democratic legislation in
the South before it was destroyed, in part by fraud, violence,
and a powerful propaganda designed to foment fear of Negro
competition and another period of Negro "domination" of the
the South. The manner in which this movement was carried out
in one state and culminated in a bloody race riot has been mas-
terfully described by Helen G. Edmonds in her *The Negro and
Fusionist Politics in North Carolina*.[72]

The Colored Farmers' Alliance grew to proportions which
are little known. In 1891 its membership, embracing at least
twenty state branches, was almost one and one-half million
souls. During the period of this movement, Negro participation
in politics received a new impetus, only to end with further and
almost complete disfranchisement. As with the nation at large,
the Populist movement served to educate the Negro in many
ways. It saw him learn anew the benficent possibilities of group
action, both along racially segregated and integrated lines. In
1891, for example, a wide-spread cotton-picker strike spread
over the South, aimed at improved wages for this type of labor.
St. Louis was hit the next year with a strike of over two thou-

sand colored longshoremen, and in 1898 over two thousand more longshoremen struck in Galveston, Texas.

H. S. Doyle, Negro preacher, was for a time one of the most ardent and open supporters of Tom Watson, the outstanding Georgia Populist. As Populists sought to win the vote of the southern Negro, especially in the year 1892, many Afro-Americans joined the movement. As Fusionists gained control of several states and cities, Negro voting and office-holding were made easier and took an upswing. "Never before or since," writes C. Vann Woodward, "have the two races in the South come so close together as they did during the Populist struggles."[73] The Granger Movement had not experienced much success in the South because of the great racial strife of the 1870's. The populist movement, however, was partly responsible for the election to Congress of several Negro Congressmen, especially in North and South Carolina. In Congress their efforts centered largely on matters designed to improve the lot of their race. Other than these efforts they were loyal party men.

Confronted by poor white defection to the Populist party in the early 1890's, Bourbon Democrats started courting the Negro vote. Thus for a time both Democrats and Populists were courting the Negro vote. In the 1880's the white Southern Farmers' Alliance cooperated for a time with the Colored Farmers' Alliance and in 1886 a cooperative union was formed. Representative George W. Murray of South Carolina, only Negro member of the 53rd Congress, voted in favor of free silver. He asserted that all Afro-Americans were in favor of free silver.[74]

The Populist Revolt, representing as it did a somewhat acute protest of poor whites in the South against their economically depraved status, sorely frightened the Southern ruling class. Perhaps for the first time, some poor whites became dimly aware that the grievances of Negroes often coincided with their own, and that perhaps the two groups should be allies rather than antagonists. But this alliance was to be short-lived indeed. The vast majority of poor whites were too immature in their social and economic thought to effect a genuine and lasting alliance. The dead hand of Old South paternalism had robbed them of the needed maturity to lead such an alliance, and in the reaction which followed, they too, were often robbed of their right to vote.

Repeatedly during the disfranchisement movement of the 1890's Negro leaders stated that they were not against educational or property qualifications for voting so long as these tests were applied equally to the races. During the 1920's, James Weldon Johnson restated this position. Johnson declared:

> The Negro in the matter of the ballot demands only that he should be given the right as an American citizen to vote under the identical qualifications required of other citizens. He cares not how high those qualifications are made—whether they include the ability to read and write, or the possession of five hundred dollars, or a knowledge of the Einstein Theory—just so long as these qualifications are impartially demanded of white men and black men.[75]

In 1890 Mississippi adopted the first of the South's ingenious disfranchisement constitutions. Most of the states quickly followed, and by 1915 the Negro voter in the South was for all practical purposes an extinct species. Despite the decline of Negro voters, the 1890 Mississippi Disfranchisement Convention refused to put its new constitution to the test of a state-wide vote, and instead put it into effect without this approval. James Weldon Johnson pointed out that fanning the Negro question by politicians not only kept Negroes from voting and led to race riots, but made whites afraid of free discussion and politically apathetic. Johnson declared:

> With a free vote in the South the specter of Negro domination would vanish into thin air. There would naturally follow a breakup of the South into two parties. There would be political light, political discussion, the right to differences of opinion, and the Negro vote would naturally divide itself. No other procedure would be probable. The idea of a solid party. a minority party at that, is inconceivable.[76]

In a speech delivered before the Fifty-First Congress, John Mercer Langston contended that when the Republican Party in the South was "killed," democracy was killed for whites as well as Negroes.[77] There were numerous southern whites, Langston avers, who did not want to belong to the Democratic Party. Langston said:

> When I stand here today, speaking for the cause of the people of my state, . . . I am pleading for her people, both white and black, I am speaking for white men as well as for Negroes; for white men in my State are proscribed, and they are denied a free ballot.

Afro-American participation in the Populist movement in such large numbers reveals again the Americanization of the race. Practically none of America's major movements and interests have been without the Negro's active participation. This largest of the nation's minorities, comprising a significant one-tenth of the total population, ever has been a part of the warp and woof of the national history and character, and few, if any, studies of the history of the nation can be complete without cognizance of the Negro's contribution.

The NAACP

The Niagara Movement, fore-runner of the NAACP, was an organization of professional men founded during the summer of 1905 near Buffalo, New York. The foundation convention, attended by twenty-nine persons from fourteen states, named the organization after the nearby Niagara Falls. The main instigator of this movement was W. E. B. DuBois,[78] although he modestly later claimed that: "The honor of founding the organization belongs to F. L. McGhee; C. C. Bently, . . . and W. M. Trotter."[79] Reflecting some of the *raison d'ete* which brought the American Federation of Labor into existence, the organizers felt that many efforts at group action among Negroes had failed because they lacked a likeminded membership with unity and definiteness of aim, thus the Niagara Movement was limited to educated professional and business persons. The organization's declaration of principles made it clear that what it sought was political, social, and civil equality for the race. In 1906 the Niagara Movement met at Harper's Ferry, at Boston in 1907, and Oberlin, Ohio in 1908. The next year it merged with the NAACP, which was incorporated in 1911.

Angered and aroused by the attack which the Monroe Trotter - DuBois leadership was making against his efforts,

Booker Washington resurrected in 1906 the old Afro-American Council. This organization had been started in 1890 and led by T. Thomas Fortune, J. C. Price, and Washington as a sort of Republican National Negro Committee. Washington now hoped to use it to make statements to the nation on race relations which would mitigate the often harsh, uncompromising, and bitter ones emanating from DuBois, Trotter, and their following. Opposition to the Booker T. Washington "machine" and its program of compromise were vital factors in producing the Niagara Movement. Striking also is the fact that this movement was, in a number of ways, a prototype of the NAACP.

Included with DuBois in founding the NAACP were such outstanding persons as Mary W. Ovington, Ida Wells-Barnett, Francis J. Grimke, Oswald Garrison Villard, John Dewey, Lincoln Steffens, William Dean Howells, Stephen S. Wise, and William E. Walling. Both DuBois and Lincoln Steffens were outstanding "Muckrakers," and the presence of other journalists and writers as Walling, Villard, and Howells reveals that the NAACP was a characteristic product of the Progressive Movement which flourished under Presidents Roosevelt, Taft, and Wilson. The interracial character of this organization also reflects another general fact about the Progressive Movement, that is, it was not strictly a class or sectional movement. As first Director of Publicity and Research, and founder and long-time editor of its journal, the *Crisis,* Dr. DuBois was a key figure in the growth and success of this organization.

From its beginning the NAACP has been thoroughly of the American tradition. Indeed, by its emphasis on legal action to abolish segregation and discrimination this organization is based on the very heart of the American tradition. Also, the NAACP has never been hostile to labor or capitalism, has refused to be drawn into politics, hence, among other things, has never found itself arrayed against the foreign policy of the United States. Partly because of its deep rooted Americanism, the NAACP has found itself severely criticized by Communists, who have felt that it was "bourgeois" and too conservative. As odd as it sometimes may seem, Communists have charged repeatedly that the NAACP leadership was Uncle

Tomish and selling the cause of the Afro-American down the river.

Led by Arthur and Joel Spingarn, by 1923 the legal defense committee of the NAACP had won three important decisions. In the 1915 case of *Guinn vs. the United States,* the Supreme Court ruled the "grandfathers clause" to be unconstitutional, two years later in *Buchanan vs. Warley,* the Court declared that city ordinances requiring compulsory residential segregation of the races are unconstitutional, and in 1923, in *Moore vs. Dempsey* the Court reversed for the first time a state murder conviction on the ground that Negroes had been systematically excluded from the jury.

This organization has summed up its *raison d'etre* as follows: "The NAACP exists to defend the full civil, legal, political rights of . . . colored Americans and to obtain for them full equality of opportunity with all other citizens. To make [colored Americans] physically free from lynchings, mob violence and peonage; mentally free from enforced ignorance; politically free from being held voteless; and socially free from insult."[80]

The NAACP has represented the most advanced thought of the race. It was supported at first largely by the educated urban Negro, but others supported financially while often thinking it either too conservative or too radical. As recent as 1934 the NAACP was largely middle-class dominated. Of its composition at that time, Wilson Record has observed "few lower-class Negroes—laborers and sharecroppers—participated in its activtiies. Even after several years of depression the 'talented tenth' psychology was still dominant within the NAACP leadership. This make-up was reflected in its program."[81] As to why he supported the NAACP for more than a quarter of a century, Benjamin Mays, long-time president of Morehouse College, stated in 1955: "I support it because as a decent, law-abiding citizen, I am entitled to respect and the protection of the law which the Federal Constitution guarantees to me. The NAACP uses the machinery of the Constitution and the courts to help me achieve the status of man."[82] A number of Afro-Americans have looked behind the front-line leadership of W. E. B. DuBois and Walter White to give much of the credit for the organization's success to such expert legal minds as those of Thurgood Marshall, Charles Houston, William Hastie, Leon Ransom, and Spottswood Robinson, and others.[53] Walter White, descendant of the Atlanta, Georgia aristocracy, at the age of 13 was shocked at seeing bloody scenes of that city's race riot of 1906. These scenes made an indelible impression on his mind. After he became head of the NAACP in 1934, posing as a poor white, Walter White investigated first-hand over two-score lynchings and served as a chief spokesman for that organization and his race until he died in 1955.

Founded in 1910, a portion of the platform of *The Crisis* stated:

> The object of this publication is to set forth those facts and arguments which show the danger of race prejudice, particularly as manifested today toward colored people. It takes its name from the fact that the editors believe that this is a critical time in the history of the advancement of men. Catholicity and tolerance, reason and forbearance can today make the world-old dream of human brotherhood approach realization. . . . The magazine will be the organ of no clique or party and will avoid personal rancor of all sorts. In the absence of proof to the contrary it will assume honesty of purpose on the part of all men, North and South, white and black.[54]

By 1918 the monthly circulation of this journal had reached over one hundred thousand copies. Indicative of his consciousness of and resentment at the Booker T. Washington philosophy, DuBois at that time contended that *The Crisis* had placed before the country "a clear-cut statement of the legitimate aims of the American Negro."[55] DuBois conceived of this as a "high class" journal "for the nine million American Negroes and—for the whole Negro world," which would "tell them of the deeds of themselves and their neighbors, interpret the news of the world to them, and inspire them toward definite ideals."[56]

Of the NAACP, Garveyism, and other movements evident among early twentieth century Afro-Americans, in 1925 Locke wrote:

Each generation, however, will have its creed, and that of the present is the belief in the efficacy of collective effort, in race co-operation. This deep feeling of race is at present the mainspring of Negro life. It seems to be the outcome of the reaction to proscription and prejudice; an attempt, fairly successful on the whole, to convert a defensive into an offensive position, a handicap into an incentive. It is radical in tone, but not in purpose and only the most stupid forms of opposition, misunderstanding or persecution could make it otherwise. Of course, the thinking Negro has shifted a little toward the left with the world-trend, and there is an increasing group who affiliate with radical and liberal movement. But fundamentally for the present the Negro is radical on race matters, conservative on others, in other words, a 'forced radical,' a social protestant rather than a genuine radical.[87]

By the 1950's not only were Afro-Americans taking great pride in such things as the rise of Asia and Africa's colored population abroad, but also in the growing recognition being given the importance of their ballot and considerable purchasing power at home. Almost every local, state, and federal election served as repeated boosts to their egos as they could see that in such cities as Chicago, New York, Detroit, and Philadelphia, as well as in several states, the Negro sometimes held in close elections the balance of political power. By 1955 so optimistic and encouraged were some persons about the progress of their race, that they believed that 1963, the one hundredth anniversary of the Emancipation Proclamation, would find their race in the "promised land" of full citizenship. Others, not so optimistic, set the year 2000 as a target date. When in 1957 colored ministers throughout the South organized the Southern Christian Leadership Conference and set a drive to get more Negroes into the status of registered voters, and to begin credit unions in their churches, the movement was launched with considerable enthusiasm and optimism. Yet in the May 9, 1959 issue of the *Pittsburgh Courier,* George S. Schuyler, while praising the objects of the movement, questioned whether it had not "petered out." Schuyler was still voicing his long-held conviction that the credit union and similar ideas designed to give the race greater economic independence and security were of far more importance than the vote drive or the 1959 student's "March-on-Washington idiocy and the phoney issue of New York's segregated schools." Yet when in 1960 a wave of student sit-down demonstrations at segregated lunch counters swept the South and nation the SCLC appeared to be working with the Congress of Racial Equality which had very dramatically and effectively joined the anti-segregation movement.

By 1960 Afro-American spokesmen were at times critical of their group for the apathy which led members of the race to fail to take advantage of privileges already won and readily available. In those southern cities and rural areas where no bars to Negro voting existed, a vast number of Negroes, due to ignorance, indolence, or the feeling, "One Negro's vote doesn't count!," failed to register to vote. In such an outstanding southern city as New Orleans, Louisiana, although most of the eligible Negro voters were unregistered, by 1960 Negro fraternities, sororities, ministers, and other "leaders" had made no concerted attack on the problem. Less noticeable, but also significant, was the continuing failure of Negro college teachers to attend national and regional meetings of scholarly societies. Although no bars existed few could be seen at the meetings of The National Council for the Social Studies, American Historical Association, and similar organizations, and it seemed to be increasingly evident that legal desegregation was a first step only.

SOME ATTTITUDES OF NEGROES TOWARD AMERICAN PRESIDENTS

An important aspect of the political and general intellectual history of the United States is the attitudes which Negro Americans have held toward various occupants of the presidency. Since a fair-sized volume probably could be written on the subject, the following résumé provides only a sketch of the "mind of the Negro" in this regards. Perhaps a larger study ought to include a rather thorough opinion poll of Negroes, a poll designed to get at their attitudes toward the beliefs and feelings about each of the presidents. Certainly for the present century any thorough study of Negro attitudes toward various presidents would have to include a more thorough analysis of the voting record than is herein attempted.

Presidents Before 1860

Of the first three presidents, Negro Americans have paid scant attention to John Adams, while showing ambivalence of attitude and feeling toward George Washington and Thomas Jefferson. Because Washington and Jefferson were slave-holders and held some biased views about Negroes highly similar to those of Abraham Lincoln, these two men have not been quite the heroes to some Negroes that they have been to white Americans. Perhaps because he was a slave-holder and made no vigorous defense of Negro rights, the same is true even of the "leveler" Andrew Jackson. Herein can be discerned the fact that, so much can slavery, prejudice and discrimination narrow the view of a people; Negro Americans have been obsessed with race to such an extent that many have tended to base their estimation of presidents on the latter's publicized position or lack of position on the "race question." That this is not wholly true, however, is seen in the fact that while Jefferson the slave-holder has been somewhat of a villain in Negro thought, Jefferson—author of the Declaration of Independence and the anti-slavery clause of the Northwest Ordinance, acquaintance of Benjamin Banneker and great friend of education—has been a hero in Negro thought. Too, although they criticized Washington and Jefferson for being slave-holders, Negro abolitionists often referred to both along with Benjamin Franklin, Anthony Benezet, and John Woolman as friends of freedom among the colonial leaders.

After comparing Jefferson's authorship of the Declaration of Independence with the reminder that, after penning this document Jefferson remained a slave-holder for fifty years, southern born and Harvard trained Archibald Grimké declared:

> This inconsistency between the man's magnificence in profession and his smallness in practice, between the grandeur of what he promised and the meanness of what he performed, taken in conjunction with his cool unconsciousness of the discrepancy, is essentially and emphatically an American trait, a national idiosyncrasy.[1]

Grimké leveled the same criticism against George Washington because this president owned over two hundred slaves and willed that they be manumitted only after his wife's death. Of the Declaration of Independence and the Constitution, Grimké stated:

> The muse of history, dipping her iron pen in the generous blood of the Negro, has written large across the page of that Preamble, and the face of the Declaration of Independence, the words, 'sham, hypocrisy.'[2]

From the Declaration of Independence, Afro-Americans have focussed their attention mainly on the words—"We hold these truths to be self-evident that all men are created equal; that they are endowed by their Creator with certain unalienable rights; that among these are life, liberty, and the pursuit of happiness."

Not only has the fact that a number of the presidents of the ante-bellum era were slaveholders interested Negroes greatly, but there has been considerable speculation to the effect that a number of those who were slave-holders sired illegitimate off-spring by their slave women. In *Clotel, or The President's Daughter,* the first novel penned by a Negro American, William Wells Brown related the trials and tribulations of a mulatto girl who was presented as the illegitimate off-spring of Thomas Jefferson.[3] Similar rumors have been levelled at other presidents.

In addition to the Declaration of Independence, as would be expected, Washington and Jefferson have been closely associated in Negro thought with the Revolutionary War and the United States Constitution.[4] William Cooper Nell, William Wells Brown, George Washington Williams and other early Negro historians, as well as more recent writers in this area, were very much interested in revealing the wide participation of Negro soldiers in the Revolutionary War, as well as that the first colonial to pour out his life's blood in the struggle against Britain was Crispus Attucks, a Negro.[5] Approximately 5,000 Negroes fought with the colonists in the Revolutionary War, in almost every capacity in almost every battle, on land and sea, and were integrated with the white troops. Doubtless the manner in which both sides made strong bids for the services of the bondsmen, with each promising them freedom, served to heighten the Negro's sense of importance and to make the promise of freedom seem more certain. The literate progeny of these troops have shown keen cognizance of, and pride in, such facts as these, and Negro historians generally have criticized Washington for his early reluctance to use colored troops. Too, these scholars and other Negro spokesmen have compared, with some cynicism and bitterness, the exalted liberal protestations of the Revolutionary War era with the nation's failure to follow this with a quick end to the institution of slavery. "There are too many young men being flogged as slaves," Charles Lenox Remond declared in 1841, "whose father receives a pension for his services in the Revolutionary War."[6]

Perhaps the high hopes of Negroes can be accounted for partially in such a fact as that, due largely to the post-war liberalism, there was a rapid increase of the free Negro population between 1790 and 1830. While the first census showed 59,000 free Negroes in the country, that of 1830 showed

319,000. Too, at the beginning of the war in 1775 the Quakers had organized the nation's first anti-slavery society, and after the war there was a great increase of abolitionist sentiment, with such leaders as Benjamin Franklin, Theodore Dwight, Noah Webster, and Benjamin Rush taking pronounced stands against the institution. The liberal trend of the times is also evidenced in the increase of rights, privileges, and opportunities granted free Negroes during and immediately following the war. In some states, these rights already had been substantial throughout the colonial period, and were to increase until after 1831 when they were to decline greatly as, for all elements in the national populace, democracy was dramatically eclipsed in the 1830-60 period.

By setting up a government whose continuance depended greatly on compromise, the Founding Fathers unwittingly gave to slavery a longer life for it soon became clear that in their devotion to the cause of the union the nation's leaders would extend the principle of compromise even to freedom itself. But if the nation-at-large had not held freedom and democracy in such high esteem, the black man probably would not have resented slavery so deeply. Negroes have been highly critical of the Founding Fathers for not using the occasion of the 1787 convention to rid the nation of slavery. As recent as the second decade of the twentieth century, one student of Negro history would say of the Founding Fathers:

> If the children's teeth today are set on edge on the Negro question, it is because the fathers ate the sour grapes of race-wrong, ate those miserable grapes during their whole life, and dying, transmitted their taste for oppression, as a bitter inheritance to their children, and children's children, for God knows how many black years to come.[7]

This is a sentiment which Archibald Grimké, George Washington Williams, W. E. B. Du Bois and numerous other Negroes have expressed.[8] Until the end of the Civil War, Negroes engaged in a lively debate as to whether the Constitution was a pro- or anti-slavery document. Typical of the latter sentiment were the following statements by Frederick Douglass and James

Forten. In a speech delivered July 5, 1852 at Rochester, New
York, Douglass said of the Constitution:

> In that instrument I hold there is neither warrant,
> license, nor sanction of (slavery); but interpreted,
> as it ought to be interpreted, the Constitution is a
> *glorious liberty document.* Read its preamble, con-
> sider its purposes. Is slavery among them? . . . What
> would be thought of an instrument drawn up . . .
> for the purpose of entitling the city of Rochester
> to a tract of land, in which no mention of land was
> made?[9]

Förten opined:

> It cannot be that the authors of our Constitution in-
> tended to exclude us from its benefits, for just emerg-
> ing from unjust and cruel emancipation, their souls
> were too much affected with their own deprivations
> to commence the reign of terror over others. . . .
> They felt that they had no more authority to enslave
> us, than England had to tyrannize over them. . . .
> Actuated by these sentiments they adopted the glori-
> ous fabric of our liberties, and declaring 'all men'
> free, they did not particularize white and black, be-
> cause they never supposed it would be made a
> question whether *we were men or not.*[10]

In contrary vein, at an 1851 state convention of Ohio Negroes
Charles H. Langston agreed with H. Ford Douglass that the
Constitution was a pro-slavery document.[11] Robert Purvis,
Henry Highland Garnet, and C. L. Remond are among the
Negro abolitionists who held similar views.

Like John Adams, the three presidents James Madison,
James Monroe, and John Quincy Adams have held little unique
significance in Negro thought. Perhaps surprisingly, in view
of the nullification controversy and the common-man emphasis
associated with his name, about the only special interest which
Negroes have shown in Andrew Jackson has been to refer repeatedly to the remarks of praise which he made about the
Negro troops who fought under him at New Orleans. Also
because of their lack of publicized position on the race question, or because they were not directly involved in any special
and dramatic controversies in this area, Martin Van Buren,

William Henry Harrison, John Tyler, James K. Polk, Zachary Taylor, Millard Filmore, and Franklin Pierce have been of slight unique consequence in Negro thought. It seems somewhat curious that, despite the prominence of the slavery issue in the Missouri Compromise and Texan and Mexican War questions, this generalization applies also to John Quincy Adams and James K. Polk. Perhaps this, and the consideration that even James Buchanan is only slightly prominent, as a villain, in Negro thought, are due in part to the fact that throughout the 1830-1861 period the role of the nation's chief executive *vis-a-vis* the slavery issue was often eclipsed by dramatic incidents involving abolitionists and their opponents in and out of congress. Throughout this period no man stood to be elected to the presidency who was closely identified with either of these two extreme camps, and when elected, to protect their own and their party's chances in subsequent elections, where possible the presidents usually avoided strong stands on the slavery issue. This was an age of compromise on the "race question."

Abraham Lincoln

The name of no president of the United States is as dear to Negro Americans as that of Abraham Lincoln. Not only the Emancipation Proclamation, but even his poverty-stricken childhood and sad and homely face served to endear Lincoln to the hearts of black men who, often looking upon themselves as belonging to an ugly-duckling race, saw a kinship with Lincoln in this regard.[12] Afro-Americans felt a kinship with Lincoln, too, because, like themselves, he was "a man of sorrow and acquainted with grief."[13] Yet, as the following survey indicates, Afro-Americans have not been unanimous in their feelings about and estimation of the Great Emancipator.

Today a great enigma and object of considerable myth to many persons, Lincoln has been accused of having been everything from a "nigger lover" of the "stripe" of Thaddeus Stevens and Charles Sumner, to a person who was anti-Negro. As with so many extreme views which his era has produced, no doubt the truth about Lincoln's attitude and feelings toward Negroes lies somewhere between these two antithetical views.

That he believed all people, of whatever creed or hue, to be entitled to freedom there can be little doubt. Furthermore, he believed that the basic political ideas on which the nation was founded, as well as the tenets of the Christian religion, supported his views on the matter. Because he believed, however, that physical appearances, innate and cultural differences, and stubborn human prejudices would always produce racial strife and friction, Lincoln supported various plans to colonize the Negro outside the United States. When in April, 1862 the slaves of the District of Columbia were emancipated, the bill bringing this about provided funds to aid in colonizing any freedmen who might wish to emigrate. In his second annual message to congress Lincoln reported that many Negroes had made requests to be colonized outside the United States. Earlier he had asked Negro leaders to support his colonization plan. Lincoln consistently opposed compulsory colonization, however, and was always polite and courteous to colored delegations and petitioners who opposed his colonization plans.

In his feelings that the nation would be best off with an all-white population, Lincoln is reminiscent somewhat of the one hundred percentism, ever a part of intense nationalism which saw sixteenth century Spain expel the Moors, Louis XIV revoke the Edict of Nantes and persecute Jansenists in the seventeenth century, and Adolf Hitler's twentieth century purge of the Jews. Of course, unlike the latter, Lincoln had no base ulterior motive in this lily-whiteism. In his failure to comprehend the manner in which cultural differences between racial groups may be made to disappear, Lincoln failed to anticipate the twentieth century faith in, and possibilities of, social engineering. Yet, in his recognition of the persistent trouble which color prejudice could cause the nation, time has proven him an excellent prophet.

In 1862 Philadelphia Negroes sent to President Lincoln a petition against his plan to colonize the race outside the United States. After excoriating slaveholders, this statement averred, "We believe that the world would be benefited by giving the four million slaves their freedom, and the lands now possessed by the blood of our kinsmen. These masters 'toil' not, neither do they spin.' They destroy, they consume, and give to the world in return but a small equivalent."[14] Although, as Miles Mark Fisher has shown, slaves of the 1820-1860 period were greatly agitated in favor of the movement to colonize Negroes, in general free Negroes, strongly resisted the movement.[15]

Despite Lincoln's view to the contrary, during the war Negro leaders fought for more than giving the franchise to literate Negroes only. They wanted the principle of universal manhood suffrage applied to their group. As 1864 was a presidential election year, political action was a dominant concern. The National Convention of Negroes, held that year at Syracuse, New York, had 144 delegates with approximately one-half of the southern states represented. This body asserted its faith that Negroes would soon be accorded the "full measure of citizenship." Yet the delegates revealed a considerable fear that the South might be accepted back into the Union and allowed to keep slavery. They alluded to the 1787 Constitutional Convention when slavery was under fire from those who then wished its termination, but it managed to survive and spread. Referring to the two major parties, the delegates declared that while the Democratic party "is our bitterest enemy, and positively and actively reactionary, the Republican Party is negatively and passively so in its tendency."[16]

Because of his reluctance to accept Negro troops, devotion to colonization, and hesitation in issuing an emancipation proclamation, early in the war Negroes had regarded Lincoln as a questionable friend. Yet, whenever he presented himself before Afro-Americans during the war, they shouted themselves hoarse in praise of his devotion to "their" cause, for they knew that, whatever his shortcomings, he was against slavery. In a speech which is quoted in The Liberator of February 14, 1862, John S. Rock, noted abolitionist, said: "While Mr. Lincoln has been more conservative than I had hoped to find him, I recognize in him an honest man, striving to redeem the country from the degradation and shame into which Mr. Buchanan and his predecessors have plunged it." This sentiment was general among Negro abolitionists of the day.

Bondsmen regarded Lincoln as the long-awaited Moses whom God had promised would lead them out of bondage.

Throughout the war they prayed for his success. "Indulgent father," prayed one Negro, "we thank Thee that Thou didst ever make a Linkum. O spare his life and bless our Union army."[17] One ex-slave reported, "I never seed Mr. Lincoln, but they told me 'bout him; I thought he was partly God."[18] Another ex-slave declared that he was a first cousin of Abraham Lincoln. "Him and my father was first cousins . . . . My father was a Mudd. Abe Lincoln and him was brother and sister's children."[19] During the Civil War at least one slave mother named her baby "Lincoln."[20]

Just before midnight, December 31, 1862 the Emancipation Proclamation was issued. This document prompted Julia Ward Howe to see "the glory of the coming of the Lord,' and fired the determination of the Union troops to new heights. Probably the masses of Negroes, still in the Confederate South, were days later in receiving news of the official act. But for those who resided in Union territory, the moment was eagerly awaited. Frederick Douglass states that in Boston, Massachusetts a crowd gathered in Tremont Temple to await the news. There was considerable doubt in the minds of the group that the President would go through with his announced plan to issue the proclamation. "We were waiting and listening as for a bolt from the sky, which would rend the fetters of four millions of slaves," Douglass stated. "We were watching as it were, by the dim light of the stars for the dawn of a new day." Douglass called the proclamation "the immortal paper, which though special in its languages, was general in its principles and effect, making slavery forever impossible in the United States,"[21] and declared that in their happiness at the issuance of the proclamation, "We forgot all delay, and forgot all tardiness, forgot that the President had bribed the rebels to lay down their arms by a promise to withhold the bolt which would smite the slave-system with destruction."[22] The Negro ever has been aware of the tremendous amount of hate from all sides that was levelled at Lincoln, and generally the Negro has been sympathetic and has understood.

The dreary rainy morning that Lincoln passed from this world on the top floor of a Washington rooming house found a multitude of ex-bondsmen gathered across the street weeping as though their hearts would break. Of all the people around the dying President, Gideon Welles said of this crowd of ex-bondsmen—"Their hopeless grief affected me more than anything else." Only the death of Franklin D. Roosevelt, and reaction to the procession which carried his body from Georgia northward, elicited anything like this sorrow over the passing of an American president. Many Negroes feared that the assassination of Lincoln meant that their protector was gone and they would be pushed back into slavery. Frederick Douglass called his assassination "the crowning crime of slavery . . . a new crime, a pure act of malice."[23] "It was," he averred, "the simple gratitification of a hell-black spirit of revenge." To Afro-Americans John Wilkes Booth is one of history's archfiends and assassins.[24]

In 1876, on the occasion of the unveiling of the Freedmen's Monument to Lincoln, in Washington, D. C., Douglass stated:

> It must be admitted, truth compels me to admit, . . . Abraham Lincoln was not, in the fullest sense of the word, either our man or our model. In his interest, in his associations, in his habits of thought, and in his prejudices, he was a white man.

> He was preeminently the white man's President, entirely devoted to the welfare of the white man. He was ready and willing at any time during the first years of his administration to deny, postpone, and sacrifice the rights of humanity in the colored people to promote the welfare of the white people of this country.[25]

"The race to which we belong,' Douglass stated, "were not the special objects of his consideration." To the whites present, Douglass said: "You are the children of Abraham Lincoln. We are at best his stepchild; children by adoption, children by force of circumstances and necessity." Yet Douglass could declare of his race that during the war years—"Our faith in him was often taxed and strained to the uttermost, but it never failed. . . . We were at times grieved, stunned, and greatly bewildered; but our hearts believed while they ached and bled." This faith in Lincoln was possible, he said, because the Negro was able through it all "to make reasonable allowance for the circumstances of his position." Thus:

> By a broad survey, in the light of the stern logic of great events, and in view of that divinity which shapes our ends, rough hew them how we will, we came to the conclusion that the hour and the man of our redemption had somehow met in the person of Abraham Lincoln.. . . . It was enough for us that Abraham Lincoln was at the head of a great movement, which, in the nature of things, must go on until slavery should be utterly and forever abolished in the United States.[26]

Douglass admitted that for Lincoln to have been radically anti-slavery would have driven too many Americans from him and killed all chance of success in his effort to save the Union and contain slavery. "Viewed from the genuine abolition ground, Mr. Lincoln seemed tardy, cold, dull, and indifferent; but measuring him by the sentiment of his country, a sentiment he was bound as a statesman to consult, he was swift, zealous, radical, and determined."[27] Douglass ended by calling Lincoln "our friend and liberator."[28]

Although Frederick Douglass critized Lincoln for seemingly putting every other consideration before the immediate interests of the Negro race, M. C. B. Mason did not feel that Lincoln's tactics revealed any real disinterest in the Negro race. Mason quoted Lincoln's famed statement to Horace Greeley— "If I could save the Union without freeing any slave, I would do it; and if I could save it by freeing all the slaves, I would do it; and if I could do it by freeing some and by leaving others, I would also do that." Of this statement, Mason declared:

> Here was statesmanship of an unusual order. Lincoln knew that the one great central idea around which all the patriotism of the North might in the end declare allegiance, was the preservation of the Union. This secured, slavery in the very nature of the case would be ultimately abolished.

In defense of their claim that he was against slavery, numerous Negro orators have quoted Lincoln's statement—"If slavery is not wrong, nothing is wrong."[30] Again differing with Douglass' view that Lincoln was not sincerely against slavery, Bishop

Alexander Walters stated that, "A careful study of this sincere, just and sympathetic man will serve to show that from his earliest years he was against slavery."[31] The bishop supported his position with numerous references to anti-slavery statements and opinions given by Lincoln between 1839 and 1861, and concluded that Lincoln was "a giant in intellect, a peerless diplomat, a fearless advocate of the rights of humanity and a wise ruler."[32] With several other Afro-Americans, Bishop Walters felt that Lincoln not only freed the Negro but the nation as well, and he felt that this justified calling him "the savior of his country, the Emancipator of its people."[33]

As indicated, since his death numerous Negro orators and poets have extolled Lincoln's virtues, and some would ascribe to him benign motives and feelings which he never had. These latter persons would sometimes become convinced that Lincoln backed their race's freedom, not so much because of his convictions about human rights as because of his faith in the ability of Negroes to prove their right to equality of treatment and opportunity. Thus it is that in his "To Our Boys," written in the 1920's, the Poet Irvin W. Underhill would exhort colored youth to—

> Come out and face life's problem,
>   boys, With faith and courage
> too, and justify that wondrous
>   faith, Abe Lincoln had in you.

In their thoughts about Lincoln since 1865 many Negroes have been concerned with the question of whether the race has justified its emancipation. The answer has been a rather unanimous "Yes." At a 1916 memorial meeting in New York honoring Booker T. Washington, Robert Russa Moton declared: "Booker T. Washington's life and work would have alone justified Abraham Lincoln's ideas and actions regarding emancipation."[34] Speaking on the occasion of the 100th anniversary of Lincoln's birth, M. C. B. Mason asked Afro-Americans:

> What is the lesson he leaves us? To be honest, industrious and true, to be useful and intelligent citizens, to make ourselves absolutely necessary to the life of every community in which we live, to acquire property and lands, to keep out of the saloon, out of the

police courts, to be sober, industrious, to be patient, to be bold, to endure and to be in our virtuous lives a standing argument for the wisdom of his action by which our liberty was secured.[35]

In the 1920's, Edward Smythe Jones, poverty-stricken southern-reared Negro boy who wrote a poem to free himself from jail in Cambridge, Massachusetts, would pen as one of his best creations, "The Sylvan Cabin: A Centenary Ode on the Birth of Abraham Lincoln." In the same period, in his poem "Daybreak," George Marion McClellan would show an awareness that while Lincoln "gave" the race a first emancipation, another was needed which could come only from within the race.

Presidents Since 1865

Negro historians have had few kind words and little sympathy for Andrew Johnson. Perhaps the most vigorous attack on Johnson's personality, views, and acts is to be found in the chapter entitled, "The Transubstantiation of A Poor White" in W. E. B. Du Bois' book, *Black Reconstruction*.[36] The consensus appears to be among Negro historians and other thinkers that Johnson was a traitor to the Lincoln "liberalism" on race, hence traitor to the political party which was the Negro's best friend.

Despite their antipathies toward Andrew Johnson, and despite the great military achievement left by U. S. Grant which resulted in their freedom, and despite the fact that Radical Reconstruction reached its greatest heights during his tenure in the presidency, Grant has been neither especial hero nor villain in Negro thought. Although they probably would have concluded otherwise had he been a zealous crusader for Negro rights, apparently Negroes have accepted the general American verdict which the scandals and other examples of political ineptness have placed on Grant.

During his campaign for the presidency, Rutherford B. Hayes declared that, if elected—

Let me assure my countrymen of the Southern States that, if I shall be charged with the duty of organizing an Administration, it will be one which will regard and cherish their truest interests, the interests of the

white and the colored people, both and equally, and
which will put forth its best efforts in behalf of a civil
policy which will wipe out forever the distinction between the North and the South in our common
country.

Although Hayes could well endeavor to "wipe out forever the
distinction between the North and the South," clearly this
was as impossible so soon after 1865 as was that other promise
to "regard and cherish . . . equally . . . the interests of the
white and the colored people." Perhaps Hayes and his successors in the presidency to the year 1933 did not wish to
side with either southern whites or Negroes on the "race question." Still, it is axiomatic that in a fight between grossly un-
even opponents, not to take sides is really to support the stronger
of the antagonists. The laissez-faire policy followed by presidents and many liberal whites, North and South, did not eliminate their weight from the struggle, nor did it eliminate their
responsibility for the outcome.

Although Negroes appear to have said little about James
A. Garfield, Frederick Douglass was a severe critic of Chester
A. Arthur. Annullment in 1883 of the 1875 Civil Rights Act
by the Supreme Court did nothing to increase his popularity
with Negroes. T. Thomas Fortune called the court's decision
a baptism "in ice water," and John Mercer Langston felt that
it was a "stab in the back."[37]

Disappointment with the Republican party's laissez-faire
attitude toward the "Negro problem" caused a considerable
number of Negroes to support Grover Cleveland in the 1884
election. Although Cleveland gave assurances that he would
not seek to undo the Fourteenth and Fifteenth Amendments,
in both of his administrations he, too, followed a policy of
laissez-faire where the "race problem" was concerned. When
Cleveland became President-elect, many colored Americans
voiced concern as to whether the Democrats would be reactionary on racial matters. Frederick Douglass counselled a wait-
and-see attitude, aand stated that he had no fears that Democrats would wish to restore slavery.[38] P. B. S. Pinchback of
Louisiana approved of Cleveland's election and denied that the
race would retrogress under his administration. Blanche K.

Bruce also spoke out to counter the charge that the return of
Democrats to national power meant an intensification of anti-
Negroism. Bruce went so far as to assert that "Mr. Blaine's
charges of intimidation and violence at the polls are entirely
false."[39] In his Inaugural Address, the new President seems to
have aimed at alleviating some of these fears. To their dismay,
however, Negroes were soon aware that, on the race issue.
Cleveland would be true to the federal pattern of the times.
With many northern whites, Negroes joined in the condemnation of Cleveland for some of his seemingly pro-southern acts
such as the veto of the pension bill and the famed Battle; Flag
Order.

A temporary reversal of the federal laissez-faire policy on
the race issue took place during the administration of Benjamin
Harrison when the Blair bill for federal aid to education and
the Lodge "Force Bill" became the focal points of the sectional struggle. After acrimonious debate, during which the
South raised the cry of "states rights" and the specter of intensified violence over the race issue, both bills were defeated.
To T. Thomas Fortune defeat of the Force Bill constituted Republican "treachery."[40]

"The last decade of the nineteenth century and the opening of the twentieth century," states Rayford W. Logan,
"marked the nadir of the Negro's status in American society."[41]
Logan asserts that "The nadir was reached, however, not . . .
because of lack of attention (to the Negro's plight, but) precisely because of the efforts made to improve it."[42] Logan. believes that the seeming militancy of President Harrison's first
annual message to congress, defeat of the Republican-backed
civil rights legislation, and the resultant southern counter-at-
tack helped to bring about the nadir.[43] Logan ably has shown
that, in general, the northern press of the 1876-1900 period
approved of and supported the retreat from defense of equal
citizenship rights for the Negro. Even such periodicals as
Atlantic Monthly, Harpers, and Scribner's, he declares, often
yielded to the common temptation to caricature, stereotype,
and ridicule Negroes. Too, this historian feels that the "let's be
friends" pronouncements toward the South made by the presidents of this period probably encouraged the southern states to

adopt and pass their disfranchising and discriminating constitutions and laws of the era. Especially is he condemnatory of President McKinley for not speaking out against the Louisiana adoption of the Grandfather Clause and against the Wilmington, North Carolina race riot.

At the beginning of his term, President McKinley had voiced the sentiment of most presidents since 1876. McKinley stated:

> It will be my constant aim to do nothing, and permit nothing to be done, that will arrest or disturb this growing sentiment of unity and cooperation (between the sections), this revival of esteem and affiliation which now animates so many thousands in both the old antagonistic sections, but I shall cheerfully do everything possible to promote and increase it.[44]

W. E. B. Du Bois was active in the Anti-Imperialist League which had supported Bryan against McKinley.[45] With other groups, Massachusetts Negroes spoke out in petition in 1899 on McKinley's failure to take a stand in defense of the rights of colored Americans.[46]

Only a few colored troops saw actual combat action in the Spanish-American war, but their bravery and gallantry received high praise. There were those in both races who claimed that the Ninth and Tenth Cavalry units saved the famed Rough Riders from certain defeat at Las Guasimas. Even Theodore Roosevelt voiced praise for these units. However, in the April, 1899 issue of *Scribner's Magazine* Roosevelt implied that without white officers, Negroes were poor soldiers. This remark angered many persons.

Colored Americans had some misgivings about the nation's designs on Cuba and the Philippines. On this, Lewis H. Douglass, son of the celebrated abolitionist, wrote:

> It is a sorry, though true, fact that whatever this government controls injustice to dark races prevails. The people of Cuba, Porto Rico, Hawaii and Manila know it well as do the wronged Indian and outraged black man in the United Statees. . . .
>
> It is hypocrisy of the most sickening kind to try to make us believe that the killing of Filipinos is for

the purpose of good government and to give protection to life and liberty and the pursuit of happiness.[47]

During Theodore Roosevelt's first term Negroes were considerably gladdened by his denunciation of lynchings, opposition to "Lily-Whitism," and such incidents as the famous luncheon with Booker T. Washington and support of the Negro postmistress of Indianola, Mississippi. Despite the criticism of some white southerners that he was too pro-Negro, in 1904 Roosevelt and the Republican party sought to woo colored voters. This courtship was short-lived. Most Negro spokesmen were strong in their denunciation of the pro-southern flavor of Roosevelt's speeches during his 1905 tour of the South. When, for example, in Jacksonville, Florida Roosevelt gave voice to the Booker Washington dictum that if Negroes attended properly to their duties, their rights would take care of themselves, some Negroes severely denounced the president.[48] Of these speeches Rayford Logan states that Roosevelt "outdid Booker T. Washington" and "surpassed Hayes" in playing up to the white South. Washington himself was slow to criticize the President until Roosevelt's highly unpopular handling of Negro soldiers accused of participating in the Brownsville riot, and even then most of Washington's efforts were directed toward minimizing the animosity which his race felt toward Roosevelt, Taft, and the Republican party.[49] Clearly, during his second term as president Theodore Roosevelt was markedly less friendly to the Negro than he had been during his first term.

During the early days of his administration, William Howard Taft continued the practice of touring the South in an effort to foster good relations with the section. As was the case with his predecessors, remarks made during his tour, intended to placate southern whites, did little to endear Negroes to the new president. Taft got into further trouble with Negroes when, in an address at Wilberforce University, Ohio, he spoke in favor of segregated education. Although Taft appointed the first Negro to a sub-cabinet position, William H. Lewis as Assistant Attorney-General, his total number of Negro appointments were markedly lower than had been the case with Roosevelt, and Taft did not consult Booker Washington on patronage as much as Roosevelt had done. During Taft's administration, Negro and white liberals became convinced that the federal government had abdicated its responsibilities for protecting Negro rights and supporting the economic struggles of the freedmen and, among other things, they organized the National Association for the Advancement of Colored People and the Urban League to effect these ends. Of Taft's devotion to American caste, Archibald Grimké stated: "He proved himself a master workman in following the lines of caste, in putting into place a new stone in the edifice."[50]

In 1912 Negroes were still voting largely the Republican ticket, and in this election they split their votes between Taft and Roosevelt. Very few voted for Woodrow Wilson, and conspicuous among these were a few intellectuals.[51] Previous to this date Frederick Douglass had voiced the sentiment of many Negroes when he declared that, "The Republican party is the ship, all else the sea." By 1912, however, many Negroes were sorely disappointed at, among other things, what seemed to them Taft's "lily-white" patronage policy. That year Bishop Reverdy C. Ransom accused Taft of having abandoned the Roosevelt liberalism, and of having remained silent on the problem of lynching through his four years in office. The animosity of Negroes was not directed at Taft alone, but even more so at the Republican party for its "do-nothing" attitude on the race problem, and a number of intellectuals were convinced that even Theodore Roosevelt and his Bull Moose party were giving their race the cold-shoulder. These men were inclined to be impressed with Woodrow Wilson's scholarly background, and felt that he was a new refreshing type of politician. This feeling was increased when Wilson wrote Bishop Alexander Walters that he wished "to see justice done the Negro people in every matter; and not mere grudging justice, but justice with liberality and cordial good feeling."[52]

In addition to Bishop Walters, among the outstanding Negroes who turned their backs on the Republican party to support Wilson were W. E. B. Du Bois and Monroe Trotter, both of whom, like Bishop Walter, had supported William Jennings Bryan in 1908, and all of whom urged their race not to follow any single party blindly and slavishly. While Wilson's academic achievements constituted a factor in his support by Negro intellectuals, disappointment with the laissez-faire policy of the Republicans toward race was probably the most influential factor. Although, as president, Wilson did little directly on the "race problem" to justify this support, and some of his ardent supporters turned to bitter critics, significant events occurred during his two terms to elevate the faith of Negroes. One such event came in 1915 when the Supreme Court declared the Oklahoma Grandfather Clause unconstitutional. It was not long after his election, however, that Negroes had become convinced that on the race issue the President's southern background might be showing. They resented particularly his markedly fewer federal appointments than had been the case with Roosevelt and Taft, and his devotion to the cause of maintaining segregation in the nation's capital. Great disappointment with Wilson filled many Negroes with bitterness and dismay. In a letter to Walter L. Cohen of Louisiana Emmett J. Scott revealed this mood. "The truth of the matter is," said Scott late in 1916, "both you and I have proved to our own satisfaction, that there is nothing in politics of a substantial character for the black man."[53] It is widely believed that in 1916 most Negro voters supported the Republican candidate Charles Evans Hughes.[54]

Like the Spanish-American War and the later World War II, World War I had sharply focused attention on the plight of colored colonials, and quickened the desire for freedom and a better material life in India, the Indies, Africa, and the world over. Thus, more Americans came to view the domestic race problem as part of an international one. As the Afro-American became more aware of the millions of humankind elsewhere who were segregated, discriminated against, and lynched, he felt less lonely in his own degradation and more hopeful for an early end to practice of the white supremacy doctrine. As with the rest of the nation, Woodrow Wilson loomed large in the picture of a better deal which this war stirred in the mind of the Negro. Afterwards, when the postwar reaction made them special objects of renewed and intensified lynchings, riots, and other forms of oppression, they often

were to contrast the lofty idealism with the bitter reality which
ensued. As in the 1820-1860 era and in the period since 1876,
the 1920's saw the occupants of the presidency again deeming
it wise to maintain a hands-off policy on the race question, and
Negro Americans again felt considerable disappointment and
bitterness at the occupants of the presidency for not using the
power and prestige of the office directly to improve race relations and to help lift their group to a higher economic and
cultural level. Contrasting in 1922 the high hopes with which
Negroes had entered the war with their disillusionment afterwards, Mordecai W. Johnson referred to the postwar slander,
abuse, and lynchings. Then he added:

> From those terrible days until this day the Ne-
> gro's faith in the righteous purpose of the Federal
> Government has sagged. Some have laid the blame on
> the parties in power. Some have laid it elsewhere. But
> all the colored people, in every section of the United
> States, believe that there is something wrong, and not
> accidentally wrong, at the very heart of the Govern-
> ment.[55]

Negro voters supported Warren G. Harding almost solidly
in the election of 1920, but the disaffection was soon to come.
In a speech delivered at Birmingham, Alabama, October 26,
1921 President Harding appeared to agree with the separate-
but-equal doctrine. For this the *Boston Guardian,* most militant
Negro paper of the day, tore into the new president. Writing
for this paper, William A. St. Clair accused the President of
catering to the whims of southern whites and averred that the
speech was "fraught with the most dangerous, pernicious, destructive and hell-born doctrines that have ever been uttered
in the fifty years of our development, not only by a president
of the United States, but by any responsible Cabinet Minister."[56]
Kelly Miller and W. E. B. Du Bois were also in the forefront
among critics of the President's speech. Among other things,
a number of spokesmen felt that the President's thinking was
objectionable when he said in the speech, "There is a fundamental, eternal and inescapable difference between the Negro
and the white man." Yet, Robert Russa Moton along with
Walter Cohen, Perry Howard, R. R. Church, Henry L. John-

son and other Negro political leaders praised the address.[57] Of both Harding and Calvin Coolidge, Negroes felt that their pronouncements against lynchings always were too vague and too late. E. L. Tatum ably has summed up the reaction of Negroes to Coolidge. On this, Tatum notes:

> During the Coolidge regime the Negro had very little against which to register political complaint... The Negro was employed and was making more money . . . than ever before in peacetime. There were fewer race riots than in the period 1920-1924, and the number of Negroes lynched had declined. The Negro credited the Republicans and Mr. Coolidge with this.[58]

While in 1924, a few Negroes voted for LaFollette, the Progressive candidate, most stayed with the Republican party. The Negro press was almost solidly behind Coolidge.[59]

Although they liked his liberal record and were impressed because Al Smith, like themselves, represented a minority group, and although they shared his opposition to the Ku Klux Klan and to Prohibition, and although they had doubts about Hoover because of his great wealth and tendency to cater to southern whites, the Negro "bolt" of the Republican party in 1928 was not sufficient to defeat Hoover. Still, the great enthusiasm which Negroes showed for Al Smith in this election was a foretaste of the large-scale exodus from the Republican party which they were to make eight years later.[60]

When the Great Depression struck, Negroes held no unique position in the general condemnation of Hoover's policy of patience and fortitude. Their dire plight during the early years of the depression caused a few persons to believe that the race was slipping from its precarious perch on the limb of freedom back to the wretchedness of slavery. In 1932 the Negro vote for Franklin D. Roosevelt was small compared to the great host which voted for him in 1936.[61] It took the huge relief program of the New Deal to complete the break with Republicanism which had been long in the making, but when they finally became committed to the Roosevelt personality and program and policies, the new president came to be viewed by Afro-Americans as the reincarnation of Abraham Lincoln.[62] Indeed, it is possible that their affection for Roosevelt as a person was even greater in some ways than had been the case with Lincoln, for while Lincoln was an admitted white-supremacist who wanted to colonize Negroes outside the United States, Roosevelt avowed that he believed in racial equality and took dramatic steps to demonstrate his avowal. Negroes were highly flattered that among his core of professional advisers Roosevelt saw fit to have a "Black Cabinet" led by such race spokesmen as Mrs. Mary M. Bethune, William H. Hastie, and Robert L. Vann, and the interest which Mrs. Roosevelt showed in the plight of oppressed peoples heightened the esteem which Negroes felt for the President.

Like many white Americans, when Roosevelt died in 1945 many Negroes felt that they had lost a close personal friend. But unlike the death of Lincoln, they no longer wondered what would happen to them with their benefactor gone. In 1945 Negroes felt their own strength and little despaired that anyone would be able to take their gains from them, and President Truman's forthright policy of racial equality soon caused them to know that while they had lost one friend, they had gained another. For many persons, not until the ex-president's 1960 statements against student "sit in" demonstrations was this ardour to cool.

By 1952 the growing obstinacy and opposition of some southern whites to Negro progress, together with the mild stand on the race question by the national Democratic party, and its failure to pass civil rights legislation joined with other issues to cause a considerable number of Negroes to go over to the Republican party. Although the celebrated May 17, 1954 Supreme Court decision against compulsory segregation in public schools based on race, and the enactment of a federal civil rights bill made Dwight Eisenhower a hero to many Afro-Americans, his vacillation in the matter of the Affair-Little Rock, and his failure to speak out more often and in bolder fashion against lynchings, bombings, and other manifestations of race hate and general southern white opposition to federal law had, by 1960, tarnished considerably this earlier image.

A NEW CENTURY

Although in 1900 there were almost nine million Negroes in the United States, only one-tenth of this number lived outside the South. The 1900 census showed a total of approximately sixty percent of the Negro population to be engaged in agriculture, mostly on a share-crop basis. Although by 1910, twenty-five percent of Negro farmers owned their own farms, the seventy-five percent who were largely sharecroppers still lived the crudest type of hand-to-mouth existence. One of the key areas where this extreme poverty was long felt was that of health. Until recently, the death rate from tuberculosis, pellagra, and other diseases of malnutrition, has been very high among southern Negroes. Less conspicuous, but of equal significance perhaps, was the loss of energy and labor consequent upon this condition. How much disease and malnutrition have contributed to the popular picture of the Negro peon as lazy, stupid, and no-account probably can never be known.

Unfortunately for race relations, by the turn of the century, only ten percent of the nation's Negroes lived in the North, and less than one percent in the West. In most of its aspects, the race problem was still peculiarly a southern problem. Among southern Negroes only twenty percent lived in urban areas. The census of 1910 revealed that 54.6 percent of the colored race were still employed in agriculture, but by 1930 this figure had dropped to 36.1 percent so employed. In the cityward trek reflected in these statistics, the Negro again was following a national trend. In the brief period between 1910-1920, the Negro population changed from one-quarter to one-third urban, and almost ninety percent of all employed Negroes were working in domestic service or farming. Despite the optimism which Booker Washington, John Hope and others had where the future possibilities of Negro business were concerned, the general plight of the race in America brought pessimism and despair in the breast of many Negroes. Still, that by the turn of the century a "new Negro" was emerging was evident. Proof of this was to be seen in such things as the effort to es-

tablish a race theater devoted to more serious themes than minstrelsy, in the slow but sure drift away from the Republican
Party which had ceased to champion racial rights, the formation of a national Negro political party, and the considerable
opposition to Booker Washington's leadership. During the first
two decades of the present century W. E. B. DuBois, Monroe
Trotter, and others urged Afro-Americans in the South to
abandon the Washington-promoted views that voting, office-
holding, civil rights and the liberal arts are not of primary importance, and that militant social action is somehow sinful.
During this period Negroes began to abandon the shame which
some had felt for slavery and their folk culture. Too, this is
the period which saw the emergence of a body of Negro scholars and the greater consciousness of the scientific spirit and
method in DuBois, Carter Woodson, and others. These are the
two decades when the first really able colored poets and novelists were flowering, and when some Negro colleges began to
take seriously the business of being institutions of higher learning in something other than name. It is in these two decades
that the Negro consciousness and envy of the mulatto reaches
its apogee and begins to go into limbo, and that the spirituals
and blues came onto the American scene as recognized forms of
music art and began to win the acceptance of cultured persons.
It is during these decades, as the founding of the National
Negro Business League in 1900 attests, that the race gets a
keener awareness of its economic potential in the world of
business, while in religion there is a beginning of the abandonment of fundamentalism and a demand for better educated
preachers. Too, there was a demand for school teachers who
would possess greater social consciousness, and a keener realization that the Negro would have to rely less on philantropic
whites and more upon himself. Finally, the founding of the
Association for the Study of Negro Life and History and the
launching of the Negro history movement revealed an increased
race pride, awareness and appreciation of social forces, of Africa,
and of a sense of mission and destiny. Yet, probably at no
other time in his history in this nation has the Negro experienced so much fear-mingled-with-hope as he did in the 1900-

1914 period. The overthrow of Radical Reconstruction; rampant racism in Congress, on the political hustings, as well as in Ivy-drenched halls of learning; the generally worsening plight of the nation's white as well as agrarian and urban working classes; plus a tremendous wave of European emigration to the U. S. A. all joined to produce a great fear in the breasts of Afro-Americans. Numerous Negro leaders began to formulate programs which they urged the race to pursue diligently if it wished to "survive," and there was rather constant talk of committing racial suicide unless the Negro group altered some of its ways and emphases. Survival became almost as large a theme with the Negro as it sometimes was during the days of slavery.

It is this atmosphere of fear, plus the hope which all America evidenced in the Populist and Progressive movements, which bred such phenomena as the National Negro Business League, Booker Washington's Gospel of Work, the Carter Woodson-led Negro History Movement, the DuBois-led Talented Tenth Movement, the Washington-led Industrial Education Movement, the independent Negro Labor Movement, the growth of the Negro Press, an emerging interest in Socialism and Communism, the strengthened puritanism and evangelical nature of much Negro preaching and religious thinking, the archaism evident in a renewed interest in Negro spirituals and dialect, and the birth of the Blues. By 1900, the Negro race in the United States was, in some ways, retreating into itself. Many of the "emergency" programs designed to save the race from seeming threatened extinction "accepted" segregation in one form and degree or another. Many of the earlier antebellum and immediate post-bellum dreams of entering the mainstream of American life with equality of citizenship now seemed all but displaced by a strengthened note of defeatism.

Already, however, by 1900 DuBois, Trotter, and others were sensing that the race's salvation could not lie in any program based on racism, and that however great the odds, the Negro must continue to push toward economic, political, and cultural integration.

In 1901, ex-slave turned New York-journalist and historian, John Edward Bruce, began publication of a militant

journal entitled *The Voice of the Negro*, the same year, interestingly enough, that the erudite Monroe Trotter began issuing
his militant *Boston Guardian*. Two years later the equally militant and uncompromising W. E. B. DuBois, who, like Trotter
was a Harvard graduate, published a group of trenchant essays
under the title *Souls of Black Folk,* which eloquently assailed
the nation's treatment of its Negro minority. Here DuBois especially denounced lynching, the peonage of share-cropping,
and Booker T. Washington, and called for absolute equality
of citizenship for his race. Within two years, DuBois and Trotter
would be leading the Niagara Movement, but many other persons, not so militant were not so hopeful. In his poem "It's a
Long Way," William Stanley Braithwaite wrote:

> Its work we must, and love we must,
> And do the best we may,
> And take the hope of dreams in trust
> To keep us day by day.

In a poem entitled "Life," Paul Lawrence Dunbar probably
spoke for the masses of Negroes when he said:

> A crust of bread and a corner to sleep in,
> A minute to smile and an hour to weep in,
> A pint of joy to a peck of trouble,
> And never a laugh but the moans come double,
> And that is life.

In his sole volume of poetry, J. Mord Allen, contemporary of
Paul Lawrence Dunbar, caught the spirit of the Negroes'
rugged determination and long slow upward climb. In his "The
Psalm of the Uplift," Allen wrote:

> 'Tis ours to do
> And dare and bear not to flinch;
> To enter where is no retreat;
> To win one stride from sheer defeat;
> To die—but gain an inch.

Had those persons who despaired in 1890-1914 been able to
foresee such events as the downfall of colonialism in the coming two world wars and the New and Fair Deals on the domestic
scene, they doubtless would have despaired less and shed fewer
tears. In what seemed to many to be the freedman's darkest
hour, the forces which were to bring a new day in race rela-

tions actually crystallized. This crystallization and beginning of an upward spiral in race relations was due in considerable part to the very conditions which brought despair to the hearts of many, that is, the depths to which race relations had sunk. Where the democratic ideal is concerned, the American spirit appears to have limits beyond which it cannot be pushed regardless of the class, race, or creed which may be the object of the pushing. This limit was reached by 1909, and having touched this limit, the vital forces in the national spirit, recoiling in dramatic fashion, reopened the crusade for equality of citizenship which had in a sense been temporarily closed down since 1876-77. The recoil, like the 1830-1876 crusade, was inter-racial in nature.

Doubtless, the mere fact of entering a new century inspired Negroes with optimism about their future, much as the coming of each January 1st brings new hope to many individuals. Despite the lowly estate which the masses of freedmen occupied on January 1, 1900, as they looked back over the nineteenth century they had considerable cause to rejoice, for despite the slowness of their operation, the mills of the gods had in some ways ground exceedingly well where the Afro-American was concerned. The single fact that slavery was gone forever was itself adequate enough to lift every heart in song. Roscoe Conkling Bruce stated:

> Perhaps the most significant fact in recent Negro history is the rapid growth in this rising people . . . of self-consciousness and race pride. If this self-consciousness degenerates on occasion into hypersensitiveness and insolence, you must remember that . . . the rose . . . does not flourish under a millstone; the cactus may.[1]

In the same period, Reverdy C. Ransom asked:

> What kind of an American does the Negro intend to be? . . . He does not intend to be an alien in the land of his birth, nor an outcast in the home of his fathers. He will not consent to his elimination as a political factor; he will refuse to camp forever on the borders of the industrial world; as an American, he will consider that his destiny is united by

indissoluble bonds with the destiny of America forever; he will strive less to be a great Negro in this
Republic and more to be an influential and useful
American. . . . he will assert himself not as a Negro, but as a man; he . . . will never mar the image
of God, reproach the dignity of his manhood, or
tarnish the fair title of his citizenship.[2]

But these were often brave voices crying out in a wilderness of
despair, and in 1900 DuBois was sure of the goal but not of the
road; though he was soon to identify with the Niagara and
NAACP movements, he would later march as resolutely into
the Marxist camp. During this period, DuBois wrote: "The
Negro race in America is today in a critical condition. Only
united concerted effort will save us from being crushed."[3]
Proud, defiant, brave and strong, Trotter never faltered for a
moment in his aim, and though he was to be accused of being
estranged from other leaders of his race, and an impractical
maladjusted idealist, who can now doubt that Trotter's long-
term vision was clearer than those who pursued mythical programs of salvation which were based on accepting and making
the most of segregation and second-class citizenship? Today,
in an integrating America, most of the programs born in this
fear-ridden period of 1890-1912 are either dead or dying,
while the Trotter program, based on non-acceptance of compromise or retreat from the ideal of full and integrated citizenship is more virile than ever. That Trotter was not alone in
his uncompromising stand is clear, for example, at a state-wide
meeting held in Macon, in February of 1906, five hundred
Afro-Americans attended a session of the Georgia Equal Rights
Convention. The delegates heard the Chairman contend for
the right to vote, because voting "is in itself an education,"
which will soon make anyone unqualified to vote a fit person
to do so. "Voteless working men are slaves," he stated, and
continued: "If we are good enough to be represented by five
Georgia Congressmen in the Councils of the nation, we are
surely good enough to choose those representatives; and if we
are not good enough to be represented, at least, as human beings, we are too good to be misrepresented by our enemies."

The Chairman also scored the systematic exclusion, of Negroes from juries, and the cruel lease system for convicts.[4]

In their reaction to the racial clashes which occurred near the opening of the century may be seen some dominant strands of Negro thought, although it occurred earlier and was of comparable scope. The Wilmington, North Carolina race riot had no brilliant observer to immortalize it in the manner that W. E. B. DuBois did with the Atlanta race riot which broke out in late September, 1906. Negroes gave a large share of the blame for the latter riot to the race baiting of John Temple Graves, then editor of a prominent Atlanta paper. Dubbed a "Massacre" by Negro papers, this violence saw ten colored persons killed and many more injured, while two whites lost their lives. Negro militancy against the growing infringements on their civil and political rights, in both city and state, was a prime target of the white hatred.[5] Booker T. Washington spoke out forthrightly against this unfortunate occurrence. In characteristic fashion, he assumed that blame for the incident lay with both races, and he suggested that "the best white people and the best colored people come together in council," to devise means for correcting the trouble. Also characteristically, he said, that the riot "should not discourage our people, but should teach a lesson from which all can profit . . . we should bear in mind that while there is disorder in one community there is peace and harmony in thousands of others."[6] One of Washington's most pronounced virtues was the manner in which he always accentuated the positive aspects of situations, while playing down the negative ones. This was a virtue which the race sorely needed in his day. But if Washington was conciliatory, Frederick Douglass' son Lewis, was not. He deplored the fact that more whites were not killed in the riot. "Our people must die to be saved," he wrote, "and in dying must take as many along with them as it is possible to do with the aid of firearms and all other weapons."[7] Doubtless, in the conclusion to his "A Litany at Atlanta," W. E. B. DuBois caught one mood of many Negroes in this period. Here DuBois lamented:

Our voices sink in silence and in night.
Hear us, good Lord.

> In night, O God of a godless land
>   Amen!
> In silence, O Silent God.
>   Selah!

Pondering the crimes "of the white man against the black," DuBois again wrote:

> Sit not longer blind, Lord God, deaf to our prayer and dumb to our dumb suffering. Surely Thou, too, art not white, O Lord, a pale, bloodless, heartless thing!

In this "Litany at Atlanta," perhaps DuBois touched another dominant strand in the Negro thought of the time with his repeated prayer for direction in the race's effort to go forward. On this he wrote:

> What meaneth this? Tell us the plan;
> Give us the sign . . . The way, O God,
> Show us the way and point us the path.

Chapter XIX

CAPITALISM, SOCIALISM, AND COMMUNISM IN NEGRO THOUGHT

The Capitalist System

Although as slaves they were long capitalism's greatest victims, in general Afro-Americans have been avid supporters of the capitalistic system. They were scarcely emancipated from chattel slavery before many adopted as their greatest heroes the mighty captains of American agriculture, finance and industry. The business success of some members of the free Negro class in New Orleans, Charleston, Philadelphia, and other cities provided the race with examples of the blessings and possibilities of free enterprise even before the demise of the Old South. By 1900 the post-bellum emergence of a sizeable number of Negro enterpreneurs, operating mostly in the fields of banking and insurance, together with the preachments of white American capitalists, gave further strength to the Negro's faith in the free enterprise profit system. Effects of the education, growing wealth, social maturity and the trek cityward were to be clear and unmistakable in the decades following World War I. U. S. Census data reveals that in 1870 the nation's Negro urban population was only 750,000, but by 1900 this figure had increased to two million; by 1930 the latter figure had doubled, while in 1950 nine million Negroes were urban dwellers. One effect of urbanization was the accelerated development and growth of Negro business. In 1898 there were only 1,900 colored business enterprises in the United States; by 1930 this number had grown to 70,000, most of which were small personal service enterprises started on small capitalization. Because they were mostly in areas where the practice of racial segregation was keenest, these businesses were sometimes referred to as "defensive enterprises."[1]

Especially during the 1920's did Negro capitalists begin to make their presence seen and felt. These individuals drew their customers almost exclusively from black America, but their inspiration and ideals were drawn from the nation's top financiers and industrialists. Banking and insurance represented the major businesses. In 1888 freedmen had organized in Washington, D. C. the Capital Savings Bank, and by 1934, Afro-Americans had formed approximately one hundred thirty-four banks, most of which failed so rapidly that by the beginning of 1906 only seven Negro banks were operating. It has often been shown that Negro banking has suffered from the fact that there has never been a significant number of Negro businesses which could serve as reliable creditors. E. F. Frazier has pointed out that in Negro thought there has been shown a distrust of the honesty of some colored bank officials.[2] Negro insurance companies grew primarily out of burial and fraternal societies. In 1950 there were approximately fifty Negro insurance companies in the United States.

Some of the outstanding entrepreneus were John Merrick and C. C. Spaulding of Durham, North Carolina; Joseph E. Walker of Memphis, Tennessee; A. F. Herndon of Atlanta, Georgia; Richard R. Wright of Philadelphia, Pennsylvania; S. W. Rutherford of Washington, D. C.; Maggie L. Walker of Richmond, Virginia; and Anthony Overton and Jesse Binga of Chicago, Illinois. Perhaps the business woman of most renown was Sarah Breedlove Walker, founder of the Madame C. J. Walker Laboratories of Indianapolis, Indiana, which specialized in barber and beauty supplies. These successful business men and women were a great source of pride, as well as envy among Afro-Americans. One trustworthy compiler of statistics has noted that by 1922 Negroes had acquired:

> 22,000,000 acres of land, 600,000 homes, and 45,000 churches. After less than sixty years of freedom, Negroes operated 78 banks, 100 insurance companies, and 50,000 other business enterprises with a combined capital of more than $150,000,000. Besides all this, there are within the race 60,000 professional men, 44,000 school teachers, and 400 newspapers and magazines; while its general illiteracy has been reduced to twenty-six per cent.[3]

In 1898 John Hope, then a teacher at the institution, addressed the Fourth Atlanta University Conference, and urged members of the race to start their own businesses and to patronize them in preference to white-owned ones. He said this should be done even if patronage was given at the sacrifice of paying higher prices for inferior goods and services. In some degree, this has been a rather constant plea of the National Negro Business League, but Afro-Americans often have not heeded it. Like most Americans, they usually have sought the best goods and services at the cheapest possible prices. Some have felt that it would be foolish to weigh down the already underprivileged race with the burden of higher prices to enrich Negro businessmen, who themselves too often were lacking in race pride and the spirit of sacrifice. Still the National Negro Business League managed to have some 320 branches after only seven years of existence. One of the resolutions adopted at the Atlanta University Conference of 1898 declared:

> The mass of the Negroes must learn to patronize business enterprises conducted by their own race, even at some slight disadvantage. We must cooperate or we are lost.

In 1900 Booker Washington and others organized in Boston the National Negro Business League for the purpose of promoting racial business enterprises. The organization grew rapidly. W. E. B. DuBois, who had directed the business bureau of the Afro-American Council, furnished Washington with a roster of prospective members of the organization. Perhaps no group among Afro-Americans has preached the self-help rags-to-riches theme more than the National Negro Business League. At the national meetings, for years individual success stories were paraded before its audiences. Booker Washington, long-time president of the league, was a main instigator of this theme. In his book, *Black Bourgeoisie,* E. Franklin Frazier has pointed to the considerable exaggeration in the claims of what Negro business is, has done, and can do, and to the large number of ministers of the gospel, teachers, and other non-business people who were often represented as being business persons. Washington often said that in his experience the "black man who was succeeding in business, who was a taxpayer, and who possessed intelligence and high character . . . was treated with the highest respect by the members of the white race."[4] In 1928 the league launched a program whereby Negro retail stores would organize community-sized groups known as the Colored Merchants Association in order to pool wholesale buying. Though launched with much optimism about the boost to Negro business which the step would effect, the movement had little success. The role of Booker T. Washington in serving as the main spirit behind the formation of the National Negro League is characteristic of his social philosophy. As stated earlier, Washington may be called an economic determinist. The league was, and is, the Negro counterpart of the Chamber of Commerce and National Association of Manufacturers.[5] For a time, wrote R. R. Moton in 1929, "it seemed that the mental and spiritual progress of the race had far outstripped its progress in material things, with the result that the aspirations of Negroes seemed to be cultivated quite beyond their own capacity for their realization, and so producing a discontent and irritability that threatened to make the whole effort toward full American citizenship abortive. However true that may have been a generation ago, the balance between these two lines of progress has been largely restored."[6]

Many Afro-Americans have been eager advocates of temperance and economy. Realizing that theirs always has been a low paid group, and that the race started with little by way of real property, leaders from the abolitionists to Booker T. Washington, George Schuyler, Martin Luther King and others constantly have exhorted the race to practice frugality and temperance. Still, elation over the novelty of acquiring many aspects of Occidental culture long denied them, plus the general secularistic outlook of the modern age, often has caused actual practice to deviate very noticeably from these preachments. Frazier stated in 1948 that a "sporting complex" and thriftlessness were widespread among Negroes, traits which he believes are due in part to the fact that many have been employed as workers in domestic and personal services where they saw and came to imitate the leisure-time habits of white Americans.

In Chapter VII of his book *Black Bourgeoisie,* Dr. Frazier ably has shown that a number of persons connected with Negro business and life have preached the doctrine that the best way for the race to win equality of treatment and opportunity was to establish and maintain many Negro businesses. Because of the smallness of these businesses in terms of number, capitalization, and of employees, Frazier labels this doctrine "mythical," and illustrates that, both as to economic value and jobs afforded, business enterprises owned and operated by and for Negroes have been only a fractional part of the total American business. Thus, he concludes, Booker Washington, the National Negro Business League, and others who have championed race owned and operated business enterprises as a solution to the "race problem" erected and pursued a myth which Negro newspapers and magazines have supported and perpetuated.[7] Frazier contends that there is also a myth of Negro wealth. He thinks that in the late 1950's the Negro market had reached no more than one-half of the fifteen billion dollar figure which erroneously had been given wide popularity, and that not only do most Negro "millionaires" not have the wealth attributed to them, but that a considerable number of the so-called wealthy actually derived their cash from the numbers lottery or such activities as those of Father Divine and Elder Solomon Lightfoot. Frazier shows that in its desire to create a high society and millionaires, the Negro press too often creates "mountains out of mole hills."

Afro-Americans often have complained among themselves that service is too often poor in their stores, cafes, cafeterias, and other businesses. There seems to be a strong and general dislike among many Negroes for serving one another, which doubtless is a heritage from the servant role which the race was forced to play during slavery and since. As a reaction against this role, many also look down on most occupations which cast them in the position of servant. Although for a long time domestic service positions were the major vocations of urban Negroes, most have hoped to educate their children for white collar positions, even though the latter might pay considerably smaller salaries. In his little book, *Miseducation of the Negro*,[8] Carter Woodson cried out against this attitude, and pointed out that in part because of it, the race was losing its hold on a number of job areas. Effects of this attitude are seen today in the fact that although cooks, maids, and butlers who reside with their employers in some areas may have higher net incomes and other advantages than persons working at such occupations as secretary or social worker, few college trained Negroes want the former positions.

At least one colored American has deplored the fact that men of his race generally are not participants in the ownership, managerial, or manufacturing ends of the brewery and distillery businesses of which, with the rest of the nation, Negroes are good customers, and that although the race purchases many automobiles, there are few Negro dealers and auto salesmen.[9] In 1956 Mordecai Johnson of Howard University deplored the sparsity of Negroes in baking, pastry, clothing (wholesale or retail) sale and manufacturing, butchers, laundry, tailor, and millinery shops. He concluded "The Negro people, just a bit over eighty years from slavery, are a child people in their ability to organize the ordinary things that have to do with effective existence."[10] As early as 1900 white workers were displacing Negroes in the barbering, cooking, butler, maid, laundering, and other areas of employment. John Hope, eminent Negro educator, was among those who felt that neither industrial education nor labor unions would return the Negro to his "old-time advantages," and, as indicated, the only solution which he could see was the creation of a capitalist class with sufficient Negro-owned and operated businesses to provide employment for many thousands. John Hope felt that because the Afro-American lived in a society dominated by the corporation and the business ethos, he could not "escape" that society's "most powerful motive and survive."[11]

The National Urban League was organized in 1910 and incorporated in 1913. Among the initial supporters of the organization were E. R. A. Seligman, Julius Rosenwald, R. R. Moton, Booker T. Washington, and Kelly Miller. Its genesis had as a major precipitant a study made of economic and social conditions among New York Negroes. The organization's first executive officers were George Edmund Haynes and Eugene Kinckle Jones. One competent observer who has summed up the work of the Urban League states:

> The Urban League is chiefly concerned with the Negro's advancement in industry—his opportunity to get work on the basis of efficiency and as far as pos-

sible without discrimination; his opportunity to improve and to be promoted on the job; and to promote
the idea of equal pay for the same calibre of work
done. The League is also concerned with the making
of scientific investigations to set forth the facts pertaining to the Negro as a worker to stipulate his industrial and economic needs.   It seeks to improve
urban conditions among Negroes in matters of health,
recreation, delinquency, and crime. It endeavors to
get the doors of organized labor opened to the Negro.
Like Booker T. Washington, the National Urban
League expresses the Negro's desire to be economically secure.[12]

In the post World War II period the Urban League had
branches in twenty-nine states which employed over four hundred trained persons. The Urban League, like the NAACP, has
steered clear of political action and has been largely middle
class in leadership, orientation, and following. Wilson Record
has observed that, "Like the NAACP," the Urban League "was
not instrumentally or ideologically equipped to tackle the bigger problems of employment, housing and welfare in the Negro
community."[13]   In Black Bourgeoisie, E. Franklin Frazier has
inferred that, in part because wealthy whites long have been
associated with its management and support, the Urban League
is a conservative organization. This organization, he states,
has at times been anti-labor and was slow to support the C.I.O.

The conciliatory and conservative spirit of Negro business
probably found no better advocate than John Merrick, co-
founder of the world's largest Negro-owned business -- the
North Carolina Mutual Life Insurance Company—who was
especially conservative on racial matters. Like Washington, he
counselled that the race should stay away from those activities
most likely to stir up the antagonism of the white man.
Of the South he said: "We (Negroes) have the same privileges
that other people have. Every avenue is open to us to do business as it is to any other people." He held politics and politicians in low esteem. On this, he wrote: "What difference does it
make to us who is elected? We got to serve in the same different
capacities of life for a living." Unwittingly perhaps he explained much of his own conservatism when he wrote: "Now

don't the writers of the race jump on the writer and try to solve my probem. Mine is solved. I solved mine by learninig to be courteous to those that courtesy was due, working and trying to save and properly appropriate what I made."[14] Merrick had started out in business the operator of a small barber shop which catered to many white wealthy patrons, and members of the Duke family of Durham had helped start him on the road to a larger success.

In his book *Black Bourgeoisie*, E. Franklin Frazier recently has stated that in the Post World War era the dominant group among Negroes is a sizeable middle class, which formal education and the white collar trend of American society have created, that is "super-patriotic" where support and promulgation of the conservative side of the national thought is concerned. Frazier contends that the mentality of the black bourgeoisie exhibits an ambivalence in that it admires and apes the white bourgeois world, but at the same both fears and hates American whites; that while this class pretends to have race pride, it belies this in such ways as holding light complexions in great esteem, speaking contemptuously of the Negro masses, failing to support programs and organizations which are designed to raise the masses, and having contempt for Africa and Africans.[15] Frazier avers that while the pre-depression era generation of Negro businessmen were still influenced by the genteel tradition of manners and morals, and "still felt some identification with the Negro masses," the new Black Bourgeoisie "has tended to break completely with the traditions of the Negro" and "has lost much of its feeling of racial solidarity with the Negro masses."[16] The new black bourgeoisie, he asserts, has little genuine pride of race and actually despises itself as well the Negro masses.[17] To this the objection might be raised that the Negro proletariat does not furnish its own leaders no more than did the pre-1917 Russian proletariat. Studies have shown that in most modern revolutions, leadership usually comes from the middle class, and so it has been with the Negro. This bourgeois leadership of the Negro masses betokens much more identificaton and sympathy between the colored bourgeoisie and proletariat than Frazier admits. Professor Frazier decries this class's over-interest in sports and poker and the lack of interest in things cultural. He asserts that gambling, largely in the form of poker, is now the middle class Negro's substitute for religion.[18] Frazier states that the colored bourgeoisie has been uprooted from its folk background, and has contempt for the Negro's history, as well as for the Negro folk, hence lacks a cultural tradition and is isolated both from the Negro folk and from white America.[19] This isolation has served to intensify the inferiority feelings common to practically all Negroes, and has resulted in the creation of an unreal world—thought to be copied from wealthy white America—whose focal point is Negro "society." In this unreal world the myths of Negro business and wealth, along with an obsessive interest in the sportive life, material possessions, gambling, sex, and liquor, and contempt for real culture or high standards of conduct or performance thrive. Although there is much truth in Professor Frazier's criticism's *Black Bourgeoisie* lacks balance because the author fails to indicate the positive side of this class and reveals too much personal animosity toward it.

Afro-American participation in the organized labor movement has a lengthy history. Nine Negroes were delegates to the 1869 convention of the National Labor Union held in Philadelphia, in which one, Isaac Myers, made a moving speech in which he pleaded for unity between the white and colored members. Colored Americans generally have deplored the racial discrimination and prejudice which have divided the nation's labor front.[20]

As in politics, the long failure of the major unions to accept and recognize Negro labor caused the latter sometimes to connect with minor movements. In December, 1869 colored Americans organized the Negro National Labor Union in Washington, D. C. With membership open to all persons regardless of sex or color, a special appeal was made to the white masses of the South to unite with Negro labor. A similar appeal was made to white minority groups of the North.[21] In a petition to Congress, this convention pointed out that the regular processes of supply and demand did not work to control wages paid Afro-Americans in the South. This, it was pointed out, was because planters "absolutely regulate the price of labor by combining against the laborer," and "resistance by organized effort is impossible," because "the earnings of the laborer leave him no surplus, and when he ceases to labor he begins to starve."

During the 1880's, around 75,000 Negroes were members of the Knights of Labor. At the 1883 National Convention of Colored Men, meeting in Louisville, Kentucky, Frederick Douglass said: "What labor everywhere wants, what it ought to have and will some day demand and receive, is an honest day's pay for an honest day's work. As the laborer becomes more intelligent, he will develop what capital already possesses—that is the power to organize and combine for its own protection. Experience demonstrates that there may be a wage slavery only a little less galling and crushing in its effects than chattel slavery." Wilson Record observes that the Communist movement in this country led Negroes, "to see that the solution of the complex problem of discrimination was intimately tied up with the success of the labor movement, thus impressing upon them the importance of organizing Negroes into militant trade unions."[22]

Although necessity, plus ignorance, has caused the race to bear the label of "strike-breaker," Negroes generally have been warm supporters of the labor movement in the United States. That they were long excluded from much direct participation made them at times critical of the restricted brand of democracy which the unions preached. John R. Lynch, prominent Reconstruction Congressman from Mississippi, stated in 1886 what has been the traditional attitude of many members of his race toward labor unions. "Colored men," wrote Lynch, "should not identify themselves with any organization that seeks the accomplishment of its purposes through a resort to lawlessness and violence."[23] Here he specifically mentioned communism, socialism, and anarchy as faiths which the colored man should not accept or countenance. "The laboring people in this country," he continued, "can secure all the rights to which they are justly entitled without violating law, and there is no better way to bring about this result than through organization." The legitimate object of unions he saw as the calling of public attention "to the condition and wants of the laboring people with a view to creating a sentiment that will enforce a recog-

nition of their just and reasonable demands." Lynch made it
plain that Negroes should support no unions which discrimi-
nate on account of race or color. Failing at times to understand that the American Federation of Labor's long practice
of excluding unskilled workers from membership was one significant source of their exclusion, many Negroes have been convinced that this union was biased against Negroes *per se*. On
the other hand, these persons have believed that the CIO always has been very friendly to Negroes, and some persons were
quite surprised when, in 1959 A. Philip Randolph pointed to
the goodly amount of race prejudice still within the nations
labor organization.

In the post World War II period, the American Communist
Party pushed a program to get management-union labor contracts which would specifically guarantee rights of Negro workers. Partly because these proposals threatened further to divide
unions along racial lines, colored workers opposed them. In
1960 A. Philip Randolph and other Negro leaders in the union
field were not only voicing strong protests against the sparsity
of Afro-Americans in labor's higher councils, but were taking
positive actions to gain for the Negro a greater voice and representation at labor's policy-forming level.

Socialism and Communism

That he has received less recognition of his claim to equal
citizenship rights than most other Americans might pre-dispose
one to think that the Negro has been favorably responsive to
Socialist and Communist ideology. This has not been the case.
Speaking of the then seven million colored Americans, in 1886
Alexander Clark stated: "They have cause . . . for reviewing
themselves upon the cruelties of old systems, [but] under stress
of burning wrongs and the opportunity of retributive justice,
they demonstrate their ability to 'stand still and see the salvation of God!'"[24] Rather than be "misled by the ambiguity of
terms and possibly become involved in the plots of anarchists
and other evil designing men," stated Clark, the Negro would
continue his trust "in that genius of American liberty which
struck the shackles from four millions of our people."[25] Also,
in the spirit of Booker Washingtotn and others of his era, Clark

was against the "strike or the boycott, the mob or the riot."[26] Since a number of colored spokesmen of this period thought that strikes and boycotts were as wrong and harmful as the courts often said they were illegal, one wonders how much the strike-breaking of which some members of the race were accused was due to economic circumstances and how much to their attitude toward labor.

Long before W. E. B. DuBois became an avowed Marxist, T. Thomas Fortune had arrived at similar economic convic-tions. Fortune, an ex-slave from Florida, was a noted New York editor who during the second half of his life became a conservative supporter of Booker Washington. In 1884 For-tune wrote that race prejudice and other social ills which plagued the nation arose from one source—the capitalist sys-tem. Partly because he was an economic determinist like Wash-ington, even in 1884 Fortune favored concentration on indus-trial education.[27] In his agreement with some of the famous preachments of Henry George, Fortune said: "In the discussion of the land and labor problem I but pursue the theories advo-cated by more able and experienced men, in the attempt to show that the laboring classes of any country pay all the taxes, in the last analysis, and that they are systematically victimized by legislators, corporations and syndicates."[28] Fortune's view of the post-bellum South coincides remarkably with the views which DuBois later popularized with his volume entitled *Black Reconstruction*. In his Preface to a book on economics Fortune wrote: "The primal purpose in publishing this work is to show . . . that the future conflict in [the South] will not be racial or political in character, but between capital on the one hand, and labor on the other."

Socialism began to make a significant impact on American society near the turn of the century. This is also the period when the agrarian revolt, Progressive movement, and the sub-sequent liberalism of World War I quickened the aspirations and hopes of the Afro-American for complete equality. Even from the beginning of the socialist vogue, a number of Negroes saw in this ideology and its proponents an ally in their quest for social justice, and especially did this outlook become signifi-cant with the conservative reaction which characterized the

'twenties. With the renewal of large-scale violence in race relations, DuBois and other leaders became convinced that only
by conceiving of his struggle as a part of the cause of a world
proletariat could the Negro in America hope to make significant
progress. Communism had its genesis in the United States shortly after World War I. Hopeful of a world revolution, the
Lenin-led Bolsheviki who captured control of Russia in November, 1917 launched the Third International and their well-
known tactics designed to weaken and destroy capitalist states.
As the Negro was one of the most exploited groups in the
United States, and a part of the vast colored population of the
world, most of which was subjected to colonialism, the Kremlin
early jumped on the race and color questions as the Achille's
heel of the Western democracies.

The Socialist Party never succeeded in winning a large
number of converts among colored Americans. In part this is
because, as with native whites, Negroes were suspicious of ideas
at such variance with the deeply rooted and popular free enterprise system of the day. Also, the Socialist Party made no especial efforts to attract Negroes. Unlike the Communist Party,
Socialists conceived of the race problem in no unique terms;
Negro labor was simply a part of the totality of labor. While
the Negro was very race conscious, the Socialist Party had no
ideology to cater to this ethnocentrism. Despite this, however,
Ben Fletcher and a few other colored persons became prominent in the socialistic Industrial Workers of the World.

New York City became the center of those who embraced
socialism. With the *Messenger Magazine* as their principal
organ, Chandler Owen and A. Philip Randolph became prominent in the movement. Randolph later became an arch foe of
all protagonists of the Marxist dogma. R. R. Moton saw a
materialistic reason why colored Americans should not join
groups of the extreme left wing. "The race has developed to
the place," he opined, "where it cannot afford to be rash or
radical in advocating public policies."[29]

The depression saw a number of cooperatives launched
among Negroes, and by 1950 at least eleven of these were still
in operation. The period witnessed a considerable increase in
radicalism, both of the right and left-wing variety. The former

continued to be represented by Zionists, while Communists and radical non-Communists now made up the left. During this period a number of Negro artists and intellectuals had their tryst with the party. One evidence of the growing radicalism was seen in the fact that the "conservative" leadership of such men as Walter White, W. E. B. DuBois, and Roy Wilkins came under increased attack.[30]

A few Afro-Americans have had trips to Russia financed for them by Communists. These trips were for the purpose of studying Communism either formally or informally. Among such persons have been W. E. B. DuBois, Paul Robeson, William L. Patterson and James W. Ford. For about three decades, Ford was one of the most prominent Negro Communists in the United States, and in 1932 he was the party's candidate for the Vice-Presidency of the United States. After World War II his prominence in the party declined, and Henry Winston, Benjamin Davis, and Edward E. Strong took over the limelight. Wilson Record, after studying carefully the relations of the Communist party with Negroes, concluded that "The degree of loyalty which the Negro has given to the conservative society which discriminates against him is impressive."[31] At another point, this same observer called this record, "a striking paradox that the most convincing demonstration of loyalty to the American system has come from a group which has reaped the least from it."[32] In 1948 it is estimated that there were no more than two hundred Negro members of the Communist party.[33]

Late in 1925 the party had organized in Chicago the American Negro Labor Congress as a means of bringing about eventual control of colored labor in the United States. The Congress fostered a program of setting up colored branches in all of the major industrial centers. These branches would be made up not only of industrial workers but other segments of Negro labor. However, the dominant race organizations such as the Urban League and NAACP refused to cooperate with this effort because it was obviously Communist-led. During this same period Communists set up the International Labor Defense, an organization aimed at legal action. Inasmuch as the civil rights of Afro-Americans were more flagrantly violated than any other segment of the social order, this body found ready grist in cases involving Negroes. Among the most notable cases were the Herndon, Scottsboro, Willie McGhee, Martinsville Seven, and Trenton Six Cases. William L. Patterson, head of the Civil Rights Congress, early became an Executive Secretary of the International Labor Defense.

From the very beginnings of Communist activity in the United States, most Afro-Americans understood that this organization is extra-American and aimed at fostering a distinctly alien ideology, and throughout its history the party has antagonized Afro-Americans by fostering programs which would increase rather than decrease the differentiation of treatment and segregation of the race.

In the 1920's Leslie Pinckney Hill declared of his race:
We will not waver in our loyalty.
No strange voice reaches us across the sea;
No crime at home shall stir us from this soil.
Ours is the guerdon, ours the blight of toil,
But raised above it by a faith sublime
We choose to suffer *here* and bide our time.[34]

During the 1930's there was a marked decline in the number of lynchings, and a seeming improvement in race relations. In the thirties, as earlier, Negroes criticized one another because of what was felt to be apathy in the face of segregation and discrimination. Especially were college presidents, principals, school teachers, and preachers the objects of this charge, and a sizeable number of Afro-Americans felt that the race should object to the very popular "Amos and Andy" radio show, and boycott movies in which Negroes were depicted in servile or clownish roles. In 1932 the court decision in *Nixon vs Condon* which over-ruled state sponsored white primaries, and the ruling which ordered a new trial for the Scottsboro boys were hailed by many Negroes as very significant steps forward. The 1935 Supreme Court decision against systematic exclusion of Negroes from juries (*Norris vs. Alabama*) was considered another significant step forward in the quest for greater justice in the courts. Inasmuch as the case which brought this decision, that of the nine Scottsboro boys, had been given international publicity and resulted in most of the defendants being freed, this was considered a very special victory. Communists, through the International Labor Defense, had wrested the Scottsboro case from the NAACP and thrown the weight of the world party apparatus behind the defense of the boys. Obviously seeking to further the party's own popularity, the Communists saved the lives of the boys and endeared themselves to many persons.

It was during this period that Communists decided to carry their campaign into the southland. Up to this date their concentration had been largely on winning over the northern Negro. These efforts had met with practically no success, but the ardent race consciousness and pride which had characerized the Harlem Renaissance and Garvey movements of the 1920's, together with the failure of efforts to organize northern Negroes, caused the party in 1928 to push the idea of a separate and self-sufficient southern black *emperium in imperio*. This scheme immediately; stirred up a veritable hornets nest of protest from Afro-Americans, the vast majority of whom were thoroughly tired of schemes to "colonize" them either in this country or elsewhere. To push this plan, branches of the party were organized in the major urban and industrial areas of the South, and through the Trade Union Unity League efforts were made to control the section's colored labor. Also, unions of tenant farmers and share-croppers, centering in Louisiana and Alabama, were formed. During the early thirties strikes of cotton-pickers met with some small success, but after 1936 the Sharecroppers Union was abandoned by the party.

In November, 1930 the party organized the League of Struggle for Negro Rights. This organization grew out of the defunct American Negro Labor Congress which the party had set up earlier. Elected first president of the League was Langston Hughes, noted author and a leader of the Harlem Renaissance, while among the Vice-Presidents were William L. Patterson, Benjamin J. Davis, Robert Minor, and James W. Ford. The League "proposed to correct all the wrongs of all the Negroes in the United States, and do it immediately."[35]

The National Negro Congress was conceived in Washington, D. C. in 1935 as another of the many efforts of Afro-Americans to organize and present a united front in the quest for social justice. The organization was hardly begun, however, before it was captured by Communists. At the organizational meeting in Chicago, in February, 1936, eight hundred seventeen delegates from twenty-eight states were present and a program of struggle for civil rights, peace, broader economic opportunities, and a workers political party were proposed.[36] The Congress set up local councils in various cities to work with civic, labor, and other groups. Headquartered in Washington, D. C., the organization held a second national meeting in Philadelphia, in May, 1937 which was widely attended. At first the movement was rather warmly received and supported by Negroes, but by the third national meeting held in Washington, D. C. in April, 1940, as Communists were plainly in full control, this support quickly dissolved.[37] At this meeting the composition of the delegates itself was questionable. Of the 1,264 delegates, only 888 were Negroes, and almost three-fourths of the delegates were from northern states. Communists immediately ousted A. Philip Randolph from his long tenure in the presidency, elected Max Yergan to this office, and passed resolutions denouncing all efforts of the U.S.A. to interfere in the war against Hitler. Until American entry into the war, states Record, Yergan and the National Negro Congress proved willing tools of the Communist Party.

During the period 1935-39, American Communists, obsessed and occupied with the threat which Hitler, Mussolini, and Tojo posed for Russian security, paid much less attention to the Negro's struggle for social justice and equality. Indeed, as Communists everywhere sought friends for Russia, they were much less critical of all capitalist countries. Although the 1939-1942 period of the Moscow-Berlin pact saw an increased attack on Franklin D. Roosevelt and all who proposed any action against Hitler, the invasion of Russia by Germany saw a sharp renewal of the friendly and conciliatory Communist attitude. During this period of the party's obvious use of Machiavellian opportunism, Afro-Americans came to see clearly that to Communists, their race's interests and efforts were secondary and subordinate to those of the Russian state. Russian aid given Italy during the "rape of Ethiopa" also served to strengthen this conviction.[38]

In February, 1937 the party, through the National Negro Congress launched the Southern Negro Youth Congress in Richmond, Virginia, an organization which was aimed especially at enlisting southern youth in the party's efforts. Though it had a larger aim, this organization remained throughout its history of about a decade, "primarily an agency of Negro student, church, and political groups centered in a few of the larger urban communities of the South."[39]

After Red capture of the National Negro Congress, the launching of their attack on Franklin D. Roosevelt, and the stand against intervention against Hitler which followed the Munich conference and the Moscow-Berlin Non-Aggression Pact, disillusionment with Communism reached a high peak. Wilson Record points out that between 1939-1941, "probably half of the several thousand Negro Communists dropped out of the organization, and despite the fact of accelerated recruitment efforts, no substantial numbers of Negroes have since joined or supported the party."[40] During the 1930's, Benjamin Mays wrote:

> The Negro's firm faith in God has saved him, up to this point from violent revolutionary methods of achieving his rights. His faith in God has not only served as an opiate for the Negro, but it has suggested and indicated that pacific and legal methods are to be used in achieving them. It is not too much to say that unless liberal prophetic religion moves more progressively to the left in the effort to achieve complete citizenship rights for the Negro, he will become more irreligious and he will become more militant and communistic in his efforts to attain to full manhood in American life. It is significant to note that prior to 1914, one finds no idea of God that imply doubt and repudiation. Since the War, and particularly since 1920, there is a wave of cynicism, defeat, and frustration in the writings of young Negroes where God is discussed.[41]

Mays does not show adequately in his study of *The Negro's God* that the race has drawn much of its faith, optimism, and gradualism from the larger American culture. Mays tended to look too much for explanations of Negro attitudes and beliefs in the colored man himself rather than in the general American culture.

The modern emphasis on economics as a prime motor force in history is one reason why the Communist movement has attracted many intellecuals. During the era of Booker T. Washington, and earlier, this emphasis on economics was clearly evident. Garveyism rode the same wave, as did the Father Divine and similar movements, but most Negroes have known that for them progress was to be slow. Most have been gradualists and evolutionists, with no faith in radicalism.

Although both white and colored American Communists have been small in number, according to Wilson Record and others, their contribution to the national life has been significant. Although difficult, if not impossible to measure, their demands that Negroes organize and agitate more, and that white America should accept a greater measure of racial integration in the political, economic, and social realms did not fall altogether on stony ground. Too, they urged many Negroes to give up their romantic conceptions of life and society and to end their slavish abherence to either the Republican or Democratic party. Communism also encouraged a reinterpretation of some aspects of Negro history, provided some fresh ideas and themes for creative writers, and compelled some organizations to adopt broader, more militant policies. In summarizing the efforts of the Communist party to win Negroes to its fold during the depression period, Wilson Record points out that there were never over 2,500 in the party. He continues:

> The Party failed to build any mass organizations with sustaining possibilities among American blacks. It did not succeed in appreciably weakening those 'reformist' organizations to which it was bitterly opposed. It drew only a few Negroes into Communist-sponsored trade unions. Its special Negro organizations made very limited headway. Its widely-heralded efforts to build up a radical Negro leadership did not come off. It alienated the bulk of the Negro intellectuals; it insulted rather than persuaded the Negro artists, by demanding that they conduct themselves

as Negroes, and Communist Negroes at that rather than as creative human beings.[42]
Drake and Cayton have testified as to one important reason why some Afro-Americans became admirers of Communism during the 1930's. "The Reds," they stated, 'won the admiration of the Negro masses by default. They were the only white people who seemed to really care what happened to the Negro."[43] Cayton points out that one source of admiration for Communism has been Russia's strong stand against racial prejudice, both within the Soviet Union and throughout the world.[44]

The Party long has tried unsuccessfully to penetrate the national offices of both the NAACP and the Urban League. Both groups learned early in their careers that Communist organizations are primarily instruments to promote the expansion and strength of the Soviet Union.[45] Wilson Record has concluded that Negro membership in the Communist party has never exceeded 8,000 members,[46] and that in 1951 this number had dwindled to 4,000. This, too, was a part of the national pattern, caused by a growing realization that hiding behind the cloak of an ideology was the ugly reality of Russian imperialism and expansionism. By 1947, when the Truman Doctrine declared these facts, most Afro-Americans had come to realize that the basic choice was not really between loyalty to one or more systems of economic and social belief and practice, but between two nations locked in a fateful ideological and power struggle, and as always in the past, they chose loyalty to the nation of their birth and forebears. Colored Americans joined in denouncing Russian aggression in Berlin, Greece, Korea and other areas. While they were equally united in their denunciation of Americans who were shown to have acted as spies for Russia, most joined in denouncing the manner of attacking native Communists which came popularly to be called "McCarthyism." Prominent among Negroes who, having been party members or followers, reversed their attitude and convictions have been Langston Hughes, George Schuyler, Richard Wright, Max Yergan, and Manning Johnson. In a highly significant statement on Communism, made before the House Un-American Activities Committee, Jackie Robinson was unequivocal in his denunciation of this ideology and movement. But he minced no words in stating that colored Americans were equally opposed to "any other influence that kills off democracy" as it pertains to Negroes and all groups.[47]

The 1948 Progressive party candidacy of Henry Wallace and Glen Taylor caused a great deal of interest among colored Americans. The great emphasis which the party platform placed on civil rights, the prominence of outstanding Negroes in the party, plus the fact that as Wallace toured the South he frequently resided in the homes of Negroes made the party popular. That this popularity did not run deep is evident in the relatively small Negro vote which Wallace received. Negroes were firmly wedded to the New-Fair Deal administrations, and suspicious of the strong Communist influence on the Progressive Party. Too, the Democrats, by including a strong civil rights plank in their platform, stole much of the thunder of the Progressives, and probably no more than twenty thousand Negro votes were cast for Wallace. In Harlem, both Truman and Dewey ran ahead of him, and the trend was similar in Chicago, as well as in almost all major cities.[48] The post-World War II peace movement which centered around the Stockholm Peace Appeal and the Progressive Party attracted some backing. Perhaps the top colored supporters of the movement were Paul Robeson and W. E. B. DuBois. Negroes voiced no significant criticism of such issues and measures as the Marshall Plan, Berlin Airlift, or Point Four Program, and, as often has been the case, their failure to make many significant public statements did not indicate lack of interest or concern, but rather agreement with the pattern of national leadership.

THE PHILOSOPHY OF NEGRO HISTORY

The Problem of Purposes or Objectives of Negro History

An examination of the writings of such early Negro historians as William Cooper Nell, James W. C. Pennington, Robert Benjamin Lewis, James Theodore Holly, Joseph T. Wilson, William Wells Brown, and George Washington Williams reveals that written Negro History had its beginnings in America primarily as an attempt to justify emancipation.[1] Here it is of interest to compare the purposes which motivated the earliest Negro historians with those of their white contemporaries. Posing recently the question, "What is written history good for?", Henry Steele Commager informs us that:

> The generation that had rejoiced in the stately histories by Bancroft, Motley, Prescott, and Parkman had not been troubled by this question. It had been content with the richness of the narrative, the symmetry of the pattern, the felicity of the style that was to be found in these magisterial volumes.[2]

As indicated, such was not the case with the Beginning School of Negro historians, who were as much interested in the *uses* of their history as they were in its discovery. Here it can be seen that Negro History originated from an urge to social reform as well as the urge to scholarship. The conception of its nature, purposes or goals, and of values to be derived from the study and teaching of this discipline have been shaped, to a large extent, by this duality of urges. If we follow the practice of the many modern educators who "divide subjects or areas into two kinds called 'tool studies' and 'content studies',"[3] we find that always Negro History has been viewed as both a "content study" and a "tool study."

Of the scholarship goal, George Washington Williams declared in his celebrated study—"Not as a blind panegyrist of my race, nor as a partisan apologist, but from a love for *'the truth of history,'* I have striven to record the truth, the whole truth, and nothing but the truth."[4] Similarly, Article II of the Constitution of the Association for the Study of Negro Life

441

and History, published when this organization had been in existence only two years, gave as the Association's object, "The collection of sociological and historical documents and the promotion of studies bearing on the Negro."[5] Of the social reform goal, in 1841 James W. C. Pennington voiced a sentiment which practically every Negro historian has echoed. Giving the purpose of his *Textbook of the Origin and History of the Colored People*,[6] Pennington declared in his Preface, "Prejudices are to be uprooted, false views are to be corrected." In 1936 L. D. Reddick stated before the Association's annual meeting in Richmond, Virginia that one of the purposes of Negro History is "to inculcate a dynamic pride in . . . Negroes."[7] "It is clear," Reddick continued, "that Negro History has the generalized objective which it shares with all scholarship of seeking the advancement of knowledge plus the specific design as a lever of what might be termed 'racial progress'."[8] In 1940 Professor W. B. Hesseltine stated that this Association "has assumed the task of inspiring pride in the achievements of the [Negro] race,"[9] and in 1957 John Hope Franklin wrote that "Negro history . . . can and, in time, will provide *all America* with a lesson in the wastefulness, nay, the wickedness of human exploitation and injustice that have characterized too much of this nation's past."[10] There may be no better evidence of the social reform goal of Negro History than the language of the section entitled, "Why the Negro in History," which Carter Woodson penned for the 1926 brochure on Negro History Week. Here Dr. Woodson wrote:

> Let truth destroy the dividing prejudices of nationality and teach universal love without distinction of race, merit or rank. With the sublime enthusiasm and heavenly vision of the Great Teacher let us help men to rise above the race hate of this age unto the altruism of a rejuvenated universe.[11]

In its social uplift role the Association for the Study of Negro Life and History has been following the pattern of practically all organizations in the Afro-American *or any other minority group* which is segregated and discriminated against. The organizations of oppressed groups are not usually at liberty to have singularity of purpose, and it is to the credit of this Association that, with the primary and permanent role of promoting scholarship, it has mixed the social protest role.

In writings of the past the present writer has suggested that (1) the Beginning School of Negro Historians had an inordinate faith in the role of education, both as a cause of race prejudice when misused, and as a corrective of this prejudice when correctly applied. This prejudice was rooted in an actual *de facto* and *de jure* situation. Furthermore, the 1876-1912 bias against the Negro which American historiography displayed was not due solely to the romanticist leanings of the new Southern historiography, nor to the writings of such Europeans as Houston Stewart Chamberlain and Count Joseph Arthur de Gobineau. This bias drew considerable sustenance from the urban-Eastern-inspired aristocratic tone which dominated American historiography from 1865-1893. The twentieth century shift to a more favorable view of the Negro in history is in part the result of a general shift in American historiography from an aristocratic to a democratic bias. (2) Further, the present writer has averred that an *improper mixing* of the scholarship and social protest urges, may be detrimental to Negro historiography. There can be no quarrel with using Negro History to teach colored youths to respect themselves and their race, or to instill in American whites a greater respect for this nation's largest ethnic minority. This might well be called "applied Negro History" and is a valid endeavor. However, while the scholar may be inspired to do research on a topic in this area by many motives, social uplift among them, once he begins his research and writing he is the pure scientist who should be guided by only the desire to discover, understand, and relate the truth as objectively and fully as he can. Ideal historical writing is not tendential and polemical, and only when his task of finding and relating the truth about the Negro in history is completed is the scholar free to enter upon the role of the applied social scientist, who brings the truth to bear on whatever problems may need resolution. Chattel slavery and racial segregation and discrimination have caused the Negro historian periodically to lay down his scholar's mantle for that of the applied social scientist much more than has been the case with the American historian of the majority group.

The present writer has differed with some noted scholars regarding some of the reasons they assigned as primary justifications for Negro History. Spinoza insisted that the philosopher must try to see things "under the aspect of eternity" and, in this view, the only end to which Negro History is absolutely necessary is to the fullest knowledge and understanding of human history. In the final analysis the cause of Negro History is circumscribed by neither time nor circumstance, for it is the cause of knowledge and truth. Although it is understandable that the early makers of Negro historiography saw its meaning, significance, and value largely in terms of social usefulness, never should it be forgotten that when all past and present social problems are solved, Negro History will still have all of the uses peculiar to any other body of knowledge. By 1960 it did not appear that the purpose or objectives of Negro History had changed much since the Association was organized in 1915. While the scholarship goal is permanent, the social uplift goal remained because race prejudice, segregation, and discrimination remained. Yet, where other aspects of this discipline are concerned, it would seem that at least two important changes had occurred since 1915 which should be reflected in the philosophy of Negro History. These changes affect its nature and scope as well as interpretation. By reference to two other areas of historical specialization this may be illustrated.

Evaluating the present state of Occidental research into Chinese history, one critic stated recently that "the field is characterized more by basic 'factual' research than by sweeping interpretive writing."[12] On this, the critic continued:

> This is largely due to the recency of the assault on Chinese history by the American and European academic communities. Confronted with a vast and virgin field of investigation, many scholars have naturally been inclined to concentrate on particularities rather than generalities.[13]

Scientific Negro historiography is also of rather recent origin, and has been characterized more by "basic 'factual' research than by sweeping interpretive writing." Carter Woodson often said that in his day the great need of the area was for basic factual research. By 1960, however, the time had probably

come when Negro History should be subjected to more comparative studies and to broader interpretive emphases.

Germaine to the second point is the comment which another scholar made recently about research and writing in state
and local history. "Local history," he said, "has altered with the
times, but the change has been so gradual and imperceptible
that it seems not to have been noticed even by its practition-
ers."[14] Continuing, this scholar stated:

> Crisply put, the change is this: local history is becom-
> ing less localized. It is widening out, extending its
> horizons, reaching for far-flung comparisons and
> points of reference. It is looking toward regional and
> interregional areas of interest.
>
> . . . .
>
> The truth is, the world has shrunk, and in shrinking,
> the local at times . . . becomes even more signifi-
> cant.[15]

Have not these same developments implications for the present
philosophy of Negro History? Does not the rise to world power
of the U. S. A., the shrinking of the globe, and the increased
internationalism have implications where today's philosophy of
Negro History is concerned? Do not these developments mean,
in part, that Negro History is perhaps more important than
ever, and where interpretation is concerned, do not these developments call for a "widening out" of Negro History, an
extending of its horizons, and reaching for far-flung compari-
sons and points of reference?

Today's student of Negro History has been well prepared
for these emphases. Carter Woodson, W. E. B. DuBois, Charles
H. Wesley and other makers of modern Negro historiography
have long contended that the approach to history should be
broad. Dr. Woodson often declared that "Negro History Week"
was more properly a "History Week," for, he stated, "there is
no such thing as Negro History or Jewish History or Chinese
History in the sense of isolated contributions."[16] "The relations
and interrelations of races," he declared, "the close communication of peoples, and the wide-spread diffusion of ideas have
made it necessary for one group so to depend upon the other
and so to profit by the achievements of the other that it is

difficult to have any particular cultutre ear-marked."[17] "History, then," he concluded, "is the progress of mankind rather than of racial or national achievement."[18]

The Problem of Interpretation

In the matter of interpretation, probably the biggest pitfalls for the student of Negro History have been the moral, Great Man, and economic emphases. The Beginning School, comprised of such men as Nell, Pennington, Lewis, Holly, Wilson, Brown, and Williams, viewed history almost exclusively as an affair in which, using individuals as tools, the forces of God and the Devil were in conflict, with the latter inexorably doomed. In this view the Civil War came as God's way of ending slavery and as punishment to the nation because of its wrong-doing. This interpretation, even if related to the tone of Abraham Lincoln's Second Inaugural Address, is erroneous in its simplicity. The same is true of that view which makes personalities always the prime determinants of events.

Frederick Jackson Turner's epic 1893 paper read before the American Historical Association has been taken as the event which signalled a "massive shift of American historiography" from an urban-Eastern-inspired aristocratic bias "to a pro-democratic orientation."[19] Yet, because the nineteenth century Negro historian had generally been out of step with the "patrician liberalism" of the 1865-1893 period, the shift for Negro historiography was not nearly so massive as it was for American historiography in general. Still, the appearance in 1896 of W. E. B. DuBois' book on the suppression of the African slave trade, and the beginning of Dr. Woodson's work a few years later, ushered in a new Negro historiography which was not only superior in literary presentation, but in interpretation as well. In spite of this, however, there was to begin in the 1930's a searching re-appraisal of the matter of interpretation in the whole of Occidental historiography.[20] For Negro historiography the re-appraisal appears to have been triggered by the appearance in 1935 of W. E. B. DuBois' book, *Black Reconstruction,* the Marxian thesis of which several able scholars would erroneously hail as a highly welcome and long-overdue fresh frame of reference for Negro History. When this book appeared,

Rayford W. Logan wrote that its "fresh interpretation" is "as significant as was Charles A. Beard's *Economic Interpretation of the Constitution of the United States.*"[21] As we shall see, a few other persons were similarly impressed, but the fact was soon to be grasped by most scholars that the Marxian thesis therein was not one of the multitudinous merits of the book *Black Reconstruction.*

The Revolt Against Classical Liberalism

One year after the appearance of this book, Dr. L. D. Reddick, at the twenty-first annual meeting of the Association, issued a call for "A New Interpretation for Negro History."[22] This history, he stated, is quite different from the study of the Negro in that Negro History has a *purpose* which is built upon a *faith.*"[23] Feeling called upon to elaborate on this position, Dr. Reddick continued:

At the sound of such words—purpose, faith—our theoretical objector may again rush forward to protest that the validity of history as history is destroyed if it is urged forward by any purpose other than the search for truth or sustained by any faith save that invested in the methods and procedures. This objection, quite fortunately, is over-ruled by the evidence that despite what the authors themselves may say, all history has been written with an 'other' purpose. . . .
In the better works, the thesis is implied more often than stated; still it is never absent. It seems humanly impossible to escape point of view.[24]

Holding that there was in 1936 little difference between the philosophy of Negro historians before or since Dr. Woodson's work, Reddick declared that these historians should end their preoccupation with the "slavery theme" and with the Negro in the U. S. A. and turn more to Africa and South America as they were beginning to do. Also, he said, they should end their bondage to the "philosophy of liberalism" which emphasized individualism, rationalism, tolerance, laissez-faire, and progress. This philosophy, he declared, "has included many of the true factors" in the nation's historical development, but "has been superficial in relating these factors and in determining the forces which have been influential."[25] In giving his own preferred frame of reference and interpretation, this scholar, obviously influenced by Charles A. Beard and W. E. B. DuBois,[26] gave great stress to the role of economic factors. Reddick had considerable to say about the Civil War as essentially a "conflict of economic systems," the role of "economic interests" on Reconstruction, and the effects of a "rather blatantly aggressive industrialism" on events since 1865. He contended that while up to 1936 the "social philosophy of the Negro historians" had been "sadly lacking in a grasp of the dynamic forces" hence had turned out to be "the rather naive Emersonian gospel of self-reliance, simple optimism and patient regard for destiny," when his own economic perspective is taken American history begins "to assume a pattern astonishingly intelligible."[27] In continuation he urged young scholars not to "fall into the errors of their literary fathers." In conclusion, he stated:

> Since point of view is inescapable, it is . . . essential that frame of reference should be large, generous, and socially intelligent; that the developments in Negro life be seen in connection with those of the general pattern, of other racial, minority and laboring groups.[29]

And:

> If Negro History is to escape the provincial nature of its first phase, it will surely re-define the area of subject matter in terms of a larger focus; recast its catalog of determinative influences affecting Negro life and re-examine the social philosophy implicit throughout the work.[30]

Two years after this call was issued for a new interpretation for Negro History, an academic colleague, who was teaching less than one hundred miles from where Dr Reddick was employed,[31] read a paper at the annual meeting of the Association which revealed a major source of the Reddick proposals. In a discourse entitled, "The Interpretation of the Thought of the Contemporary Negro from the Standpoint of the Theory of the Sociology of Knowledge," Dr. W. T. Fontaine referred glowingly to Professor Reddick's "new interpretation" and declared that this was part of a new "toughmindedness" in Negro thought which showed "an opposition to the thought patterns, concepts and techniques of the democratic-liberal-scientific

Weltanschauung."[32] Like Dr. Reddick, Professor Fontaine had nothing but praise for the Marxist thesis of DuBois' *Black Reconstruction*. Fontaine mentioned with apparent favor the "agnosticism of the late Weldon Johnson, DuBois and Just, the atheism of Schuyler and Hughes, and the contra-accultura-tive 'black God' religion of Father Divine," as well as new departures in thought among certain distinguished Negro scholars,[33] and took polite jibes at the sometimes "conservatism" of Alain Locke[34] and Charles S. Johnson.[35] Again like Dr. Reddick, Fontaine deplored "the uncritical acceptance of the liberal-democratic *Weltanschauung* by the American Negro," which he called "a supreme example of a *situationally determined* knowledge."[36] Fontaine made it clear that he preferred that the Negro reject the liberal-democratic view in favor of a militant rationally determined outlook and, several times, he expressed the conviction that the new trend in Negro thought which he favored was largely the product of "a defense psychology thrust upon it by social conditions."

It is fairly clear by now that in some of its aspects the revolt against moderation, objectivity, and faith in progress which Reddick and Fontaine evidenced in the thirties was itself a temporary phenomenon. This radicalism in historical inter-pretation was part and parcel of the radicalism which saw a number of Negro and white intellectuals flirt with communism, and a general pushing to the fore of pessimism, iconoclasm and nihilism in the thought and actions of Occidental man. Much of this had too much of the heavy hand of prevailing but tem-porary social conditions upon it, and today in historical thought, as well as in social action, the vogue is back to many elements of that democratic-liberal-scientific *Weltanschaung* which we might best never have shifted from.

Although the rejection-without-qualification of the liberal philosophy mentioned above was extreme in some respects, it was far from being completely in error. Not only was this re-jection in line with a larger movement among Afro-American scholars, but the reading of such a discourse as R. R. Palmer's "The Waning of Classical Liberalism," shows that this thinking was in line with a movement which was affecting the whole of

Occidental culture.[39] As Professor Palmer shows, Classical Liberalism had been visibly on the wane since about 1880 and in many ways this philosophy was given the *coup de grace* by World War I and the Great Depression. By the time Dr. Reddick read his paper before the Association the mighty weight of social circumstances had demonstrated clearly that *some elements* of the old liberalism had become antiquated and harmful. Of these no-longer-useful elements the most pronounced were probably the faith in automatic progress and the faith that science and knowledge were inherently benign. When these faults of the liberal philosophy are considered, it can be seen that Professor Reddick's judgment that not only was a revised or enlarged interpretation for Negro History in order, but that the same need existed for the whole of American and Occidental historiography, was essentially correct. Yet, reacting against malevolent factors and trends in modern technology, corporateness, war, depressions, and poverty, and against certain ideas implicit or explicit in Social Darwinism, Freudianism, and Behavioristic Psychology, the opponents of Classical Liberalism sometimes went too far. The old liberalism contained many elements which were not just "situationally determined," as Dr. Fontaine would say, but which are or ought to be of value as long as men claim to be civilized.

In their insistence that in nineteenth century Negro historiography the list of determinative influences was too narrow, and that point of view is inescapable, Drs. Reddick and Fontaine were correct. But too much easily can be made of this latter point. That Edward Gibbon was a rationalist, Leopold Von Ranke a conservative, and Heinrich von Treitschke a nationalist, as Reddick points out, does not legislate these faults into any general acceptance. Productions as objective and free from bias as is humanly possible ever must be the scholar's goal, and Negro History possesses no exception to this.

CHAPTER XXI

THE MIND OF THE NEGRO WRITER
· AND ARTIST

Due to the proscriptions of slavery, for over two centuries of their existence in North America, the masses of Negroes were unable to make a direct contribution as producers of literature. Until emancipation in 1865, colored men of letters were drawn almost exclusively from the small class of free Negroes and that of fugitive slaves. During the Colonial Period the scientific writings of Benjamin Banneker and the poetry of Phillis Wheatley and Jupiter Hammon, and the limited historical writings of Paul Cuffee and Prince Saunders were among the most outstanding productions.[1] The abolitionist movement provided the first major stimulus to the development of Negro literature, giving birth to the Beginning School of Historians,[2] the press, poetry, a spate of slave narratives, and the first novel.[3] In practically all of these works the writers echoed the well-known thought of William Lloyd Garrison, Wendell Phillips, Benjamin Lundy and other abolitionists of the majority group who, in a number of instances, served as sponsors of the neophyte writers. The best-known product of this tutelage was Frederick Douglass. In 1882 the most outstanding historian which the race had produced, concluded: "Thus far the Negro has not gone, as an author, beyond mere narration. But we may soon expect a poet, a novelist, a composer, and a philosophical writer."[4] This prediction was to prove a correct one.

Inasmuch as the thought of the historians is discussed elsewhere in this work, the main burden of the present chapter is that literature and art which came into existence largely since emancipation.

Pre-Renaissance Era Novels

Before 1865 Frances E. W. Harper, Martin Delany, William Wells Brown, and Frank J. Webb, all produced works of fiction. Their stories generally centered around the abolitionist crusade, a movement in which all of these writers were engaged at the time their works were produced. William Wells Brown is generally regarded as the first Negro novelist. His most famed work, first appearing in London, England as *Clotel, or the President's Daughter*[5] was the tragic tale of a supposed mulatto daughter of Thomas Jefferson, ex-President of the United States. Four years after this work appeared, Webb's *The Garies and Their Friends* was published, also in London. The theme again was miscegenation and the tragedies experienced by mulattoes. Delany and Mrs. Harper wrote short stories which appeared in *The Anglo-African Magazine* in 1859.

For several decades after emancipation, like Negro historians, the novelists were essentially propagandists, justifying the emancipation of their race. The trend toward glorification of the Old South, with its concomitant degrading of the Negro personality, as found in the writings of Joel Chandler Harris, Ruth McEnery Stuart, Maurice Thompson, Grace Elizabeth King, Walter Hines Page, and especially Thomas Dixon, constituted the primary targets of Negro novelists. Under the spell of the nineteenth century romantic movement, and of a psychological need to justify the "Lost Cause" and relegation of Negroes to an inferior status, these cast Negroes in the pattern of sub-humanity which ante-bellum planters had used to excuse the institution of slavery. The embodiment of all of the hated stereotypes about the race came in Thomas Dixon's volumes entitled *The Leopard's Spots: A Romance of the White Man's Burden,* which appeared in 1902, and his *The Clansman: An Historical Romance of the Ku Klux Klan* (1905). From a close study of Negro novelists Blyden Jackson states that to be accepted as any other American is an "infinitude of longing" held by "virtually every Negro."[6] What the Negro wants, Jackson writes, is "to be accepted as everyone else—not always to be the strangers at the feast, the untouchables."[7] Commenting on the essentially propagandistic nature of Negro novels before 1920, Hugh Gloster asserts that they are "more polemic than fiction."[8] Still, some novelists of the post-bellum epoch produced stories which confirmed the ante-bellum depiction of their race. Charles W. Chesnutt's, *The Conjure Woman* (1899) was a collection of stories patterned after the Uncle Remus tales of Joel Chandler Harris. Also in the plantation tradition are Paul Laurence Dunbar's *Folks From Dixie* (1898), *The*

Strength of Gideon (1900), *In Old Plantation Days* (1903), and *The Heart of Happy Hollow* (1904). Some Afro-American novelists before 1914 wrote on altogether non-racial themes. Examples here are Alice Moore's, *Violets and Other Tales* (895), and *The Goodness of St. Rocque and Other Stories* (1899); and George W. Ellis, who in 1917 published his *The Leopards Claw* which dealt with the life of the English aristocracy.

For many years a theme of colored novelists has been the plight of the mulatto. Because of the nature of the origins of this class, and because of its unique position as a border line ethnic type, mulattoes have long constituted an interesting theme of Negro thought. Among white authors, George Washington Cable may be said to have begun the keen interest of novelists in this class. Samuel Langhorne Clemens, Rebecca H. Davis, William Dean Howells, Albion W. Tourgee, and other writers of the period dealt with the mulatto, and these writers almost in unison called the mulatto the highest type of Negro and explained his superiority in terms of the Caucasian blood in his veins. Knowing that mulattoes also often possessed superior cultural advantages from most dark-skinned persons, many Negroes resented this explanation. Thus the treatment of mulattoes by colored novelists generally explained their achievements in terms of superior cultural advantages while at the same time playing up the nature of the relationships which bred this class, and depicting the sometimes unfortunate consequences of being near-white.

Negro novelists of this period were deeply concerned with painting a brighter picture of the colored man's nature and aspirations than white writers of the period were wont to do. To the colored novelist, the shortcomings of his race were due to no inherent inadequacies, but to lack of opportunity and to omnipresent prejudice and discrimination. Hugh Gloster ably has summarized the treatment which these novelists gave to the matter of miscegenation. Gloster states:

> Sometimes characters venerate parents who are a highborn white gentleman and a colored woman, and generally no condemnation is made of such a relationship if the man is as honorable as Southern mores will

permit. Liasons between white women and Negro men, however, are usually avoided; and though suspense is occasionally stimulated by the suggestion of such affairs, it normally develops that the woman has Negro blood and thus is free to marry her colored lover.[9]

These novelists also showed "warmer friendliness" toward "blue-bloods than for poor whites."[10] William M. Ashby's *Redder Blood* (1915) is a story which deals with intermarriage and the pitfalls encountered by mulattoes who wish to pass for white. Probably the interest which Negro authors of this period show in mulattoes springs in part from their observation that mulattoes constituted a large portion of their "better" class, and from envy of this "better class" and the desire to present them as evidence of what the race could achieve when given ample opportunities.

Blyden Jackson and other critics have concluded that previous to the 1920's, apart from James Weldon Johnson's *Autobiography of An Ex-Coloured Man*, among Negroes Charles W. Chesnutt was the only novelist "worthy of the name."[11] Chesnutt's stories, appearing in 1887, were the first by an Afro-American to be printed in *The Atlantic Monthly*. In 1899 his first book, *The Conjure Woman* appeared. So objectively does he treat the suffering inherent in slavery that for years many Americans thought the work was authored by a white person. He skillfully and subtly pointed up the fact that slaves were not the idyllically happy creatures that the master class had painted them to be. In 1899 also appeared a biography of Frederick Douglass authored by Chesnutt, and *The Wife of His Youth and Other Stories of the Color Line*, in which the mulatto theme figured prominently. These stories dealt not only with slavery, but with the Reconstruction period also. The next year appeared his *The Marrow of Tradition*, which is the tragedy of a mulatto physician, Dr. William Miller. Chesnutt's last novel, *The Colonel's Dream*, appeared in 1905. Gloster points out that in his last two novels, Chesnutt "prescribes no panacea for the ills which he exposes; and the implication is that he was not very hopeful for harmonious race relations in the Southern states."[12] Gloster also states that, like so many writers of his race before World War I, "Chesnutt sometimes seems to accept the racial myths of his time."[13]

In his *Negro Tales,* published in 1912, Joseph S. Cotter also dealt with the miscegenation-mulatto theme. In his muckraking novel of the same period entitled *The Quest of the Silver Fleece* (1911), W. E. B. DuBois ably depicts the small southern town, scores miscegenation and the evils of share-cropping; and the prejudice, Uncle Toming, ignorance, and poverty too often evident in the deep South. In *The Uncalled* (1898), *The Love of Landry* (1900), and *The Fanatics* (1901), Paul Laurence Dunbar treated white characters solely, thus presaging the more recent efforts of such books as Willard Motley's *Knock on Any Door,* Anne Petry's, *The Narrows,* and the many volumes by Frank Yerby. In the same period in which Dunbar was writing, Charles W. Chesnutt also wrote stories with all white characters. Of Dunbar's stories, a competent critic has written—"Catering to the demands of publishers and readers of his time, Dunbar generally evaded themes . . . [of racial uplift] and usually specialized either in the treatment of white American life or in the perpetuation of the plantation tradition."[14] Of Dunbar's four novels, three deal with white characters. His fourth, *The Sport of the Gods,* is written in the plantation tradition, and the same is true of his collections of short stories. His treatment of Harlem in *The Sport of the Gods* inspired Carl Van Vechten's celebrated effort entitled *Nigger Heaven.* Gloster terms Dunbar's fiction "acquiescent and uncontroversial."[15]

Hope's Highway (1918) by Sarah Lee Brown Fleming treats the struggles of Afro-Americans in founding their own schools. The story has a World War I background, while F. Grant Gilmore's, *The Problem: A Military Novel* (1915) has a Spanish-American War setting and is high in praise of the Negro soldier. With an avowedly propagandist and racial uplift motive in mind, J. W. Grant published his *Out of the Darkness, or Diabolism and Destiny* in 1909, in which he treats the lives of a Negro physician, a minister, and a lawyer. When he brings up the Booker Washington-DuBois controversy, Grant sides with DuBois. In doing so, he asks the question: "What are houses, land and money to men who are *women?*"

In his *Imperium in Imperio* (1899), *Overshadowed* (1901), *Unfettered* (1902), *The Hindered Hand* (1905), and *Pointing the Way,* Sutton E. Griggs, embittered by the violently anti-Negro writings of Thomas Dixon, indulged in a counter-propaganda. Griggs has been called the "most outspoken among the glorifiers and defenders of his race in twentieth century American fiction."[16] He wrote of the new fearless, usually dark-skinned person whom he believed had taken the place of the Uncle Tom, and proposed in his stories actual group strategy for racial uplift. His *Imperium in Imperio* has been called "the first political novel by an American Negro,"[17] and his *Pointing the Way* also treats this theme. In his writings he mercilessly flays Jim Crow, miscegenation, and the racial formula of Booker Washington. Especially in *Overshadowed* is Washington bitterly attacked. Though often pessimistic himself, Griggs proposed political independence, education, landownership, character, and cooperation with southern whites as the best means of solving the race problem. On this political theme, to Frances Ellen Watkins Harper, ante-bellum poet, novelist, and abolitionist, goes the credit for producing the first novel about Reconstruction to be written by a colored person. Her *Iola Leroy, or Shadows Uplifted* (1892) was also the first novel to be published by a member of her race in the post bellum period. In this work Mrs. Harper treated the mulatto theme and admitted that she aimed at racial uplift. She adopted cultured mulattoes and advised that they seek to lead their race into the path of social justice. She hoped that her novel would inspire youth to high aim, and awaken in white Americans "a stronger sense of justice."

With her *Contending Forces: A Romance Illustrative of Negro Life North and South,* Pauline E. Hopkins admitted that she had been motivated by the desire, "in an humble way to raise the stigma of degradation from my race." She, too, treated the miscegenation-mulatto theme, while in his *The Autobiography of An Ex-Coloured Man,* James Weldon Johnson breaks with the traditional southern setting and the then wellworn theme of attacking prejudice and stereotypes, and artistically depicts many aspects and levels of Negro life, in many ways heralding the coming of the writers of the Harlem Renaissance. But the Renaissance was still in the distance and the shadow of the plantation still strong. In 1896 appeared J. McHenry Jone's, *Hearts of Gold*, which treats the miscegenation-mulatto theme and depicts the well-demeaned cultured Negro as a counter-argument to the stereotyped degraded freedman. *The Climbers: A Story of Sun-Kissed Sweethearts* (1912) by Yorke Jones, is another story which holds up the cultured person as a counterweight to the degraded type which white southern writers of the period delighted in depicting. The collection of short stories which James E. McGirt published in 1907 under the title, *The Triumphs of Ephraim* are written in the plantation tradition. In 1913 Oscar Micheaux published the first of his novels under the title, *The Conquest: The Story of a Negro Pioneer*. This work, dedicated to Booker Washington, agreed with the latter's racial formula in most essentials. Micheaux treats the problem of inter-marriage and castigates members of his race for their love of luxury items and for not showing greater initiative. Especially did he think they were overlooking golden opportunities in the western part of the United States. Two years later, Micheaux published *The Forged Note: A Romance of the Darker Ages*. Here again he is condemnatory of southern Negroes for what he thinks is their excessive concern with pleasure, luxury items, and vice. In 1917 he published the last of his novels under the title, *The Homesteader*, which had a setting in South Dakota. In *Neither Bond Nor Free* (1902), G. Langhorne Pryor, like Sutton E. Griggs, in order to combat the notion that mulattoes represent the highest type in his race, is highly commendatory of the dark-skinned person. But unlike Griggs, Pryor accepted and championed the Booker Washington formula of racial adjustment.

In *Lillian Simmons, or the Conflict of Sections*, Otis M. Shackleford deals with racial tensions in the North which resulted from the migrations of southern-born members of his race. He ably outlines the resentment and shame which many old residents of the North had toward the newcomers because of their poverty, illiteracy, and the racial troubles which sprang from their pouring into northern communities. Shackleford

accepted the Booker Washington racial formula of concentration on playing down the issue of social and political equality.
Like most novels of the 1865-1920 period, educated, cultured,
and professional persons loom large among the characters of
this story. It is evident that Mr. Shackelford, like so many of
his contemporaries, wished to present the better type of colored
person as a counter argument against the derogatory stereotypes of the race. In both *Bebbly, or the Victorious Preacher*
(1910) and *J. Johnson, or the Unknown Man: An Answer to
Mr. Thos. Dixon's Sins of the Fathers* (1915), Thomas H. B.
Walker holds up cultured Negroes as a counter-argument to the
stereotypes.   In the latter story, the miscegenation-mulatto
theme is prominent. Of similar pattern is Henry F. Downing's,
The American Cavalryman: A Liberian Romance (1917).
This is one of the earliest novels to pay considerable attention
to Africa, and another story of this year which reflects the
growing world consciousness of Afro-Americans, and which
also has an African setting, is Clayton Adam's, *Ethiopia, the
Land of Promise: The Book with a Purpose*. The "purpose" in
the book was to show the "much-abused Ethiopian race" to be
"men and women endowed with hearts as feeling, with motives
as pure, and with aims as high as are those that govern the acts
of the children of other races." In 1910 Robert L. Waring published *As We See It*, a story which compliments the educated
and cultured Negro, accepts the Booker Washington formula
of race adjustment, and heaps villification and hatred on the
southern poor white.

Poetry, Drama, and the Press

Frances Ellen Watkins Harper has been called the most
popular Negro poet of the abolitionist era. Born in the free
class, in Baltimore, Maryland, she early moved to Ohio and
became a school teacher. After a short while, she gave up this
work to enter the abolitionist movement and to work with the
Underground Railroad. She continued to write able verse long
after the war ended.[18] Surveying early poetry produced by his
race, one critic of Paul Laurence Dunbar asserted:

> Behind Dunbar, there is nothing that can stand the
> critical test. . . . With Dunbar we have our first au-

thentic lyric utterance, an utterance more authentic
. . . for its faithful rendition of Negro life and
character than for any rare or subtle artistry of expression. . . .

The two chief qualities in Dunbar's works are,
however, pathos and humor, and in these he expresses
that dilemma of soul that characterized the race between the Civil War and the end of the nineteenth
century.[19]

Dunbar reflects the growing secular spirit. In a poem entitled
"Religion," he stated:

> I am no priest of crooks nor creeds,
> For human wants and human needs
> Are more to me than prophets' deeds;
> And human tears and human cares
> Affect me more than human prayers.
>
> Go cease your wail, lugubrious saint;
> You fret high Heaven with your plaint,
> Is this the Christian's boasted bliss?
> Avails your faith no more than this?
>
> Take up your arms, come out with me,
> Let Heav'n alone; humanity
> Needs more and Heaven less from thee,
> With pity for mankind look 'round;
> Help them rise—and Heaven is found.[20]

Robert Kerlin said of Dunbar:

[He] revealed to the Negro youth of America the
latent literary powers and the unexploited literary
materials of their race. . . . Upon all his people he
was a tremendously quickening power, not less so
than his great contemporary at Tuskegee [Booker
Washington]. [Dunbar] was the prophet . . . of a
new generation, . . . as he was the poet of a vanishing generation.[21]

Dunbar's *forte* was accurate rendition of dialect. However, the
rise to national prominence of James Weldon Johnson which
started in 1913 gave to the poetry of this period a superior type
of intellectualism and universality, qualities which stand out in
the subsequent verse of such writers as Angelina Grimké,

Georgia Douglass Johnson, Anne Spencer; Claude McKay, Leslie Pinckney Hill, Charles B. Johnson, Fenton Johnson, Joseph Cotter, Everett Hawkins, Lucien Watkins, Roscoe Jameson and others. In this same 1865-1920 period in literature, William Stanley Braithwaite published his *Lyrics of Life and Love* (1904) and *The House of Falling Leaves* (1908).

The half decade immediately preceding the opening of the 1920's saw Negro poetry reach a new high with the initial works of Claude McKay. Despite this and later achievements, Nick Aaron Ford, writing in 1950, deplored that "despite one hundred and ninety years of effort, no American Negro poet has achieved a status comparable to such first-rate white poets as Robert Frost or Edwin Arlington Robinson."[22] The chief weakness of colored writers, Ford stated, has been in "craftsmanship and design rather than theme."[23] As to the paucity of literary works produced by the Negro, still another observer, writing in the same year as Ford, also deplored this shortcoming. "Today in an honest anthology of the best in American fiction, drama and poetry," he asserts, "there might be no Negro entry."[24] But if another observer is correct, there is great promise for the future. "Negroes take to poetry as they do to music," Arna Bontemps has stated.[25] Following this same conviction, an outstanding colored poetess states:

> The Negro poet has impressive advantages. Ready-made subjects—which he may twist as he wills. Great drives. And that inspiriting emotion, like tied hysteria, found only in the general territory of great drives.[26]

This same critic feels that "Every Negro poet has 'something to say.' Simply because he is a Negro; he cannot escape having important things to say."[27]

Langston Hughes has given an explanation for the lack of achievement which the Negro has shown in dramatic writing. "We haven't made too much progress as writers in the theare," he asserts, "mainly because it's pretty hard to have professional contacts. Such contacts are indispensable to success in modern playwriting."[28] "The Negro dramatist," states another eminent authority, "has been interested in the subject of Negro drama from the point of view of oppression, exploitation, humiliaticn, illegitimacy, folklore, and natural mimicry."[29] In other words, as with novels, historical writings, and so much else, the contribution in this area has suffered from being too narrowly propaganda for racial uplift.

Like so much of Negro life, the history of this groups' contribution to dramatics goes back to ante-bellum plantations. White Americans have been most interested in the humorous side of Negro acting, hence the black-faced comic or minstrel-man has long been popular. Especially was the minstrel tradition dominant until the close of the nineteenth century, and on to the period of the Great Depression. However, in the early years of the present century Rosamond and James Weldon Johnson, Robert Cole, and others, began to write for the serious stage, and with such actors as Bert Williams, George Walker, and Sam Jack, light comedy became a vogue. From the beginning, however, there has been a counter-tradition in the race's dramaturgy. By the second decade of the nineteenth century, New York was enjoying serious productions by the African Players, and Ira Aldridge, first outstanding Negro Shakespearean actor, and Victor Sejour were thrilling European audiences with their acting. Aiding the growth of this drama was the development of Negro theatres in several northern urban centers, and the "Little Theatre" movement which later began to grow in many cities and colleges.

While most Americans are prone to state that William Lloyd Garrison's paper, *The Liberator,* was the first paper to champion militant and radical abolitionism, they overlook the fact that *Freedom's Journal,* started by John B. Russwurm and Samuel E. Cornish deserves this title. The latter paper was begun in 1827, three years before Garrison launched *The Liberator,* and it was suspended only when Russwurm was expatriated to Africa in 1830. Seven years later Cornish became editor of the *Weekly Advocate,* which Phillip A. Bell of New York was just launching. By the outbreak of the Civil War, approximately a score of periodicals had been launched by Afro-Americans, most of them born in the forties and fifties. Perhaps best known of all is Frederick Douglass' *North Star* which was begun in 1847, and renamed *Frederick Douglass' Paper* in 1850.

This periodical lasted until 1864, a much longer duration than most of those started in the ante bellum period. Four magazines were started in the same period. The first issue of the first Negro newspaper in this country, the aforementioned *Freedom's Journal*, said in its editorial—"We wish to plead our own cause. Too long have others spoken for us." The same sentiment was given by Douglass as his reason for launching the *North Star*. The existence of these journals is refutation of the oft-repeated assertion that the Negro did not fight for his own freedom, but that it was given to him by white persons. The Negro was in the thick of the abolitionist fight from beginning to end. Indeed, the Negro comprised the very first abolitionist group.

Growth of the press is reflected in the fact that in 1870 there were approximately ten Negro periodicals in the nation, by 1880 this figure had doubled, and in 1890 the number had grown to 154. Among the most outstanding papers by the latter date were the *Philadelphia Tribune,* the *Washington Bee,* the *Cleveland Gazette,* and the *New York Age.* Like many white periodicals of this period, the personalities and opinions of the editors stood out boldly. With the colored press the too often sensational slant of the news, cheap paper, poor pictures, faulty grammar and proof reading, and curious assortment of advertising testified to the poor training, education, and poverty of the editors as well as to similar conditions which were fairly typical of the colored reading public for which these papers were meant to be sources of race pride and militant awakening. Everywhere these editors thought of themselves as leaders of and spokesmen for the race. In the epic *American Dilemma*, Gunnar Myrdal made the mistake of taking them at their own word. Myrdal concluded that the Negro press is "the greatest single power in the Negro race." What he apparently did not know is that until recent years, often southern Negroes have been afraid of the militancy and outspokenness of their editors. Lower class persons sometimes have regarded these editors as "overly intellectual" self-seeking individuals who wanted to make money by capitalizing on racial problems, while the more sophisticated, made conservative frequently by the fact that they held public jobs, wished the editors would tone down their protests and demands—so as not to "stir up trouble."

Almost exclusively, the press has been interested in news which involves colored people directly, and it frequently has exaggerated the importance of this news. Even in sports, white athletic groups have come in for attention only when they either had colored members or when they were competing against Negroes. Not until a colored woman found the body of Charles Lindbergh's baby did this sensational kidnapping come in for attention by this press. Especially since World War I, the increased internationalism of the Afro-American has tended to broaden the "colored community" to a world setting, a fact which prompted Frederick G. Detweiler to conclude that the horizon of the Negro editor is "at least as wide as that of a small-town white editor and often wider."[30] This world-focus on race has caused this press to join colonial peoples everywhere as they have sought to overthrow European rule.[31] The press constantly has reflected the belief that not even northern whites were free from prejudice and false notions regarding the race. "Our friends," commented the first Negro editorial, "are actually living in the practice of prejudice, while they abjure it in theory, and feel it not in their hearts." This was a reason given as to why there should be a segregated race literature and separate race action.[32]

The following papers were founded during the year indicated: *California Eagle*, Los Angeles, 1870; Savannah *Tribune*, Georgia, 1875; *The Conservator*, Chicago, 1878; *The Planet*, Richmond, Virginia, 1884; New York *Age*, 1885; and the Cleveland *Gazette*, 1883. That northern Negroes felt freer and more able to protest than those in the South may be reflected in the fact that of the approximately thirty newspapers which existed in 1880, only seventeen were published in the South, although over eighty per cent of the race lived there. The two decades starting with 1890 saw the most successful of all race newspapers launched. In 1884 the *Philadelphia Tribune* was launched, the Baltimore *Afro-American* in 1892, the Norfolk *Journal and Guide* in 1900, the *Chicago Defender* in 1905, the *Amsterdam News* in 1909, and the *Pittsburgh Courier* in 1910.[33] By 1948 the total circulation of the *Chicago Defender*, the *Afro-American*, *Pittsburgh Courier*, and *Journal and Guide* was near the million mark. By 1959 almost four hundred Negro periodicals were regularly issuing from the presses of the nation. P. L. Prattis, outstanding journalist, states that the traditional function of the press has been "to speak up for the rights of Negroes, to wage war against those who would have kept Negroes in chains."[34] This, he states, "is, and always has been a necessary" service,[35] but, he believes that in the twentieth century progress in race relations is causing some colored Americans to lose interest in their papers.[36] Thus, he opines these papers in order to survive must change their objectives, and "be for and of the people, white people and black people."[37]

On the tendency of the Negro press to sensationalize news of such matters as segregation and instances of Jim Crow, one observer has pointed out that this tendency "acts as a kind of counter-weght to the tendency of many white papers to highlight the reverse situation—Negro crimes against whites."[38] This same writer analyzed two Harlem newspapers of the post World War II era, the *People's Voice,* formerly edited by Adam Clayton Powell, Jr., who founded it in 1942, and the *Amsterdam News.* From this analysis he concluded that the most common techniques used by the colored press "to assert the Negro's fundamental right to equal opportunity and socio-economic status" have been:

1. Protest (attacks on discrimination, Jim Crow, etc.);

2. Playing up achievements of Negroes, both past and contemporary, and

3. Identifying Negroes with liberal and progressive movements, both among white Americans and the world's rising masses and colonials.

In their volume *Black Metropolis,* Horace Cayton and St. Clair Drake present similar conclusions from their study of the *Chicago Defender,* while studies made by Howard University graduate students have revealed that the *New York Age,* long a leader in the Afro-American press, fitted these generalizations. The *Age,* too, emphasized news about affluent and otherwise successful Negroes. The same was true of the *Washington Bee* and other papers.[39]

Intellectual Growth and Reaction

March, 1897 saw the founding of The American Negro Academy, which had Washington, D. C. as the center of its activities. This organization had a fairly long and interesting career centered around stimulating and producing scholarly studies. Like most Negro organizations, racial uplift was a dominant theme with this group. Also characteristically, ministers of the gospel played a leading part in its founding and history. Most outstanding from this field were Alexander Crummell, first president of the Academy, L. B. Moore, J. A. Johnson, and F. J. Grimké. Also prominent in the launching of the organization were several college teachers, one of whom was to become the most renown of all colored scholars, W. E. B. DuBois. Though none of the members approached DuBois in training or later reputation, W. H. Crogman and Kelly Miller became authors of considerable recognition. The Academy claimed as its objectives, the "promotion of literature, science and art [and] the fostering of higher education, the publication of scholarly work and the defense of the Negro against vicious assault." Most of its publications appear to have been concerned with the latter two motives. Alexander Crummell felt that the low cultural level of the race was the key to the Negro's problem in the United States. "As a race in this land," he wrote, "we have no art; we have no science; we have no philosophy; we have no scholarship." He deplored the doctrine which Booker Washington was then championing, that the acquisition of property and wealth was the "source of power." To Crummell the "source of power" lay in the direction of achievement in the liberal arts, and the educated person of talent was to be the main source of racial uplift and respect. A few years hence DuBois and Woodson were loudly to champion these same views in favor of developing a "talented tenth" as the salvation of the Afro-American.[01]

In 1910 students at Howard University protested against the preoccupation with Negro spirituals which their assembly programs evidenced. Especially chaffing to students were the occasions on which these dialect songs were sung in the presence of Caucasians. This feeling was general with educated individuals, and colored arrangers of the spirituals began to modernize and correct their grammar and diction. Paradoxically, the wide acceptance of the spirituals and dialect poetry of Paul Laurence Dunbar were two sources of the new race pride which the Negro was manifesting. Some members of the middle class also resented the dialect in Dunbar's poems. Contrary to popular opinion, though Negro poets of the 1920s were too earnest, too conscious of its servile connotations and too interested in themes for which dialect verse was unsuited to devote a great deal of time to it, they did not spurn it altogether. Even the sophisticated James Weldon Johnson devoted a section of his first book to poems in dialect. Perhaps in most societies where the culture of a minority group is taking on the character of that of the majority, there are those among the minority who oppose the relinquishing of elements peculiar to its culture. Among Afro-Americans this penchant is seen in the controversy over dialect songs and poetry, in the proposal by Carter Woodson, Benjamin Brawley and others that the "Negro genius" be sought and cultivated—even through a separate type of formal education—, in the re-awakened fundamentalist tendencies in Negro religious denominations and the rise of holiness churches and in Negroes who favored the continuance of segregation, as well as in the resurgent zionism.

In the thought of the Negro writer of the Progressive and World War I eras are to be found practically all of the themes which agitated and impelled the writers of the majority group. Negroes of this period did not have to become reformers, for at least within the confines of the ever-dominant racial theme, most Negro writers always had been muckrakers, and in the 1901-1917 period the pens of W. E. B. DuBois, William Monroe Trotter and others would provide fitting rivals for the strictures of Ida Tarbell, Upton Sinclair, Frank Norris, and Lincoln Steffens.

The Negro Renaissance: Origins and Scope

The 1920s witnessed the beginning of an outburst of literary and artistic talent which has been dubbed the Negro Renaissance. Washington, D. C., location of the nation's most outstanding Negro university, was a center of the Negro

Renaissance which was second in importance to no city save New York, where the movement was centered in Harlem. Cultural capital of Afro-Americans since the 1890s, during the 1920s New York city attracted further national and international attention through the artistic, literary, and political activities of its Negro population.

The recognition of their achievements in art and literature by the March, 1925 issue of the *Survey Graphic* not only inspired Afro-Americans, but went far toward gaining greater acceptance of their creative endeavors. Among other such works, the anthology *Ebony and Topaz,* edited by Charles S. Johnson and published in 1927, placed before the reading public writings by twenty of the race's leading creative and scholarly spirits, who also had *Crisis* and *Opportunity,* organs of the NAACP and Urban League respectively, among the more significant supporters of the Renaissance. Of one dominant characteristic of the movement, Alain Locke states that—"pride of race supplanted the bitter wail of unjust persecution."[41] "For Negroes themselves," states Gloster, "the Renaissance was the period of new opportunities and bright hopes, when their abilities and attainment were at long last receiving attention and reward from the majority group."[42] Some major sources of this Renaissance were:

1. The Negro History movement launched by Woodson in 1915.
2. The northern and urban exodus, and the militant protest which it sustained.
3. The growing educational and economic attainments of the race and the nation-at-large.
4. The democratic and international ideologies propagated and disseminated by World War I.
5. The primitivist movement of the period, which partly reflected the frustration of "the lost generation," and partly the growing interest in anthropological and archeological studies. The new-found appreciation for things African was a tremendous source of inspiration to the growing race pride of colored Americans.

Novels of the Renaissance period reveal quite clearly the frustration that the "Lost Generation" of Americans felt as they attempted to "return to normalcy" in a nation which had shifted from an agrarian-rural base to an industrial-urban one. During the twenties the thought of the Negro revealed new emphases. Up to this point the colored American had been forced to have rather narrow, definite and fixed goals which probably made easier a sense of hope and direction. Those goals were primarily economic survival and secondarily the elimination of prejudice, discrimination, lynching, and all forms of social injustice, hence it may be said that the Negro mind, to 1920, was largely monistic and alternately, or often at the same time, defensive and aggressive. World War I saw a de-emphasis of the racial theme and many more Afro-Americans joined the nation-at-large in the sometimes noisy quest for an outlook on and an approach to life which would harmonize with the changed economic, cultural and social realities. Serious Negro thought of the 1920's is much more identical with that of the nation-at-large than it had been previously and this identification was to become even more pronounced during and after the thirties. This new trend was clearly evident in the writings of William Stanley Braithwaite and others. In addition to the polish and urbanity which were pronounced, there seems to be little obvious race consciousness in his poetry. Along with writing *Lyrics of Life and Love* (1904), *The House of Falling Leaves* (1908), and *Sandy Star and Willie Gee* (1922), Braithwaite began in 1913 to edit and evaluate annual anthologies of magazine verse. Yet, despite these new departures, more than with any previous generation, Negro writers of the 1920s were concerned with their personal philosophies of life and with art as an escape from the realities of social conditions which their sensibilities often found revolting. Afro - Americans became more critical of themselves than they had been in any previous period, and few segments of the group escaped criticism. Educators, clerics, politicians, businessmen, even the NAACP itself, came under attack where they left themselves vulnerable. De-emphasis of race, and growing self-criticism are among the more reliable signs that by the 1920's Negro literature and thought were reaching a considerable degree of maturation.

Novels, Poetry and Drama of the Renaissance Era

The primitivist movement, which emphasized the exotic

and sensual aspects of Negro life, was best represented in such writings as those of Arna Bontemps, Claude McKay, and Wallace Thurman. The emphasis which these writers placed on Harlem was continued, minus the exotic and sensual emphasis, in the novels of Countee Cullen, Rudolph Fisher, and others. Fisher's novels are *The Walls of Jericho,* Published in 1928, and *The Conjure Man Dies,* which appeared four years later. In the former work Fisher criticized the NAACP for being too much, in his opinion, an impractical, statistical-minded fact-finding agency, and he advocated less race consciousness on the part of both Negroes and Whites. The second work uses a murder-mystery pattern to depict Harlem life. Countee Cullen's most outstanding novel, *One Way to Heaven* (1932), which is centered in Harlem, effectively depicts the more prosaic and less exotic aspects of life in this teeming colored community.

Carl Van Vechten's, *Nigger Heaven,* published in 1926, is generally credited with being a precipitating factor of one aspect of the Negro Renaissance. In this highly successful work, Van Vechten played up the sensual, animalistic, exotic side of the race. Harlem and the night club represented the focal point of his interest, and he purported to see savage Africa in the dance orchestras and songs of these clubs. *Nigger Heaven* caused an influx of curious and fun-seeking Whites into Harlem's night spots, of which the Cotton Club on Lenox Avenue was probably the most popular. Colored people were both flattered by, and resented, this heightened interest in their lives. While James Weldon Johnson praised the book as high and representative art, W. E. B. DuBois was caustic in his condemnation of what he termed another caricature and degrading stereotype which amounted to nothing more than "cheap melodrama."[43] Van Vechten, who was already a highly successful and respected critic before this work was penned, deliberately set out to utilize *Nigger Heaven* as a means of informing racial bigots that, like all other races, Negroes, too, are human beings. Like many of the colored writers who preceded him, Van Vechten sought to propagandize and educate toward the end of better race relations. "His attack was not directed against the masses but against the upper classes who influence and direct the masses."[44] He wanted to dramatize to the world the genius of the colored artist, entertainer, and intellectual as proof of the humanity of the race. Beginning with intellectuals of both races, Van Vechten sought to introduce the too-often segregated groups to each other, and the interracial salon approach which he utilized, along with his writing, was a hallmark of New York's social life in the twenties.[45] That Van Vechten was not himself a faddist in this connection is adequately proved by the continuing interest which he has maintained in introducing the Negro artist and intellectual to American whites. He has made a specialty of putting before the public high-class photographs of these artists and intellectuals. Throughout the 1940's and since he has made his collections available to thousands. Yale, Howard, and Fisk Universities have permanent collections which he gave.[46] Probably the fact that white Americans could give attention to aspects of the life of sepia America other than those which centered around crime, lynching, and 'keeping the Negro in his place," so flattered the race until most were willing to overlook the creation of another stereotype which the volume *Nigger Heaven* represented, for, regardless of how viewed, the new stereotype was a decided advance over those which less friendly persons had put forth, and which represented to many the general picture of the colored man.[47]

Although there is less evidence that novelists of the 1920's were writing with outright propaganda in mind, *Fire in the Flint* (1924) by Walter White, *Dark Princess* (1928), by W. E. B. DuBois, and *Slaves Today* (1931) by George Schuyler are definitely in the old tradition of Negro novels. Also in the earlier tradition, propaganda-wise, were Herman Dreer's, *The Immediate Jewel of His Soul* (1919), William Pickens', *The Vengence of the Gods* (1922), and Joshua H. Jones', *By Sanction of Law* (1924). In *The Immediate Jewel of His Soul* Dreer reproves Afro-Americans for not giving better support to the NAACP, and demands full citizenship for his race. *In the Vengeance of the Gods*, Pickens flays the argument that the white race is superior to the colored. Jones' *By Sanction of Law* has been called "perhaps the only American interracial romance in which the colored wooer of a white woman has no misgivings because of African blood."[48] *Dark Princess* by DuBois has an international cast of characters and reflects the growing world consciousness of Afro-Americans. Hugh Gloster calls this story "the only novel by an American Negro which makes an exhaustive study of the place of black folk among the darker races of the earth."[49]

Reflecting the interest aroused by the Negro History Movement, Arna Bontemps produced two historical novels near the end of the Harlem Renaissance, in one of which, *God Sends Sunday* (1931), he centered a Van Vechten-style story around his native New Orleans. Jessie Fauset's novels are *The Chinaberry Tree* (1931); *There is Confusion* (1924); *Comedy: American style* (1933); and *Plum Bun* (1929). Miss Fauset's distinct contribution was to prove that upper class individuals constituted good artistic material, and so skillful was she in this effort that she became the first nationally acclaimed Afro-American novelist. Taking her cue from the earlier trend, Miss Fauset sought to serve the racial cause by showing that upperclass persons are essentially like the best white people. Her *Comedy: American Style* has been termed "the most penetrating study of color mania in American fiction."[50] She depicts the members of the middle class as being persons who are "limited to a small passion for pretty things and more or less unwittingly given to the idealization of Nordicism."[51] Continuing the trend of treating the western United States which was started earlier by Oscar Micheaux and William M. Ashby, Langston Hughes produced in 1936 his *Not Without Laughter,* basing the story on his own direct experiences and observations. Hughes chose a small town western setting because he believed such to be "more truly American" than the traditional Harlem or southern centers, but even in this setting, prejudice and segregation loom large in the lives of the characters.[52]

Continuing the trend of interest in locales outside the United States which was seen earlier in such writers as Henry F. Downing and Clayton Adams, during the Renaissance Claude McKay and Eric Walrond produced stories with West Indian settings, while George Schuyler's *Slaves Today: A Story of Liberia,* based on first-hand observation and published in 1931, takes up the cudgel against the sufferings of natives of Africa.

Schuyler sought to "arouse enlightened world opinion against this brutalizing of the native population in a Negro republic." In 1928, McKay published his *Home to Harlem,* which was severely criticized by some colored people because it emphasized the animalistic sides of their life.[53] McKay's next novel, published in 1929 under the title of *Banjo,* dealt with Negro life in French slums. His *Gingertown* (1932), and *Banana Bottom* (1933), are volumes which depict life in Harlem and Jamaica. McKay's stories are often based on personal experience and he was the most successful colored devotee of the so-called Van Vechten Vogue. Eric Walrond's contribution to this body of literature, a volume entitled *Tropic Death* (1926), is a collection of stories centered around Negro life in the Caribbean. Walrond is objective and offers no panacea for the ills which he artistically portrays. Nella Larsen's novels are *Quicksand* (1928) and *Passing* (1929). Her theme is the old one of the tragedies inherent in miscegenation and crossing the color line. The primary difference, however, is that with Miss Larsen these themes are more artistically handled than ever before. In *Passing* she points out such dangers as the risk of exposure, the fear that one's children will be born with dark complexions, and the sometimes never-forgotten desire to return to and be with Negroes. She has one of the characters state:

> It's funny about 'passing.' We disapprove of it and at the same time condone it. It excites our contempt and yet we rather admire it. We shy away from it with an odd kind of revulsion, but we protect it.

George Schuyler's *Black No More,* published in 1931, represents the highest point of the Renaissance penchant in which Afro-Americans, casting aside much of their intense ethnocentrism, stopped defending and apologizing for their race and began to criticize it broadly and soundly. Schuyler, in all of his writings, seems to be a rugged individualist and a born iconoclast. He typifies the growing emancipation of the Negro mind. Scoring both colored and white, North and South, *Black No More* is excellent satire that probably deserves to be rescued from oblivion. Wallace Thurman's *The Blacker the Berry,* published in 1929, treats color consciousness within his race, and the Harlem life of the Renaissance literati. In his second novel,

Infants of the Spring (1932), he also deals with the life of this group, and is much more critical of the superficiality of many aspects of the Renaissance movement. *Cane,* published by Jean Toomer in 1923, has been termed "one of the more significant productions of the Negro Renaissance," and "possibly the first time in American Negro fiction [that one] handles inflammatory interracial themes without abandonment of the artist's point of view." The novel is also unique in that Toomer turned to rural Georgia for a setting. Walter White's novels, *Fire in The Flint* (1924), *Flight* (1926), and *Rope and Faggot: A Biography of Judge Lynch* (1929) were all written with the cause of racial uplift in mind. In *Flight,* White continued the growing tendency of the Negro novelist to criticize his own race. Especially is he severe with his criticism of high society in Atlanta, Georgia, his hometown. The author decried the obsession of this elite with light complexions, "good" hair, bridge, and private parties, and he saw the lower class, dark-skinned persons as the superior specimens in the race. *Fire in The Flint* and *Rope and Faggot* are both trenchant treatments of lynching and mob violence. Of *Fire in the Flint* White later stated that it was written partly to champion the Negro middle class of professionals and intellectuals.[55] As stated earlier, Miss Fauset's four novels, appearing between 1924-1933, also dealt with the race problem from the point of view of the middle class. Blyden Jackson is somewhat caustic in his criticism of *Fire in the Flint.* "Sadly disappointing as a novel," he states, "it is most unabashed as a polemic. It trumpets its race-consciousness to the world, but one looks through it in vain for any semblance of well-wrought fiction."[56]

Claude McKay, leading Negro poet of the twenties, has been called "a genius meshed in . . . dilemma." "His work," this critic continues, "is caught between the currents of the poetry of protest and the poetry of expression; he is in turn the violent and strident propagandist, using his poetic gifts to clothe arrogant and defiant thoughts, and then the pure lyric dreamer, contemplating life and nature with a wistful sympathetic passion."[57] McKay's "If We Must Die" is typical of his courage and defiance. Robert Kerlin has noted that throughout Negro

poetry runs "an appeal sometimes plaintively uttered, an appeal
to mankind for fundamental justice and for human fellowship
on the broad basis of kinship of spirit."[58] This appeal, Kerlin
concluded, "contains every element of reasonableness." Although
they were fairly prolific during the 1920s, Negro poets produced very little humorous verse. "Pathos," Kerlin avers, "is
indeed the characteristic note of the great body of Negro
verse."[59] During the twenties white Americans tended to view
the poetry of the Negro as the "prattle of a gifted child," while
most Negroes "showed little appreciation for poetry."[60] For the
colored poet, this was "a day of individual literary patronage
when a rich 'angel' adopted a struggling poor artist and made
an exotic plaything out of any 'really brilliant Negro.'"[61] Like
the novelists of earlier decades, colored poets of this period were
greatly concerned with justifying the race's humanity, a theme
evident in Countee Cullen's *Copper Sun,* Claude McKay's
Harlem Shadows, Langston Hughe's *Color,* and James Weldon
Johnson's *God's Trombones.* These were the most outstanding
volumes of poetry published during the period.

"Between 1917 and 1935," notes Frederick W. Bond,
"plays by Negro writers became more and more numerous.
These playwrights weakened their drama, however, because of
too much sensationalism and propaganda." "'Sugar Cane,' by
Frank Wilson, and 'Mulatto,' by Langston Hughes, are definite
examples," Bond concludes.[62] In 1921 Willis Richardson, a
government clerk, had his play "The Deacon's Awakening,"
produced at St. Paul, Minnesota and in May, 1923, his "The
Chip Woman's Fortune," was produced by the Ethiopian Art
Players of New York. The latter group, sponsored by Raymond
O'Neil and Sherwood Anderson, flourished in the twenties.
Richardson also compiled a collection of plays entitled *Plays
and Pageants from the Life of the Negro,* and in 1935 he and
Mary Miller published *Negro History in Thirteen Plays,* a
volume which deliberately avoided the use of dialect. Other
noteworthy colored writers for the stage were Hall Johnson,
Miller and Lyle, and Dennis Donohue. In 1933 Donoghue attempted to use the Scottsboro case as the basis for a play entitled "Legal Murder." The following year Randolph Edmond's
play, "Nat Turner," won him a scholarship at the Yale School

of Drama. Subsequent plays by Edmonds have been widely used in schools and colleges and he has been a leader of the Little Theater movement which flourished at Negro colleges. Acting roles saw Charles Gilpin starred in Eugene O'Neill's "Emperor Jones," a role which Paul Robeson later played. This smashing success, the first full-length Negro play, was quickly followed by O'Neill's, "All Gods Chillun Got Wings," and such works by Paul Green as "White Dresses," "In Abraham's Bosom," and "The No 'Count Boy." Rose McLendon and Florence Mills were the favorite colored actresses. Some of the plays in which Rose McLendon starred were "Rose Marie," "Deep River," "Mulatto," "In Abraham's Bosom," and the Du Bose and Heyward hit, "Porgy and Bess." As with Gilpin, her acting was warmly praised by several of the nation's top artists and critics. Bert Williams the comic actor was popular, and in the role of "The Lord" in Marcus Connelly's play "Green Pastures," Richard B. Harrison won fame and plaudits for his fine acting. During the Depression era Rex Ingram was to star in the movie version of this play. In the same period Ethel Waters rose to fame as Aunt Hagar in another DuBose Heyward production entitled "Mamba's Daughters." As did O'Neil, Green, and other writers of the twenties and thirties, during the earlier abolitionist era white Americans had utilized the race theme to produce for the stage the propagandist "Star of Emancipation" in 1841, "The Branded Hand" in 1845, and "Uncle Tom's Cabin," beginning in 1852.

As stated, during the twenties Afro-Americans became aware of the classic beauty of much of the primitive African art, a knowledge of which slavery had robbed their ancestors in this country. Also, the extent to which Negroes had figured as subjects in, and producers of Occidental art was a pleasantly surprising discovery to many. Locke concluded that early African art was "without peer among the primitive art traditions of the world,"[63] and decried the fact that, "there have been notably successful Negro artists, but no development of a school of Negro art."[64] He believed that the new-found race pride would produce such a school.[65] Some of the most outstanding scientists of the period were Ernest E. Just, zoologist; Julian H. Lewis and William A. Hinton, pathologists; Daniel

Hale Williams, heart surgeon; Elmer Imes, physicist; Charles
Drew, surgeon; and George Washington Carver, genius in agriculture. A number of colored Americans criticized Carver because he was not an outspoken champion of racial equality,
because he did not exploit his discoveries monetarily, and felt
that the great recognition which he received from white Americans was due too much to his meek and docile personality
traits.[66]

Seeing the numerous changes which had been wrought in
many Afro-Americans by 1925, Alain Locke was wont to write
of a "New Negro." Locke's use of this expression sometimes
obscured the fact that his focus was on the intellectual and
artist almost exclusively. Of the class which commanded his
attention, he stated:

> Their work already shows that, being less subject to
> the hypersensitive inhibitions and defense mechanisms
> of their elders, they plunge more naturally into the
> core substance of Negro life and experience and catch
> its characteristic idioms more deftly. Though avowedly
> racial, for the most part, in their work, they also
> range with greater sense of freedom through all the
> provinces of what they sense to be a common human
> art.[67]

But even Locke was wont to admit that the "New Negro" was
not completely new. On this he wrote:

> The Old Negro, we must remember, was a creature
> of moral debate and historical controversy. His has
> been a stock figure perpetuated as an historical fiction
> partly in innocent sentimentalism, partly in deliberate
> reactionism. The Negro himself has contributed his
> share to this through a sort of protective social mimi-
> cry forced upon him by the adverse circumstances of
> dependence.[68]

Locke continued: "Recall how suddenly the Negro spirituals revealed themselves; suppressed for generations under the
stereotypes of Wesleyan hymn harmony, secretive, half-asham-
ed, until the courage of being natural brought them out—and
behold, there was folk-music. Similarly the mind of the Negro
seems suddenly to have slipped from under the tyranny of social
intimidation and to be shaking off the psychology of imitation

and implied inferiority. By shedding the old chrysalis of the Negro problem ·we are achieving something like a spiritual emancipation. Until recently, lacking self-understanding, we have been almost as much of a problem to ourselves as we still are to others."[69]

Locke points out that a great stimulus to the rise of the "New Negro" was the great migrations to the northern cities which came in the late nineties and during World War I. The New Negro was an urban product. "Up to the present," Locke continued, "one may adequately describe the Negro's 'inner objectives' as an attempt to repair a damaged group psychology and reshape a warped social perspective. Their realization has acquired a new mentality for the American Negro."[70] Locke opined—

> As it matures we begin to see its effects; at first nega-tive,iconoclastic, and then positive and constructive. In this new group psychology we note the lapse of sentimental appeal, then the development of a more positive self-respect and self-reliance; the repudiation of social dependence, and then the gradual recovery from hyper-sensitiveness and 'touchy' nerves, the repudiation of the double standard of judgment with its special philanthropic allowances and then the stur-dier desire for objective and scientific appraisal; and finally the rise from social disillusionment to race pride, from the sense of social debt to the responsibili-ties of social contribution, and offsetting the necessary working and commonsense acceptance of restricted conditions, the belief in ultimate esteem and recogni-tion.[71]

During the 1920's and thirties, the Negro history move-ment, launched by Carter Woodson in 1915, became something of a mass movement. It found expression in scholarly books and journals, novels, poems, college and high school courses, plays, the very popular Negro History Week, and the begin-ning of numerous private and public manuscript and book collections. Also during the twenties James Weldon John-son's song, "Lift Every Voice and Sing," became a "national Negro anthem" which many Negroes, perhaps significantly, called the "Negro National Anthem." The song revealed con-

siderable race pride and an objective attitude toward the slavery-dominated past. The statement, "Lest our feet stray from
the places our God where we met Thee," revealed concern
about the changes which urbanization and sophistication were
bringing to the Negro.

One immediate effect of the Depression was the demise of
the Harlem phase of the Renaissance. As unemployment made
itself felt, the large-scale private parties, night club life, and
frenzied buying of novels and poetry were no longer possible.
With that of other Americans, Negro thought became more
influenced by Marxist and socialist dogma, and turned to themes
of the economic ills which were reflected in such phenomena as
bread lines, soup kitchens, and evictions. Hard times and depression, save for the Renaissance period, were no new themes
for the always-underprivileged Negro. Arising from his lowly
position on the economic scale, these ever had been reflected in
his literature and thought; the Depression only intensified these
themes and in addition to its characteristic race consciousness,
Negro thought now became class or proletarian conscious—
hence less race conscious. Economic equality as a goal assumed
new importance alongside the old social and political considerations.

Among the chief Negro fictionists of the depression period
were Richard Wright, Langston Hughes, Arna Bontemps and
Zora Neal Hurston. Of the Renaissance writers, Bontemps and
Hughes appear to have been the most successful in changing
to the new themes which the depression introduced. Reflecting
the thoroughness of this change, it has been pointed out that
between 1933-1942, not one novel by a colored American con-
cerns itself directly with the theme of Negroes passing for
white.[72] Among fictionists, several new names rose to the fore,
and Arna Bontemps, John H. Hill, and John H. Paynter wrote
novels based on actual historical incidents in the Negro's past,
a trend which was part of the Negro History movement. Bon-
temp's books were entitled *Black Thunder* and *Drums at Dusk*,
the former a fictionalized account of the celebrated Gabriel insurrection plot which took place in Virginia in the year 1800,
while *Drums at Dusk* dealt with the Haitian revolution.

In 1933 John H. Hill published his *Princess Malah,* based

on the life and adventures of an American Indian who possessed Negro blood. Like the stories by Bontemps, *Princess Malah* was an effort to win greater respect for colored Americans. John H. Paynter's novel, *Fugitives of the Pearl*, published in 1930, has a background of slaves, abolitionists, and free persons, all of whom were obsessed with bringing about an eventual overthrow of slavery. Reflecting the interest in the hosts of unfortunates who became uprooted and displaced persons during the depression years, William Attaway published in 1939 his *Let Me Breathe Thunder*. This story of non-Negro Hobo youths also points up the growing tendency of colored writers to get away from the old racial theme. Basing his story on personal experiences, in 1932 Victor Daly published the first full length story by an Afro-American which dealt with experiences of colored soldiers during World War I. As might be expected, prejudice and discrimination loom large in this novel.

Jessie Fauset's novel, *Comedy: American Style,* which appeared in 1933, treats the theme of Negroes who want to "pass" for white, while with *Aunt Sara's Wooden God,* published in 1938, Mercedes Gilbert also returns to the tragic mulatto theme, but writes much more objectively and artistically than earlier novelists who sought to exploit that topic. Another work of merit which appeared during this period was Langston Hughe's volume of short stories entitled, *The Ways of White Folks* (1934). In 1935 George Wylie Henderson published *Ollie Miss,* the first novel by a colored American which presents a thorough-going treatment of the southern sharecropping system. In Zora Neale Hurston is encountered the first colored American to base her fiction on good training and research in anthropology. Showing a keen interest in folklore, Miss Hurston published *Jonah's Gourd Vine* in 1934, and *Their Eyes Were Watching God* in 1937. In these works Miss Hurston reveals herself as a masterful portrayer of the lives of lower class southern Negroes, and unlike many Afro-American writers of fiction, she gives little or no message for racial uplift.[73] During this period Waters Turpin turned to the seemingly prosaic theme of chronicling family history. Using eastern Maryland as a setting, Turpin published *These Low Grounds* in 1937 and *O Canaan* in 1939.

One of the best known names among Negro writers of fiction is Richard Wright. With little formal education, Wright emigrated from the South to become one of the most effective of all writers in exposing the racial ills of that section. In *Black Boy* published by Harpers in 1942, Wright has given a vivid account of his early life. Although he first began to receive serious attention as a writer in 1936, and although his first volume of fiction, entitled *Uncle Tom's Children,* a collection of short stories was published in 1938, it was not until the appearance of *Native Son* in 1940 that Wright's name was emblazoned across the literary horizon. Clearly designed to shock, the brief and tragic life of Bigger Thomas is without doubt one of the great stories in modern fiction. To then Marxist-minded Wright, not Bigger Thomas but capitalistic American society was the real fomenter of the murders which Bigger committed; poverty, race prejudice, and discrimination made him sub-human. Bigger stated that segregation and discrimination creates a situation which is "just like living in jail." "Half the time," he continues, "I feel like I'm on the outside of the world peeping in through a knot-hole in the fence." Over a decade later, after having embraced and rejected Communism, Wright ends *The Outsider* on a similar note.

The New Deal, and the forces which produced it, cast the Negro poet, and most other persons engaged in literary expression, into the mainstream of American life. The theme with poets, as with novelists, was no longer exclusively racial, but now dealt with the broader aspects of social protest. To the old themes of protest against segregation and discrimination were added new ones which cried out against slums, poverty, unemployment, poor health and inadequate educational facilities. Poetry took on a stronger note of militancy. In this mood, Sterling Brown published in 1932 his *Southern Road;* in 1935 Frank Marshall Davis published *Black Man's Verse,* and two years later, *I Am the American Negro;* while the labor movement received attention in *Black Labor Chant* by David W. Cannon which appeared in 1939. During the thirties Negro poets, like colored novelists, came of age, broadening their perspective beyond the cramping confines of race, while at the same time revealing greater technical skills.

One competent observer has stated that during the thirties and forties the three most outstanding Negro critics "whose ideas on literature were dominant," were Alain Locke, Benjamin Brawley, and Sterling Brown.[74] In this period, more race artists were winning fame as composers, singers, and players of serious music. In the first decade of the twentieth century the Theodore Drury Opera Company had successfully performed such works as "Faust," "Aida," and "Carmen." Singing in these roles in subsequent years were such notables as Azalia Hackley, Lillian Evanti, Dorothy Maynor, Marian Anderson, Catarina Jarboro, Sidney Woodward, Todd Duncan, Clarence Muse, and Roland Hayes. Among outstanding composers of the period were John T. Layton, Samuel Coleridge Taylor, Clarence White, R. Nathaniel Dett, H. Lawrence Freeman, Charles L. Cook, William L. Dawson, Harry T. Burleigh, and William Grant Still, whose musical compositions and arrangements reflect both the strengthened race pride and increased internationalism of thought. Dett's arrangements of spirituals came at a time when the race was no longer ashamed of its "plantation melodies." In such orchestral works as "Bandanna Sketches," and "Ouanga," Clarence Cameron White treated moods of non-American colored people, while his "From the Cotton Field," like the operatic compositions, "Marty," "Plantation," and "The Octoroon," by H. Lawrence Freeman, also reveal that some Negroes were beginning to find in the slave period more of pride and inspiration than shame. The same is true of Shirley Graham's musical drama "Tom Tour" and of Dawson's "Negro Folk Symphony" and his "African-American Symphony." Not until 1935 did Negro artists find any success at Hollywood studios and they and other spokesmen have been highly critical of the movie and radio industries for giving the race meager and stereotyped roles.

The forties and afterwards have seen a continuation of the maturation as well as the introspection and self-criticism which had been so prominent in the previous two decades. The introspection led many writers and critics to review again the shortcomings and dominant characteristics of the race's literature. A number of these impressions and conclusions follow.

William Gardner Smith feels that a most prominent fact about Negro literature is that, "The Negro writer is . . . invariably bitter."[75] Smith indicates that, because a writer is "a man of sensitivity," it would be erroneous to equate the mind of the colored novelist with the race mind in general. "The sensitivities of the Negro writer," he believes, react "more strongly against the ignorance, prejudice and discrimination of American society than do those of the average Negro in America." Like most observers of this literature, Smith is convinced that the colored novelist has produced more propaganda than art, and with Hugh Gloster and others he also points out the difficulty which colored novelists have had in adding to their "weighty diatribes the leaven of humor." "Too often," in these novels, he concludes, "we witness the dull procession of crime after crime against the Negro, without relief in humor or otherwise."[76] Hugh Gloster aptly has summed up the impact of race on the colored writer. His summary states:

In the first place, it [obsession with race] has retarded his attainment of a cosmic grasp of the varied experiences, humorous as well as tragic, through which individuals pass in this life. Second, it has diminished his philosophical perspective to the extent that he has made only meager contributions to national and world ideologies. Third, it has usually limited his literary range to the moods and substance of race in the United States. Fourth and finally, it has helped certain critics and publishers to lure him into the deadly trap of cultural segregation by advising him that the black ghetto is his proper milieu and that he will write best when he is most Negroid.[77]

N. P. Tillman has stated that obsession with race has made the colored writer "so thoroughly a part of his subject that he has been usually unable to view it objectively."[78] Sterling Brown, Langston Hughes, Blyden Jackson, Hugh Gloster, Alain Locke, L. D. Reddick, and numerous other scholars have pointed out the hyper-sensitivity which has caused Afro-Americans generally to steer clear of certain types and areas of self-criticism. "Why," Locke asks, "has there been this protective silence about the ambivalences of the Negro upper classes, about the dilemmas of intra-group prejudice and rivalry, about the dramatic inner paradoxes of mixed heritage, both biological and cultural, or the tragic breach between the Negro elite and the Negro masses, or the conflict between integration and vested-interest separatism in the present-day life of the Negro?"[79] Here Locke is pointing up a main tendency in Negro thought and expression, that is, the penchant for exposing and playing up only the *favorable* aspects of their life and achievement, or else exposing and playing up the unfavorable only when the white man can be directly blamed for it. The rest, the colored American creative artist usually has chosen to let "moulder in closed closets like family skeletons."[80] Locke might have added that a similar penchant has been an understandable, but regrettable, tendency to see only the black side of the Caucasian and not to view the white American and his problems *vis-a-vis* race with greater objectivity and sympathy. An eminent Negro social scientist also has deplored abuse of the racial theme. "Moods of pessimism," he asserts, "racial breast-beating, portrayal of the ugliness of life as if it were the reality of Negro group existence, all have been over-used as vehicles of the racial theme."[81] Locke has given a similar criticism. Until very recently, he points out, Negro creative expression "was inevitably imitative and marked with a double provincialism of cultural immaturity and a racial sense of subordination. It ran a one-dimensional gamut from self-pity through sentimental appeal to hortatory moralizing and rhetorical threat—a child's gamut of tears, sobs, sulks and passionate protest."[82] Ulysses Lee declares that, in large part because of the demands of Negro readers, colored critics have had to "judge the works with which they are concerned less as literature than as new evidence of advance and achievement, to be shared and gloried in by all members of the race."[83] Still the opinion has been given that, everything considered, the propaganda in Negro literature is not altogether to be deplored, rather, a main objection is to the unskillful use of propaganda which has been such a marked characteristic of the race's literature. Thus in 1950 Nick Aaron Ford called for "the use of social propaganda subordinated so skillfully to the purposes of art that it will not insult the average intelligent reader."[84] Ford quoted Albert Guerard, Granville Hicks, and Tolstoi to bolster his assertion that propa-

ganda is a "legitimate ingredient of [all] serious literature."[85]
In the same vein, another critic opined recently:

> One of the great weaknesses of Negro fiction as
> a whole has been that its utopianism, like its propa-
> ganda and didacticism, has lacked sufficient guile as
> art. The Negro writer has tended to mix but two
> formulas in the expression of his interest in bringing
> to pass the brave new world. Either he has tried to
> paint the brave new world, or he has tried to show
> what that world is not.[86]

William Gardner Smith feels that being a Negro has a
number of compensations for the novelist. Because racial oppression weighs so heavily on the colored novelist, Smith feels
that his writings, "however poor artistically, must almost invariably contain some elements of social truth."[87] Because he is
"denied many freedoms, robbed of many rights, the Negro—
and the Negro writer—," asserts Smith, "rejects those aspects
of both American Capitalism and Russian Communism which
trample on freedoms and rights."[88] and thus he is capable of a
greater objectivity than is possible for most white writers who
are strict devotees of one or the other of these isms.   Smith
predicted in 1950 that a disproportionate percentage of the outstanding writers of the next decade would be Negroes.[89] Many
persons believe that the Negro's strong mooring in religion accounts for his passion for right, justice, and democracy. Also to
be reckoned with here, however, is the fact that in varying
degrees, at different periods of the nation's development, these
have been basic American passions, and to the Negro devotion to
these ideals has been, in part, a defensive mechanism. As Locke
stated: "There is, of course, a warrantably comfortable feeling
in being on the right side of the country's professed ideals. We
realize that we cannot be undone without America's undo-
ing."[90] "More and more," he stated, "an intelligent realization
of the great discrepancy between the American social creed
and the American social practice forces upon the Negro the
taking of the moral advantage that is his." Locke believed that
"Democracy itself is obstructed and stagnated to the extent
that any of its channels are closed," and that "the choice is not
between one way for the Negro and another way for the rest,

but between American institutions frustrated on the one hand and American ideals progressively fulfilled and realized on the other."[91]

Perhaps most observers of the race relations scene in the United States will agree that there is taking place, in this century, a veritable revolution in both the social position as well as the thought and attitudes of many colored Americans. The change in position has been from "isolation and attempted self-sufficiency to integration and the fight for a common humanity."[92] The change in attitude has been an abandonment of the Booker Washington philosophy of general acceptance of less than first class citizenship, but, as repeated often in this study, both the present position and attitude have long been goals of the race with which the militant tradition of the Negro never has compromised.

Evidence of the Negro's diminishing race consciousness is seen in William Gardner Smith's portrayal of G.I.'s doing occupation duty in post World War II Europe. Of this portrayal, Malcolm Cowley has noted that Smith's characters are "Americans before they are Negroes." On this point, Cowley continues:

> A foreigner might draw a curious lesson from *Last of the Conquerors*: that the two races in this country have developed identical cultures which are kept apart only by force and fear. Except when questions of race are involved, the Negroes act, speak and think exactly like the whites—and even write like them, so that one could read whole chapters of this novel without suspecting that they were written by a Negro about Negroes.[93]

With this diminishing race consciousness, which began to make itself manifest during the 1920's, there came a debate, sometimes rather heated, as to whether Negro writers should or can successfully abandon racial themes. Prominent among the "nayes" were the voices of Sterling Brown and other editors of the volume entitled *The Negro Caravan*. In this work, these editors stated: "Negro authors, as they mature, . . . must assume the responsibility of being the ultimate portrayers of their own." A number of Afro-Americans have criticized the writings of Frank Yerby as being superficial and lacking in the elements of true art. Although Yerby openly admits that he writes to please his audience and to gain sales, many of these critics contend that his "failure" to produce works of consummate art is proof of the inability of Negro writers to do high class work on non-racial themes. Persons who contend that these writers should abandon the racial theme contend that Afro-Americans need to prove that they can handle themes other than the "easy" ones of race, and that the preoccupation with racial subjects strengthens segregation and group consciousness, when integration and human consciousness should be the goals. Sterling Brown, Hugh Gloster, Nick Aaron Ford, and other outstanding Negro writers and critics feel that inasmuch as a person writes best about that which he knows best, this argument is misleading.[94] In the debate as to whether to abandon racial themes, Hugh Gloster casts a negative vote. He counsels, however, that colored novelists should not write solely about race. "To accept the principle that racial experience is the only natural province of the Negro writer," he avers, "is to approve an artistic double standard that is just as confining and demoralizing in American literature as is segregation in American life."[95]

The past three decades have seen a considerable increase in Negro magazines, both scholarly and lay. Some that were started in this period were the *Negro History Bulletin*, the *Negro College Quarterly*, the *Quarterly Review of Higher Education Among Negroes, Phylon*, the *Negro Digest, Ebony, Headlines, Our World, Color, Pep*, and *Bronze Confessions*. As to whether, in the face of growing racial integration, the Negro press should give up its narrow and militant race crusading, at least one observer has said: "Not yet."[96] This observer gives as his reason that, "the Negro community" in any given city is still "fully institutionalized." Thus, "the Negro newspaper must remain always partly exclusive in terms of the closed community which it serves."[97]

Like most other endeavors of the race, its fiction is still relatively young in its development. Thus, just as colored historians have not yet exploited adequately many themes in the race's past, so the novelists have left gaps in their coverage of life. Writing in 1941, the editors of *The Negro Caravan* noted these gaps as follows:

> The Negro working class, the various strata of the Negro middle class; urban life in both the South and North (outside Harlem) are some of [the neglected] areas. Even the fields covered—the rural South and Harlem—still call for interpreters. . . . There is little fiction dealing with College life, with the Negro professional class, with the Negro church, business, white-collar employment, or with Negroes in entertainment and athletics.[98]

Many observers have noted the general paucity of Negro literature in practically *all* areas. L. D. Reddick has opined that perhaps one explanation for this situation is that the colored community has an oral tradition. "Even Negro intellectuals," he notes, "tend to read and talk, rather than read and write."[99] G. Chandler Lewis has pointed out that the youthfulness of the race's literature is an explanation for many of its shortcomings.[100]

Among the better novels of the 1940's and 1950's were Willard Savoy's *Alien Land* (1949); Chester Himes' *Lonely Crusade* (1947); J. S. Redding's *Stranger and Alone* (1950; V. S. Reid's *New Day* (1950); Peter Abraham's *Wild Conquest* (1950); and William Gardner Smith's *Anger at Innocence* (1954). The works by Abraham and Reid continue the interest in fictionalizing history which was started during the period of the Harlem Renaissance and the 1930's. Alden Bland's *Behold A Cry* (1947), is the story of Ed Tyler's philanderings against a background of Chicago race riots and union organization. Sex is his "elixir of life" with his mistress Mamie, and Phom, his wife, and his kids. *Picketing Hell,* by Adam Clayton Powell, Sr. (1942), is a humorous story of a Negro minister, while Oscar Micheaux's *The Masquerade* (1947) is a miscegenation story very reminiscent of Chesnutt's *The House Behind the Cedars.* Among the best of works produced by Micheaux are his *The Wind from Nowhere* (1946), and *The Case of Mrs. Wingate* (1948). The latter story depicts a Georgia white woman who falls in love with a Negro barber, whom she sends to Harvard University, after which they marry and

live in New York. A story which treats of an interesting aspect of the lives of many urban Negroes is *The Policy King*
(1945), written by Lewis A. Caldwell. John Lee's *Counter
Clockwise* (1940), is the story of a mulatto female who, after
being rejected by her wealthy white lover, commits suicide,
while Willard Savoy's *Alien Land* (1948), is another story
that treats the theme of Negro's passing for white. Author of
the successful *The Street* (1946), Ann Petry followed that
story with *Country Place* (1947), a tale of love and romance
with a New England setting. Her next effort, *The Narrows*,
also had a New England and non-racial setting, while Zora
Neale Hurston's *Seraph on the Sewanee* is a love and romance
story which has a happier ending than *Country Place*.

Rising to prominence during the post-World War II period,
Frank Yerby represents a culmination of the long and steady
drift by colored Americans away from racial themes. With a
keen eye toward the likes and dislikes of the reading public,
Yerby has been more successful financially than any other
Negro novelist. His first work, *The Foxes of Harrow* (1946),
was a best-seller with Louisiana as the setting and was made
into a popular and successful movie. In rapid succession he has
followed this effort with *The Vixens* (1947), a tale from the
Reconstruction period; *Pride's Castle* (1949), which treats late
nineteenth century industrialism; *The Golden Hawk* (1947),
a story of Spanish buccaneering; *Floodtide* (1950), a Spanish-
American War background; and numerous other stories, all
highly successful. One of Yerby's first efforts to gain serious
attention, a story published in 1944 under the title of "'Health
Card," was a bitter and vehement denunciation of America's
prejudiced treatment of the Negro. Though his best-seller novels
are all on non-racial themes, a competent critic has noted that
"in all of his [Yerby's] non-racial writings he has substituted
a racial symbol, the symbol of rejection."[101]   On this point,
continues this critic—

> He finds in the social rebels of the white race, in men
> and women who because of birth, or manner of live-
> lihood, or disregard of social and moral properties have
> become pariahs among their own people, an archtype
> of racial rejection.   But these white rejectees fight

back. They build industrial empires, or pile up huge mountains of illicit wealth, or become swashbuckling pirates who defy the laws of the smug and the respectable.[102]

Hugh Gloster has expressed the general attitude of critics toward the novels of Frank Yerby. These works, Gloster observes, are "ideologically and esthetically unimportant but nevertheless noteworthy as the first series of best-seller triumphs by an American Negro in the field of general fiction."[103] Still another critic holds that his works are in the "tradition of nineteenth century romantic fiction, overwritten, turgid, and in its total effect, tends to reinforce aristocratic biases which should have died a century ago."[104]

Thomas D. Jarrett, able observer of Negro literature, feels that—"too much has been said about the Negro novelist's having come of age rather than about what is still required of him before he can attain maturity in the realm of fiction writing."[105] Jarrett concludes that "to date he [the Negro novelist] has not arrived," though "there are indications that he will arrive in the not too distant future." Writing in the same vein in 1953, Blyden Jackson concluded:

> Some day in America there may well be no Negro literature in the sense that there is now. Negroes will write about Negroes, or not write about them as the spirit moves—and as, indeed, they have already, in several notable instances, done—and it will be considered only a matter of the most passing interest. For, then, being a Negro will itself be only a matter of the most passing interest.[106]

Between 1930-1950 at least ten books of poetry by new Negro poets received "serious critical comment in leading literary magazines and columns."[107] Beginning with the late 1940's, this poetry has shown "an emphasis placed on technique rather than subject matter, and a moving toward intellectual themes of psychological and philosophical implications which border on obscurantism."[108] While the new poetry of the post-Depression period reflects America's growing concern with social problems, as witness even the title of Bruce McWright's *From the Shaken [Ivory] Tower,* Negro poets have not reflected in any pronounced way the post-World War II religious revival as it is portrayed by such verse-makers as Robert Lowell and W. H. Auden.[109] During the 1940's poetry by Afro-Americans continued to reflect the militancy and interest in broad social problems which had characterized the first Depression decade. Among the major publications of verse in this period were: Robert Hayden's, *Heart-Shape in the Dust* (1940); Margaret Walker's, *For My People* (1942); Melvin Tolson's, *Rendezvous with America* (1944); Gwendolyn Brook's, *A Street in Bronzeville* (1945); Rober Haydn and Myron O'Higgin's, *The Lion and the Archer* (1948); and Gwendolyn Brook's, *Annie Allen* (1949). With the latter work, Miss Brooks became the first American Negro writer of verse to win a Pulitzer prize. A "keynote" of Negro poetry in the 1950's has been the "global perspective."[110]

In drama, during the 1940's Richard Wright's *Native Son* was adapted for the stage. Also Langston Hughes adapted his story *Mulatto* to the stage in a play entitled "The Barrier," and Owen Dodson wrote "Divine Comedy" and "Bayou Legend." By 1960 Lorraine Hansberry's play, "A Raisin in the Sun," centered around events in the life of a Chicago Negro family, had become a major success and Langston Hughes was meeting with some success as a playwright. The Little Theater movement, centered in colleges, appeared to have lost momentum, and an able critic called the literary efforts of the movement's top figure, Randolph Edmonds, "turgid and loose, too much given to hackneyed situations and bombastic, set speeches."[111] This same critic deplored the dearth of dramatic writings by Negroes, and compared this paucity of effort with the success which white writers of the period were having with such plays as "Anna Lucasta," "Deep are the Roots," "St. Louis Woman," and "Lost in the Stars."

The growing success of Afro-Americans on the concert stage is seen in the fact that in 1954, Marian Anderson became the first colored person to sing a major role with the Metropolitan Opera Company, and Robert McFerrin, Ellabella Davis, Leontyne Price, and other singers were winning wide acceptance and acclaim. "A crude measure of their acceptance as major artists," writes Bardolph of Negro artists, "is afforded by the fact that by 1941 . . . . three Negroes (Marian Anderson, Paul Robeson, and Dorothy Maynor) were among the ten most highly paid concert artists in America, and a fourth (Roland Hayes, by then in his fifties) followed close behind."[112] Hopefully, the post-World War II period has seen a similar integration in practically every area of the nation's life, and this has caused colored Americans generally to feel that, for them, hence the nation unavoidably, the gap which has existed between the American ideal and reality is, in some ways, about to be bridged.

In a study published in 1944, W. T. Fontaine sought to ascertain whether social determination was evident in the writings of Negro scholars.[113] Specifically he wanted to know if there is any correlation between the knowledge and conclusions put forth by these scholars and the position which their race generally occupies in the social order. His answer was in the affirmative. Fontaine based his conclusion on an analysis of the scientific methods and conclusions about race of E. Franklin Frazier, Charles S. Johnson, Allison Davis, W. M. Cobb, Horace Mann Bond, Martin Jenkins, Carter G. Woodson, Charles Wesley, W. E. B. DuBois, L. D. Reddick, and Ernest E. Just. Fontaine declared that all of these writers were environmentalists to a large extent,, and that they utilized this approach because it rendered conclusions favorable to their race. Fontaine found that—

> The thought style of the parties of the Left was most frequently analytical.   These parties sought by a counter-thought to break down the morphological classifications [of "parties of the Right"] into units so as to recombine the units in a manner affording intellectual support for its social goals.[114]

All of the Negro scholars studied, Fontaine asserted, are environmentalists and analytical. They discount all morphological categories such as race, blood, race morality, and race soul. "The Negro scholar," he writes, "does not look upon the exceptional Negro as a sporadic incident; he is rather a sort of terminus toward which all Negroes are moving, some more retarded than others by environmental handicaps." "The relation of environment to 'defense' of race," he continues, "is made obvious by the fact that it enables ascription of the shortcomings of Negroes to external handicaps, and it counter attacks the arguments of those who point to innate capacity . . . As with the [Negro] biologist, so with the sociologist, anthrologist, educational psychologist, and historian, environmentalism holds sway."[115]Fontaine asserts that this "mental fix," often unconscious and determineed by "such psycho-social factors as resentment, aggression, rage, and a desire for equality," leads to the following epistemological consequences for the knowledge of Negro scholars:

1. Absence of the awareness and, consequently of the analysis of certain aspects of the problems that arise when experience is extended to comprehend the mentality of the opposite group.
2. An instantaneous and aggressive 'drive' to reject the opponent's knowledge even before considering its implications as support for the position of his group.
3. Failure to evaluate his conclusions critically and systematically from the perspective of the opponent . . .;
4. Preclusion from experience of a great vista of relevant data which, if not obtained by conscious, systematic role-taking, may come into experience only through laborious, random thinking.[116]

While he holds that recent scholars have outgrown the "narrow racist" perspective such as was characteristic of the imaginative writers of the "Negro Renaissance," Fontaine criticizes the efforts of twentieth century colored historians to bring about a reconstruction of history so as to give the race a more consequential place in it. "Preoccupation with a racially pointed 'reconstruction'," he holds, "blinds the historian to the fact that his extravagant praise of the trivial makes his knowledge as well as his group the easy target of the 'debunker.' . . . The historian would de better to 'paint his gray in gray' rather than in a false gold easily tarnished by the heart of satire."[117] "That the majority of Negro psychologists and social scientists are environmentalists," declared E. F. Frazier in rejoinder, "simply means that they have taken over the viewpoint prevailing to-day."[118] E. B. Reuter also attacked Fontaine's conclusions. "It is exceptional rather than usual," Reuter averred, "for students of social reality to rise to a truly objective level of analysis. [This] proposition assimilates the Negro scholar to rather than differentiates him from the current level of scholarly procedure."[119] Even more convincingly, Reuter wrote:

> It may very well be that the Negro scholar occupies the position that he does because the weight of evidence makes any other position untenable. The great majority of white scholars occupy substantially the same position . . . In the absence of conclusive evidence, we may not assume that white scholars reach a position on the basis of evidence and that Negro scholars reach the same position because of their social bias. This is not to deny that there are many Negro students who are unable to recognize and discount their biases, but the Negro group has no monopoly on undisciplined and incompetent scholars.[120]

In recent decades, many persons have written and talked conspicuously of the state of maturity of the Negro mind, but only in broad outline have these persons hinted at what their criteria of maturity are, and the criteria indicated does not encompass the totality of indices of maturity of even such a popular work as H. A. Overstreet's, *The Mature Mind*. Furthermore, among Negro critics too little attention seems to have been given to consideration of the extent to which the larger *American mind is yet mature*. For just as it is recognized that a whole is equal to the sum of its parts, it is as much accepted that seldom is a part greater than the whole. In 1954 Henry Steele Commager wrote that American civilization had become 'urban, but it was not yet an urbane civilization."[121] Further, he stated: "That the American mind was more mature in the midtwentieth than in the mid-nineteenth or even the mid-eighteenth century was by no means clear."[122] Yet, viewed by any criteria, as would be expected, the Afro-American still reveals some cultural shortcomings, one of which is the paucity of good novels, plays, poems, musical compositions, paintings, and other works of art created and enjoyed, and the still oftentimes too narrow concern with race. Growing out of this, in part, is the lack of original. contribution in such areas as economic, political, historical, or philosophical theory. Not only has there been almost no original contribution in these areas, but there has been a strong neglect of them. Even intellectuals among Afro-Americans have done considerably less discussing of such matters as Kantism, Darwinism, Marxism, the Single Tax, tariff, or Turner's Frontier Thesis than has been the case with the majority race. Too, by 1960 perhaps not a dozen Afro-Americans had earned the doctorate degree in either Economics, Geography, Anthropology, Philosophy, Mathematics, or Physics, and, apart from the field of Education, it is probable that in no single academic discipline had as many as fifty Negroes earned this degree.

Atlanta University through its scholarly journal *Phylon,* was endeavoring to present an annual resumé and critique of the literature produced by Afro-Americans. Each year these critiques, written largely by professors of English literature, gave a commendable picture of the tortuous progress of the Negro novel and commented on the considerable lack of effort being made by Negroes where poetry and playwriting is concerned. Of the novelists the total impression given by the resumés is that, compared with the 1920s and thirties, apart from the continuing efforts of such established writers as Richard Wright, Willard Motley and Frank Yerby, the novel as produced by Negroes since 1945 was in the doldrums. A serious weakness of the critiques was the failure to give adequate attention to the scholarly writings by Negroes, as it was largely in the area of scholarly writing that distinctive literary works were being produced by Afro-Americans in the fifties. In the field of History Rayford Logan's, *The Negro in American Life and Thought,* Benjamin Quarles', *The Negro in the Civil War,*[123] and John Hope Franklin's, *The Militant South* were particularly noteworthy efforts, while perhaps the present writer's *The Desertion of Man: A Critique of Philosophy of History*[125] introduced a new dimension to historical writings by Negroes. Also of noteworthy distinctiveness was the praiseworthy analysis of the history and nature of capitalism by Olivier C. Cox.[126] In the field of English leading publishers brought out textbooks by Nick Aaron Ford and Edward Farrison, Hugh Gloster, and N. Tillman, which constituted a new dimension of achievement for Negro scholars in this area.

An evidence of the Afro-American's efforts to live up to

the best in American culture may be seen not only in the membership of persons in the nation's scholarly associations, but also in the development of segregated scholarly and professional organizations. Just as the Negro church, business, and other areas have felt the need to organize into district, state, regional, and national groups, so have Negro teachers, scholars, and other professional persons. At the national level such groups as the National Teachers Association, Association of Social Science Teachers, Association for the Study of Negro Life and History, Negro Medical Association, Negro Dental Association, and the national guild of Negro lawyers were by the 1950s almost a half-century old, and the integration trend was having no noticeable negative effect on the size of their membership or the quality of their annual programs. These organizations had never confined their interests and activities to their professions, but ever had included efforts to raise Negro citizenship to the plane of equality. Despite this "distraction" from their central pursuits, through learned papers, discussions, and publications these organizations have been significant means of stimulating and elevating the Negro professional man and enriching the professional and cultural life of the nation. Because race prejudice has too often caused the Negro scholar and professional man to be refused a hearing by the larger community, by giving an opportunity for expression in their meetings, discussions, and journals, these organizations have kept the Afro-American from being as cramped and thwarted in his development as he otherwise might have been. Indeed, these meetings and journals have served as similar outlets for many white scholars and professional persons, both beginners and the well-established.

FOOTNOTES

INTRODUCTION

THE· TASK

[1] New York: Harcourt, Brace, 1939.

[2] New Haven: Yale University Press, 1950.

[3] New York: A. A. Knopf, 1951

[4] On this practice, see the volume *A History of Civilization*, Brinton, et. alia., (New York. Prentice Hall, 1955).

[5] Cf. rev. ed., Boston: Houghton-Mifflin, 1940.

[6] London: Macmillan, 1920.

[7] Carl Becker, *The Heavenly City of the Eighteenth Century Philosophes* (New Haven: Yale University Press, 1932).

[8] New Haven: Yale University Press, 1950.

[9] New York: Harpers, 1943.

[10] New York: Ronald Press, 1940.

[11] New York: Prentice-Hall, 1950.

[12] Chicago: University of Chicago Press, 1939.

[13] New York: Vanguard Press, 1927.

[14] New York: Columbia University Press, 1931.

[15] Washington, D. C.: Associated Publishers, 1940.

[16] Washington, D. C.: Associates in Negro Folk Education, 1936.

[17] Earl E. Thorpe,·*Negro Historians in the United States* (Baton Rouge, La.: Fraternal Press, 1958).

[18] See Carter Woodson, *History of the Negro Church* (Washington, D. C.: Associated Publishers, 1921.·

[19] See Langston Hughes and Arna Bontemps, eds., *The Poetry of the Negro* (New York: Doubleday, 1939), and James Weldon Johnson, ed., *The Book of American Negro Poetry* (New York: Harcourt, Brace, 1931). There are a number of anthologies in this area.

[20] See Horace Mann Bond, *The Education of the Negro in the American Social Order* (New York: Prentice-Hall, 1934).

[21] Washington, D. C.: Associated Publishers, 1926.

[22] New York: Citadel Press, 1950.

[23] New York: Cornell University Press.

[24] R. Bardolph, "The Distinguished Negro in America, 1770-1936," *American Historical Review*, Vol. 60, No. 3, April, 1955, p. 527.

[25] Ibid.

[26] Ibid.

[27] Robert Anderson, *From Slavery to Affluence*: *Memories of Robert Anderson, Ex-Slave* (Hemingsford, Nebraska: 1927).

[28] Cf. his *The Negro Family in the United States*, revised and abridged ed. (New York: Citadel Press, 1948), Chs. 13, 15, 16, 17, and 18.

CHAPTER I

THE FRONTIER AND SLAVERY

[1] See, for example, Pieter Geyl, "The American Civil War and the Problem of Inevitability," in his *Debates with Historians* (New York: Philosophical Library, 1956).

[2] For related viewpoints, see F. J. Turner, *The Frontier in American History* (New York: Henry Holt, 1921); Walter P. Webb, *The Great Frontier* (Boston: Houghton Mifflin, 1952), and the same author's "The World Frontier," in *The Frontier in Perspective*, Walker D. Wyman and Clifton B. Kroeber, eds. (Madison: University of Wisconsin Press, 1957), pp. 115-116. Just as the Turner Thesis suggested the Webb Thesis, so is the present writer indebted to Webb for suggesting many of the ideas presented in this essay.

[3] Eric Williams, *Capitalism and Slavery* (Chapel Hill: University of North Carolina Press, 1944).

[4] See his, "The World Frontier," *loc. cit.*.

[5] In his *Capitalism and Slavery*, p. 29.

[6] *Ibid.*, p. 7.

[7] U. B. Phillips, *Life and Labor in the Old South* (Boston: Little. Brown, 1929), p. 25.

[8] In his "The Southern Frontier, an Interpretation," Professor T. P. Abernethy seems to be guilty of the short view. (See Wyman and Kroeber, eds., *The Frontier in Perspective*, pp. 129-142.)

[9] Walter P. Webb, *The Great Frontier*, p. 82.

[10] Herbert Aptheker, *Negro Slave Revolts* (New York: Columbia University Press, 1943).

[11] It may be doubted whether such a degree of prosperity could have been achieved by an essentially agrarian society.

[12] Adam Smith, *The Wealth of Nations* (New York: 1937), p. 365.

[13] Webb, *The Great Frontier*, p. 49.

[14] *Ibid.*, pp. 49-50.

[15] Eric Williams, *Capitalism and Slavery*, p. 7.

[16] Walter P. Webb, *The Great Frontier*, chapter on "The Prospect of a Corporate Individualism."

[17] Geoffrey Barraclough, *History in a Changing World* (Norman, Oklahoma: University of Oklahoma Press, 1955), p. 149.

[18] *Ibid.*, p. 152.

[19] *Ibid.*, p. 183.

[20] Wilbur J. Cash, *The Mind of the South* (New York: A. A. Knopf, 1941).

[21] For one aspect of this truth, see Miles Mark Fisher, *Negro Slave Songs* (New York: Cornell University Press, 1949).

[22] See Earl E. Thorpe, "Frederick Douglass, Booker Washington, and W. E. B. DuBois," *Negro History Bulletin*, January, 1957; and the same

author's, "The Booker Washington—W. E. B. DuBois Controversy," *Quarterly Review of Higher Education Among Negroes*, October, 1955.

[23] Pieter Geyl, *Debates With Historians*, pp. 216-217.

[24] *Ibid.*, See also H. R. Floan, *The South in Northern Eyes*, 1832-1861 (Austin: University of Texas Press, 1958).

CHAPTER II

AFRICA IN THE THOUGHT OF NEGRO AMERICANS /

[1] E. Franklin Frazier, *Black Bourgeoisie* (Glence, Ill.: The Free Press, 1957), p. 235.

[2] Margaret Just Butcher, *The Negro in American Culture*. Mentor Book (New York: New American Library, 1957), p. 220.

[3] *Ibid.*, p. 19 Since by this date Jeefferson already had taken strong stands against slavery, as in the Northwest Ordinance, it may be doubted that this letter had an original influence in moulding his liberalism. Rather, both Banneker and Jefferson (and Phillis Wheatley) were products of the European Enlightenment which was anti-slavery.

[4] Herbert C. Renfro, *Life and Works of Phyllis Wheatley*, (Washington, D. C.: Robert L. Pendleton, 1916), p. 27. See also Benjamin Mays, *The Negro's God*, (Boston: Chapman and Grime, 1938), p. 104; E. D. Seeber "Phyllis Wheatley," *Journal of Negro History*, XXIV, July, 1939, pp. 259-262; *Dictionary of American Biography*, XX, p. 36; William Wells Brown, *The Black Man* (New York, 1863), pp. 138ff.

[5] H. G. Renfro, *op. cit.*, p. 27.

[6] Cf. Arthur P. Davis, "Personal Elements in the Poetry of Phyllis Wheatley," *Phylon*, 2nd Qtr., 1953, pp. 191-198.

[7] *Ibid.*

Chapel Hill: University of North Carolina Press.

[9] Margaret Just Butcher, *op. cit.*

[10] New York: Cornell University Press, 1953.

[11] E. Franklin Frazier, *The Negro Family in the United States*, rev. and abridged ed. (New York: Citadel Press, 1948), p. 15. For some contrary evidence see Newbell Puckett, *Folk Beliefs of the Southern Negro* (Chapel Hill: University of North Carolina Press, 1926).

[12] Kenneth Stampp, *The Peculiar Institution* (New York Knopf, 1956), p. 363.

[13] Ibid.

[14] *Ibid.*, p. 362.

[15] Alain Locke, "Who and What is a Negro," *Opportunity*, March, 1942.

[16] Wilson Record, *The Negro and the Communist Party* (Chapel Hill: University of North Carolina Press).

[17] Quoted in Vernon Loggins, *The Negro Author* (New York: Columbia University Press, 1931), p. 54.

[18] See Earl E. Thorpe, *Negro Historians in the United States* (Baton Rouge, Louisiana: Fraternal Press, 1958), Chapter II.

[19] *Freedom's Journal*, New York, March 16, 1827.

[20] Quoted in Carter G. Woodson, *Negro Orators and Their Orations* (Washington, D. C.: The Associated Publishers, 1925), p. 36.

[21] Ibid., p. 33.

[22] Ibid., p. 628.

[23] Quoted in Herbert Aptheker, ed. *Documentary History of the American Negro* (New York: Citadel Press, 1951), p. 71.

[24] Ibid., Section IIff.

[25] Bishop W. T. Vernon, in address before the Kansas Day Club, 1905, quoted in C. G. Woodson, *Negro Orators and Their Orations*, p. 618.

[26] Ibid., p. 76.

[27] J. Sella Martin, in Woodson, *Negro Orators*, p. 261.

[28] Cf. Earl E. Thorpe, Op. Cit., pp. 30ff.

[29] George W. Williams, *History of the Negro Troops in the War of the Rebellion*, 1861-1865 (New York: Harpers, 1888), p. 363.

[30] Cf. Wright, *The Free Negro in Maryland*, p. 325.

[31] See, for example, letter written by Abraham Camp, An Illinois free Negro on July 13, 1818, to Elias Caldwell, Secretary of the Colonization Society, reprinted in Aptheker, *Documentary History*, p. 70.

[32] Ibid., p. 70.

[33] Ibid., p. 71.

[34] Cf. M. M. Fisher, *Negro Slave Songs*, pp. 111-113ff.

[35] In C. Woodson, ed.., *Negro Orators*, p. 52.

[36] Ibid., p. 53.

[37] Theodore S. Wright addressing New York State Antislavery Society, September 20, 1837, quoted in C. Woodson, ed., *Negro Orators*, p. 88.

[38] Ibid., p. 90.

[39] In *The Liberator*, February 14, 1862.

[40] Ibid., September 22, 1932.

[41] Ibid., February 12, 1831.

[42] Published by the author in Philadelphia in 1852. Delany was the co-founder and assistant editor of Frederick Douglass' *North Star*.

[43] *The Liberator*, March 5, 1852.

[44] See *Congressional Record*, 49th Cong., 1st Sess., p. 3138.

[45] In J. W. E. Bowen, ed., *Africa and the American Negro* (Atlanta: 1896), pp. 195-197.

[46] Perhaps the contempt for their spirituals and other folk art and literature by Negroes reveals no basic contempt for Africa, but is a universal reaction to folk literature and art. Because of "its disingenuous simplicity," declares Alain Locke, "folk art is always despised and rejected at first; but generations after, it flowers again and transcends the level of its origin."

(In his *The New Negro,* New York: Albert and Charles Boni, 1925, p. 199).

[47] See the discussion of these Congresses in W. E. B. DuBois, *Dusk of Dawn* (New York: Harcourt Bace, 1940); and comment on them in Mordecai W. Johnson's Havard University Commencement Address, delivered June 22, 1922, quoted in C. G. Woodson, ed., *Negro Orators and Their Orations,* p. 661. .

[48]2Langston Hughes, *The Big Sea; An Autobiography* (New York: Knopf, 1940), p. 325.

[49] See his poems "The Return," and "Bethesda," for example.

[50] Carter G. Woodson, *Miseducation of the Negro* (Washington, D. C.: Associated Publishers), p. 1.

[51] St. Clair Drake and Horace R. Cayton, *Black Metropolis* (New York: Harcourt, Brace, 1945), pp. 751ff; Gunnar Myrdal, *An American Dilemma* (New York: Harpers, 1944), p. 748; E. F. Frazier, *Black Bourgeoisie,* p. 235.

[52] Cf. E. F. Frazier, *Black Bourgeoisie;* Gunnar Myrdal, *op. cit.*

[53] Quoted in Carter G. Woodson, ed., *op. cit.,* pp. 605-606

[54] New York, Dodd, Mead, 1937.

[55] See address by William Hamilton to the New York African Society, delivered January 2, 1809, quoted in Aptheker, *Documentary History,* p. 53.

[56] R. R. Moton, *What the Negro Thinks,* p. 239.

[57] *The Liberator,* February 25, 1842.

[58] Speech before Legislative Committee of the Massachusetts House of Representatives, quoted in *The Liberator,* February 25, 1842.

[59] *Proceedings* of this Convention (Pittsburgh: 1854).

[60] Hugh Gloster, *Negro Voices in American Fiction* (Chapel Hill: University of North Carolina Press), p. 256.

[61] *What the Negro Thinks,* pp. 234-235.

[62] *Sketches of the Higher Classes of Colored Society in Philadelphia* (1841), p. 13.

[63] From 1856 address of Negroes to the Ohio Senate and House of Representatives.

[64] *Freedom's Journal,* New York, March 16, 1827.

[65] David Walker, *Appeal,* p. 15. See also Rebecca C. Barton, *Race Consciousness and the American Negro* (Copenhagen, Denmark: 1934); and Sterling A. Brown, "The American Race Problem as Reflected in American Literature," *Journal of Negro Education,* VIII, July, 1939, pp. 275-290.

[66] See, for example, Edward Smythe Jones' poem, "An Ode to Ethiopia: To the Aspiring Negro Youth," and John Hope Franklin's discussion of Negro reaction to Mussolini's invasion of Ethiopia in his *From Slavery to Freedom* (New York: A. A. Knopf, 1947).

[67] Washington, D. C.: Associated Publishers, 1936.

[68] Washington, D. C.: Associated Publishers, 1939.

[69] Charles Wesley, "The Reconstruction of History," *Journal of Negro History*, XX, 4, October, 1935, pp. 421-22.

[70] New York: Henry Holt, 1915.

[71] New York: Harcourt, Bruce, 1939.

[72] New York: Viking Press, 1947.

[73] W. E. B. DuBois, *The World and Africa*, p. vii.

[74] George Schuyler, *Slaves Today* (New York: Brewer, Warren and Putnam).

[75] Cf. Earl E. Thorpe, *Negro Historians in the United States*, Ch. VI.

[76] New York: Harpers, 1954.

[77] New York: Doubleday, 1954.

[78] Margaret Just Butcher, *The Negro in American Culture*, p. 166.

CHAPTER III

SOME ATTITUDES OF NEGROES TOWARD SLAVERY
AND FREEDOM

[1] 1843 address of Henry Highland Garnet to American slaves, see either Carter G. Woodson, ed., *Negro Orators and Their Orations* (Washington, D. C.; Associated Publishers, 1925) or Herbert Aptheker, ed., *Documentary History of the American Negro* (New York: Citadel Press, 1951).

[2] See H. Aptheker, op. cit., p. 317.

[3] Hosea Easton, *A Treatise on the Intellectual Character, and Civil and Political Condition of the Colored People of the United States* (Boston: 1837), p. 33.

[4] Henry Highland Garnet, while pastor of the Fifteenth Street Presbyterian Church in Washington, D. C., delivered an address in the House of Representatives at the request of the Chaplain, Reverend William H. Channing. This note is an excerpt reproduced in Alice Moore Dunbar, *Masterpieces of Negro Eloquence* (New York: The Bookery Publishing Co., 1914), pp. 110ff.

[5] C. G. Woodson, ed., *op. cit.*, p. 15.

[6] Ibid.

[7] Quoted in *The Liberator*, Nov. 19, 1841.

[8] Ibid.

[9] Ibid., May 29, 1846.

[10] Frederick Douglas, *My Bondage and My Freedom* (New York: 1855), Appendix.

[11] In C. Woodson, ed., *op. cit.*, p. 553.

[12] *Ibid.*, p. 490.

[13] *Ibid.*, p. 64ff.

[14] Margaret Just Butcher, *The Negro in American Culture*, paperback ed., p. 15.

[15] In C. Woodson, ed., *op. cit.*, p. 65.

[16] In *The Liberator*, July 9, 1841.

[17] Frederick Douglass, *op. cit.*

[18] *The Liberator*, May 29, 1846.

[19] *Ibid.*

[20] *Ibid.*

[21] *Ibid.*

[22] *Ibid.*

[23] See H. Aptheker, ed., *op. cit.*, p. 231.

[24] Cf. letter by Douglass to his former master, in *The Liberator*, Sept. 22, 1848.

[25] Letter from William Wells Brown, London, England to Enoch Price, St. Louis, Missouri, printed in *The Liberator*, Dec. 14, 1849.

[26] Hosea Easton, *op. cit.*, p. 43.

[27] In C. Woodson, ed., *op. cit.*, p. 86.

[28] Fisk University, *Unwritten History of Slavery*, Social Science Documents (Nashville, Tennessee, 1945), p. 295.

[29] *Ibid.*, p. 259.

[30] In his *Up From Slavery*, pp. 7-15.

[31] B. A. Botkin, ed.., *Lay My Burden Down* (Chicago, Illinois: University of Chicago Press, 1945), pp. 187-188.

[32] Fisk University, *op. cit.*, p. 12.

[33] B. A. Botkin, ed., *op. cit.*, pp. 223-224.

[34] *Ibid.*, p. 226.

[35] Quoted in T. W. Knox, *Camp-Fire and Cotton-Field*, p. 373.

[36] C. Woodson, ed., *op. cit.*, p. 518.

[37] In *Congressional Record*, 51 Cong., 2 Sess., pp. 1479-1483.

[38] C. Woodson, ed., *op. cit.*, p. 492.

[39] *Ibid.*, p. 74.

CHAPTER IV

NEGRO THOUGHT ON CRUELTY AND PLEASURE DURING BONDAGE

[1] Miles Mark Fisher, *Negro Slave Songs in the United States* (New York: Cornell University Press, 1953), p. 137.

[2] *Narrative of the Life and Adventures of Henry Bibb, an American Slave*, p. 175.

[3] Kenneth Stampp, *The Peculiar Institution* (New York: A. A. Knopf, 195), p. 99.

[4] Fisk University, *Unwritten History of Slavery*, Social Science Documents (Nashville, Tennessee, 1945), p. 300.

[5] *Ibid.*, p. 216. .

[6] See B. A. Botkin, ed., *Lay My Burden Down* (Chicago, Illinois: University of Chicago Press, 1945), pp. 164, 165, 194, 195.

[7] Fisk University, *op. cit.*, p. 276.

[8] *Ibid.*, p. 161.

[9] *Ibid.*, p. 95. .

[10] *Ibid.*, p. 118, 276.

[11] B. A. Botkin, ed., *op. cit.*, and Fisk University, *op. cit.*, p. 262.

[12] B. A. Botkin, ed., *op. cit.*, p. 169. .

[13] *Ibid.*, p. 288; Fisk University, *op. cit.*, pp. 31, 45, 193.

[14] *Ibid.*, p. 129.

[15] *The Liberator*, September 22, 1848.

[16] Fisk University, *op, cit.*, p. 185.

[17] B. A. Botkin, ed., *op. cit.*, p. 185.

[18] Fisk University, *op. cit.*, p. 131.

[19] *Ibid.*, p.. 197.

[20] See Herbert Aptheker, *American Negro Slave Revolts* (New York: Columbia University Press, 1943), p. 513.

[21] Frederick Douglass, *My Bondage and My Freedom*, p. 264.

[22] Kenneth Stampp, *op. cit.*, p. 100.

[23] *Ibid.*, esp. Ch. III, "A Troublesome Property."

[24] See also Raymond A. and Alice H. Bauer, "Day to Day Resistance to Slavery," *Journal of Negro History*, XXVII, 1942, pp. 388-419; Herbert Aptheker, *op. cit.*, Ch. VI.

[25] K. Stampp, *op. cit.*, p. 108. See also Harriet Martineau, *Society in America* (New York: 1937), II, p. 113; Drew, *The Refugee*, p. 1781.

[26] K. Stampp, *op. cit.*, p. 92.

[27] Cf. her *Journal of a Residence on a Georgia Plantation in 1838*, p. 379. Frederick L. Olmsted made a similar observation in his *A Journey in the Back Country*, p. 474.

[28] See Herbert Aptheker, *Documentary History of the American Negro* (New York: Citadel Press, 1951), pp. 1, 4, 5, 12, 14ff.

[29] Fisk University, *op. cit.*, pp. 263, 264, 268; B. A. Botkin, ed., *Lay My Burden Down*, pp. 122, 269.

[30] Fisk University, *op. cit.*, p. 155.

[31] *Ibid.*, p. 132.

[32] *Ibid.*, pp. 95, 97.

[33] *Ibid.*, p. 278.

[34] *Ibid.*, p. 295.

[35] *Ibid.*, p. 143.

[36] B. A. Botkin, ed., *op. cit.*, p. 126.

[37] Fisk University, *op. cit.*, pp. 84, 191.

[38] *Ibid.*, p. 207.

[39] B. A. Botkin, ed., *op. cit.*, pp. 60, 119-20, 179.

[40] *Ibid.*, p. 172.

[42] Kenneth Stampp, *op. cit.*, p. 361.

[41] Fisk University, *op. cit.*, p. 187, 229-230.

[43] *Ibid.*, p. 364.

[44] *Ibid.*

[45] *Ibid.*, p. 370.

[46] *Ibid.*, p. 361.

[47] *Ibid.*, pp. 333-34.

[48] Cf. Northrup, *Twelve Years A Slave*, pp. 186ff. .

[49] Frederick Douglass, *op. cit.*, p. 118.

[50] Steward, *Twenty-two Years A Slave*, p. 101.

[51] Frederick Douglass, *op. cit.*, pp. 69-72, 74-75, and 129-32.

[52] Fannie Kemble, *op. cit.*, p. 239.

[53] Wilbur J. Cash, *The Mind of the South* (New York: A. A. Knopf, 1944); John Hope Franklin, *The Militant South* (Cambridge: Harvard University Press, 1956).

CHAPTER V

HOSTILITY, REVENGE, AND PROTEST AS ELEMENTS IN NEGRO THOUGHT

[1] Revenge as an element in Negro thought is the major concern of the present treatise. The complicated nature of the picture of Negro aggression and revenge can be seen in part when the question is asked—"Revenge against whom?", for this revenge is sometimes aimed at the southern white man, sometimes all whites, sometimes at "the South," sometimes at "the nation," or Jews and other minority groups, and even at members of the Negro group. Herein we have not always attempted to designate the exact object or objects of the revenge, and obviously we have not dealt with that purely private revenge which has no discernible connection with the historic social circumstances of the Negro masses. Of Negro aggression, Charles S. Johnson once wrote: "The different types of hostility may be classified as personal hostility, group hostlity, and impersonal hostility." (in his *Patterns of Negro Segregation*. New York: Harpers, 1943, p. 294).

[2] John Fiske, *Old Virginia and Her Neighbors*, II, p. 196.

[3] James Schouler, *History of the United States Under the Constitution*, II (New York: Dodd Mead, 1894-1913), rev. ed., op. 264-67.

[4] See J. G. Randall, *The Civil War and Reconstruction* (Boston: D. C. Heath, 1937), p. 53; Claude H. Van Tyne, *The War of Independence* (Boston: Houghton Mifflin, 1929), p. 203; Ulrich B. Phillips, *The Course of the South to Secession*, p. 10, and his *Life and Labor in The Old South* (Boston: Little Brown, 1929), p. 196, and his *American Negro Slavery* (New York: D. Appleton, 1918), p. 341. See also Appendix of W. E B. DuBois, *Black Reconstruction* (New York: Harcourt Brace, 1935).

[5] John Dollard, *Caste and Class in a Southern Town* (New York: Doubleday, 1957), 3d ed., p. 293.

[6] Herbert Aptheker, *American Negro Slave Revolts* (New York: Columbia University Press, 1943).

[7] Martin R. Delany, *The Condition, Elevation, Emancipation and Destiny of the Colored People of the United States, Politically Considered* (Philadelphia: the author, 1852).

[9] Herbert Aptheker, *American Negro Slave Revolts* (New York: Columbia Univerosity Press, 1943).

[10] Wilson Record, *The Negro and the Communist Party* (Chapel Hill: University of North Carolina Press, 1953).

[11] *Congressional Globe*, 41 Cong., 2 Sess., Pt. 3, pp. 1986ff.

[12] Quoted in Carter G. Woodson, ed., *Negro Orators and their Orations* (Washington, D. C.: Associated Publishers, 1926), p. 622; hereinafter referred to as *Negro Orators*.

[13] *Ibid.*

[14] New York: Harpers.

[15] Benjamin Mays, *The Negro's God* (Boston: Chapman and Grimes, 1938), pp. 24-25.

[16] Robert R. Moton, *What the Negro Thinks* (New York: Doubleday, 1929), p. 64.

[17] *Ibid.*, p. 27.

[18] In Mason Crum, *Gullah: Negro Life in the Carolina Sea Islands* (Durham: 1940), p. 80.

[19] In Kenneth Stampp, *The Peculiar Institution* (New York: Knopf, 1956), p. 88.

[20] *Ibid.*, p. 99, quoting *The Farmer's Register*, V (1837), p. 32.

[21] Hortense Powdermaker, "Channeling the Negro's Aggressions," *American Journal of Sociology* (May, 1943), pp. 754-756. Powdermaker calls the recent dying out of this meek type of Negro "a psychological revolution" which has been brought about by such factors as decline of religious faith among Negroes, rising literacy, emergence of alternative patterns of behavior through labor unions, political action, and protest oganizations, and the fact that in an industial-urban economy, as against the old rural pattern, whites can no longer offer the same degree of economic security as a reward for subservience.

[22] One of the best books on Negro history is entitled *From Slavery to Freedom.*

[23] Gunnar Myrdal, *An American Dilemma* (New York: Harpers, 1944), p. 763. Edgar Thompson has written—"Punishment and the frustration of normal human wishes generated hatred and bitterness in the slave." (In his *Race Relations and the Race Problem*. Durham, N. C.: Duke University Press, 1939, p. 131).

[24] Arnold M. Rose, *The Negro's Morale: Group Identification and Protest* (Minneapolis: University of Minnesota Press, 1949), p. 112.

[25] *Ibid.* See also Gordon Allport, *The Nature of Prejudice* (Boston: Beacon Press, 1954).

[26] Helen V. McLean, "Race Prejudice," *American Journal of Ortho-*

psychiatry, XIV, 4, Oct. 1944, p. 71. Hortense Powdermaker states that Negroes "would be abnormal" if they did not hate whites. She declares that the Negro "lives in an interracial situation which is a constant stimulus to aggressive thoughts and fantasies." (In her "Channeling the Negro's Aggressions," *loc. cit.,* p. 754),

[27] John Dollard, *Caste and Class in a Southern Town,* p. 267.

[28] In Arnold M. Rose, ed., *Race Prejudice and Discrimination* (New York: Knopf, 1953), pp. 278-280.

[29] On p. 131 of his *Race Relations and the Race Problem,* Edgar Thompson has observed that Negro crimes against whites have "aroused the fear and the racial antagonism of the whites to a high pitch."

[30] See section "Boomerangs From the Urge to Revenge," below.

[31] John Hope Franklin has noted: "The times that overseers and masters were killed by slaves in the woods or fields were exceedingly numerous, as the careful reading of almost any Southern newspaper will reveal." (in his *From Slavery to Freedom,* New York: Knopf, 1956 ed., p. 207).

[32] "Self-mutilation and suicide were popular forms of resistance to slavery" declares John Hope Franklin. (*Ibid.,* p. 206). Suicide by starving or drowning or hanging appear to have been most popular forms used. Slaves had no real access to guns. Modern psychiatry knows that there is an element of revenge in suicide. (See Karl Menninger, *Man Against Himself.* New York: Harcourt Brace, 1938).

[33] See Booker T. Washington, *A New Negro for A New Century,* p. 206.

[34] Robert T. Kerlin, ed., *Negro Poets and their Poems* (Washington, D. C.: Associated Publishers, 1935), p. 9.

[35] A major reason for the persistence of the secret meetings lies in the fact that slaves were happiest away from members of the dominant group.

[36] Karl Menninger affirms this view, while quarreling with Sigmund Freud's theory of the origin and nature of religion. (See K. Menninger, *Love Against Hate,* pp. 190-191).

[37] For example, almost each week in the *Pittsburgh Courier* Ollie Harrington's "Bootsie" places some act or thought of prejudiced whites in a ridiculously humorous pose.

[38] Arnold Rose, *The Negro's Morale,* p. 117. See also John H. Burma, "Humor as a Technique in Race Conflict" *American Sociological Review,* XI, Dec., 1946; Hortense Powdermaker, "Channeling the Negro's Aggressions," p. 753; Langston Hughes, *The Best of Negro Humor* (Chicago: Negro Digest, 1945).

[39] Cf. Bernard E. Wolfe, "Uncle Remus and the Malevolent Rabbit," *Commentary,* VIII, 1, July, 1949, pp. 31-41; Sterling Brown, "Negro Folk Expression," *Phylon,* XI 4th Qtr., 1950, pp. 322-23; R. Bradford, *Ol Man Adam An' His Chillun* (New York: 1928).

[40] Arnold Rose, *The Negro's Morale,* p. 19.

[41] *Ibid.,* p. 20.

[42] B. E. Wolfe, "Uncle Remus and the Malevolent Rabbit," *loc. cit.,* p. 38.

[43] See A. Davis, et alia, *Deep South*, p. 396, and *Mississippi Valley Historical Review*, XXIII, pp. 55-74.

[44] See Mrs. Guion Johnson, *Ante-Bellum North Carolina* (Chapel Hill: University of North Carolina Press, 1937), p. 496; W. P. Harrison, *The Gospe Among Slaves* (Nashville: 1893), p. 103.

[45] Quoted in K. Stampp *op. cit.*, p. 98.

[46] *Ibid..*, p. 125.

[47] *Ibid.*

[48] From a "Letter to the American Slaves," statement adopted by a New York Convention of fugitive slaves, Sept., 1850 in response to the Fugitive Slave Act which had just been passed by Congress.

[49] *The Liberator*, Sept. 22, 1848.

[50] *Ibid.*, April 27, 1860.

[51] Hortense Powdermaker, "Channeling the Negro's Aggression," p. 75.

[52] In W. D. Weatherford and C. S. Johnson, *Race Relations* (New York: 1934), p. 265.

[53] In Alice Moore Dunbar Nelson, ed., *Masterpieces of Negro Eloquence* (New York: Bookery Pub. Co., 1914), p. 42.

[54] *The Liberator*, July 10, 1857.

[55] Carter G. Woodson, ed., *Negro Orators*, p. 65.

[56] From speech by Douglass' in Boston, reprinted in *The Liberator*, June 8, 1849.

[57] From resolution adopted Sept. 17, 1850 in Springfield, Massachusetts, printed in *The Liberator*, Oct. 4, 1850.

[58] *Ibid.*

[59] Frederick Douglass, *Lectures on American Slavery by Frederick Douglass* (Buffalo: 1851).

[60] Frederick Douglass, *My Bondage and My Freedom* (New York: Miller, Orton and Mulligan, 1855), p. 191.

[61] *The Liberator*, June 8, 1849.

[62] In H. Aptheker, ed., *Doc. Hist.*, p. 319.

[63] *The Liberator*, April 10, 1857, and May 18, 1860.

[64] *Ibid.*

[65] *Ibid.*, July 10, 1857.

[66] *Ibid.*, Aug. 13, 1858.

[67] *Ibid.*

[68] Speech given at 1843 National Negro Convention, Buffalo, New York.

[69] See Carter G. Woodson, ed., *Negro Orators*, pp. 242ff.

[70] For letters to Brown from Negroes see James Redpath, *Echoes of Harper's Ferry*, pp. 418-19.

[71] *The Liberator*, Nov. 11, 1859.

[72] New York: Harcourt Brace, 1935.

[73] Bell I. Wiley, *Southern Negroes* (New Haven: Yale University Press, 1938), p. 83.

[74] Herbert Aptheker, *The Negro in the Civil War* (New York: International Publishers, 1938), pp. 44-45.

[75] In Fisk University, *Unwritten History of Slavery*, Social Science Documents (Nashville, Tennessee, 1945), p. 253.

[76] *Ibid., p.* 144.

[77] See B. A. Botkin, ed., *Lay My Burden Down* (Chicago, Illinois: University of Chicago Press, 1945).

[78] In his *Caste and Class in a Southern Town*, p. 137.

[79] *Ibid.,* p.138.

[80] One group of ex-slaves sang jubilantly:

Mammy, don't you cook no more,

You are free, you are free!

[81] In learning to read, despite proscriptions, in part the bondsman was getting revenge against those who sought to keep him in ignorance.

[82] On economic progress and white collar job as revenge see John Dollard, *Caste and Class in a Southern Town,* chapter entitled "Negro Aggression Against Whites."

[83] *Ibid.,* p. 301.

[84] *Ibid.,* p. 303.

[85] *Ibid.*

[86] *Ibid.,* pp. 309-311.

[87] Cf. Charles S. Johnston, *Patterns of Negro Segregation,* pp. 296, 303, 304-5, 309; and Arnold M. Rose, *The Negro's Morale,* pp. 51-52.

[88] In his *The Negro's Morale,* p. 73.

[89] In his *Patterns of Negro Segregation,* pp. 294, 304.

[90] John Dollard says: "There is undoubtedly the element of revenge" in rape of white women by Negroes. In rape "the Negro is wreaking on a symbolic member of the white caste the impotent rage which he so frequently feels at the seduction of his own women by white men. This point has not escaped the attention of white observers." (in his *Caste and Class in a Southern Town,* p. 296).

[91] See, for example, The Emancipation League, *Facts Concerning The Freedmen,* p. 4ff; W. C. Garrett, "The Freedmen at Port Royal," *North American Review,* Vol. 101, July, 1865; "The Southern Negroes," *New York Times,* August 7, 1887, p. 3; and "The Georgia Freedmen," *New York Tribune,* Sept. 4, 1875, p. 1.

[92] See, for example, Fisk University, *Unwritten History of Slavery,* p. 142..

[93] 93Cf. *Congressional Globe,* 42 Cong., 1 Sess., pp. 559ff.

[94] See speech in *Congressional Globe,* 41 Cong., 2 Sess., p. 3520.

[95] See also speech in *Congressional Globe,* 41 Cong., 3 Sess., pp. 1059-1060.

[96] *Congressional Record,* 44 Cong., 1 Sess., p. 3669.

[97] Cf. *Congressional Globe,* 42 Cong., 1 Sess., pp. 389ff. and 2 Sess., Appendix, pp. 490-92.

[98] See *Congressional Record,* 43 Cong., 1 Sess., pp. 216, 937.

[99] *Congressional Record*, 51 Cong., 2 Sess., pp. 2691-2696.

[100] *Congressional Record*, 51 Cong., 2 Sess., pp. 1479ff.

[101] B. A. Botkin, ed., *Lay My Burden Down*, p. 117.

[102] *Ibid.*, pp. 262, 264.

[103] *Ibid.*, p. 262.

[104] For examples of the various arguments which Afro-Americans gave both for and against—mainly for—the exodus, see the more than seventeen hundred pages of testimony on the movement in United States *Senate Report 693*, 46 Cong., 2 Ses., Pts. I, II, III; Arna Bontemps and Jack Conroy, *They Seek A City* (New York: Doubleday, 1945); Gunnar Myrdal, *An American Dilemma*, Ch. 8.

[105] Arnold M. Rose, *The Negro's Morale*, p. 38.

[106] *Ibid.*

[107] New York: Knopf, 1952.

[108] New York: Random House, 1957.

[109] On this, Roi Ottley states: "Close track is kept [by Negroes] of Negroes who have been successful in all fields, but especially in those in which Negroes excel in competition with white men." (in his *'New World A-Coming*, Boston: Houghton Mifflin, 1943, p. 189).

[110] Arnold Rose, *The Negro's Morale*, p. 114.

[111] *Ibid.*, p. 108.

[112] Cf. Leon J. Saul, *The Hostile Mind: The Sources and Consequences of Rage and Hate* (New York: Random House, 1956).

[113] Helen V. McLean states that the Negro's "angry hostility against white men leads to anxiety and guilt." (in her "Psychodynamic Factors in Racial Relations," in Arnold M. Rose, ed., *Race Prejudice and Discrimination*, p. 473).

[114] Arnold Rose, *The Negro's Morale*, p. 113.

[115] On this, Myrdal has written: "There are no reasons to assume that Negroes are endowed with a greater innate propensity to violence than other people. The excess of physical assaults—and altercations—within the Negro community is rather to be explained as a misplaced aggression of a severely frustrated subordinate caste." (in his *An American Dilemma*, p. 764).

[116] John Dollard, *Caste and Class in a Southern Town*, pp. 267-286. See also E. Franklin Frazier, *Black Bourgeoisie* (Glencoe, Illinois: Free Press, 1957), pp. 85, 235.

[117] Arnold Rose, *The Negro's Morale*, p. 29. On this point see also Gunnar Myrdal, *An American Dilemma*, p. 766. One of the most anti-Negro Negroes was the well-educated northern mulatto William H. Thomas whose bitter book, *The American Negro: A Critical and Practical Discussion* was published by Macmillan in 1901.

[118] Gunnar Myrdal, *An American Dilemma*, p. 764.

[119] Gunnar Myrdal, *An American Dilemma*, p. 764. On revenge against whites as an element in the assaults and murders which Negroes inflict on one another see also Arnold M. Rose, *The Negro's Morale*, pp. 89-90; Benjamin E. Mays, *Pittsburgh Courier*, June 28, 1947, p. 7; Richard

Wright, *Black Boy* (New York: Harpers, 1937), p. 221; and Hortense Powdermaker, "Channeling the Negro's Aggression," *loc. cit.*, p. 653.

[120] See Karl Menninger, *Man Against Himself.*

[121] In E. S. Schneidman and N. L. Farberow, eds., *Clues to Suicide* (New York: McGraw-Hill, 1957), it is pointed out that suicide "is more common among privileged groups in American society than among downtrodden," and among urban than among rural groups. (p. 60). The bonds men's plight must have made many of them wish often to be taken out of this vale of tears.

[122] One eminent writer in this area has noted: "Repressed emotions . . . discharge themselves by the somatic short cut into the sympathetic and parasympathetic systems without appearing in consciousness." (Frank G. Slaughter, *Medicine for Moderns.* New York: Grosset and Dunlap, 1947, pp. 57-58).

[123] *Ibid.,* p. 219.

[124] *Ibid.,* p. 44.

[125] *Ibid.*

[126] Cf. Karl Menninger, *Man Against Himself.*

[127] On the psychosomatic element in these ailments see Frank G. Slaughter, *op. cit.*, and Karl Menninger, *op. cit.*

[128] See Martin Luther King, *A Stride Toward Freedom* (New York: 1958), and Lawrence D. Reddick, *Crusader Without Violence* (New York: Appleton-Century, 1959).

[129] In *The Liberator,* March 12, 1858. Further evidence of glorification of the Negro physiognomy is to be found in the following poems by Negroes—Helene Johnson's, "Sonnet to a Negro in Harlem"; Gladys Casely Hayford's, "The Palm Wine Seller"; Gwendolyn B. Bennett's, "To A Dark Girl"; Countee Cullen's "Atlantic Waiter"; and Andrea Razafkerief's, "The Negro Woman," all in Robert Kerlin, ed., *Negro Poets and Their Poems.* See also in this same volume Lucian B. Watkins' poem, "Ebon Maid and Girl of Mine."

CHAPTER VI

THE NEGRO'S CHURCH AND GOD

[1] William Pickens, "The Kind of Democracy the Negro Race Expects," in Carter Woodson, ed., *Negro Orators and Their Orations* (Washington, D. C.: Associated Publishers, 1925), p. 657.

[2] *Ibid.,* p .670.

[3] Miles M. Fisher, *Negro Slave Songs in the United States* (New York: Cornell University Press, 1953), p. 137.

[4] Frederick Douglass, *My Bondage and My Freedom* (New York: Miller, Orton and Mulligan, 1855), p. 159.

[5] Frederick Douglass, *Lectures on American Slavery by Frederick Douglass* (Buffalo: 1851).

[6] *Ibid.*

[7] *Ibid.*

[8] In his *Life and Times of Frederick Douglass* (Hartford: 1882), p. 179. Douglass conceived and planned his own escape during one of these meetings.

[9] *Ibid.*

[10] Robert R. Moton, *What the Negro Thinks*, (New York: Doubleday, 1929), p. 86.

[11] Kenneth Stampp, *The Peculiar Institution* (New York: A. A. Knopf, 1956), p. 375.

[12] *Ibid.*, p. 375.

[13] Kelly Miller, *Out of the House of Bondage* (New York: Neale Publishing Co., 1914).

[14] Sterling Brown, "Negro Folk Expression," *Phylon*, XI, 4th Qtr., 1950, p. 319. See also N. N. Puckett, *Negro Folk Expression*, Preface; and F. W. Bond, *The Negro and the Drama* (Washington, D. C.: Associated Publishers, 1940).

[15] Benjamin Mays, *The Negro's God* (Boston: Chapman and Grimes, 1939), p. 19.

[16] M. M. Fisher, *op. cit.*, p. 137.

[17] *Ibid.*, p. 108.

[18] *Ibid.*, p. 179.

[19] B. Mays, *op. cit.*, pp. 24, 28.

[20] *Ibid.*, p. 24.

[21] *Ibid.*, p. 126.

[22] M. M. Fisher, *op. cit.*, p. 144.

[23] R. R. Moton, *op. cit.*, p. 233. See also Alain Locke, ed., *The New Negro* (New York: Albert and Charles Boni, 1925), p. 199.

[24] Frederick Douglass, *My Bondage and My Freedom*, p. 90.

[25] *Ibid.*

[26] *Ibid.*, p. 134.

[27] Daniel A. Payne, *Recollection of Seventy Years* (Nashville: AME Publishing House, 1888).

[28] Fisk University, *Unwritten History of Slavery*, Social Science Documents (Nashville, Tennessee, 1945), pp. 121; 57, 204, 209.

[29] Cf. B. A. Botkin, ed., *Lay My Burden Down* (Chicago, Illinois: University of Chicago Press, 1945), section "What the Preacher Said," pp. 25ff.

[30] *Ibid.*, p. 178.

[31] Fisk University, *op. cit.*, p. 84.

[32] *Ibid.*, p. 150.

[33] *Ibid.*, p. 152.

[34] B. A. Botkin, ed., *op. cit.*, pp. 120, 164; Fisk University, *op. cit.*, p. 100.

[35] A. Crummell, *Sermon* (Boston: T. R. Marion and Son, 1865), p. 8.

[36] B. A. Botkin, ed., *op. cit.*, p. 46.

[37] Benjamin Mays and J. W. Nicholson, *The Negro's Church* (New York: Institute of Social and Religious Research, 1933), pp. 69-70.

[38] *Ibid..*, pp. 64ff. Many of the sermons studied reveal a sensitivity to economic, social, and political needs.

[39] B. Mays, *The Negro's God*, p. 23.

[40] Cf. Herbert Aptheker, *Documentary History of the American Negro* (New York: Citadel Preeses, 1951), p. 76, testimony of Rolla, one of the plotters with Vesey.

[41] *Ibid.*, p. 205.

[42] T. Thomas Fortune, *Black and White: Land, Labor and Politics in the South* (New York: 1884).

[43] In C. Woodson, ed., *Negro Orators*, p. 214.

[44] In his *My Bondage and My Freedom*.

[45] *Ibid.*, Appendix.

[46] In C. Woodson, ed., *Negro Orators*, pp. 214-15.

[47] *Ibid.*, pp. 91-92.

[48] *Ibid.*, p. 120.

[49] H. Aptheker, ed., *op. cit.*, p. 385.

[50] *Ibid.*, p. 387.

[51] Cf. Charles H. Nichols, Jr., "Slave Narratives and the Plantation Legend," *Phylon*, 3d Qtr., X, p. 205. See also W. J. Cash, *The Mind of the South* (New York: A. A. Knopf, 1944), pp. 4-94. In this classic picture of the South, Cash has reached a similar conclusion about the bulk of the planter class.

[52] C. H. Nichols, *loc. cit.*, quoting Miss Martineau's *Society in America*. II, p. 117.

[53] Booker T. Washington, *A New Negro for a New Century*, p. 206.

[54] Andrea Razafkeriefo, "The Negro Church."

[55] Wilson Record, *The Negro and the Communist Party* (Chapel Hill: University of North Carolina Press, 1953), p. 7.

[56] F. Douglass, *Why Is the Negro Lynched* (Bridgewater: Printed by John Whitby and Sons, 1885).

[57] B. T. Washington, *The Future of the American Negro* (Boston: Small, Maynard and Co., 1899), p. 177.

[58] D. A. Payne, *op. cit.*, p. 68.

[59] Kelly Miller, *Race Adjustment* (Washington, D. C.: The Neale Publishing Co., 1909), p. 157.

[60] *The Christian Recorder*, June 18, 1891.

[61] Lida K. Wiggins, *The Life and Works of Paul Laurence Dunbar* (Washington, D. C.: Mulliken-Jenkins Co.), p. 209.

[62] James Weldon Johnson, *Saint Peter Relates An Incident* (New York: Viking Press, 1935), pp. 96ff.

[63] On Negro religion of this period cf. also W. C. Gannett, "The Freedmen at Port Royal," *North American Review*, July, 1865, 101:9; Edward

King, *The Great South*, pp. 779ff.; Walter Lynwood Fleming, *The Sequel of Appomattox*, Ch. 32; David Macrae, *The Americans at Home*, II, p. 90ff.

[64] See Fisk University, *op. cit.*, p. 25.

[65] *Ibid.*, pp. 46, 47, 157, 160.

[66] In C. Woodson, ed., *op. cit.*, pp. 703-4.

[67] Robert Kerlin, ed., *Negro Poets and Their Poems* (Washington, D. C.: Associated Pubs.), p. 261.

[68] *Ibid.*, p. 148.

[69] B. Mays, *The Negro's God*, p. 219.

[70] Countee Cullen, *The Black Christ* (New York: Harpers, 1929). See, by the same author, *Color* (New York: Harpers, 1924), esp. his poem "Heritage" in which the author wishes that God was a Negro (pp. 3, 39-40).

[71] W. E. DuBois, *Darkwater* (New York: Harcourt, Brace, 1920), pp. 275-276.

[72] In White and Jackson, eds., *Poetry by American Negroes* (Durham, North Carolina: Trinity College Press, 1924), p. 1957.

[73] In C. G. Woodson, ed.., *op. cit.*

[74] Kelly Miller, *The Everlasting Stain* (Washington, D. C.: Associated Publishers, 1924), p. 80.

[75] *Ibid.*, pp. 46-47, 351-352.

[76] Robert R. Moton, *Finding a Way Out* (New York: Doubleday, Doran and Co., 1920), p. 15.

[77] In C. G. Woodson, ed., *op. cit.*, p. 574.

[78] See also Sterling D. Spero and Abram L. Harris, *The Black Worker*: William A. Nolan, *Communism Versus the Negro* (Chicago: Henry Regnery Co., 1951); James W. Ford, *The Negro and the Democratic Front* (New York: International Publishers, 1938).

[79] Carter G. Woodson, *The Rural Negro* (Washington, D. C.: Association for the Study of Negro Life and History, 1930), p. 152.

[80] *Ibid.*, p. 166.

[81] Carter G. Woodson, *The Mis-Education of the Negro* (Washington, D. C.: Associated Publishers, 1933), p. 70.

[82] B. Mays, *The Negro's God*, p. 213.

[83] *Ibid.*, p. 216.

[84] *Ibid.*, p. 218.

[85] *Ibid.*, pp. 68, 88.

[86] *Ibid.*, p. 68.

[87] *The Messenger*, December, 1919, p. 4..

[88] Quoted in B. Mays, *The Negro's God*, p. 237.

[89] *Ibid.*, p. 220, referring to Nella Larsen's *Quicksand* (New York: A. A. Knopf, 1928).

[90] *Ibid.*, p. 209, referring to Walter White's *Fire in the Flint* (New York: A. A. Knopf), p. 72. White shows in this novel that he felt that religion, as often practiced then, was too often an opiate for Negroes. See also J. Fauset, *Plum Bun* (New York: F. A. Stowes Co., 1928).

CHAPTER VII

ANTE-BELLUM CLASSES AND FAMILY LIFE AMONG NEGROES

[1] E. Franklin Frazier, *The Negro Family in the United States*, 1948 ed., p. 65.

[2] Henry Bibb, *The Life and Adventures of Henry Bibb, An American Slave* (New York: 1849), p. 38.

[3] Fisk University, *Unwritten History of Slavery*, Social Science Documents (Nashville, Tennessee, 1945), p. 222.

[4] Kelly Miller, *Out of the House of Bondage* (New York: Neale Publishing Co., 1914).

[5] Fisk University, *op. cit.*, p. 84.

[6] *Ibid.*, p. 217.

[7] *Ibid.*, p. 176.

[8] William Wells Brown, *William Wells Brown, A Fugitive Slave* (Boston: 1847), p. 13.

[9] Frederick Douglass, *The Life of Frederick Douglass, An American Slave* (Boston: 1845), pp. 2-3.

[10] *The Liberator*, Sept. 22, 1848.

[11] Cf. B. A. Botkin, ed., *Lay My Burden Down* (Chicago, Illinois: University of Chicago Press, 1945), pp.. 122ff.

[12] Kenneth Stampp, *The Peculiar Institution* (New York: A. A. Knopf, 1957), p. 351.

[13] Helen Catterall, ed., *Judicial Cases*, I, p. 357; II, pp. 63-64, 117, 119, 167.

[14] Kenneth Stampp, *op. cit.*, p. 359.

[15] *Ibid.*, p. 360.

[16] *Ibid.*, p. 361.

[17] See Fisk University, *op. cit.*, pp. 251-252.

[18] *Ibid.*, pp. 169-174.

[19] *Ibid.*, p. 208.

[20] J. M. Herskovits, *The American Negro*, pp. 51-61; Frederick Law Olmsted, *A Journey in the Seaboard Slave States* (New York: 1856), p. 421; Gunnar Myrdal, *An American Dilemma*, Chapter 32.

[21] R. R. Moton, *What the Negro Thinks* (New York: Doubleday, 1929), p. 228.

[22] Henry Bibb, *The Narrative of the Life and Adventures of Henry Bibb, An American Slave* (New York: 1863), pp. 39-40.

[23] E. B. Reuter, *The Mulatto in the United States*, pp. 271-73; C. G. Woodson, *The Negro Professional Man and the Community* (Washington, D. C.: 1934), pp. 81-82; E. F. Frazier, *The Negro Family in the United States*, 1948 ed.., pp. 320-321.

[24] Wilson Record, *The Negro and the Communist Party* (Chapel Hill: University of North Carolina Press), p. 294.

[25] Frances A. Kemble, *Journal of a Residence on a Georgia Plantation* (New York: 1863).

[26] *The Liberator*, February 25, 1842.

[27] In "An Address to the Slaves of the United States," given at the 1843 National Negro Convention, Buffalo, New York.

[28] David Ruggles, answering the attack on abolitionism by a white New York physician.

[29] Austin Steward, *Twenty-two Years a Slave, and Forty Years a Freeman* (Rochester, New York: Allings and Cory, 1857), pp. 30ff.

[30] Fisk University, *op. cit.*, p. 221.

[31] *Ibid.*, p. 201.

[32] Kenneth Stampp, *op. cit.*, p. 337, Fannie Kemble, *op. cit.*, pp. 193-94.

[33] Frederick L. Olmsted, *op. cit.*, p. 421.

[34] E. Franklin Frazier, *op. cit.*, Ch. III.

[35] Fisk University, *op. cit.*, p. 65.

[36] E. Franklin Frazier, *op. cit.*, p. 361.

[37] Kenneth Stampp, *op. cit.*, pp. 343-346.

[38] *Ibid.*, p. 347. On slave promiscuity see also Frederick Douglass, *My Bondage and My Freedom*, p. 86.

[39] Cf. J. C. Colcord, *Broken Homes: A Study of Family Desertions* (New York: 1919); E. F. Frazier, *op. .cit.*, Ch. XV.

[40] E. F. Frazier, *op. cit.*, p. 32.

[41] *Ibid.*, pp. 103-193, 113.

[42] Cf. Herbert J. Aptheker, *American Negro Slave Revolts* (New York: Columbia University Press), pp. 114-115.

[43] *Ibid.*, pp. 244-246.

[44] *Ibid.*, pp. 357-358.

[45] E. F. Frazier, *op. cit.*, p. 138.

[46] See John Hope Franklin, *The Free Negro in North Carolina*, and by the same author, *From Slavery to Freedom*. See also Charles S. Sydnor, "The Free Negro in Mississippi Before the Civil War," *American Historical Review*, XXXII, July, 1927.

[47] R. R. Wright, *The Negro in Pennsylvania* (Philadelphia: University of Pennsylvania, 1918), p. 31. The first Negro Masonic Order in the United States was chartered from London in 1787.

[48] Fisk University, *op. cit.*, p. 225.

[49] See protest to Charleston, South Carolina legislators, in Herbert J. Aptheker, *Documentary History of the American Negro* (New York: Citadel Press, 1950), pp. 26-28, and 1793 and 1794 protests to the same body, *Ibid.*, pp. 30-31.

[50] Rev. Theeodore S. Wright, addressing New York Anti-Slavery Society, Sept. 20, 1837, in C. G. Woodson, *Negro Orators and Their Orations*, p. 93.

[51] *Ibid.*, p. 78, Rev. Peter Williams at St. Phillip's Church, New York, July 4, 1830.

[52] *Freedom's Journal*, New York, March 16, 1827.

CHAPTER VIII

SOME SOURCES OF THE NEGRO'S FAITH IN HIMSELF
AND IN AMERICAN DEMOCRACY

[1] *Congressional Record*, 43 Cong., 1 Sess., II, Pt. 1, pp. 565-567.

[2] In C. G. Woodson, ed., *Negro Orators and Their Orations* (Washington, D. C.: Associated Publishers, 1925), p. 707.

[3] *Ibid.*, pp. 198-99.

[4] *Ibid.*, p. 221.

[5] *Ibid.*, p. 497.

[6] Kelly Miller, *Out of the House of Bondage* (New York: Neale Publishing Company, 1914).

[7] C. G. Woodson, ed., *op. cit.*, pp. 569-571.

[8] *Ibid.*

[9] *Ibid.*, p. 624.

[10] *Ibid.*, p. 537.

[11] Kelly Miller, *op. cit.*

[12] *The Liberator*, Dec. 1, 1852.

[13] *Ibid.*, July 20, 1838.

[14] *An Address, Delivered on the Celebration of the Abolition of Slavery, in State of New York*, July 5, 1827, by Nathaniel Paul (Albany, New York: 1827), p. 15.

[15] In C. G. Woodson, ed., *op. cit.*, p. 517.

[16] *Ibid.*, p. 623.

[17] J. C. Price, *The Race Problem Stated*.

[18] *The Liberator*, June 22, 1833.

[19] *The Liberator*, Oct. 16, 1840.

[20] *The Liberator*, Nov. 30, 1849.

[21] *The Liberator*, Dec. 14, 1849.

[22] Frederick Douglass, *Lectures on American Slavery by Frederick Douglass* (Buffalo, New York, 1851).

[23] *The Independent*, New York, Sept. 7, 1899, LI, pp. 2425-2427.

[24] Thomas Hamilton, *The Anglo-African Magazine*, editorial of the initial issue, Jan., 1859.

[25] In his 1875 address to the Convention of Colored Newspaper Men, Cincinnati, Ohio.

[26] In C. G. Woodson, ed., *op. cit.*, pp. 488-501.

CHAPTER IX

ASPECTS OF THE THOUGHT OF FREE NEGROES
DURING THE 1850's

[1] Frederick Douglass, *My Bondage and Freedom*.

[2] *Ibid.*

[3] Quoted in H. Aptheker, *Documentary History of the American Negro* (New York: Citadel Press, 1951), p. 317. See also pp. 299-305.

[4] Helen Boardman, *Common Ground*, VII (1947)7.

[5] In Carter G. Woodson, ed., *Negro Orators and Their Orations*. (Washington, D. C.: Associated Publishers, 1925), p. 650.

[6] *The Liberator*, April 5, 1850.

[7] C. G. Woodson, ed., *op. cit.*, p. 218.

[8] In H. Aptheker, ed., *op. cit.*, p. 316.

[9] *Ibid.*, p. 318.

[10] *Ibid.*, p .319.

[11] *The Liberator*, Dec. 19, 1851.

[12] *Ibid..*, Dec. 10, 1852.

[13] *Ibid.*

[14] See C. G. Woodson, *op.cit.*, pp. 150ff.

[15] *The Liberator*, June 23, 1854.

[16] *Ibid.*, Jan. 25, 1856.

[17] See account in H. Aptheker, ed., *op. cit.*, pp. 378-380.

[18] *The Liberator*, April 10, 1857.

[19] *Ibid.*

[20] *Ibid.*, May 18, 1860.

[21] Philip S. Foner, ed., *The Life and Writings of Frederick Douglass*, 4 vols. (New York: 1950-1955), II, p. 411.

[22] *The Liberaor*, July 10, 1857.

[23] *Ibid.*

[24] *Ibid.*, July 9, 1858.

[25] Archibald Grimke, *The Shame of the Republic*.

[26] *The Liberator*, March 12, 1858.

[27] *The Anglo-African*, May, 1859, I, p. 160.

[28] J. B. Shannon, "Southern Sectionalism and National Politics," *Social Science*, June, 1957, p. 141.

THE ABOLITIONIST—CIVIL WAR ERAS

[1] Richard Bardolph, "The Distinguished Negro in America, 1770-1936," *American Historical Review*, Volume 60, No. 3, April, 1955, p. 533. See also his "Social Origins of Distinguished Negroes, 1770-1865," *Journal of Negro History*, Volume 40, No. 3, July, 1955, p. 230.

[2] R. Bardolph, "Social Origins of Distinguished Negroes, 1770-7865," *loc. cit.*, p. 231.

[3] *The Liberator*, Nov. 19, 1841.

[4] Frederick Douglass, *My Bondage and My Freedom* (New York: 1855).

[5] Robert Purvis, in 1838 appeal to the Pennsylvania legislature not to take the ballot away from its free Negro population.

[6] *The Liberator*, April 5, 1850.

CHAPTER X

THE NEGRO AND AMERICAN WARS

[1] Quoted in *The Liberator*, April 1, 1842.

[2] William Whipper, Columbia, Pennsylvania, in *The Colored American*, Sept. 9, 16, 23, 30, 1837, editorial entitled "Non-Resistance to Offensive Aggression."

[3] *Ibid.*

[4] Quoted in Carter G. Woodson, ed., *Negro Orators and Their Orations* (Washington, D. C.: Associated Publishers, 1925), pp. 691-92; hereinafter referred to as *Negro Orators.*

[5] Carter G. Woodson, *The Negro in Our History*, 6th ed. (Washington, D. C.: Associated Publishers, 1931), pp. 120-121.)

[6] See George W. Williams, *History of the Negro Race in America from 1619 to 1880* (New York: Putnam and Sons, 1883).

[7] Cf. C. G. Woodson, *The Negro in Our History*, pp. 126-128; John Hope Franklin, *From Slavery to Freedom* (New York: A. A. Knopf, 1947), discussion of Negro soldiers in Revolution and Spanish-American wars, and World Wars I and II. ·

[8] George Washington Williams, *History of the Negro Race in America*, I, p. 369. See also his *History of the Negro Troops in the War of the Rebellion*, 1861-1865 (New York: Harpers, 1888), section entitled "The Cloud of Witnesses."

[9] *From Slavery to Freedom*, p. 172.

[10] *History of the Negro Race in America*, II, p. 27.

[11] Cf. petition, dated August 1, 1853, signed by William C. Nell and many other Negroes, which was presented to the Massachusetts Constitutional Convention as quoted in *The Liberator*, Aug. 5, 1853.

[12] Boston: R. F. Wallcut, 1851.

[13] In his *The North Star*, March 17, 1848.

[14] In Frederick Douglass, *The Life and Times of Frederick Douglass*, pp. 373-376.

[15] In *The Liberator*, Febr. 14, 1862.

[16] Editorial, *The North Star*, March 2, 1863.

[17] In B. A. Botkin, ed., *Lay My Burden Down* (Chicago, Illinois: University of Chicago Press, 1945), p. 211.

[18] In *Congressional Record*, 43 Cong., 1st Sess., II, Pt. 1, pp. 565-567.

[19] *The Liberator*, Febr. 14, 1862.

[20] *Ibid.*

[21] B. A. Botkin, ed., *op. cit.*, pp. 158, 196.

[22] *Ibid.*, p. 192.

[23] Fisk University, *Unwritten History of Slavery*, Social Science Documents (Nashville, Tennessee, 1945), p. 84.

[24] Fisk University, *op. cit.*, p. 206.

[25] Bell I. Wiley, *Southern Negroes* (New Haven: Yale University Press, 1938), p. 108.

[20] In Herbert Apthekekr, *American Negro Slave Revolts* (New York: Columbia University Press, 1943), p. 358.

[27] Herbert Aptheker, *The Negro in the Civil War* (New York: International Publishers, 1938), pp. 44-45.

[28] Cf. W. E. B. DuBois, *Black Reconstruction* (New York: Harcourt, Brace, 1937).

[29] *The Liberator*, Febr. 14, 1862.

[30] See Robert Russa Moton, *What the Negro Thinks*.

[31] In Carter Woodson, ed., *Negro Orators*, p. 347.

[32] *Ibid.*, p. 248.

[33] *Ibid.*, p. 124.

[34] *The Liberator*, Nov. 19, 1841.

[35] In Carter Woodson, ed., *Negro Orators,* pp. 248-249.

[36] *Ibid.*, p. 346.

[37] Cf. G. W. Williams, *History of Negro Troops in the War of the Rebellion*: John R. Lynch, *Congressional Record*, 43 Cong., 1st Sess., II, Pt. V, pp. 4782-3.

[38] In C.. Woodson, ed., *Negro Orators*, p. 567.

[39] *Ibid.*, p. 553.

[40] Quoted in C. Woodson, ed., *Negro Orators*, pp. 546-7.

[41] *Ibid.*, p. 587. .

[42] Archibald Grimke, *The Shame of the Republic*.

[43] Cf., for example, the writings of Frederick Douglass and William Wells Brown, in *The Liberator*, January 29 and October 7, 1865.

[44] *The Liberator*, September 9, 1864.

[45] Cong. James T. Rapier of Alabama, speaking to 43d Congress in defense of the Civil Rights Bill.

[46] Archibald Grimke, *op. cit.*

[47] Quoted in C. Woodson, ed., *Negro Orators*, p. 250.

[48] *Ibid.*, p. 251.

[49] *Ibid.*, p. 248.

[50] Reprinted in *The Life and Times of Frederick Douglass*.

[51] Cf. Bell I. Wiley, *Southern Negroes*, pp. 325-341.

[52] *Ibid.*, pp. 307-310.

[53] Fisk University, *op. cit.*, p. 218.

[54] B. A. Botkin, ed., *op. cit.*, p. 200.

[55] *Ibid.*, p. 188.

[56] Bell I. Wiley, *op. cit.*, p. 344.

[57] Cf. Thomas Wentworth Higginson, *Army Life in a Black Regiment*, p. 133; Bell I. Wiley, *op. cit.*, p. 315; Thomas W. Knox, *Camp Fire and Cotton Field* (New York: 1865).

[58] Cf. Ulrich B. Phillips, *Life and Labor in the Old South*, p. 234; Bell I. Wiley, *op. cit.*, Chs. I and IV; I. S. Staples, *Reconstruction in Arkansas*, p. 183.

[59] New York: Harcourt, Brace, 1935.

[60] Bell I. Wiley, *op. cit.*, p. 17 and Ch. IV.

[61] *Ibid.*, p. 83.

[62] *Ibid.*, p. 64. See also Mrs. I. Morgan, *How It Was* (Nashville: 1892), p. 90; J. A. Wyeth, *With Sabre and Scapel*, p. 54; and Dolly S. Lunt, *A Woman's War-Time Journal* (New York: 1918), p. 32.

[63] Fisk University, *op. cit.*, p. 175.

[64] *Ibid.*, p. 268.

[65] Bell I. Wiley, *op. cit.*, Ch. VII "Military Laborers," esp. pp. 132-33.

[66] Fisk University, *op. cit.*, p. 138.

[67] *Ibid.*, p. 218.

[68] B. A. Botkin, ed., *op. cit.*, p. 223.

[69] Fisk University, *op. cit.*, p. 232.

[70] See David Macrae, *The Americans at Home*, II, p. 97.

[71] Bell I. Wiley, *op. cit.*, Ch. I; Orland Kay Armstrong, *Old Massa's People*, p. 301; E. L. Pierce, *The Freedmen of Port Royal South Carolina*, pp. 307ff.

[72] See William W. Davis, *The Civil War and Reconstruction in Florida*

[73] *The Independent* (New York: April 28, 1898, Vol. 50, pp. 535-536.

[74] *The Richmond Planet*, July 30, 1898.

[75] In *The American Citizen*, Kansas City, Kansas, Nov. 17, 1899.

[76] In W. Richardson, ed., *Message and Papers of the Presidents* (1911), VIII, pp. 6248ff.

[77] See petition in Aptheker, *Documentary History*, pp. 787-791. W. E. B. DuBois was active in the Anti-Imperialist League which supported Bryan against McKinley. For other evidence of support of Bryan by Negroes see Aptheker, *Documentary History*, pp. 818-19.

[78] In H. Aptheker, ed., *Documentary History*, p. 545.

[79] R. R. Moton, *What the Negro Thinks*, pp. 152-53. Moton goes on to point out that the Negro was disillusioned when he found out that these ideals were not to be applied to him.

[80] In C. Woodson, ed., *Negro Orators*, p. 659.

[81] *Ibid.*, p. 693.

[82] Archibald Grimke, *op. cit.*

[83] *The Liberator*, October 7, 1864.

[84] See letters in the Carter Woodson Collection, Library of Congress. Many of these letters were earlier published in *The Journal of Negro History*, Volume IVff.

[85] Alain Locke, ed., *The New Negro* (New York: Albert and Charles Boni, 1925), p. 7.

[86] See article by Wright in *Charities* (New York: October 7, 1905, IV, pp. 69-73.

[87] Cf. Moton's *Finding A Way Out* (New York: Doubleday, 1920). See also W. E. B. DuBois, "Returning Soldiers," *Crisis*, XVII, May, 1919, p. 14.

[88] In his poem "Facts."

[89] In C. Woodson, ed.., *Negro Orators*, pp. 700-701. .

[90] *Ibid.*, p. 692.

[91] Archibald Grimke, *op. cit.*

[92] Rev. Francis J. Grimke, in C. Woodson, ed., *Negro Orators*, p. 701.

[93] *Ibid.*, p. 699.

[94] *Ibid.*, p. 700.

[95] *Ibid.*, p. 703.

[96] R. R. Moton, *What the Negro Thinks*, p. 66.

[97] *Congressional Record*, 44th Cong., 1st Sess., p. 165.

[98] R. R. Moton, *What the Negro Thinks*, p. 246.

[99] *Christian Recorder*, August 11, 1892.

[100] Claude McKay, "The Lynching."

[101] Rayford W. Logan, *The Negro in the United States* (Anvil Book).

[102] Wilson Record, *The Negro and the Communist Party*, p. 205.

[103] For expressions of Negro views, cf. Horace M. Bond, "Should the Negro Care Who Wins the War," *Annals of the American Academy of Political and Social Science*, Sept. 1942, pp. 81-84; Drake and Cayton, *Black Metropolis*, pp. 745-761; John Hope Franklin, *From Slavery to Freedom*; Walter White, *A Man Called White*, pp. 102-119; R. Logan, ed., *What the Negro Wants*, esp. chapters by Mary M. Bethune, Rayford W. Logan, and Charles Wesley.

[104] Cf. *Negro Digest*, IX, Nov., 1940, pp. 29ff; John Hope Franklin, *op. cit.*, pp. 448, 560.

[105] Cf. Sterling Brown, "Negro Folk Expression," *Phylon*, VI, 4th Qtr., 1950, p. 327.

[106] *Pittsburgh Courier*, October 14, 1944, p. 6.

[107] *Ibid.*, November 4, 1944, p. 4.

[108] Cf. Earl Conrad, *Jim Crow America* (New York: Duell, Sloan and Pearce, 1947), pp. 79ff. See also H. H. Moon, "How the Negroes Voted," *Nation*, Nov. 25, 1944, pp. 640-641; Z. N. Hurston, "Negro Voter Sizes Up Taft," *Saturday Evening Post*, Dec. 8, 1951, p. 29, and *Readers Digest*, Febr., 1952, pp. 109-113.

[109] New York: Farrar, Strauss, and Co., 1948.

[110] Cf. his review, "In Love with Germany," in *New Republic*, Sept. 25, 1948, p. 33.

CHAPTER XI

THE DAY FREEDOM CAME

[1] In this vein see such works as J. A .Bishop, *The Day Christ Died* (New York: Harpers, 1957); and Jim Bishop, *The Day Lincoln Was Shot* (New York: Harpers, 1955).

[2] Quoted in Alice Moore Dunbar, ed., *Masterpieces of Negro Eloquence*, p. 42.

[3] Quoted in *The Liberator*, September 22, 1848.

[4] In *The Life and Times of Frederick Douglass, Written by Himself.*

p.p. 387-389. Scores of such meetings of Negro people and their friends were held on this evening.

[5] Fisk University, *Unwritten History of Slavery*, Social Science Documents, Nashville, Tennessee, 1945), p. 267. E. A. Botkin, ed., *Lay My Burden Down* (Chicago: University of Chicago Press, 1945); also relates many such instances.

[6] Cf. Fisk University, *op. cit.*, p. 282.

[7] Botkin, ed., *op. cit.*, p. 225.

[8] *Ibid.*, p. 134.

[9] Fisk University, *op. cit.*, p. 306. .

[10] Quoted in E. L. Pierce, "The Freedmen at Port Royal," *Atlantic Monthly*, XII, 1863.

[11] In his *Up From Slavery*. See also Bell I Wiley, *Southern Negroes* (New Haven: Yale Univ., 1938), pp. 21-23.

[12] Quoted in Mrs. Roger Pryor, *Reminiscenses of Peace and War* (New York: Macmillan (Co., 1904), p. 385.

[13] Botkin, ed., *Lay My Burden Down*, p. 241.

[14] *Ibid.*, p. 197.

[15] *Ibid.*, p. 224.

[16] Quoted in Elizabeth W. Allison Pringle, *Chronicles of Chicora Wood* (New York: Scribner's Sons, 1923), pp. 269ff.

[17] Botkin, *Lay My Burden Down*, p. 226.

[18] *Ibid.*

[19] *Ibid.*, p. 236. See also Bell I Wiley, *Southern Negroes*.

[20] E. A. Botkin, ed., *Lay My Burden Down*, p. 267.

[21] *Ibid.*, p. 268..

[22]

[23] Richard Wright, *Black Boy* (New York: Harpers, 1945).

[24] Carl Rowan, *South of Freedom* (New York: Knopf, 1952).

CHAPTER XII

THE AFRO-AMERICAN AND SOME OF HIS BENEFACTORS

[1] In C. G. Woodson, ed., *Negro Orators and Their Orations* (Washington, D. C.: Associated Publishers, 1925), p. 156.

[2] George Washington Williams, *History of the Negro Race in America From 1619 to 1880* (New York: Putnam and Sons, 1883), II, p. 91.

[3] *The Liberator*, Dec. 29, 1837.

[4] *Ibid.*

[5] Jack Abramowitz, "Crossroads of Negro Thought, 1890-1895," *Social Education*, XVIII, No. 3, March, 1854, pp. 117-120.

[6] *The North Star*, Dec. 3, 1847.

[7] *Ibid.*

[8] See C. Woodson, ed., *op. cit.*, p. 92.

[9] *Ibid.*, p. 533.

[10] *The Liberator*, Sept. 24, 1841.

[11] *Ibid.*, April 3, 1840.

[12] John A. Copeland, *Voice from Harper's Ferry* (Boston: 1861).

[13] *The Liberator*, Nov. 11, 1859.

[14] See Benjamin Quarles, *Frederick Douglass* (Washington, D. C.: Associated Publishers, 1948), Ch. X, "Douglass and John Brown."

[15] See Fisk University, *Unwritten History of Slavery*, Social Science Documents (Nashville, Tennessee, 1945), p. 237.

[16] *Ibid.*

[17] George Washington Williams, *op. cit.*, p. 214.

[18] *Ibid.*, p. 546.

[19] For letters to Brown, see James Redpath, *Echoes of Harper's Ferry*, pp. 418-419.

[20] *Congressional Record*, 43 Cong., 1 Sess., 1 Sess., pp. 73-74, 3412.

[21] See C. Woodson, ed., *op. cit.*, p. 513.

[22] *Ibid.*

[23] *Ibid.*, p. 503.

[24] *Ibid.*

CHAPTER XIII

SHADOW OF THE PLANTATION, 1865-1900

[1] See, for example, speech by Dr. John S. Rock, quoted in *The Liberator*, February 14, 1862.

[2] *Ibid.*, May 16, 1862.

[3] *Ibid.*, Dec. 12, 1862.

[4] Cf., for example, Charles S. Johnson, *Shadow of the Plantation*; A. A. Taylor, *The Negro in South Carolina During Reconstruction*; David Macrae, *Americans at Home*, II, pp. 70ff; Whitelaw Reid, *After the War*, p. 532; Rupert S. Holland, ed., *Letters and Diary of Laura M. Towne*, 1862-1884, p. 33; Claude G. Bowers, *The Tragic Era*.

[5] Fisk University, *op. cit.*, p. 23.

[6] Irwin D. Rinder, "A Sociological Look Into the Negro Pictorial," *Phylon*, Summer, 1959, pp. 169-177.

[7] Glencoe, Illinois: Free Press, 1957.

[8] Fisk University, *op. cit.*, p. 233.

[9] See George Washington Williams, *History of the Negro Race in America From 1619 to 1880* (New York: Putnam and Sons, 1883), and John Hope Franklin, *From Slavery to Freedom* (New York: A. A. Knopf, 1947).

[10] In C. Woodson, ed., *op. cit.*, pp. 154, 156.

[11] *The Liberator*, Nov. 30, 1849.

[12] See Helene Johnson's, "Sonnet to a Negro in Harlem," Gladys Casely

Hayford's, "The Palm Wine Seller," Gwendolyn B. Bennett's, "To A Dark Girl," Countee Cullen's, "Atlantic City Waiter," Andrea Razafkeriefa's "The Negro Woman," all in Robert Kerlin, et., *Negro Poets and Their Poems*. In the same volume see also "Ebon Maid and Girl of Mine," by Lucian B. Watkins.

[13] Karl Menninger, *Love Against Hate* (New York: Harcourt, Brace, 1942), p. 172. .

[14] Quoted in B. A. Botkin, ed., *Lay My Burden Down* (Chicago, Illinois: University of Chicago Press, 1945), pp. 231, 233.

[15] *Ibid.*, p. 247.

[16] See Fisk University, *Unwritten History of Slavery*, Social Science Documents (Nashville, Tennessee, 1945), p. 276.

[17] See Walter Lynwood Fleming, *Documentary History of Reconstruction*, pp. 79ff., James G. Randall, *The Civil War and Reconstruction*, pp. 724ff.; E. L. Pierce, *The Freedmen of Port Royal*, p. 309; Susan B. Smedes, *Memorials of a Southern Planter*, pp. 287ff.

[18] B. A. Botkin, ed.., *op. cit.*, p. 237.

[19] *Ibid.*, p. 241.

[20] Fisk University, *op. cit.*, p. 151.

[21] Robert Russa Moton, *What the Negro Thinks* (New York: Doubleday, 1929), p. 30.

[22] Quoted in Carter G. Woodson, ed., *Negro Orators and Their Orations* (Washington, D. C.: Associated Publishers, 1925), p. 569.

[23] *Ibid.*, p. 490.

[24] *Journal of Social Science*, Vol. XI (May: 1880).

[25] John Mercer Langston, *Lectures and Addresses of John Mercer Langston*, pp. 141ff.

[26] C. G. Woodson, ed., *op. cit.*, p. 256.

[27] John Mercer Langston, *op.cit.*, pp. 141ff.

[28] *Congressional Globe*, 42 Cong., 2 Sess., Appendix, pp. 15-17.

[29] C. G. Woodson, ed., *op.cit.*, p. 513.

[30] *Ibid.*, p. 622.

[31] See Archibald Grimke, *The Shame of the Republic*.

[32] *Ibid.*

[33] Kelly Miller, *Out of the House of Bondage* (New York: Neale Publishing Co., 1914).

[34] Robert S. Henry, *The Story of Reconstruction*, p. 30.

[35] Cf. Walter Lynwood Fleming, *Civil War and Reconstruction in Alabama*, pp. 444ff.; and "What Shall We Do With the Negro," *The Nation*, Vol. 7 (Nov. 12, 1868), p. 366.

[36] C. G. Woodson, ed., *op. cit.*, p. 588.

[37] Bell I. Wiley, *Southern Negroes* (New Haven: Yale University Press, 1938), p. 240.

[38] Fisk University, *op. cit.*, pp. 203, 205.

[39] *New York Tribune*, "Condition of the Colored People," September 1, 1870.

[40] Fisk University, *op.cit.*, p. 60.

[41] *Ibid.*, p. 175.

[42] B. A. Botkin, ed., *op. cit.*, pp. 112-113.

[43] *Ibid.*, p. 112.

[44] Fisk University, *op. cit.*, p. 192.

[45] *Ibid.*

[46] *Ibid.*, p. 295.

[47] *Ibid.*, p. 35.

[48] *Ibid.*, p. 229.

[49] See O. W. Blackwell, "The New Departure in Negro Life," *Atlantic Monthly*, Nov., 1883; "Life in the South," *New York Tribune*, Feb. 21, 1881; and P. A. Bruce, *The Plantation Negro As A Freedman* (New York: 1889).

[50] Cf. Israel Gerver, *The Changing Position of the Negro and Other Minorities in the United States* (New York: 1949), pp. 5-6.

[51] Philip A. Bruce, *op. cit.*, p. 4. Also cf. petition to Congress of Sylvester Gray which was referred, on March 23, 1860 to the Committee on Public Lands of the U. S. Senate.

[52] For some further evidence of the interest of the freedmen in acquiring education, land and the ballot see *The Liberator*, Dec. 12, 1862, Jan. 29, 1864, April 1, 1864, and Feb. 24, 1865.

[53] *Senate Miscellaneous Document No. 3*, 41 Cong., 2 Sess.

[54] In C. Woodson, ed., *op. cit.*, p. 474.

[55] See James W. Wright, *The Free Negro in Maryland*, 1634-1860 (New York: 1921), pp. 242-244; W. E. B. DuBois, *The Philadelphia Negro* (Philadelphia: 1899), pp. 66ff.

[56] *Congressional Record*, 45 Cong., 1 Sess., Appendix, p. 98.

[57] R. Kinzer and E. Sagarin, *The Negro in American Business* (New York: 1950), p. 110.

[58] *The Liberator*, May 26, 1865.

[59] *Ibid.*

[60] The Representatives were Richard H. Cain, Henry P. Cheatham, Robert C. DeLarge, Robert B. Elliott, Jeremy Haralson, John Hyman, Jefferson Long, John R. Lynch, Thomas E. Miller, Charles E. Nash, James E. O'Hara, Joseph Rainey, Alonzo J. Ransier, James T. Rapier, Robert Smalls, Benjamin S. Turner, Josiah R. Walls, George H. White, James M. Turner, and George W. Murry. Outstanding at the state level were Francis L. Cardoza, Jonathan Jasper Wright, P. B. S. Pinchback, Oscar Dunn, and others. For a time Francis L. Cardoza served as Secretary of State for South Carolina and later as state treaesurer. Louisiana had threee Negro lieutenant-governors. Some diplomats of the period were Frederick Douglass, John Mercer Langston, John Henry Smyth, J. E. W. Thompson, William F. Powell, Henry W. Furness, E. E. Smith and Ernest W. Lyon. These men served as ministers to the Negro republics of Haiti and Liberia.

[61] Samuel Denny Smith, *The Negro in Congress*, p. 78.

[62] *Congressional Globe*, 42 Cong., 2 Sess., pp. 1442-1443.

[63] In C. Woodson, ed., *op. cit.*, p. 498.

[64] *Ibid.*

[65] Samuel Denny Smith, *op. cit.*, p. 76.

[66] *Congressional Record*, 43 Cong., 2 Sess., pp. 958ff.

[67] *Congressional Record*, 43 Cong., 1 Sess., pp. 4782-4786.

[68] *Ibid.*

[69] In C. Woodson, ed., *op.cit.*, p. 500.

[70] *Congressional Record*, 43 Cong., 1st Sess., pp. 565-567.

[71] *Ibid.*, pp. 4782-84.

[72] *Ibid.*

[73] *Ibid.*, II, Pt. V, 43 Cong., 1 Sess., pp. 4782-4786.

[74] *Ibid.*

[75] *Ibid.*, Pt. 1, 43 Cong., 1 Sess., pp. 565-567.

[76] *Ibid.*, 43 Cong., 2 Sess., pp. 958ff.

[77] *Ibid.*

[78] *Ibid.*, II, Pt. 1, 43 Cong., 1 Sess., pp. 565-567.

[79] See S. D. Smith, *The Negro in Congress*, p. 115. See also Richard Bardolph, "The Distinguished Negro in America, 1770-1936," *American Historical Review*, Vol. 60, No. 3, April 1955, and by the same author, "Social Origins of Distinguished Negroes, 1770-1865," *Journal of Negro History*, Vol. 40, No. 3 ,July, 1955.

[80] Robert Russa Moton, *What the Negro Thinks*, p. 140.

[81] *New York Tribune*, July 4, 1871 and Dec. 5, 1867; Walter Lynwood Fleming, *Documentary History of the Civil War and Reconstruction*, II, pp. 76ff., Fisk University, *op. cit.*, p. 124.

[82] *Congressional Record*, II, Pt. 1, 43 Cong., 1 Sess., pp. 407-410.

[83] John Mercer Langston, *op. cit.*, pp. 209-231.

[84] *Ibid.*

[85] Archibald Grimke, *The Shame of the Republic*.

[86] Kelly Miller, *Out of the House of Bondage* (New York: Neale Publishing Company (1914).

[87] *Journal of Social Science*, May, 1880, Vol. XI.

[88] Cf. article in San Francisco *Examiner*, March 3, 1890, p. 1; and Mozell Hill, "The All Negro Communities of Oklahoma: The Natural History of a Social Movement," *Journal of Negro History*, XXXI, July, 1946, pp. 254-268. For still another movement of the period, see J. Fred Rippy, "A Negro Colonization Project in Mexico, 1895," *Journal of Negro History*, VI, Jan., 1921, pp. 66-73.

[90] On Singleton's role in this movement see Herbert Aptheker, *Documentary History of the American Negro* (New York: Citadel Press, 1951), pp. 308-383.

[91] *Journal of Social Science*, May, 1880, Vol. XI. For Booker Washington's ideas on the exodus see *Journal of Negro Education*, XVII, 1948, p. 463.

[92] *Journal of Social Science*, May, 1880, Vol. XI.

[93] Cf. Gunnar Myrdal, *An American Dilemma* (New York: Harpers,

1944), pp. 185-86, 746-49, 805-807; Guy B. Johnson, "Negro Radical Movements," *American Journal of Sociology*, XLIII, pp. 577-71; and Bell I. Wiley, *Southern Negroes* (New Haven: 1938).

[94] *Journal of Social Science*, May, 1880, Vol. XI.

[95] Cf. Greener's paper, "The Emigration of Colored Citizens From the Southern States," read before American Social Science Association, Sept. 12, 1874, quoted in C. Woodson, ed., *op. cit.*, pp. 473ff.

[96] Rayford W. Logan, *The Negro in American Life and Thought* (New York: Dial Press, 1954), p. 12.

[97] *Congressional Record*, April 27, 1882, 47 Cong., 1 Sess., pp. 3384-3387.

[98] James T. Rapier, *loc. cit.*

[99] *Congressional Record*, 45 Cong., 3 Sess., pp. 1307, 1314.

[100] *Ibid.*, 43 Cong., 1 Sess., pp. 1442, 1443, 4967.

[101] In C. G. Woodson, ed., *op. cit.*, p. 541.

[102] Rayford W. Logan, *op. cit.*, p. 12.

[103] Sterling Brown, "Negro Folk Expression," *Phylon*, XI, 4th Qtr. 1950, p. 318.

[104] James Weldon Johnson, *Along This Way*, p. 149.

[105] In A. Locke, ed., *The New Negro* (New York: Albert and Charles Boni, 1925), p. 31. Italics supplied.

[106] *Congressional Record*, 56th Cong., 1st Sess., pp. 2150-2151.

[107] From memorial to Congress of the National Association of Colored Men, meeting in Detroit, Michigan, 1896, in *Senate Document* No. 61, 54th Cong., 1st Sess.

CHAPTER XIV

THE NEGRO AND EDUCATION AND SEGREGATION

[1] See 1787 petition of Boston Negroes to the Massachuetts legislature for adequate schooling for their children, quoted in Herbert Aptheker, ed., *Documentary History of the American Negro* (New York: Citadel Press, 1951), pp. 19-20. For a good discussion of ante-bellum Negro schools see George Washington Williams, *History of the Negro Race in America from 1619 to 1880* (New York: Putnam and Sons, 1883), II, Ch. XII.

[2] Frederick Douglass, *Lectures on American Slavery by Frederick Douglass* (Buffalo: 1851).

[3] H. Aptheker, ed., *op. cit.*, pp. 72-73.

[4] Se editorial, *Freedom's Journal*, New York, March 16, 1827.

[5] Cf. autobiographical statement of Turner, quoted in H. Aptheker, *op. cit.*, p. 122.

[6] *Ibid.*, p. 151.

[7] *Proceedings*, National Negro Convention (Rochester, New York: 1853).

[8] Quoted in Julia Griffiths, ed., *Autographs For Freedom*, II (Rochester, New York: 1854).

[9] See A. A. McPheeters, "Interest of the Methodist Church in the Education of Negroes," *Phylon*, X, 4th Qtr., 1949, pp. 343-350.

[10] See his "Seventy Years of the Negro College, 1860-1930," *Phylon*, X, 4th Qtr., 1949, p. 307. .

[11] *Ibid.*, p. 110.

[12] Cf. Bell I. Wiley, *Southern Negroes*, pp. 274-275.

[13] Cf. Walter L. Fleming, *Civil War and Reconstruction*, pp. 458ff.; Philip A. Bruce, *The Plantation Negro As A Freedman*, pp. 7ff.

[14] *Congressional Globe*, 42 Cong., 2 Sess., pp. 808ff. Representative R. H. Cain of South Carolina held a similar attitude toward education. (See speech, *Congressional Record*, 45 Cong., 3 Sess., pp. 683-688.

[15] *Congressional Record*, 43 Cong., 1 Sess., II, Pt. V, pp. 4782-86.

[16] *Ibid.*

[17] *Congressional Globe*, 42 Cong., 2 Sess., Appendix, pp. 15-17.

[18] *Ibid.*

[19] Quoted in Carter G. Woodson, ed., *Negro Orators and Their Orations* (Washington, D. C.: Associated Publishers, 1925), p. 624.

[20] *Ibid.*, p. 655, speech by William Pickens.

[21] *Ibid.*, p. 586, speech by Roscoe Conkling Bruce.

[22] *Congressional Record*, 43 Cong., 1 Sess., II, Pt. V, pp. 4782-4786.

[23] *Congressional Record*, 42 Cong., 2 Sess., Appendix, pp. 15-17.

[24] *Congressional Record*, 43 Cong., 2 Sess., pp. 958ff.

[25] John Mercer Langston, *Lectures and Addresses of John Mercer Langston*, pp. 141-161.

[26] *Ibid.*, 43 Cong., 1 Sess., pp. 1311ff; *Ibid.*, pp. 346, 576ff. for statements by Congressmen Rainey, A. J. Ransier, Richard H. Cain, Benjamin S. Turner and others.

[27] *Ibid.*, 45 Cong., 3 Sess., pp. 683ff. Also on education of the freedmen see D. C. Darrow, Jr., "A Georgia Plantation," *Scribner's Monthly*, April, 1881; S. Barrow, "What the Southern Negro is doing for Himself," *Atlantic Monthly*, June, 1891; "Mental Capacity and Attainments of the Negro," *New York Tribune*, Aug. 12, 1874; "Education of the Freedmen," *Debow's Review*, July, 1866; Horace Mann Bond, *Education of the Negro in the American Social Order*.

[28] In H. Aptheker, ed., *op. cit.*, p. 151.

[29] Cf. Robert R. Moton, *What the Negro Thinks*, p. 105.

[30] *The Negro Yearbook*, 1937-38, p. 2.

[31] John Mercer Langston, *Lectures and Addresses of John Mercer Langston*, pp. 141-161.

[32] *Ibid.*

[33] In his *What the Negro Thinks*.

[34] William Pickens, "The Kind of Democracy the Negro Race Expects," in C. G. Woodson, ed., *Negro Orators and Their Orations*, p. 656-657.

[35] R. R. Moton, *What the Negro Thinks,* p. 111.

[36] Cf. his "Role of Private Colleges for Negroes," *Phylon,* X, 4th Qtr., 1949, p. 327.

[37] *Ibid.,* pp. 326-327. See also Oliver C. Cox, "Negro Teachers, Martyrs to Integration?" *Nation,* Vol. 176, April 25, 1953, p. 347; Albert N. D. Brooks, "Negro History, A Foundation for Integration," *Negro History Bulletin,* Vol. 17, Jan., 1954, pp. 96ff.; Walter White, "What Negroes Want Now," *United States News,* Vol. 36, May 28, 1954, pp. 54-59; Roy N. Wilkins, "Segregation gets an O.K. if treatment is Equal," *U. S. News,* Vol. 33, Dec. 12, 1952, pp. 30-31; A. C. Powell, Jr., "What the Negro Wants," *U. S. News,* Vol. 33, Sept. 5, 1952, p. 52-59; H. L. Moon, "New Emancipation, the Atlanta Conference," *Nation,* Vol. 178, June 5, 1954, pp. 484-485; E. F. Frazier, "Human, all Too Human; How Some Negroes Have Developed Vested Interests in the System of Racial Segregation," *Survey Graphic,* Vol. 36, Jan., 1947, pp. 74-75.

[38] R. R. Moton, *op. cit.,* p. 140.

[39] *Ibid., p.* 90.

[40] *Ibid.*

[41] *Ibid.,* pp. 92-93. See also T. C. Cochran, "Negro Conceptions of White People," *American Journal of Sociology,* Vol. 56, March, 1951, pp. 458-467.

[42] R. R. Moton, *op. cit.,* p. 138.

[43] *Ibid.,* p. 96.

[44] *Ibid.,* p. 67.

[45] *Ibid.,* pp. 217-218.

[46] In his column, "My View," *Pittsburgh Courier,* Louisiana ed., Aug. 13, 1955, p. 6.

[47] In their *Black Metropolis,* p. 128.

[48] J Curtis Dixon, "Changing School Patterns in the South," reprinted in *Proceedings of the Southern Association of Secondary Schools and Colleges,* 1955, p. 182.

[49] Quoted in *Phylon,* 3d Qtr., 1951, pp. 215-216.

[50] Rev. Randolph R. Claiborne, Jr., quoted in the *Pittsburgh Courier,* Louisiana ed., Aug. 13, 1955, p. 4.

[51] *Ibid.*

[52] *Loc. cit.,* p. 217.

[53] *Ibid.,* p. 218.

[54] Cf. editorial, *The Carolina Times* (Durham, North Carolina), Mar. 17, 1956.

[55] Quoted in Carter G. Woodson, ed., *Negro Orators and Their Orations* (Washington, D. C.: Associated Publishers, 1925), p. 439.

CHAPTER XV
THE WASHINGTON - DU BOIS CONTROVERSY

[1] G. W. Grimke, *Journal of Negro History*, XXXX, July, 1955, p. 283, reviewing Rayford W. Logan's, *The Negro in American Life and Thought* (New York: Dial Press, 1954).

[2] Rayford W. Logan, *op.cit.*, p. 275.

[3] *Ibid.*

[4] Quoted in Alice M. Bacon, *The Negro and the Atlanta Exposition* (Baltimore: 1896), pp. 12-16. Subsequent quotes from this address are also taken from this source.

[5] *Ibid.*

[6] *Ibid.*

[7] Letter from Douglass to his former master, printed in The *Liberator*, Sept. 22, 1848.

[8] T. Thomas Fortune, *Black and White: Land, Labor and Politics In the South* (New York: 1884).

[9] E. D. Washington, ed., *Selected Speeches of Booker T. Washington* (New York: Doubleday, 1932), p. 6.

[10] Booker T. Washington, *Working With the Hands* (New York: Doubleday, 1904), p. 58.

[11] E. D. Washington, ed., *op. cit.*, p. 7.

[12] B. T. Washington, *The Future of the American Negro* (Boston: Small, Maynard and Co., 1899), p. 53.

[13] Cf. Herbert Aptheker, ed., *Documentary History of the American Negro* (New York: Citadel Press, 1951), pp. 663ff.

[14] From *Frederick Douglass' Paper*, in *African Repository*, XXIX (Washington, D. C.: 1853).

[15] Quoted in Carter G. Woodson, ed., *Negro Orators and their Orations* (Washington, D. C.: Associated Publishers, 1925), p. 593.

[16] *Ibid.*, pp. 593-594.

[17] *Ibid.*

[18] See W. H. Councill, "The Future of the Negro," *Forum*, XXVII, July, 1899, p. 570; and Earl E. Thorpe, "William Hooper Councill," *Negro History Bulletin*, XIX, January, 1956, pp. 85ff..

[19] E. D. Washington, ed., *op. cit.*, p. 189.

[20] *Ibid.*, p. 7. See also August Meier, "Toward a Reinterpretation of Booker T. Washington," *Journal of Southern History*, XXIII, pp. 220ff. Meier declares of Washington—"His ultimate ends were stated so vaguely and ambiguously that southern whites mistook his short-range objectives for his long-range goals." (p. 220).

[21] *Ibid.* See also letter which Washington sent to the disfranchisement Constitutional Convention in Louisiana of 1898, in H. Aptheker, ed., *op. cit.*, pp. 781-784.

[22] Cf. Samuel R .Spencer, Jr., *Booker T. Washington* (Boston: Little, Brown and Co., 1955), p. 117.

[23] *Ibid.*, p. 129.

[24] *Ibid.*, pp. 130, 163.

[25] See review by G. W. Grimke, *Journal of Negro History*, XXXX, July, 1955, p. 283.

[26] In Carter G. Woodson, ed., *Negro Orators and Their Orations*, p. 529.

[27] In *Black-Belt Diamonds: Gems from the Speeches, Addresses, and Talks to Students of Booker T. Washington* (New York: Fortune and Scott) p. 40).

[28] In Carter G. Woodson, ed., *Negro Orators and Their Orations*, p. 493.

[29] *Ibid.*, p. 611.

[30] In Carter G. Woodson, ed., *Negro Orators and Their Orations*, p. 584.

[31] *Ibid.*

[32] Jack Abramowitz, "Crossroads of Negro Thought, 1890-1895," *Social Education*, XVIII, 3, March, 1954, p. 120.

[33] *Ibid.*, p. 119.

[34] See John H. Franklin, *From Slavery to Freedom* (New York: A. A. Knopf, 1948), pp. 387-390.

[35] Chicago: A. C. McClurg and Co., 1904. See also Elliot M. Rudwick, "The Niagara Movement," *Journal of Negro History*, XXXXII, 3, July, 1957, pp. 177ff.; Wilson Record, "Negro Intellectual Leadership in the NAACP: 1910-40," *Phylon*, 4th Qtr., 1956; and Elliott M. Rudwick, "W. E. B. Du Bois: in the Role of Crisis Editor," *Journal of Negro History*, XLIII, 3, July, 1958, pp. 214-240.

[36] See W. E. B. Du Bois, *Souls of Black Folk*, essay entitled "The Talented Tenth."

[37] *Ibid.*, p. 52.

[38] See *By Booker T. Washington* (New York: Doubleday, Doran and Co., 1929), p. 214.

[39] Cf. W. E. B. DuBois, *Dusk of Dawn* (New York: Harcourt, Brace, 1945).

[40] B. T. Washington, *My Larger Education* (New York: Doubleday, 1911), pp. 120ff.

[41] In this connection, see the excellent unpublished Ph.D. dissertation by Blyden Jackson, "Of Tragedy in Negro Fiction," University of Michigan, 1952.

[42] See H. Aptheker, ed.., *op. cit.*, p. 881.

[43] S. R. Spencer, *op. cit.*, pp. 164-165.

[44] *Ibid.*, pp. 162-163.

[45] *Ibid.*, Chapter X. See also "William Monroe Trotter, 1782-1934," by Charles W. Puttkammer and Ruth Worthy," *Journal of Negro History*, XLIII, 4, Oct.., 1950, p. 302.

[46] *Ibid.*, pp. 167-168ff. See also chapter herein entitled, "Some Attitudes of Negroes Toward American Presidents."

[47] New York: The Social Science Press, 1954.

[48] S. R. Spencer, *op. cit.*, p. 200.

[49] *Ibid.*, p. 152.

[50] See chapter herein entitled "Hostility, Revenge, and Protest as Elements in Negro Thought."

[51] See Benjamin Quarles, *Frederick Douglass* (Washington, D. C.: The Associated Publishers, 1948), pp. 23, 34.

[52] Samuel R. Spencer, Jr., *Booker T. Washington and the Negro's Place in American Life* (Boston: Little, Brown, 1955), pp. 23-26; 28ff.

[53] Cf. W. E. B. DuBois, *Suppression of the African Slave Trade to the United States of America,* 1954 reprint (New York: The Social Science Press), "Apologia."

[54] In W. E. B. DuBois, *Dusk of Dawn* (New York:) Harcourt, Brace. 1940); and evident throughout his *Black Reconstruction* (New York: Harcourt, Brace, 1935).

[55] W. E. B. DuBois, *Suppression of the African Slave Trade to the United States of America,* "Apologia."

[56] Cf. his *Dusk of Dawn.*

[57] Benjamin Quarles, *op.cit.,* p. 162.

[58] *Ibid.,* p. 75.

[59] *Ibid.,* p. 162.

[60] *Ibid.,* p. 168.

[61] B. .Quarles, *op. cit.,* p. 336, quoting the Rochester *Democrat and Chronicle* of August 7, 1883.

[62] *Douglass' Paper* in *African Repository* (Washington, D. C.), XXIX, May, 1853, p. 137.

[63] Quoted in Alice M. Bacon, *The Negro and the Atlanta Exposition* (Baltimore: 1896), pp. 12-16.

Chapter XVI

NORTH AND SOUTH IN NEGRO THOUGHT

[1] Cf. Herbert Aptheker, ed., *Documentary History of the American Negro* (New York: Citadel Press, 1951), p. 227.

[2] In C. G. Woodson, ed., *Negro Orators and Their Orations* (Washington, D. C.: Associated Publishers, 9125), p. 66.

[3] *The Liberator,* July 9, 1841.

[4] Archibald Grimke, *The Shame of the Republic.*

[5] Kenneth Stampp, *The Peculiar Institution* (New York: A. A. Knopf, 1957), p. 379.

[6] *Ibid..,* p. 377.

[7] *Ibid.,* p. 381. On this point see also Drew, *The Refugee,* pp. 30, 86, 156-57; Williams Wells Brown, *Narrative,* pp. 102-130.

[8] Fisk University, *op. cit.,* p. 215.

[9] *Ibid.,* p. 225.

[10] W. E. B. Du Bois, *Black Reconstruction* (New York: Harcourt, Brace).

[11] Kelly Miller, *Out of the House of Bondage* (New York: Neale Publishing Co., 1914).

[12] B. A. Botkin, ed., *Lay My Burden Down* (Chicago: University of Chicago Press, 1945), p. 169.

[13] Robert Russa Moton, *What the Negro Thinks* (New York: Doubleday, 1929).

[14] *Ibid.*, p. 39.

[15] B. A. Botkin, ed., *op. cit.*, p. 109.

[16] *Ibid.*, pp. 110, 118, 238.

[17] Kelly Miller, *op. cit.*

[18] *Ibid.*

[19] In R. A. Carter, *Feeding Among the Lillies*, pp. 272-288.

[20] *Congressional Record*, 43d Cong., 1st Sess., p. 410.

[21] *Ibid.*, 44 Cong., 1 Sess., p. 5542.

[22] James Weldon Johnson, "O Southland!"

[23] C. G. Woodson, ed., *Negro Orators*, p. 491.

[24] William H. Lewis, in C. Woodson, ed., *op. cit.*, p. 599.

[25] *Ibid.*, p. 48.

[26] Frederick Douglass, *Lectures on American Slavery by Frederick Douglass* (Buffalo: 1851).

[27] Archibald Grimke, *op.cit.*

[28] *The Liberator*, Febr. 25, 1842.

[29] *Ibid.*, Nov. 18, 1842.

[30] *Ibid.*, Nov. 6, 1863.

[31] *Ibid.*

[32] *The North Star*, March 2, 1863, editorial.

[33] C. G. Woodson, ed., *op. cit.*, p. 43.

[34] Frederick Douglass, 1846 speech in England, reprinted in Appendix of his *My Bondage and Freedom*.

[35] In C. G. Woodson, ed., *op.. cit.*, p. 517.

[36] *Ibid.*, p. 705.

[37] Cf. his *The Negro Family in the United States*, p. 213. See also George W. Lee, *Beale Street* (New York: Vail-Ballou Press, 1943); Sterling A. Brown, "The Blues," *Phylon*, XIII, 4th Qtr., 1952, pp. 286-292; Charles S. Johnson, et alia, *Shadow of the Plantation* (Chicago: University of Chicago Press, 1934); Edwin R. Embree, *Brown America* (New York: The Viking Press, 1935).

[38] Alain Locke, *The New Negro*, (New York: Albert and Charles Boni, 1925), p. 8.

[38] Cf. A. T. Andreas, *History of Chicago: From the Earliest Period to the Present Time*, 3 vols. (Chicago: 1884), I, pp. 70-71.

[40] Langston Hughes, *The Big Sea* (New York: 1940), p. 225.

[41] A. Lcke, ed., *The New Negro*, pp. 8-9.

[42] Cf. Gunnar Myrdal, *An American Dilemma* (New York: Harpers, 1940), Ch. XXI.

[43] Carl Van Vechten, "The Negro in Art: How Shall He be Portrayed?" *The Crisis*, XXI, 1926, p. 219.

[44] Cf. T. J. Woofter, Jr., *Negro Problems in Cities* (New York: 1923); E. F. Frazier, *The Negro Family in the United States*, 1948 ed., Ch. XVII.

[45] E. F. Frazier, *The Negro Family in the United States*, p. 257ff.

[46] *Ibid.*

[47] Ruth Reed, *op. cit.*, p. 49.

[48] E. F. Frazier, *The Negro Family*, 1948 ed., pp. 228-229.

[49] R. R. Moton, *What the Negro Thinks*, p. 238.

[50] *Ibid.*, p. 22.

[51] R. R. Moton, *op. cit.*, p. 259.

[52] *Ibid.*, p. 55.

[53] *Freedom's Journal*, New York, March 16, 1827.

[54] R. R. Moton, *op. cit.*, p. 32.

[55] *Ibid.*, pp. 187, 185.

[56] *Ibid.*, pp. 188-189.

[57] A. Locke, ed., *The New Negro*, p 5.

[58] Randolph Edmonds, *Six Plays For a Negro Theatre* (Boston: 1934), p. 111.

CHAPTER XVII

SOME SOURCES AND PATTERNS OF PUBLIC BEHAVIOR

[1] *The Liberator*, Oct. 22, 1831.

[2] Letter from William Wells Brown, London, England to Enoch Price, St. Louis, Missouri, in *The Liberator*, Dec. 14, 1849.

[3] *The Liberator*, July 9, 1841.

[4] Quoted in C. G. Woodson, ed., *Negro Orators and Their Orations* (Washington, D. C.: Associated Publishers, 1925), p. 571.

[5] *The Liberator*, Febr. 25, 1842.

[6] *Ibid.*

[7] William Wells Brown, London, England, letter of Nov., 1849 to Wendell Phillips, in *The Liberator*, Nov. 30, 1849.

[8] *Proceedings* (Rochester: 1853).

[9] C. G. Woodson, ed., *op. cit.*, p. 349.

[10] *Ibid.*, p. 538.

[11] *Ibid.*, p. 656.

[12] John Mercer Langston, *Lectures and Addresses of John Mercer Langston*, pp. 141-161.

[13] *Freedom's Journal*, New York, March 16, 1827.

[14] *The Liberator*, April 19, 1834.

[15] *Ibid.*, Aug. 1, 1835.

[16] See, for example, speech delivered by W. E. B. DuBois before April,

1960 meeting of the Association of Social Science Teachers, Johnson C. Smith University, Charlotte, North Carolina.

[17] In Woodson, ed., *op. cit.*, p. 97.

[18] *Ibid.*, p. 98.

[19] *Proceedings* (Rochester: 1853).

[20] *The Liberator*, Dec. 10, 1852.

[21] Letter from Remond to Charles B. Ray, June 30, 1840, London, England, in *The Liberator*, Oct. 16, 1840.

[22] *Ibid.*, Febr. 25, 1842.

[23] See, for example, *The Liberator*, Nov. 4, 1842, protest resolutions drawn by Boston Afro-Americans on October 27, 1842.

[24] *Ibid.*, May 18, 1860..

[25] Francis Cardoza, speaking before a meeting of Charlestonians, March 21, 1867, quoted in *New York Daily Tribune*, March 26, 1867.

[26] *Congressional Globe*, 42 Cong., 2 Sess., p. 1443.

[27] *Congressional Record*, 43 Cong., 1 Sess., II, Pt. V, pp. 4782-4786.

[28] See Walter L. Fleming, *Civil War and Reconstruction in Alabama*, pp. 775ff, and *New York Tribune*, Aug. 19, 1868.

[29] See Walter L. Fleming, *op. cit.*, pp. 562ff; J. S. Reynolds, *Reconstruction in South Carolina*, pp. 370ff; and other state histories of the period.

[30] Cf. speech by South Carolina Congressman Robert C. DeLarge, in *Congressional Globe*, 42 Cong., 1 Sess., Appendix, p. 230.

[31] Cf., for example, the testimony of Henry Adams, a leader of the 1879 mass migrations from the South, in *Senate Report 693*, 46 Cong., 2 Sess., Pt. 2, pp. 101-11.

[32] Speech by Sydenham Porter, of Livingston, Alabama, July 18, 1868, in *Testimony Taken by the Joint Committee to Inquire Into the Condition of Affairs in the Late Insurrectionary States* (Washington, D. C.: Government Printing Office, 1872).

[33] The *Daily Advertiser*, Montgomery, Ala., Aug. 8, 1872.

[34] William Still, *An Address on Voting and Laboring* (Philadelphia, 1872)..

[35] Wilson Record, *The Negro and the Communist Party* (Chapel Hill: University of North Carolina Press), p. 312.

[36] R. R. Moton, *op. cit.*, p. 136.

[37] *Ibid.*, p. 162.

[38] Frederick Douglass, at 1883 National Negro Convention, Louisville, Kentucky.

[39] James T. Rapier, *loc. cit.*

[40] In J. W. E. Bowen, ed., *Africa and the American Negro* (Atlanta: 1896), p. 98.

[41] Quoted in *The Negro Problem* (New York: 1903), p. 124.

[42] John Q. Johnson, *Report of the Fifth Tuskegee Negro Conference* (Baltimore: 1896).

[43] In *The Christian Recorder*, June 18, 1891.

⁴⁴ J. Max Barber, ed., *The Voice of the Negro*, July, 1904.

⁴⁵ See C. G. Woodson, ed., *op. cit.*, p. 252.

⁴⁶ James T. Rapier, *loc. cit.*

⁴⁷ R. R. Moton, *op. cit.*, p. 135.

⁴⁸ See report in New York *Daily Tribune*, Jan. 15, 1881. On the freedmen see also Henderson H. Donald, *The Negro Freedman* (New York: H. Schuman, 1952); Allan Nevins, *The Emergence of Modern America, 1865-1878*; Claude G. Bowers, *The Tragic Era* (Cambridge, Mass.: 1929); Walter L. Fleming, *Documents Relating to Reconstruction* (Morgantown, West Virginia: 1904), and his *Documentary History of Reconstruction*, 2 vols.. (Cleveland: 1906-07).

⁴⁹ *Congressional Record*, 47 Cong., 1 Sess., June 7, 1882, p. 4656.

⁵⁰ See *Appleton's Annual Cyclopedia* (New York: 1889), p. 721.

⁵¹ See Herbert J. Aptheker, ed., *Documentary History of the American Negro* (New York: Citadel Press, 1950).

⁵² See C. G. Woodson, ed., *op. cit.*, pp. 411-417.

⁵³ T. Thomas Fortune, *Black and White: Land, Labor and Politics in the South* (New York: 1884).

⁵⁴ *The Birth of the Afro-American National League* (Chicago: 1890).

⁵⁵ From Address to the People of the United States adopted by the 1890 Convention of Colored Americans, Washington, D. C., and submitted to the United States Senate; published as *Senate Miscellaneous Document No. 82, 51 Cong., 1 Sess.*

⁵⁶ In *The A.M.E. Church Review* (Philadelphia) July, 1887, Ill., pp. 497-505.

⁵⁷ R. R. Moton, *What the Negro Thinks*, p. 237.

⁵⁸ In C. Woodson, ed., *op.cit.*, p. 530.

⁵⁹ *Ibid.*, p. 567., speech by William H. Lewis, delivered before the Massachusetts House of Representatives, Febr. 12, 1913.

⁶⁰ *Ibid.*, p. 497, speech by J. C. Price.

⁶¹ James T. Rapier, *loc. cit.*

⁶² *Ibid.*, p. 254.

⁶³ *Congressional Record*, 43 Cong., 1 Sess., II, Pt. 5, pp. 4782-4786.

⁶⁴ Editorial, *The Crisis*, July, 1917, p. 114.

⁶⁵ See E. F. Frazier, *The Negro Family in the United States*, 1948 ed., pp. 308-309.

⁶⁶ *Ibid.*, p. 151.

⁶⁷ *Proceedings*, published at Frederick Douglass' press, Rochester, 1853.

⁶⁸ R. R. Moton, *op. cit.*, pp. 147-148.

⁶⁹ R. R. Moton, *op.cit.*, p. 155.

⁷⁰ *Senate Document No. 61, 54 Cong., 1 Sess.*

⁷¹ R. R. Moton, *op. cit.*, p. 255.

⁷² Chapel Hill: University of North Carolina Press, 1950.

⁷³ See C. Vann Woodward, *Tom Watson: Agrarian Rebel.*

⁷⁴ *Congressional Record*, 53 Cong., 1 Sess., pp. 858ff.

⁷⁵ In C. Woodson, ed., *op. cit.*, p. 669. .

[76] *Ibid.*, pp. 667ff.

[77] *Congressional Record*, 51 Cong., 2 Sess., pp. 1479-1483 .

[78] Cf. manuscript, "Du Bois, Letter Launching the Niagara Movement," in H. Aptheker, ed., *op. cit.*, pp. 900-901.

[79] Cf. *The Voice of the Negro* (Atlanta), Sept., 1905.

[80] National Association for the Advancement of Colored People, *The NAACP: Its History, Achievement, Purposes* (New York: Published by the NAACP, 1933).

[81] Wilson Record, *op. cit.*, p. 92.

[82] B. Mays, "My View," *Pittsburgh Courier*, Louisiana ed., Aug. 13, 1955, p. 6.

[83] Walter White's writings include: *Fire in the Flint* (1924); *Flight* (1924); *Rope and Faggot* (1929); *A Rising Wind* (1945); *A Man Called White* (1948); and *How Far The Promised Land?*

[84] Editorial, *The Crisis,* I, 1910, p. 10.

[85] See *Phylon*, X, 4th Qtr., 1949, p. 305.

[86] In his *A Pageant in Seven Decades* (Atlanta: 1938), p. 27.

[87] Alain Locke, ed., *The New Negro* (New York: Albert and Charles Boni, 1925), p. 11.

CHAPTER XVIII

SOME ATTITUDES OF NEGROES TOWARD
AMERICAN PRESIDENTS

[1] Quoted in Carter G. Woodson, ed., *Negro Orators and their Orations* (Washington, D. C.: Associated Publishers, 1925), p. 672, hereinafter referred to as *Negro Orators*.

[2] *Ibid.*, p. 675.

[3] See section on Brown in Vernon Loggins, *The Negro Author* (New York: Columbia University Press, 1931).

[4] See section on this period in Woodson, ed., *Negro Orators*.

[5] See Earl E. Thorpe, *Negro Historians in the United States* (Baton Rouge, Louisiana: Fraternal Press, 1958), Ch. II.

[6] C. Woodson, ed., *Negro Orators*, p. 128.

[7] *Ibid.*, p. 675.

[8] Cf. Earl E. Thorpe, *op. cit.*, p. 34. Also on Washington see Walter H. Mazyck, *George Washington and the Negro* (Washington, D. C.: Associated Publishers, 1932).

[9] C. Woodson, *Negro Orator*, p. 220.

[10] *Ibid.*, pp. 44-45.

[11] See Herbert J. Aptheker, *Documentary History of the American Negro* (New York: Citadel Press, 1950), p. 319; hereinafter referred to as *Doc. Hist.*

[12] See, for example, Raymond Garfield Dandridge's reference to Lincoln

in his poem "De Innah Part," in Dandridge's, *The Poet and Other Poems* (Cincinnati, Ohio: 1920).

[13] Kelly Miller, *Out of the House of Bondage* (New York: Neale Publication Company, 1914).

[14] Aptheker, ed., *Doc. Hist.*, pp. 474-475.

[15] Cf. Miles Mark Fisher, *Negro Slave Songs* (New York: Cornell University Press, 1949). See also John Hope Franklin, *From Slavery to Freedom* (New York: A. A. Knopf, 1955 ed.), Ch. XIV.

[16] Aptheker, ed., *Doc. Hist.*, p. 516.

[17] Bell I. Wley, *Southern Negroes* (New Haven: Yale University Press, 1938), p. 290.

[18] Quoted in B. A. Botkin, ed., *Lay My Burden Down* (Chicago, Illinois: Chicago University Press, 1945), p. 240.

[19] Quoted in Fisk University, *Unwritten History of Slavery* (Social Science Document, Nashville, Tennessee, 1945), p. 93.

[20] *Ibid.*, p. 230.

[21] Quoted in Woodson, *Negro Orators*, p. 522. See also Earl E. Thorpe, "The Day Freedom Came," *Negro History Bulletin*, October, 1958.

[22] *Ibid.*

[23] Quoted in Woodson, *Negro Orators*, p. 526.

[24] *Ibid.*, p. 519.

[25] *Ibid.*

[26] *Ibid.*, p. 521.

[27] *Ibid.*, p. 523.

[28] *Ibid.*, p. 527.

[29] *Ibid.*, p. 551.

[30] See, for example, speech by W. T. Vernon, 1905, quoted in Woodson, *Negro Orators*, p. 621, also p. 557.

[31] *Ibid.*, p. 557.

[32] *Ibid.*, p. 588.

[33] *Ibid.*, p. 555.

[34] *Ibid.*, p. 602.

[35] *Ibid.*, p. 554. Also on Lincoln see James H. Hubert, *The Life of Abraham Lincoln, Its Significance to Negroes and Jews* (New York: W. Mallett, 1939).

[36] New York: Harcourt, Brace, 1935. See also, Earl E. Thorpe, *op.cit.*, p. 97. For a general study of the political thought of the Negro between 1865-1900 see Elsie M. Lewis, "The Political Mind of the Negro, 1865-1900," *Journal of Southern History*, XXI, May, 1955, pp. 189-202.

[37] Quoted in Rayford W. Logan, *The Negro in American Life and Thought* New York: Dial, 1954, p. 41.

[38] New York *Freemen*, No. 22, 1884.

[39] *New York Times*, November 23, 1884.

[40] Quoted in Rayford W. Logan, *The Negro in the United States*, Anvil Book (New York: D. Van Nostrand, 1957), p. 46.

[41] Rayford W. Logan, *The Negro in American Life and Thought*, p. 52.

[42] *Ibid.*

[43] *Ibid..*, see also his Chapter IV.

[44] In W. Richardson, ed., *Messages and Papers of the President*, VIII (1911) pp. 6248ff. .

[45] For this and other evidence of support of Bryan by Negroes see H. Aptheker, ed., *Doc. Hist.*, pp. 818-19.

[46] *Ibid.*, pp. 787-791.

[47] *The American Citizen* (Kansas City, Kansas), November 17, 1899.

[48] See Jerome Dowd, *The Negro in American Life* (New York: Century Co., 1826), pp. 513-13.

[49] Rayford Logan, *The Negro in the United States*, p. 61. On the storm of animosity directed by Negroes at Roosevelt and Taft because of the Brownville riot see E. L. Thornbrough, "The Brownsville Episode and the Negro Vote," *Mississippi Valley Historical Review*, XLIV, Dec., 1957, pp. 469-493. On Roosevelt's relation with Booker Washington see August Meier, "Toward a Reinterpretation of Booker T. Washington," *Journal of Southern History*, XXIII, May, 1957, pp. 220ff.

[50] Quoted in Carter Woodson, ed., *Negro Orators*, p. 686.

[51] Elbert L. Tatum, *The Changed Political Thought of the Negro* (New York: Exposition Press, 1951), p. 85.

[52] Quoted in W. E. B. DuBois, "The Republicans and the Black Voter," *The Nation*, June 5, 1920, p. 757.

[53] Quoted in K. L. Wolgemuth, "Woodrow Wilson's Appointment Policy and the Negro," *Journal of Southern History*, XXIV, November, 1958, p. 471,

[54] E. L. Tatum, *op. cit.*, p. 94: J. G. Van Deusen, *The Black Man in White America* (Washington, D. C.: Associated Publishers, 1938, Ch. IX).

[55] Quoted in Carter Woodson, ed., *Negro Orators*, p. 660.

[56] Quoted in Jerome Dowd, *The Negro in American Life*, p. 513. For further condemnation of the speech see *Crisis* magazine, November, 1921; Baltimore *Afro-American*, November 2, 1921.

[57] For further praise of the speech by Negroes see *New York News*, November 3, 1921.

[58] E. L. Tatum, *op. cit.*, p. 98.

[59] *Ibid..*, pp. 98-99.

[60] Cf. "Why the Negro Should Vote for Hoover," *Crisis*, October, 1932.

[61] See editorial, "The Negro Votes Shifted from the Traditional Alignment," *Opportunity*, January, 1933.

[62] See editorial, "How the Negro Voted in the Presidential Election," *Opportunity*, December 1936, p. 359.

A NEW CENTURY

[1] Roscoe Conkling Bruce, quoted in Carter Woodson, ed., *Negro Orators and Their Orations* (Washington, D. C.: Associated Publishers, 1925), p. 591.

[2] *Ibid.*, p. 538.

[3] Quoted in *Phylon*, X, 4th Qtr., 1949, p. 305.

[4] Cf. *The Voice of the Negro* (Atlanta), March, 1906.

[5] For evidence of the way in which hatred of the Negro was deliberately aroused see J. Max Barber, ed., *The Voice of the Negro*, Nov., 1906, pp. 470-472.

[6] *Ibid.*, Oct. 4, 1906.

[7] *New York Age*, Sept. 27, 1906.

CHAPTER XIX

CAPITALISM, SOCIALISM, AND COMMUNISM IN NEGRO THOUGHT

[1] Abram L. Harris, *The Negro as Capitalist* (Philadelphia: 1836), pp. 53ff.

[2] E. Franklin Frazier, *Black Bourgeoisie* (Glencoe, Illinois: The Free Press, 1957), p. 242.

[3] Robert Russa Moton, "The Negro's Debt to Lincoln," in Carter G. Woodson, ed., *Negro Orators and Their Orations* (Washington, D. C.: Associated Publisheers, 1925), p. 576; hereinafter referred to as *Negro Orators*.

[4] *Proceedings of the National Negro Business League*, 1900.

[5] See article by Booker T. Washington in *World's Work* (New York), October, 1902, IV, pp. 2671-76.

[6] Robert Russa Moton, *What the Negro Thinks*. p. 31.

[7] E. Franklin Frazier, *The Negro Family in the United States*, 1948 ed., p. 366.

[8] Washington, D. C.: Associated Publishers, 1923.

[9] See George S. Schuyler, "Views and Reviews," in *Pittsburgh Courier*, Louisiana ed., August 13, 1955, p. 6.

[10] *The Postwar Outlook for Negroes in Small Business, the Engineering Professions, and Technical Vocations* (Howard University: Washington, D. C.: 1946).

[11] Cf. Abram L. Harris, *The Negro as Capitalist*, pp. 49ff.

[12] Benjamin Mays, *The Negro's God* (Boston: Chapman and Grimes, 1939), pp. 11-12.

[13] Wilson Record, *The Negro and the Communist Party* (Chapel Hill: University of North Carolina Press, 1953), p. 95.

[14] Quoted in W. K. Boyd, *The Story of Durham* (Durham: Duke University Press, 1927), pp. 282-283.

[15] *Black Bourgeoisie*, pp. 26ff.

[16] *Ibid.*, p. 126.

[17] *Ibid.*, p. 131.

[18] Ibid., pp. 209-10.

[19] *Ibid.,* pp. 24ff. On attitudes of Negroes toward business, see also Booker T. Washington, *The Negro in Business.* (Boston: Hertel, 1907).

[20] For Myer's speech, see *New York Times,* August 19, 1869.

[21] Cf. *The New Era* (Washington, D. C., January 13, 1870 and April 21, 1871.

[22] Wilson Record, *op. cit.,* p. 305..

[23] Quoted in *The A.M.E. Church Review* (Philadelphia) Oct., 1886, III, pp. 165-167.

[24] *Ibid.,* III, July, 1886, pp. 53-54.

[25] *Ibid.*

[26] *Ibid.*

[27] See Introduction to his *Black and White: Land, Labor and Politics in the South.*

[28] *Ibid.,* Preface.

[29] R. R. Moton, *op. cit.,* p. 140.

[30] Wilson Record, *op. cit.,* pp. 112ff.

[31] *Ibid.,* p. 302.

[32] *Ibid.,* p. 313.

[33] *Ibid..,* p. 26.

[34] Leslie Pinckney Hill, "Self-Determination: The Philosophy of the American Negro."

[35] Wilson Record, *op. cit.,* pp. 78-79.

[36] Cf. James W. Ford, *The Negro and the Democratic Front* (New York: International Publishers, 938); and Richard Wright, "Two Million Black Voices," *New Masses,* XVIII, No. 9, Febr. 25, 1936, p. 15.

[37] Wilson Record, *op. cit.,* pp. 154-161.

[38] See *The Crisis,* XLII, No. 10, Oct., 1935, p. 305.

[39] Wilson Record, *op. cit.,* p. 163.

[40] *Ibid.,* p. 207.

[41] B. Mays, *The Negro's God,* pp. 243-244.

[42] Wilson Record, *op. cit.,* p. 118.

[43] Cf. their *Black Metropolis* (New York: Harcourt, Brace, 1945), p. 736.

[44] *The Negro Digest,* III, No. 2, Dec., 1944, pp. 67-68.

[45] Wilson Record, *op. cit., pp.* 93-94.

[46] *Ibid.,* pp. 299, 193-200. Cf. also Yergan's *Democracy and the Negro People Today* (New York: National Negro Congress, 1940); A. Philip Randolph, "Why I Would Not Stand for Reelection," *American Federationist,* XLVIII, No. 1, July, 1940, p. 24; *The Negro Digest,* III, No. 2, Dec., 1944, p. 63.

[47] Cf. *Hearings Before the Committee on Un-American Activities,* House of Representatives, 81st Cong., 1st Sess., 1949, p. 464.

[48] Cf. "Henry Wallace," *The Crisis,* LV, No. 10, Oct., 1948; and *ibid.,* p. 297.

CHAPTER XX

THE PHILOSOPHY OF NEGRO HISTORY

[1] See Earl E. Thorpe, *Negro Historians in the United States* (Baton Rouge, La.: Fraternal Press, 1958), esp. Chapter I; the 1931 paper, "Perspectives in History" by Professor Evarts B. Greene, (*Journal of Negro History*, hereinafter referred to as *JNH*, XVII); L. D. Reddick, "A New Interpretation for Negro History," *JNH*, XXII, Jan., 1937. Over one-half or ten of the fourteen articles in the Oct., 1940 issue of this journal were devoted to an evaluation of Negro History and what has been termed the Negro History Movement. In this connection, see also, this journal, XX, No. 1, Jan., 1935 and No. 4, Oct., 1935. It is, perhaps, regrettable that the Presidential Address at each annual meeting of this Association is not published as a permanent record which would reveal shifts and changes in philosophy, as is the case with many historical societies.

[2] Henry Steele Commager, *The American Mind* (New Haven: Yale University Press, 1950), p. 278.

[3] Louis O. Kattsoff, *Elements of Philosophy* (New York: Ronald Press, 1953), p. 66.

[4] George Washington Williams, *History of the Negro Race in America, 1619-1880* (New York: G. P. Putnam's Sons, 1883), p. x.

[5] *JNH*, II, p. 443.

[6] Hartford, Connecticut.

[7] *JNH*, XX, 1937, p. 19.

[8] *Ibid.*

[9] In Hesseltine's "A Quarter-Century of the Association for the Study of Negro Life and History," *JNH*, XXV, 4, Oct., 1940, p. 442.

[10] John Hope Franklin, "The New Negro History," *JNH*, XLII, 2, April, 1957, pp. 89-197.

[11] *JNH*, II, 1926, p. 24.

[12] C. A. Hucker, *Chinese History: A Bibliographic Review* (Washington, D. C.: The American Historical Association, 1958), p. 1.

[13] *Ibid.*

[14] Philip D. Jordan, *The Nature and Practice of State and Local History* (Washington, D. C.: American Historical Association, 1958), p. 4.

[15] *Ibid.*, pp. 4, 16.

[16] *JNH*, XIII, p. 12.

[17] *Ibid.*

[18] Charles H. Wesley, "The Reconstruction of History," *JNH*, XX, 4, Oct., 1935, pp. 421-422.

[19] Charles G. Sellers, Jr., *Jacksonian Democracy* (Washington, D. C.: American Historical Association, 1958), pp. 3-5.

[20] On the continuing re-appraisal of historical interpretations, see Geoffrey Barraclough, *History in a Changing World* (Norman, Oklahoma: University of Oklahoma Press, 1955).

[21] Review by Rayford W. Logan, *JNH*, *XXI*, 1, Jan., 1936, p. 62.

[22] L. D. Reddick, "A New Interpretation for Negro History," *loc.cit.*

[23] *Ibid.*, p. 17.

[24] *Ibid.*

[25] *Ibid.*, pp. 23-25.

[26] Both of whom he refers to, calling DuBois "brilliant" and Beard "the most eminent of American historians."

[27] *Ibid.*, pp. 26-27.

[28] *Ibid.*, p. 27.

[29] *Ibid.*

[30] *Ibid.*, p. 28.

[31] At the time Dr. Reddick was teaching at Dillard University in New Orleans, while Dr. Fontaine was employed by Southern University at Baton Rouge.

[32] *Journal of Negro History*, XXV, No. 1, Jan., 1940, pp. 6-13.

[33] Ralph Bunche, Allison Davis, E. E. Just, and Abram Harris.

[34] "Alain Locke sometimes understands."

[35] "A much better compiler than interpreter," and "Dr. Johnson seems to be profoundly lacking in a sense of history."

[36] *Ibid.*, p. 6.

[39] R. R. Palmer, *A History of the Modern World*, 2nd ed. (New York: A. A. Knopf, 1956), pp. 607-612.

CHAPTER XXI

THE MIND OF THE NEGRO ARTIST
AND WRITER

[1] See Earl E. Thorpe, *Negro Historians in the United States* (Baton Rouge, Louisiana: Fraternal Press, 1958), Chs. I, II.

[2] *Ibid.*

[3] *Ibid.* See also Vernon Loggins, *The Negro Author* (New York: Columbia University Press, 1931); Herman Dreer, *American Literature by Negro Authors* (New York: Macmillan, 1949), Robert A. Bone, *The Negro Novel in America* (New Haven: Yale University Press, 1959); Hugh Gloster, *Negro Voices in American Fiction* (Chapel Hill: University of North Carolina Press), 1948.

[4] George Washington Williams, *History of the Negro Race in America from 1619 to 1880* (New York: Putnam and Sons, 1883), I.

[5] London: 1853.

[6] Blyden Jackson, "Of Tragedy in Negro Fiction," unpublished Ph.D. dissertation, University of Michigan, 1952, p. 92.

[7] *Ibid.*

[8] Hugh Gloster, *op. cit.*, p. 99.

[9] *Ibid.*

[10] *Ibid.*

[11] Blyden, Jackson, *op. cit.*, p. 219. See also Hugh Gloster, *op. cit.*, p. 34.

[12] Hugh Gloster, *op. cit.*, p. 43.

[13] *Ibid.*, p. 46.

[14] *Ibid.*

[15] Ibid., p. 56. See also Lida Keck Wiggins, comp., *The Life and Works of Paul Laurence Dunbar* (Napierville, Ill.: J. L. Nichols and Co., 1907); and Benjamin Brawley, *Paul Laurence Dunbar* (Chapel Hill: University of North Carolina Press, 1936).

[16] Hugh Gloster, *op. cit.*, p. 56.

[17] *Ibid.*, p. 58. .

[18] Cf. B. Brawley, *Early American Negro Writers*, p. 228; William Wells Brown, *The Black Man*, pp. 152ff; Vernon Loggins, *op. cit.*, pp. 235ff.

[19] Benjamin Mays, *The Negro's God* (Boston: Chapman and Grimes, 1939), pp. 133-34.

[20] L. K. Wiggins, ed., *op. cit.*, p. 160.

[21] Robert Kerlin, ed., *Negro Poets and Their Poems* (Washington, D. C.: Associated Publishers), pp. 39, 41.

[22] In his "A Blueprint for Negro Authors," *Phylon*, XI, 4th Qtr., 1950, p. 374.

[23] *Ibid.*

[24] N. P. Tillman, "The Threshold of Maturity," *Phylon*, XI, 4th Qtr., 1950, p. 388.

[25] "Negro Poets, Then and Now," *Ibid.*, p. 355.

[26] Gwendolyn Brooks, "Poets Who Are Negroes," *Ibid.*, p. 312.

[27] *Ibid.*

[28] *Ibid.*, p. 309.

[29] F. W. Bond, *The Negro and the Drama* (Washington, D. C.: Associated Publishers, 1940), p. 108.

[30] Cf. "The Negro Press Today," *American Journal of Sociology*, November, 1938, p. 398.

[31] See especially Gunnar Myrdal, *An American Dilemma* (New York: Harpers, 1944), p. 915.

[32] Cf. *Freedom's Journal*, New York, March 16, 1827. At first an ardent abolitionist, Russworm soon became a convert to emigration. In 1828 he emigrated to Liberia where he became an influential educational leader. He is known as the first Negro college graduate. Russwurm graduated from Bowdoin College in 1826. See G. Parris, "John B. Russwurm," *Negro History Bulletin*, November, 1941, p. 38. William H. Brewer, "John B. Russwurm," *Journal of Negro History*, XIII, Oct., 1928, pp. 413-422; and *The Dictionary of American Biography*, XVI, p. 253.

[33] See I. Garland Penn, *The Afro-American Press* (Springfield, Mass.: Wiley and Co., 1891).

[34] P. L. Prattis, "Race Relations and the Negro Press," *Phylon*, XIV, 4th Qtr., 1953, p. 373.

[35] *Ibid.*

[36] *Ibid.*, p. 381.

[37] *Ibid.*, p. 383.

[38] Richard Robbins, "Counter-Assertion in the New York Negro Press," *Phylon*, X, 2d Qtr., 1949, p. 135.

[39] Also on the Negro press see Roi Ottley, *The Lonely Warrior* (Chicago: Regnery Co., 1955), a biography of Robert S. Abbott, founder of the *Chicago Defender;* Dorothy H. Cunningham, "An Analysis of the *A.M.E. Church Review,* 1884-1900," unpublished M.A. thesis, Howard University, Washington, D. C.; John Syrjamaki, "The Negro Press in 1938," *Sociology and Social Research,* October, 1939; Vishnu V. Oak, "What of the Negro Press," *Saturday Review of Literature,* March 6, 1943; L. M. Jones, "Editorial Policy of Negro Newspapers of 1917-18 as compared with that of 1941-42," *Journal of Negro History,* January, 1944; Harry McAlpin, "The Negro Press in Politics," *New Republic,* Oct. 16, 1944; Gunnar Myrdal, *op. cit.,* Ch. 42.

[40] Cf. Alexander Crummel, *Civilization the Primal Need of the Race* (Washington, D. C.: 1898).

[41] Alain Locke, ed., *op. cit.,* p .22.

[42] In his *Negro Voices in American Fiction,* p. 116.

[43] Cf. *Opportunity,* IV, 1926, pp. 316-217; and *The Crisis,* XXXIII, 1926, pp. 8-82; and Carl Van Vechten, *Nigger Heaven* (New York: A. A. Knopf, 1926).

[44] George S. Schuyler, "Carl Van Vechten," *Phylon,* XI, 4th Qtr., 1950, p. 362.

[45] *Ibid.*, p. 364.

[46] *Ibid.*, pp. 366-367.

[47] *Ibid.*, p. 366.

[48] Hugh Gloster, *op. cit.,* p. 125.

[49] *Ibid.*, p. 153.

[50] *Ibid.*, p. 138.

[51] Blyden Jackson, "Of Tragedy in Negro Fiction," *loc. cit.,* p. 116.

[52] Cf. *The Amsterdam News,* July 9, 1930.

[53] Cf. review by Dewey R. Jones, *The Chicago Defender,* March 17. 1928; and W. E. B. DuBois, *The Crisis,* XXXV, 1928, p. 202.

[54] H. Gloster, *op.cit.,* p. 128.

[55] See his autobiography, *A Man Called White* (New York: 1948), p. 65.

[56] In his unpublished Ph.D. Dissertation, "Of Tragedy in Negro Fiction," p. 216.

[57] W. S. Braithwaite, "The Negro in American Literature," in A. Locke, ed., *The New Negro,* p. 40.

[58] Robert Kerlin, ed., *Negro Poets and Their Poems,* pp. 318-19.

[59] *Ibid.*, p. 267.

[60] Margaret Walker, "New Poets," *Phylon*, XI, 4th Qtr., 1950, p. 345.

[61] *Ibid.*, p. 346.

[62] F. W. Bond, *The Negro and the Drama*, p. 200.

[63] In *The New Negro*, p. 8.

[64] *Ibid.*, p. 264.

[65] Cf. Albert C. Barnes, "Primitive Negro Sculpture and Its Influence on Modern Civilization," in *Opportunity*, VI, 1928, pp. 140 and 147.

[66] See E. Franklin Frazier, *The Negro in the United States*, p. 561.

[67] A. Locke, *The Negro in Art*, p. 10.

[68] A. Locke, ed., *The New Negro*, p. 3.

[69] *Ibid.*, p. 4.

[70] *Ibid.*, p. 10.

[71] *Ibid.*

[72] Hugh Gloster, *op. cit.*, p. 209.

[73] Miss Hurston's folklore investigations have been reported in *Mules and Men*, 1935; *Moses: Man of the Mountain*, 1939; and *Tell My Horse*, 1938. See also A. Burris, review of *Jonah's Gourd Vine*, in *The Crisis*, XLI, 1934, p. 166; H. M. Gloster, "Zora Neale Hurston: Novelist and Folklorist," *Phylon*, IV, 2d Qtr., 1943, pp. 153-158; Arthur P. Davis, review of *Black No More*, in *Opportunity*, IX, February, 1931, pp. 89-90; and Dewey R. Jones, review of *Slaves Today*, in *Opportunity*, X, January, 1932, p. 27.

[74] Ulysses Lee, "Criticism at Mid-Century," *Phylon*, 4th Qtr., 1950, p. 330; F. W. Bond, *The Negro and the Drama*, pp. 126, 133, 160-161.

[75] In his, "The Negro Writer: Pitfalls and Compensations," *Phylon*, XI, 4th Qtr., 1950, pp. 297, 298.

[76] *Ibid.*

[77] In his "Race and the Negro Writer," *Phylon*, XI, 4th Qtr., 1950, p. 369.

[78] *Ibid.*, p. 387.

[79] In his "Self-Criticism: the Third Dimension in Culture," *Phylon*, XI, 4th Qtr., 1950, p. 394; also pp. 309, 298, 328, 339-40, 380ff.

[80] *Ibid.*

[81] Ira De A. Reid, "The Literature of the Negro: A Social Scientist's Appraisal," *Phylon*, XI, 4th Qtr., 1950, p. 390.

[82] *Ibid.*, p. 391.

[83] *Ibid.*, p. 329.

[84] *Ibid.*, p. 375.

[85] *Ibid.*, p. 376.

[86] Blyden Jackson, *op. cit.*, pp. 211-212.

[87] William Gardner Smith, "The Negro Writer: Pitfalls and Compensations," *loc. cit.*, p. 300.

[88] *Ibid.*, p. 303.

[89] *Ibid.*

[90] A. Locke, ed., *The New Negro*, pp. 12, 13.

91 *Ibid.*

92 Ira De Reid, "Negro Movements and Messiahs, 1900-1949," *Phylon,* X, 4th Qtr., 1949, p. 362. See also George S. Schuyler, *Phylon,* XI, 4th Qtr., 1950, p. 362.

93 See Cowley's review of this work, *loc. cit.,* p. 33.

94 Cf. Nick Aaron Ford, "A Blueprint for Negro Authors," *Phylon,* XI, 4th Qtr., 1950, p. 375; J. Saunders Redding. "The Negro Writer— Shadow and Substance," *Phylon,* XI, 4th Qtr., 1950, p. 371.

95 In *Phylon,* XI, 4th Qtr., 1950, p. 371.

96 Richard Robbins, "Counter-Assertion in the New York Negro Press," *loc. cit.,* p. 133.

97 *Ibid.* See also R. E. Wolseley, "Vanishing Negro Press," *Common-Weal,* Vol. 52, Sept. 22, 1950, pp. 577-579; H. McAlpin, "Negro Press and Politics," *New Republic,* III, Oct. 16, 1944, p. 493; F. G. Detweiler, *The Negro Press in the U. S.* (University of Chicago Press, 1922); Irvine G. Penn, *The Afro-American Press and Its Editors* (Springfield, Mass.; Wiley and Co., 1891); A. S. Pride, "Emergent Africa and the Negro Press," *Nation,* Vol. 177, Nov. 7, 1953, pp. 369-370.

98 Sterling Brown, et alia, eds., New York: 1941, pp. 144-45.

99 In *Phylon,* XI, 4th Qtr., 1950, p. 382.

100 *Ibid.,* p. 385. See also Langston Hughes, "The Negro Artist and the Racial Mountain," *The Nation,* CXXII, 1926, p. 694; Sterling Brown, "The Negro Author and His Publisher," *The Quarterly Review of Higher Education Among Negroes,* IX, July, 1941, pp. 140-146.

101 Nick Aaron Ford, in *Phylon,* XI, 4th Qtr., 1950, p. 377.

102 *Ibid.*

103 In *Phylon,* XI, 4th Qtr., 1950, p. 370.

104 Charles H. Nichols, Jr., in *Phylon,* XI, 4th Qtr., 1950, p. 379.

105 In his "Toward Unfettered Creativity: A Note on the Negro Novelist's Coming of Age," *Phylon,* 4th Qtr., XI, 1950, p. 313.

106 Blyden Jackson, *op. cit.,* p. 221. See also Fred De. Armond, "A Note on the Sociology of Negro Literature," *Opportunity,* III, Dec., 1925, pp. 369-371; Alain Locke, "American Literary Tradition and the Negro," *The Modern Quarterly,* III, May-July, 1926, pp. 215-222; James Weldon Johnson, "The Dilemma of the Negro Author," *American Mercury,* XV, Dec., 1928, pp. 477-481; James Weldon Johnson, "Race Prejudice and the Negro Artist," *Harper's Magazine,* CLVII, Nov., 1928, pp. 769-776; Sterling Brown, *The Negro in American Fiction* (Washington, D. C.: The Associates in Negro Folk Education, 1937); and by the same author, *Negro Poetry and Drama* (Washington, D. C.: The Associates in Negro Folk Education, 1937); John Chamberlain, "The Negro as Writer," *The Bookman,* LXX, 1930, p. 607; Rebecca C. Barton, *Race Consciousness in American Negro Literature* (Copenhagen, 1934); Nick Aaron Ford, *The Contemporary Negro Novel* (Boston: Meador Publishing Co., 1936); and Ralph Ellison's *Invisible Man* (New York: Random House, 1952).

107 Margaret Walker, "New Poets," *Phylon,* XI, 4th Qtr., 1950, p. 345.

[108] *Ibid.,* p. 350.

[109] *Ibid.,* p. 353.

[111] Charles H. Nichols, Jr., *loc. cit.,* p. 379.

[112] R. Bardolph, "The Distinguished Negro in America, 1770-1936," *American Historical Review,* Vol. 60, p. 544.

[113] W. T. Fontaine, "Social Determination in the Writings of Negro Scholars," *American Journal of Sociology,* Vol. 49, Jan. 1944, pp. 302-313.

[114] *Ibid.,* p. 304.

[115] *Ibid.,* pp. 306, 308.

[116] *Ibid.,* p. 310.

[117] *Ibid.,* pp. 311-312.

[118] *Ibid.,* p. 314.

[119] *Ibid.,* p. 315.

[120] *Ibid.*

[121] In his *The American Mind,* p. 407. See this entire chapter on 'The' Twentieth Century American."

[122] *Ibid.,* p. 409.

[123] New York: Harpers.

[124] Cambridge: Harvard University Press.

[125] Baton Rouge, Louisiana: Ortlieb Press, 1958.

[126] Oliver C. Cox, *Foundations of Capitalism* (New York: Philosophical Library, 1959).

www.ingramcontent.com/pod-product-compliance
Lightning Source LLC
Chambersburg PA
CBHW041254040426
42334CB00028BA/3006